W9-ASF-498

# PRACTICING TEXAS POLITICS

GOLEMON LIBRARY
Ranger College
College Circle
Ranger, TX 76470

GOLEMON LIBRARY
Ranger College
College Circle
Ranger, TX 76470

# PRACTICING TEXAS POLITICS

**LYLE C. BROWN**
Baylor University

**TED A. LEWIS**
Cy-Fair College

**JOYCE A. LANGENEGGER**
Blinn College
–Bryan Campus

**ROBERT E. BILES**
Sam Houston State University

**SONIA R. GARCÍA**
St. Mary's University

## THIRTEENTH EDITION

GOLEMON LIBRARY
Ranger College
College Circle
Ranger, TX 76470

Houghton Mifflin Company    Boston   New York

**Publisher:** Suzanne Jeans
**Senior Sponsoring Editor:** Traci Mueller
**Executive Marketing Manager:** Nicola Poser
**Marketing Associate:** Karen E. Mulvey
**Development Editor:** Christina Lembo
**Editorial Assistant:** Tiffany Hill
**Senior Project Editor:** Fred Burns
**Editorial Assistant:** Katherine Roz
**Senior Art and Design Coordinator:** Jill Haber Atkins
**Cover Design Director:** Tony Saizon
**Senior Photo Editor:** Jennifer Meyer Dare
**Composition Buyer:** Chuck Dutton
**New Title Project Manager:** James Lonergan

Cover Image Description: Barn With Texas Flag Painted On Roof, Eddy, Texas, USA.
Cover Image credit: © Masterfile/Jeremy Woodhouse
Map on inside front cover: "Counties of Texas" from the 2006–2007 Texas Almanac.
Copyright © 2006, The Dallas Morning News, L.P. Foldout map found between pp. 192
and 193. Used by permission.

Copyright © 2008 by Houghton Mifflin Company. All rights reserved.

No part of this work may be reproduced or transmitted in any form or by any
means, electronic or mechanical, including photocopying and recording, or by any
information storage or retrieval system without the prior written permission of the
copyright owner unless such copying is expressly permitted by federal copyright law.
With the exception of non-profit transcription in Braille, Houghton Mifflin is not
authorized to grant permission for further uses of copyrighted selections reprinted in
this text without the permission of their owners. Permission must be obtained from
the individual copyright owners as identified herein. Address requests for permission
to make copies of Houghton Mifflin material to College Permissions, Houghton
Mifflin Company, 222 Berkeley Street, Boston, MA 02116-3764.

Printed in the U.S.A.

Library of Congress Control Number: **2006931647**

Instructor's examination copy:
ISBN-10: 0-618-73030-3
ISBN-13: 978-0-618-73030-8

For orders, use student text ISBNs
ISBN-10: 0-618-64292-7
ISBN-13: 978-0-618-64292-2

5 6 7 8 9—VH—10 09 08

# Brief Contents

# Contents

### Selected Readings

## 8 The Executive   301

### Selected Readings

## ★ 9  Public Policy and Administration   342

### Selected Readings

## ⭐ 10  Laws, Courts, and Justice    382

## ⭐ 11 Finance and Fiscal Policy   436

### Selected Readings

# Preface

This thirteenth edition of *Practicing Texas Politics* describes and analyzes state and local politics as practiced within the Lone Star State. Published for college and university students early in the twenty-first century, our textbook gives readers a realistic and up-to-date picture of how the state and its cities, counties, and special districts are governed. Approximately 85 percent of *Practicing Texas Politics* consists of text material written jointly by co-authors who critically examine public policymaking within Texas. Each chapter features one or two selected readings.

## ★ The Co-authors

The newest member of our team of co-authors is Robert E. Biles, who has taught American and Texas politics since 1972 to students at Sam Houston State University, at universities in Colombia and Ecuador, and in Texas prisons. He brings local government experience as a school board member, party county chair, and county election supervisor, as well as service on state advisory committees, membership on the state board of a citizens lobbying organization, and staff work for the U.S. Senate Foreign Relations Committee. His publications include books and articles on Texas, Latin America, and women in politics. Ted Lewis draws on his personal experience in Texas politics to explain the organization and functions of political parties and the actions of politicians. Sonia García provides valuable insights based on her teaching and research concerning women's organizations. Joyce Langenegger is a law school graduate. She practiced law for several years before obtaining a graduate degree in political science and becoming a college instructor. Her background and experience have strengthened our coverage of the Texas judicial system and public finance. Lyle Brown has studied and taught in Mexico, has published articles on Mexican politics and U.S.-Mexican relations, and has been a co-author of *Practicing Texas Politics* since the first edition in 1971.

### Important Features of This Edition

The thirteenth edition of *Practicing Texas Politics* gives special attention to political developments since 2004. To include descriptions and analyses of recent political events and governmental changes, the narrative has been significantly rewritten. Topics given special attention include population changes documented by the 2005 federal census estimate; the debate over illegal immigration; recent state constitutional amendments, including 2005's Proposition 2; attempts to generate revenue for economic development at the local level; party primaries and the general elections in 2004 and 2006; the roles of interest groups and political action committees (PACs) in state affairs; the importance of interest group lobbying and the results of Republican majorities in both chambers of the 79th Texas Legislature; actions by Governor Rick Perry and other executive officials in recent years, including the special sessions on school finance called by the governor; changes in the state's administrative agencies; issues facing Texas's courts and penal institutions; and the politics of taxing and spending in the Perry era, with special emphasis on the impact of Hurricanes Katrina and Rita on the state of Texas and the school finance crisis.

To provide a wide range of views on current issues, we have included a number of selected readings. Every reading has a brief introduction to prepare readers for what follows. Examples of a reading from each of the eleven chapters are as follows: (1) Kellie Dworaczyk reports on the role of states in enforcing immigration laws and on state responses to issues concerning undocumented aliens; (2) José Roberto Juárez, Jr., sheds light on the importance of English language rights claimed by Anglo-American settlers before Texas's independence was won; (3) Alexander Briseno explains how term limits can have a negative impact on municipal government; (4) Paul Burka examines divisions and conflicts among Texas Republicans; (5) Laylan Copelin reports on electronic voting systems and the potential for error and fraud; (6) Lisa Sandberg addresses the influence of "revolving door lobbyists" on members of the Texas Legislature; (7) Lyle C. Brown and Jerry Wilkins discuss recent legislative and congressional redistricting in Texas, related electoral results, and the influence of Tom DeLay; (8) Mike Ward describes features of the Texas Enterprise Fund and changes recommended by critics; (9) Thomas Korosec discusses the conflict that developed when East Texas residents, fearing loss of jobs and land, opposed Dallas-Fort Worth's plans to build two new reservoirs; (10) the Supreme Court of Texas Gender Task Force suggests eight ways for lawyers and judges to avoid gender bias in courtrooms; and (11) the board of editors for the *Fort Worth Star-Telegram* highlights the negative impact of chronic underfunding on state parks in Texas.

This thirteenth edition includes two new features, "Point/Counterpoint" and "Learning Checks," which are found in each of the text's eleven chapters. Previously available only in the text's brief edition, "Point/Counterpoint" examines a key controversial issue in Texas politics from both sides of the debate. "Learning Checks," which appear at the end of most sections in each chapter, consist of a few factual questions designed to test students' grasp of the major points that were just presented, with answers to the questions provided at the end of each chapter. "Learning Checks" offer a quick way for students to confirm that they are attending properly to each section; students who want more test practice can then go online to access the book's ACE practice tests (see below).

Each chapter also includes features from previous editions that have been well received by both instructors and students. The feature "Points to Ponder" provides interesting (and sometimes little-known) facts about Texas in order to stimulate student curiosity about the state. "How Do We Compare?" compares Texas with the three other most populous U.S. states (California, Florida, and New York); with the four U.S. states bordering Texas (Arkansas, Louisiana, New Mexico, and Oklahoma); and, for some subjects, with the four Mexican states bordering Texas (Chihauhua, Coahuila, Nuevo León, and Tamaulipas).

In addition, the thirteenth edition includes a number of helpful pedagogical aids designed to facilitate student learning. For the first time, this edition features a vibrant, full color design that clearly highlights the maps, diagrams, photographs, cartoons, and tables that appear throughout the book. This edition also includes a marginal glossary, which defines key terms directly on the pages of the text where they are found, as well as a brief outline on the opening page of each chapter. A map of Texas and its borders is printed on the inside front cover of the text to familiarize students with their surroundings, and a list of Texas governors is located on the inside back cover for easy reference and review.

As in previous editions, each chapter includes a bulleted summary, a list of discussion questions, a list of Internet resources featuring URLs for agencies and organizations relevant to the chapter, and endnotes that document information provided in the text and suggest additional reading for further study. Also as before, students can access a listing of key terms at the end of each chapter (now with page references), and they can look up definitions arranged alphabetically in the glossary at the end of the text.

## Instructor Ancillary Package

The thirteenth edition of *Practicing Texas Politics* offers an extensive package of supplementary materials for instructors:

- Each chapter of the **Instructor's Resource Manual**, revised for this edition by David Ligon of Tyler Junior College, provides a complete lecture outline, suggested class activities, and a listing of numerous audiovisual and Web resources. This manual is available on the text's ONLINE TEACHING CENTER at http://college.hmco.com/PIC/brownPTP13e. Please contact your Houghton Mifflin sales representative to obtain the user name and password for the site.
- The **Test Bank**, revised for this edition by David Ligon of Tyler Junior College, is available electronically and as Word files on the **HM Testing CD-ROM** and, for those using course management systems, in **Blackboard** and **WebCT**. The CD-ROM and course cartridges are available from your Houghton Mifflin sales representative.
- Text-specific **PowerPoint Slides**, which include chapter outlines and figures from the thirteenth edition, are available for download at the ONLINE TEACHING CENTER (http://college.hmco.com/PIC/brownPTP13e).

- **In-Class Clicker Quizzes,** PowerPoint slides for use with Personal (or Classroom) Response Systems, are available for download at the ONLINE TEACHING CENTER (http://college.hmco.com/PIC/brownPTP13e). Half of the questions in the slides are available to students as a pre-class quiz on the ONLINE STUDY CENTER (http://college.hmco.com/PIC/brownPTP13e), and you can use these questions in combination with questions that they have not seen to motivate students to study before class.
- Instructors looking for additional coverage of natural disasters, including Hurricane Katrina and FEMA, may package *Practicing Texas Politics* with a new ***Politics of Natural Disasters* supplement** written by William L. Waugh of Georgia State University. This free packaging option analyzes the natural disasters that occur most often in the United States, the government policy created to deal with them, and the future of emergency management. Please contact your Houghton Mifflin sales representative for more information.

## ★ Student Ancillary Package

The text's ONLINE STUDY CENTER website, accessible at http://college.hmco.com/PIC/brownPTP13e, contains a wealth of study aids and resources for students, including assets previously available via the *Study Guide* that are now online free of charge. These study resources, carefully revised and updated by Lyle C. Brown, Joyce Langenegger, and Janet Adamski, include summaries of the text and readings, learning objectives, flashcards, pre-class quizzes to prepare students for class discussion, ACE practice tests, Internet research projects, and an updated bibliography of books and articles for further reading and research. A number of these items can be printed off the site for students wishing to review material "on the go."

## ★ Acknowledgments

We are indebted to many political scientists as well as scholars in other disciplines. They have shared generously the results of their research and have stimulated our effort to produce a better textbook for classroom use. In particular, we thank Nancy Bond, Tarleton State University; William E. Carroll, Sam Houston State University; Laura De La Cruz, El Paso Community College; Yolanda Garza Hake, South Texas College; Amy S. Glenn, Tyler Junior College; and John David Rausch, Jr., West Texas A&M University, who served as reviewers for this edition of our textbook. They provided many useful comments and suggestions for which we are grateful.

We are also indebted to many personal friends, government officials and their staffs, political activists, lawyers, and journalists who have stimulated our thinking. Likewise, we owe much to librarians and archivists who located hard-to-obtain facts, photos, and new readings. Special appreciation is expressed for help from Michael Hernandez, a graduate student at St. Mary's University. We also appreciate the professional assistance rendered by the editorial, production, and marketing staff of Houghton Mifflin Company. Without the benefit of their publishing experience, this textbook and its ancillaries would be of much less value to students and instructors.

Of course, expressions of appreciation are due to secretaries and others who helped to produce this new edition of our book and to spouses and other family members who have learned to cope with the irregular working hours of authors struggling to meet deadlines. Last and most important, we dedicate this book to Texas students and political science instructors who, we hope, will continue to be the chief beneficiaries of our efforts to describe and analyze the practice of Texas politics.

Lyle C. Brown
Joyce A. Langenegger
Sonia R. García
Ted A. Lewis
Robert E. Biles

## Chapter 1

# The Environment of Texas Politics

★ **Political Behavior Patterns**

★ **The Land**

★ **The People**

★ **Searching for New Economic Directions**

★ **Meeting New Challenges: Social and Economic Policy Issues**

© 2006 John Branch/
*San Antonio Express-News.* Reprinted with
permission.

*You ask me what I like about Texas*
*I tell you it's the wide open spaces!*
*It's everything between the Sabine and the Rio Grande.*
*It's the Llano Estacado,*
*It's the Brazos and the Colorado;*
*Spirit of the people down here who share this land!*[1]

Texas is a big state with nearly 80,000 miles of highways. As the preceding cartoon illustrates, Texans often face the dual frustration of traffic delays caused by ongoing construction and the increasing costs of highway maintenance. In both square miles and population, Texas is among the largest states in the nation.

In 2005, the Census Bureau estimated a rapidly growing U.S. population. Texas ranked second among the 50 states with a population of more than 22 million, up from nearly 17 million in 1990 and almost 21 million in 2000. California ranked first with close to 36 million; New York was third with less than 20 million. This increased population for the Lone Star State included more than 16 million men and women of voting age (18 years or older). Of course, some of them could not legally cast ballots because they lacked qualifications concerning residence, voter registration, or U.S. citizenship. Nevertheless, most Texans are involved in political activities, even if they limit their actions to talking about politics or merely listening while others talk, and everyone is affected by the words and deeds of politicians, government officials, and public employees.

Legislative actions, executive decisions, and court proceedings, as well as popular elections and lobbying activities, are parts of the political struggle that determine, in the words of political scientist Harold Lasswell, "who gets what, when, and how."[2] **Politics** involves conflict between political parties and other groups that seek to elect government officials or to influence those officials when they make public policy, such as enacting and interpreting Texas laws.

## ⭐ Political Behavior Patterns

This book focuses on politics as it is practiced within Texas and on the diverse and rich cultural heritage of the Lone Star State. Our analysis of the politics of Texas's state and local governments today is intended to help readers understand political action and prepare them for informed participation in the political affairs of the state and its counties, cities, and special districts. In addition, we will introduce readers to important political actors, most of them high-ranking party activists or government officials who have been elected or appointed to public office. In politics, as in athletics, people need to be able to identify the players to understand the game.

### Government, Politics, and Public Policy

**Government** may be defined as a public institution with the authority to allocate values in a society. In practice, values are allocated when a state or local government formulates, adopts, and implements a public policy, such as raising taxes to pay for more police protection or better streets and highways. At the state level, each **public policy** is a product of political activity that may involve both conflict and cooperation among legislators, between legislators and the governor, within the courts, and among various governmental agencies, citizens, and **aliens** (persons who lack U.S. citizenship, including undocumented people who have entered legally but have stayed after their authorized visa has expired).

Policymaking involves political action intended to meet particular needs or achieve specific objectives. For example, a legislator might receive a proposal to promote public health by reducing or eliminating the use of pesticides alleged to cause cancer. This proposal could come from the governor or another

**politics** The process by which individuals and political parties nominate and elect public officials and formulate public policy.

**government** A public institution with authority to allocate values by formulating, adopting, and implementing public policies.

**public policy** Government action designed to meet a public need or goal as determined by a legislative body or other authorized officials.

**alien** A person who is neither a national nor a citizen of the country where he or she is living.

<table>
<tr><td>

**Points to Ponder**

</td><td>

Texans have had a large impact on national politics during the latter part of the twentieth century and today. Consider the following:

- Three men who have claimed Texas as their residence have occupied the Oval Office within the past 50 years: Lyndon B. Johnson (1963–1969), George H. W. Bush (1989–1993) and George W. Bush (2001–current).
- Texans have served in key positions as cabinet secretaries, advisers, and diplomats.
- Texans have served in the federal judicial branch as district judges and appellate judges, and one has served as a Supreme Court Justice (Tom C. Clark, 1949–1967).
- Texans who have served in key positions in Congress include Senate Majority Leader (Lyndon B. Johnson, 1953–1961), Speaker of the U.S. House of Representatives (John Nance Garner, D-Uvalde, 1931–1933; Sam Rayburn, D-Bonham, 1940–1947, 1949–1953, and 1955–1961; and Jim Wright, D-Fort Worth, 1987–1989), as well as numerous party leaders, whips (assistant leaders), and key committee chairs.
- When Tom DeLay (R-Sugar Land) was forced to resign his position as House majority leader in early 2006 after an indictment for criminal conspiracy and increasing ethical questions, it marked the first time since 1925 that Texas did not have a member in leadership position in either house of Congress.

</td></tr>
</table>

government official, from a nongovernmental organization such as the environmentalist Sierra Club, or from any interested person. Next, the proposal would be incorporated into a bill and submitted to the Texas Legislature by a state senator or representative favoring a new policy. Then, in committee hearings and on the floor of the Senate and the House of Representatives, the bill would be discussed and debated in the presence of lobbyists representing interest groups, journalists reporting the news, and concerned citizens. When the bill is passed by the legislature and signed by the governor, the pesticide proposal would become law. Next, the new public policy must be implemented, or put into operation. That responsibility might be assigned by law to the Texas Department of Agriculture or another governmental agency. But the policy measure could be challenged in court. Judges might uphold all or part of the legislation or nullify it entirely if it violates a provision of the Texas Constitution or the U.S. Constitution. In sum, politics is the moving force that produces public policy, which in turn determines what government does and who is affected.

## Political Culture

**political culture**
Attitudes, habits, and general behavior patterns that develop over time and affect the political life of a state or region.

Politics is influenced by **political culture**, which consists of the values, attitudes, traditions, habits, and general behavioral patterns that develop over time and shape the politics of a particular region. Political culture is the result of both remote and recent political experiences. According to political scientist Daniel Elazar, "Culture patterns give each state its particular character and

*The Texas State Capitol in Austin (Texas House of Representatives)*

help determine the tone of its fundamental relationship, as a state, to the nation."[3] Professor Elazar has identified three distinct cultures that exist in the United States: moralistic, individualistic, and traditionalistic.

The **moralistic culture** originated in New England with Puritanism. In the moralistic culture, the people view government as a public service. The role of government is to improve conditions for the people and to create a just society. The people expect government to provide goods and services to advance the public good. Citizens play an important role in politics in the moralistic culture. They see it as their duty to become active in governmental decision making through participation in town councils and other representative bodies or by closely monitoring the actions of their leaders. Government is viewed as a participatory endeavor, not simply the province of self-serving individuals. The people generally have high expectations of their government because they hold it accountable. Today, this culture has spread across the northern states and to the Pacific Northwest.

The **individualistic culture**, the second culture to emerge, grew out of westward expansion throughout the nineteenth century. Originally, many people migrated west to pursue economic opportunities not available to them in the East. The frontier areas in which they settled had no government to provide goods and services for them. They became more self-reliant, and the notion of the "rugged individualist" emerged. The business community also advanced the individualistic culture. They viewed government as an adversary that taxed and regulated them; therefore, they wanted to limit its size and scope. In contrast to the moralistic culture, individualistic culture does not

**moralistic culture** This culture influences people to view political participation as their duty and to expect that government will be used to advance the public good.

**individualistic culture** This culture looks to government to maintain a stable society but with minimum intervention in the lives of the people.

consider government a vehicle for creating a just society and believes government intervention into public life should be limited. Today, the individualistic culture is found in a majority of the midwestern and western states.

The **traditionalistic culture**, the third culture to emerge, developed about the same time as the individualistic culture. However, the traditionalistic culture grew out of the Old South and is rooted in feudal-like notions of society and government that developed in the context of the agrarian plantation economy. Economically, the South differed from the North and the West in that it was based primarily on agriculture and, to a large extent, on the labor of African American slaves. As a result, property and income were unequally dispersed. Governmental policymaking fell to a few elite citizens who belonged to established families or influential social groups. Policies were designed to preserve the social order, and a one-party system developed. The poor and minorities were often disenfranchised. Even in the early twenty-first century, those in lower socioeconomic categories show a high degree of **political inefficacy** and lower voter turnout. In the traditionalistic culture, government is a vehicle to maintain the status quo and its hierarchy. Today the traditionalistic culture remains dominant throughout the South.

### Texas Political Culture

The foundations of Texas's political culture were laid and developed under the flags of six national governments: Spain, France, Mexico, the Republic of Texas, the Confederate States of America, and the United States. Unlike most of the other 49 states, Texas was not a U.S. territory before statehood. As an independent republic (1836–1845), Texas was given diplomatic recognition by the governments of the United States, England, France, Holland, and Belgium. With a popularly elected president and congress, the republic maintained its own army and navy, operated a postal system, printed paper money, administered justice through its courts, and provided other governmental services.

**Texas Individualism**    Daniel Elazar asserts that the political culture of Texas is strongly individualistic in that government is supposed to maintain a stable society but intervene as little as possible in the lives of the people. He identifies the state's politics with economic and social conservatism, strong support of personal politics, distrust of political parties, and minimization of the latter's importance.

An important source of Texas's conservatism is the nineteenth-century **frontier experience**. In the early nineteenth century, having obtained land grants from Spain, Anglo settlers moved to Texas individually or with such leaders as Stephen F. Austin. Many of these settlers had been unsuccessful in business or wished to escape their pasts, and Texas provided them with new opportunities. After securing independence from Mexico in 1836, the Republic of Texas developed its own economy, military, and education system. The Texas republic's main success was its endurance. Texans, unlike other Americans who received military help from the federal government, had dis-

**traditionalistic culture** A product of the Old South, the traditionalistic culture uses government as a means of preserving the status quo and its leadership.

**political inefficacy** The inability to influence the nomination and election of candidates and the decision making of governing bodies. In Texas, this has been a major problem for minorities and low-income groups.

**frontier experience** Coping with danger, physical hardships, and economic challenges tested the endurance of nineteenth-century Texans and contributed to the development of individualism.

placed Native Americans from a large region by themselves, established farms and communities, and persevered through extreme economic hardships.[4] These achievements have been enlarged over time by historians and fiction writers emphasizing the violent aspects of Texans' struggle for independence from Mexico and their clashes with Native Americans who unsuccessfully resisted the westward movement of Anglo settlers. Thousands of Native Americans and settlers—men, women, and children—were slain on the Texas frontier from the 1820s to the mid-1870s. This period of frontier warfare lasted longer in Texas than in other states.

After the Texas frontier was secured, there remained the task of bringing law and order to the land. In some areas, range wars, cattle rustling, and other forms of violence continued to menace law-abiding citizens into the twentieth century. As a result of these experiences, many Texans grew accustomed to the use of force in settling disputes and struggling for survival. In 1995, when the legislature legalized the carrying of concealed handguns by licensed owners, some people interpreted the action as another influence of frontier days, when many Texans carried concealed weapons or bore pistols openly in holsters. Two assumptions underlie the concealed weapons law: first, that Texans do not need to rely on law enforcement for protection and, second, that citizens of the Lone Star State have a right to possess and carry weapons. Guns-rights groups have helped to advance these presumptions. Today, shootings and other violence may be as common in Texas's inner cities and elsewhere as they were on the state's frontier in the nineteenth century.

Elements of the individualistic culture persist in other examples as well. Compared with other heavily populated states, Texas has a limited government with restricted powers: a legislature that meets biennially, with salaries that can be increased only after approval by Texas voters; a governor who has limited budgetary, appointment, and removal powers; and an elected judiciary with multiple levels of courts. Texas has a climate favorable to business. It remains one of the few states without a personal or corporate income tax. Government spending for social services on a per capita basis is consistently among the lowest in the nation. Public education in Texas is poorly funded and has remained a source of court battles and legislative sessions for several years. Including independent school districts, Texas has more than 3,000 special districts that perform a single service or groups of related services not performed by city or county governments. Participation in politics and voter turnout remain low. Turnout of the voting age population falls below 50 percent for presidential elections, and consistently below 30 percent for gubernatorial elections. Public perception of government and elected officials remains negative. In 1998, George W. Bush became the first Texas governor elected to a second consecutive four-year term (although he resigned two years into his second term, following his election as U.S. president in 2000).

**Texas Traditionalism**   The traditionalistic culture of Texas also can be traced to the early nineteenth century. The plantation system thrived in the rich, fertile soil of East Texas, and cotton was by far the state's largest money crop. Before Texas's entry into the Confederacy, much of its wealth was concentrated in a few families. Although only a quarter of the state's population and a third of the farmers owned slaves, slave owners had 60 to 70 percent of the wealth and controlled state politics.[5] After the Civil War (1861–1865), "**Jim Crow**" laws limited blacks' access to public services. In the late nineteenth and early twentieth centuries, literacy tests, grandfather clauses, poll taxes, and "all-white primaries" further restricted voting rights.

Today, many Texans are descendants of migrants from traditionalistic states of the Old South, where conservatism, elitism (upper-class rule), and one-party politics were long entrenched. Although urbanization and industrialization, together with an influx of people from other states and countries, are changing the cultural patterns of Texas's population, Elazar insists that the traditionalistic influence of the Old South still lingers. He notes that many Texans have inherited southern racist attitudes, which for decades were reflected in state laws that discriminated against African Americans and other minority groups. In 2000, however, two Civil War plaques were removed from the Texas Supreme Court building as demanded by the National Association for the Advancement of Colored People. One plaque bore a likeness of the Confederate battle flag, and the other displayed the official Confederate seal. Similar symbols of Texas's role in the Confederacy remain in public places throughout the state and are a source of continuing controversy.

The traditionalistic influence of Mexico is discernible among Mexican American Texans affected by a political culture featuring the elitist *patrón* (protecting political boss) **system** that dominates certain areas of South Texas. For more than three decades, however, the old political order of that region has been challenged—and, in many instances, defeated—by a new generation of Mexican Americans.[6] Compared with other areas of the state, however, voter turnout remains much lower in counties along the Mexican border.

The traditionalistic culture can also be seen in the state's social and economic conservatism. Religious groups have influenced government policies on matters such as blue (Sunday closing) laws, liquor laws, pari-mutuel betting, and the state lottery. City councils have drawn public criticism for publicly financing corporate ventures or providing certain businesses with property tax abatements. Powerful families continue to play an important role in state politics and influence public policies.

**A Changing Culture?**    Beginning in the mid-1970s, Texas experienced a large population influx from other areas of the nation and, more recently, from other countries. With regard to Elazar's appraisal of Texas's conservative political culture, important questions arise: How long will particular sociocultural influences last? Aren't past cultural influences being replaced by new ones? Will Texas's cultural identities, inherited largely from the nineteenth century, survive indefinitely in the face of widespread urbanization, industrialization, education, communication, and population change? Will a moralistic culture ever take root and flourish in the Lone Star State?

**Jim Crow** "Jim Crow" laws were ethnically discriminatory laws that segregated African Americans and denied them access to public services for many decades after the Civil War.

***patrón* system** A type of boss rule that has dominated areas of South Texas.

## How Do We Compare ... in Area?

Throughout the book, we use this feature to compare Texas with the other three most populous U.S. states, and with Texas's four neighboring U.S. states. Some How Do We Compare boxes include information about the Mexican states bordering Texas: Chihuahua, Coahuila, Nuevo León, and Tamaulipas.

### Land and Inland Water Area Combined

| Most Populous U.S. States | Area (sq. miles) | U.S. States Bordering Texas | Area (sq. miles) | Mexican States Bordering Texas | Area (sq. miles) |
|---|---|---|---|---|---|
| California | 163,707 | Arkansas | 53,182 | Chihuahua | 95,400 |
| Florida | 65,758 | Louisiana | 54,813 | Coahuila | 58,522 |
| New York | 54,475 | New Mexico | 121,593 | Nuevo León | 25,126 |
| Texas | 267,339 | Oklahoma | 69,903 | Tamaulipas | 30,734 |

---

**Learning Check 1.1**      **(Answers on p. 39)**

**1.** True or False: Texas's estimated population of more than 22 million ranks it third among the 50 states, behind California and New York.

**2.** What two types of political culture are found in Texas?

---

# The Land

Like people everywhere, Texans are influenced by their geography as well as by their history. Thus, Texas's mountains, plains, seacoasts, climate, mineral deposits, and other geographic features affect the state's economy, its political culture, and the part the Lone Star State plays in national and international affairs. By the twenty-first century, Texans had cleared the land to establish and operate thousands of farms and ranches, built hundreds of towns and cities, organized many banks and businesses, and produced much of the nation's oil and natural gas, cotton and mohair, fish and meat, wheat and sorghum, fruits and vegetables, computers and computer chips.

## The Politics of Geography

From the start, Texas politics and public policy have been molded in part by the state's size. Its large area and diverse physical geography create strong regional interests. Regardless of where we live, however, most citizens of the Lone Star State strongly identify with our state and are proud to be called Texans.

- The longest highway in Texas is US 83. It extends from the Oklahoma state line in the Panhandle to the Mexico border at Brownsville. It is 899 miles long.
- The shortest highway in Texas is Loop 168 in downtown Tenaha in Shelby County. This road is 0.074 mile long, or about 391 feet.

**Points to Ponder**

**Size**   With more than 267,000 square miles of territory, Texas is second only to Alaska in area. The Lone Star State is as large as the combined areas of New York, Pennsylvania, Ohio, Illinois, New Hampshire, Connecticut, Vermont, Rhode Island, Massachusetts, and Maine.

It's an 800-mile trip flying south in a straight line from the northwestern corner of the Texas Panhandle to the state's southern tip on the Rio Grande near Brownsville. Almost equally long is the distance from Newton County's Louisiana border (south of the Sabine River's Toledo Bend Reservoir) to the New Mexican border near El Paso. Such great size requires about 222,000 miles of roadways in the state, including nearly 80,000 miles of major highways constructed and maintained under the supervision of the Texas Department of Transportation. No other state has so many miles of roadways.

Because of the state's vast size and geographic diversity, Texas developed a concept of five areas—North, South, East, West, and Central Texas—as five potentially separate states. In fact, the congressional resolution by which Texas was admitted to the Union in 1845 specifies that up to four states "in addition to said state of Texas" may be formed out of its territory and that each "shall be entitled to admission to the Union." Various plans for carving Texas into five states have been proposed to the Texas Legislature. Few Texans have taken them seriously.

**Regions**   Geographically, Texas is at the confluence of several major physiographic regions of North America. The four principal **physical regions** of the state are the Gulf Coastal Plains, the Interior Lowlands, the Great Plains, and the Basin and Range Province. (For a map showing these regions, see Figure 1.1.)

The **Gulf Coastal Plains** region in East Texas is an extension of the Gulf Coastal Plains of the United States, a region that stretches westward from the Atlantic coast and then southward into Mexico. The internal boundary of the Gulf Coastal Plains follows the Balcones Fault, so named by Spanish explorers because the westward-rising hills resemble a line of balconies. Immediately east of the fault line is the Blackland Belt. Fifteen to 70 miles in width, this strip of black soil stretches southward from the Red River, which marks the eastern half of the Oklahoma border, to the Mexican border. The international boundary follows the Rio Grande in its southeastern course from El Paso to Brownsville and the Gulf of Mexico. (Mexicans call this international stream the Rio Bravo, which means "brave river" or "fierce river.") For several months in 2001, however, the Rio Grande ceased its flow into the Gulf of Mexico because it ran dry downstream from Brownsville.

Within the Gulf Coastal Plains region lies the Coastal Prairies area. Bordering the Gulf of Mexico, between the Piney Woods of East Texas and the Rio Grande Plain of South Texas, this flat area has been the scene of great industrial growth since World War II, particularly in the section between Beaumont and Houston. Here are the state's chief petrochemical industries, based on oil and natural gas. In contrast to the arid plains of West Texas, this is the greenest region of the state, with certain areas receiving more than 50 inches of rain annually.

**physical region** An area identified by unique geographic features, e.g., the Gulf Coastal Plains and the Great Plains.

**Gulf Coastal Plains** Stretching from the Louisiana border to the Rio Grande, Texas's Gulf Coastal Plains area is an extension of the Gulf Coastal Plains of the United States.

*Figure 1.1* Texas Geographic Regions
*Source: Texas Almanac and State Industrial Guide 2006–2007.* Reprinted with permission of the *Texas Almanac*, published by *The Dallas Morning News.*

The **Interior Lowlands** region encompasses the North Central Plains of Texas. This territory is bounded by the Blackland Belt to the east, the Cap Rock Escarpment to the west, the Red River to the north, and the Colorado River to the south. Farming and ranching are important activities within this largely prairie domain. The major cities in the region are Abilene, Dallas, Fort Worth, and Wichita Falls.

In 1999, after decades of controversy and negotiation stemming from the Adams-Onís Treaty between the United States and Spain (1819), the governments of Texas and Oklahoma entered into the Red River Boundary Compact. It established the south bank of the river where vegetation begins as the boundary between the two states.

Immediately west of the Interior Lowlands and rising to higher altitudes, the Texas **Great Plains** area is a southern extension of the Great High Plains of the United States. From Oklahoma at the northern boundary of the Panhandle, this area extends southward to the Rio Grande. The Panhandle–South Plains portion of the region is known principally for its large-scale production of

**Interior Lowlands** This region covers the North Central Plains of Texas extending from the Dallas–Fort Worth Metroplex westward to the Abilene area and northward to the Wichita Falls area.

**Great Plains** A large area in West Texas extending from Oklahoma to Mexico, the Great Plains is an extension of the Great High Plains of the United States.

cotton and grain sorghum. These irrigated crops draw their water from the Ogallala Aquifer, formed thousands of years ago by runoff from the Rocky Mountains. This underground, water-bearing rock formation extends northward from Texas to North Dakota, underlying parts of eight states. The chief cities of the Panhandle–South Plains are Lubbock and Amarillo.

Centered in Nevada, the **Basin and Range Province** region of the United States enters western Texas from southern New Mexico. The only part of the Lone Star State classified as mountainous, this rugged triangle provides Texans and many non-Texans with a popular vacation area that includes the Davis Mountains and Big Bend National Park. The state's highest mountains, Guadalupe Peak (8,749 feet) and El Capitan (8,085 feet), are located here. Among the few cities in this large area are the small city of Alpine (site of Sul Ross State University) and the big city of El Paso (on the north bank of the Rio Grande, just across the border from Mexico's more populous Ciudad Juárez).

### Economic Geography

Although geographic factors do not directly determine political differences, geography greatly influences the economic pursuits of a region's inhabitants, which in turn shape political interests and attitudes. Geography has encouraged rapid population growth, urbanization, and industrialization in East Texas; in arid West Texas, it has produced a sparsely populated rural and agricultural environment. In the course of its economic and political development, the Lone Star State has been influenced greatly by three land-based industries: cattle, cotton, and oil.

**Cattle**    The origin of Texas's cattle ranching may be traced to Gregorio de Villalobos, who transported Spanish-Moorish cattle from Spain to Mexico in the early years of the conquest. Subsequently, Francisco Vásquez de Coronado and other Spanish explorers and settlers brought livestock into Texas. Later, cattle from Mexico interbred with cattle brought by Anglo settlers to produce the hardy Texas longhorn that thrived on the open range. Although "Mexican" cattle of the long-horned variety provided the basic strain, folklorist J. Frank Dobie explained that an infiltration of cattle of mongrel American blood contributed to the evolution of the Texas longhorn. Dobie estimated the Texas longhorn evolved as the result of 80 percent Spanish influence and 20 percent mongrel influence.[7]

Plentiful land and minimal government interference encouraged huge cattle empires established by determined entrepreneurs such as Richard King and Mifflin Kenedy. Today the famous King Ranch is composed of four separate units that total more than 825,000 acres or almost 1,300 square miles in Kleberg County (with the county seat at Kingsville, near the ranch headquarters) and five other South Texas counties.[8] Ownership of the Kenedy Ranch's 370,000 acres has been contested by more than 700 descendants of José Manuel Ballí, who claim that Kenedy acquired this land illegally. Early in 2003, a state district judge in Corpus Christi ruled against the claims of the Ballí family. However, by 2006 this decision was under appeal.

**Basin and Range Province** An arid region in West Texas that includes the Davis Mountains, Big Bend National Park, and El Paso.

■ Brownsville is closer to Mexico City than to the Panhandle town of Texline.
■ Texarkana is closer to Chicago, Illinois, than to El Paso.
■ El Paso is closer to Los Angeles on the Pacific Coast than to Port Arthur on the Gulf Coast of Texas.
■ Port Arthur is closer to Jacksonville, Florida, on the Atlantic Coast than to El Paso.

**Points to Ponder**

After the Civil War, an estimated 5 million cattle ranged over Texas's nearly 168 million acres of land. During the 25 years following that war, approximately 35,000 men drove about 10 million cattle and 1 million horses north along the Chisholm and Goodnight-Loving Trails to Kansas railheads. By the late 1880s, when the railroads were built closer to Texas ranches, the cattle drives ended and large ranches developed. In time, the political and economic impact of the beef business leveled off in the wake of newly emerging industries. Although Texas cattle production has declined in recent years, Texas still has more cattle than any other state: about 13.6 million, including more than 300,000 dairy cows. In fact, livestock and their products account for about two-thirds of Texas agricultural cash receipts. Texas ranks first nationally in all cattle, beef cattle, and cattle feed production. It also leads the nation in the production of sheep, goats, wool, and mohair.

**Cotton** Although popular culture romanticizes the nineteenth-century cowboys and cattle drives, cotton formed the backbone of the state's economy in that era. Before Spaniards brought cattle into Texas, cotton was already growing wild in the region. The rich, fertile soil led to its easy cultivation, begun by Spanish missionaries. In the 1820s, the first hybrid, or improved, cotton was introduced into Texas by Colonel Jared Groce, known as the founder of the Texas cotton industry. Groce and other Anglo Texans first cultivated cotton in East and Central Texas, where crop conditions most closely resembled those in the Old South. Before the Civil War, when slaves performed much of the field labor, cotton production spread. During that war, revenue from the sale of Texas cotton to European buyers aided the Confederacy. As more frontier land was settled, cotton production moved westward and increased in volume.

Currently, the High Plains region of West Texas accounts for about 60 percent of the state's annual cotton yield. With more than 6.4 million acres of Texas farmland devoted to cotton production (about 40 percent of the country's cotton acreage), the annual harvest usually exceeds 4.5 million bales of lint and 1.5 million tons of cottonseed. The annual value of this crop has ranged from $1.0 billion to $1.7 billion in recent years. Much of Texas cotton is exported.

In addition to cotton's contribution to the Texas economy, other important cash crops today include corn, grain sorghum, hay, rice, cottonseed, peanuts, soybeans, and pecans. Texas is also among the leading states in production of fresh market vegetables and citrus.

**Oil**    Long before Europeans arrived, Native Americans used oil seeping from the Texas soil for medicinal purposes. Early Spanish explorers in the sixteenth and seventeenth centuries used it to caulk their boats. In the late nineteenth century, thousands of barrels had been produced from crudely dug wells in different areas of the state. However, before the twentieth century, Texas petroleum was an unknown quantity of limited commercial value. Not until 1901, when the **Spindletop Field** was developed near Beaumont, did petroleum usher in the industry that dominated the state's economy for nearly a century. After the Spindletop boom, other wells were drilled across Texas. Over the next 50 years, Texas evolved from a predominantly agricultural culture into an industrial society. Oil brought industrial employment on a grand scale to rural Texas. It offered tens of thousands of Texans an immediate and attractive alternative to life down on the farm or ranch. Many of the major oil companies, such as Gulf Oil Corporation, Humble (later ExxonMobil Corporation), Magnolia Petroleum Company, Sun Oil Company, and the Texas Company (later Texaco and more recently ChevronTexaco), were created or quickly grew to corporate size. In 1919, the legislature gave the **Railroad Commission of Texas** limited regulatory jurisdiction over the state's oil and natural gas industry.[9]

At its peak in the early 1980s, the Texas petroleum industry employed a half million workers earning more than $11 billion annually, and it was estimated that oil and natural gas production accounted for almost one-third of the state's economy. By that time, the state's oil business had expanded into gasoline refineries, petrochemical plants, and factories for manufacturing a wide range of tools and equipment used in drilling, transporting, and refining operations. Meanwhile an increasing number of banks willingly financed these costly enterprises. In 1982, an oil price slump began that produced a near panic in the industry, and the number of operating drilling rigs plunged from more than 1,000 to near zero by 1986. At that time, the price of oil dropped to less than $10 per barrel, its lowest level in more than a decade. As a result, many oil operators, businesspeople in related industries, and real estate developers failed to meet their loan obligations; hundreds of banks and savings and loan institutions became insolvent and closed. From 1987 to 1989, more Texas financial institutions failed than at any other time since the Great Depression.[10] Many other banks and savings and loan institutions merged with healthier financial institutions often controlled by out-of-state interests.[11] At the same time, tens of thousands of laborers, technicians, engineers, managers, and others lost their jobs and joined the ranks of the unemployed or left Texas to find jobs elsewhere.

In the century-long development of the Texas oil industry, its political impact has been inevitable. Because of the large amounts of oil money contributed to candidates for public office and collected as revenue from taxes and lease holdings by state and local governments, Texas politics could hardly escape the industry's influence. From the mid-1980s until 1999, however, cheap oil and falling production plagued Texas's petroleum industry—except

**Spindletop Field**
Located near Beaumont, this oil field sparked a boom in 1901 that made Texas a leading petroleum producer.

**Railroad Commission of Texas**  A popularly elected, three-member commission primarily engaged in regulating natural gas and petroleum production.

for the brief period of the Gulf War (1990–1991), sparked by Iraq's invasion and brief occupation of oil-rich Kuwait. Consequences of hard times in the Texas oil patch included reduced revenues for state and local governments and less election campaign money contributed by political action groups connected to the industry. As a result, the Texas economy diversified and became less dependent on oil as a major source of revenue for the state. Although petroleum prices have risen steadily since 1998 (more than $70 per barrel in mid-2006), oil is not expected to regain its former level of influence over the Lone Star State's economy and politics.

Texas has 4 of the 10 largest U.S. oil fields in terms of production, but today the oil and gas industry accounts for less than 6 percent of the state's economy. About 200,000 Texans work in this industry, and more than 200,000 others depend on energy-related industries for their employment. Most oil and gas jobs (including those in refineries and other petrochemical plants) pay relatively high wages and salaries. Meanwhile, awareness is growing that oil-based fuels burned in automobiles, trucks, buses, and airplanes are the world's principal source of air pollution. In addition, immeasurable harm to the world's oceans has resulted from oil spills in the Gulf of Mexico and other waters around the globe. Groups such as the Sustainable Energy and Economic Development (SEED) Coalition, the Lone Star Chapter of the Sierra Club, the Texas Campaign on the Environment, and the Texas Clean Air Working Group (a project of the Texas Conference of Urban Counties) have identified alternative fuel strategies for the Lone Star State. During his state of the union address in 2006, President Bush, a former Texas oilman, derided America's "addiction" to oil and offered a proposal to limit U.S. dependence on foreign oil as more Americans express concern about the rising cost of gasoline and home heating fuel. In announcing his Advanced Energy Initiative, the president proposed a 22 percent increase in clean-energy research at the Department of Energy. This could promote investment in zero-emission coal-fired power plants, revolutionary solar and wind technologies, and clean and safe nuclear energy.

---

**Learning Check 1.2**      **(Answers on p. 39)**

1. What are the four principal physical regions located in Texas?
2. In 1901, which oil field ushered in the oil industry that would dominate Texas's economy for nearly a century?

---

## ⭐ The People

Texas has a large, ethnically diverse population. In every decade since 1850, it has grown more rapidly than the overall population of the United States. Like the population of the nation, Texas's population is aging as the post–World War II baby-boom generation (persons born between 1946 and 1964) reaches middle age. The Bureau of the Census estimates that the population of Texans over the age of 64 will exceed 5 million by 2030. Nearly half of all Texans are

| How Do We Compare . . . in Population? | | | |
|---|---|---|---|
| *2005 Population Estimate as Reported by U.S. Census Bureau* | | | |
| **Most Populous U.S. States** | **Population** | **U.S. States Bordering Texas** | **Population** |
| California | 36,132,147 | Arkansas | 2,779,154 |
| Florida | 17,789,864 | Louisiana | 4,523,628 |
| New York | 19,254,630 | New Mexico | 1,928,384 |
| **Texas** | **22,859,968** | Oklahoma | 3,547,884 |

either African Americans or Latinos (also called Hispanics).[12] The remainder are predominantly Anglos (non-Hispanic whites), with a small but rapidly growing number of Asians and fewer than 70,000 Native Americans (also called American Indians).

### Demographic Features

According to the federal census estimate of 2005, Texas's population totaled 22,859,968—an increase of 34.6 percent from the 1990 total of 16,986,510, and an increase of almost 10 percent from the 2000 census total of 20,851,820. (At the national level, the total population estimate in 2005 was 296,410,404—an increase of 19 percent from the U.S. population of 248,709,873 in 1990 and an increase of 5 percent from the 2000 census total of 281,421,906.) Texas also had three of the fastest-growing metropolitan areas in the nation from 2000 to 2005. McAllen-Edinburg-Mission grew by 17.6 percent, Laredo grew by 16.5 percent, and Austin-Round Rock grew by 14.0 percent.

Although the U.S. Census Bureau estimated that the 2000 census missed about 3.3 million Americans (1.2 percent), the administration of President George W. Bush decided to use raw totals rather than figures based on statistical sampling. Latinos and African Americans, especially those in big cities, are most likely to be undercounted. Because creation of congressional and legislative districts, as well as allocation of federal grants and state tax money, are affected by census figures, areas with large minority populations tend to receive less representation and lower funding.[13] Additionally, by relying on raw census totals, Texas loses billions of dollars in federal programs and aid.

**Population Distribution**   Just as Texas's physical geography makes the state a land of great contrasts, so does the distribution of its inhabitants. Densely populated humid eastern areas contrast with sparsely populated arid regions in the west. At one extreme is Harris County (containing Houston and most of its suburbs). Located in the southeastern part of the state, Harris has more than 3.6 million inhabitants. At the other extreme is Loving County, on the New Mexican border, where the 2005 census estimate counted only 52 people. Today, Texas's four most populous counties (Harris, Dallas, Bexar, and Tarrant) have a combined population of greater than 9 million, more than 40 percent of all

Texans. These four urban counties (along with Travis County) are located within the Texas Triangle, which is roughly outlined by segments of Interstate Highways 35, 45, and 10.

In the 1980s and 1990s, **population shifts** within Texas matched the national pattern: movement from rural to urban areas and from large cities to suburbs. Regions where the economy depended largely on oil and agriculture either decreased in total population or grew more slowly than the state as a whole. While the movement from rural to urban areas and growth of exurbs (extra-urban areas beyond suburbs) has continued into the twenty-first century, there has also been a repopulation of inner cities as cities such as Houston, Dallas, Fort Worth, and Austin have revitalized their downtowns and attracted new urban residents.

**Population Changes**   To provide today's public policymakers and businesspeople with demographic information that will allow them to plan for the future, state demographer Steven H. Murdock and his associates (now in the Institute for Demographic and Socioeconomic Research at the University of Texas at San Antonio) prepared alternative scenarios of population growth. According to Murdock, if the number of people migrating to Texas each year between 2000 and 2040 were offset by an equal number of people leaving, the state's population would still increase to over 26 million by 2040. If the rates of net migration from other countries and other states decreased to one half of those for 1990-2000, Texas would have nearly 35.8 million people by 2040. Finally, if the rates of net migration remained the same as those for 1990-2000, the figure for the year 2040 would be more than 45 million.

Murdock believes that the most likely scenario is the one that places Texas's population at 35.8 million people by 2040. Three justifications are given for this projected figure. First, the period from 1990 to 2000 was a period of expansive growth in the Texas economy. A general slowdown in the U.S. and Texas economies since 2000 is likely to slow population growth. Recovery will occur, but it is uncertain when this will happen. Second, the 2000 census count showed U.S. and Texas populations substantially larger than anticipated. Although the Census Bureau has not fully determined the reasons, it is likely that the 2000 count included some persons missed in 1990. Since migration measures classify such persons as 1990–2000 migrants, and the scenarios are based on 1990–2000 migration patterns, it is possible that migration rates are too high for some groups, for some periods, and for some counties. This suggests the use of a more moderate rate-of-growth scenario. Finally, although the scenarios use trends in births and deaths, they assume constant levels of migration. This assumption is used because of the lack of historical data to effectively study these rates over time. However, the overall direction of trends and differences among racial/ethnic groups seems likely to continue, suggesting the need for the use of a more moderate rate-of-growth scenario.[14]

**population shifts** Within Texas, changes in population density have featured demographic movements from rural to urban areas and from large cities to suburbs and back.

**Urbanization**    Migration of people from rural regions to cities results in **urbanization**. Urban areas are composed of one or more large cities and their surrounding suburban communities. A suburb is a relatively small town or city, usually outside the boundary limits of a central city. For a century after statehood, Texas remained primarily rural. Then came urbanization, which progressed at an accelerated rate. Whereas Texas was 80 percent rural at the beginning of the twentieth century, by 1970 it was 80 percent urban. Today, Texans living in metropolitan areas constitute more than 85 percent of the state's population. Suburbs adjoining or near central cities spread into rural areas and surrounding counties.

**Metropolitanization**    **Suburbanization** on a large scale creates a metropolitan area, a core city surrounded by a sprawl of smaller cities and towns. Like most states, Texas is experiencing suburbanization on a very large scale. Between 1980 and 2000, Texas suburbs experienced explosive growth. **Metropolitanization** concentrates large numbers of people in urban centers, which become linked in a single geographic entity. Though socially and economically integrated, a metropolitan area is composed of separate units of local government, which include counties, cities, and special districts.

Since 1910, federal agencies have defined metropolitan areas (MAs) for census purposes. In general, an MA is a core area containing a large population nucleus together with adjacent communities economically and socially integrated with that core. Standard definitions of metropolitan areas were first issued in 1949 by the then Bureau of the Budget (predecessor of the Office of Management and Budget), under the designation *standard metropolitan area* (SMA). In 1959, the term was changed to *standard metropolitan statistical area* (SMSA). The word *standard* was dropped and the term changed to *metropolitan statistical area* (MSA) in 1983. The collective term *metropolitan area* (MA) became effective in 1990. The term *core-based statistical area* (CBSA) became effective in 2000 and refers collectively to metropolitan and micropolitan statistical areas. Each CBSA must contain at least one urban area of 10,000 or more population. Effective June 6, 2003, the Office of Management and Budget established new sets of statistical areas. Today, criteria for these designations are as follows:

- **Micropolitan statistical area:** has at least one urban cluster with a population of at least 10,000, but less than 50,000
- **Metropolitan statistical area:** the basic unit, comprising a freestanding urbanized area with a total population of at least 50,000
- **Combined statistical area:** a geographic entity consisting of two or more adjacent core-based statistical areas (CBSAs)
- **Metropolitan division:** a county or group of counties within a CBSA that contains a core with a population of at least 2.5 million

By mid-2006, the United States (including Puerto Rico) had 582 micropolitan statistical areas (42 in Texas), 369 metropolitan statistical areas (27 in

**urbanization** Migration of people from rural areas to cities.

**suburbanization** Growth of relatively small towns and cities, usually incorporated but outside the corporate limits of a central city.

**metropolitanization** Concentration of people in urban centers that become linked.

**micropolitan statistical area** An area that has at least one urban cluster with a population of at least 10,000, but less than 50,000.

**metropolitan statistical area** A freestanding urban area with a minimum total population of 50,000.

**combined statistical area** A geographic entity consisting of two or more adjacent core-based statistical areas.

**metropolitan division** County or group of counties within a core based statistical area that contains a core with a population of at least 2.5 million.

Texas), 125 combined statistical areas (8 in Texas), and 29 metropolitan divisions (2 in Texas; one consisting of Dallas–Plano–Irving, and the other consisting of Fort Worth–Arlington).

Cities are eager to obtain the highest possible statistical designation because many congressional appropriations are made accordingly. For example, to qualify for mass transit funds, an area must be an MSA. The business community also uses data on population concentrations for market analysis and advertising.

Texas's rate of population growth is consistently greater in the MSAs than throughout the state as a whole. Most of these population concentrations are in the eastern part of the state and the Rio Grande Valley of South Texas. Texas's MSAs contain more than 80 percent of the state's population but less than 20 percent of the 254 counties. It is politically significant that these 48 counties potentially account for about four out of every five votes cast in statewide elections. Thus, governmental decision makers are answerable primarily to people living in one-fifth of the state's counties. The remaining four-fifths, constituting the bulk of the state's area, have one-fifth of the people. Urban voters, however, are rarely of one mind at the polls; they do not tend to overwhelm rural voters by taking opposing positions on all policy issues.

## Racial/Ethnic Groups

When answering questions on ethnicity and race for the 2000 census, 32 percent of all Texas respondents indicated that they were Hispanic or Latino (without identifying race), 1.1 percent claimed a heritage of two or more races, and 66.9 percent said they were neither Hispanic nor Latino and were of one race. Racial categories within the last group were as follows:

| | |
|---|---|
| White: | 52.4 percent |
| Black or African American: | 11.3 percent |
| Asian: | 2.7 percent |
| American Indian and Alaska Native: | 0.3 percent |
| Native Hawaiian and other Pacific Islander: | 0.1 percent |
| Some other race: | 0.1 percent |

In 1980, two-thirds of all Texans were called Anglos (that is, white people not identified as Hispanics or Latinos). By 2004, less than half of the Texas population could be classified as Anglo. By 2006, more than 60 percent of births in the state were minority births, with Latino births accounting for half of all newborn. Murdock projected the following population percentages for the year 2010 if the rates of net migration from other countries and other states decrease to one-half of those for 1980–1990: Anglo, 47.4; Hispanic, 37.3; African American, 11.3; and other (Asian and Native American), 4.0. In this scenario, Anglos would constitute the largest group; but they would be outnumbered by the combined total of other groups. In a similar scenario, Murdock projected the following population percentages for the year 2040:

Anglo, 32.2; Hispanic, 52.6; African American, 9.5; and other, 5.7. At this point, Hispanics would constitute a majority.[15]

**Anglos**    As commonly used in Texas, the term *Anglo* is not restricted to persons of Anglo-Saxon lineage. Traditionally, the term applies to all whites except Latinos. By 1800, Anglo settlements began to appear in East Texas. Before the Civil War, more than half of the state's Anglo residents had migrated from Alabama, Arkansas, Georgia, Kentucky, Louisiana, Mississippi, Missouri, and Tennessee.[16] Most remained in the eastern half of the state as farmers. Although the first non–Spanish-speaking immigrants to Texas were largely of English ancestry, some were of Scottish, Irish, or Welsh ancestry. Additional European settlers included French, Scandinavian, and Eastern European peoples, together with a scattering of Italians, Greeks, and others.

A significant number of German immigrants established settlements in the Hill Country west and north of San Antonio before the Civil War. It has been estimated that as many as 24,000 German immigrants and descendants were settled in the Hill Country by 1860. Most opposed slavery on principle, while others simply had no need for slaves. As a result, 14 counties in Central Texas voted 40 percent or higher against secession in 1861. The area was scarred by what a historian called "a civil war within a Civil War,"[17] as hundreds of Union and Confederate sympathizers were killed in armed confrontations. Although Anglo migration into the state declined during the Civil War and Reconstruction, it resumed by the 1870s. By the turn of the twentieth century, the largest migration came from the border states, the Northeast, and the Midwest.

According to the 2000 census, more than 52 percent of Texas's population is composed of "non–Hispanic whites." However, according to census estimates, when that percentage dropped to slightly less than 50 percent in 2004, Texas joined Hawaii, New Mexico, California and the District of Columbia as a majority-minority state. Population projections show that the percentage of Anglos in the state will decline and the percentage of other racial/ethnic groups will increase.

**Latinos**    Until 1836, Texas history was part of the history of Spain and Mexico. From 1836, when Texas acquired independence from Mexico, until 1900, immigration from Mexico all but ceased. **Latinos** remained concentrated in settlements such as Goliad, Laredo, and San Antonio, founded during the eighteenth century. However, most of the Latino population was located within the regions of Central and South Texas. In South Texas, they composed a majority of the population despite the increased number of Anglo arrivals after the Mexican War of 1846–1848 (which followed admission of Texas into the Union). In the years after the Civil War, Latinos moved west, migrating along with Anglo settlers to displace Native Americans from their lands and to convert the prairies into cattle and sheep ranches.

Early in the twentieth century, the rise of commercial agriculture created the need for seasonal laborers. Consequently, many Latinos picked cotton,

**Anglo**  A term commonly used in Texas to identify non–Latino white people.

**Latino**  This is an ethnic classification of Mexican Americans and others of Latin American origin. When applied to females, the term is *Latina*.

fruits, and vegetables. Others found work as day laborers or used their skills as ranch hands or shepherds. Although Texas became more urbanized following World War I, Latinos remained mostly an agrarian people. After World War II, however, increased numbers of Latinos left agricultural work and sought employment opportunities in the industrializing cities. Most of them experienced improvements in wages and working conditions in unskilled or semiskilled positions, though a growing number of Latinos entered managerial, sales, and clerical professions.[18] In the second half of the twentieth century, Texas's Latino population was enlarged by a relatively high birth rate and a surge of both legal and illegal immigration from Mexico and other countries in the Western Hemisphere. In the 1980s, Texas's Latino population became more diverse in terms of country of origin following an increase in immigrants from Central America, South America, and the islands of the Caribbean.

By 2005, Texas Latinos numbered about 7.8 million, slightly more than one-third of the state's population. More than 76 percent of Texas Latinos are of Mexican origin. Texas ranks second in the nation in the number of Latino residents; only California, with about 12.5 million in 2005, has more. In 24 Texas counties, more than 61 percent of the population is Latino. Texas's Spanish-surnamed citizens are gaining economic strength. Latinos typically have larger families and are younger than the Anglo population. Immigration from Mexico and other Spanish-speaking countries is expected to continue throughout the twenty-first century. Latino political influence is also increasing. Between 1846 and 1961, only nineteen Latino politicians were elected to seats in the Texas Legislature. However, since 1961, Latinos have won elections to local, statewide, and national positions. In 1984, with the election of Raul Gonzalez to the Texas Supreme Court, the first Latino won a statewide office. By 2006, Texas had more than 2,200 Latino elected officials, the largest number of any state in the United States. This figure represents approximately 40 percent of all Latino elected officials in the country. Organizations such as the League of United Latin American Citizens (LULAC) and the Southwest Voter Registration Education Project have worked to increase voter registration and turnout among Latinos in recent years. In November 2006, six Latinos were elected to the U.S. House of Representatives, while 37 were elected to the Texas Legislature: 6 senators and 31 representatives.

**African Americans**   The first **African Americans** entered Texas as slaves of Spanish explorers in the sixteenth century. By 1792, it was reported that Spanish Texans included thirty-four blacks and 414 mulattos.[19] Some of them were free men and women. About the time slavery was abolished in Mexico, Anglo settlers brought larger numbers of black slaves from the United States to Texas. In addition, a few free African Americans came from northern states before the Civil War. By 1847, African Americans accounted for one-fourth of the state's population. During Reconstruction, there was a small wave of freemen migration into Texas. Many African Americans also moved from the state's rural areas to large cities. They often resided in "freedmantowns" that

**African American** A racial classification indicating African ancestry.

became the distinct black neighborhoods on the outskirts of these cities. Some of these freedmantowns have been preserved by various historical associations. Black labor also contributed substantially to the economic development of Texas cities and helped the state's transition from its agrarian roots to an increasingly industrialized society. In 1880, the African American population in Texas numbered about 400,000.

By 2005, Texas had 2.5 million African Americans, more than 11 percent of the state's population. Although the African American population has continued to grow, it is at a much slower rate than other ethnic groups. Today, Texas has the third largest number of African Americans in the nation after New York and California. Most are located in southeast, north central, and northeast Texas, concentrated in large cities. In recent years, a significant number of Africans have immigrated to the United States and settled in Texas. Their search for employment and their desire for a higher standard of living have prompted this migration. More than half of the state's African Americans reside in and around Houston (approximately 650,000), Dallas (464,000), Fort Worth (213,000), San Antonio (107,000), and Beaumont (86,000) in Jefferson County. Although African Americans do not constitute a majority in any Texas county, according to 2005 census estimates, Jefferson County has the largest percentage of African Americans, 34.4 percent.

Like Latinos, as the African American population in Texas increased, so did its political influence. From the years following Reconstruction until 1958 (when Hattie White was elected to the Houston Independent School District Board of Trustees), no African American had held elective office in the state. In 1972 Barbara Jordan became the first African American since Reconstruction to represent Texas in Congress, and in 1992 Morris Overstreet became the first African American to win a statewide office when he was elected to the Texas Court of Criminal Appeals. Although his bid was ultimately unsuccessful, Ron Kirk became the first African American Texan to be nominated by a major party (Democratic) for a U.S. Senate seat in 2002. Today African American Texans hold local, statewide, and national offices. Three African Americans, Al Green (D-Houston), Eddie Bernice Johnson (D-Dallas), and Sheila Jackson Lee (D-Houston), were re-elected to the U.S. House of Representatives in November 2006, and 16 African Americans were elected to the Texas Legislature: 2 in the Senate and 14 in the House of Representatives.

**Asian Americans**  Few members of Texas's three largest ethnic populations (Anglo, Latino, and African American) are aware that the Lone Star State is home to one of the largest **Asian American** populations in the nation; approximately 800,000. Most of Texas's Asian American families have immigrated to the United States from Southeast Asia (Cambodia, Laos, and Vietnam in particular), but a growing percentage are American born. Compared with Latinos and African Americans, however, Asian Americans are newcomers to Texas. When

**Asian American**  A term used to identify people of Asian ancestry (e.g., Chinese, Japanese, Korean).

*State Representative Hubert Vo (D-Houston) at his desk in the Texas House of Representatives (AP-Wide World Photos)*

Vietnamese-born Hubert Vo (D-Houston) defeated 11-term incumbent representative Talmadge Heflin (R-Houston) in the 2004 general election, he became the first Vietnamese American to be elected to the Texas House of Representatives. He joined Martha Wong (R-Houston) as the two representatives of Asian ancestry in the Texas Legislature. While Vo was re-elected, Wong lost her bid for re-election in November to Democrat Ellen Cohen.

Most Asian Americans live in the state's largest urban centers, Houston and the Dallas–Fort Worth Metroplex. The 2000 Census placed two Texas counties among the top fifty in the nation with the highest concentration of Asian Americans by percentage: Fort Bend, with 39,706 Asian Americans (11.2 percent of the population) ranks 22nd, and Collin, with 34,047 (6.9 percent) ranks 43rd. Although many are unskilled laborers, about half of Texas's first-generation Asian Americans entered this country with college degrees or completed degrees later. The intensity with which the state's young Asian Americans focus on education is revealed by enrollment data for the University of Texas at Austin. Although Asian Americans account for less than 3 percent of the total population of the state, they comprised 14.3 percent of the enrollment at the University of Texas at Austin and 17.5 percent of the enrollment at the University of Texas at Dallas in the fall 2005 semester.

**Native Americans**    The Lone Star State owes part of its cultural heritage to **Native Americans**, who were called *indios* by Spanish explorers and American Indians by Anglo settlers. Today, relatively few Texans are identified as Native Americans, but some counties (Cherokee, Comanche, Nacogdoches, Panola, Wichita), cities and towns (Caddo Mills, Lipan, Nocona, Quanah, Watauga, Waxahachie), and other places have names that remind us that Native Americans were here first. In fact, the state's name comes from the word *tejas,* meaning "friendly," which was also the tribal name for a group of Indians within the Caddo Confederacy.

Before 1900, members of more than 50 Native American tribes or nations roamed the prairies or had permanent settlements within the territory that became Texas. The Comanches, who displaced the Lipan Apaches, were the most important tribe in shaping Texas history. Excellent horsemen, they were an obstacle to the northward expansion of Spaniards and the westward expansion of Anglos. By contrast, the Tonkawa were a peaceful tribe who lived in Central Texas and often allied with the Anglos against the Comanches and the Wichitas, another important South Plains tribe. In East Texas, the Caddo lived in organized villages that had a complex and sophisticated political system.

Estimates of the number of Native Americans in Texas when the first Spaniards arrived range from 30,000 to 150,000. Traveling in the Lone Star State in 1856, after three decades of Anglo-Indian warfare, one observer estimated the state's Native American population at about 12,000.[20] By 2005, Texas's Native Americans numbered less than 70,000. Most reside in towns and cities, where they work in a variety of jobs and professions.

Only a few Native Americans live on Texas reservations. About 1,000 members of the Alabama and Coushatta tribes reside on a 4,351-acre reservation in Polk County in the Big Thicket region of East Texas. Far across the state, near Eagle Pass on the United States–Mexican border, live a few hundred members of another Indian group, the Kickapoo tribe. The governments of Mexico and the United States allow them to move back and forth between Texas and the Mexican state of Coahuila. A third Native American group, the 1,400-member Tigua tribe, inhabits a 100-acre reservation near El Paso.

---

**Learning Check 1.3**        **(Answers on p. 39)**

1. Which four counties have a combined population of more than 40 percent of the state's population?
2. True or False: The fastest growing ethnic group in Texas is Latinos.

---

**Native American**  A descendent of the first Americans, who were called *indios* by Spanish explores and Indians by Anglo settlers who arrived later.

# ⭐ Searching for New Economic Directions

Once identified in the popular mind with cattle barons, cotton kings, and oil millionaires, the image of the Lone Star State is changing. Because the petroleum industry is not expected to regain its former leading role in Texas business, restructuring the state's economy has been vigorously pursued since the 1980s.

In so doing, business and government leaders have launched new industrial programs within the context of rapid national and international change. Today, Texas is part of middle-class America, with its share of professionals and businesspeople employed by varied enterprises: law firms; universities; federal, state, and local government bureaucracies; real estate and insurance companies; wholesale and retail sales firms; and manufacturing, communication, and transportation industries. However, a continuing struggle to provide jobs and market goods and services requires effective public policies, an educated and productive labor force, an adequate supply of capital, and sound management practices.

For more than a half century, petroleum production and related enterprises led Texas's industrial development. Then, devastated by plunging oil prices in the mid-1980s, the entire Texas petroleum industry declined sharply. Even by the 1990s, with the price of oil on the rebound, Texans understood the danger of being overly reliant on one industry and recognized the need to develop an economically diverse economy. New industries have quickly spread across the state, affecting the Texas economy and now playing an important role in the national economy. In 2006, for the first time, Texas had more *Fortune* 500 companies than any other state. In *Fortune*'s 2006 listing of the 500 largest private corporations in the United States, 56 were headquartered in Texas cities. New York was second with 55 and California was third with 52. Among the 20 cities having 5 or more of the *Fortune* 500 corporations, New York City led with 41, Houston was second with 23 and Dallas was fourth with 11.[21]

### Energy

A natural offspring of the state's expansive oil and gas industries, the four largest private corporations in Texas, as identified in *Fortune*'s 2006 listing, were energy and energy related. Two of these corporations, Exxon-Mobil (second) and ConocoPhillips (sixth) were among the six largest corporations in the United States.

Another energy-related corporation headquartered in Texas, the Enron Corporation, consistently placed high on the *Fortune* list throughout the 1990s. Headquartered in Houston and founded in 1985 when Houston Natural Gas merged with Inter-North, based in Omaha, Nebraska, Enron provided the first nationwide natural gas pipeline system. During the 1990s, Enron moved into commodities trading, starting with natural gas and expanding into electricity, and ultimately becoming the world's largest trader in electricity.

That success ended abruptly when the corporation declared bankruptcy in December 2001.[22] Through a variety of accounting tricks (with the assistance of accounting firm Arthur Anderson), undisclosed partnerships, and the formation of limited-liability companies, Enron had reported inflated profits and reduced debt. Managers misled their employees, investors, and the general public regarding the company's financial condition. After declaring bankruptcy in

2001, Enron's stock plummeted from almost $80 to less than $1 per share. Investors lost billions of dollars. Thousands of employees lost their jobs and their retirements, while Enron executives reaped multimillions through undisclosed partnerships and by selling off stock before the collapse. It was one of the largest bankruptcies in U.S. history.

By 2006, 16 top Enron officials had pled guilty and another 5 were found guilty by juries of charges including securities fraud; conspiracy to commit wire fraud; insider trading; and conspiracy to falsify books, records, and accounts. In 2006, former CEO and founder Ken Lay and former CEO Jeff Skilling stood trial for their involvement in the scandal. A jury found Lay guilty of one count of conspiracy, three counts of securities fraud, and two counts of wire fraud. In a separate bench trial, a district judge convicted Lay on three counts of making false statements to banks and one count of bank fraud. However, before his appeal could be heard, Lay died of a heart attack. Skilling was convicted on 19 counts against him, including conspiracy, insider trading, making false statements to auditors, and securities fraud.

### High Technology

The term *high technology* applies to research, development, manufacturing, and marketing of a seemingly endless line of electronic products. Among these are computers, calculators, digital watches, microwave ovens, telecommunications devices, automatic bank tellers, aerospace guidance systems, medical instruments, and assembly-line robots. Although high-technology businesses employ less than 6 percent of Texas's labor force, these enterprises contribute about 10 percent of all wages paid to private-sector employees. Most "high-tech" jobs are in manufacturing. Approximately 85 percent of all high-tech employment in Texas is centered in Austin, Dallas, El Paso, Fort Worth, Houston, and San Antonio. Major high-tech manufacturers include Motorola, Dell Computer, Hewlett-Packard, Texas Instruments, and Applied Materials (which produces machinery for manufacturing semiconductors).

The occupational structure of many high-tech companies differs from those of most other industrial firms. High-tech enterprises employ larger percentages of professional, technical, and managerial personnel. More than one-third of all high-tech jobs are in these categories, and wages and salaries are well above average. Reports of the American Electronic Association show that Texas has continued to rank second only to California in the size of its high-tech workforce. By 2006, more than 465,000 Texans held high-tech jobs paying nearly twice as much as the average for other private-sector positions. At the request of Governor Rick Perry and other leaders in government and business, the 79th Texas Legislature in 2005 created the Texas Emerging Technology Fund, providing $200 million for research and development activities in emerging technology industries. The Texas Emerging Technology Fund is designed to expand the state's high-tech industry, encourage relocation of high-tech companies from other states (especially California), and challenge

**high technology**
Technology that applies to research, development, manufacturing, and marketing of computers and other electronic products.

Texas's community colleges and universities to educate more students for high-tech careers.

## Biotechnology

The history of biotechnology dates back more than 6,000 years, when the Egyptians began using yeast to leaven bread, brew beer, produce wine, and make cheese. Today biotechnology ("biotech") exerts a growing influence on the state's economy. This multibillion-dollar industry produces many new medicines and vaccines, exotic chemicals, and other products designed to benefit medical science, human health, and agricultural production. In the past two decades, biotech-related jobs have increased four times faster than the overall increase in employment in Texas. The Lone Star State employs more than 56,000 workers in this industry.

In 1999, a Summit on Biotechnology for Agriculture, Food, Fiber, and Health convened in Austin to develop a strategic plan that would make Texas a national leader in agricultural biotechnology and allied technologies. Texas A&M University has become a recognized national leader in the biotechnology revolution in agriculture and hosts an annual conference for biotechnology educators each fall. Supported by Monsanto and other biotech companies, scientists at Texas A&M University have played an important role in research leading to production of genetically modified organism (GMO) crops, such as corn, soybeans, and cotton. However, Greenpeace and other environmental groups have opposed the marketing of gene-altered products without long-term safety tests and have called for labeling of all foods containing GMOs.[23]

## Services

One of the fastest-growing economic sectors in Texas is the service industry. Employing one-fourth of all Texas workers, this sector continues to provide new jobs more rapidly than all other sectors. Service businesses include health-care providers (hospitals and nursing homes); personal services (hotels, restaurants, and recreational enterprises such as bowling alleys and video arcades); and commercial services (printers, advertising agencies, data processing companies, equipment rental companies, and management consultants). Other service providers include education, investment brokers, insurance and real estate agencies, banks and credit unions, and numerous merchandising enterprises.

Influenced by an aging population, the availability and use of new medical procedures, and the rapidly increasing cost of prescription drugs and other medical services, health services employment has steadily risen. In 2005, education and health services created more than 33,200 jobs in the state, with an annual growth rate of 2.9 percent.

Most service jobs pay lower wages and salaries than employment in manufacturing firms that produce goods. Thus, journalist Molly Ivins warns, "the dream that we can transform ourselves into a service economy and let all the widget-makers go to hell or Taiwan is bullstuff. The service sector creates jobs all right, but they're the lowest paying jobs in the system. You can't afford a house frying burgers at McDonald's, even if you're a two-fryer family."[24]

### Agriculture

Endowed with a wide range of climates, hundreds of thousands of acres of arable land, and adequate transportation and harbor facilities, Texas's farmers and ranchers are well equipped to produce and market huge amounts of food and fiber. Today, Texas ranks second in the nation in agricultural production. It leads the country in total acreage of agricultural land and numbers of farms and ranches, as well as in production of beef, grain sorghum, cotton, wool, and mohair (from Angora goats).

Gross income from the products of Texas agriculture amounts to more than $14 billion annually, making agriculture the second largest industry in Texas. The estimated value of agricultural assets in the state (such as land, buildings, livestock, and machinery) is more than $80 billion. The nation's second largest exporter of agricultural products (behind California), the Lone Star State leads the country in exported cotton, much of which goes to Korea and Taiwan. Mexico is the largest buyer of Texas's farm and ranch products, and Japan is a major consumer of Texas-grown wheat and corn. Beef is the state's most important meat export.

Despite these impressive statistics, farming and ranching provide less than 2 percent of the state's jobs and total income. Furthermore, most agricultural commodities are shipped abroad or to other parts of the United States without being processed in Texas by Texans. Consequently, Texas needs industrial development for processing food and fiber to derive maximum economic benefit from the products of its farms and ranches.

The number and size of Texas farms and ranches have changed greatly over the past eight decades. These developments largely reflect the availability of laborsaving farm machinery and the use of chemicals to kill weeds, defoliate cotton before harvesting, and protect crops from insects and diseases. In the 1930s Texas had more than 500,000 farms and ranches, with an average size of 300 acres. By 2006, the number of farms and ranches had dropped to about 230,000, and the average size had grown to approximately 564 acres.[25]

Most small farms are operated by part-time farmers, many of whom can farm only because a spouse has nonfarm employment. Although agribusiness adds more than $80 billion to the Texas economy each year, the combined net annual income of all Texas farmers is under $3.1 billion. A large majority net less than $20,000 per year after production costs. When farm commodity prices are low (because of overproduction and weak market demand) or crops are poor (sometimes as a result of too much rain but usually because of drought), many farmers end the year deeply in debt. Some are forced to sell their land—usually to larger farm operators and sometimes to corporations. But some rich corporate executives, professional people, and politicians purchase agricultural property (especially ranchland) because such ownership is a status symbol they can afford—even though their land provides little or no income. Some use their agricultural property ownership to qualify for various exemptions and reductions for state or local sales and property taxes and for federal income tax deductions. Economic pressures cause loss of much farm and ranchland near expanding cities to urban sprawl. According to the U.S. Department of Agriculture, every minute, a half acre of Texas farmland is converted into part of a road, shopping mall, or subdivision.

## Trade

In 1993, the U.S. Congress approved the **North American Free Trade Agreement (NAFTA)**, to which the United States, Canada, and Mexico are parties. By reducing and then eliminating tariffs over a 15-year period, the agreement has stimulated U.S. trade with both Canada and Mexico. Because more than 60 percent of U.S. exports to Mexico are produced in Texas or transported through the Lone Star State from other states, an expanding foreign trade produces more jobs for Texans, more profits for the state's businesses, and more revenue for state and local governments.

**Maquiladoras** (partner plants) on the Mexican side of the border typically use cheap labor to assemble imported parts for a wide range of consumer goods (for example, computers and television sets) and then export these goods back to the United States. Only the value added in Mexico is subject to U.S. import taxes. Consequently, Texas border cities (especially Brownsville, McAllen, Laredo, and El Paso) attract many manufacturers who set up supply and distribution facilities in Texas that serve the maquiladoras in Mexico.[26] A report made by the director of the United Nations Development Fund for Women revealed that labor policies at maquiladora assembly plants, including late shifts and turning away employees for tardiness, endanger women in Ciudad Juarez, a Mexican city across the border from El Paso, where hundreds of women and girls have disappeared or have been raped and murdered in recent years.[27]

NAFTA is not without its critics. Texas's garment industry has been adversely affected, especially in border counties. Most clothing manufacturers have closed their plants and moved to Mexico, Central America, the Caribbean islands, or Asia. Likewise, some Texas fruit and vegetable producers have been hurt by Mexican competition. Increased trucking on highways between Mexico and Canada has contributed to air pollution in Texas and causes serious traffic problems that make travel more dangerous for all drivers and passengers and slows transportation of goods.

Since 1995, a succession of political and economic crises in Mexico has raised serious questions concerning the future of NAFTA. In fact, the survival of Mexico's political system has been jeopardized by assassinations of public figures, kidnappings of wealthy businesspeople, drug-related corruption of government officials, attacks on tourists, widespread unemployment and hunger in both urban and rural areas, and acts of armed rebellion (especially in the southern states of Chiapas, Oaxaca, and Guerrero).[28]

**North American Free Trade Agreement (NAFTA)** An agreement among the United States, Mexico, and Canada designed to expand trade among the three countries by reducing and then eliminating tariffs over a 15-year period.

**maquiladora** An assembly plant that uses cheap labor and is located on the Mexican side of the U.S.–Mexican border.

The election of President Vincente Fox in 2000 raised hopes for expanding political democracy, reducing poverty, and suppressing crime and corruption in Mexico.[29] After dominating Mexican politics for 71 years, the Institutional Revolutionary Party (PRI) lost the presidency to Fox and his National Action Party (PAN). Fox's victory demonstrated Mexico's capacity for peaceful political change, but his country's serious economic and social problems were not easily solved. By the end of his six-year term, President Fox had experienced only limited economic success. Slow growth of the Mexican economy has led more Mexican citizens to migrate. Late in 2005, it was reported that the Mexican economy lost 180,000 jobs between 2001 and 2005, forcing many Mexican citizens to leave Mexico for job opportunities available in Texas and other border states. A more prosperous and stable Mexico would help reduce the flow of jobless workers to Texas and other parts of the United States, while increasing the volume of trade between the two countries.[30] In July 2006, Mexico's voters selected PAN candidate Felipe Calderón to succeed Fox.

---

**Learning Check 1.4**　　　**(Answers on p. 39)**

1. True or False: The four largest private corporations in Texas are in the high technology industry.
2. What is the term for "partner plants" on the Mexican side of the border that use cheap labor to assemble imported parts for a wide variety of consumer goods and then export these goods back to the United States?

---

## ★Meeting New Challenges: Social and Economic Policy Issues

As we continue to move deeper into the twenty-first century, Texans are greatly affected by public policy decisions concerning the state's economy and its entire social order. The most important of these decisions relate to immigration and Texas's workforce, protection of the ecological system, job-creating economic development, technological changes in communications and industry, and restructuring and financing of public schools and institutions of higher education in the state.[31]

Social and economic influences on government, politics, and policymaking have been recognized since the days of ancient Greece. In recent years, Texas has experienced a wave of uncontrolled immigration and rapid economic change. Both of these developments pose problems for policymakers.

### Immigration: Federal and State Problems

Since Texas became part of the Union, the meandering Rio Grande boundary with Mexico has been the source of many controversies. Controlling the flow of aliens across the river, deciding how long they may remain within U.S. territory, determining what labor (if any) they may perform, and other immigration policy matters are issues that affect state, national, and international politics. Persons who enter the United States in violation of federal immigration laws are called **undocumented aliens**. Although they supply Texas employers with cheap labor, some compete with U.S. citizens for jobs and require costly social services for themselves or for their children who come into this country or are born here. As with immigration issues involving other racial and ethnic groups today and in earlier periods of American history, passions and prejudices produce explosive politics.

In response to heavy political pressure and 14 years of debate and political maneuvering, the U.S. Congress enacted into law the Immigration Reform and Control Act of 1986. This federal statute was designed to restrain the flow of illegal immigrants into the United States by penalizing employers who knowingly hire undocumented aliens and by appropriating funds to provide more enforcement personnel for the U.S. Immigration and Naturalization Service (INS), especially border patrol officers, whom Latinos refer to as *la migra*. Despite this act, hundreds of thousands of undocumented aliens continue to enter Texas each year. Many are arrested, detained, and subsequently expelled from the country. Others voluntarily return to Mexico and other countries after earning money to support their families. However, many thousands of undocumented aliens remain in Texas and often arrange for family members to join them. Some undocumented aliens are shamelessly exploited by employers, merchants, and landlords. Others receive fair wages and humane treatment. All, however, live and work in fear of arrest and deportation.

In the 1990s, an anti-immigration groundswell developed throughout most parts of the United States. Central to the controversy was the issue of costs and benefits resulting from both legal and illegal immigration. In 1994, Texas joined other states in suing the federal government to recover various costs (for example, health, welfare, education, and law enforcement) incurred from illegal immigration. Meanwhile, immigration issues continued to attract the attention of social scientists, special-interest groups, politicians, the general public, and policymaking officials at all levels of government in Texas and throughout the country.

With the approach of congressional and presidential elections in 1996, the matter of undocumented aliens became a "hot-button" issue that some politicians exploited. Before the November election, the U.S. Congress enacted the Immigration Control and Financial Responsibility Act of 1996, which was cosponsored by Representative Lamar Smith, a Republican from San Antonio. In addition to increasing the number of border patrol officers, the law increased penalties for immigrant smuggling and sped up the deportation of illegal immigrants who used false documents or committed other crimes while in the United States.

In the wake of the terrorist attacks of September 11, 2001, the United States Congress passed the Enhanced Border Security and Visa Entry Reform Act of 2002, which President George W. Bush signed into law. The act concerns tracking international students accepted by educational institutions, the issuance of visas, and other details regarding foreign nationals. It authorizes an additional 200 inspectors and 200 investigators for the Immigration and

**undocumented alien** A person who enters the United States in violation of federal immigration laws.

*As many as half a million people march through downtown Dallas for the rights of illegal immigrants.* (Smiley N. Pool/©2006 The Dallas Morning News)

Naturalization Service in each of the fiscal years 2003 through 2006. In addition, the act increases the pay and training of INS personnel, including border patrol agents. The act also provides an additional $150 million for improved border control technology, provides for creation of electronically maintained visa files available to immigration inspectors, and requires the INS to integrate all of its data systems into one system. In June 2003, INS was folded into the U.S. Department of Homeland Security's new Bureau of Immigration and Customs Enforcement. (For a detailed study of the role of the states in immigration enforcement, see Selected Reading 1.1, "The Role of States in Immigration Enforcement.")

Despite legal obstacles to immigration, low wages and widespread unemployment in Mexico motivate masses of Mexican workers to cross the border in search of jobs. At the same time, many businesspeople, farmers, and ranchers in Texas and elsewhere are willing to violate U.S. law (and run the risk of incurring fines) by hiring undocumented aliens. They do so because other labor is unavailable or because illegal immigrants will work harder for lower wages.

Texas (and national) politicians often face the difficult task of balancing constituents' demands for increased border security against the demands of a growing Latino constituency pushing for immigration reforms. In 2004, President Bush proposed a plan to restructure America's immigration laws and allow more than 8 million illegal immigrants to obtain legal status as temporary workers. Many political observers saw the plan as an attempt to appeal to a growing Latino voter base, and it faced harsh criticism from members of Bush's party, stalling for months without enactment. Then, in late March of 2006, the debate heated up again as President Bush, President Fox, and Canadian Prime Minister Stephen Harper held a two-day summit in Cancun, Mexico, to discuss North American border security. As Congress prepared to consider new legislation addressing undocumented immigrants, hundreds of thousands of Mexicans and Americans held protests calling for immigration reform, hundreds of Texas high school students walked out of classes, and partisan differences over this issue intensified. By the end of 2006, Congress has adjourned without passing any meaningful immigration reform.

## Water

With the state's population expected to double by the middle of the twenty-first century, Texas faces a formidable challenge in meeting the water needs of its citizens. The state's current dependable water supply will meet only about 70 percent of projected demand by the year 2050. As the population continues to shift from rural to urban areas, and with the migration of people from other states to Texas cities, urban demands will increasingly compete with rural communities and agricultural interests for the same water. To meet this challenge and to provide necessary flows of water for maintaining the environment, Texas will need to rely on water conservation and alternative water management strategies.[32]

After a devastating drought in the 1950s, the Texas Legislature created the **Texas Water Development Board (TWDB)** in 1957 and mandated statewide water planning. Since then, the TWDB and the Texas Board of Water Engineers have prepared and adopted seven state water plans, including *Water for Texas— 2002*. This plan differs from previous plans in that its development involved public participation (nearly 900 public meetings were held across the state) at each step in the process, and local and regional input contributed to decisions to produce 16 regional water plans to form the basis of the State Water Plan. *Water for Texas—2002* makes several recommendations for development, management, and conservation of water resources and for preparation and response to drought conditions so that sufficient water may be available for the foreseeable future.[33]

**Texas Water Development Board (TWDB)** A board that conducts statewide water planning as mandated by state law.

# ▶ POINT/COUNTERPOINT ◀

## Recognition of the *Matricula Consular* by the State of Texas

**THE ISSUE**    The 11 Mexican consular offices in Texas issue the *matricula consular* (consular registration) to Mexican nationals—both undocumented and legal—living in the state. Many U.S. banks accept this photo identification card for the purpose of opening an account; and, at the beginning of 2004, 13 state governments recognized it as valid identification. Although the governments of 18 Texas cities and 6 counties recognize the *matricula consular*, in 2003 the 78th Legislature rejected proposals that would have required the Texas Department of Public Safety to accept it as proof of identity for a driver's license.

### Arguments for Recognition

1. *Identification.* The *matricula consular* would help state officials and agencies determine the identity and residence of holders who are now unidentifiable.

2. *Public Safety.* Law enforcement officers could more easily identify card-bearing crime suspects, witnesses, and victims.

3. *Immigration.* Neither a *matricula consular* nor a driver's license, which is required for obtaining auto insurance, is proof of U.S. citizenship or legal residency; so undocumented aliens with these ID cards could still be arrested and deported.

### Arguments Against Recognition

1. *Identification.* The *matricula consular* is too susceptible to fraud, and we have no central database for tracking recipients of these cards.

2. *Public Safety.* Homeland security would be compromised by ID cards that criminals and terrorists could use to move around the state and engage in financial transactions to support their activities.

3. *Immigration.* State recognition of the *matricula consular* would encourage illegal immigration and give cardholders a quasi-legal status that would hinder enforcement of U.S. immigration laws.

This Point/Counterpoint is based on Kellie Dworaczyk, "Should Texas Recognize Mexican-Issued Identity Cards Held by Immigrants?" *Interim News* No. 78-20 (Austin: House Research Organization, Texas House of Representatives, 20 January 2004), 1–6.

## Environmental Protection

Poor air quality and impure water are causing many Texans serious health problems. Some effects of environmental pollution are revealed in observations concerning fish and wildlife populations. For example, Texas (along with California, Hawaii, and Florida) leads all other states in the number of endangered fish and wildlife species.

Bordered by Florida, Alabama, Mississippi, Louisiana, and Texas, the Gulf of Mexico covers nearly 700,000 square miles, or seven times as much area as the Great Lakes. Industries in each of these states and Mexico release toxic chemicals directly into the gulf or into rivers that flow into it. Also contributing greatly to the gulf's environmental problems is the continuing flow of nitrate-laden rivers that draw their water from the chemically fertilized farms

**Texas ranks**

- #1 in toxic and hazardous waste
- #1 in toxic manufacturing emissions
- #1 in cancerous manufacturing emissions
- #1 in toxic air emissions
- #1 in cancerous air emissions
- #1 in carbon dioxide emissions
- #1 in "hazardous air pollutants" emissions
- #1 in toxic water emissions
- #1 in clean water permit violations
- #1 in number of environmental rights complaints

**Yet only**

- #18 in per capita spending on air quality
- #38 in water-quality planning
- #46 in per capita spending on environmental protection of open spaces
- #49 in per capita spending on water quality

*Source:* Texans for Public Justice and *Texas Monthly,* "Where We Rank," May 2005.

**Points to Ponder**

of rural areas and the lawns and gardens of cities large and small. With declining catches of fish, shrimp, and oysters from gulf waters, Texans must do with less seafood or import it from abroad at high prices. Of course, an obvious solution to the problem would be environmental protection measures designed to clean up the Gulf of Mexico and restore its productivity.[34]

### Education and Economic Development

Along with a poor record of environmental protection, Texas gets low marks in other critical areas that affect its residents' quality of life and economic welfare. More well-paying jobs, along with rising productivity, depend largely on a well-educated Texas workforce. Teachers are the key element in any educational system, but from year to year the Lone Star State confronts shortages of certified personnel to instruct its 4 million elementary and secondary school students. Included within this total are more than a half million students with limited English proficiency.

Although estimates of the teacher shortage vary, the Texas Education Agency reports that about one-fifth of the state's 250,000 teachers quit teaching each year. Some retire, but most of them abandon their profession for reasons that include inadequate pay and benefits, low prestige, and time-consuming chores such as grading that often must be done at night and on weekends. Contributing to their decision to seek other careers is stress over student performance on standardized tests and classroom problems affected by the poverty and troubled home life of many students. A Sam Houston State University study showing that 28 percent of Texas teachers surveyed were "moonlighting" or working after school hours and on weekends in other jobs indicated educators' own struggles with economic problems.[35] Although the public tends to overlook the needs of teachers, many Texans complain about students' high dropout rates, low levels of academic achievement, and inadequate preparation for work or college.

Success in dealing with educational needs will be especially important in determining Texas's ability to compete nationally and internationally in business as well as in science and technology. The urgency of this matter is suggested in studies that rank Texas near the bottom of the nation in the literacy of its residents. Employers are particularly concerned that one out of every three Texans cannot read and write well enough to fill out a simple job application. Moreover, the state loses many billions of dollars annually because most illiterate Texans are doomed to unemployment or low-paying jobs and thus generate little or no tax revenue.

### Poverty and Social Problems

Although many of America's public figures stress the importance of family values, serious social and economic problems affect homes throughout the country. The Lone Star State has alarming numbers of children living in poverty and in single-parent homes, births to unwed teenagers, juvenile arrests, and violent acts committed by teenagers and preadolescents. More than one of every five Texas children lives in poverty, and many children at all levels of society suffer from abuse and neglect. Estimates of the number of homeless people (including many children) vary widely, but at least 100,000—and perhaps more than 200,000—Texans cannot provide themselves with shelter in a house or apartment. In 2006, more than one-third of Texas workers were earning less than $20,000 a year, which was below the federal poverty level for food stamps for a family of four.

Texas's limited response to its peoples' social and economic needs continues to excite debate. Some Texans argue that any public assistance for the poor is too much. They believe government assistance encourages dependence and discourages self-reliance, personal initiative, and desire to work. Other Texans advocate greatly increased government spending to help people unable to care for themselves and their families because of mental or physical health problems, lack of job opportunities, or age. Between these extremes are Texans who support a limited role for government in meeting human needs but call for churches and other nongovernmental organizations to play a more active role in dealing with social problems. Texas voters, however, tend to support candidates for public office who promise lower taxes, tighter government budgets, fewer public employees, and reduction or elimination of social services. As a result, the Lone Star State continues to rank near the bottom of the 50 states in governmental responses to poverty and social problems.

**Learning Check 1.5**    (Answers on p. 39)

1. True or False: The Immigration Reform and Control Act of 1986 has been effective at controlling undocumented aliens.
2. True or False: More than one-third of Texas workers are earning below the federal poverty level.

## ⭐ Looking Ahead

As the process of economic development and diversification goes forward in Texas, some of the state's cherished values are being sorely tried. Many jobs are lost as others are created, and old industries decline or die as new ones are established. Meanwhile, the lives of all Texans are affected—some for better and others for worse. Critical environmental problems—including air, water, and soil pollution—must be resolved at the same time the state's water supply is declining.

Natural disasters such as hurricanes, tornadoes, floods, and droughts will continue to trouble individuals, businesses, and governments at all levels. Further, as indicated by federal census statistics, together with economic and social data from other sources, Texas policymakers must deal with an expanded aging population and a high incidence of poverty. Above all, both ordinary citizens and public officials must realize that their ability to cope with public problems now and in the years ahead depends largely on how well homes and schools prepare young Texans to meet the crises and demands of an ever-changing state, nation, and world.

The following chapter "Federalism and the Texas Constitution" examines the position of the states within the federal Union and looks at the constitutional development of the Lone Star State, especially its much-amended Constitution of 1876.

## ⭐ Chapter Summary

- The political culture of Texas is both individualistic and traditionalistic. The individualistic culture is rooted in the state's frontier experience and includes economic and social conservatism, strong support of personal politics, distrust of political parties, and minimization of parties' importance. The traditionalistic culture grew out of the Old South, where a one-party system developed, policies were designed to preserve the social order, and the poor and minorities were often disenfranchised. Today, these two cultures can still be found in the values, attitudes, traditions, habits, and general behavior patterns of Texans and in governmental policies of the Lone Star State.
- With more than 267,000 square miles of territory, Texas ranks second in size to Alaska among the 50 states. Cattle, cotton, and oil have at

different times dominated the Texas economy and influenced the state's politics. Today, Texas is a highly industrialized state in which high-technology products are of increasing importance.

■ Texas has a population of more than 22 million (2005 data). More than 80 percent of all Texans live in the state's most highly urbanized counties. The three largest groups are Anglos, Latinos (mostly Mexican Americans), and African Americans. Texas has a small but growing population of Asian Americans, and fewer than 70,000 Native Americans.

■ Although the state's petroleum industry has declined in importance, Texas has become a leading manufacturer of computers and other high-tech products. Agriculture continues to be important in the state's economy but employs relatively few Texans. Service businesses provide many low-paying jobs.

■ Challenges Texas faces include the need for measures that will more effectively address immigration, protect the environment, develop educational programs to meet the demands of an industrial society, and formulate policies for combating poverty and social problems.

## Key Terms

- politics, *p. 3*
- government, *p. 3*
- public policy, *p. 3*
- alien *p. 3*
- political culture, *p. 4*
- moralistic culture, *p. 5*
- individualistic culture, *p. 5*
- traditionalistic culture, *p. 6*
- political inefficacy, *p. 6*
- frontier experience, *p. 6*
- Jim Crow, *p. 8*
- *patrón* system, *p. 8*
- physical regions, *p. 10*
- Gulf Coast Plains, *p. 10*
- Interior Lowlands, *p. 11*
- Great Plains, *p. 11*
- Basin and Range Province, *p. 12*
- Spindletop Field, *p. 14*
- Railroad Commission of Texas, *p. 14*
- population shifts, *p. 17*
- urbanization, *p. 18*
- suburbanization, *p. 18*
- metropolitanization, *p. 18*
- micropolitan statistical area, *p. 18*
- metropolitan statistical area, *p. 18*
- combined statistical area, *p. 18*
- metropolitan division, *p. 18*
- Anglo, *p. 20*
- Latino, *p. 20*
- African American, *p. 21*
- Asian American, *p. 22*
- Native American, *p. 24*
- high technology, *p. 26*
- North American Free Trade Agreement (NAFTA), *p. 29*
- maquiladora, *p. 29*
- undocumented alien, *p. 31*
- Texas Water Development Board (TWDB), *p. 33*

## Learning Check Answers

**1.1**

1. False. Only California, with an estimated population of almost 36 million, is more populous than Texas.
2. Texas has elements of the individualistic culture and the traditionalistic culture.

**1.2**

1. The four principal physical regions of the state are the Gulf Coastal Plains, the Interior Lowlands, the Great Plains, and the Basin and Range Province.
2. In 1901, the Spindletop Field near Beaumont ushered in the oil industry in Texas.

**1.3**

1. Harris, Dallas, Bexar, and Tarrant counties have a combined population of more than 9 million, which is more than 40 percent of all Texans.
2. True. The fastest-growing ethnic group in Texas is Latinos. By 2006, more than 60 percent of births in the state were minority births, with Latino births accounting for half of all newborns. Additionally, with migration trends, it is estimated that Latinos could constitute a majority within 35 years.

**1.4**

1. False. The four largest private corporations in Texas, as identified in *Fortune*'s 2006 listing, were energy and energy related.
2. "Partner plants" on the Mexican side of the border that use cheap labor to assemble goods and then export these goods back to the United States are called maquiladoras.

**1.5**

1. False. The Immigration Reform and Control Act of 1986 has been largely ineffective in controlling undocumented aliens. Despite this act, hundreds of thousands of undocumented aliens continue to enter Texas each year.
2. True. In 2006, more than one-third of Texas workers were earning less than $20,000 a year, which was below the federal poverty level for food stamps for a family of four.

## Discussion Questions

1. In what ways is Texas's political culture (individualism and traditionalism) reflected in politics, policies, and the people's attitudes about, and expectations of, government today?
2. What political advantages accompany Texas's rank as second most populous state in the nation?

3. What challenges does Texas government face in the state's growing urban population in cities such as Houston, San Antonio, Dallas, and Fort Worth? How can government respond to these challenges?
4. What challenges does Texas government face with the state's shrinking rural population? How can government respond to these challenges?
5. How have various ethnic and racial groups contributed to the state's culture and economic development?
6. What challenges does Texas government face with the state's racial and ethnic diversity? How can government respond to these challenges?
7. What industries are essential to sustain and continue to develop the Texas economy in the twenty-first century?
8. What social services are essential to sustain and continue to develop the Texas economy in the twenty-first century?

## Internet Resources

Free Trade Area of the Americas: **www.ftaa-alca.org**
The Handbook of Texas Online: **www.tsha.utexas.edu/handbook/online**
North America Free Trade Agreement: **www.nafta-sec-alena.org**
Texas Department of Agriculture: **www.agr.state.tx.us**
Texas oil industry: **www.rrc.state.tx.us**
Texas State Data Center: **txsdc.utsa.edu**
Texas State Library and Archives Commission: **www.tsl.state.tx.us/lobby/ reffirst.htm**
United States Census Bureau: **www.census.gov**
Window on State Government: **www.window.state.tx.us**

## ★ Notes

1. Gary P. Nunn. "What I Like About Texas," from *What I Like About Texas* (Campfire Records, 1997). Lyrics by Gary P. Nunn. Copyright © Nunn Publishing Co. Reprinted by permission.
2. Harold Lasswell, *Politics: Who Gets What, When, How* (New York: McGraw-Hill, 1936).
3. Daniel Elazar, *American Federalism: A View from the States*, 3d ed. (New York: Harper & Row, 1984), 84–126, 134.
4. See "A Brief Sketch of Texas History," *Texas Almanac 2006–2007* (Dallas: Dallas Morning News, 2006), 56–57.
5. Ibid., 45.
6. For a case study of the *patrón* system, see J. Gilberto Quezada, *Border Boss: Manuel B. Bravo and Zapata County* (College Station: Texas A&M University Press, 1999).
7. For more on Texas longhorns, see J. Frank Dobie, *Longhorns* (Austin: University of Texas Press, 1980). Results of the most recent research on the origin of

longhorn cattle are found in T. J. Barragy, *Gathering Texas Gold: J. Frank Dobie and the Men Who Saved the Longhorn* (Corpus Christi, Tex.: Cayo de Grullo Press, 2003). Barragy disputes assertions in Don Worcester's popular *The Texas Longhorn: Relic of the Past, Asset for the Future* (College Station: Texas A&M University Press, 1987) that English Bakewell Longhorns and other British breeds played a significant role in the genetic makeup of Texas Longhorns.

8. See Don Graham, *Kings of Texas: The 150-Year Saga of an American Empire* (Hoboken, N.J.: John Wiley & Sons, 2003); Jane Clements Monday and Betty Bailey Colley, *Voices from the Wild Horse Desert: The Vaquero Families of the King and Kenedy Ranches* (Austin: University of Texas Press, 1997); Armando C. Alonzo, *Tejano Legacy: Rancheros and Settlers in South Texas, 1734–1900* (Albuquerque: University of New Mexico Press, 1998); Andrés Tijerina, *Tejano Empire: Life on the South Texas Ranchos* (College Station: Texas A&M University Press, 1998); and Daniel D. Arreola, *Tejano South Texas: A Mexican American Cultural Province* (Austin: University of Texas Press, 2002).

9. For an account of the history of the early years of the oil industry in Texas, see Roger M. Olien and Diana Davids Olien, *Oil in Texas: The Gusher Age, 1895–1945* (Austin: University of Texas Press, 2002).

10. "Boom, Bust and Back Again: Bullock Tenure Covers Tumultuous Era," *Fiscal Notes* (December 1990): 6–7.

11. For details concerning Texas's economy in the 1980s, see M. Ray Perryman, *Survive and Conquer: Texas in the '80s: Power, Money, Tragedy, Hope!* (Dallas: Taylor Publishing, 1990).

12. For a personal view of Hispanic (or Latino) culture, see Richard Rodriguez, "What Is a Hispanic?" *Texas Journal of Ideas, History and Culture* 22 (Summer 2000): 32–41.

13. See Daryl Janes, "Politics and Purse Strings: Why the Census Counts," *Fiscal Notes* (March 2000): 3–4.

14. See Steven H. Murdock et al., "2005 Population Projections: State of Texas Projections of the Population of Texas and Counties in Texas by Age, Sex and Race/Ethnicity for 2000–2040, produced by the Population Estimates and Projections Program," Texas State Data Center, Office of the State Demographer, University of Texas at San Antonio (June 2004) http://txsdc.utsa.edu/tpepp/2004_txpopprj_txtotnum.php.

15. Ibid.

16. Terry G. Jordan, "The Imprint of Upper and Lower South on Mid-Nineteenth Century Texas," *Annals of the American Association of Geographers* 57 (December 1967): 667–690.

17. Kent Biffle, "If At First You Don't Secede," *Dallas Morning News*, 3 November 2002.

18. Arnoldo De León, "Mexican Americans," in *The Handbook of Texas Online* (2002), **www.tsha.utexas.edu/handbook/online/articles/view/MM/pqmue.html.**

19. Alwyn Barr, *Black Texans: A History of Negroes in Texas, 1528–1971* (Austin: Jenkins, 1973).

20. Frederick Law Olmsted, *A Journey Through Texas* (New York: Dix, Edwards, 1857; reprint, Burt Franklin, 1969), 296. For more information on Texas Indian tribes, see Richard L. Schott, "Contemporary Indian Reservations in Texas: Tribal Paths to the Present," *Public Affairs Comment* (Lyndon B. Johnson School of Public Affairs, University of *Texas at Austin*) 39:3 (1993), 1–9; and David LaVere, *The Texas Indians* (College Station: Texas A & M University Press, 2004).

21. *Fortune*, 17 April 2006, F-32.

22. Carol J. Loomis, "Got Energy Trading Contracts?" *Fortune*, 15 April 2002, 190. Several Texas politicians were tied to Enron through campaign contributions, and Enron's lobbyists were active in Austin and Washington. Dozens of books concerning Enron have been published, with more to come. For example, see Robert Bryce and Molly Ivins, *Pipe Dreams: Greed, Ego, and the Death of Enron* (New York: Public Affairs Press, 2002); Brian Cruver, *Anatomy of Greed: The Unshredded Truth from an Enron Insider* (New York: Avalon, 2002); Loren Fox, *Enron: The Rise and Fall* (Hoboken, N.J.: Wiley, 2002); Mimi Swartz and Sherron Watkins, *Power Failure: The Inside Story of the Collapse of Enron* (New York: Doubleday, 2003); Bethany MacLean and Peter Elkind, *The Smartest Guys in the Room: The Amazing Rise and Scandalous Fall of Enron* (New York: Penguin, 2003); and Kurt Eichenwald, *Conspiracy of Fools: A True Story* (New York: Broadway Books, 2005).

23. For criticism and questions concerning genetic engineering for food production, see Nate Blakeslee, "Banking on Biotech: Is the Latest Food Science from Aggieland a Lemon?" *Texas Observer*, March 30, 2001, 6–9, 14; Sandra Kill Leber, "Biotechnology: Curse or Cure?" *State Government News* (January 2000): 23–26; and Ronnie Cummins, "Exposing Biotech's Big Lies," *BioDemocracy News* 39 (May 2002). www.organicconsumer.org/newsletter/blod39.cfm. Concerning the use of GMOs to reduce risks of chronic diseases, see Edward A. Hiler, "Houston Has a Stake in High-Tech Agriculture, Too," *Houston Chronicle,* 18 June 2001.

24. Molly Ivins, "Top to Bottom Reform of Financial Structures Essential," *Dallas Times Herald,* 3 June 1990.

25. These statistics were provided by the Texas Agricultural Statistics Service, Texas Department of Agriculture.

26. For a case study of an assembly-line manufacturing job that passed (with big pay cuts) from Paterson, New Jersey, to Blytheville, Arkansas, to the Mexican border city of Matamoros (across the Rio Grande from Brownsville, Texas), see William M. Adler, *Mollie's Job: A Story of Life and Work on the Global Assembly Line* (New York: Scribner, 2000).

27. "UNIFEM Head Decries Feminization of Poverty," *UN Wire*, 3 December 2002, at **www.unwire.org/UNWire/20021203/30674_story.asp**; and Amnesty International, "Demand Justice for the Women and Girls of Ciudad Juarez and Chihuahua, Mexico," 20 February 2006, at **www.amnestyusa.org/women/juarez/**.

28. See Denise Dresser, "Mexico: Uneasy, Uncertain, Unpredictable," *Current History* 96 (February 1997): 51–54.

29. See Lucy Conger, "Mexico's Long March to Democracy," *Current History* 100 (February 2001): 58–64; Carlos E. Casasillas and Alejandro Mújica, "Mexico: New Democracy with Old Parties?" *Politics* 23 (September 2003): 172–180; Julia Preston and Samuel Dillon, *Opening Mexico: The Making of a Democracy* (New York: Farrar, Straus and Giroux, 2004); and Jeffrey Davidow, *The U.S. and Mexico: The Bear and the Porcupine* (Princeton, N.J.: Marcus Weiner Publishers, 2004). Davidow was United States Ambassador to Mexico, 1998–2002.

30. Guillermina Guillén, "Political Decisions Stopped Development of Mexico," *The Universal*, 7 September 2005. See also Peter Andreas, "Politics on the Edge: Managing the U.S.-Mexican Border," *Current History* 105 (February 2006): 64–68; Jorge G. Castenada, "NAFTA at 10: A Plus or a Minus?" *Current*

*History* 103 (February 2004): 51–55; and Sidney Weintraub, "Scoring Free Trade: A Critique of the Critics," *Current History* 103 (February 2004): 56–60.

31. For 150 indicators assessing Texas's environment, education, economy, human services, public safety, and democracy, see Paul Robbins and Andrew Wheat, eds., *The State of the Lone Star State: How Life in Texas Measures Up* (Austin: Texans for Public Justice, 2000). For each indicator, Texas's ranking is compared with rankings of the five highest and five lowest states.

32. For an excellent overview of the state's water problems, see Ann Walther, *Texas at a Watershed: Planning Now for Future Needs*, Focus Report No. 75-13 (Austin: House Research Organization, Texas House of Representatives, 15 April 1997); see also Ted Holladay, *Groundwater Management Issues in Texas*, Focus Report No. 79-4 (Austin: House Research Organization, Texas House of Representatives, June 6, 2006).

33. Jan Gertson, Mark MacLeod, and C. Allan Jones, *Efficient Water Use for Texas: Policies, Tools, and Management Strategies*, report prepared for Environmental Defense by Texas Agricultural Experiment Station, Texas A&M University, College Station, Texas (September 2002).

34. For information on all aspects of Texas's environmental problems, see Mary Sanger and Cyrus Reed, comps., *Texas Environmental Almanac*, 2d ed. (Austin: University of Texas Press, 2000); and Texas Center for Policy Studies at www.TexasCenter.org.

35. Connie Mabin, "Survey: Many Texas Teachers Moonlight to Make Ends Meet," *Austin American-Statesman*, 29 April 2000.

## 1.1 The Role of States in Immigration Enforcement*

### *Kellie Dworaczyk*

*This report, as prepared by the Texas House Research Organization, examines the states' roles in enforcing immigration laws and outlines their responses to issues surrounding illegal immigration. It details proposals that have been considered in other states and summarizes areas of disagreement over these policy areas.*

The ability of states to influence illegal immigration is being explored as state legislatures consider or enact laws concerning workplace requirements, access to benefits, voting requirements, college tuition, identification, and other areas related to immigration policy. Since the attacks of September 11, 2001, the illegal immigration debate also has included the role state law enforcement agencies should play in dealing with unauthorized immigrants and border security.

Some argue that the problems resulting from illegal immigration are so serious that states, in concert with federal efforts, should take all possible steps to stem the flow of unauthorized immigrants. These problems, they say, include the high costs of providing services and the appropriateness of allowing unauthorized immigrants to enjoy rights and privileges that should be reserved for citizens and legal residents. Others argue that enforcing immigration policy is a federal responsibility and that state action in this area is inappropriate. Still others contend that federal immigration policy should be completely revamped, such as by enacting a guest worker program, and that piecemeal state action in this area is counterproductive.

Governors in two states—Arizona and New Mexico—declared states of emergency in 2005 over immigration

issues, and recent opinion polls reflect the public's interest in this topic. Seventy-nine percent of those surveyed in November 2005 for a Scripps-Howard Texas Poll said that that the government is not doing enough to stop unauthorized immigration. Eighty-four percent of those surveyed said they considered unauthorized immigration from Mexico to be a serious problem. These numbers are similar to the results of a Washington Post-ABC News national poll conducted in December 2005 in which about 80 percent of those surveyed said the government was not doing enough to keep illegal immigrants from coming into the United States.

President Bush has called for changes to immigration policy and laws, including changes in the way the federal government handles immigrants caught crossing the border illegally and increases in manpower, technology, and physical barriers designed to prevent illegal border crossings. In addition, the president has proposed increased enforcement of requirements barring the employment of illegal workers and the establishment of a temporary worker program. Federal lawmakers are responding to this debate by considering several proposals that would amend current law dealing with border security, enforcement of laws designed to discourage illegal residency in the United States, technology and infrastructure—including a security fence along the border—workplace requirements, and more.

This report outlines states' responses to issues surrounding illegal immigration. It details proposals that have been considered in other states and summarizes the debate over these policy areas.

**Estimates of Illegal Immigration.**  A report by the Pew Hispanic Center used U.S. census data to estimate that as of March 2005 the undocumented population in the United States has reached nearly 11 million, including more than 6 million Mexicans, which translates to roughly 3.7 percent of the U.S. population as a whole. In March 2004, according to the Pew report, approximately 29

---

*Kellie Dworaczyk, *The Role of the States in Immigration Enforcement*, Focus Report No. 79-12 (Austin: House Research Organization, Texas House of Representatives, 24 February 2006). Kellie Dworaczyk is a research analyst for the House Research Organization. Online at **http://www.hro.house.state.tx.us/focus/immigration 79-12.pdf**

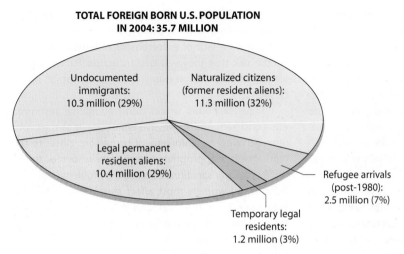

**TOTAL FOREIGN BORN U.S. POPULATION IN 2004: 35.7 MILLION**

Undocumented immigrants: 10.3 million (29%)

Naturalized citizens (former resident aliens): 11.3 million (32%)

Legal permanent resident aliens: 10.4 million (29%)

Temporary legal residents: 1.2 million (3%)

Refugee arrivals (post-1980): 2.5 million (7%)

*Figure 1*  Legal status of immigrants in United States, 2004  *Source:* Pew Hispanic Center.

percent of the foreign-born population in this country was unauthorized (see Figure 1). Over the past decade, according to the report, an average of 700,000 to 800,000 unauthorized immigrants arrived annually. However, some of these immigrants leave the United States, some die, and some obtain legal status, resulting in an average net growth of unauthorized migrants of about half a million persons annually. Although most of the undocumented population are young adults, about one-sixth of the population is under the age of 18.

With 14 percent of the nation's undocumented population, Texas ranks second among states to California, with 24 percent of the undocumented population (see Table 1). This puts the unauthorized migrant population at roughly 6 percent of the Texas population.

## State Legislation and Proposals

At least 22 states considered proposals relating to illegal immigration in 2005, according to the National Immigration Law Center. These proposals covered a broad range of policy areas, including workplace requirements, access to public benefits, driver's license and identification card requirements, voter registration requirements, college tuition standards, and law enforcement issues.

## Workplace Requirements

Under federal law, employers are prohibited from knowingly hiring aliens not authorized to work in the United States. According to the Congressional Research Service (CRS), the law prohibits hiring or continuing to employ an alien knowing he or she is unauthorized to work and hiring any worker without following specific record-keeping requirements. The law lists acceptable documents that employees can present to prove their legal

*Table 1*   Estimates by State of Undocumented Immigrant Population, 2002–2004

| California | 2,400,000 |
|---|---|
| Texas | 1,400,000 |
| Florida | 850,000 |
| New York | 650,000 |
| Arizona | 500,000 |
| Illinois | 400,000 |
| New Jersey | 350,000 |
| North Carolina | 300,000 |
| All other | 3,150,000 |

*Source:* Pew Hispanic Center.

status, and employers are required to complete Employment Eligibility Verification (I-9) forms for each employee.

U.S. Immigration and Customs Enforcement, part of the federal Department of Homeland Security, is authorized to conduct investigations to determine whether employers are complying with the law. Employers who do not comply can be subject to civil fines, and some violations can result in imprisonment. The state of Texas currently has no role in sanctioning employers who break federal law by hiring illegal workers.

Some state legislative proposals have sought to discourage illegal immigration by authorizing state sanctions on employers who hire unauthorized workers or by enacting other workplace requirements. These proposals include imposing state fines on employers who hire illegal workers, prohibiting the receipt of state contracts by employers who violate federal immigration law, and revoking licenses of employers who hire workers illegally.

In 2005, according to the NCSL, Arizona, Connecticut, Georgia, New York, and South Carolina considered proposals to impose fines and revoke licenses of employers who hire unauthorized workers, but none were enacted. That same year, at least six states also considered, but did not enact, proposals that would have prohibited the awarding of government contracts to firms that employ unauthorized workers.

Proposals to deny workers' compensation claims for unauthorized workers were introduced in two states. In a bill dealing with workers' compensation issues, Wyoming amended its statutes to define "employee" to be someone an employer believes to be a citizen or permanent resident, according to the NCSL. Another proposal would hold employers responsible for the costs of providing uncompensated medical care for employees who are not in the United States lawfully.

Arizona enacted legislation in 2005 that prohibits cities, towns, and counties from constructing and maintaining a work center if any part of the center facilitates the knowing employment of an unlawful alien.

**Supporters of state-imposed sanctions on employers say** state laws to sanction employers who hire illegal workers are needed because federal law has proven ineffective. Employers often ignore federal law and hire illegal workers with impunity. Some employers feel that due to a lack of enforcement of federal law, there is little risk that they will be sanctioned for employing illegal workers and see any fines as a cost of doing business.

State sanctions would bring additional resources and consistent and aggressive enforcement to the problem and allow for enforcement by persons closer to the work site. It is appropriate to use state resources to enforce employer sanctions because the problems resulting from illegal workers most affect states, employers, and legal workers on the local level. It is only fair to address the problem of illegal immigration on the demand side as well as the supply side. Industries should not rely or be built on illegal labor.

**Opponents of state-imposed sanctions on employers say** it is unnecessary for states to impose sanctions on employers for hiring undocumented workers because federal laws already prohibit such hiring, and sanctions already exist for breaking these laws. States should not impose employer sanctions on top of existing federal sanctions because doing so could lead to a patchwork of requirements for employers and to uneven or unfair enforcement of federal law. Texas should not spend its finite resources duplicating federal efforts when the state has other pressing financial needs. Rather than making state employers, in effect, deputy immigration agents, perceived problems with illegal immigration should be dealt with by changing federal law or beefing up enforcement efforts.

In some industries federal sanctions have proved ineffective because undocumented workers are essential, and state sanctions would fare no better. The enforcement of additional or overly punitive sanctions against employers could damage the Texas economy, and certain sectors, such as the construction industry, might experience particular harm. Before imposing additional employer sanctions, the labor problem in certain industries should be addressed through a guest worker program or similar initiative. In addition, labor laws could be better enforced so that the rights of all workers were recognized and economic incentives for hiring undocumented workers were eliminated.

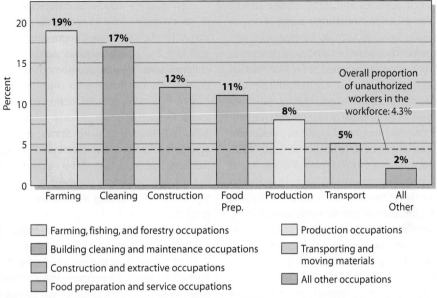

*Figure 2*    Proportion of Unauthorized Workers Within Various Occupations, 2004    *Source:* Pew Hispanic Center.

The availability of counterfeit documents and the difficulties employers have in judging the authenticity of those documents also would make state sanctions as ineffective as federal sanctions have proved in some cases. It would be unfair to sanction an employer who misjudged the integrity of a document provided by an unauthorized worker.

### Access to Benefits

U.S. citizens and some legal immigrants are eligible for federal and state benefits, including food stamps, Medicaid, the Children's Health Insurance Program (CHIP), and cash assistance. Because there is a federal funding component to all of these programs, the eligibility requirements generally are guided by federal law, although the eligibility determination process may differ from state to state. In Texas, the application forms ask for both a declaration of citizenship or legal immigrant status and a Social Security number. The Texas Health and Human Services Commission has verification and other checks built into the enrollment process for some programs and requires proof of citizenship for others.

The federal Emergency Medical Treatment and Active Labor Act of 1986 requires emergency room physicians to assess and stabilize any patient, regardless of ability to pay or immigration status. Because of this law, hospitals with emergency facilities often treat undocumented immigrants. If patients are unable to pay out-of-pocket for their care, these charges often go unreimbursed.

Some local governments in Texas and elsewhere have established locally funded health plans, in part to avoid costlier emergency room charges by providing services in other settings. Some counties also have chosen to restrict their programs to U.S. citizens or legal residents, but others stipulate only that an applicant must be a "resident" to be eligible. There was some concern that county and hospital district programs could not offer services to undocumented immigrants, but a provision in HB 2292 by Wohlgemuth, enacted by the 78th Legislature in 2003, allows local authorities to include all residents in a local medical assistance plan.

Some argue that states and local entities should gather statistics on the use by illegal immigrants of certain public benefits and services such as emergency room medical care and local public health programs. Others say that gathering this information could serve as a form of intimidation that might discourage some eligible persons from seeking needed care.

In the first half of 2005, fifteen states considered proposals to restrict illegal immigrants' access to public benefits, but only one bill became law, according to NCSL. Virginia enacted a law that prohibits non-citizens and people residing illegally in the United States from receiving state or local public benefits, unless required by federal law. The law has exemptions for some state-funded medical assistance for certain immigrant children and long-term care patients. Applicants can receive temporary benefits by signing an affidavit attesting to U.S. citizenship or legal residency and following up with the required proof. Many of the proposals in other states would have required applicants for benefits to show proof of citizenship or would have prohibited undocumented immigrants from receiving local public benefits unless required by federal law.

In 2004, Arizona voters approved a ballot initiative, Proposition 200, which requires state and local government employees to verify the identity, eligibility, and immigration status of applicants for "state and local public benefits that are not federally mandated." State and local government employees are required to report to federal immigration authorities violations of federal immigration laws by applicants for public benefits. Failure to make the required report is a misdemeanor. Another provision in the law deals with voter registration and identification. After initial legal challenges, the public benefits portions of the law are being implemented in four state benefit programs: general assistance under the Arizona Department of Economic Security; the sight conservation program, which provides eye examinations, glasses, and other services for the prevention or correction of eye problems to individuals 21 or more years of age who are receiving certain other benefits programs; the neighbors helping neighbors program that provides certain low-income Arizonans with assistance in paying utility bills, conserving energy, and weatherization; and the state's program for utility repair, replacement, and deposit assistance.

All resident school-age children in Texas are eligible to attend public schools, regardless of their immigration status. The U.S. Supreme Court's decision in *Plyler v. Doe,* 457 U.S. 202 (1982) requires public schools to accept children who are undocumented immigrants without charge. In addition, the high court struck down a Texas statute that withheld from local school districts any state funds for education of children who were not "legally admitted" into the United States and that authorized school districts to deny enrollment to such children. It ruled that the law violated the equal-protection clause of the U.S. Constitution by depriving a "disfavored group" of the means of obtaining an education without adequate justification.

***Supporters of state requirements to prove citizenship for public benefits say*** that these provisions merely enforce current laws, most of which already restrict benefits to U.S. citizens. Requiring proof of citizenship prevents fraud in benefit programs and would not deny benefits to anyone who is lawfully eligible to receive them. It is unfair for taxpayers to continue to pay the high cost of providing public benefits to those who are not eligible to receive them.

***Opponents of state requirements to prove citizenship for public benefits say*** that these measures are unnecessary. Undocumented immigrants already are ineligible for numerous public benefits, and there are penalties for fraud and making false claims. Other benefits, such as education and emergency medical care, are federally mandated for all, regardless of immigrant status. State and local employees should not enforce federal immigration law by making judgments on the citizenship status of applicants for public benefits. Unauthorized immigrants come to the United States seeking jobs, not benefits.

## Proof of Citizenship for Voter Registration

In 2005, according to the National Immigration Law Center, several states considered, but did not enact, legislation that would have required persons to submit proof of U.S. citizenship to register to vote. While all states require voters to be U.S. citizens, only Arizona has a requirement that voters produce proof of citizenship before being able to register, according to NCSL. The Arizona requirement was part of Proposition 200, approved by voters in 2004, that also requires voters to show proof of identity at the polling place. The voter registration component currently is being implemented while the requirement to show identification when voting is being implemented for Arizona's elections this year [2006].

In Texas, the voter registration application requires applicants to check a box indicating U.S. citizenship and requires a signature attesting that the voter understands that giving false information is a crime. Election Code, ch. 17 establishes a procedure for challenging a voter on the elements of the voter registration application. HB 516 by B. Brown, which died in committee during the 78th Legislature in 2003, would have specified a list of documents for use in establishing U.S. citizenship and required voter registration applications to include a copy of such a document.

**Supporters of requiring proof of citizenship for voter registration say** that states should be willing to enforce current laws that restrict voting to U.S. citizens and to protect this right by ensuring that only citizens are voting. Any burden on citizens or local voting officials would be minimal, and protecting the integrity of the vote would be well worth any minor inconvenience. Having fair, honest elections is important enough to require a one-time demonstration of citizenship.

**Opponents of requiring proof of citizenship for voter registration say** that the burden required to prove citizenship for voter registration would depress legal votes, especially among low-income, minority, elderly, or disabled voters. These individuals might not have the required documents nor the ability to bear the expense or clear bureaucratic hurdles necessary to obtain them. In addition, this requirement would place a burden on local election officials who would have to evaluate and store the documents. Requiring proof of citizenship is unnecessary because there is no evidence that a problem exists with noncitizens voting, and remedies exist in current law to address such a problem if it arises.

## In-State College Tuition

In 2005, New Mexico became the ninth state to permit unauthorized immigrants to pay tuition at public colleges and universities at in-state resident rates. It joined Texas, California, Illinois, Kansas, New York, Oklahoma, Utah, and Washington. Also in 2005, the Arizona Legislature enacted legislation prohibiting in-state tuition to unauthorized immigrants, but it included other provisions relating to unauthorized immigration that the governor found objectionable in vetoing the bill. Alaska and Mississippi specifically prohibit allowing unauthorized immigrants to pay in-state resident tuition.

In 2001, Texas became the first state to enact legislation that allows undocumented immigrants to pay in-state college tuition at any public institution. In order to qualify for in-state rates, a student first must have lived in Texas with a parent or guardian for at least three years before graduating from a public or private high school and must declare an intention to seek status as a legal resident as soon as the student is eligible. According to the Texas Higher Education Coordinating Board (THECB), about 3,700 such students were enrolled in Texas higher education institutions in the autumn of 2004 out of a population of approximately 1.2 million students.

Opponents of the Kansas in-state tuition law sued the state because they said it violated a federal immigration law that prohibits states from allowing illegal immigrants to pay in-state tuition. They say that sec. 1623 of the Illegal Immigration Reform and Immigration Responsibility Act of 1996 (8 U.S.C.) is designed to ensure that any state that offers discounted, in-state college tuition rates to illegal aliens also must offer those same discounted tuition rates to all U.S. citizens and nationals, regardless of what state they live in.

U.S. Dist. Judge Richard D. Rogers, in *Day* v. *Sebelius*, 376 F. Supp. 2d 1022 (D. Kan. 2005), ruled that the plaintiffs had no standing to challenge the Kansas in-state tuition provision. He determined that the plaintiffs could show no potential harm or injury to themselves since their own nonresident status would not change regardless of whether resident tuition applied to illegal immigrants. He also ruled that as private individuals, the plaintiffs had no authority to seek to enforce federal immigration law, which is under the exclusive jurisdiction of the U.S. Department of Homeland Security (DHS). The plaintiffs have appealed the ruling, and separate complaints have been filed with the DHS challenging the tuition laws in Texas and New York.

According to the Texas Civil Rights Review, each year, 65,000 immigrants without legal status graduate from

U.S. high schools. While federal law prohibits illegal immigrant students from receiving federally backed financial aid, undocumented students in Texas are eligible for state financial aid under the same conditions that other students must meet, except that undocumented students cannot qualify for work study or the "B-on-Time" program, through which students who graduate "on time" from a four-year university with a 3.0 grade-point-average may receive loans.

Lawmakers in the U.S. Congress have proposed legislation to provide undocumented students a way to obtain legal status. The Development, Relief and Education for Alien Minors (DREAM) Act—S. 2075 by Durbin—would allow undocumented students who arrived in the United States before the age of 16, lived here at least five years, and graduated from high school or had been accepted to college to apply for six years of conditional legal status that would become permanent if the student went on to college or military service. The proposed legislation also would allow states to define residency for higher education purposes.

***Supporters of in-state tuition for unauthorized immigrants say*** that it is good public policy to further the education of immigrants who already are integrated into local communities and want to contribute to the local and national economy. State laws granting in-state tuition for undocumented immigrants open the doors of higher education to those who need it most and do not violate federal law because the requirements set for in-state tuition apply to all students, whether they reside in the country illegally or not. Without the opportunity to qualify for in-state tuition, many undocumented immigrants cannot obtain an affordable college education because they are not eligible to receive federal financial aid. Undocumented immigrants who have grown up in the United States and graduate from U.S. high schools should not be punished for the actions of parents who brought them illegally to this country.

***Opponents of in-state tuition for unauthorized immigrants say*** that state laws granting in-state tuition for illegal aliens reward illegal activity and encourage more illegal immigration. In addition, they contend that such laws violate federal law because they discriminate against U.S. citizens and legal immigrants because states are not permitted to treat nonresidents who are U.S. citizens worse, with respect to college benefits, than it treats illegal aliens who are physically present in the state. As a result, they say, numerous illegal aliens are paying in-state rates to attend Texas colleges and universities, while U.S. citizens who do not reside in Texas are required to pay higher, out-of-state tuition rates.

## Identification and Driver's Licenses

In the first part of 2005, at least 27 states considered proposals relating to identification documents and immigrants, and nine bills were enacted, according to NCSL. Some of these proposals related to documents necessary to obtain state driver's licenses. Texas is not among the approximately 40 states that require applicants to prove legal U.S. residency to obtain a driver's license.

Texas Transportation Code, sec. 521.142 requires applicants for driver's licenses to state their full name and place and date of birth and to present proof of identity to the Department of Public Safety (DPS). Texas Administrative Code, Title 37, sec. 15.24 lists three categories of acceptable identification documents. An applicant must present one type of document from a list of "primary" identification or one type from a list of "secondary" identification, plus one or more types of supporting identification. Primary identification includes a valid or expired Texas driver's license or identification card, a U.S. passport, U.S. military identification cards, and certain U.S. immigration documents. Secondary identification–defined as recorded government documents whose authenticity can be verified—includes an original or certified copy of a U.S. or Canadian birth certificate and driver's licenses issued by other states. Supporting materials include public school records, marriage licenses, utility bills, voter registration cards, Social Security cards, and consular documents issued by a state or national government, including a Mexican-issued *matrícula consular*.

In addition, DPS obtains Social Security numbers from all applicants who have been issued a number. License and identification card applicants who state that they have not applied for or received a Social Security number must sign an affidavit attesting to these facts.

HB 1137 by W. Smith, enacted by the 79th Legislature in its 2005 regular session, allows DPS to enter into reciprocal agreements with foreign countries so that certain persons can obtain Class C commercial driver's licenses.

Such a person is required to hold a license issued by the other country that is similar to a Texas Class C license. A non-U.S. citizen must present to DPS documentation authorizing the person to be in the United States before the person may be issued a driver's license under a reciprocal agreement.

Title II of the federal REAL ID Act of 2005 includes provisions imposing minimum standards for state-issued driver's licenses that are to be put to a "federal use." Federal agencies will be prohibited from accepting as identification state-issued driver's licenses or identification cards after May 11, 2008, if they do not meet the new standards. To comply, a state issuing a driver's license will have to verify that the applicant is a U.S. citizen or a legal resident of this country as well as confirm the applicant's Social Security number. The rules to implement the law currently are being written.

**Supporters of requiring driver's license applicants to prove citizenship say** states that require only proof of identity, rather then legal U.S. residence, reward illegal behavior by making it easy for illegal aliens to obtain driver's licenses. States should not wait for the federal REAL ID deadline in 2008 to require that applicants for driver's licenses or identification cards prove legal residency in the United States.

**Opponents of requiring driver's license applicants to prove citizenship say** that driving in some states, including Texas, often is a necessity because many areas do not have adequate mass transit systems. Driving is a lifeline to work, health care, education, and more. It is far better for all drivers—including undocumented immigrants—to be licensed and insured than for them to drive illegally. Current law does not "reward" illegal immigrants. A driver's license is not proof of citizenship, and granting one should not be contingent on a person's immigration status. States should not be involved in enforcing immigration laws at driver's license bureaus.

### The Role of Local Law Enforcement

**Current Law**  Violations of federal immigration laws include both criminal and civil penalties. Traditionally, state and local law enforcement's authority for enforcing immigration laws has been limited to criminal provisions of the federal laws. The enforcement of civil provisions,

which include the apprehension and removal of deportable aliens, has been viewed by many as an exclusively federal responsibility, according to the Congressional Research Service (CRS). The mere illegal presence of someone in the United States is a civil immigration violation, according to CRS, and entering the United States illegally is a misdemeanor criminal offense. Texas, like many states, generally does not authorize law enforcement officers to make arrests for misdemeanors committed outside their presence.

The question of the authority of state and local law enforcement officers to enforce federal immigration law is complicated by numerous other factors, including statutory exceptions and judicial interpretation. Amendments to federal laws have authorized states to enforce civil immigration violations in limited circumstances, according to NCSL. For example, the federal Illegal Immigration Reform and Immigrant Responsibility Act of 1996 (IIRIRA) allows states and localities to play a role in enforcing federal civil immigration laws if the state has entered into a voluntary written agreement with the federal government. The law requires, among other things, that local law enforcement officers be educated and trained about federal immigration law, and the agreement must list the specific powers and duties of the local law enforcement officers. Alabama, Florida, and the Los Angeles County Sheriff's Department each have entered into an IIRIRA agreement with the federal government, and a handful of other states and local entities are considering or pursuing such agreements.

State and local officials also have specific authority to enforce federal immigration law under provisions in the Anti-Terrorism and Effective Death Penalty Act of 1996, which allow them to arrest and detain aliens who are present unlawfully in the United States and previously were deported or left the country after a felony conviction in this country. In addition, state and local law enforcement authorities under IIRIRA can enforce certain civil immigration provisions if there is a "mass influx" of foreign nationals as determined by the U.S. Attorney General, the situation requires an immediate response from the federal government, and federal officials obtain the consent of the state and local supervising department.

**Local Policies**  While there is debate over the role of local law enforcement officers in enforcing federal

**Waco Tribune-Herald/Herschberger/Herschberger Cartoon Service**

IN SEARCH OF THE TEXAS CONSTITUTION...

The Texas Constitution, adopted in 1876, serves as the Lone Star State's fundamental law. This document outlines the structure of Texas's state government, authorizes the creation of counties and cities, and establishes basic rules for governing. It has been amended frequently over 13 decades (as illustrated by the cartoon at the beginning of the chapter). Lawyers, newspaper editors, political scientists, government officials, and others who consult the state constitution tend to criticize it for being too long and for lacking organization. Yet despite criticism, Texans have expressed strong opposition to, or complete lack of interest in, proposals for wholesale constitutional revision.

The Texas Constitution is the primary source of the state government's policymaking power. The other major source of its power is membership in the federal Union. Within the federal system, state constitutions are subject to the U.S. Constitution.

# The American Federal Structure

Federalism can be defined as a structure of government characterized by the division of powers between a national government and associated regional governments. The heart of the American federal system lies in the relationship between the U.S. government (with Washington, D.C. as the national capital) and the governments of the 50 states. Since 1789, the U.S. Constitution has prescribed a federal system of government for the nation, and since 1846 the state of Texas has been a part of that system.

Political scientist David Walker emphasizes the important role that states play in federalism: "The states' strategically crucial role in the administration, financing, and planning of intergovernmental programs and regulations—both federal and their own—and their perennial key position in practically all areas of local governance have made them the pivotal middlemen in the realm of functional federalism."[1]

Described by North Carolina's former governor Terry Sanford as "a system of states within a state," American federalism has survived two centuries of stresses and strains. Among the most serious threats were the Civil War from 1861 to 1865, which almost destroyed the Union, and economic crises such as the Great Depression that followed the stock market crash of 1929.

## Distribution of Powers

Division of powers and functions between the national government and the state governments was originally accomplished by listing the powers of the national government in the U.S. Constitution and by adding the **Tenth Amendment**. The latter asserts: "The powers not delegated to the United States by the Constitution, nor prohibited by it to the States, are reserved to the States, respectively, or to the People." Although the Tenth Amendment may seem to endow the states with powers comparable to those delegated to the national government, Article VI of the U.S. Constitution contains the following clarification: "This Constitution, and the laws of the United States which shall be made in pursuance thereof; and all treaties made, or which shall be made, under the authority of the United States, shall be the supreme law of the land; and the judges in every State shall be bound thereby, anything in the Constitution or laws of any State to the contrary notwithstanding." Referred to as the **national supremacy clause**, it emphasizes that the U.S. Constitution and acts of Congress, as well as U.S. treaties, must prevail over state constitutions and laws enacted by state legislatures.

**Delegated and Implied Powers**     Article I, Section 8, of the U.S. Constitution lists powers specifically delegated to the national government. Included are powers to regulate interstate and foreign commerce, borrow and coin money, establish post offices and post roads, declare war, raise and support armies, provide and maintain a navy, levy and collect taxes, and establish uniform rules of naturalization. Added to these **delegated powers** is a clause that gives

**Tenth Amendment** The Tenth Amendment of the U.S. Constitution declares that "the powers not delegated by the Constitution, nor prohibited by it to the States, are reserved to the States, respectively, or to the people." Although not spelled out in the U.S. Constitution, these reserved powers include police power, taxing power, proprietary power, and power of eminent domain.

**national supremacy clause** Article VI of the U.S. Constitution states: "This Constitution, and the Laws of the United States which shall be made in Pursuance thereof; and all Treaties made, or which shall be made, under the Authority of the United States, shall be the supreme Law of the Land...."

**delegated powers** Specific powers entrusted to the national government by Article 1, Section 8, of the U.S. Constitution (e.g., regulate interstate commerce, borrow money, and declare war).

the national government the power "to make all laws which shall be necessary and proper for carrying into execution the foregoing powers, and all other powers vested by this Constitution in the government of the United States, or in any department or officer thereof." Since 1789, Congress and the federal courts have used this grant of **implied powers** to expand the authority of the national government. For instance, the U.S. Supreme Court, in a case originating in Texas, gave significant leeway to Congress to legislate in matters traditionally reserved to the states. In this case, the Court allowed Congress to set a minimum wage for employees of local governments.[2]

**Limitations on the States**    As members of the federal Union, Texas and other states are constrained by limitations imposed by Article I, Section 10, of the U.S. Constitution. For example, they may not enter into treaties, alliances, or confederations or, without the consent of Congress, make compacts or agreements with other state or foreign governments. Furthermore, they are forbidden to levy import duties on another state's products. From the outcome of the Civil War and the U.S. Supreme Court's landmark ruling in *Texas* v. *White* (1869), Texans learned that states cannot secede from the Union. In the *White* case, the Court ruled that the national Constitution "looks to an indestructible union, composed of indestructible states." More recently, the states learned that a state legislature cannot limit the number of terms for members of the state's congressional delegation. The U.S. Supreme Court held that term limits for members of Congress could be constitutionally imposed only if authorized by an amendment to the U.S. Constitution.[3]

Other provisions in the U.S. Constitution prohibit states from denying anyone the right to vote because of race, gender, failure to pay a poll tax, or age (if the person is 18 years of age or older). The Fourteenth Amendment forbids states from denying anyone the equal protection of the laws or the privileges and immunities of citizens of the United States. Furthermore, no state may deprive persons of life, liberty, or property without due process of law.

**Guarantees to the States**    The U.S. Constitution provides all states with an imposing list of **constitutional guarantees**, which include the following:

- States may be neither divided nor combined with another state without the consent of the state legislatures involved and Congress. (Texas, however, did retain power to divide itself into as many as five states under the terms of its annexation to the United States.)
- Each state is guaranteed a republican form of government (that is, a representative government with elected lawmakers).
- To serve the ends of federalism, the framers of the U.S. Constitution gave the states an important role in the affairs of the central government. Accordingly, each state is guaranteed that it will have two senators in the U.S. Senate and at least one member in the U.S. House of Representatives. Because of population growth, as determined by the 2000 census, Texans now elect 32 representatives.

**implied powers**  Powers inferred by the constitutional authority of the U.S. Congress "to make all laws which shall be necessary and proper for carrying into execution the foregoing [delegated] powers, and all other powers vested by this Constitution in the government of the United States, or in any department or officer thereof."

**constitutional guarantees**  Included among the U.S. Constitution's guarantees to members of the Union are protection against invasion and domestic violence, territorial integrity, a republican form of government, representation by two senators and at least one representative in the U.S. Congress, and equitable participation in the constitutional amendment process.

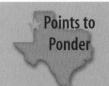

**Points to Ponder**

- The Twenty-Seventh Amendment to the U.S. Constitution became effective in 1992 but was actually proposed in 1789.
- The congressional joint resolution proposing this amendment was discovered in 1982 by Gregory D. Watson, an undergraduate student at the University of Texas at Austin, while he was researching a paper on the Equal Rights Amendment.
- This forgotten proposal would prevent congressional pay raises until after an intervening congressional election had been conducted.
- At the time of Watson's discovery, only nine states had ratified the proposal. Since the joint resolution contained no time limit, completion of ratification by the required three-quarters of the state legislatures was still possible.
- Watson received a grade of C for his paper, but he was motivated to undertake a 10-year personal crusade that led to ratification by the necessary number of states (including Texas, which ratified it in May 1989).

- As provided by the U.S. Constitution, Texas and the other states participate in presidential elections through the electoral college. A state has one electoral vote for each of its U.S. senators and each of its U.S. representatives.
- All states participate equally in approving or rejecting proposed amendments to the U.S. Constitution. Approval requires ratification by either three-fourths of the state legislatures (used for all but the Twenty-First Amendment, which repealed Prohibition) or by conventions called in three-fourths of the states.
- Each state is entitled to protection by the U.S. government against invasion and domestic violence, although Texas may also have its own militia (National Guard units).
- Finally, Texas is assured that trials by federal courts for crimes committed in Texas will be conducted in Texas.

## Interstate Relations and State Immunity

Two provisions in the U.S. Constitution that affect federal–state relations are Article IV and the 11th Amendment.

Article IV of the U.S. Constitution provides that "citizens of each state shall be entitled to all **privileges and immunities** of citizens in the several states." This means that residents of Texas who visit another state are entitled to all the privileges and immunities of citizens of that state. It does not mean, however, that such visiting Texans are entitled to all the privileges and immunities to which we are entitled in our home state. Nearly two hundred years ago, the U.S. Supreme Court defined "privileges and immunities" broadly as follows: protection by government, enjoyment of life and liberty, right to acquire and possess property, right to leave and enter any state, and right to the use of courts. Although corporations are legal persons, they are not protected under the privileges and immunities clause.

Article IV also states that "full faith and credit shall be given in each State to the public acts, records, and judicial proceedings of every other State." The

**privileges and immunities** Article IV of the U.S. Constitution guarantees that "citizens of each state shall be entitled to the privileges and immunities of citizens of the several states." According to the U.S. Supreme Court, this means that citizens are guaranteed protection by government, enjoyment of life and liberty, the right to acquire and possess property, the right to leave and enter any state, and the right to use state courts.

**full faith and credit clause** means that any legislative enactment, state constitution, deed, will, marriage, divorce, or civil court judgment of one state must be officially recognized and honored in every other state. This clause does not apply to criminal cases. A person convicted in Texas for a crime committed in Texas is not punished in another state to which he or she has fled. Such cases are handled through extradition, whereby the fugitive would be returned to the Lone Star State at the request of the governor of Texas. Furthermore, for some felonies, the U.S. Congress has made it a federal offense to flee from one state to another for the purpose of avoiding arrest.

One of the more recent controversies regarding the full faith and credit clause revolves around whether states must recognize same-sex marriages. In 1996, the Clinton administration passed the Defense of Marriage Act. This law allows states or political divisions such as cities to deny any marriage between persons of the same sex recognized in another state. Although several challenges to the law's constitutionality have been presented to the U.S. Supreme Court, the Court has declined to review any such cases, and all lower court rulings have upheld the law's constitutionality.

In 2003, the Texas Legislature passed a law prohibiting the state or any agency or political subdivision (such as a county or city) from recognizing a same-sex marriage or civil union formed in Texas or elsewhere. The leadership of the state legislature, as well as Governor Rick Perry, expressed support for President Bush's call in February 2004 for a proposed U.S. constitutional amendment that would ban gay marriage. Then, in November 2005, Texas joined 15 other states with similar constitutional amendments banning same-sex marriages since 2002.[4] Although it became the sixteenth state to approve the ban, Texas was among the first to define marriage as "the union of one woman and one man." Many opponents believed the constitutional amendment was unnecessary, given the existing state law. Supporters of the amendment, in contrast, believed that it was necessary to amend the constitution to preempt any constitutional challenges to the state law.

The Eleventh Amendment also affects federal–state relations. It states: "The Judicial power of the United States shall not be construed to extend to any suit in law or equity, commenced or prosecuted against one of the United States by citizens of another state. . . ." Recent U.S. Supreme Court rulings have ensured that a state may not be sued by its own citizens, or those of another state, without its consent, nor can state employees sue the state for violating federal law.[5] This assurance of sovereign immunity, however, is not absolute. When Texas was sued in federal courts on behalf of several families for the state's failure to provide federally required Medicaid programs, the lower federal courts ordered the state to correct the problem after the plaintiffs and state officials agreed to a consent decree (an agreement by both parties to avoid further litigation). Texas appealed to the U.S. Supreme Court, arguing that "sovereign immunity" did not allow federal courts to enforce the consent decree. The Supreme Court ultimately held that this was not a sovereign immunity case because the suit was against state officials (not the state) acting in violation of federal law. The Eleventh

**full faith and credit clause** It means that most government actions of another state must be officially recognized by public officials in Texas.

Amendment does not bar enforcement of a consent decree; enforcement by the federal courts is permitted to ensure enforcement of federal law.[6]

### State Powers

Nowhere in the U.S. Constitution is there a list of state powers. As mentioned, the Tenth Amendment simply states that all powers not specifically delegated to the national government, nor prohibited to the states, are reserved to the states or to the people. The **reserved powers** of the states are therefore undefined and often very difficult to specify, especially when the powers are concurrent with those of the national government, such as the taxing power. Political scientists, however, view reserved powers in broad categories:

- Police power (protection of the health, morals, safety, and convenience of citizens, and provision for the general welfare)
- Taxing power (raising revenue to pay salaries of state employees, meet other costs of government, and repay borrowed money)
- Proprietary power (public ownership of property such as airports, energy-producing utilities, and parks)
- Power of eminent domain (taking private property for highway construction or other public use at a fair price)

Needless to say, states today have broad powers, responsibilities, and duties. They are, for example, responsible for the nation's public elections—national, state, and local; there are no nationally operated election facilities. State courts conduct most trials (both criminal and civil). States operate public schools (elementary and secondary) and public institutions of higher education (colleges and universities), and they maintain most of the country's prisons.

More recently, the Katrina disaster along the Gulf Coast highlighted the responsibility of state and local governments to provide an array of services for the evacuees who fled primarily from Louisiana to Texas, and to Houston in particular. The disaster, as well as the Congressional investigation following the aftermath, also raised the question as to which level of government should provide the initial response to natural disasters. During Congressional hearings, Texas governor Rick Perry, along with other state governors, voiced his opposition to assigning the first response to the U.S. military, especially given the slow and inadequate response by the federal government during Katrina.

One broad state power that recently raised controversy was the power of eminent domain. Customarily, government entities have used the power of eminent domain to appropriate private property for public projects, such as highways, parks, and schools, so long as the property owners are paid a just compensation. In 2005, the U.S. Supreme Court expanded this power under the Fifth Amendment, allowing local governments to seize private homes for private development; the Court, however, left the door open for a state to set its own rules.[7] In response, in the summer of 2005, Governor Rick Perry added to the agenda of a special legislative session limits on government entities condemning private property where the primary purpose is for economic development.

**reserved powers** The Tenth Amendment of the U.S. Constitution declares that "The powers not delegated by the Constitution, nor prohibited by it to the States, are reserved to the States, respectively, or to the people." Although not spelled out in the U.S. Constitution, these reserved powers include police power, taxing power, proprietary power, and power of eminent domain.

Exceptions, however, were made for public projects, and to protect Arlington's efforts to build a proposed Dallas Cowboys stadium.

Although most state powers are recognizable, identifying a clear boundary line between state and national powers remains often complicated. Take, for example, the issue of interstate commerce. Not until *United States* v. *Lopez* (1999), a case that originated in Texas, did the U.S. Supreme Court indicate that the U.S. Congress had exceeded its powers to regulate interstate commerce when it attempted to ban guns in public schools. Operation of public schools has traditionally been considered a power of state and local governments, and the Court used the *Lopez* case[8] and other recent rulings to rein in the power of the federal government. (This time period is often referred to as the era of New Federalism.) In 2005, however, in another interstate commerce case, the Court drew a line when it came to regulating the use of marijuana for medical purposes of terminally ill patients. Based on a California initiative, the Court struck down the state's ability to make an exception to the illegalization of marijuana, contending that Congress had the sole power to regulate local and state activities that substantially affect interstate commerce.[9] Although the measure would have protected noncommercial cultivation and use of marijuana that did not cross state lines, the federal government contended that it would handicap enforcement of federal drug laws. In this regard, the Court ruled that the federal government is primarily responsible for regulating narcotics and other controlled substances.

### Federal-State Relations: An Evolving Process

Since the establishment of the American federal system, states have operated within a constitutional context modified to meet changing conditions. At the same time, the framers of the U.S. Constitution sought to provide a workable balance of power between national and state governments that would sustain the nation indefinitely. The fact that the American federal system has endured more than 200 years of stresses and strains attests to the foresight of its framers. The ultimate test of endurance occurred during the Civil War, which pitted North against South in a struggle to settle the issue of states' rights versus national supremacy regarding slavery. The Union army's victory in 1865 did not end federalism. The national government's policymaking authority after the Civil War was not necessarily broader than before, although for a period of time, Texas was subject to military rule. Each state's position within the nation remained essentially intact, but southern states could no longer legalize slavery.

Between 1865 and 1930, Congress acted vigorously to regulate railroads and interstate commerce. With the onset of the Great Depression of the 1930s, the federal government's role began to expand to policy areas typically within the realm of state and local governments. The federal government used grants of money to the states to influence state policymaking. Concurrently, the number and size of **federal grants-in-aid** grew as Congress gave states more financial assistance. As federally initiated programs multiplied, the national

**federal grants-in-aid**
Money appropriated by the U.S. Congress to help states provide needed facilities and services.

government's influence on state policymaking widened accordingly, and the states' control lessened in many areas. Beginning in the 1980s, and particularly in the 1990s and later, state and local governments gained more freedom to spend federal funds as they choose. In some areas, however, such as public assistance programs, they have been granted less money to spend.

This latest development in federal–state relations has been called **devolution**. The underlying concept in devolution is to bring about a reduction in the size and influence of the national government by reducing federal taxes and expenditures and by shifting many federal responsibilities to the states. Because one feature of devolution involves sharp reductions in federal aid, states are compelled to assume important new responsibilities with substantially less revenue to finance them. Texas and other states have been forced to assume more responsibility for formulating and funding their own programs in education, highways, mental health, public assistance (welfare), and other areas. In some cases, federal programs are shared, whereby the states must match federal monies to benefit from a program, such as the Children's Health Insurance Program (CHIP).

Another important feature of devolution is Congress's use of **block grants** to distribute money to state and local governments. Block grants are fixed sums of money awarded according to an automatic formula determined by Congress. Thus, states that receive block grants have greater flexibility in spending. For example, welfare programs have been primarily a federal responsibility, beginning with the Franklin D. Roosevelt administration's (1933–1945) response to widespread unemployment and poverty of the Great Depression. However, the Clinton administration (1993–2001) and a Republican-controlled Congress forced states to assume more responsibility to provide welfare programs and supplied federal funding in the form of block grants.[10] President George W. Bush continued these trends and added a new twist to devolution by giving federal financial assistance to faith-based organizations that provide social services to the poor. Also, after Hurricanes Katrina and Rita in 2005, the federal government agreed to provide community development grants designed to respond to natural disasters. (After Texas received close to a half million Hurricane Katrina evacuees, public officials raised concerns that the state would not receive its fair share of federal monies for the costs incurred.)

Despite the focus on devolution, recently enacted federal laws, such as the No Child Left Behind Act of 2001, suggest that the Bush administration is aggressively pursuing policies that once again expand the federal government's role. This law, which among other things requires federal testing in public schools, expands the national government's reach into a traditional area of state and local responsibility. In response to compliance pressures, the National Teachers Association and various school districts from three states, including Texas, sued the U.S. Department of Education for failing to provide adequate money to comply with the initiative and for forcing states and local school districts to incur the unfunded costs. A federal judge dismissed the suit stating that Congress had already allocated significant funding and that the federal government had the power to require states to meet educational standards in exchange for these funds.[11]

**devolution** Devolution exists when the federal government's financial and administrative responsibilities shift to state and local governments, especially in the area of social services.

**block grants** Congressional grants of money that allow the state considerable flexibility in spending for a program, such as providing welfare services.

Learning Check 2.1        (Answers on p. 84)
1. True or False: The Tenth Amendment specifically identifies states' powers.
2. Does devolution give states more or less freedom to make decisions?

## ★ The Texas Constitution: Politics of Policymaking

Political scientists and legal scholars generally believe that a constitution should not attempt to solve specific policy problems. Instead, it should indicate the process by which problems will be solved, both in the present and in the future. Presumably, if this principle is followed, later generations will not need to adopt numerous amendments. The Texas Constitution establishes the state's government, defines governing powers and imposes limitations thereon, and identifies our civil liberties and civil rights. In many areas, however, it also mandates specific policies in great detail.

The preamble to the Texas Constitution states, "Humbly invoking the blessings of Almighty God, the people of the state of Texas do ordain and establish this Constitution." These words begin the 28,600-word document that became Texas's seventh Constitution in 1876. By the end of 2006, that same document had been changed by no fewer than 439 amendments and had grown to more than 90,000 words.

The major flaws of the present Texas Constitution are its unwieldy length and its disorganized explanation of provisions. It has grown by amendment chiefly because the framers spelled out policymaking powers and limitations in minute detail. This, in turn, made frequent amendments inevitable, as constitutional provisions were altered to fit changing times and conditions. For more than a century, the Texas Constitution has continued to grow through an accumulation of amendments, most of which are essentially statutory (resembling a law made by the legislature). The resulting document more closely resembles a code of laws than a fundamental instrument of government. To fully understand the present-day Texas Constitution, we will examine the historical factors surrounding its adoption, as well as previous historical periods and constitutions.

### Historical Developments

The Texas Constitution provides the legal basis on which the state functions as an integral part of the federal Union. But the document is also a product of history and an expression of the dominant political philosophy of Texans living at the time of its adoption.

Generally, constitution drafters have been pragmatic people performing an important task. Despite the idealistic sentiment commonly attached to constitutions in the United States, however, the art of drafting and amending constitutions is essentially political in nature. In other words, these documents reflect the drafters' views and political interests as well as the political environment of their time. With the passing of years, our Texas Constitution reflects the political ideas of new generations of people who amend or change it.

## How Do We Compare ... in State Constitutions?

*Comparison of Age and Length of State Constitution of Various U.S States*

| Most Populous U.S. States | Year of Adoption | Approximate No. of Words | U.S. States Bordering Texas | Year of Adoption | Approximate No. of Words |
|---|---|---|---|---|---|
| California | 1879 | 54,600 | Arkansas | 1874 | 59,500 |
| Florida | 1968 | 52,000 | Louisiana | 1974 | 54,100 |
| New York | 1894 | 51,500 | New Mexico | 1911 | 27,200 |
| **Texas** | **1876** | **90,000** | Oklahoma | 1907 | 74,000 |

| Mexican States Bordering Texas | Year of Adoption | Approximate No. of Words |
|---|---|---|
| Chihuahua | 1950 | 23,900 |
| Coahuila | 1918 | 29,400 |
| Nuevo León | 1917 | 20,700 |
| Tamaulipas | 1921 | 13,600 |

*Sources:* The Book of States, 2006 ed., vol. 38 (Lexington, Ky.: Council of State Governments, 2006), 9; Instituto de Investigaciones Jurídicas de la Universidad Nacional Autónoma de México at **info4.juridicas.unam.mx**.

The **constitutional history of Texas** began nearly two centuries ago, when Texas was a part of Mexico. Each of its seven constitutions has reflected the political situation that existed when the document was drafted.[12] In this section, we see the political process at work as we examine the origins of these constitutions and note the efforts to revise and amend the current Texas Constitution.

**The First Six Texas Constitutions**   In 1824, three years after Mexico gained independence from Spain, Mexican liberals established a republic with a federal constitution. Within that federal system, the former Spanish provinces of Tejas and Coahuila became a single Mexican state that adopted its own constitution. Thus, the Constitution of Coahuila y Tejas, promulgated in 1827, marked Texas's first experience with a state constitution.

Political unrest among Anglo Texans, settled in Mexico's northeastern area, arose almost immediately, however. Factors that led Texans to declare independence from Mexico included their desire for unrestricted trade with the United States, Anglo attitudes of racial superiority, anger over Mexico's abolition of slavery, increasing numbers of immigrant settlers, and insufficient Anglo representation in the 12-member Texas-Coahuila legislature.[13] (See Selected Reading 2.1, "The American Tradition of Language Rights: The Forgotten Right to Government in a 'Known Tongue,'" for a different view of the new Texian settlers and the role of language.)

On 2 March 1836, at Washington-on-the-Brazos (between present-day Brenham and Navasota), a delegate convention of 59 Texans issued a declaration of independence from Mexico. The delegates then drafted the Constitution of the Republic of Texas, modeled largely after the U.S. Constitution. During this same period, in an effort to retain Mexican sovereignty, General Antonio López de Santa Anna defeated the Texians (as Texans identified themselves at the time) and Tejanos (Mexicans in Texas who also wanted independence from

**constitutional history of Texas** Texas constitutional history began with promulgation of the Constitution of Coahuila y Tejas within the Mexican federal system in 1827 and the Constitution of the Texas Republic in 1836. Texas has since been governed under its state constitutions of 1845, 1861, 1866, 1869, and 1876.

Mexico) in San Antonio in the siege of the Alamo that ended on 6 March 1836. Shortly afterward, Sam Houston's troops crushed the Mexican forces in the Battle of San Jacinto on 21 April 1836. Part of Texas's unique history is its existence as an independent nation for close to ten years.

After his victory over Santa Anna, Texas voters elected Sam Houston as president of their new republic; they also voted to seek admission to the Union. Not until 1845, however, was annexation authorized by a joint resolution of the U.S. Congress. Earlier attempts to become part of the United States by treaty had failed. Texas president Anson Jones called a constitutional convention, whose delegates drew up a new state constitution and agreed to accept the invitation to join the Union. In February 1845, after Texas voters ratified both actions of the constitutional convention, Texas obtained its third constitution and became the twenty-eighth state of the United States.

These events, however, set the stage for war between Mexico and the United States (1846–1848), especially with regard to where the boundary lines would be drawn. Historians argue that U.S. expansionist politicians and business interests actively sought this war. When the Treaty of Guadalupe Hidalgo between Mexico and the United States was signed in 1848, Mexico lost more than half its territory and recognized the Rio Grande as Texas's southern boundary. Negotiations also addressed the rights of Mexicans left behind, many of whom owned land in the region. Under the treaty, Mexicans had one year to choose to return to Mexico or remain in the newly annexed part of the United States; it also guaranteed Mexicans all rights of citizens. For all intents and purposes, these residents became the first Mexican Americans of Texas and the United States.

The Constitution of 1845 lasted until the Civil War began. When Texas seceded from the Union, it adopted the Secession Constitution in 1861, with the aim of making as few changes as possible in government structure and powers. Only changes necessary to equip the government for separation from the United States were included. Following the Confederacy's defeat, however, the Reconstruction Constitution of 1866 was drafted amid a different set of conditions. Here, the framers sought to restore Texas to the Union with a minimum of changes in existing social, economic, and political institutions. Although the Constitution of 1866 was based on the Constitution of 1845, it nevertheless recognized the right of former slaves to sue in the state's courts, to enter into contracts, to obtain and transfer property, and to testify in court actions involving blacks (but not in court actions involving whites). The Constitution of 1866 protected the personal property of African American Texans, but it did not permit them to vote, hold public office, or serve as jurors.

The relatively uncomplicated reinstatement of Texas into the Union ended abruptly when the Radical Republicans gained control of the U.S. Congress following the election of November 1866. Refusing to seat Texas's two senators and three representatives, Congress set aside the state's reconstructed government, enfranchised former slaves, disenfranchised prominent whites, and imposed military rule across the state. U.S. Army officers replaced civil authorities. As in other southern states, Texas functioned under a military government.

Under these conditions, delegates to a constitutional convention met in intermittent sessions from June 1868 to February 1869 and drafted yet another state constitution. Among other things, the new constitution centralized more power in state government, provided compulsory school attendance, and guaranteed a full range of rights for former slaves. This document was ratified in 1869. Then, with elections supervised by federal soldiers, Radical Republicans gained control of the Texas Legislature. At the same time, Edmund Jackson Davis (commonly identified as E. J. Davis), a former Union army general, was elected as the first Republican governor of Texas.

Historians have described the Davis administration (January 1870 to January 1874) as one of the most corrupt in Texas history. The governor imposed martial law in some places and used police methods to enforce his decrees. His administration was characterized by extravagant public spending, property tax increases to the point of confiscation, gifts of public funds to private interests, intimidation of newspaper editors, and control of voter registration by the military. In addition, hundreds of appointments to various state and local offices were made. Although the Constitution of 1869 is associated with the Reconstruction era and the unpopular administration of Governor Davis, the machinery of government created by this document was quite modern. The new fundamental law called for annual sessions of the legislature, a four-year term for the governor and other executive officers, and gubernatorial appointment (rather than popular election) of judges. It abolished county courts and raised the salaries of government officials. These changes centralized more governmental power in Austin and weakened local government.

Democrats gained control of the legislature in 1872. Then, in perhaps the most fraudulent election ever conducted in Texas, Governor Davis (with

E. J. Davis and some of the Constitutional Convention delegates of 1875 (Left: Portrait by William Henry Huddle/Texas State Library and Archives Commission; right: Texas State Library and Archives Commission)

42,633 votes) was badly defeated in December 1873 by Democrat Richard Coke (with 85,549 votes). When Davis refused to leave his office on the ground floor of the Capitol, Democratic lawmakers and Governor-elect Coke are reported to have climbed ladders to the Capitol's second story where the legislature convened. When President Grant refused to send troops to protect him, Davis left the Capitol under protest in January 1874. But he locked his office and kept the key. Governor Coke's supporters had to use an ax to open the office door. In that same year, Democrats wrested control of the state courts from Republicans. The next step was to rewrite the Texas Constitution.

**Drafting the Constitution of 1876**   In the summer of 1875, Texans elected 75 Democrats and 15 Republicans (6 of whom were African Americans) as delegates to a constitutional convention; however, only 83 attended the gathering in Austin. The majority of the delegates were not native Texans. More than 40 percent were members of the **Texas Grange** (the Patrons of Husbandry), a farmers' organization committed to strict economy in government (reduced spending) and limited governmental powers. Its slogan of "retrenchment and reform" became a major goal of the convention.[14] So strong was the spirit of strict economy among delegates that they refused to hire a stenographer or to allow publication of the convention proceedings. As a result, no official record was ever made of the convention that gave Texas its most enduring constitution.

In their zeal to undo Davis administration policies, the delegates on occasion overreacted. Striking at Reconstruction measures that had given Governor Davis control over voter registration, the overwrought delegates inserted a statement providing that "no law shall ever be enacted requiring a registration of voters of this state." Within two decades, however, the statement had been amended to permit voter registration laws.

As they continued to dismantle the Davis administration machinery, the delegates restricted the powers of the three branches of state government. They reduced the governor's salary, powers, and term (from four to two years); made all executive offices (except that of secretary of state) elective for two-year terms; and tied the hands of legislators with biennial (once every two years) sessions, low salaries, and limited legislative powers. All judgeships became popularly elected for relatively short terms of office. Justice of the peace courts, county courts, and district courts with popularly elected judges were established. In addition, public services were trimmed to the bone. Framers of the new constitution limited the public debt and severely curbed the legislature's taxing and spending powers. They also inserted specific policy provisions. For example, they reinstated racially segregated public education and repealed the compulsory school attendance law, restored precinct elections, and allowed only taxpayers to vote on local bond issues.

Texas's most enduring constitution was put to a popular vote in 1876 and was approved by a more than two-to-one majority. Although Texans in the state's largest cities—Houston, Dallas, San Antonio, and Galveston—voted against it, the much larger rural population voted for approval.

**Texas Grange** Known as the Patrons of Husbandry, this farmers' organization was well represented in the constitutional convention that produced the Constitution of 1876.

**Distrust of Government and Its Consequences**    Sharing in the prevailing popular distrust of and hostility toward government, the framers of the **Texas Constitution of 1876** sought with a vengeance to limit and thus control policymaking by placing many restrictions in the state's fundamental law. The general consensus of the time held that a state government could exercise only those powers listed in the state constitution. Therefore, instead of being permitted to exercise powers not denied by the U.S. Constitution, Texas lawmakers are limited to powers spelled out in the state's constitution.

## Today: After More Than a Century of Usage

The structural disarray and confusion of the Constitution of 1876 compound the disadvantages of its excessive length and detail. Unlike the Texas Constitution, the U.S. Constitution has only 26,000 words and only 27 constitutional amendments. Yet with all its shortcomings, the Texas Constitution of 1876 has endured for more than 130 years.

It was inevitable that filling the Texas Constitution with many details and creating a state government with restricted powers would soon lead to constitutional amendments. In fact, many substantive changes in Texas government require an amendment. For example, an amendment is needed to change the way the state pays bills, to abolish certain unneeded state and county offices, or to authorize a bond issue pledging state revenues. Urbanization, industrialization, the communication revolution, population explosion, increasing demands for programs and services, and countless social changes contribute to pressures for frequent constitutional change.

Most amendments apply to matters that should be resolved by statutes enacted by the Texas Legislature. Instead, an often uninformed and usually apathetic electorate must decide the fate of many frequently complex policy issues. In this context, special interests represented by well-financed lobbyists and the media often play influential roles in constitutional policymaking. Policymakers are also likely to influence the success or defeat of constitutional amendments. Governor Rick Perry, for instance, has played a pivotal role in advocating for specific constitutional amendment proposals. As the most visible policymaker in Texas, his public support or nonsupport of key propositions can sway voters.

One amendment supported by Governor Perry, Proposition 12 submitted to voters in 2003, resulted in intensive lobbying activity and media coverage, as public debate focused on setting limits for medical malpractice awards.[15] Despite opposition by plaintiffs' lawyers and some public interest groups, 51 percent of the voters (751,896) supported the amendment while 49 percent (718,647) opposed it.

In 2005, Governor Perry also supported Proposition 2, which signified a new direction in the substantive nature of constitutional amendment proposals on the ballot. The controversial nature of Proposition 2, which sought to ban same-sex marriages, produced unprecedented media coverage and interest

**Texas Constitution of 1876**  Texas's lengthy, much-amended constitution, a product of the post-Reconstruction era.

*Opposing signs urge voters to support or reject 2005's Proposition 2.* (Ralph Barrera/*Austin American-Statesman/* World Picture News)

group activity. As mentioned previously, the amendment proposal defined marriage as the "union of one man and one woman." It also prohibited the state and all political subdivisions from "creating or recognizing any legal status identical or similar to marriage," and contained language allowing the appointment of guardians, rights to property, hospital visitation, and the designation of life insurance beneficiaries without the necessity of legal marriage. Despite opposition from most of Texas' leading newspapers (in cities such as Austin, Houston, Dallas, Fort Worth, El Paso, and San Antonio), the measure overwhelmingly passed with 76 percent of the voters (more than 1.7 million) supporting it and 24 percent (more than 500,000) opposing it. Although the vote margin varied from county to county, only one county disapproved the constitutional amendment; Travis County (Austin) opposed the measure by a margin of close to 27,000 votes (81,170 in opposition to 54,246 in support).[16]

Oftentimes, Texas voters are expected to evaluate numerous constitutional amendments. (Table 2.1 provides data on amendments proposed and adopted from 1879 through 2005.) Along with Proposition 12 in 2003, for example, the 78th Legislature proposed 21 other amendments. Subjects included granting tax exemptions on property owned by religious groups for expansion, freezing property taxes for elderly and disabled homeowners, permitting wineries to sell wine for consumption both on and off premises, and allowing homeowners to establish home equity lines of credit. All 22 proposals were submitted to voters on 13 September 2003 rather than the traditional November election day. Voters approved all of these constitutional amendment proposals, most with comfortable majorities.

## How Do We Compare . . . in State Constitutional Amendments?

### Comparison of Number and Frequency of State Constitutional Amendments, 2005

| Most Populous U.S. States | No. of Amendments Added Since Adoption of Current Constitution | Average No. of Amendments Submitted to Voters Through 2005 | U.S. States Bordering Texas | No. of Amendments Added Since Adoption of Current Constitution | Average No. of Amendments Submitted to Voters Through 2005 |
|---|---|---|---|---|---|
| California | 513 | 4.1 | Arkansas | 91 | .7 |
| Florida | 104 | 2.8 | Louisiana | 129 | 4.2 |
| New York | 216 | 2.0 | New Mexico | 151 | 1.6 |
| **Texas** | **439*** | **3.4** | Oklahoma | 171 | 1.8 |

*Source:* The Book of States, 2006 ed., vol. 38 (Lexington, Ky.: Council of State Governments, 2006): 9.

*signifies as of November 2006.

In November 2005, only nine proposals were submitted to voters. These proposals ranged from denying bail for defendants with pre-trail release violations to adding members to the State Commission on Judicial Conduct and expanding the line of credit advances under reverse mortgages.[17] Two of the nine proposals, however, failed: one related to lengthening terms of office from two to six years for local transit boards and another related to authorizing the legislature to define commercial interest rates. The latter measure received wide support from business leaders and a bipartisan vote in the state legislature. It would have eliminated interest rate caps on commercial loans above $7 million, and provided business owners with more flexibility to obtain loans in Texas and to do business in Texas. In addition to constitutional amendments that apply to all parts of Texas, some examples of policymaking by constitutional amendment affect categories of counties or a single county.[18]

To modernize the Texas Constitution, one amendment adopted in 1999 authorized elimination of certain "duplicative, executed, obsolete, archaic and ineffective provisions of the Texas Constitution." Among resulting deletions were references to the abolished poll tax and the governor's authority "to protect the frontier from hostile incursions by Indians." Voters approved a similar amendment to eliminate several obsolete or duplicative provisions in 2001. Despite these measures, the Texas Constitution still has problems.

The following were among the joint resolutions proposing constitutional amendments considered but rejected in the 79th Legislature's regular session in 2005:

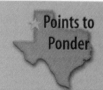

**Points to Ponder**

- Placing a moratorium on executing persons convicted of capital offenses
- Prohibiting authorization or funding of a school voucher program
- Establishing an independent redistricting committee
- Authorizing the operation of video lottery games
- Authorizing a uniform statewide property tax to benefit public education
- Requiring recorded votes in the state legislature

**Learning Check 2.2**     **(Answers on p. 84)**

**1.** How many different constitutions has Texas had throughout its history?
**2.** True or False: Our present-day constitution has been amended just under 100 times.

## ★ Constitutional Amendments and Revision

Each of the 50 American state constitutions provides the means for changing the powers and functions of government. Without a provision for change, few constitutions would survive long. A revision may produce a totally new constitution to replace an old one. Courts may alter constitutions by interpreting the wording of these documents in new and different ways. Finally, constitutions may be changed by formal amendment, the chief method by which the Texas Constitution has been altered.

Because Texas's registered voters have an opportunity to vote on one or more proposed amendments nearly every year—and sometimes twice in a single year—an understanding of the steps in the **constitutional amendment process** is important. Article XVII, Section 1, provides a relatively simple procedure for amending the Texas Constitution. The basic steps in that process are as follows:

- A joint resolution proposing an amendment is introduced in the House or in the Senate during a regular session or during a special session called by the governor.
- Two-thirds of the members in each chamber must adopt the resolution.
- The secretary of state prepares an explanatory statement that briefly describes the proposed amendment, and the attorney general approves this statement.
- The explanatory statement is published twice in Texas newspapers that print official state notices.
- A copy of the proposed amendment is posted in each county courthouse at least 30 days before the election.
- The voters must approve the proposed amendment by a simple majority vote in a regular or special election.
- The governor, who has no veto power in the process, proclaims the amendment.

The Texas Legislature decides whether a proposed amendment will be submitted to the voters in the November general election of an even-numbered year or in a special election scheduled for an earlier date. The 77th Legislature submitted 19 proposed amendments to voters in November 2001, and it placed an additional amendment before voters in November 2002. In contrast, the 78th Legislature proposed 22 amendments in its 2003 regular session, and it submitted all of them to the voters in September of that year. The 79th Legislature presented voters with nine constitutional amendments in November 2005.

Increasing influence of interest groups in the legislative process has produced efforts to give Texans the powers of **initiative** and **referendum** at the state

**constitutional amendment process** Article XVII, Section 1, of the Texas Constitution stipulates that an amendment must be proposed by a two-thirds vote of members in each chamber of the legislature and approved by a simple majority of voters in a general or special election.

**initiative** Although not used at the state level in Texas, this is a process whereby individuals or groups may gather signatures required for submitting a proposed constitutional amendment or a proposed statute to a popular vote.

**referendum** The referendum process allows voters to gather signatures needed to challenge at the polls (and potentially to overturn) a law enacted by their state legislature. In Texas this process occurs at the local level. At the state level, bonds secured by taxes and state constitutional amendments must be approved by voters.

*Table 2.1*     Texas Constitution of 1876: Amendments Proposed and Adopted, 1879–2005

| Year Proposed | Number Proposed | Number Adopted | Year Proposed | Number Proposed | Number Adopted |
|---|---|---|---|---|---|
| 1879 | 1 | 1 | 1949 | 10 | 2 |
| 1881 | 2 | 0 | 1951 | 7 | 3 |
| 1883 | 5 | 5 | 1953 | 11 | 11 |
| 1887 | 6 | 0 | 1955 | 9 | 9 |
| 1889 | 2 | 2 | 1957 | 12 | 10 |
| 1891 | 5 | 5 | 1959 | 4 | 4 |
| 1893 | 2 | 2 | 1961 | 14 | 10 |
| 1895 | 2 | 1 | 1963 | 7 | 4 |
| 1897 | 5 | 1 | 1965 | 27 | 20 |
| 1899 | 1 | 0 | 1967 | 20 | 13 |
| 1901 | 1 | 1 | 1969 | 16 | 9 |
| 1903 | 3 | 3 | 1971 | 18 | 12 |
| 1905 | 3 | 2 | 1973 | 9 | 6 |
| 1907 | 9 | 1 | 1975 | 12 | 3 |
| 1909 | 4 | 4 | 1977 | 15 | 11 |
| 1911 | 5 | 4 | 1978 | 1 | 1 |
| 1913 | 7 | 0 | 1979 | 12 | 9 |
| 1915 | 7 | 0 | 1981 | 10 | 8 |
| 1917 | 3 | 3 | 1982 | 3 | 3 |
| 1919 | 13 | 3 | 1983 | 19 | 16 |
| 1921 | 5 | 1 | 1985 | 17 | 17 |
| 1923 | 22 | 1 | 1986 | 1 | 1 |
| 1925 | 4 | 4 | 1987 | 28 | 20 |
| 1927 | 8 | 4 | 1989 | 21 | 19 |
| 1929 | 7 | 5 | 1990 | 1 | 1 |
| 1931 | 9 | 9 | 1991 | 15 | 12 |
| 1933 | 12 | 4 | 1993 | 19 | 14 |
| 1935 | 13 | 10 | 1995 | 14 | 11 |
| 1937 | 7 | 6 | 1997 | 15 | 13 |
| 1939 | 4 | 3 | 1999 | 17 | 13 |
| 1941 | 5 | 1 | 2001 | 19 | 19 |
| 1943 | 3 | 3 | 2002 | 1 | 1 |
| 1945 | 8 | 7 | 2003 | 22 | 22 |
| 1947 | 9 | 9 | 2005 | 9 | 7 |
| | | | Totals | 637 | 439 |

*Source:*  Texas Legislative Council.

**Points to Ponder**

- State law, as well as federal law, requires the secretary of state to publish explanatory statements twice for each proposed constitutional amendment in English and Spanish in Texas newspapers.
- Typically, in the past, these notices were published in both languages in the English-language press.
- In 2003, the U.S. Department of Justice and the Texas secretary of state entered into an agreement whereby only a Spanish-language version of the explanatory notice would be mailed to each registered voter with a Hispanic surname instead of publishing the notice in Spanish in the newspapers to provide an efficient and economical method of reaching monolingual Spanish speakers.
- Many bilingual Texans with Hispanic surnames were upset when they received this communication. They believed that government officials should not infer or assume that people with Hispanic surnames are unable to read English or, for that matter, are fluent in Spanish.

level (see the chapter "Local Governments" for a discussion of how these powers work locally). If adopted, the initiative process would bypass the legislature and allow individual Texans or groups to gather signatures required for submitting proposed constitutional amendments and statutes (ordinary laws) to direct popular vote. The referendum process would allow Texas voters to gather signatures to challenge and potentially overturn statutes enacted by state lawmakers. As of 2005, voters in 19 states were empowered to propose and enact laws; and in 18 states they could propose constitutional amendments.[19] Since 1997, no serious legislative efforts to amend the Texas Constitution to authorize the initiative and referendum processes at the state level have emerged. However, as part of her gubernatorial campaign in 2006, independent candidate Carole Keeton Strayhorn publicly supported giving Texans the power to initiate constitutional amendments and state laws, with or without legislative approval.

## Constitutional Revision

Attempts to revise Texas's Constitution of 1876 began soon after its adoption. A legislative resolution calling for a constitutional revision convention was introduced in 1887 and was followed by others. Limited success came in 1969, when an amendment removed 56 obsolete constitutional provisions. Not since the 1970s, however, have major efforts been made to revise the state's constitution.

**constitutional revision** Extensive or complete rewriting of a constitution.

### The Revision Efforts of the 1970s

The most comprehensive movement to achieve wholesale **constitutional revision** began in 1971. In that year, the 62nd Legislature adopted a joint resolution proposing an amendment authorizing the appointment of a study commission and naming the members of the 63rd Legislature as delegates to a constitutional convention. Except for the Bill of Rights, any part of the Texas Constitution of 1876 could be changed or deleted. Submitted to the voters in 1972 as a proposed constitutional amendment, the resolution was approved by a comfortable margin of more than a half million votes (1,549,982 for to 985,282 against).

A six-member committee (composed of the governor, the lieutenant governor, the speaker of the House, the attorney general, the chief justice of the Texas Supreme Court, and the presiding judge of the Court of Criminal Appeals) selected 37 persons to serve as members of the Constitutional Revision Commission. The commission prepared a draft constitution based on opinions and information gathered at public hearings conducted throughout the state and from various authorities on constitutional revision. One-fourth the length of the present constitution, the completed draft was submitted to the legislature on November 1, 1973.

On January 8, 1974, members of both houses of the Texas Legislature met in Austin as a **constitutional revision convention**. Previous Texas constitutions had been drafted by convention delegates popularly elected for that purpose. When the finished document was put to a vote, the result was 118 for and 62 against, three votes short of the two-thirds majority of the total membership needed for final approval. (Approval required a total of at least 121 votes.) Attempts to reach compromises on controversial issues proved futile.

The Constitutional Convention of 1974 perhaps provided the best demonstration of the politics surrounding Texas constitution making. First, the convention was hampered by a lack of positive political leadership. Governor Dolph Briscoe maintained a hands-off policy throughout the convention. Lieutenant Governor Bill Hobby similarly failed to provide needed political leadership; and the retiring speaker of the House, Price Daniel Jr., pursued a nonintervention course. Other members of the legislature were distracted by their need to campaign for reelection.

The primary reason the convention failed to agree on a proposed constitution was the phantom "non-issue" of a right-to-work provision. A statutory ban on union shop labor contracts was already in effect. Adding this prohibition to the constitution would not have strengthened the legal hand of employers to any significant degree. Nevertheless, conservative, anti-labor forces insisted on this provision, and a pro-labor minority vigorously opposed it. The controversy aroused much emotion and at times produced loud and bitter name-calling among delegates on the floor and spectators in the galleries.[20]

Stung by widespread public criticism of the 1974 convention's failure to produce a proposed constitution for public approval or rejection, the 64th Legislature resolved to submit a proposal to Texas voters. In 1975, both houses of the legislature agreed on a constitutional revision resolution comprising 10 articles in 8 sections to be submitted to the Texas electorate in November of

**constitutional revision convention** A body of delegates who meet to make extensive changes in a constitution or to draft a new constitution.

that year. The content of the articles was essentially the same as that of the final resolution of the unsuccessful 1974 convention.

The revision proposed in 1975 represented years of work by men and women well informed about constitution making. Recognized constitutional authorities evaluated the concise and orderly document as one of the best-drafted state constitutions ever submitted to American voters. Although new and innovative in many respects, the proposal did not discard all of the old provisions. In addition to retaining the Bill of Rights, the proposed constitution incorporated such basic principles as limited government, separation of powers, and bicameralism (a two-house legislature).

Nevertheless, Texas voters demonstrated a strong preference for the status quo by rejecting each proposition. Voters in 250 of the state's 254 counties rejected all eight proposals. A mere 23 percent of the estimated 5.9 million registered voters cast ballots, meaning that only about 10 percent of the state's voting-age population participated in this important referendum. When asked to explain the resounding defeat of the eight propositions, Bill Hobby, then lieutenant governor, responded, "There's not enough of the body left for an autopsy."

### Recent Revision Attempts

After the revision debacle of 1975, two decades passed before the next attempt to revise the constitution. In 1995, Senator John Montford (D-Lubbock) drafted a streamlined constitution that incorporated many of the concepts contained in the failed 1975 proposal. Montford's plan also called for a voter referendum every 30 years (without legislative approval) on the question of calling a constitutional revision convention. But Montford resigned from the Texas Senate to become chancellor of the Texas Tech University System in 1996; and with such issues as tax changes, welfare reform, and educational finance pressing for attention, the 75th Legislature did not seriously consider constitutional revision in 1997.

In 1998, Senator Bill Ratliff (R-Mount Pleasant) and Representative Rob Junell (D-San Angelo) launched another attempt to revise the constitution.[21] With assistance from San Angelo State University students and others, they prepared a complete rewrite of the much-amended 1876 document. Subsequently, Ratliff and Junell introduced another draft for consideration by the 76th Legislature in 1999. It failed to muster enough support for serious consideration in committee and never received a floor vote in either legislative chamber. This proposal would have trimmed the 80,000-word document to about 19,000 words. Significant changes included expanding powers of the governor, repealing the current partisan election method of selecting state judges, and increasing salaries of the House speaker and the lieutenant governor.[22]

With redistricting and budgeting issues dominating the regular session in 2001, the 77th Legislature gave constitutional revision little attention. Similarly,

## POINT/COUNTERPOINT

### Should the Texas Constitution Be Rewritten?

**THE ISSUE**   Over the past several decades, proponents and opponents to a wholesale constitutional rewrite have debated the merits of the issue. The opponents continue to argue for the status quo, whereas the proponents argue that now, more than ever before, a rewrite is necessary. A 2003 editorial in the *Dallas Morning News* stated that since this is a new century, the leadership of the Texas Legislature should "lead the way on a renewed effort to give the state a new and streamlined constitution." Some of the arguments that have been raised are as follows:

### Arguments For Rewriting the Constitution

1. It is excessively long and outdated.
2. Voter turnout for constitutional amendment elections tends to be very low.
3. Voters are asked to decide on complex proposals that are not (or cannot be) adequately summarized in brief explanatory statements.
4. Expanding the powers of the government would better serve the needs of Texans.

### Arguments Against Rewriting the Constitution

1. Despite its flaws, the Texas Constitution remains a functioning document.
2. The amendment process allows changes when needed.
3. Special interests would in all likelihood control constitutional revision.
4. A comparison of state constitutional revision attempts suggests that constitutional revision can be a high-risk endeavor and does not ensure success.

For a review of constitutional revision attempts by various states, see James M. Burns et al., *State & Local Politics: Government by the People*, 11th ed. (Upper Saddle River, N.J.: Prentice Hall, 2004): 47–50.

with a budget crisis and congressional redistricting at hand, wholesale constitutional revision was not on the agenda for the 78th Legislature in 2003. School funding took center stage during the 79th Legislature's regular and special sessions, and nothing was accomplished for constitutional revision in 2005 or 2006.

### Piecemeal Revision and Turnout for Voting on Amendments

Since extensive constitutional reform has proved futile, Texas legislators have sought to achieve some measure of government reform by other means, including legislative enactments and piecemeal constitutional amendments. In 1977, for example, the 65th Legislature enacted into law two parts of the 1975 propositions defeated at the polls. One established a procedure for reviewing state administrative agencies; the other created a planning agency within the Office of the Governor. In 1979, the 66th Legislature proposed six amendments designed to implement parts of the constitutional revision package rejected in 1975. Three were adopted by the voters and added to the Texas Constitution. They accomplished the following:

■ Established a single property tax appraisal district in each county (discussed in the chapter "Local Governments")

■ Gave criminal appellate jurisdiction to 14 courts of appeals that formerly had exercised civil jurisdiction only

■ Allowed the governor restricted removal power over appointed statewide officials[23]

Proposals for important constitutional changes in recent years have been unsuccessful in the House and the Senate. For example, during the regular session of the 77th Legislature in 2001, Representative Rob Junell (D-San Angelo) submitted a proposal that was considered and approved by the House Select Committee on Constitutional Revision. Among other items, the proposal would have changed the terms of office for state senators and House members. It would also have created a Texas Salary Commission to set salaries for elected and appointed officials of the executive, judicial, and legislative branches. This proposal, however, died because it was never brought up for a floor vote in the House.[24]

Part of the problem with piecemeal revision relates to the typically low voter turnout for constitutional amendment elections in odd-numbered years. Roughly 8.3 percent of Texas voters participated in the 1999 election—about 950,000 of the state's 11.4 million registered voters. Statewide turnout in the 2001 special constitutional election for voting on 19 proposed amendments was less than 7 percent. This amounted to merely 800,000 of Texas's 12 million registered voters. In 2002, given the gubernatorial contest and other competitive races, turnout was higher (36 percent), but only a single amendment was on the ballot. A year later, despite the controversy surrounding some of the 22 proposed amendments, voter turnout in this special election dropped to 12 percent (under 1.5 million voters). In 2005, given the controversial amendment to ban same-sex marriages, turnout increased to close to 18 percent (which translated to more than 2 million among registered voters).

---

**Learning Check 2.3          (Answers on p. 85)**

1. When was the last time voters were presented with a constitutional revision proposal from the state legislature?
2. True or False: Amending the Texas Constitution requires two-thirds of the members of each chamber of the state legislature adopting a proposed amendment, and three-fourths of the voters approving it in a constitutional amendment election.

---

## ★ The Texas Constitution: A Summary

Chiefly because of its length, complete printed copies of the Texas Constitution are not readily available to the public. Until publication of its Millennium Edition (2000–2001), the *Texas Almanac* was the most widely used source for the text of this document. That edition and subsequent editions, however, refer persons seeking the text of the Texas Constitution to the Internet. (See this chapter's "Internet Resources.")

Although *Practicing Texas Politics* does not include the entire text of the Texas Constitution, each chapter looks to Texas's basic law for its content. The rest of this chapter presents a brief synopsis of the document's 17 articles.[25]

## The Bill of Rights

We begin by examining Article I, the Texas Constitution's **Bill of Rights**. The Bill of Rights is made up of 30 sections that cover a multitude of topics, including protection against arbitrary governmental actions, the rights of accused and convicted criminals and victims of crime, and equal rights for women. Article I also includes philosophical observations that have no direct force of law.

**Arbitrary Governmental Actions**    Eleven of Article I's sections provide protections for people and property against arbitrary governmental actions. Guarantees such as freedom of speech, press, religion, assembly, and petition are included. The right to keep and bear arms, prohibitions against taking of property by government action without just compensation, and protection of contracts are also incorporated. Most of these rights found in the Texas Constitution are also protected under the U.S. Constitution. Thus, with their basic rights guaranteed in both national and state constitutions, Texans, like people in other states, have a double safeguard against arbitrary governmental actions. (Some civil rights advocates believe, however, that, banning same-sex marriages in our Texas Constitution indicates less legal protection and fewer safeguards for gays and lesbians against discrimination.)

One of these constitutional rights centers on freedom of religion. Although both our state and federal constitutions protect freedom of religion, the wordings are different. The Texas Bill of Rights, Section 6, states, "All men have a natural and indefeasible right to worship Almighty God according to the dictates of their own conscience. No man shall be compelled to attend, erect or support any place of worship, or to maintain any ministry against his consent . . . and no preference shall ever be given to any religious society or mode of worship." Under the U.S. Constitution, the First Amendment (as applied to the states under the Fourteenth Amendment) provides that states "shall make no law respecting an establishment of religion, or prohibiting the free exercise thereof."

Cases on religious freedom have gone from Texas all the way to the U.S. Supreme Court. Recent cases centered on student-led prayer before school football games and a Ten Commandments monument placed on the Capitol grounds. The Court, which has interpreted the Establishment Clause to require a separation of church and state, struck down school prayer before a football game, contending that the message conveyed amounted to an endorsement of religion on the school grounds.[26] (See the Selected Reading 2.2, "They Haven't Got A Prayer," for a view of the circumstances before and after the ruling.) In contrast, the Court upheld the Ten Commandments display, concluding that it is an historical monument among other historical monuments on the state grounds.[27]

**Bill of Rights** Composed of 30 sections in Article I of the Texas Constitution, it guarantees protections for people and their property against arbitrary actions by state and local governments. Included among these rights are freedom of speech, press, religion, assembly, and petition. The Texas Bill of Rights is similar to the one found in the U.S. Constitution.

**Criminals and Victims**    Thirteen sections of the Texas Constitution's Bill of Rights relate to the rights of persons accused of crimes and to the rights of individuals who have been convicted of crimes. For example, one section concerns the right to release on bail; another prohibits unreasonable searches and seizures; and a third declares that "the right to trial by jury shall remain inviolate." These provisions relate closely to similar language in the national Bill of Rights.

The Texas Constitution is even more protective of certain rights than is the U.S. Constitution. An additional set of rights added by constitutional amendment in 1989 guarantees the "rights of crime victims." This provision, developed in the early 1980s when a presidential task force explored the inequality of rights for crime victims, establishes victims constitutional rights. Generally, this amendment gives victims such rights as the right to restitution, the right to information about the accused (conviction, sentence, release, etc.), the right to be protected from the accused throughout the criminal justice process, and the right of respect for the victim's dignity and privacy throughout the process.

**Equal Rights for Women**    Another example where the Texas Constitution provides more protection than the U.S. Constitution relates to equal rights for women. Attempts nationwide to add the proposed Equal Rights Amendment (ERA) to the U.S. Constitution failed between 1972 and 1982 (even though the amendment was approved by the Texas Legislature). Nevertheless, the **Texas Equal Legal Rights Amendment (ELRA)** was added to Article 1, Section 3, of the Texas Constitution in 1972. It states: "Equality under the law shall not be denied or abridged because of sex, race, color, creed or national origin." This constitutional amendment was proposed and adopted after several unsuccessful attempts dating back to the 1950s.[28] Interestingly, the constitution has a provision that states: "All free men have equal rights."

**Additional Protections**    Additional protections in the Texas Constitution include prohibitions against imprisonment for debt, outlawry (the process of putting a convicted person outside of the protection of the law), and transportation (punishing a convicted citizen by banishment from the state). Monopolies are prohibited by a provision of the Texas Bill of Rights but not by the U.S. Constitution. Interpretation of the Texas Constitution by the Texas Supreme Court has also provided additional rights, such as the Court's interpretation of Article VII, Section 1, requiring the state legislature to provide support and maintenance for an efficient system of free public schools. In 1989, the high court first held that the state legislature has a constitutional requirement to create a more equitable public school finance system.

The Texas Supreme Court revisited school finance in 2005 and declared the school finance system unconstitutional. However, rather than focusing on the system's continued and persistent inequities, the Court focused on whether the state-imposed property tax cap amounted to a statewide property tax, which the Texas Constitution forbids. (Property taxes can be collected only at the local level.) Because more than 80 percent of all school districts have reached this cap, and state funding has continued to decline, the Court held that school boards had

**Texas Equal Legal Rights Amendment** Added to Article 1, Section 3, of the Texas Constitution, it guarantees that "Equality under the law shall not be denied or abridged because of sex, race, color, creed or national origin."

effectively lost control of tax rates. Equally important, the Court rejected district court judge John Dietz's 2004 ruling that more money in the system was necessary to comply with the Texas constitution's requirement to provide the "general diffusion of knowledge."[29] (For more on school finance see the chapter "Finance and Fiscal Policy.")

**Philosophical Observations**   Three sections of the Texas Bill of Rights contain philosophical observations that have no direct force of law. Still stinging from what they saw as the "bondage" years of Reconstruction, the angry delegates to the constitutional convention of 1875 began their work by inserting this statement: "Texas is a free and independent state, subject only to the Constitution of the United States." They also asserted that all political power resides with the people and is legitimately exercised only on their behalf and that the people may at any time "alter, reform, or abolish their government." To guard against the possibility that any of the rights guaranteed in the other 28 sections would be eliminated or altered by the government, Section 29 proclaims that "everything in this 'Bill of Rights' is excepted out of the general powers of government, and shall forever remain inviolate."

## The Powers of Government

Holding fast to the principle of limited government, the framers of the Constitution of 1876 firmly embedded in the state's fundamental law the familiar doctrine of **separation of powers**. In Article II, they assigned the lawmaking, law-enforcing, and law-adjudicating powers of government to three separate branches, identified as the legislative, executive, and judicial departments, respectively.

Article III is titled "Legislative Department." Legislative powers are vested in the bicameral legislature, composed of the House of Representatives with 150 members and the Senate with 31 members. A patchwork of more than 60 sections, this article provides vivid testimony to more than 125 years of amendments directly affecting the legislative branch. For example, in 1936, an amendment added a section granting the Texas Legislature the authority to levy taxes to fund a retirement system for public school, college, and university teachers. Today, public school teachers and personnel employed by public universities and community colleges benefit from pension programs provided by the state.

Article IV, "Executive Department," states unequivocally that the governor "shall be the Chief Executive Officer of the State" but then shares out the executive power with four other popularly elected officers independent of the governor: the lieutenant governor, the attorney general, the comptroller of public accounts, and the commissioner of the General Land Office. (A state treasurer was originally included in this list, but a constitutional amendment abolished the office.) With this and other provisions for division of executive power, some observers consider the Texas governor no more than first among equals in the executive department.

**separation of powers**
The assignment of law-making, law-enforcing, and law-interpreting functions to separate branches of government.

Through Article V, "Judicial Department," Texas joins Oklahoma as the only states in the country with two courts of final appeal: one for civil cases (the Supreme Court of Texas) and one for criminal cases (the Court of Criminal Appeals). Below these two supreme appellate courts are the courts authorized by the Texas Constitution and created by the legislature: the intermediate appellate courts (14 courts of appeals) and hundreds of courts of original jurisdiction (district courts, county courts, and justice of the peace courts).

### Suffrage

Article VI, titled "**Suffrage**" (the right to vote), is one of the shortest articles in the Texas Constitution. Before 1870, states had the definitive power to conduct elections. Since that time, amendments to the U.S. Constitution, acts of Congress, and U.S. Supreme Court rulings have vastly diminished this power. Within the scope of current federal regulations, the Texas Constitution establishes qualifications for voters, provides for citizen voter registration, and governs the conduct of elections. In response to federal-level changes, this article has been amended to abolish the payment of a poll tax or any other form of property qualification for voting in the state's elections, and to change the minimum voting age from 21 to 18.

### Local Governments

The most disorganized part of the Texas Constitution concerns units of **local government**: counties, municipalities (cities), school districts, and other special districts. Although Article IX is titled "Counties," the provisions concerning county government are scattered through four other articles. Moreover, the basic structure of county government is defined not in Article IX on counties but in Article V on the judiciary. Article XI on municipalities is equally disorganized and inadequate. Only four of the sections of this article relate exclusively to municipal government. Other sections concern county government, taxation, public indebtedness, and forced sale of public property.

Along with counties and municipalities, the original text of the Constitution of 1876 referred to school districts but not to other types of special-district governments. Authorization for special districts, however, crept into the Texas Constitution with a 1904 amendment that authorizes the borrowing of money for water development and road construction by a county "or any defined district." Since then, special districts have been created to provide myriad services such as drainage, conservation, urban renewal, public housing, hospitals, and airports.

### Other Articles

The nine remaining articles also reflect a strong devotion to constitutional minutiae. Titles of these articles are as follows: Education, Taxation and Revenue, Railroads, Private Corporations, Spanish and Mexican Land Titles, Public

**suffrage** The right to vote.

**local government** The Texas Constitution authorizes these units of local government: counties, municipalities, school districts, and other special districts. These "grassroots governments" provide a wide range of services that include rural roads, protection of persons and property, city streets, and public education.

Lands and Land Office, Impeachment, General Provisions, and Mode of Amendment. The shortest is Article XIII, Spanish and Mexican Land Titles. The entire text was deleted by amendment in 1969 because its provisions were deemed obsolete. The longest article is Article XVI, General Provisions. Among other provisions, it prohibits bribing of public officials and authorizes the legislature to regulate the manufacture and sale of intoxicants.

---

**Learning Check 2.4**        **(Answers on p. 85)**

1. True or False: The Texas Constitution contains constitutional rights not found in the U.S. Constitution.
2. Article II of the Texas Constitution assigns powers to which branches of government?

---

## Looking Ahead

The Constitution of 1876 was written by a convention composed largely of Democrats; and, until recently, amendments were proposed by Democrat-controlled legislatures. Now that Texas Republicans dominate both houses of the legislature and have a record of winning statewide elections by large majorities, will GOP leaders launch a drive for a convention that would write the state's eighth constitution?

Later chapters will demonstrate how the Texas Constitution affects the structure, functions, and procedures of the three branches of the state's government; the operation of political parties and interest groups within the state; and the financial arrangements for state and local units of government in Texas.

It is important to note that counties, municipalities, and special districts do not derive their powers and responsibilities from the federal government. Rather, these low-level governments receive their legal authority from state constitutional provisions and/or acts of the Texas Legislature. The chapter "Local Governments" examines the structure and operation of these various forms of local government.

## Chapter Summary

- The American federal system features a division of powers between a national government and 50 state governments. Powers not delegated (nor implied, as interpreted by federal courts) to the federal government are reserved to the states or to the people under the Tenth Amendment. A balance of power between the national and state governments has evolved over time.
- The Texas Constitution is the fundamental law that sets forth the powers and limitations of the state's government. Texas has had seven constitutions, each reflecting the political situation that existed when the document was drafted. The Constitution of 1876 has endured despite its excessive length, confusion, and statutory detail.

- Today's Texas Constitution is the country's second longest and, at the end of 2006, had 439 amendments. Most amendments are statutory in nature, so the document resembles a code of laws.
- Changing the Texas Constitution requires an amendment proposed by a two-thirds majority vote of the members in each legislative chamber and approved by a simple majority of the state's voters in a general or special election. Despite several efforts to revise the Texas Constitution, only piecemeal revisions have occurred.
- The Texas Constitution is composed of 17 articles. Included are the Bill of Rights, an article on suffrage, articles on the three branches of state government, and provisions concerning the powers of state and local governments.

## Key Terms

- Tenth Amendment, *p. 57*
- national supremacy clause, *p. 57*
- delegated powers, *p. 57*
- implied powers, *p. 58*
- constitutional guarantees, *p. 58*
- privileges and immunities, *p. 59*
- full faith and credit clause, *p. 60*
- reserved powers, *p. 61*
- federal grants-in-aid, *p. 62*
- devolution, *p. 63*
- block grants, *p. 63*
- constitutional history of Texas, *p. 65*
- Texas Grange, *p. 68*

- Texas Constitution of 1876, *p. 69*
- constitutional amendment process, *p. 72*
- initiative, *p. 72*
- referendum, *p. 72*
- constitutional revision, *p. 74*
- constitutional revision convention, *p. 75*
- Bill of Rights, *p. 79*
- Texas Equal Legal Rights Amendment (ELRA), *p. 80*
- separation of powers, *p. 81*
- suffrage, *p. 82*
- local government, *p. 82*

## Learning Check Answers

**2.1**
1. False. The Tenth Amendment does not specifically identify the powers of the states.
2. Devolution gives the states more freedom to make decisions.

**2.2**
1. Texas has had seven constitutions throughout its history.
2. False. Our present-day Texas Constitution has been amended more than 400 times.

**2.3**

1. November 1975 was the last time that voters were presented with a constitutional revision proposal from the state legislature; recent attempts have failed.
2. False. Amending the Texas Constitution requires two-thirds of the members of each chamber of the state legislature to adopt a proposed amendment, and only a simple majority of the voters to approve it in a constitutional amendment election.

**2.4**

1. True. The Texas Constitution does contain additional constitutional rights, such as the Equal Legal Rights Amendment, not found in the U.S. Constitution.
2. The Texas Constitution assigns power to the legislative, executive, and judicial branches.

## Discussion Questions

1. What recent examples reflect an evolving nature of federalism?
2. Given the state's police power, how does government protect the health, morals, and safety of its citizens? Can you think of specific policies?
3. How does Texas's constitutional history continue to influence the state's present-day constitution and government?
4. What were your initial impressions of some of the constitutional amendments considered or proposed by the Texas Legislature? Are these the kinds of issues that should be placed in the Texas Constitution?
5. In your opinion, should the Texas Constitution be rewritten?
6. What recommendations would you offer for revision of the Texas Constitution?

## Internet Resources

FindLaw: U.S. Constitution: **www.findlaw.com/casecode/constitution**
National Governors Association: **www.nga.org**
Texas Constitution: **www.capitol.state.tx.us/txconst/toc.html**
Texas Legislature Online: **www.capitol.state.tx.us**
Texas Office of State-Federal Relations: **www.osfr.state.tx.us**
Texas Office of the Secretary of State: **www.sos.state.tx.us**
Texas State Historical Association Online: **www.tsha.utexas.edu**

## Notes

1. David B. Walker, *The Rebirth of Federalism* (New York: Chatham House, 2000), 260.
2. See *Garcia v. San Antonio Metropolitan Transit Authority*, 469 U.S. 528 (1985).
3. See *U.S. Term Limits v. Thornton*, 514 U.S. 115 (1995).
4. See Kristen Mack, "Activists Collide over Proposition 2," *Houston Chronicle*, 9 October 2005; and Paul Burka, "The M Word," *Texas Monthly*, January 2006, pp. 14-16.
5. See *Kimel v. Florida Board of Regents*, 528 U.S. 62 (2000); *Alden v. Maine*, 527 U.S. 706 (1999); and *Seminole Tribe v. Florida*, 517 U.S. 44 (1996).
6. See *Frew v. Hawkins*, 540 U.S. 431 (2004). See also Carlos Guerra, "High Court Orders Texas to Honor its Word—and Pay Up," *San Antonio Express-News*, 15 January 2004.
7. See *Kelo v. New London*, 545 U.S. 469 (2005).
8. See *United States v. Lopez*, 514 U.S. 549 (1995).
9. See *Gonzalez v. Raich*, 545 U.S. 1 (2005).
10. See Sanford F. Schram, "Welfare Reform: A Race to the Bottom?" *Publius: The Journal of Federalism* 28 (Summer 1998): 1–8. (Special issue: "Welfare Reform in the United States: A Race to the Bottom?" edited by Sanford F. Schram and Samuel H. Beer.)
11. For a concise study examining the influence of this influential law, see Frederick M. Hess and Michael J. Petrilli, *No Child Left Behind* (New York: Peter Long, 2006). For more information regarding the law, see the web site for the National Education Association at **www.nea.org/esea/more.html**. See also Toni Locy, "Judge Dismisses Suit Against No Child Left Behind Law," *Houston Chronicle*, 24 November 2005.
12. For a more detailed account of early Texas constitutions, see John Cornyn, "The Roots of the Texas Constitution: Settlement to Statehood," *Texas Tech Law Review* 26, no. 4 (1995): 1089–1218. The author served as a member of the Texas Supreme Court and as the state's attorney general before being elected to the U.S. Senate in 2002.
13. See Leobardo F. Estrada, F. Chris Garcia, Reynaldo Flores Macias, and Lionel Maldonado, "Chicanos in the United States: A History of Exploitation and Resistance," in *Latinos and the Political System*, edited by F. Chris Garcia (Notre Dame, Ind.: University of Notre Dame Press, 1988), 28–64.
14. New light on writing Texas's seventh constitution is presented in Patrick G. Williams, "Of Rutabagas and Redeemers: Rethinking the Texas Constitution of 1876," *Southwestern Historical Quarterly* 106, no. 2 (2002): 230–253.
15. Janet Elliott, "Low Turnout Is Expected Despite Advertising Blitz," *Houston Chronicle*, 3 September 2003. See also Max B. Baker, "Tempers Flare at Rally: Groups Clash Over Move to Limit Damages," *Fort Worth Star-Telegram*, 6 September 2003.
16. Jane Elliott, "Gay Marriage Ban Put in Texas Constitution," *Houston Chronicle*, 9 November 2005. See also *Summary Report of the 2005 Constitutional Election Results* at **www.sos.state.tx.us**.
17. See House Research Organization, Texas House of Representatives, "Constitutional Amendments," at **www.hro.house.state.tx.us/frame4.htm#const**.

18. "Mark Collette, "Land, Ho!" *Fort Worth Star-Telegram*, 23 October 2005. See also Gary Scharrer, "Proposition 8 Would Clear Up Cloudy Land Titles," *San Antonio Express-News*, 21 October 2005.

19. *The Book of States*, 2006 ed., vol. 38 (Lexington, Ky.: Council of State Governments, 2006), 307.

20. Texas has a right-to-work law enacted in 1947 by the 50th Legislature. The law bans the union shop arrangement whereby newly hired workers must join a union after employment.

21. See Jim Lewis, "Getting Around to a New Constitution," *County* (January/February 1999): 11–13. For a profile of Representative Rob Junell and his collaboration with Senator Bill Ratliff, see Janet Elliott, "Maverick in the Middle," *Texas Lawyer* (January 1999): 19–20.

22. For the text of the Ratliff-Junell draft constitution, refer to *Texas Legislature Online* at **www.capitol.state.tx.us** and search by bill number for the 76th Regular Session, HJR1 or SJR1.

23. For an analysis of amendments proposed between 1976 and 1989, see James G. Dickson, "Erratic Continuity: Some Patterns of Constitutional Change in Texas Since 1975," *Texas Journal of Political Studies* 14 (Fall–Winter 1991–1992): 41–56.

24. For the text of Junell's constitutional proposal, refer to *Texas Legislature Online* at **www.capitol.state.tx.us** and search by bill for the 77th Legislature, HJR 69.

25. For a more detailed analysis of the contents of the Texas Constitution, see Janice C. May, *The Texas State Constitution: A Reference Guide* (Westport, Conn.: Greenwood Press, 1996); and George D. Braden, *Citizen's Guide to the Texas Constitution* (Austin: Texas Advisory Commission on Intergovernmental Relations, 1972).

26. See *Santa Fe* v. *Doe*, 530 U.S. 290 (2000).

27. *Van Orden* v. *Perry*, 545 U.S. 677 (2005).

28. For details concerning the struggle for equal legal rights, see Rob Fink, "Hermine Tobolowsky, the Texas ELRA, and the Political Struggle for Women's Equal Rights," *Journal of the West* 42 (Summer 2003): 52–57; and Tai Kreidler, "Hermine Tobolowsky: Mother of Texas Equal Rights Amendment," in *The Human Tradition in Texas*, edited by Ty Cashion and Jesús de la Teja (Wilmington, Del: SR Books, 2001), 209–220.

29. Jason Embry, "School Tax System Unconstitutional: State Supreme Court Wants a Fix by June 1," *Austin American-Statesman*, 23 November 2005. See also Gary Scharrer, "Justices Warn that Changes will have to be Significant," *San Antonio Express-News*, 23 November 2005.

## Selected Readings

## 2.1 The American Tradition of Language Rights: The Forgotten Right to Government in a "Known Tongue"*

### *José Roberto Juárez, Jr.*

*Scholars have long debated the various factors leading Texians to declare independence from Mexico. One factor not adequately explored is the role of language. This reading sheds light on the importance of language rights for the early Anglo-American settlers of Texas.*

### Language Rights and the Struggle for Independence from Mexico: The Multiple Causes of Independence

The reasons that led some of the Anglo-American immigrants and native Tejanos to declare their independence from Mexico were many and varied. Among the reasons cited in the Texas Declaration of Independence were military abuses, the inadequacies of the Mexican justice system, the failure of the Mexican Republic to abide by the federalist guarantees of the Mexican Constitution of 1824, and the failure of the Mexican government to make Texas its own separate state. Other reasons not cited by the Texians included a desire to protect their purported "right" to own slaves, and Manifest Destiny, the belief held by many Americans in the nineteenth century that the United States was destined to extend from the Atlantic Ocean to the Pacific Ocean. Others have attributed the break to "differences in folkways and mores, in the culture patterns of the two groups." Like most historical phenomena, there is no single cause that explains why a group of immigrants who had entered a foreign country less than fifteen years before felt compelled to declare their independence. In

the rush to consider other explanations, however, the role that language played in this effort has been minimized. . . .

Before proceeding, the limits of my argument should be noted. I do not claim that language discrimination was the principal motive leading the Texians to declare their independence from Mexico. Given the interplay among Texians and Tejanos, and the wide variety of motivations among the players, any attempt to identify one motive as *the* motive is ludicrous. Nonetheless, Mexico's failure to provide even greater access to government in the English language did play a significant role in motivating many Anglo-American immigrants to seek independence from Mexico. Notwithstanding the fact that these Anglo-Americans were recent immigrants to a foreign country, they believed they had a fundamental right of access to governmental services in a language they could understand.

This belief was manifested prior to any attempt to declare independence from Mexico. In 1832, the Texians pledged their support to Antonio López de Santa Anna in his struggle for the presidency of Mexico. In return for this pledge of support, the immigrants asked for reforms. At a convention held at San Felipe de Austin in October, 1832, a committee was appointed to petition the state government "to pass a law authorizing the people of Texas (whose native language is English) to have all their transactions, and obligations, written in the English language, except those which have an immediate connection with Government." Two days later, the Anglo-American immigrants requested bilingual education. . . . The proposal authorizing government in English was ultimately rejected by the Convention. Instead, the Convention sought to organize a state government separate from Coahuila. This was the first of several attempts to establish Texas as a state separate from Coahuila; one of the reasons the immigrants sought a separate state government was to obtain more multilingual governmental services. Ultimately, none of the Convention's proposals were ever presented to the Mexican government.

---

*José Roberto Juárez, Jr. was a professor at St. Mary's University School of Law, San Antonio, and is now the dean of the Sturm College of Law at the University of Denver. Edited excerpt from José Roberto Juárez, "The American Tradition of Language Rights: The Forgotten Right to Government in a 'Known Tongue,'" *Law & Inequality: A Journal of Theory and Practice* 13, no. 2 (1995): 495–518. Abridged and reprinted by permission of the author. (Note: Readers should refer to the original source for all the footnotes and references.)

Dissatisfied with the outcome of the 1832 Convention, some of the Anglo-American immigrants soon called for another convention. The circular calling for the convention at San Felipe de Austin asserted a right of access to the Mexican justice system in English:

> The laws which ought to be inforced [sic], if any such there be, are locked up in a language known to a few only, and, therefore, for all practical purposes, [are] utterly beyond our reach. . . .
>
> The accurate observer, on taking a survey of our situation, must pronounce the decisive opinion, that we are without *remedy* for wrongs; that we are without *redress* for grievances; and that we must remain without them, until they are provided by the deliberate, and *declared will* of a majority of the people, assembled by delegation, in Public Convention.

Stephen F. Austin prepared an address for the Central Committee which was presented to the convention in April, 1833. Austin began by noting the fundamental right of the Anglo-American immigrants to present their petitions to the government:

> The people of Texas ought therefore to rely with confidence on the government for protection, and to expect that an adequate remedy will be applied to the many evils that are afflicting them.
>
> [T]he *right* of the people of Texas to represent their wants to the government, and to explain in a respectfull [sic] manner the remedies that will relieve them cannot therefore be doubted or questioned. It is not merely a right, it is also a sacred and bounden duty which they owe to themselves and to the whole Mexican nation. . . .

One could conclude from Austin's remarks that if individuals have a fundamental right to address the government, that right is meaningless if they do not have access to the government in a language they speak. But reliance on implication for an understanding of the role of language at the 1833 Convention is unnecessary, for the participants explicitly stated the importance of communication with the government in their own language:

> The unnatural annexation of what was formerly the province of Texas to Coahuila by the constituent congress of the Mexican nation, has forced upon the people of Texas *a system of laws which they do not understand.* . . .
>
> A total disregard of the laws has become so prevalent, both amongst the officers of justice, and the people at large, that reverence for laws or for those who administer them has almost intirely [sic] disappeared and contempt is fast assuming its place, so that the protection of our property[,] our persons and lives is circumscribed almost exclusively to the moral honesty or virtue of our neighbor. . . .

The Texians in 1833 did not yet seek independence; they claimed they wished to remain a part of the Mexican nation. But they also claimed the fundamental right to communicate with their government in their own language. . . .

## Language Rights as a Factor in the Attempt to Make Texas a Separate State of Mexico

The Texas Declaration of Independence asserted that the failure of the Mexican government to establish Texas as a separate state had deprived the Texians of their right to government in a "known tongue." . . .

In considering the problems the framers of the Texas Bill of Rights were attempting to remedy, the Texas courts must consider the failure of the Mexican government to establish Texas as a separate state. The analysis cannot end there, however. The reasons the Anglo-American immigrants gave for seeking a separate state must also be considered. One of the most important forces behind the move for statehood was the failure of the Mexican state of Coahuila and Texas to address the needs of immigrants who did not speak the national language. . . .

While the Anglo-Americans insisted on the right to communicate with the government in their own language, the assertion of this right did not mean that government should be conducted *only* in English. Austin believed Texas would be made a separate state only if the native Tejano population supported the move. Tejanos would not have supported an effort by recently-arrived immigrants to condemn natives to government in a language they did not understand. The efforts of the Texians were bilingual. . . .

While Mexico did not agree to make Texas a separate state, further concessions were made to address the needs of monolingual English-speaking immigrants. Stephen F. Austin had asserted that "[w]ith only two measures Texas would be happy—judges who understand English even if only in provisional cases and the trial by jury." In May, 1833, the state legislature responded to these requests. Judges were required to provide interpreters in civil and criminal cases "commenced or contested in the state by persons unacquainted with the language of the country."

In 1834, a Department of Brazos was established. Article 11 of the decree establishing the new Department gave English full equality with Spanish in local government in Texas: "The Castilian and English shall be lawful languages in Texas; both may be used in the acts of the public administration as the case may require, except in communications with the supreme power, which shall be made expressly in Castilian."

One month later, the state legislature responded to the immigrants' continuing complaints about the judicial system by establishing a bilingual court system for Texas. Judges who were not "acquainted with both the legal idioms of Texas" were required to appoint an interpreter at a salary of $1000 per year. Criminal trials were required to be conducted in the language of the accused party, so long as the accused spoke either English or Spanish. If jurors who spoke the language of the accused could not be found in that district, the case had to be transferred to the nearest district where such jurors could be found. A party appealing a case to the state supreme court with a written record in English was given the right to have the record translated into Spanish at his own cost by a translator appointed by the judge. The law was ordered published in both English and Spanish.

Mexico attempted to respond to the needs of her new monolingual English-speaking immigrants by providing for bilingual services far greater than any provided by the State of Texas or by the United States today. . . .

## The Declaration of Independence

On December 11, 1835, the General Council called for an election on February 1, 1836 to elect delegates to a con-

vention at Washington-on-the-Brazos. Consistent with Stephen F. Austin's earlier guarantee that the rights of Tejanos would be protected, the elections for delegates in Béxar to the convention at Washington-on-the-Brazos were held in Spanish. Three Tejanos were elected as delegates: Lorenzo de Zavala (representing Harrisburg), and Francisco Ruíz and Antonio Navarro (representing Béxar).

The Convention at Washington-on-the-Brazos began on March 1, 1836. On the second day of the convention, a Declaration of Independence was adopted by the delegates. The Texas Declaration of Independence began with a list of the circumstances that had driven the Texians to declare independence from Mexico: "When a government has ceased to protect the lives, liberty, and property of the people, from whom its legitimate powers are derived, and for the advancement of whose happiness it was instituted. . . ." Language is not explicitly cited in this introduction, but in fact it was one of the principal complaints the Texians had about the Mexican justice system. The Texians had complained about the inability to enforce laws published in Spanish, and how this had created an atmosphere of lawlessness. Thus this complaint regarding the lack of protection of Texian lives, liberty, and property must be read in the context of the complaints that had previously been presented to the Mexican government. Inaccessibility to the Mexican judicial and legal system because of language problems was a perennial complaint of the Texians. Later in the Declaration of Independence, the Texians directly asserted the right to communicate with their government in their own language. . . . The Mexican government's refusal to establish Texas as a separate state from Coahuila has been well-recognized as a cause of the independence movement. But often overlooked is the role that language played in this desire to establish a separate state. It was not language differences alone which were complained of; rather, it is that the Coahuila-dominated state government was unwilling to address the needs of the English-speaking immigrants in Texas by expanding multilingual governmental services. This is one of the principal complaints registered in the text of the Texas Declaration of Independence. . . .

The Texas Declaration of Independence did not merely assert these complaints as grievances. It asserted a fundamental right to have these grievances remedied. . . . The Texians practiced what they preached. Immediately after the draft of the Constitution for the Republic of Texas was presented to the Convention, de Zavala moved to appoint an interpreter to translate "the constitution and laws of this government into the Spanish language." The motion was approved on March 10, 1836. . . .

By 1836, the influx of Anglo-American immigrants had made Tejanos a minority in their own land. One might expect that the Texians would ignore the Tejano minority and conduct government in English, the language of the majority of the population.

But such was not the case. The government of the Republic of Texas recognized the Tejanos as citizens, and respected the language rights of the Tejano minority. The Texians who, when they had been the minority had asserted a right to communicate with the Mexican government in English, now provided opportunities for the Tejanos to communicate with the government of the Republic of Texas in Spanish.

## 2.2 They Haven't Got a Prayer*

### *Pamela Colloff*

*Freedom of religion is protected by both our state and federal constitutions. However, when it comes to school prayer, the U.S. Supreme Court has influenced this controversial issue. This reading sheds light on the circumstances surrounding the Supreme Court's decision to strike down school prayer at football games in Santa Fe, Texas, a small community outside Galveston.*

On the first friday night of football season, Santa Fe High School's bleachers were packed with straw-haired girls and sunburned boys in baseball caps and parents in T-shirts that said "Fix Your Eyes on God." Beneath them, a spectacle was unfolding that seemed far grander than anything a Santa Fe Indians–Hitchcock Bulldogs game would normally merit. TV trucks and camera crews were descending from all directions on this small-town stadium, having come not for the sport, but for the symbolism: This was the first game since the U.S. Supreme Court had handed down a devastating decision against the Santa Fe school district, striking down its long-standing tradition of school-sponsored prayer at football games. The ruling had touched a wellspring of emotion in Santa Fe, and as game-time neared, it was clear that the town's indignation ran deep. . . . Faith and football have always gone hand in hand in Texas, where the gridiron is king, and especially in Santa Fe, a devout, largely Baptist town in western Galveston County where residents keenly feel God's presence. A rural community of around ten thousand people, Santa Fe has become ground zero in the fight for school prayer, its June defeat before the Supreme Court having lent its barren stretches of salt grass and marshland an air of martyrdom. The battle that has raged here—turning friend against friend, neighbor against neighbor—has centered on the right to pray. But the prayer controversy is also part of a larger struggle over how great a role religion should play in public life, and in Santa Fe many think it should play a very large role indeed. . . .

### The Origins of the Case

The battle over prayer began here when two mothers sued the Santa Fe school district in 1995 for what they saw as an undue presence of religion in the public schools: Gideons were distributing Bibles in the hallways, teachers were teaching religious songs to their pupils, and graduation ceremonies had taken on the air of Sunday worship services. Only one sentence in the fifteen-page petition mentioned prayer at football games, but it became the key issue in subsequent appeals and the sole complaint to be heard by the Supreme Court. The town's five-year fight culminated with the *Santa Fe* v. *Doe* ruling, in which the high

*"They Haven't Got a Prayer" by Pamela Colloff from *Texas Monthly* (November 2000): Vol. 28; Issue 11, p. 116. Edited and reprinted with permission from the November 2000 issue of *Texas Monthly*.

court held that students could no longer deliver prayers over school loudspeakers before football games: The practice violated the separation of church and state, the court ruled, and was inherently coercive. Though students' right to pray on their own before, during, and after games is still protected by law, the decision has stirred deep emotions. This fall, it has triggered a grassroots movement for prayer in the stands across parts of Texas and the South, where pre-game prayer over the loudspeaker is tradition, as much a part of Friday nights as the opening kickoff. . . .

Fundamentalist and evangelical churches had always played an important, if low-key, role in Santa Fe. But as the town grew from 5,413 residents in 1980 to 8,628 people in 1990, church rolls swelled, and the Ministerial Alliance—a coalition of local church leaders who would figure prominently in the push for school prayer—became more powerful, and more political. Several school board positions were soon filled with self-described Christian conservatives, who called the separation of church and state doctrine a "myth" and a misinterpretation of the Constitution. By the time the lawsuit was filed, the town's mood had begun to shift. . . .

Word soon leaked that a lawsuit was in the works, and in 1994, the school board held a meeting to discuss whether to fight it. By that time the school district had begun to make changes, reprimanding a teacher who had disparaged a Mormon girl's religion and, in one case, instructing a teacher not to lead students in religious songs. The ACLU, however, took the position that the previous practices were part of a larger pattern of behavior in which the district gave a platform to religion. . . .

In April 1995 the ACLU filed *Jane Doe* v. *Santa Fe Independent School District*, a wide-ranging civil rights lawsuit that sought to "remind [the school district] of the value of the separation of church and state and the need to prevent the government from endorsing one religion over another." It cited eleven infractions—from Bible distribution, to a baccalaureate service led by a Baptist minister, to prayer before football games—that had "the primary effect of advancing, sponsoring, promoting, endorsing and/or encouraging religion and foster[ing] excessive entanglement by Santa Fe Independent School District with religion." Identified only as Jane Does, the plaintiffs were described in court filings as two mothers—one Catholic, one Mormon—who each had two children attending Santa Fe schools. . . .

Attorney Anthony Griffin took on the Does' case in 1995 for the ACLU and would argue on their behalf before the Supreme Court. . . . Raised a Baptist, Griffin had no reservations about taking on the case—despite heated criticism from his brother, who is an evangelist, and several devout co-workers, who regularly held prayer circles at the office in support of the opposing side—because he felt he was fighting for religious freedom. "Students may pray on their own anytime, anywhere," said Griffin. "But at Santa Fe football games, students were being coerced to participate in a religious exercise that was clearly sponsored and encouraged by the school. Religious belief and expression is flourishing in this country because we have avoided others' mistakes; we have not allowed our government to endorse religion or to interfere in religion. In Santa Fe the will of the majority was being imposed on the minority." U.S. district court judge Sam Kent heard testimony from both the Does' and school administrators and ruled in 1996 that the district had violated the First Amendment by having allowed school-sponsored prayer and the distribution of Bibles on school property. Though the district had erred, Kent ruled, it was acting in good faith to correct such policies, and he declined to award any damages to the Does. Both sides appealed to the Fifth U.S. Circuit Court of Appeals, which delivered a ruling last February that proved to be a devastating blow to prayer proponents in Santa Fe. Student-led prayer was appropriate at graduation ceremonies, the three-judge panel ruled, since it is "a significant, once-in-a-lifetime event," but football games, they added with scant understanding of Texas tradition, are "far less solemn and extraordinary." Prayer before football games was unconstitutional, the court ruled, stating, "Football games are hardly the sober type of annual event that can be appropriately solemnized with prayer." . . .

Five years after the Does filed suit, the battle that rocked this small Texas town to its core made its way to the Supreme Court, where nine justices sat in judgment this past March. At issue was a very narrow portion of the original case: Whether the school district's pre-game policy endorsed prayer and violated the First Amendment or merely allowed a neutral forum for free expression in which a student could choose to say, or not say, a prayer before a football game. Aided by Texas attorney general John Cornyn, Jay Sekulow, the chief counsel of the American Center for Law and Justice, which was founded by televangelist Pat Robertson, represented the school district, arguing that its policy neither favored nor disfavored religious expression. Anthony Griffin, representing the Does for the ACLU, contended that the policy was adopted solely for the purpose of perpetuating public prayer at football games, and that, in practice, it coerced students at school-sponsored events to participate in religious exercises. "It endorses religion and its whole purpose is religion," Griffin said, adding, "They weave a web, and seek to have this court ignore its history."

## U.S. Supreme Court Rules

Reaffirming its earlier rulings against school-sponsored prayer, the Supreme Court ruled 6–3 in favor of the Does this past June. In the majority decision, Justice John Paul Stevens wrote that the district "asks us to pretend that we do not recognize what every Santa Fe High School student understands clearly—that this policy is about prayer. The District further asks us to accept what is obviously untrue: that these messages are necessary to 'solemnize' a football game and that this single-student, year-long [prayer leader] position is essential to the protection of student speech. We refuse to turn a blind eye to the context in which this policy arose, and that context quells any doubt that this policy was implemented with the purpose of endorsing school prayer." The policy, cautioned Stevens, "encourages divisiveness along religious lines" and "has the improper effect of coercing those present to participate in an act of religious worship." He judged the policy to be lacking in secular purpose and therefore an unconstitutional government practice. "We recognize the important role that public worship plays in many communities," Stevens wrote. "But such religious activity in public schools, as elsewhere, must comport with the First Amendment."

Echoing the sentiments of many in Santa Fe, Chief Justice William Rehnquist wrote in his dissenting opinion that the ruling "bristles with hostility to all things religious in public life." The court's reasoning was flawed and contradictory, he wrote, observing that "sporting events often begin with a solemn rendition of our national anthem, with its concluding verse 'And this be our motto: in God is

our trust.' Under the Court's logic, a public school that sponsors the singing of the national anthem before football games violates the [First Amendment]." It is these subtle legal distinctions that rile school prayer supporters, who see the courts as irrational arbiters of that which is sacrosanct and who will not rest easy until the wall separating church and state has been breached. But it is such distinctions that protect religious freedom. As Justice Stevens concluded, "nothing in the Constitution as interpreted by the Court prohibits any public school student from voluntarily praying at any time before, during, or after the schoolday. But the religious liberty protected by the Constitution is abridged when the State affirmatively sponsors the particular religious practice of prayer."

In the end, it was not school prayer in Santa Fe that proved so troubling as what the fight for school prayer wrought—branding those who disagreed as infidels. Perhaps the greatest irony of this town's five-year crusade is that by fighting relentlessly for school prayer, Santa Fe revealed the true dangers of its argument, laying bare the need to keep religion out of government and, just as importantly, to keep government out of religion.

But between these two extremes, voluntary student prayer—as long as it is free of government intervention and truly student-led—can have a place in public schools. Indeed, despite considerable hand-wringing after the Supreme Court ruling, student prayer is very much alive and well, as was evident one morning in Santa Fe this September, when nearly seventy students gathered at dawn to give thanks to God. The sky was still a dusky gray when they massed around the school flagpole: Some knelt in supplication, while others bowed their heads, a few raising their hands skyward. Together, they stood in silent reflection, they joined in singing "Amazing Grace," their reedy, uncertain voices slowly gathering strength. As students began straggling toward school from the parking lot, a few threw down their backpacks and entered the circle. In the shadow of a doorway, one teacher stood and watched, wiping tears away. At last, here was a prayer gathering that was truly and solely student-led. It was a moment for which all of Santa Fe could say amen.

---

An extensive bibliography of books and articles for this chapter is posted on Selected Sources for Reading, available online at http://college.hmco.com/PIC/brownPTP13e. For use with any chapter, see Resources for Further Research online at http://college.hmco.com/PIC/brownPTP13e.

*Chapter 3*

# Local Governments

SARGENT©2003
*Austin American-Statesman.* Reprinted with permission of UNIVERSAL PRESS SYNDICATE. All rights reserved.

For most Texans, when we think about government, we think about the national government. Yet local government has the greatest effect on our daily lives. Most of us drive every day on city streets or county roads, drink water provided by the city or a special district, attended schools run by the local school district, play in the city or county park, eat in restaurants inspected by local health officials, and live in houses or apartments that required local permits and inspections to build.

Many of our contacts with local government are positive—potholes are filled, trash is picked up regularly, ballfields are groomed for baseball games—but other experiences are less positive. As in the cartoon that begins the chapter, our streets and freeways seem increasingly congested, and the current solution is to build more toll roads that we must pay to use. Many schools are overcrowded, and the property taxes to support them seem high. To confront these problems and make local governments more responsive to our needs and wishes, we need to understand how they are organized and what they do.

Local government comes in many forms. In Texas, we have municipalities (about 1,200 city and town governments), counties (254), and special districts (more than 3,000). The special district most students know best is the school district, but we also have special districts for water, hospitals, conservation, housing, and a multitude of other services. Each local government covers a certain geographical area and has legal authority to carry out one or more government functions. Most collect revenue such as taxes or fees, spend money while providing services, and are controlled by officials ultimately responsible to voters. These local, or grassroots, governments affect our lives directly.

## ★ Local Politics in Context

Who are the policymakers for grassroots governments? How do they make decisions? What challenges do they face daily? Putting local politics in context first requires an understanding of American federalism.

### Local Governments and Federalism

Texas's local governments, like those of other states, are at the bottom rung of the governmental ladder. Cities, counties, and special-district governments are creatures of the state of Texas. They are created through state laws and the Texas Constitution, and they make decisions permitted or required by the state. Local governments may receive part of their money from the state or national governments, and they must obey the laws and constitutions of both.

At the local level, federalism is more than just dealing with the state and national governments. The territory of local governments often overlaps. Your home, for example, may be in a county, municipality, school district, community college district, and hospital district—all of which collect taxes, provide services, and hold elections. Local governments need to deal with each other—sometimes as friends, occasionally as adversaries. For example, the city and the school district generally cooperate to ensure that students travel safely to and from school. But a city may first negotiate with and later sue a rural water district over the size of water pipe being laid in areas the city plans to annex. Clearly, federalism, often called **intergovernmental relations**, is important to how local governments work. (For more on federalism see the chapter "Federalism and the Texas Constitution.")

**intergovernmental relations** Relationships between different governments. They may be on the same or different levels.

### Grassroots Challenges

When studying local governments, it is also important to keep in mind the challenges these governments face daily. More than 80 percent of all Texans reside in cities, and residents of these heavily populated urban and suburban areas have immediate concerns they want addressed: fear of crime, decaying infrastructures (streets, roads, and bridges), controversies over public schools, and, since September 11, 2001, the threat of terrorism.

Texas cities are also becoming increasingly diverse, and many African American and Latino Texans are seeking access to public services and local power structures long dominated by Anglos. Making sure that all communities receive equal access to public services is a key challenge for grassroots-level policymakers, community activists, and political scientists.

Grassroots government also faces the challenge of widespread voter apathy. Many times, fewer than 10 percent of a community's qualified voters participate in a local election. But the good news is that voter interest increases when people understand that they can solve grassroots problems in Texas through political participation. Opportunities to participate in local politics begin with registering and then voting in local elections. (See "The Politics of Elections" chapter for voter qualifications and registration requirements under Texas law.) Some citizens may even seek election to a city council, county commissioners court, school board, or other policymaking body. Other opportunities to be politically active include homeowners' associations, neighborhood associations, other community or issue-oriented organizations, voter registration drives, and election campaigns of candidates seeking local offices. By gaining influence in city halls, county courthouses, and special-district offices, individuals and groups may address grassroots problems through the democratic process.

### How Do We Compare . . . In Employees and Spending at State and Local Levels?

In this chapter's "How Do We Compare?" features, rather than compare Texas to other large and neighboring states, we compare our state government to our local governments.

|  | State Government | | Local Government | |
| --- | --- | --- | --- | --- |
|  | Number | Texas's Rank Among the 50 States | Number | Texas's Rank Among the 50 States |
| Government Employees | 280,542 | 2 | 987,274 | 2 |
| Government Employees per 10,000 Population | 119 | 44 | 446 | 6 |
| Average Annual Earning of Full-Time Employee | $36,972 | 33[a] | $31,620 | NA |
| Per Capita Government Expenditure | $3,456 | 49 | $3,550 | 21 |
| Per Capita Government Debt | $1,105 | 46 | $4,545 | 9 |

*Sources:* Legislative Budget Board, *Texas Fact Book, 2006,* www.llb.state.tx.us, and U.S. Census Bureau, *Statistical Abstract of the United States, 2006,* www.census.gov.

[a]Ranking for state and local together.
NA: Not available

# Municipal Governments

**municipal government**
A local government for an incorporated community established by law as a city.

Perhaps no level of government influences the daily lives of citizens more than **municipal** (city) **government.** Whether taxing residents, arresting criminals, collecting garbage, providing public libraries, or repairing streets, municipalities determine how millions of Texans live. Knowing how and why public policies are made at city hall requires an understanding of the organizational and legal framework within which municipalities function.

**general-law city** Municipality with a charter prescribed by the legislature.

## Legal Status of Municipalities

**home-rule city** Municipality with a locally drafted charter.

**ordinance** A local law enacted by a city council or approved by popular vote in a referendum election.

**recall** A process for removing elected officials through a popular vote. In Texas, this power is available only at the local level, not at the state level.

**initiative** A citizen-drafted measure proposed by a specific number or percentage of qualified voters, which becomes law if approved by popular vote. In Texas, this process occurs only at the local level, not at the state level.

**referendum** A process by which issues are referred to the voters to accept or reject. Voters may also petition for a vote to repeal an existing ordinance. In Texas, this process occurs at the local level. At the state level, bonds secured by taxes and state constitutional amendments must be approved by the voters.

City government powers are outlined and restricted by municipal charters, state and national constitutions, and statutes. Texas has two legal classifications of cities: **general-law cities** and **home-rule cities.** A community with a population of 201 or more may become a general-law city by adopting a charter prescribed by a general law enacted by the Texas Legislature.[1] But a city of more than 5,000 people may be incorporated as a home-rule city, with a locally drafted charter adopted, amended, or repealed by majority vote in a citywide election. (Once chartered, a general-law city does not automatically become a home-rule city just because its population rises above 5,000, nor does home-rule status change when a population declines to 5,000 or less. Local voters must decide the legal designation of their city.)

Texas has about 900 general-law cities, most fairly small. Some of the approximately 350 home-rule cities are small, but larger cities tend to have home-rule charters.

The principal advantage of home-rule cities is greater flexibility in determining their organization and how they operate. Citizens draft, adopt, and revise their city's charter through citywide elections. The charter establishes powers of municipal officers, sets salaries and terms of offices for council members and mayors, and spells out procedures for passing, repealing, or amending **ordinances** (city laws). In 2001, for example, the voters of Houston approved a contentious city charter amendment banning the city council from offering benefits, such as health insurance, to same-sex domestic partners of city workers.

Home-rule cities may exercise three powers not held by the state government: recall, initiative, and referendum. **Recall** provides a process for removing elected officials through a popular vote. In 2004, for example, voters in Kingsville (south of Corpus Christi) recalled their mayor and two council members. An **initiative** is a citizen-drafted measure proposed by a specified number or percentage of qualified voters. If approved by popular vote, an initiative becomes law without city council approval, whereas a **referendum** repeals an existing ordinance. Ballot referenda and initiatives require voter approval and, depending on city charter provisions, may be binding or nonbinding on municipal governments. Initiatives and referenda can be contentious, as in 1999, when Houston voters defeated an initiative that would have repealed the city's affirmative action rules for hiring women and minorities and for awarding city contracts, or in 2000, when San Antonio voters approved an initiative allowing fluoridation of their drinking water.

## Forms of Municipal Government

The four principal forms of municipal government used in the United States and Texas—strong mayor-council, weak mayor-council, council-manager, and commission—have many variations. The council-manager form prevails in more than 80 percent of Texas's home-rule cities, and variations of the mayor-council system operate in many general-law cities.

Citizens often ask, "How do you explain the structure of municipal government in my town? None of the four models accurately depicts our government." The answer lies in home-rule flexibility. For instance, Brownsville and Harlingen in the Rio Grande Valley have a mayor and city commission structure. Various combinations of the forms discussed in the following sections are permissible under a home-rule charter, depending on community preference, provided they do not conflict with state law. Informal practice also may make it hard to define a city's form. For example, the council-manager form may work like a strong-mayor form if the mayor has a strong personality and the city manager is timid.

**Strong Mayor-Council**    Among larger American cities, the **strong mayor-council form** continues as the predominant governmental structure. Among the nation's ten largest cities, only Dallas and San Antonio operate with a structure (council-manager) other than some variation of the strong mayor-council system. In New York, Chicago, Philadelphia, and Detroit, the mayor is the chief administrator as well as the political head of the city. Houston and El Paso also have the strong mayor-council form of government. Many people see the strong mayor-council system as the best form for large cities because it provides strong leadership and is more likely than the council-manager form to be responsive to the full range of the community. In the early twentieth century, however, it began to fall out of favor in many places, including Texas, because of its association with the corrupt political machines that once dominated many cities. Now, most of Texas's larger home-rule cities have chosen other forms of government (mostly council-manager).

In Texas, cities operating with the strong mayor-council form have the following characteristics:

- A council composed of members elected from single-member districts
- A mayor elected at large, with power to appoint and remove department heads
- Budgetary power (for example, preparation and execution of a plan for raising and spending city money) exercised by the mayor, subject to council approval before the budget may be implemented
- A mayor with the power to veto council actions

**strong mayor-council form**  A type of municipal government with a separately elected legislative body (council) and an executive head (mayor) elected in a city-wide election with veto, appointment, and removal powers.

Houston's variation of the strong mayor-council form features a powerful mayor aided by a strong chief of staff, a citizens' assistance office, and an elected controller with budgetary powers (see Figure 3.1). This arrangement allows the mayor to delegate much administrative work to the chief of staff, whom the mayor appoints and may remove. Duties of the chief of staff include coordinating the activities of city departments, the mayor's office, and council members' offices.

**Weak Mayor-Council**    As the term **weak mayor-council form** implies, this model of local government gives the mayor limited administrative powers. Popular elections choose members of the city council, some department heads, and other municipal officials. A city council has power to override the mayor's veto. The mayor's position is weak because the office shares appointive and removal powers over municipal government personnel with the city council.

Instead of being a chief executive, the mayor is merely one of several elected officials responsible to the electorate. The trend is away from this form. None of the 10 largest cities in Texas has the weak mayor-council form, though some small general-law and home-rule cities in Texas and other parts of the country use it. For example, Conroe, a city with a population of about 43,000 in Montgomery County north of Houston, has a weak-mayor council form of government.

**Council-Manager**    When the cities of Amarillo and Terrell adopted the council-manager form in 1913, a new era in Texas municipal administration began. Today, most home-rule cities in Texas (about 220) follow the **council-manager form** (sometimes termed the commission-manager form). Figure 3.2 illustrates how this form is used in San Antonio. The council-manager form has the following characteristics:

- A mayor, elected at large, who is the presiding member of the council but generally has few formal administrative powers
- City council or commission members elected at large or in single-member districts to make general policy for the city
- A city manager who is appointed by the council (and can be removed by the council) and is responsible for carrying out council decisions and managing the city's departments

Under the council-manager form, the mayor and city council make decisions after debate on policy issues such as taxation, budgeting, annexation, and services. The actual role of the city manager varies considerably, but most city managers exert strong influence. City councils generally rely on their managers for preparation of annual budgets and policy recommendations. Once a policy is made, the city manager's office directs an appropriate department to implement it. Typically, city councils hire professionally trained managers. Successful applicants usually possess graduate degrees in public administration and can earn competitive salaries. City managers for Dallas, Austin, and San Antonio are among the highest paid in the country—all earning over $200,000 per year.

**weak mayor-council form**   A type of municipal government with a separately elected mayor and council, but the mayor shares appointive and removal powers with the council, which can override the mayor's veto.

**council-manager form**   A system of municipal government in which an elected city council hires a manager to coordinate budgetary matters and supervise administrative departments.

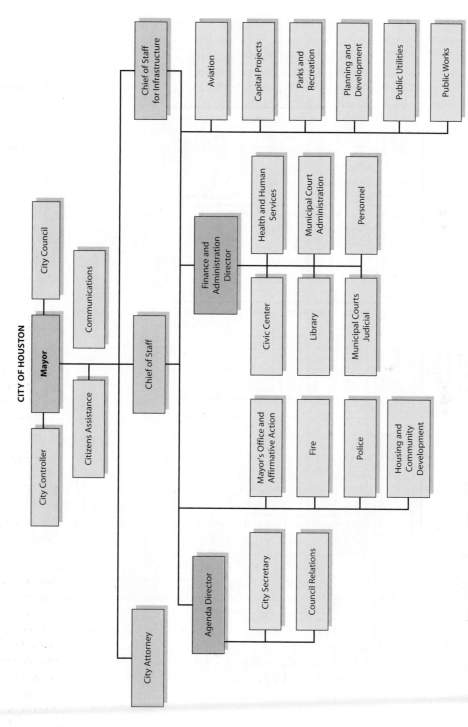

*Figure 3.1* Strong Mayor–Council Form of Municipal Government: City of Houston

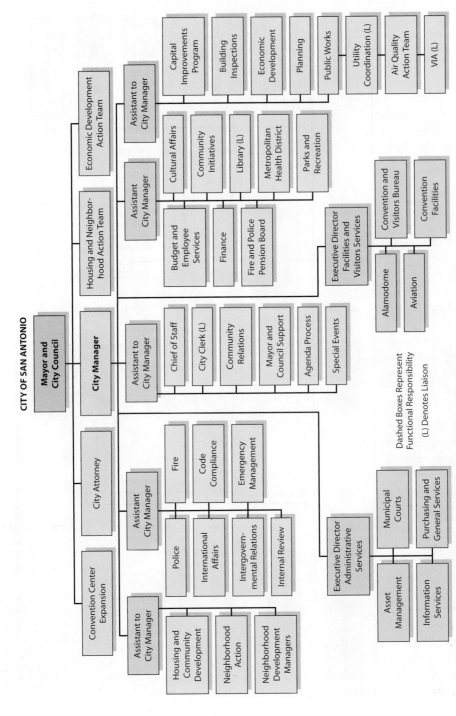

*Figure 3.2*    Council-Manager Form of Municipal Government: City of San Antonio

Obviously, a delicate relationship exists between appointed managers and elected council members. In theory, the council-manager system has a weak mayor and attempts to separate policymaking from administration. Councils and mayors are not supposed to "micromanage" departments. However, in practice, elected leaders experience difficulties in determining where to draw the line between administrative oversight and meddling in departmental affairs.

A common major weakness of the council-manager form of government is the lack of a leader to whom citizens can bring demands and concerns. The mayor is weak, the city council is composed of many individuals, and the city manager is supposed to "stay out of politics." Thus, council-manager cities tend to respond more to elite and middle-class concerns than to those of the working class and ethnic minorities. (The business elite and the middle class have more organizations and leaders who have access to city government and know how to work the system.) Only a minority of council-manager cities have mayors who regularly provide strong political and policy leadership. One of these exceptions is San Antonio, where mayors generally are strong leaders. The council-manager form seems to work well in cities where most people are of the same ethnic group and social class and share common goals. Obviously, few central cities fit this description, but many suburbs do.

**Commission**　Today, none of Texas's home-rule cities operates under a pure **commission form** of municipal government. First approved by the Texas Legislature for Galveston following a destructive hurricane that demolished that city in 1900, this form lacks a single executive, relying instead on elected commissioners that form a policymaking board.

In the commission form, each department (for example, public safety, finance, public works, welfare, or legal) is the responsibility of a single commissioner. Most students of municipal government criticize its dispersed administrative structure and lack of a chief executive. Texas municipalities with a variation of the commission form of government designate a city secretary or another official to coordinate departmental work. Some general-law cities, such as Gorman (in Eastland County), have a commission form of government.

### Municipal Politics

Election rules make a difference in who wins and what policies are more likely to win. This section examines several election rules that affect local politics and then looks at the nature of local politics in Texas.

All city and special district elections in Texas are **nonpartisan**. That is, candidates are listed on the ballot without party labels. This was done to reduce the role of political parties in local politics, and it succeeded for a long time. However, party politics is again becoming important in some city elections, such as those in the Houston metropolitan area. Nonpartisan elections have at least two negative consequences. First, without political parties to stir up excitement, voter turnout tends to be low compared to state and national

**commission form**　A type of municipal government in which each elected commissioner is a member of the city's policymaking body, but also heads an administrative department (e.g., public safety with police and fire divisions).

**nonpartisan election**　An election in which candidates are not identified on the ballot by party label.

elections. Those who do vote are more likely to be Anglos and middle class, which cuts down on the representation of ethnic minorities and the working class. San Antonio, for example, has a majority Latino population, but the greater Anglo voter turnout has meant that most San Antonio mayors are Anglo. The two exceptions were Mexican Americans who could appeal to both Anglos and Latinos. A second problem is that nonpartisan elections tend to be more personal, less issue oriented. Thus, voters tend to vote for personalities, not issues. In smaller cities and towns, local elections are often decided by who has more friends and neighbors.

Like the state legislature, city councils must **redistrict** (redraw their districts) after every 10-year census. After the 2000 Census, Texas's city council districts had to be redrawn because of shifts in population within cities and between districts. Under federal law, a city's council districts must have approximately the same population, and any changes in districting must be approved by the U.S. Department of Justice. The growth of the Latino population in urban areas has increased the number of districts in which Latino candidates have a chance of winning.

The two most common ways of organizing municipal elections are **at-large election**, in which council members are elected on a citywide basis, and **single-member district election**, in which all voters cast a ballot for a candidate who resides within their district. Texas long used at-large elections. These were challenged because they tended to over-represent the majority Anglo population and under-represent ethnic minorities—in at-large elections the majority in one race tends to be the majority in all races. This works to the disadvantage of ethnic minorities because voting remains racially polarized (that is, people tend to vote for candidates of their own race).

On the other hand, dividing a city into single-member districts creates some districts with a majority of ethnic minorities, thereby increasing the chance of electing a Latino, African American, or Asian American candidate to the city council. Prompted by lawsuits, several municipalities, including five of the largest, have adopted single-member districts or a mixed system of at-large and single-member districts. Houston, for example, has five council members elected at large (citywide) and nine from single-member districts. Increased use of single-member districts has led to more ethnically and racially diverse city councils.[2]

About 50 Texas local governments (including 40 school districts) use **cumulative voting** to increase minority representation. In this election system, voters cast a number of votes equal to the positions available and may cast them for one or more candidates in any combination. For example, if eight candidates vie for four positions on the city council, a voter may cast two votes for Candidate A, two votes for Candidate B, and no votes for the other candidates. By the same token, a voter may cast all four votes for Candidate A. In the end, the candidates with the most votes are elected to fill the four positions. Where racial minority voters are a numerical minority, this system increases the chances that they will have some representation. The largest government

**redistrict** The redrawing of districts after every 10-year census to account for shifts in population. This process occurs at local, state, and national levels.

**at-large election** Members of a policymaking body, such as some city councils, are elected on a citywide basis rather than from single-member districts.

**single-member district election** An area that elects one representative to serve on a policymaking body (e.g., city council, county commissioners court, state House and Senate).

**cumulative voting** When multiple seats are contested in an at-large election, voters cast one or more of the specified number of votes for one or more candidates in any combination. It is designed to increase representation of minorities.

## POINT/COUNTERPOINT

**Should Term Limits Be Instituted for City Council Members and the Mayor?**

**THE ISSUE** Municipal term limits are increasingly common. According to U.S. Term Limits (**www.termlimits.org**), Texas currently has about seventy cities with term limits. Critics raise strong arguments for and against term limits. The following are examples of the more common arguments.

**Arguments for Instituting Term Limits**

1. Long tenure tends to encourage corruption.
2. Term limits facilitate new approaches to solving public problems.
3. Turnover ensures election of citizen public officials instead of professional office-seekers.

*"Local limits transform political culture from one of entrenched careers to one of progression and citizen representation."*

—Danielle Fagre, former research director for the U.S. Term Limits Foundation

**Arguments Against Instituting Term Limits**

1. Turnover does not guarantee better or more honest leaders.
2. Turnover produces amateurs easily outwitted by experienced lobbyists.
3. By the time officeholders learn their job, they have to leave.

*"As an organization dedicated to protecting and enhancing the role of citizens in our representative democracy, the League strongly opposes term limits…."*

—Becky Cain, President of the National League of Women Voters

entity in the country to use cumulative voting is the Amarillo Independent School District, which adopted the system in 1999 in response to a Federal Voting Rights Act suit. The district was 30 percent minority but had no minority board members for two decades. With the adoption of cumulative voting, African American and Latino board members were elected.

Home-rule cities may also determine whether or not to institute **term limits** for their elected officials. Beginning in the 1990s, many cities, including San Antonio and Houston, amended their charters to institute term limits for their mayor and city council members. Houston has a limit of three 2-year terms for its mayor. In 2003, Houston's first African American mayor, Lee Brown, was term-limited after serving three terms. San Antonio has a limit of two 2-year terms for its mayor and city council members. Both supporters and opponents feel strongly about term limits. See the debate in the Point/Counterpoint and this chapter's Selected Reading 3.1, " 'Extreme' Term Limits—San Antonio Style," for a discussion of the impact of restrictive term limits on that city's government by its former city manager, Alexander Briseno.

**term limits** Restriction on the number of terms officials can serve in a public office

Historic San Saba County courthouse built 1910–15. Located in the city of San Saba, 90 miles northwest of Austin. (Picture courtesy of Jim Carter.)

**County Judge**   The **county judge**, who holds the most prominent job in county government and usually has a higher-status background, generally is the most influential county leader. The judge presides over the commissioners court, has administrative responsibility for most county agencies not headed by another elected official, and may exercise limited judicial functions. Much of the judge's power or influence comes from his or her leadership skills and from playing a lead role in the budget decisions of the commissioners court. The judge has essentially no formal authority over other elected county officials. The county judge need not be a lawyer. (See the chapter "Laws, Courts, and Justice" for more information on county judges, justices of the peace, and constables.)

**County Attorney and County Sheriff**   The **county attorney** represents the state in civil and criminal cases. Nearly 50 counties do not elect a county attorney because a resident district attorney performs those duties. Other counties elect a county attorney but share the services of a district attorney with two or more neighboring counties.

**county judge** An individual popularly elected to preside over the county commissioners court and, in many counties, to hear civil and criminal cases.

**county attorney** An individual elected to represent the county in civil and criminal cases, unless a resident district attorney performs these functions.

The **county sheriff,** as chief law enforcement officer, is charged with keeping the peace in the county. In this capacity, the sheriff appoints deputies and oversees the county jail and its prisoners. In a county with a population of less than 10,000, the sheriff may also serve as tax assessor-collector, unless that county's electorate votes to separate the two offices.

**County Clerk and County Tax Assessor-Collector**    A **county clerk** keeps records and handles various paperwork chores for both the county court and the commissioners court. In addition, the county clerk files legal documents (such as deeds, mortgages, and contracts) in the county's public records and maintains the county's vital statistics (birth, death, and marriage records). The county clerk may also administer elections, although counties with larger populations often have an administrator of elections.

Another county office receiving considerable statewide attention is the **county tax assessor-collector,** whose title is partially a misnomer. Since 1982, the **county tax appraisal district** assesses property values in the county. The tax-assessor-collector collects county taxes and fees and certain state fees, including the license tag fees for motor vehicles. The office also commonly handles voter registration.

**Other County Officers**    The **county treasurer** receives and pays out all county funds authorized by the commissioners court. If the office is eliminated by constitutional amendment (as in Tarrant and Bell counties), the county commissioners assign treasurer duties to the **county auditor.** A county of 10,000 or more people must have a county auditor, appointed by the county's district court judges. The auditing function involves checking the account books and records of all officials who handle county funds.

## County Finance

Increasing citizen demands for services and programs impose on most counties an ever-expanding need for money. Just as the structure of county governments is frozen in the Texas Constitution, so is the county's power to tax and, to a lesser extent, its power to spend.

**Taxation**    The Texas Constitution authorizes county governments to collect taxes on property, and that is usually their most important revenue source. Although occupations may also be taxed, none of the counties implements that provision. The commissioners court may impose higher property taxes, but only after statutory authorization by the Texas Legislature and approval by a majority of the county's voters.

**Revenues from Nontax Sources**    Counties receive small amounts of funds from various sources that add up to an important part of their total revenue. Counties may impose fees on the sale of liquor, and they share in state revenue from liquor sales, various motor vehicle taxes and fees, and traffic fines. Like other local governments, counties receive federal grants-in-aid, but this source

**county sheriff** An individual popularly elected as the county's chief law enforcement officer; the sheriff is also responsible for maintaining the county jail.

**county clerk** An individual elected to perform clerical chores for the county court and commissioners court, keep public records, maintain vital statistics, and administer public elections, if the county does not have an administrator of elections.

**county tax assessor-collector** This elected official no longer assesses property for taxation but does collect taxes and fees.

**county tax appraisal district** The district appraises all real estate and commercial property for taxation by units of local government within a county.

**county treasurer** An elected official who receives and pays out county money as directed by the commissioners court.

**county auditor** A person appointed by the district judge or judges to check the financial books and records of other officials who handle county money.

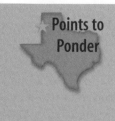

In the 2002 general election, Bexar County was the last county in the nation to count its votes because of a complicated ballot that caused problems. Optical scanning of ballots was delayed because a two-sheet ballot (printed front and back on the first sheet) was held together with a paper clip. For the constitutional amendment election of 2003, Bexar County was one of the first counties in the state and in the nation to use the touch-screen ballot method of voting. In 2005, county commissioners in one East Texas county complained that they couldn't spend federal grant money for electronic voting machines on county roads.

**Points to Ponder**

continues to shrink. With voter approval, the county may borrow money through **bonds** to pay for capital projects such as a new courthouse or jail. The Texas Constitution limits county indebtedness to 35 percent of a county's total assessed property value.

**Tax Incentives**    Like cities, a commissioners court may grant tax abatements (reductions or suspensions) on taxable property, reimbursements (return of taxes paid), or tax increment financing (TIF) to attract or retain businesses. For instance, in 2003 Bexar County offered a $22 million tax abatement for a Toyota factory to be built to produce pickup trucks in San Antonio. This tax abatement ensures that the company need not pay property taxes for 10 years. The offer was part of a complex incentive package put together by officials of the city, the local school district, and the state, as well as San Antonio's natural gas and electric power company. Once operational, the factory is expected to create 1,800 high-paying jobs and foster economic development in the region.[6]

**The Bottom Line**    Despite various revenue sources, Texas counties, like other units of local government, are pressured to raise property taxes or to balance their budgets by eliminating or reducing programs and services. Although administrative costs and demands for expanded public services continue to increase, sources of county revenue are not expanding.

**Expenditures**    The state restricts county expenditures in certain areas and mandates spending in others. Yet patterns of spending vary considerably from county to county. The county judge, auditor, or budget officer prepares the budget, but the commissioners court is responsible for final adoption of an annual spending plan. County road and bridge maintenance continues to require the largest expenditures in rural counties.

**bond** A certificate of indebtedness issued by a borrower to a lender that constitutes a legal obligation to repay the principal of a loan plus accrued interest. In Texas, both state and local governments issue bonds under restrictions imposed by state law.

Counties do not have complete control over their spending, because state and federal rules require certain county services and regulatory activities. Examples include social services, medical care for poor people, and mental health programs. When state funding tightened in 2003 to avoid new state taxes, counties had to absorb more costs, such as providing indigent healthcare and legal representation. Early in 2004, about 165 county commissioners courts adopted resolutions protesting unfunded state mandates and cuts in state funding for Medicaid and the Children's Health Insurance Program (CHIP). In addition, counties are seeking a constitutional amendment to ban unfunded mandates.

## County Government Reform

Texas counties suffer various problems: rigid structure and duties fixed in the constitution and law, inefficiency related to too many elected officials and the lack of merit systems for hiring employees, and too little money. Larger counties may establish merit systems, and half of those eligible have done so. One often-suggested reform is county home rule to give counties more ability to organize and operate in accordance with local needs and wishes. Texas is one of 13 states that do not grant home rule to counties. Until 1969, Texas had a home-rule provision in the constitution, but it was too difficult to implement. Reviving a workable version would be hard to achieve. Many, probably most, county officials prefer the present system, as do many people served by counties outside of the metropolitan areas.

## Border Counties

In recent years, there has been unprecedented population growth in Texas's counties near the Rio Grande because of the North American Free Trade Agreement (NAFTA) and immigration. Unfortunately, the population growth has outstripped the substantial economic growth, and the traditionally poor border region now has even more poor people. More than 40 counties in the Mexican border area between El Paso and Brownsville are among the most impoverished places in the country. Many of the poor live in **colonias** (depressed housing settlements often without running water or sewage systems). It is estimated that there are currently about 1,800 colonias in the U.S.–Mexican border region. Colonias, however, are not exclusive to the border region. In 2002, a "colonia-like" district was identified in Colorado County (Alleyton). More than 1 million Texans live in substandard conditions in these settlements.[7]

Minimal efforts have been made to deal with problems of the colonias. Counties were given planning and inspection powers, the Texas Secretary of State created a plan to provide water and sewage to 32 (of 1,800) colonias, voters approved a constitutional amendment for bonds to fund roads and streets within the colonias, and the federal government provided some aid. However, the state legislature's anti-tax attitude in recent years has caused funding to lag. Advocates for the border counties fear that the area's serious infrastructure, educational, and medical needs will continue to be neglected. (See the Selected Reading 3.2 "Bottoms Up" for further discussion of colonias.)

**colonia** A low-income settlement, typically located in South Texas and especially in counties bordering Mexico, that lacks running water, sewer lines, and other essentials.

---

**Learning Check 3.2**        **(Answers on p. 125)**

1. True or False: Local residents of each county can determine the structure of their own county government.
2. What is the major policymaking body in each Texas county?
3. What is usually the most important source of revenue for county governments?

## ★ Special Districts

Among local governmental units, the least known and least understood are special-district governments. They fall into two categories: school districts and noneducation special districts. Created by an act of the legislature or, in some cases, by local ordinance (for example, establishing a public housing authority), a special district usually has one function and serves a specific group of people in a particular geographic area.

### Public School Districts

Citizen concerns over public education cause local school systems to occupy center stage among special-district governments. More than 1,000 Texas **independent school districts (ISDs)**, created by the legislature, are governed by popularly elected, nonsalaried boards of trustees. The school board selects the superintendent, who by law and practice makes most major decisions about the district's educational programs. The board, generally made up of local businesspeople and professionals, tends to focus on things they know—particularly money issues such as taxes and budgets. School board elections are generally low-turnout friends-and-neighbors affairs. When they become heated, it is generally because of sharp divisions within the community over volatile cultural issues like sex education or prayer in the schools, racial and ethnic conflict, or differences over taxing and spending.

Texas has traditionally had a highly centralized educational system in which the Texas Education Agency significantly limited local district decisions. However, since 1995, school boards have been given increased local autonomy over some decisions. Districts must also comply with federal regulations in areas such as racial nondiscrimination and treatment of students with disabilities. Thus, school districts make local educational policy but in the context of substantial limits, mandates, and influences from the state and federal governments.

This shared control of public education has been highlighted in recent years by increased state and now federal requirements for testing students. Districts have been forced to spend more time and money on preparing for tests. Supporters say that testing has improved student performance and made local schools more accountable. Critics charge that students are now better at taking tests but learn less in other areas. (For a discussion of education policy, see the chapter "Public Policy and Administration.")

Since at least 1987, the major issue in Texas education has been school finance. In that year, a state district court (later affirmed by the Texas Supreme Court) held that the system for school finance violated the Texas Constitution. The basic problem was that poor districts, relying on property taxes, had to tax at a high rate to provide minimum expenditures per pupil. Wealthier districts, on the other hand, could spend considerably more with significantly lower tax rates. It was 1993 before the legislature found a solution the courts

**independent school district (ISD)** Created by the legislature, an independent school district raises tax revenue to support its public schools. Voters within the district elect a board that hires a superintendent, determines salary schedules, selects textbooks, and sets the property tax rate for the district.

would accept as constitutional. The "Robin Hood" plan placed a cap on property tax rates and required wealthier districts to share revenues with poorer districts. Not surprisingly, the wealthier districts fought hard in the courts and the legislature to change the policy.

With growing resistance to high property taxes, most districts were finding it increasingly difficult to adequately pay for their schools. In 2006, the legislature faced a deadline to change the finance system again. The Texas Supreme Court had ruled that the system amounted to a statewide property tax prohibited by the state constitution. With only days to spare, the legislature created a business tax that would allow the property taxes for many to be lowered. (For further discussion, see the chapter "Public Policy and Administration.")

## Junior or Community College Districts

Another example of a special district is the **junior college or community college district,** which offers two-year academic programs beyond high school, as well as various technical and vocational programs. Each district is governed by a board with the power to set property tax rates, issue bonds (subject to voter approval), and adopt an annual budget. Operated by 50 districts (some with two or more campuses) and three Lamar University units, Texas's 75 public junior or community colleges enroll more than 500,000 students. (See Figure 3.5 for the locations of these districts.)

Community colleges, like state universities and technical colleges, are funded by state appropriations, tuition and fees, and small amounts of federal aid and private donations. Where they differ is the support community colleges receive from property taxes raised by the local district.

A recent study commissioned by the Texas Association of Community Colleges found that community colleges stimulate the local economy and are critical to a region's economic development. The study also found that community colleges help the state to improve the health of Texans and to reduce crime, welfare costs, and unemployment.[8]

## Noneducation Special Districts

Texas has more than 2,200 **noneducation special districts** handling a multitude of problems—water supply, sewage, parks, housing, irrigation, and fire protection to name a few. There are a variety of reasons why Texas has so many special districts, but three stand out. Many local needs, such as mass transit, hospitals, and flood protection, cut across the boundaries of cities and counties. In other cases, restrictive state constitutional provisions or the unwillingness of local government leaders make it difficult for an existing government to take on new tasks. And in some cases, individuals seek to create special districts to make more money for themselves. Personal profit has been a particular motivation for the proliferation of municipal utility districts in the unincorporated Houston suburbs.

**junior college or community college district** Establishes one or more two-year colleges that offer both academic and vocational programs.

**noneducation special districts** Special districts other than school districts or community college districts, such as fire prevention or water districts, that are units of local government and may cover part of a county, a whole county, or areas in two or more counties.

**Points to Ponder**

Going to college pays off financially. Income goes up for every year of college completed and even for every hour of college credit. Nationwide, average annual income for people with a high school diploma is $29,185, with an associate's degree $35,590, and with a bachelor's degree, $53,103.

Source: Texas Higher Education Coordinating Board, *Texas Higher Education Facts 2006*, www.thecb.state.tx.us.

The structure and powers of special districts vary. Most are governed by a board, collect property taxes and fees, can issue bonds, and spend money to provide one or more services. Mass transit authorities, such as Houston's Metro or Dallas's DART, rely on a 1 percent sales tax. Depending on the board, members may be elected, appointed, or automatically sit on the board because of another position they hold. Most special districts are small and hardly noticed by the general public. A few, such as the mass transit authorities in seven of the largest metropolitan areas of the state, receive more public attention.

Special districts will remain an important part of Texas government because they provide so many necessary services. But because they are so invisible to most voters, they are the form of government most subject to corruption and abuse of power.

### Learning Check 3.3    (Answers on p. 125)

1. What are the two categories of special districts in Texas?
2. Why are special districts so important?

## Metropolitan Areas

In excess of 85 percent of Texans live in metropolitan areas, mostly central cities surrounded by rapidly growing suburbs. People living in a metropolitan area share many problems such as traffic congestion, lack of access to health care, crime, and pollution. Yet having so many different governments makes it difficult to deal effectively with problems affecting the whole area. The situation is made worse by differences between central city residents and suburbanites. Many who live in central cities need and use public facilities such as public transportation, parks, and medical care, while many suburban residents have less interest in public services, particularly public transportation. Class and ethnic differences also separate metropolitan communities, particularly the central city from the suburbs.

One way to deal with area-wide problems would be **metro government** (consolidation of local governments into one "umbrella" government for the entire metropolitan area). Examples are Toronto, Canada; Miami, Florida; and Nashville-Davidson County, Tennessee. Given the divisions within Texas metropolitan areas and the opposition of local officials, observers do not see

**metro government**
Consolidation of units of local government within an urban area under a single authority.

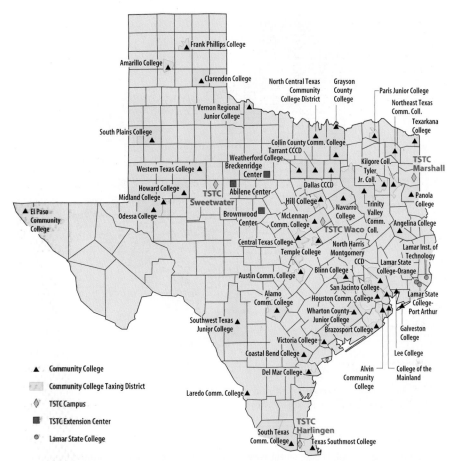

*Figure 3.5*   Texas Community, Technical, and State Colleges   *Source*: Reprinted by permission of the Texas Association of Community Colleges.

this solution as probable in Texas in the foreseeable future. Instead, we are likely to continue to rely on COGs and annexation (see below).

## Councils of Governments

Looking beyond city limits, county lines, and special-district boundaries requires expertise from planners who think regionally. In 1966, the legislature created the first of twenty-four regional planning bodies known as **councils of governments (COGs)** or, in some areas, planning/development commissions/councils. (See Figure 3.6.)

COGs are voluntary associations of local governments. They perform regional planning activities and provide services requested by member governments or directed by federal and state mandates. Their expertise is particularly useful in implementing state and federally funded programs. They also provide a forum for local government leaders to share information and coordinate their efforts.

**council of governments (COGs)**  A regional planning body composed of governmental units (e.g., cities, counties, special districts); functions include review and comment on proposals by local governments for obtaining state and federal grants.

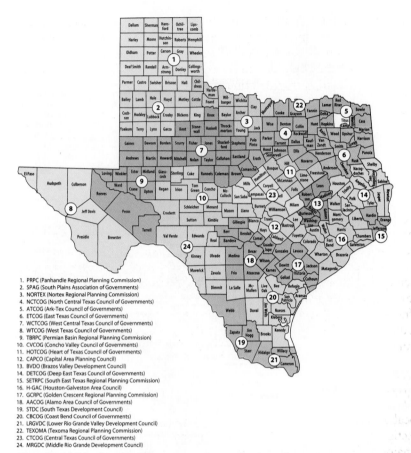

1. PRPC (Panhandle Regional Planning Commission)
2. SPAG (South Plains Association of Governments)
3. NORTEX (Nortex Regional Planning Commission)
4. NCTCOG (North Central Texas Council of Governments)
5. ATCOG (Ark-Tex Council of Governments)
6. ETCOG (East Texas Council of Governments)
7. WCTCOG (West Central Texas Council of Governments)
8. WTCOG (West Texas Council of Governments)
9. TBRPC (Permian Basin Regional Planning Commission)
10. CVCOG (Concho Valley Council of Governments)
11. HOTCOG (Heart of Texas Council of Governments)
12. CAPCO (Capital Area Planning Council)
13. BVDO (Brazos Valley Development Council)
14. DETCOG (Deep East Texas Council of Governments)
15. SETRPC (South East Texas Regional Planning Commission)
16. H-GAC (Houston-Galveston Area Council)
17. GCRPC (Golden Crescent Regional Planning Commission)
18. AACOG (Alamo Area Council of Governments)
19. STDC (South Texas Development Council)
20. CBCOG (Coast Bend Council of Governments)
21. LRGVDC (Lower Rio Grande Valley Development Council)
22. TEXOMA (Texoma Regional Planning Commission)
23. CTCOG (Central Texas Council of Governments)
24. MRGDC (Middle Rio Grande Development Council)

**Figure 3.6**    Texas Councils of Government, www.txregionalcouncil.org.    *Source*: Reprinted by permission of the Texas Association of Regional Councils.

## Municipal Annexation

**extraterritorial jurisdiction (ETJ)** The limited authority a city has outside its boundaries. The larger the city's population size, the larger the reach of its ETJ.

**annex** To make an outlying area part of a city. Within a city's extraterritorial jurisdiction, the city can annex unincorporated areas without a vote by those who live there.

In an attempt to provide statewide guidelines for home-rule cities grappling with suburban sprawl, the Texas Legislature enacted a municipal annexation law in 1963. Under the law, cities have **extraterritorial jurisdiction** (ETJ), that is, limited authority outside their city boundaries. How far out their ETJ goes depends on the city's population size, which gives central cities an advantage over the suburbs. (In most other states, central cities are surrounded by incorporated suburbs and cannot expand.) Within the ETJ, the city can regulate some aspects of development and **annex** (make the area a part of the city) unincorporated areas without a vote by those who live there.

The idea of extraterritorial jurisdiction is to improve order and planning in metropolitan growth. Timing for annexation varies. Houston tends to wait until areas have developed and will provide tax revenue, while cities in the Dallas-Fort Worth area tend to annex undeveloped areas and oversee their development. Some areas with few urban services (such as police, fire, and sewer) are happy to be annexed. But, not surprisingly, established suburban communities generally object strenuously to being "gobbled up" without their permission. Their opposition has led to small changes in the process but has not prevented annexation from continuing.

| Learning Check 3.4 | (Answers on p. 125) |
|---|---|

1. What are the two primary ways that Texas deals with problems in metropolitan areas?

## ★ Looking Ahead

The practice of local politics in Texas is as disjointed as the maze of local governments that attempt to deliver services. City hall politics, county courthouse politics, school board politics, and other special-district politics present a bewildering array of governments to frustrated taxpayers who are already skeptical and often cynical about politics in general. Where to turn for answers? One solution is to become more involved. Aided by single-member districts, newly empowered African Americans and Latinos are changing local political agendas. You can make a difference as well. The next chapter, " Political Parties," describes how citizens can work through political parties to affect elections and public policy.

## ★ Chapter Summary

- Local government is important to most Texans' day-to-day lives.
- Election rules and the way local governments are organized make a major difference in who is elected and who benefits from government.
- Texas has two legal classifications of municipalities: general-law cities and home-rule cities. Large municipalities have home-rule charters that spell out the structures and powers of individual cities.
- Four principal forms of municipal government operate in Texas: strong mayor-council, weak mayor-council, council-manager, and commission.
- Elections for cities and special districts are nonpartisan, and most are organized as at-large or single-member districts.
- Increased use of single member districts, greater pluralism, and the growing number, organization, and political activity of minority Texans are changing the face of local government.
- City governments focus primarily on delivering basic services—police and fire protection, streets, water, sewer and sanitation, and perhaps parks and recreation. They also regulate important aspects of our lives such as construction and food service sanitation.
- The two major sources of revenue for cities are property taxes and the sales tax. For counties, it is the property tax. Both cities and counties are making more use of fees and debt.

- Local governments have a difficult time because they face increasing demands for services but have limited revenue sources.
- County governments have fragmented organizational structures and powers restricted by the Texas Constitution. Counties provide an array of services, conduct elections, and enforce state laws. Actual activities vary greatly between metropolitan and rural counties.
- Various county officials are policymakers, but the major policymaker is the commissioners court, comprised of the county judge and four elected commissioners.
- The many special-district governments are separate legal entities providing services that include public schools, community colleges, and mass transit systems. They are important for the multitude of services they provide but are more subject to fraud and manipulation.
- Dealing with metropolitan-wide problems is a difficult task. To do so, Texas relies heavily on councils of government to increase cooperation and on annexation, a controversial process.

## Key Terms

- intergovernmental relations, *p. 96*
- municipal government, *p. 98*
- general-law city, *p. 98*
- home-rule city, *p. 98*
- ordinance, *p. 98*
- recall, *p. 98*
- initiative, *p. 98*
- referendum, *p. 98*
- strong mayor-council form, *p. 99*
- weak mayor-council form, *p. 100*
- council-manager form, *p. 100*
- commission form, *p. 103*
- nonpartisan election, *p. 103*
- redistrict, *p. 104*
- at-large election, *p. 104*
- single-member district election, *p. 104*
- cumulative voting, *p. 104*
- term limits, *p. 105*
- property tax, *p. 107*
- municipal bond, *p. 108*
- tax reinvestment zone (TRZ), *p. 109*
- county, *p. 110*
- commissioners court, *p. 113*
- county judge, *p. 114*
- county attorney, *p. 114*
- county sheriff, *p. 115*
- county clerk, *p. 115*
- county tax assessor-collector, *p. 115*
- county tax appraisal district, *p. 115*
- county treasurer, *p. 115*
- county auditor, *p. 115*
- bonds, *p. 116*
- colonia, *p. 117*
- independent school district (ISD), *p. 118*
- junior college or community college district, *p. 119*
- noneducation special districts, *p. 119*
- metro government, *p. 120*
- council of governments (COG), *p. 121*
- extraterritorial jurisdiction (ETJ), *p. 122*
- annex, *p. 122*

## Learning Check Answers

**3.1**

1. a. General-law and home-rule cities. b. Home-rule. c. General law.
2. a. Council-manager. b. Weak mayor-council
3. Single-member districts and cumulative voting. Reapportionment may help or hurt, depending on how lines are drawn.
4. a. Property tax and sales tax. b. No

**3.2**

1. False
2. Commissioners Court
3. Property taxes

**3.3**

1. School districts and noneducational districts.
2. Many local needs cut across boundaries of cities and counties; limitations in the state constitution and the unwillingness of some officials make it difficult to take on new tasks; and some unscrupulous people seek personal profits.

**3.4**

1. Councils of government and annexation.

## Discussion Questions

1. What is the form of municipal government for your hometown?
2. What are the advantages or disadvantages of one form of municipal government over another?
3. What are some different election rules and ways to organize government at the local level, and why do they make a difference in who is elected and which groups have more influence?
4. What are some changes taking place in urban Texas that are putting great pressure on local governments?
5. County activities vary between metropolitan and rural areas. What are some differences, and why do they exist?
6. What recommendations would you offer to the state legislature to ensure equal funding for students attending Texas's public schools?
7. Give the arguments supporting and opposing term limits. What is your position on this issue?

## Internet Resources

Austin city government: **www.ci.austin.tx.us**
Dallas city government: **www.dallascityhall.com**
El Paso city government: **www.ci.el-paso.tx.us**
Fort Worth city government: **www.fortworthgov.org**
Houston city government: **www.cityofhouston.gov**
San Antonio city government: **www.ci.sat.tx.us**
State Comptroller's Report on the Border: **www.cpa.state.tx.us/border**
Texas Association of Counties: **www.county.org**
Texas Association of Regional Councils: **www.txregionalcouncil.org**
Texas Municipal League: **www.tml.org**
Texas State Data Center: **www.txsdc.utsa.edu**
U.S. Census Bureau: **www.census.gov**

## Notes

1. See "Local Government Code," Sections 1.001–140, Chapters 6–8, *Vernon's Texas Codes Annotated* (St. Paul, Minn.: West Group, 1999).
2. See Robert Bezdek, David Billeaux, and Juan Carlos Huerta, "Latinos, At-Large Elections, and Political Change: Evidence from the Transition Zone," *Social Science Quarterly* 81 (March 2000): 207–225. (Special issue: "Hispanics in America at 2000," edited by Benigno Aquirre, Robert Lineberry, and Edward Murguia.)
3. See Sonia R. Garcia, Valerie Martinez-Ebers, Irasema Coronado, Sharon Navarro, and Patricia Jaramillo, *Politicas: Latina Trailblazers in the Texas Political Arena* (University of Texas Press, forthcoming), which provides biographical essays on the first Latina elected public officials in Texas; Stephen L. Klineberg, *The Houston Area Survey 1982-2005* (Houston: Rice University, 2005), 13; Gromer Jeffers, Jr., "Political Talent Emerges in Suburbs," *Dallas Morning News*, 29 June, 2005.
4. An interesting account of the problems facing a rural county undergoing population change is Dave Mann, "The Battle for San Jacinto," *Texas Observer*, 10 February, 2006.
5. Steve Brewer, "Redrawing of Precincts May Be Easy: Hispanic Could Be Member of Court," *Houston Chronicle*, 21 April 2001. See also Steve Brewer, "Hispanics Draw Lines on County Remapping," *Houston Chronicle*, 22 August 2001; Tom Bower, "County Redistricting May Shift Party Balance," *San Antonio Express-News*, 18 April 2001; and Alex Taylor, "Rise of Republicans Complicates Travis Redistricting Effort," *Austin American-Statesman*, 5 August 2001.
6. Tom Bower, "Toyota Incentives Gets County's OK," *San Antonio Express-News*, 21 May 2003.

7. Alison Gregor and W. Gardner Selby, "Census Finds Border Still Dirt-Poor," *San Antonio Express-News*, 27 May 2002. See also Armando Villafranca, "Not Suitable for Living," *Houston Chronicle*, 5 November 2001, and Erica Cordova, "Residents' Dream for Running Water Draws Near," *Laredo Morning Times*, 11 June, 2005.

8. Kjell A. Christopherson and M. Henry Robison, "The Socioeconomic Benefits Generated by 50 Community College Districts in Texas: Executive Summary," commissioned by the Texas Association of Community Colleges, CC Benefits, Inc., 2002.

# 3.1 "Extreme" Term Limits—San Antonio Style*

### *Alexander E. Briseno*

*Limiting the number of terms an elected official can serve in office is not an uncommon practice. However, in San Antonio, the city charter provision on term limits is among the most restrictive in the country and can be considered "extreme." This provision's impact on governance needs review after application for more than 10 years.*

## Political Climate

To understand what instigated term limits in San Antonio, it is necessary to review the city's political environment immediately prior to the adoption of this provision. The late 1980s and early 1990s were a challenging period for San Antonio as well as most cities in Texas. The economy was suffering: banking, construction, and oil and gas industries were in disarray; unemployment rates were increasing; and real estate property values were decreasing. The impact on the city of San Antonio was daunting due to increasing demands for services concurrent with declining or stagnant revenue sources. City officials responded by adopting "bad news, bad news" budgets that reduced service levels while raising the property tax rate high enough to recover lost revenues due to lower property values and still generate a net revenue increase.

Other controversial issues muddied the political landscape and deepened divisions in the ongoing community debate. The city council approved a four-year collective bargaining agreement with the San Antonio Police Officers Association and subsequently discovered that its cumulative financial impact had been inaccurately calculated by the city's negotiating team, resulting in greater fiscal woes. A hotly disputed election in 1989

approved a half-cent sales tax increase for five years to build the Alamodome, a multipurpose domed stadium, and its companion transit facility. The city council approved the land acquisition and construction of the Applewhite Reservoir, a surface-water project designed to supplement the city's sole source of water despite community concerns about its cost and viability.

Ultimately, a taxpayers' "watchdog" group organized petition drives that successfully garnered enough voter signatures to force elections in 1990 and 1991 on three major issues: a property tax rate rollback, repeal of the ordinance approving construction of the Applewhite Reservoir, and an amendment to the city charter limiting the terms of members of the city council.

The term limits provision allows an individual to be elected twice to the office of mayor or council member during his or her lifetime and then be prohibited from running for election again. As a result, 39 council members and four mayors served on San Antonio's 11-seat governing body between 1991 and 2001. By comparison, during the prior 10 years, 15 council members and 2 mayors occupied those same seats. The turnover resulting from the term limits provision has had a significant effect on the community's governance.

## City Council Service After Term Limits

Newly elected council members come into office from diverse backgrounds, with varying levels of life experience, and sometimes with a limited understanding of municipal government. Each, wittingly or unwittingly, evolves through progressive phases of learning, adapting, executing, campaigning, and completing, sometimes on an ongoing basis.

Local government in San Antonio is a complicated business. Within three months of taking office, council members are presented with a proposed consolidated annual budget of up to $1.4 billion, financing a full array of municipal services to almost 1.2 million residents deliv-

---

*Alexander Briseno served as San Antonio's city manager for almost 11 years until retiring in March of 2001. He currently serves as an appointed professor of Public Service in Residence at St. Mary's University, San Antonio, and works as a municipal consultant. This article was written especially for *Practicing Texas Politics*, and is printed by permission of the author.

ered by more than 12,000 employees on a 24/7 basis. The city government must manage basic city services ranging from public safety to infrastructure maintenance and construction. It operates enterprises including garbage collection, airports, convention facilities, parking garages, sports venues, golf courses, and retail centers. In addition, it provides many services to enhance the quality of life and well-being of the residents: libraries, parks, health facilities, cultural institutions, and social services.

The city government is also actively engaged in stimulating economic activity and investment as well as the revitalization of decaying neighborhoods. To accomplish these tasks it must manage a strong revenue stream financed by a complex assortment of taxes, fees, fines, rents, contracts, and other charges for services. Ample preparation is desirable for serving on the governing board of this corporate conglomerate, which is equivalent to a *Fortune* 1000 company. In this context, new council members are responsible for making policy decisions and must learn as much as possible about the intricacies of governance to assure high-quality, responsive, and sufficient municipal services. This learning process is best achieved over time as issues arise and are addressed; at least one to two years of experience is necessary to be minimally effective.

A new council member must also adapt to conducting business in a different and public environment. Getting to know the other 10 members of the council, their strengths and weaknesses, goals and priorities, and personalities is critical to forging successful coalitions. Familiarity with procedures for initiating policy direction, accounting for expenses, complying with ethics and election laws, contracting, and countless other activities is also important. Moreover, city business must be conducted in the light of public scrutiny actively monitored by multiple media sources; neighborhood, community, and business groups; and opponents and supporters alike. This adaptation phase is rarely concluded since the variables are dynamic and evolutionary.

During their first term, council members must then execute or "deliver" to set the stage for reelection. Sometimes uninformed campaign rhetoric of expanded services, more efficiency, and "no increased taxes" demands adherence, although it is often difficult to achieve in reality. Campaign promises become accountability measures for the electorate, and efforts to initiate and execute a campaign agenda must show progress. As a consequence of two-year terms, "making an impact" within six to 18 months is highly desirable. Frequently, elections based on a "change" agenda create conflict when implementation attempts are made, whether successfully or quashed by apparent impermeable obstacles. Intensive and sometimes frustrating, the execution phase is a prerequisite to a reelection campaign.

A year to 18 months after taking office, council members should be gearing up for the next election: organizing supporters, discouraging opponents, and soliciting campaign contributions. Then they must wage a three to six month reelection campaign, have countless time-consuming but necessary meetings and rallies with myriad interest groups and individuals, write and deliver multiple speeches, and make continuous personal outreach to voters. Watchful opponents exacerbate the need for accountability. Finally, council members must achieve all this while handling the persistent responsibilities of city business and while still learning, adapting, and executing. The campaign phase, if successful, completes the first two years in office and leads to a new term.

Council members' final two years in office are punctuated by endeavors to complete the initiatives undertaken in the first term or promised during the campaign. Returning council members are now "veterans" who guide the recently elected freshmen and serve in leadership capacities on city council committees. With two opportunities for reviewing and approving the city budget and its implicit work program under their belt, these veterans are more effective in addressing pressing municipal issues and executing their commitments. However, this effectiveness is sometimes short-lived: within a year their attention becomes focused on who will succeed them, and they become potentially "lame ducks," unaccountable to the voters.

This is not the case if they are ambitiously seeking higher office, such as the mayor's seat or state and county positions. Nevertheless, their effectiveness is frequently diminished by election calendars that may force them to resign their council seats as early as six months into their second term. Therefore, "extreme" term limits can produce officeholders who only serve as little as 30 months of their potential 48-month tenure. Their successors are appointed by the city council, creating a different breed of unelected new council member. Indeed, among the 39 San Antonio city council members who served from 1991 to 2001, eight were first appointed to the office, two of whom were never elected.

This final completion phase, marked by lame-duck stature or pursuit of higher office, caps the progression, with varying levels of success, through the other phases of learning, adapting, executing, and campaigning. Together these phases reflect the overall context for city council service under the term limits provision.

## Impact on Governance

But what are the results? What has been the impact of term limits on governance in San Antonio? Since 1991, it appears the community has experienced short-term, disjointed policy direction with limited overall vision. In addition, sources of influence have often shifted, and community leadership development has been challenged.

Continuity in completing multiyear phased projects or policy initiatives has been diminished. Each two-year council cycle witnesses from four to as many as eight council members elected for the first time. Bound by the pressure to make their own mark to get reelected, new council members often push programs or projects that render short-term, positive, or visible results to the top of the list, failing to continue the work of their predecessors and leaving the investment in engineering designs and program plans on the shelf.

As policy priorities shift, long-term planning efforts drag on for years and can best be completed by advocate council members who may rise to the mayor's office. For example, the comprehensive revision of the Master Plan, a policy guide for community growth and development that was raised as an issue in the mayoral campaign of 1991, was not effectively completed until the approval of the rewrite of the Unified Development Code in 2001. Annual goal-setting sessions have generated top-echelon priorities in many diverse areas, such as youth programs, international trade, sidewalks, neighborhood police patrol, workforce development, community revitalization, crime prevention, water quantity/quality, and infrastructure maintenance. Although new perspectives and ideas can be beneficial, these periodic shifts in municipal priorities drain resources and reduce council members' effectiveness in making a lasting impact with comprehensive strategies. This myopic, truncated vision through a four-year window ultimately can hamper San Antonio's ability to reach its potential for a better quality of life for all of its residents.

Term limits has generated a policy arena often filled with uncertainty and struggles for power and influence. Some observers see the power shifting to the bureaucracy, augmented by the strength of continuity and institutional knowledge and resistant to change, secure in the knowledge it can outlast change agents. However, this view has nurtured skepticism among incoming elected officials that borders on mistrust and detonated team-building between policymakers and the city employees who execute their policies. Indeed, council members often are leery of municipal professionals' recommendations, forcing staff personnel to invest significant time and energy revalidating themselves every two years, again sapping resources better applied to delivery of municipal services. Burdened by this lack of confidence in staff input, new council members are frequently vulnerable to the counsel of others seeking influence on policy decisions. Campaign contributors, contractors, special-interest groups, and lobbyists gain audiences and input that, although predictable in a political environment and sometimes worthwhile, may outweigh the judgment of the city's own professional cadre and can result in policy decisions flavored by private gain at the expense of the public good.

Moreover, the policy arena is further scrambled as term-limited council members vie for an edge in the anticipated competition for the mayor's chair, the only option for continued municipal elected service after two terms on the city council. Policy agendas and supportive coalitions are juggled within the governing body for months prior to the election as potential candidates poise themselves for the mayor's race. Conflicts lace policy decisions as campaign positions are staked out, and frequently policy decisions are postponed or hurried to satisfy political strategies. Indeed, the turmoil fueled by San Antonio's "extreme" term limits appears to have had a cumulative impact on governance in the community that is questionable.

The inherent turnover mobilized by the term limits provision has also challenged the community's ability to renew its leadership talent pool. This continuous demand for new elected official talent has been aggravated by minuscule council pay ($20 per meeting), demanding mayoral and council district responsibilities, and their concomitant time commitments. Experienced midcareer individuals with family obligations are often reluctant to offer their candidacy for public service in this environment. Consequently, leadership options are sometimes inordinately skewed toward inexperienced yet well-meaning and enthusiastic elected officials who are restricted from fully realizing their leadership potential before term limits forces them out of office. Council members are elected, go through a learning process in the context of the conditions outlined above, become more effective, and then move out of office to other endeavors before the community can maximize the value of their newly developed expertise. The cycle is then repeated, further depleting the reservoir of willing and capable potential leaders. Outgoing council members interested in further elected public service are then thrust into the competition for county or legislative seats, further complicating the governance scenario at other levels. Ultimately, this guaranteed turnover of leadership may be detrimental to the community.

## Conclusion

Indeed, with more than 10 years of application, the current city charter provision limiting elected service in the positions of mayor and council member to two 2-year terms—with a subsequent lifetime prohibition of running for these offices—has had a significant impact on San Antonio's governance. It has fostered a challenging maze to maneuver for elected officials to become effective in their already difficult policymaking role for cities. The community's vision has frequently narrowed to immediate fixes at the expense of nurturing comprehensive, long-term strategies for San Antonio's future. Struggles for power and influence often mark the decisionmaking process, sometimes minimizing the public good. Finally, the community's leadership talent pool is confronted with the constant need for reinvigoration.

Although term limits are common in government and periodic replacement of entrenched incumbents can inject fresh ideas into policy development, San Antonio's "extreme" term limits are frequently counterproductive. Given the electorate's apparent support for limiting elected service, a longer period of up to eight years, with the potential to return after an intermittent absence, may prove more effective. Maintaining the status quo may only serve to jeopardize San Antonio's future.

## 3.2 Bottoms Up*

### *Cecilia Balli*

*Cameron Park is the poorest community in America, a Brownsville colonia where people struggle to get by on little more than $4,000 a year. So why are its residents so optimistic?*

He calls them his "one thousand acres of excellence." In the northeastern corner of the border city, just four miles north of Mexico, Bill Hudson has reinvented Brownsville

in a way Brownsville never dared imagine itself. Using tile, stone, and stucco, the cheery blue-eyed native converted property his grandfather had purchased in 1937 into an upscale and as yet unfinished residential and retail development known as Paseo de la Resaca. There are now restaurants, shopping strips, and an events center, and when all is said and done, Brownsville will also count some two thousand new homes and a man-made waterway framed by a nine-mile hiking and biking trail. "This is six years ago," says Hudson, who looks and dresses like a Southern gentleman but is fascinated by Mexican border culture. He points at an aerial shot of a brown wasteland

*"Bottoms Up" by Cecilia Balli from *Texas Monthly,* January 2003: 116–119, 126–129. Reprinted by permission from *Texas Monthly.* A native of Brownsville, Cecilia Balli is a writer-at-large for *Texas Monthly* and a doctoral candidate at Rice University. She writes extensively on the border region.

hanging on his conference room wall and snickers. "Nada." For Hudson, Paseo de la Resaca is more than a development; it is a symbol of what could happen all along the Texas-Mexico border if only its people were willing to think big, to dream. In his view, the biggest challenge the border region faces is not drugs or immigration or low wages but what he calls "a deficit of spiritual capital, which is reflected in a resignation to mediocrity."

But even as Brownsville basks in this new identity, Paseo de la Resaca is not the only development in this part of town where people have come with visions of upward mobility. Rubbing against Hudson's excellent acres, in the shape of a slightly flawed parallelogram—and at a markedly different point on the economic spectrum—lies Cameron Park. This neighborhood of 4,895 residents is, according to the 2000 U.S. census, the poorest place in the country. The ranking is based on the median income per capita for communities of one thousand or more households. If the middle-American tries to make it on $21,587 a year and the middle-Texan lives on $19,617, the Cameron Park resident squeaks by on just $4,103. For most of the people who live here, this is the beginning of the American experience.

## A Success Story?

Cameron Park is a "colonia." The Spanish term refers literally to a "neighborhood" or a "settlement of homes," but along the Texas-Mexico border, it carries the stigma of fierce deprivation. Along the border it translates to rutted roads, crumbling homes, no running water. Along the border it means that the community is not incorporated, that it exists in legal limbo, really, because no government entity wants the responsibility of providing basic services. Colonias began to crop up in the sixties, when wily developers started selling plots of raw land that were cheap but had no infrastructure: no paved streets, no water and electricity hookups, no sewer lines. The lots were typically sold under contracts for deed, meaning that the buyer did not get title to the land until he made his final payment. By 2000, when critics of George W. Bush made conditions in the colonias an issue in the presidential race, the number of colonias in Texas had grown to almost 1,500.

The origins of Cameron Park date to 1964, when a thin, bespectacled man with a white mustache named Edward Dicker began selling off hundreds of 7,200-square-foot lots for as little as $300 each. That was well before Cameron County officials passed building codes in the early seventies that required new subdivisions to provide water and sewer services. But even after the new restrictions were passed, Dicker continued to sell. In 1979, when a Mexican journalist asked him who had authorized the sales, he replied defiantly, "Me. They're mine."

The floodgates were open. People who had crossed over the border from Mexico flocked into the neighborhood, where they squeezed into acquaintances' homes or rented trashed-out trailers while saving up to buy their own plot of land—their own little chunk of the American promise. The men took jobs as shrimpers, welders, day laborers, construction workers, or housepainters. The women became maids, home health aides, or seamstresses, or they participated in the informal economy, selling blankets, jewelry, and used clothing. Cameron Park stretched out until it became a city of sorts, one that has now displaced Indian reservations and Southern rural towns as this country's most glaring illustration of economic deprivation. After the census made Cameron Park's status official, journalists arrived from Chicago, Washington, D.C., and Germany, pressing residents on what it's like "to live in the poorest place in the nation." They cited the alarming numbers: Four-fifths of the colonia's dwellings are substandard; more than a third still lacked indoor plumbing.

And yet, these poverty statistics obscure the fact that Cameron Park is, in its own way, a success story, a down-and-out version of Paseo de la Resaca. Like Bill Hudson's Brownsville, the Cameron Park of today looks nothing like its former incarnation. As the largest of the country's 119 colonias, it has in the past eight years demanded and secured the attention of elected officials, with some $8 million in public funds having gone into making the place a symbol of what can be done in these poor settlements of the border: paved roads, water and sewer hookups, and soon to come, even curbs, gutters, sidewalks, and streetlights. How to show in a quantitative survey that Cameron Park has a bustling community center that offers a whole slew of social services? How to brag that there is now a Boys and Girls club, a sheriff's substation, a small health clinic, and a park? How to describe the shops lining its western boundary, which offer everything from birthday cakes and flowers to rotisserie chickens and tuxedo rentals? The signs of empowerment are everywhere. Undocumented immigrants speak of legalization, the documented speak about the importance of voting, and religion has taken root in the homes, where neighbors gather weekly to relate spiritual readings to their own material needs.

In other words, how to explain to demographers and statisticians and newspaper reporters that poverty is a relative thing—to rationalize why, amid the doom and the tragedy, optimism thrives?

## Activism for Social Services

"This is the way Cameron Park used to be," says 56-year-old Gloria Moreno, tapping her fingernail on a snapshot of mesquite and three-foot-tall weeds, which she pulls from a pile of photo albums documenting Cameron Park's progress since the seventies. "Like this. Like a jungle. There were snakes, there were scorpions, there were tarantulas, and at night you could hear the coyotes go like this: *auuuu!*" The worst was when it rained, says the self-described traditional Mexican wife who metamorphosed into an unflinching activist. When it rained, the children were scolded by bus drivers for climbing on with dirty shoes and had to scrape off the mud at the school's restroom sinks before entering the classroom. When it rained, the excrement rose to the top of the latrines, where the mosquitoes hovered before buzzing around the colonia and feasting on its residents. When it rained, the neighborhood erupted into a chorus of grunting automobile engines as cars and trucks fell prey to the hidden potholes and the chewy mud, their wheels spinning pitifully until the earth gave or a motor broke. If the rain came at three in the morning, the men emerged from their homes in a frenzied rush to park their trucks on the main road outside the colonia. The next morning, the repercussions: a missing battery, slashed tires.

The activism was born of sheer frustration. In its nascent stages, it was a movement shaped by men in guayaberas and cowboy hats, residents of the colonia who were inspired to action when they began to see county officials and other politicos pop into the neighborhood to drum up political support. Maybe their voice—at least their vote—mattered beyond Cameron Park. They joined forces with Valley Interfaith, a church-based, grassroots community group that was working to raise the standard of living for residents across the Rio Grande Valley. They organized meetings in the colonia, where the community president, Fidel Velasquez, diligently learned how to conduct a meeting. On the walls, they hung white paper and spelled out the rules in Spanish: We shall put our politics aside when the meeting begins; we shall not digress from the issues to discuss personal problems. But it seemed the politicians never lived up to their end of the deal. The Mexican daily newspapers, which covered Cameron Park extensively in the seventies and eighties, speculated that county officials hoped Cameron Park would not develop into a permanent neighborhood because the Brownsville Country Club was about to be constructed not far from the colonia's western boundary.

Moreno, who moved into Cameron Park in 1977, sometimes stood near the back of the room during those meetings, soaking up the lessons about how to approach and speak in front of elected officials. But when the U.S. Department of Agriculture asked the mother of eight to begin organizing nutrition classes for the colonia's residents, she initiated another kind of activism that catered particularly to the needs of women and children. After the nutrition lessons had been imparted to her neighbors, she began working the rest of the colonia by street, which wasn't easy since there were no street signs or addresses at the time. So Moreno pulled out the map she had received when she bought her property and began tracking her progress with a black marker. When an organization that provided health care asked her to find it some clients, her method became more precise; she filed each household's paperwork in separate envelopes and labeled them for future reference: "White house with red trimmings and three pines."

The huddled political meetings and street organizing began to pay off. In 1994, after residents had made frequent visits to Austin, the Texas Water Development Board and the Brownsville Public Utilities Board agreed to install water and sewer lines. Many of the homes did not meet the codes required for hookup, but state officials decided to proceed anyway. After much prodding,

Cameron County began paving the streets, and Texas A&M University's Colonias Program helped build the community center. That center serves as the clearinghouse for a number of other government and nonprofit programs, which deliver their services in Spanish, with cultural modifications if necessary. The colonia's churches—Catholic, Baptist, and Pentecostal—provide another crucial spiritual and social support system. "If Gloria and I want to do something, and if we want everybody to know," Alma Rendon, the center's 54-year-old program coordinator, says, "we call the churches and everybody hears the gossip."

## Housing Problem

Social services have transformed Cameron Park, but the biggest remaining challenge here, as in all colonias along the border, is housing. Owner-built homes, which are the norm in the community, take years to complete and sometimes don't meet building codes when they are finished. The major obstacle to securing a mortgage is that the poor have a difficult time qualifying for loans because banks require some credit history. Using low-interest loans subsidized by the federal and state governments, the nonprofit Community Development Corporation of Brownsville (CDCB) has built 130 simple wood-frame and brick homes in the colonia since 1997, but this hardly makes a dent in the housing problem. Several years ago Don Currie, the executive director of the CDCB, pushed this idea: that the government loans would go further if they could be bundled with private loans from Valley banks. The CDCB has helped organize the eight-year-old Rio Grande Valley Multibank, a group of lenders that has been making these loans for two years—with nearly flawless results. Unlike traditional mortgages, potential homebuyers do not have to meet rigorous credit standards; they only have to prove that they pay their bills on time and earn enough to meet their monthly payment. The banks protect their own risks by jointly maintaining a reserve fund in case anyone fails to make a monthly pay-

ment. Out of 145 mortgages the CDCB has overseen in Cameron Park, only one has been foreclosed on—and this because the borrower died and left no family to take over. "Our main point," Currie says, "was to show that you can lend these people money and they'll pay it back."

## Better Days Ahead?

The ultimate test of how far the neighborhood has come will be whether the City of Brownsville, which has created a doughnut hole on its map by annexing all of the land surrounding the colonia, ever decides to take it in too. It is doubtful that this will happen anytime soon.* Cities annex only areas that can provide enough tax revenue to pay for services like maintaining the streets and providing police and fire protection, and Cameron Park lacks the tax base. Time and again, city officials have sniffed at the idea, but they always conclude that the cost of providing services is too high. The colonia thus remains under the care of the county, which has neither the authority nor the funds to do what a city can do. Some residents say they would rather not pay city taxes anyway, while others point out that annexation would bring garbage control, bus service—possibly even a post office and a fire station.

One person believes with certainty the day will come. "This will be a prime neighborhood fifty years from now, prime neighborhood," says Bill Hudson, tapping at the parallelogram on his aerial map. "Cameron Park is gonna get better and better and better. It is not the bombed-out, burned-out permanent slum, and it's mostly because of the people. They are decent people." While Paseo de la Resaca may provide Brownsville's vision, this colonia will continue playing the essential role of absorbing the border's—and America's—deepest poverty. As Hudson's neighbor Seifert candidly puts it: "Thank goodness for Cameron Park."

---

*Note: As of summer 2006, there were no serious plans for Brownsville to annex Cameron Park.

---

An extensive bibliography of books and articles for this chapter is posted on Selected Sources for Reading, available online at http://college.hmco.com/PIC/brownPTP13e. For use with any chapter, see Resources for Further Research online at http://college.hmco.com/PIC/brownPTP13e.

# Chapter 4

# Political Parties

- ★ Party Structure
- ★ Political Democracy
- ★ Racial/Ethnic Politics
- ★ Women in Politics
- ★ Political Campaigns

SARGENT © 2004
*Austin American
Statesman.* Reprinted
with permission of
UNIVERSAL PRESS
SYNDICATE. All rights
reserved.

Following the 2004 general election the Republican Party in Texas continued to hold all statewide offices, as well as a majority of seats in the Texas House of Representatives and Texas Senate. Republican victories left many political observers to speculate that the Democratic Party might be destined to wander in the wilderness as Ben Sargent's cartoon depicts. This chapter examines the structure of political parties in Texas, their history, recent electoral trends, and voting coalitions. It also focuses on campaigns and the role media and money play in our electoral system.

## ⭐ Party Structure

**political party**  An
organization influenced
by political ideology
whose primary interest is
to gain control of gov-
ernment by winning
elections.

Although neither the U.S. Constitution nor the Texas Constitution mentions political parties, these organizations are an integral part of the American governmental process. A **political party** can be defined as a combination of people and interests whose primary purpose is to gain control of government by winning elections. Whereas interest groups (covered in the following chapter) tend to focus on influencing governmental policies, political parties are chiefly concerned with the recruitment, nomination, and election of individuals to governmental office. In Texas, as throughout the United States, the Democratic and Republican parties are the two leading political parties. State election laws have contributed to the continuity of the two-party system. These laws specify that a general election is won by the candidate who receives the largest number of votes (a plurality) without a runoff. Third-party candidates have little chance of winning an election by defeating the two major-party nominees.

American political parties exist on four levels: national, state, county, and precinct. In part, these levels correspond to the organization of the federal system of government in the United States. Whereas a corporation is organized as a hierarchy, with a chain of command that makes each level directly accountable to the level above it, a political party is organized as a **stratarchy** in which power is diffused among and within levels of the party organization.[1] Each major party is loosely organized, so that state and local party organizations are free to decide their positions on party issues. State- and local-level organizations operate within their own spheres of influence, separate from one another. Although these levels of the two major parties are encouraged to support national party policies, this effort is not always successful. As mandated by the Texas Election Code, Texas's two major parties are alike in structure. Each has permanent and temporary organizational structures (see Figure 4.1).

### Temporary Party Organization

The **temporary party organization** consists of primaries and conventions in which members of the major political parties select candidates for public office. Primary election voting periods may also include runoff voting. Conventions elect state-level party officers and are scheduled at precinct, county and state senatorial district, and state levels. Each convention lasts a limited time: from less than an hour to one or two days. These events are temporary because they are not ongoing party activities.

At the state level, conventions select party leaders chosen by delegates elected at the local level. Rules of the Texas Democratic and Republican parties mandate that party policy be determined at their conventions. This is done by passing resolutions, in both local and state conventions, and adopting a platform at the state conventions. A party's **platform** is a document that sets forth the party's position on current issues. In presidential election years, conventions on all levels select delegates who attend a party's national convention. Here candidates are chosen for president and vice president of the United States. All Texas political conventions must be open to the media, according to state law.

**Precinct Conventions** In Texas, **precinct conventions** occur every even-numbered year on the first Tuesday in March, which is the first primary day. At the lowest level of the temporary party organization, these conventions (both Democratic and Republican) assemble in almost all of the state's voting precincts. Precinct conventions start immediately after the polls close that evening and last approximately 30 minutes to two hours. Usually, precinct conventions

**stratarchy** A political system wherein power is diffused among and within levels of party organization.

**temporary party organization** Primaries and conventions that function briefly to nominate candidates, pass resolutions, adopt a party platform, and select delegates to party conventions at higher levels.

**platform** A document that sets forth a political party's position on issues such as an income tax, school vouchers, or public utility regulation.

**precinct convention** At the lowest level of political party organization, voters convene in March of even-numbered years to adopt resolutions and to name delegates to a county convention.

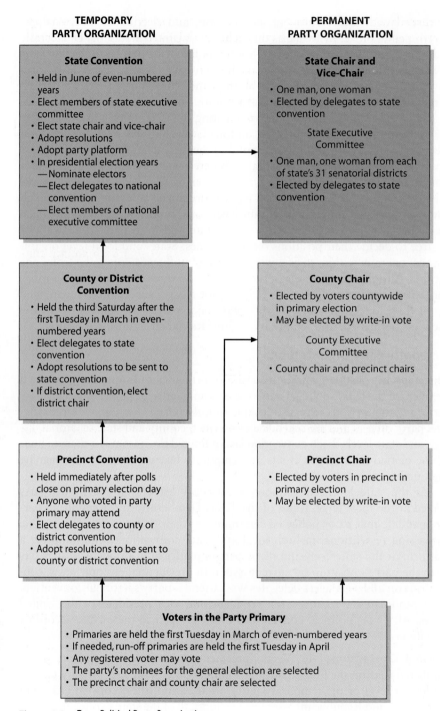

TEMPORARY
PARTY ORGANIZATION

**State Convention**

- Held in June of even-numbered years
- Elect members of state executive committee
- Elect state chair and vice-chair
- Adopt resolutions
- Adopt party platform
- In presidential election years
  — Nominate electors
  — Elect delegates to national convention
  — Elect members of national executive committee

**County or District Convention**

- Held the third Saturday after the first Tuesday in March in even-numbered years
- Elect delegates to state convention
- Adopt resolutions to be sent to state convention
- If district convention, elect district chair

**Precinct Convention**

- Held immediately after polls close on primary election day
- Anyone who voted in party primary may attend
- Elect delegates to county or district convention
- Adopt resolutions to be sent to county or district convention

PERMANENT
PARTY ORGANIZATION

**State Chair and Vice-Chair**

- One man, one woman
- Elected by delegates to state convention

State Executive Committee

- One man, one woman from each of state's 31 senatorial districts
- Elected by delegates to state convention

**County Chair**

- Elected by voters countywide in primary election
- May be elected by write-in vote

County Executive Committee

- County chair and precinct chairs

**Precinct Chair**

- Elected by voters in precinct in primary election
- May be elected by write-in vote

**Voters in the Party Primary**

- Primaries are held the first Tuesday in March of even-numbered years
- If needed, run-off primaries are held the first Tuesday in April
- Any registered voter may vote
- The party's nominees for the general election are selected
- The precinct chair and county chair are selected

*Figure 4.1*    Texas Political Party Organization

are sparsely attended. By state law, any individual who voted in the party primary is permitted to attend and participate in that party's precinct convention as a delegate. Delegates will elect a chairperson to preside over the convention and a secretary to record the proceedings. The main business of the precinct convention is to elect delegates to the county or district convention. Under long-standing rules of both the Democratic and Republican parties, precinct conventions have been authorized to elect one delegate to the county (or district) convention for every 25 votes cast in the precinct for the party's gubernatorial nominee in the last general election. Delegates to a party's precinct convention are allowed to submit and debate resolutions. These resolutions express the positions of precinct convention participants on any number of issues, ranging from immigration, to abortion, to the national debt. If adopted, a resolution will be submitted to a county or district convention for consideration.

**County and District Conventions**  State law requires that both **county conventions** and **district conventions** occur 11 days after the precinct conventions. These conventions are always held on a Saturday and usually last three or more hours. District conventions, rather than a single-county convention, are held in heavily populated counties (such as Harris, Dallas, and Bexar) that have more than one state senatorial district. Delegates to a party's county or district convention elect a chairperson to preside over the convention and a secretary to record the proceedings. The main business of county and district conventions is to elect delegates to the state convention.

Under the rules for each party, county and district conventions may select one delegate to the state convention for every 300 votes cast in the county or district for the party's gubernatorial nominee in the last general election. Under Republican Party rules, all delegate candidates are submitted by the county or district convention's committee on nominations for approval by the county or district convention participants. Rules of the Democratic Party allow state delegates to be selected by precinct delegations. If not all state delegate positions are filled in this manner, the county or district convention's nominations committee proposes the remaining state delegates, subject to selection by the county or district convention delegates. These delegates consider resolutions submitted from the party's precinct conventions. The resolutions adopted at this level the go to the party's state convention for its consideration.

**State Conventions**  In June of even-numbered years, each Texas political party must hold a biennial **state convention** to conduct party business. State conventions occur over a two-day period. Delegates to a party's state convention elect a chairperson to preside over the convention and a secretary to record the proceedings. Additionally, delegates conduct the following tasks:

**county convention**
A party meeting of precinct delegates held on the second Saturday after precinct conventions; it elects delegates and alternates to the state convention.

**district convention**
Held on the second Saturday after the first primary in counties that have more than one state senatorial district. Participants elect delegates to the party's state convention.

**state convention**
Convenes every even-numbered year to make rules for a political party, adopt a party platform and resolutions, and select members of the state executive committee; in a presidential election year it elects delegates to the national convention and names members to serve on the national committee.

- Certify to the secretary of state the names of party members nominated in the March and April primaries for Texas elective offices (or by convention if no primary was held)
- Write the rules that will govern the party
- Draft and adopt a party platform
- Adopt resolutions regarding issues too specific to be included in the party platform
- Select members of the party's state executive committee

In presidential election years, the June convention delegates also perform the following three functions:

- Elect delegates to the national presidential nominating convention (the total number for Texas is calculated under national party rules)
- Elect members from Texas to serve on the party's national committee
- Elect a slate of potential presidential electors to cast Texas's electoral votes if the party's ticket wins a plurality of the state's popular presidential vote

Texas is allowed 34 electoral votes. A state's electoral vote equals the number of its members in the U.S. Congress (for Texas, 32 representatives and 2 senators).

### Selection of National Convention Delegates

**presidential preference primary** A primary in which the voters indicate their preference for a person seeking nomination as the party's presidential candidate.

**caucus** A once-used nominating process involving selection of candidates by an informal committee of party leaders; also, a group of legislators organized according to party, racial/ethnic, or ideological identity.

Selection of delegates to a national party convention depends on their support for particular candidates for the party's presidential nomination. In a **presidential preference primary**, rank-and-file party members can vote directly for the presidential candidates of their choice. In states that, like Texas, use primaries, voting is by precinct. Delegates to the party's national convention are chosen according to the results of the primary vote. The respective national conventions nominate the parties' candidates for president and vice president.

In many states, parties select delegates to a national convention in **caucuses**. Party members assemble in caucuses at the respective precinct, county, and state levels. Here they choose national convention delegates who either are pledged to support a particular presidential candidate or are uncommitted.

**Democratic Selection**    Texas Democrats combine the two delegate-selection plans in a primary-caucus plan. At each of the conventions in presidential years, participants must identify their presidential preferences. Individuals may indicate they are uncommitted and do not want to pledge their support to any candidate. Presidential candidates are awarded delegates to local and state conventions in proportion to the number of their supporters in attendance. In 2004, John Kerry won overwhelming support by the 232 Texas delegates to the national Democratic convention. National delegates include those selected by

*Texas delegates participate in the Republican National Convention in 2004. (Paul Sancya/AP-Wide World Photos)*

state senatorial district, those selected on an at-large basis, and **superdelegates** (unpledged party and elected officials).

**Republican Selection**     The Republican Party selects national delegates from the results of the presidential preference primary. Some Republican delegates are chosen by congressional district caucuses (three from each district in 2004). Others are chosen on an at-large basis by the entire convention. Any presidential candidate who wins 50 percent or more of the popular vote in the primary in a particular congressional district or statewide is entitled to all of the district or at-large delegates, respectively. A nominating committee selects all at-large delegates. State convention delegates approve all national delegates. George W. Bush won all 138 Texas delegates in 2004.

### Permanent Party Organization

Each major political party in the United States consists of thousands of virtually autonomous executive committees at local, state, and national levels. For both Democrats and Republicans, these executive committees nationwide are linked only nominally. At the highest level, each party has a national committee. In Texas, the precinct chairs, together with the county, district, and state executive committees, comprise the permanent organization of the state parties. The role of the **permanent party organization** is to recruit candidates, devise strategies, raise funds, distribute candidate literature and information, register voters, and turn out voters on election day.

**superdelegate** An unpledged party official or elected official who serves as a delegate to a party's national convention.

**permanent party organization** In Texas, the precinct chairs, county and district executive committees, and the state executive committee form the permanent organization of a political party.

**Precinct Chair**    In Texas, the basic party official in both the temporary and permanent party structures is the **precinct chair**, elected by precinct voters in the party primaries for a two-year term. A party precinct chair's duties and responsibilities include registering and canvassing voters within the precinct, distributing candidate literature and information, operating phone banks within the precinct on behalf of the party and its candidates, and getting people to the polls. If both parties are evenly matched in strength at the polls, the precinct chairs become more vital in getting people out to vote. A precinct chair is an unpaid party official who also arranges for the precinct convention and serves on the county executive committee. These positions often go unfilled in more populous counties that have one hundred or more precincts.

**County and District Executive Committees**    A **county executive committee** is composed of all the precinct chairs and the county chair, elected by county party members in the primaries. The county chair heads the party's countywide organization. County executive committees conduct primaries and arrange for county conventions. At the local level, the **county chair** is the key party official and serves as the party's chief strategist within that county. Duties of the county chair include recruiting local candidates for office, raising funds, establishing and staffing the party's campaign headquarters within the county, and serving as the local spokesperson for the party. The Texas Election Code also provides for a **district executive committee** composed of the county chairs from each county in a given district (senatorial, representative, or judicial). District executive committees rarely meet except to nominate candidates to fill a district vacancy when one occurs.

**State Executive Committee**    For each major political party, the highest permanent party organization in the state is the **state executive committee**. As mandated by state law, an executive committee is composed of one man and one woman from each of the 31 state senatorial districts, plus a chair and a vice chair, one of whom must be a woman. For both the Democratic and Republican parties, a state executive committee with 64 members is elected at the party's state convention. On that occasion, delegates from each of the 31 senatorial districts choose two members from their district and place these names before the convention for its approval. At the same time, convention delegates choose the chair and vice chair at large. The party's state chair serves as its key strategist and chief spokesperson. The role of vice chair has traditionally been more honorary in nature. In addition to the 64 statutory members of the party's state executive committee, party rules may allow "add-on" members. An add-on member may represent recognized statewide auxiliary organizations within the party such as women's groups, racial groups, House and Senate caucus chairs, youth groups, and county chairs associations.

The party's state chair works with the party's state executive committee to recruit candidates for statewide and district offices, plan statewide strategies, and raise funds for the party at the state level. Additionally, the state executive committee of each party must canvass statewide primary returns and certify

**precinct chair** The party official responsible for the interests and activities of a political party in a voting precinct; typical duties include supervising party volunteer workers, encouraging voter registration, and getting out the vote on election day.

**county executive committee** Composed of a party's precinct chairs and the elected county chair, the county executive committee conducts primaries and makes arrangements for holding county conventions.

**county chair** Elected by county party members in the primaries, this key party official heads the county executive committee.

**district executive committee** Composed of county chairs within a district that elects a state senator, representative, or district judge, this committee meets to fill a vacancy created by the death, resignation, or disqualification of a nominated candidate.

**state executive committee** Composed of a chair, vice chair, and two members from each senatorial district, this body is part of a party's permanent organization.

the nomination of party candidates. It also conducts the state convention, promotes party unity and strength, maintains relations with the party's national committee, and raises some campaign money for party candidates (although most campaign funds are raised by the candidates themselves).

---

**Learning Check 4.1**        **(Answers on pp. 167–168)**

1. What is the difference between a party's permanent organization and temporary organization?
2. True or False: A political party's state chairperson is chosen by the temporary organization.

---

# ★ Political Democracy

Today's politics in the Lone Star State reflects Texas's political history. Traditions based on centuries of political experience and culture influence current attitudes toward parties, candidates, and issues. Nevertheless, Texans' changing demands and expectations have forced revisions in party platforms and affected the campaigns of candidates for public office. Political parties cannot remain static and survive, nor can politicians win elections unless they are in step with the opinions of the voting majority. Over the last 20 years, competition between Texas's Democratic and Republican parties has brought more women, Latinos, and African Americans into the state's political system. As a result of this competitiveness, party politics has become more democratic and more nationalized. Compared with the politics of earlier years, Texas politics today is more partisan (party centered). But both the Democratic and Republican parties experience internal feuding (factionalism) among competing groups.

## Ideology

Since the 1930s, the terms *liberal* and *conservative* have meant more to many Texas voters than the names of political parties. In view of long-standing ideological differences between liberals and conservatives, this terminology must be explained. These ideological labels almost defy definition, however, because meanings change with time and circumstances. Furthermore, each label has varying shades of meaning for different people. In Texas, because of the influences of the individualistic and traditionalistic cultures, both Democrats and Republicans tend to be conservative. But the Republican Party organization is dominated by right-wing conservatives, whereas the Democratic Party is influenced (but not dominated) by left-wing liberals. Despite the use of right-left terminology throughout the United States, the Texas Legislature has not traditionally used partisan or ideological criteria for assigning floor seats on the right and left sides of House and Senate chambers.

**Conservatism**    In its purest form, modern conservative doctrine envisions ideal social and economic orders that would be largely untouched by government.

According to this philosophy, if all individuals were left alone (the doctrine of laissez-faire) to pursue their self-interests, both social and economic systems would benefit, and the cost of government would be low. **Conservatives**, therefore, are generally opposed to government-managed or government-subsidized programs such as assistance to poor families with dependent children, unemployment insurance, and federal price support programs for the benefit of farmers producing commodities such as cotton and wheat. Today's fiscal conservatives give the highest priority to reduced taxing and spending; on the other hand, social conservatives (such as those associated with the Christian Coalition) stress the importance of their family values, including opposition to abortion and homosexuality. They support school vouchers to provide government-funded assistance to parents who choose to send their children to private schools, especially church-affiliated schools.

Attempting to distance himself from more extreme conservative Republicans, President George W. Bush used the phrase "compassionate conservatism" to describe his political philosophy when he ran for governor of Texas in 1998 and for the presidency in 2000 and 2004. Bush insists that he is "a conservative who puts a compassionate face on a conservative philosophy."[2] His ideology is sometimes described as **neoconservatism** because he is fiscally conservative but does allow for a limited governmental role in solving social problems.

**Liberalism**    **Liberals** favor government regulation of the economy to achieve a more equitable distribution of wealth. Only government, liberals insist, is capable of guarding against air, water, and soil pollution by corporations and individuals. Liberals claim that government is obligated to aid the unemployed, alleviate poverty (especially for the benefit of children), and guarantee equal rights for minorities and women. Liberalism seeks a limited role for government involvement with regard to other social issues, especially those related to issues of morality or religion. Liberals are more likely to oppose mandatory prayer in public schools, government subsidies for religious institutions, and any church involvement in secular politics. Many Texas Democrats have a **neoliberal** ideology. This position incorporates a philosophy of less government regulation of business and the economy while adopting a more liberal view of greater government involvement in social programs.

Both Texas liberals and conservatives are often ideologically inconsistent. A conservative may oppose government subsidies, such as welfare assistance for individuals, but support similar payments to corporations. Liberals may support pollution control laws for corporations but oppose antipollution measures that require installation of emission control devices for their own automobiles. Frequently, individuals who have extreme conservative or liberal ideologies accuse moderates of being ideologically inconsistent.

### An Overview of Texas Political History

From the time political parties developed in Texas until the 1960s, the Lone Star State was dominated primarily by one political party: the Democratic

**conservative** Someone who advocates minimal intervention by government in social and economic matters and who gives a high priority to reducing taxes and curbing public spending.

**neoconservatism** A political ideology that reflects fiscal conservatism but accepts a limited governmental role in solving social problems.

**liberal** One who favors government regulation to achieve a more equitable distribution of wealth.

**neoliberal** A political view that advocates less government regulation of business but supports more governmental involvement in social matters.

# ◄ POINT/COUNTERPOINT ►

## Positions of the Two Major Parties on Key Issues

**THE ISSUE** The two major parties, as identified in their platforms, differ on many major social and economic issues. Below are excerpts from each party platform, as passed at their respective state conventions in 2006, which illustrate several of these different points of view. For the complete text of each party's platform, visit **www.texasgop.org** (Republican) and **www.txdemocrats.org** (Democratic).

### The Texas Republican Party

**Bilingual Education:** The Republican Party demands the abolition of bilingual education programs in favor of an "English Immersion Program." All students must pass recognized standard tests that verify each student's English ability for their grade level before advancing.

**School Vouchers:** The Republican Party encourages the governor and the Texas Legislature to enact child-centered school funding options—which fund the student, not schools or districts—to allow maximum freedom of choice in public, private, or parochial education for all children.

**Abortion:** The Republican Party believes the unborn child has a fundamental individual right to life that cannot be infringed. Supports a human life amendment to the Constitution, opposes the use of public revenues and/or facilities for abortion or abortion–related services, supports the elimination of public funding for organizations that advocate or support abortion, and urges the reversal of *Roe* v. *Wade*.

**Social Security:** The Republican Party supports an orderly transition to a system of private pensions based on the concept of individual retirement accounts, and gradually phasing out the Social Security tax.

**Energy:** The Republican Party believes the foundation of a National Energy Strategy must be a competitive domestic oil and gas industry. Encourages Congress to stop the promulgation of unnecessary environmental legislation or regulation that causes domestic oil production to be economically not feasible.

### The Texas Democratic Party

**Bilingual Education:** The Democratic Party supports multilanguage instruction to make all children fluent in English and at least one other language and rejects efforts to destroy bilingual education.

**School Vouchers:** The Democratic Party opposes any form of private school vouchers and other inequitable, unaccountable privatization schemes that would siphon off public education funds.

**Abortion:** The Democratic Party believes in the fundamental American values of freedom, privacy, and personal responsibility. Trusts the women of Texas to make personal and responsible decisions about when and whether to bear children, in consultation with their family, their physician, and their God, rather than having these personal decisions made by politicians.

**Social Security:** The Democratic Party believes the promise of Social Security must be kept strong and certain for those who have worked and contributed to the system most of their lives. Social Security should continue to be the foundation of income security for working Americans.

**Energy:** The Democratic Party wants a safe, secure, and sustainable supply of clean energy to reduce Texas' relicance on finite petroleum resources. Supports the development of bold yet achievable national policy for energy independence and the development and use of emerging renewable energy technology to address the global need to reduce greenhouse gas emissions.

Party. In the 1970s and 1980s, Texas moved toward a competitive two-party structure. However, by the 1990s and into the twenty-first century it appears that the state has become a one-party state again, with the Republican Party in control.

### 1840s to 1870s: The Origin of the Party System

Before Texas's 1845 admission into the Union, its political parties had not fully developed. Political factions during the years that Texas was an independent republic tended to coalesce around personalities. The two dominant factions were the pro-(Sam) Houston and anti-Houston groups. Even after the Lone Star State's admission into the Union, these two factions remained. By the 1850s, the pro-Houston faction began referring to itself as the Jackson Democrats (Unionists), whereas the anti-Houston faction called themselves the Calhoun Democrats (after South Carolina senator John C. Calhoun, a states' rights and proslavery advocate). In the course of the Civil War, Texas politics became firmly aligned with the Democratic Party.

During the period of Reconstruction that followed the Civil War (1865–1873), the Republican Party controlled Texas politics. The Reconstruction acts passed by the United States Congress purged all officeholders with a Confederate past. Congress also disenfranchised all Southerners who had ever held a state or federal office before secession and later supported the Confederacy. In Texas, any man who had ever been a mayor, a school trustee, a clerk, or even a public weigher was denied the right to vote.[3] Republican governor Edmund J. Davis was elected in 1869 during this period of Radical Reconstruction. The Davis administration quickly became the most unpopular in Texas history. During his tenure in office, Davis took control of voter registration and appointed more than 8,000 public officials. From the Texas Supreme Court justices to the state police to city officials, Davis placed Republicans in office throughout the state. Davis's administration is best remembered for its corruption, graft, and excessive taxation. Following Davis's defeat for reelection in 1873 by a newly enfranchised electorate, Texas voters did not elect another Republican governor for more than one hundred years.

### 1870s to 1970s: A Dominant One-Party System

From the end of Reconstruction until the 1970s, Texas and other former Confederate states had a one-party identity in which the Democratic Party was strong and the Republican Party weak. During those years (when a gubernatorial term was two years), Democratic candidates won 52 consecutive gubernatorial elections, and Democratic presidential nominees carried the state in all but 3 of the 25 presidential elections.

During the latter part of the nineteenth century, Democrats faced a greater challenge from the Populist Party than they did from Republicans. The Populist (or People's) Party formed in Texas as an agrarian-based party, winning local elections throughout the state. From 1892 to 1898, their gubernatorial nominees received more votes than did Republicans. Although its ideas remained influential in Texas, the Populist Party became less important after

1898. Rural Texans continued to be active in politics, but most farmers and others who had been Populists shifted their support to Democratic candidates. In large measure, the Populist Party declined because the Democratic Party adopted Populist issues such as government regulation of railroads.[4]

In the early twentieth century, the Democratic Party strengthened its control over state politics. Having adopted Populist issues, Democratic candidates faced no opposition from Populist candidates. Over the next five decades, two factions emerged within the Democratic Party: conservatives and liberals. Fighting between these two factions was often as fierce as between two separate political parties. By the late 1940s and early 1950s, Republican presidential candidates began enjoying greater support from the Texas electorate. With the backing of conservative Democratic governor Alan Shivers, Republican presidential nominee Dwight D. Eisenhower successfully carried Texas in 1952 and 1956. To bolster support for Eisenhower, Shivers secured both the Democratic and Republican nominations for governor. Supporters of Governor Shivers began referring to themselves as "Shivercrats."

Evidence of the growing strength of the Texas GOP (Grand Old Party, a nickname that the Republican Party adopted in the 1870s) was sharply revealed in 1961 with the election to the U.S. Senate of Texas Republican John Tower, a political science professor at Midwestern State University in Wichita Falls. Originally elected to fill the vacancy created when Lyndon Johnson left the Senate to become vice president, Tower became the first Republican to win statewide office in Texas since 1869 and won successive elections until his retirement in 1984.

**1970s to 1990s: An Emerging Two-Party System**    Beginning in the late 1940s, a majority of conservative Democrats began to support the national Republican ticket. However, at the state and local levels, the Democratic Party remained firmly in control. Three decades later, however, the Republican Party began enjoying greater electoral support. No longer was the winner in a Democratic primary assured of victory in the general election contest in November. When Bill Clements was elected governor of the Lone Star State in 1978, he became the first Republican to hold that office since Reconstruction. In the 1980s, GOP voters elected growing numbers of candidates to the U.S. Congress, the Texas Legislature, and county courthouse offices. And they began to dominate local politics in suburban areas around the state.

The Republican Party continued to make substantial gains throughout the 1990s. With the Republican victory of U.S. senatorial candidate Kay Bailey Hutchison in the 1993 special election, the Texas GOP began a series of "firsts." Hutchison's victory included two firsts. She was the first woman to represent Texas in the U.S. Senate, and, for the first time in modern history, Texas was represented by two Republican senators.

The elections of 1994 were a preview of future elections. Elected governor in 1990, Democrat Ann Richards failed to win reelection despite her personal popularity. Republican George W. Bush (who received more than 53 percent of

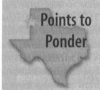

**Points to Ponder**

In the gubernatorial election of 1952, Democratic nominee Alan Shivers received more votes than did Republican nominee Alan Shivers by a three-to-one margin.

the vote and strong support from Anglo and suburban voters) beat Richards in the 1994 gubernatorial race. At the same time, Senator Hutchison easily defeated her Democratic opponent. Democrats holding four executive offices (lieutenant governor, attorney general, comptroller of public accounts, and commissioner of the general Land Office) defeated their Republican challengers. However, Republican incumbent agriculture commissioner Rick Perry had a 1-million-vote margin of victory over his Democratic opponent, and all six Republican statewide candidates below him on the ballot won. These victories gave Republicans two Railroad Commission members, two more Supreme Court justices, and two more Court of Criminal Appeals judges. Republicans also won many lower-level judgeships. For the first time, they gained control of the 15-member State Board of Education. Active support by members of the Christian Coalition resulted in Republican victories in three of the six contested races for seats on this board.

In 1996, for the first time since the primary system was established, Republican primaries were conducted in all 254 Texas counties. More of the Lone Star State's voters participated in the Republican primary than the Democratic primary. In addition, Republican victories continued in the general election of that year, as all statewide Republican candidates won. Republicans now held all three positions on the Texas Railroad Commission and gained three more Court of Criminal Appeals judgeships and four more positions on the Texas Supreme Court. Republican presidential candidate Bob Dole carried the state over President Bill Clinton. The 1992 election had made Clinton the first Democratic president elected without carrying Texas. By 1996, Clinton was certain that he could be elected without Texas's electoral votes, so his campaign effort focused on closely contested states where he was more likely to win. This decision demonstrates the acceptance by national Democratic candidates that Texas is a Republican state and that its electoral votes may not be needed for a Democratic presidential victory.

The 1998 elections gave Republicans control of all statewide offices but one. Texas Supreme Court justice Raul Gonzalez was the lone Democrat in statewide office when he announced his retirement in December 1998. The GOP sweep was complete when Governor Bush appointed a Republican to replace Gonzalez. In 1998, Bush was so popular that he received endorsements from more than 100 elected Democratic officials and almost 70 percent of the vote in the gubernatorial election. When the prospect of a Bush presidential bid in 2000 seemed likely,

Republican lieutenant gubernatorial nominee Rick Perry campaigned on the issue that a Republican should succeed Governor Bush if he resigned to become president. The 1998 elections allowed Republicans to retain control of the Texas Senate and to increase their representation in the state House of Representatives, although they did not gain control of the latter chamber. After the dismal performance of Democratic candidates, Texas Republican chair Susan Weddington advised Democrats to "turn out the lights, [because] the Democrat[ic] party [was] definitely over."

**2000 to 2006: Republican Dominance**   After their party's statewide success in 1998, Texas Republicans focused attention on national elections in 2000. Governor Bush's candidacy for the presidency was enhanced by his ability to maintain the backing of social conservatives within his party while gaining support from minority voters, women, and some Democrats. National Republican leaders seeking an electable candidate found Bush's 1998 gubernatorial victory and his inclusive strategy appealing. Although Bush did not announce that he would seek the Republican presidential nomination until after the Texas Legislature completed its 1999 regular session, Republican leaders streamed to Austin during the session. More than one-fourth of Texas Democrats told pollsters they would vote for Bush for president.

*Table 4.1*   Growth of Republican Officeholders

| Year | U.S. Senate | Other Statewide Offices | U.S. House | Texas Senate | Texas House | County Offices | District Offices | S.B.O.E.* | Total |
|------|-------------|-------------------------|------------|--------------|-------------|----------------|------------------|-----------|-------|
| 1974 | 1 | 0 | 2 | 3 | 16 | 53 | ? | — | 75+ |
| 1976 | 1 | 0 | 2 | 3 | 19 | 67 | ? | — | 92+ |
| 1978 | 1 | 1 | 4 | 4 | 22 | 87 | ? | — | 119+ |
| 1980 | 1 | 1 | 5 | 7 | 35 | 166 | ? | — | 215+ |
| 1982 | 1 | 0 | 5 | 5 | 36 | 191 | 79 | — | 317 |
| 1984 | 1 | 0 | 10 | 6 | 52 | 287 | 90 | — | 446 |
| 1986 | 1 | 1 | 10 | 6 | 56 | 410 | 94 | — | 578 |
| 1988 | 1 | 5 | 8 | 8 | 57 | 485 | 123 | 5 | 692 |
| 1990 | 1 | 6 | 8 | 8 | 57 | 547 | 170 | 5 | 802 |
| 1992 | 1 | 8 | 9 | 13 | 58 | 634 | 183 | 5 | 911 |
| 1994 | 2 | 13 | 11 | 14 | 61 | 734 | 216 | 8 | 1,059 |
| 1996 | 2 | 18 | 13 | 17 | 68 | 938 | 278 | 9 | 1,343 |
| 1998 | 2 | 27 | 13 | 16 | 72 | 1,108 | 280 | 9 | 1,527 |
| 2000 | 2 | 27 | 13 | 16 | 72 | 1,233 | 336 | 10 | 1,709 |
| 2002 | 2 | 27 | 15 | 19 | 88 | 1,443 | 362 | 10 | 1,966 |
| 2004 | 2 | 27 | 21 | 19 | 87 | 1,608 | 392 | 10 | 2,166 |

*Source:* Reprinted by permission of the Republican Party of Texas.
*State Board of Education.

In the closest presidential election of modern times, Governor Bush defeated Democratic nominee Al Gore by four electoral votes (271 to 267). After controversial recounts and protracted court battles over Florida's 25 electoral votes, George W. Bush was ultimately declared the victor in mid-December 2000 after a 5-4 ruling by the U.S. Supreme Court mostly along party lines. In the Lone Star State, Bush received 3,795,262 votes (59.3 percent) to Gore's 2,428,187 votes (37.7 percent), giving Bush Texas's 32 electoral votes. For the third straight election, all statewide Republican candidates won, including U.S. senator Kay Bailey Hutchison, who became the first candidate in Texas history to receive more than 4 million votes. Democrats did not even have candidates in most statewide contests or in many local races. In fact, the Libertarian Party and Green Party each had more candidates for statewide office than did the Democratic Party in 2000. Of the nine statewide offices up for election in 2000, the Democratic Party fielded candidates in only three contests. By contrast, the Libertarian Party ran candidates in seven of the nine races, and the Green Party had candidates in five.

As early as 2000, potential gubernatorial candidates began to solicit campaign contributions for the 2002 election. Governor Rick Perry established the Century Council, whose members pledged to donate or raise $100,000 each for Perry's 2002 campaign.[5] Meanwhile, some Democrats encouraged Tony Sanchez, a Laredo businessman with a fortune of more than $600 million and a strong supporter of George W. Bush, to seek the office. Sanchez, a political newcomer, brought two major assets to the campaign: a Latino surname and an ability to fund more than $50 million from his own resources for the gubernatorial campaign.

In September 2001, Phil Gramm announced his retirement from the U.S. Senate. Following Gramm's announcement, Texas attorney general John Cornyn declared that he would seek the Republican nomination to succeed Gramm. Several Democrats also filed for Gramm's Senate seat; but Dallas mayor Ron Kirk, an African American, emerged as the Democratic Party's nominee. To complete the Democratic line-up of candidates for the top three state offices, former comptroller John Sharp was nominated for lieutenant governor.

Sanchez, Kirk, and Sharp were dubbed the "dream team," because of their expected appeal to Latino, African American, and Anglo voters. They ran with a full slate of candidates for other statewide offices (including popular Austin mayor Kirk Watson for attorney general, state senator David Bernsen for commissioner of the General Land Office, and state representative Tom Ramsay for commissioner of agriculture). Thus, Texas Democrats presented their strongest field of candidates in 20 years. Many political analysts believed that the multiracial Democratic ticket would significantly increase minority turnout and help Democrats reclaim several statewide offices. However, on election night, the dream quickly turned into a nightmare as the GOP swept all statewide races, including contests for seats on the state's highest courts. The anticipated increase in voter turnout to support Tony Sanchez, Ron Kirk, John Sharp, and other Democratic candidates never materialized.

The 2002 election increased Republican control over the Texas Senate from a 1-seat majority to a 7-seat majority (19 to 12). And for the first time since Reconstruction, the GOP gained control of the Texas House of Representatives, winning 88 of 150 seats. Thus the stage was set to elect a Republican as speaker of the Texas House at the beginning of the 78th regular legislative session in January 2003.

With Republicans firmly in control of both houses of the Texas Legislature, U.S. representative Tom DeLay (R-Sugar Land) was determined that his job as U.S. House majority leader in Washington would be made easier with more Republican-dominated congressional districts in his state. After a contentious regular legislative session early in 2003, and three special sessions called by the governor later that year, new congressional districts were finally crafted by DeLay and the state legislature. Their work ensured that after the 2004 election Texas would have a large Republican majority in its delegation to the U.S. House of Representatives for the first time since Reconstruction. As a result, in 2004, Republicans picked up 6 seats in the U.S. House of Representatives, from a 15-seat minority to a 21-seat majority (out of 32 districts).

In addition to gaining a majority of Texas congressional seats in the 2004 general election, Republicans won all statewide elections, maintained control of the Texas Senate and the Texas House, and picked up approximately 200 more county and district-level offices. Benefiting many of the Republican candidates was the fact that at the top of the ballot, President Bush carried the state with more than 61 percent of the vote compared to Senator John Kerry's 38 percent. Inevitably, Republican candidates down the ballot were assisted by the president's coattails.

By 2006, it appeared clear that Texas was becoming a one-party state again (see Table 4.1). The Democratic Party fielded candidates for 9 of 15 statewide races in 2006, including U.S. Senate, governor, and the Cabinet (plural executive), but their chances for victory were considered slim. In fact, although they lost the statewide races and their gains were modest in comparison to those of the Democratic Party nationally, it appeared that the Texas Democratic Party might be making a comeback following the 2006 general election. Democratic candidates won all countywide races in Dallas (a Republican stronghold throughout the 1980s and 1990s) and Hays counties, and narrowed the margin of Republican control in Harris County.

### Electoral Trends

Some political scientists interpret recent polling and election results as evidence of a **dealignment** of Texas voters. These scholars explain that the large percentage of Texans who claim to be independent voters have abandoned allegiance to any political party (especially the Democratic Party) but tend to vote for Republican candidates. Other political scientists assert that the rising tide of Republican electoral victories throughout the 1990s and into the twenty-first century demonstrates that many Texans have switched their political affiliation and loyalty to the Republican Party in a **realignment** of voters.

**dealignment** Citizens abandon allegiance to a political party and become independent voters.

**realignment** Occurs when members of one party shift their affiliation to another party.

Republican candidates carried Texas in 10 of the 14 presidential elections between 1952 and 2004, including the last 7 elections in that period. Republican candidates also won 6 of 8 gubernatorial elections between 1978 and 2006. Because the GOP dominates statewide elections, intra-party competition among Republicans has increased (see this chapter's Selected Reading 4.1, "Elephants in the Room").

Texas GOP strongholds are in West Texas, the Panhandle–South Plains, some small towns and rural areas in East Texas, the Dallas–Fort Worth Metroplex, and the suburbs of Houston, San Antonio, and Austin. With the exception of Democratic El Paso, West Texas Republicanism is predominant from the Permian Basin (Midland-Odessa) through the Davis Mountains and the German Hill Country. This West Texas region, like the Panhandle–South Plains area to the north, is populated primarily by conservative farmers and ranchers, along with people connected with the oil and gas industry in Midland, Odessa, and other parts of the Permian Basin.

Although the Democratic Party has been unsuccessful in statewide election contests in recent years, it still controlled a majority of county offices in 2006. Democratic voting strength is concentrated in El Paso, South Texas, parts of East Texas, the Golden Triangle (Beaumont, Port Arthur, and Orange), portions of the diverse Central Texas region, and the lower-income neighborhoods of larger cities. **Straight-ticket voting** for all Democratic candidates on the general election ballot has declined, however, as fewer Texans (especially those in rural East Texas) choose to remain "yellow-dog Democrats." This term has been applied to people whose party loyalty is said to be so strong that they would vote for a yellow dog if it were a Democratic candidate for public office.

Republican expansion has diminished the intensity of factional politics within the Democratic Party. Nevertheless, Democrats are divided by many interests and issues, and factionalism within Republican ranks has increased.

### Third Parties

Americans commonly apply the term *third party* (or minor party) to any political party other than the Democratic or Republican Party. Both in the United States and in Texas, third parties have never enjoyed the same success as the two major parties. Major parties' success is measured by their ability to win elections. By this measure, minor parties are unsuccessful. However, third parties' success can better be measured by their ability to make the public aware of their issues, persuade the major parties to adopt those issues, and/or force the major parties to bring them into a coalition. When judged by these measures, third parties in Texas have enjoyed modest success.

During the 1890s, the Populist Party successfully promoted agricultural issues and displaced the Republicans as the "second" party in Texas.[6] In the 1970s, La Raza Unida elected a few candidates to local offices in South Texas (principally Crystal City and Zavala County offices) and forced the Democratic Party to begin to address Latino concerns. In the 1990s, Ross Perot's

**straight-ticket voting** Voting for all the candidates of one party.

**third party** A party other than the Democratic Party or the Republican Party. Sometimes called a "minor party" because of limited membership and voter support.

## How Do We Compare ... Which Party Controls the Statehouses in 2006?

| Most Populous U.S. States | Governor/Senate/House | U.S. States Bordering Texas | Governor/Senate/House |
| --- | --- | --- | --- |
| California | Republican/Democrat/Democrat | Arkansas | Democrat/Democrat/Democrat |
| Florida | Democrat/Republican/Republican | Louisiana | Democrat/Democrat/Democrat |
| New York | Democrat/Republican/Democrat | New Mexico | Democrat/Democrat/Democrat |
| Texas | **Republican/Republican/Republican** | Oklahoma | Democrat/Tie/Republican |

Reform Party had organizations in many areas in the state. Over the past 20 years, the Libertarian Party (a party that advocates minimizing government performance at all levels while maximizing individual freedom and rights) has nominated candidates for national, state, and local offices throughout Texas. In addition to these parties, other parties have nominated candidates and increased public awareness of their issues: the Greenback Party (late nineteenth century), the Prohibition Party (late nineteenth and early twentieth centuries), the Socialist and Socialist Labor parties (early twentieth century), the Progressive Party (early to mid-twentieth century), and the Green Party (starting in the late twentieth century). The Green Party has advocated environmental protection and government reform policies. In 2000, Green Party presidential candidate Ralph Nader received 2.2 percent of the popular vote in Texas. In 2002, the Green Party fielded candidates for U.S. senator, governor, lieutenant governor, attorney general, comptroller, land commissioner, agriculture commissioner, railroad commissioner, and several statewide judgeships and congressional seats. However, Green candidates (like Libertarians) won no elections and rarely received more than 3 percent of the vote. Nader failed to get on the general election ballot as an independent candidate in 2004. He did not submit 64,076 petition signatures to the secretary of state by the May 10 deadline.

### Independents

The term *independent* applies to candidates who have no party affiliation. Their success is less likely as they usually lack a ready-made campaign organization and fundraising abilities. In 2006, two candidates declared themselves independents and "threw their hats into the ring" for governor.

Carole Keeton Strayhorn had long been active in Republican politics. From her management of Republican gubernatorial nominee Clayton Williams' campaign in 1990, to her election to the Texas Railroad Commission, to her election as state comptroller in 1998 and 2002, Strayhorn had developed a reputation as a leader in the Republican Party. Additionally, her self-promoted reputation as "one tough grandma" provided Strayhorn with an easily recognizable image among

**independent** A candidate who has no party affiliation.

Texas voters. In 2002, she led all candidates of either party in number of votes received. In 2004, she emerged as a competitor with Governor Rick Perry for the Republican gubernatorial nomination in 2006. Strayhorn was particularly critical of Perry's proposal for resolving the state's school finance problem, positioning herself as a leading critic of the governor within his party. However, after internal polls showed that Strayhorn would be competitive with Perry in a general election but not in the Republican primary, Strayhorn announced in early January 2006 that she would seek the office of governor as an independent. In her announcement, she invoked the rugged individualism of Sam Houston, the last independent candidate to be elected governor of Texas. Strayhorn's image, political organization, and ability to raise funds provided her with resources most independent candidates lack.

Songwriter, author, humorist, and cigar smoker Kinky Friedman announced for governor as an independent in 2005. Since the 1970s Friedman, best known for his band, "Kinky Friedman and the Texas Jewboys," and songs like "They Ain't Makin' Jews Like Jesus Anymore," had developed a cult following. After declaring his candidacy, he was profiled nationally on programs such as *60 Minutes* and *Sunday Morning*, and frequently appeared as a guest on national political talk shows such as *Imus in the Morning* and *Real Time with Bill Maher*. Friedman's unorthodox campaign included selling "Kinky Friedman Action Figures" as a fundraiser and the announcement that Willie Nelson would serve as his "Texas Energy Czar." Nelson, an advocate of Biodiesel, a diesel fuel substitute made from soybean oil and other natural fats and vegetable oils, established several BioWillie stations across the country that sell clean-burning, American-made fuel.

To qualify for the general election ballot, each candidate was required to gather 45,540 signatures by May 11 from registered voters who had not voted in either the Democratic or Republican primary or any primary runoff in April or signed another candidate's petition. The Texas Election Code requires that signatures be submitted to the Texas secretary of state for verification. Previously, a common practice of verifying signatures had been statistical analysis by which names were randomly selected for verification. However, Texas secretary of state Roger Williams, a Rick Perry appointee, announced that he would not use the statistical analysis method, but would verify each signature. He also announced that he would not begin the process of certifying the petitions until all of the candidates had filed their petitions, and that

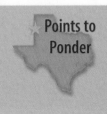

**Points to Ponder**

The origin of the phrase "to throw one's hat into the ring" is from an English idiom. In the days of fairground boxing competitions (when most men wore hats), the public was invited to try their skills against resident boxers. Those wishing to participate would throw their hats into the ring for all to see their willingness to compete. Since the competitor was without a hat, he could easily be identified as he made his way to the ring. The term was later adapted to those declaring their political candidacy when former president Theodore Roosevelt entered the presidential campaign of 1912 as an independent.

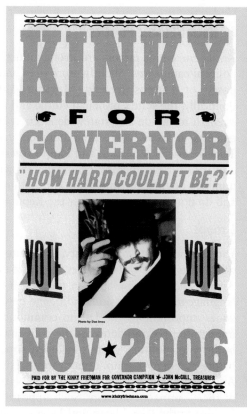

*Campaign poster for Independent Gubernatorial Candidate, Kinky Friedman (Courtesy Kinky Friedman for Governor Compaign, www.kinkyfriedman. com)*

the certification process could take up to two months. Both the Strayhorn and Friedman campaigns strongly criticized Williams' decision as a partisan move by a supporter of the governor. They both contended that by delaying the certification until July, their campaigns could have difficulty raising funds and lose valuable momentum. In early May, Strayhorn sued the secretary of state to fastrack the certification process.[7] In ruling against her claim, federal district judge Lee Yeakel said that the secretary of state's intention to examine each petition signature by signature was "reasonable and nondiscriminatory."

### Learning Check 4.2          (Answers on p. 168)

1. True or False: Before the 1980s, most elections in Texas were won by Republican candidates.
2. Who was the last independent candidate to be elected governor of Texas?

## ★ Racial/Ethnic Politics

Racial and ethnic factors are strong influences on Texas politics, and they shape political campaigns. Slightly more than half of Texas's total population is composed of Latinos (chiefly Mexican Americans) and African Americans. Politically, the state's principal ethnic and racial minorities wield enough voting strength to decide any statewide election and determine the outcomes of local contests in areas where their numbers are concentrated. Large majorities of Texas's African American and Latino voters participate in Democratic primaries and vote for Democratic candidates in general elections. However, increasing numbers of African Americans and Latinos claim to be politically independent and do not identify with either the Republican or the Democratic Party.

### Latinos

Early in the twenty-first century, candidates for elective office in Texas and most other parts of the United States recognize the potential of the Latino vote. Most Anglo candidates use Spanish phrases in their speeches, advertise in Spanish-language media (television, radio, and newspapers), and voice their concern for issues important to the Latino community (such as bilingual education and immigration). Candidates for the 2000 and 2004 presidential nomination from both major political parties included appearances in Latino communities and before national Latino organizations, such as the League of United Latin American Citizens (LULAC) and the National Council of La Raza, as a part of their campaign strategy. Such appearances recognize the political clout of Latinos in the Republican and Democratic presidential primaries as well as in the general election.

Although Mexican Americans have played an important role in South Texas politics throughout the twentieth century, not until the 1960s and early 1970s did they begin to have a major political impact at the state level. Founded in 1969 by José Angel Gutiérrez of Crystal City and others, the Raza Unida Party mobilized many Mexican Americans who had been politically inactive. It attracted others who had formerly identified with the Democratic Party. By the end of the 1970s, however, Raza Unida had disintegrated. According to Ruben Bonilla, former president of LULAC, the main reason Raza Unida did not survive as a meaningful voice for Texas's Mexican American population was "the maturity of the Democratic Party to accept Hispanics."

In the 1980s, Mexican American election strategy became more sophisticated as a new generation of college-educated Latinos sought public office and assumed leadership roles in political organizations. Among Latinos elected to statewide office in the 1980s and 1990s were Democrat Raul Gonzalez (the first Latino elected to statewide office in Texas), who served on the Texas Supreme Court from 1986 until 1999; Democrat Dan Morales, the state's attorney general for two terms from 1991 through 1998; and Republican Tony Garza, elected to the Texas Railroad Commission in 1998. After President Bush appointed Garza U.S. ambassador to Mexico in 2002, Governor Perry replaced him on the commission with Victor Carrillo early in 2003. Just as the political party affiliation of Latino elected officials is divided, so too is the Latino electorate.

Although Latinos are more likely to vote for Democratic candidates, Republican candidates such as George W. Bush have succeeded in winning the support of many Latino voters. Successful GOP candidates emphasize family issues and target heavily Latino areas for campaign appearances and media advertising. Bush also selected several Latinos for high-profile positions, most notably secretary of state (Tony Garza and Al Gonzales) and Supreme Court justice (Al Gonzales). Gonzales resigned from the Texas Supreme Court in 2001 to become White House counsel to President Bush, and later became U.S. attorney general. Governor Rick Perry also appointed a Latino secretary of state, Democrat Henry Cuellar, who served from 2001 to 2002.

The votes Bush received in the 1998 gubernatorial election have led Democrats to no longer assume they have Latino voter support in statewide electoral contests. Their voting behavior indicates that Latinos respond to candidates and issues, not to a particular political party. Often, successful Republican candidates distance themselves from their party, especially in the Latino community. In one 1998 commercial that appeared on Spanish-language television stations, Governor Bush highlighted the support he received from Democrats but never identified himself as a Republican. Although both national and state Republican Party platforms discourage bilingual education and urge stricter immigration controls, Republican candidates frequently do not endorse these positions.

Many members of the Democratic Party believe it is important to have Latino nominees for high-level statewide offices to attract Latino voters to the polls. They argue that since the majority of Latinos are more likely to support Democratic candidates, a higher voter turnout will elect more Democrats to office. In 2002, Laredo businessman Tony Sanchez Jr. became the first Latino candidate nominated for governor by a major party in Texas. Challenged for the Democratic nomination by former Texas attorney general Dan Morales, on 1 March 2002 the two men held the first Spanish-language gubernatorial debate in U.S. history. By 2006, 2 Latinos held statewide offices (railroad commissioner and Supreme Court justice), 6 Latinos were in Texas' congressional delegation, 37 Latinos served in the Texas Legislature, and Latinos held approximately 2,000 of 5,200 elected positions in Texas.

The Latino community's political impact was clear in the debate over immigration laws, as millions of Latinos in Texas took part in demonstrations or boycotts in early 2006. As the Latino population continues to grow in Texas, how each party addresses the issue of undocumented workers will in large part determine the future of its support among Latino voters.

The sheer size of the Latino population causes politicians to solicit support from this group. Latino voters can represent the margin of victory for a successful candidate. Lower levels of political activity than in the population at large, however, both in registering to vote and in voting, limit the impact of the Latino electorate.

### African Americans

In April 1990, the Texas State Democratic Executive Committee filled a candidate vacancy by nominating Potter County court-at-law judge Morris Overstreet, an African American Democrat, for a seat on the Texas Court of Criminal Appeals. Because the Republican candidate, Louis Sturns, was also African American, this historic action guaranteed the state's voters would elect the first African American to statewide office in Texas. Overstreet won in 1990 and again in 1994. He served until 1998, when he ran unsuccessfully for Texas attorney general. Governor Bush appointed Republican Michael Williams to the Texas Railroad Commission in 1999. This African American commissioner was elected to a six-year term in 2002.

The appointment of Justice Wallace Bernard Jefferson to the Texas Supreme Court in 2001 increased the number of African Americans in statewide offices to three. Justice Jefferson is the first African American to serve on the court. He and another African American, Dale Wainwright, were elected in 2002 to six-year terms on that court. Two years later, Jefferson was appointed as chief justice. In 2002, former Dallas mayor Ron Kirk became the first African American nominated by either major party in Texas as its candidate for United States senator. Although unsuccessful in the general election, Kirk's candidacy appeared to many political observers an important breakthrough for African American politicians.

Since the 1930s, African American Texans have tended to identify with the Democratic Party. With a voting-age population in excess of 1 million, they constitute about 10 percent of the state's potential voters. As demonstrated in recent electoral contests, approximately 80 percent of Texas's African American citizens say that they are Democrats, and only 5 percent are declared Republicans. The remainder are independents. More than 90 percent of the state's African Americans of voting age support Democratic candidates and tend to remain with the Democratic Party regardless of income. From 1971 to 2006, African Americans increased their membership in the Texas Legislature from 3 to 16. By 2006, more than 500 elective offices in Texas were held by African Americans.

---

**Learning Check 4.3**      **(Answers on p. 168)**

**1.** Which party have Latinos traditionally supported?
**2.** True or False: In 2006, no African Americans were holding statewide elected office.

---

## ★ Women in Politics

Texas women did not begin to vote and hold public office for three-quarters of a century after Texas joined the Union. Nevertheless, in 1990, Texas female voters outnumbered male voters, and Ann Richards was elected governor. Through 1990, however, only four women had won a statewide office in Texas, including two-term governor Miriam A. ("Ma") Ferguson (1925–1927 and 1933–1935). Mrs. Ferguson owed her office to supporters of her husband, Jim, who was impeached and removed from the governorship in 1917. After 1990, the number of women elected to statewide office increased dramatically.

Female candidates also succeeded in winning an increasing number of seats in the Texas Legislature—from 2 in 1971 to 36 in 2003. This total dropped to 35 after the death of Representative Irma Rangel (D-Kingsville). The expanded presence of women in public office is changing public policy. Increased punishment for family violence and sexual abuse of children, together with a renewed focus on public education, can be attributed in large part to the presence of women in policymaking positions.

In the early 1990s, Texas women served as mayors in about 150 of the state's towns and cities, including the first 4 in population (Houston, Dallas, San Antonio, and El Paso). As mayor of Dallas (1988–1991), Annette Strauss was fond of greeting out-of-state visitors with this message: "Welcome to Texas, where men are men and women are mayors." In 2006, women were mayors in some of the largest Texas cities: Beaumont, Dallas, Del Rio, Denton, Carrollton, Euless, Flower Mound, Killeen, Laredo, Plano, and Waco. In fact, Dallas was the largest city in America with a woman mayor.

The impact of women's voting power was evident in both 2000 and 2002, when women led all candidates on either ticket in votes received. With her reelection to the U.S. Senate in 2000, Republican Kay Bailey Hutchison became the first person to receive more than 4 million votes, and in 2002 Carole Keeton Rylander received more than 2.8 million votes in her reelection as state comptroller. Rylander changed her name to Strayhorn following her marriage in early January 2003.

However, despite their electoral victories in Texas and elsewhere across the nation, fewer women than men seek elective public office. Several reasons account for this situation, chief of which is difficulty in raising money to pay campaign expenses. Other reasons also discourage women from seeking public office. Although women enjoy increasing freedom, they still shoulder more responsibilities for family and home than men do (even in two-career families). Some mothers feel obliged to care for children in the home until the children finish high school. Such parental obligations, together with age-old prejudices, deny women their rightful place in government. Yet customs, habits, and attitudes change; new opportunities for women in public service are expanding accordingly.

**Learning Check 4.4**    **(Answers on p. 168)**

**1.** True or False: Women candidates received the most votes for a single office in the elections of 2000 and 2002.

**2.** By 2006, how many women had served as governor of Texas?

The father of western swing music, Bob Wills was one of the original Light Crust Doughboys who worked for W. Lee O'Daniel.

countered with the "Kiki" ad. The commercial featured two drug enforcement agents claiming that the drug lords who orchestrated a hit on federal drug agent Enrique "Kiki" Camarena had laundered their drug money through Tesoro Savings and Loan, a financial institution that Sanchez once owned. One political observer noted that this was the turning point in the campaign: "It was brutally negative, even by the standards of this bitterly partisan election season."[9]

Because no major statewide office was up for election and Texas was not a targeted state in the 2004 presidential election, voters across the state were subjected to fewer negative campaign ads. With President Bush, a Texan, running for reelection, neither the Bush nor Kerry campaigns spent valuable financial resources on commercials; it was a fairly safe bet that Bush would carry his home state. However, spending for campaign commercials in the 2004 presidential campaign topped $1 billion nationally, most airing in key electoral swing states such as Florida, Pennsylvania, and Ohio. Continuing the trend of negative campaigns, some of these commercials featured "Swift Boat Veterans for Truth," a group of Bush supporters whose purpose was to oppose John Kerry and criticize his military record in Vietnam.

### Campaign Reform

Concern over the shortcomings of American election campaigns has given rise to organized efforts toward improvement at all levels of government. Reformers have ranged from single citizens to members of the U.S. Congress and large lobby groups. Reform issues include eliminating negative campaigning, increasing free media access for candidates, and regulating campaign finance.

**Eliminating Negative Campaigning**    The Markle Commission on the Media and the Electorate has concluded that candidates, media people, consultants, and the electorate are all blameworthy for the increase in negative campaigns. Candidates and consultants, wishing to win at any cost, employ negative advertising and make exaggerated claims. The media emphasize poll results and the horserace appearance of a contest rather than basic issues and candidate personalities that relate to leadership potential. Voters must be the corrective force for reform. Because the bottom line of campaign reform involves educating citizens, little can be achieved quickly.

**Increasing Free Media Access**    Certainly a candidate for statewide office in Texas cannot win without first communicating with a large percentage of the state's voting population. As noted previously, television is the most important communication tool and the most expensive. One group supporting media access reform is the Alliance for Better Campaigns (**www.bettercampaigns.org**). So long as paid media advertising is a necessary part of political campaigns and media outlets generate a significant source of revenue from political campaigns, fundraising will remain important in electoral success.

## Campaign Finance

On more than one occasion, President Lyndon Johnson bluntly summarized the relationship between politics and finance: "Money makes the mare go." Although most political scientists would state this fact differently, it is obvious that candidates need money to pay the necessary expenses of election campaigns. The 1990 gubernatorial campaign established a record of $45 million spent on the primary and general election races combined, including more than $22 million by Midland oilman Clayton Williams. He narrowly lost to Ann Richards, who spent $12 million. However, that record was shattered by the 2002 gubernatorial election. Tony Sanchez's and Rick Perry's campaigns spent a combined record of more than $95 million. Sanchez outspent Perry by more than two to one ($67 million to $28 million) in the race for governor. Despite his big spending, Sanchez lost by 20 percent.[10] Even though $95 million establishes a new record for spending in a Texas race, it does not establish a national record. New York's 2002 gubernatorial contest, which cost an estimated $148 million, ranks first, followed by California's gubernatorial races in 1998 ($130 million) and 2002 ($110 million).

Many Texans are qualified to hold public office, but relatively few can afford to pay their own campaign expenses (as presidential candidates Ross Perot and Steve Forbes and gubernatorial candidates Clayton Williams and Tony Sanchez did) or are willing to undertake fundraising drives designed to attract significant campaign contributions by others (as George W. Bush has done in both his gubernatorial and presidential campaigns, and Governor Rick Perry has done in his campaigns for lieutenant governor and governor).

Candidates confront the need to raise large amounts of cash at local, state, and national levels. Successful Houston City Council candidates often require from $150,000 (for district races) to $250,000 (for at-large races), and mayoral candidates may need $2 million or more. In 2003, Houston businessman Bill White spent a record $8.6 million in his mayoral election, including $2.2 million of his own money. Some individuals and **political action committees** (**PACs**), organizations created to collect and distribute contributions to political campaigns, donate because they agree with a candidate's position on the issues. Others' motivations, however, may be questionable. In return for their contributions these donors receive access to elected officials. Many politicians and donors assert that access does not mean donors gain control of officials'

**political action committee (PAC)** An organizational device used by corporations, labor unions, and other organizations to raise money for campaign contributions.

policymaking decisions. Yet others, such as former Texas House Speaker Pete Laney, attribute the decline in voter participation to a growing sense that average citizens have no voice in the political process because they cannot afford to make large financial donations to candidates.

Both federal and state laws have been enacted to regulate various aspects of campaign financing. Texas laws on the subject are relatively weak and tend to emphasize reporting of contributions. Federal laws are more restrictive, featuring both reporting requirements and limits on contributions to a candidate's political campaign by individuals and PACs.

In 1989, chicken magnate Lonnie "Bo" Pilgrim handed out $10,000 checks on the Senate floor, leaving the "payable to" lines blank, as legislators debated reforming the state's workers' compensation laws. Many were surprised to find that Texas had no laws prohibiting such actions. Two years later the Texas Legislature passed laws prohibiting political contributions to members of the legislature while they are in session, and in 1993 Texas voters approved a constitutional amendment establishing the **Texas Ethics Commission**. Among its constitutional duties, the Texas Ethics Commission requires financial disclosure from public officials. However, unlike the Federal Election Campaign Act, Texas has no laws that limit political contributions.

Further restricting the amount of money that can be contributed to campaigns is another area of possible reform. Efforts in this area, however, have been unsuccessful. In 2002, Congress passed the long-awaited **Campaign Reform Act**, signed into law by President Bush. This federal law includes the following reforms:

- It prohibits **soft money**—that is, donations made to national political parties.
- It increases individual **hard money** (or direct) contribution limits.
- It restricts corporations' and labor unions' ability to run "electioneering" ads featuring the names and/or likenesses of candidates close to election day.[11]

Plaintiffs such as Texas Congressman Ron Paul (R-Clute) and others challenged the constitutionality of this act, claiming it was an unconstitutional restraint on freedom of speech. In 2003, in a sharply divided decision, the U.S. Supreme Court upheld the constitutionality of the "soft money" ban in *McConnell* v. *FEC*. Additional reform efforts include making contributor information more easily available to citizens. Candidates and treasurers of campaign committees are required to file periodically with the Texas Ethics Commission (**www.ethics.state.tx.us**). With limited exceptions, these reports must be made electronically. Sworn statements list all contributions received and expenditures made during designated reporting intervals. Candidates who fail to file these reports are subject to a fine.

During the 78th regular session in 2003, the Texas Legislature passed House Bill 1606, which Governor Perry later signed into law. Supported by

**Texas Ethics Commission** Enforces state standards for lobbyists and public officials, including registration of lobbyists and reporting of political campaign contributions.

**Campaign Reform Act** Enacted by the U. S. Congress and signed by President Bush in 2002, this law restricts donations of "soft money" and "hard money" for election campaigns, but it has been challenged in federal courts.

**soft money** campaign money donated to national political parties rather than to candidates.

**hard money** Campaign money contributed directly by individuals.

such public interest groups as Common Cause Texas, Public Citizen, and Campaigns for People, this statute strengthens the Texas Ethics Commission, curbs conflicts of interest, and requires greater disclosure of campaign contributions. Specifically, the law requires officials of cities with more than 100,000 population and trustees of school districts with enrollments of 5,000 or more to disclose the sources of their income, as well as the value of their stocks and their real-estate holdings. Additionally, candidates for state political offices must identify employers and occupations of people contributing $500 or more to their campaigns and publicly report "cash on hand." The measure also prohibits lawmakers from lobbying for clients before state agencies. "This bill eliminates several chronic ethics loopholes and gives the Ethics Commission some teeth," said Tom "Smitty" Smith, Texas director of Public Citizen, a government watchdog group. "It's a big step forward."[12]

In practice, both federal and state campaign finance laws have largely failed to cope with influence buying through transfers of money in the form of campaign contributions. It may well be that as long as campaigns are funded by private sources, they will remain inadequately regulated.

In late 2005, a Travis County grand jury indicted U.S. House majority leader Tom DeLay for conspiracy to violate Texas election law, money laundering, and conspiracy to commit money laundering. In September 2002, Texans for a Republican Majority, a political action committee formed by DeLay, accepted $190,000 in corporate contributions and contributed them to the Republican National Committee (RNC). The RNC then donated $190,000 to seven Republican candidates running for the Texas House of Representatives. Under Texas law, corporate donations may not be used in state campaigns to influence voters. Upon a motion by DeLay's attorney, a state district judge dismissed the charge of conspiracy to violate election law. However he allowed the charges of money laundering and conspiracy to commit money laundering to stand. Facing a criminal trial and the possibility of losing in the November general election, DeLay resigned his seat in the U.S. House of Representatives in mid-2006. (For more on this subject, see Selected Reading 7.2.)

---

**Learning Check 4.5**     **(Answers on p. 168)**

1. True or False: Most Texas voters learn about candidates through newspaper editorials.
2. Which commission requires financial disclosure from public officials?

---

## ★ Looking Ahead

Under the freedom-of-speech guarantee in the First Amendment of the U.S. Constitution, Americans have a right to give money to the candidates of their choice. The U.S. Supreme Court has ruled that campaign contributions may be limited, but independent expenditures in support of a specific candidate may not. Furthermore, in *Buckley* v. *Valeo* (1976), the U.S. Supreme Court held that candidates may not be prohibited from spending their own money on their campaigns. These guaranteed rights in turn weaken political parties. When PACs can collectively contribute millions of dollars to a candidate for a statewide office, the candidate no longer needs to remain obligated to a party.

It is interesting to speculate on how candidates and voters would respond to or be affected by public funding of Texas elections. First, challengers would be placed on a more equal financial footing with incumbents. Private financing favors incumbents in raising campaign money. Texas legislators are well aware of this, and they will surrender their advantage only in the face of strong public pressure. Second, public funding would run counter to Texas tradition. The Lone Star State has never tried it, and many citizens are undisturbed by big-money domination of politics.

For the foreseeable future, Texas will continue to allow wealthy individuals and powerful interest groups to buy political favors from government under the guise of making campaign contributions. The following chapter explores elections and election laws in Texas.

## ★ Chapter Summary

- Political parties serve two functions: administering party primaries and conducting party conventions. These are activities of the party's temporary organization. The permanent party organization includes autonomous executive committees at the local, state, and national levels that direct party activities.
- Texas voters and political parties represent various political ideologies, including conservatism and liberalism. The two major political parties are Republican and Democratic. Minor, or third, parties also often appear on general election ballots.
- Historically, Texas was a one-party state, dominated by the Democratic Party following Reconstruction through the 1960s. Beginning in the 1970s and 1980s, the state moved toward a competitive two-party structure. In the 1990s and into the twenty-first century, however, it appears that the state became a one-party state again, with the Republican Party in control.
- Recent elections reflect two major trends. The Republican Party now dominates statewide electoral contests. Democratic candidates are successful only in district and local races.
- An increasing number of African Americans and Latinos have won office in recent years at both state and local levels of government. African American voters consistently favor Democratic candidates. Latino voters, although tending to favor Democratic candidates, have given strong support to some Republican candidates.

■ Gender-based politics grew in importance during the final decades of the past century as women became more politically active and had a direct influence on public policy decisions.

■ Political campaigns reflect the influence of the media (especially television), mudslide (negative) campaigning, and money. Both federal and state laws regulate election campaigns, with federal law requiring disclosure of donor information and limiting contributions. State law establishes reporting requirements. A possible solution to money's influence on Texas politics is public funding of campaigns.

## Key Terms

- political party, *p. 136*
- stratarchy, *p. 137*
- temporary party organization, *p. 137*
- platform, *p. 137*
- precinct convention, *p. 137*
- county convention, *p. 139*
- district convention, *p. 139*
- state convention, *p. 139*
- presidential preference primary, *p. 140*
- caucus, *p. 140*
- superdelegate, *p. 141*
- permanent party organization, *p. 141*
- precinct chair, *p. 142*
- county executive committee, *p. 142*
- county chair, *p. 142*

- district executive committee, *p. 142*
- state executive committee, *p. 142*
- conservative, *p. 144*
- neoconservatism, *p. 144*
- liberal, *p. 144*
- neoliberal, *p. 144*
- dealignment, *p. 151*
- realignment, *p. 151*
- straight-ticket voting, *p. 152*
- third party, *p. 152*
- independent, *p. 153*
- sound bite, *p. 161*
- political action committee (PAC), *p. 163*
- Texas Ethics Commission, *p. 164*
- Campaign Reform Act, *p. 164*
- soft money, *p. 164*
- hard money, *p. 164*

## Learning Check Answers

**4.1**

1. The role of the permanent party organization is to recruit candidates, devise strategies, raise funds, distribute candidate literature and information, register voters, and turn out voters on election day. The temporary party organization consists of primaries and conventions in which members of the major political parties select candidates for public office.

2. True. Although the state chair presides over the party's permanent organization at the state level, he or she is selected by delegates to the party's state convention, its temporary organization at the state level.

**4.2**

1. False. From the end of Reconstruction until the 1970s, Texas and other former Confederate states had a one-party identity in which the Democratic Party was strong and Republican Party weak.
2. Sam Houston was the last independent candidate to be elected governor of Texas.

**4.3**

1. Although more Latinos today are likely to split their tickets, traditionally they have supported the Democratic Party.
2. False. In 2006, three African Americans were holding statewide elected positions: Michael Williams (Texas Railroad Commission) and state Texas Supreme Court justices Wallace Bernard Jefferson and Dale Wainwright.

**4.4**

1. True. With her reelection to the U.S. Senate in 2000, Republican Kay Bailey Hutchison became the first person to receive more than 4 million votes, and in 2002 Carole Keeton Rylander (later Strayhorn) received more than 2.8 million votes in her reelection as state comptroller.
2. Two: Miriam A. ("Ma") Ferguson (1925–1927 and 1933–1935) and Ann Richards (1991–1995).

**4.5**

1. False. Most Texas voters learn about candidates through television commercials.
2. The Texas Ethics Commission. However, unlike the Federal Election Campaign Act, Texas has no laws to limit political contributions.

## Discussion Questions

1. How has Texas's political culture in the past been reflected in the development of Texas political parties? How is it reflected today?
2. In what ways does the structure of political parties in Texas encourage participation in partisan politics? In what ways does it discourage participation?

3. What challenges face the Democratic Party in Texas in the twenty-first century? What challenges face the state's Republican Party?
4. Can third parties be successful in Texas? How?
5. With the increasing political importance of women and of racial and ethnic minorities, how has Texas politics changed? What changes can we anticipate in the future?
6. What electoral reforms are suggested to improve all levels of government? Which of these reforms have the best chance of succeeding?

## Internet Resources

Green Party of Texas: **www.txgreens.org**
Independent Texans: **www.independenttexans.org**
Texas Democratic Party: **www.txdemocrats.org**
Texas Ethics Commission: **www.ethics.state.tx.us**
Texas Libertarian Party: **www.tx.lp.org**
Texas Reform Party: **www.texasreformparty.org**
Texas Republican Party: **www.texasgop.org**
Texas Young Republican Federation: **www.tyrf.org**
Young Democrats of Texas: **www.texasyds.org**

## Notes

1. Samuel Eldersveld, *Political Parties: A Behavioral Analysis* (Chicago: Rand McNally, 1964).
2. Paul A. Gigot, "GOP's Clinton? George W. Bush Says No Way," *Wall Street Journal*, 30 October 1998.
3. T. R. Fehrenbach, *Lone Star: A History of Texas and Texans* (New York: Macmillan, 1999), 400.
4. Mike Kingston and Robert Piocheck, "A Brief Sketch of Texas History," *The Texas Almanac 2004–2005* (Dallas: Dallas Morning News, 2004), 46–47.
5. Wayne Slater, "Governor Lines Up Millions in Pledges," *Dallas Morning News*, 25 February 2001.
6. For more information on the Populist Party in Texas, see Alwyn Barr, *Reconstruction to Reform: Texas Politics, 1876–1906* (Austin: University of Texas Press, 1971).
7. John Moritz, "Strayhorn Sues to Get Petitions Certified Faster," *Fort Worth Star Telegram*, 1 May 2006.
8. George N. Green, "O'Daniel, Wilbert Lee [Pappy]." *The Handbook of Texas Online* at **www.tsha.utexas.edu/handbook/online/articles/view/OO/fo'4.html**.

9. S. C. Gwynne, "Grand Illusion: Rich, Moderate, and Hispanic: For a While, Tony Sanchez Seemed Like a Competitive Candidate for Governor. Then the Smoke Cleared," *Texas Monthly*, December 2002, p. 46.

10. W. Gardner Selby, "Sanchez Campaign Fueled Record," *San Antonio Express-News*, 15 January 2002.

11. 2 U.S.C. § 431 (2002), The "Bipartisan Campaign Reform Act of 2002."

12. Quoted in "House Panel OK's Disclosure Rules," *Waco Tribune*, 17 April 2003.

## 4.1  The Elephants in the Room*

### *Paul Burka*

*As the Republican Party continues to dominate Texas politics, with Republicans holding all statewide offices and the majority in both houses of the Texas Legislature, intraparty divisions have occurred. The 2006 Republican Primary elections across the state often featured bitter contests over the ideological control of the party. This reading examines some of these divisions and conflicts within the Republican Party.*

Just home from a weekend trip in early November, state representative Tony Goolsby, of Dallas, went to his office and left his wife, Toppy, to check their voice mail messages. A few minutes later, Toppy called him. Most of the messages were routine, but there was one he needed to hear—an automated political poll. The first question was no surprise: Do you support Proposition 2, the constitutional amendment to defend traditional marriage? "Answer yes or no," the robo-voice instructed. The next question took Tony completely by surprise. "If the election were held today, would you vote to reelect your state representative, Tony Goolsby?" It was the last thing he expected to hear—well, almost the last thing. *He* certainly hadn't authorized the poll. There could be only one explanation: An unknown enemy was probing to see if he was vulnerable to a challenge. And then came the absolute last thing he expected to hear. "This poll was authorized and paid for by the Republican Party of Texas." Was it possible that his own party was interested in defeating him?

As it turned out, Goolsby wasn't the only Republican legislator whose constituents were polled about their representative by the state GOP. Others included Carter Casteel, of New Braunfels; Charlie Geren, of Fort Worth; Toby Goodman, of Arlington; Delwyn Jones, of Lubbock; Tommy Merritt, of Longview; and Todd Smith, of Euless.

*Paul Burka is senior executive editor at *Texas Monthly* magazine. "The Elephants in the Room" by Paul Burka, *Texas Monthly*, January 2006: pp. 126–127, 194–196. Reprinted with permission from the January 2006 issue of *Texas Monthly*.

Smith, in particular, was outraged about the party's participation in the poll. He says he confronted Jeff Fisher, the executive director of the Texas GOP, who claimed that the poll about Prop 2 was taken statewide, in every legislative district. But were other Republican lawmakers singled out? "Show me the list of the state representatives whose constituents were polled," Smith said. Fisher refused. "Tell me how the list was compiled." Again, he refused. "Why did you poll in my district?" This time Fisher answered: "To help you in case you have a Democratic opponent," a response Smith characterized to me as "lying to my face." His district is so solidly Republican that David Dewhurst, running for lieutenant governor in 2002 as a virtual unknown, got 65 percent of the district's vote against veteran Democrat John Sharp. "What I want to know is where all this is leading," Smith told me. "Who is calling the shots?"

Where this is leading is toward all-out war in the 2006 Republican primary. Many Republicans outside the Capitol—especially on the far right—are angry about the failure of Republicans inside the Capitol to enact the conservative agenda on school finance, spending, and other litmus-test issues. In 2003, the first session of Republican rule in 130 years, everything had gone according to plan: budget cuts, tort reform, congressional redistricting, and new restrictions on abortion. Then, in 2005, the majority couldn't pass a school finance bill, provide property tax relief, impose budget restraints on local government, pass a school voucher program, or otherwise advance the ideological agenda embraced by Governor Rick Perry and such friends of the GOP as the influential Texas Public Policy Foundation, Republican National Committee member Bill Crocker, major donor James Leininger, and the authors of various conservative Internet newsletters. For months, speculation about a purge of Republican lawmakers who put the interests and desires of their constituents ahead of party orthodoxy has run rampant. If the anger of the ideologues can be transmitted to the GOP primary electorate (which, everyone agrees, is more conservative than the larger group of voters who identify themselves as Republicans), the March primary could become a witch hunt for incumbents derisively labeled RINOs, as in Republicans in Name Only.

But Tony Goolsby, Todd Smith, and the rest of the group that got such unwelcome attention from the state party are hardly RINOs. On the vast majority of votes, especially social issues ranging from gay marriage to abortion, they seldom stray. They see themselves as mainstream Republicans beholden to no one except the voters who sent them to Austin, and they simply aren't going to support a school finance bill or a school voucher bill that's unpopular back home. (Goolsby, for example, polls his district by mail every election cycle on their views about vouchers, and the smallest negative response has been 56 percent.)

It is an odd story: Having devoured the Democrats, the Republicans have turned on one another. The consequences for the state have been severe. This became evident during the fight over school finance last spring, when Speaker Tom Craddick and Kent Grusendorf, the Republican chairman of the House Public Education Committee, kept pushing a bill that tossed out the old system and imposed a series of mandates, often unfunded, on school districts in the name of reform. Republican lawmakers were squeezed between the viewpoint of the leadership, which was openly hostile to the education community on ideological grounds, and that of the education community back home, which itself was openly hostile to the leadership on policy grounds. This squeeze, along with the much-remarked-upon infighting between Perry, Dewhurst, and Craddick (and sometimes Comptroller Carole Keeton Strayhorn), prevented Republicans from producing a plan that had broad backing inside and outside the Capitol. Now, with the self-sabotage at fever pitch and primary season approaching, the big question being asked in Texas political circles is, What should a real Republican stand for?

Last summer I came across a Midland Web site called Jessica's Well (**jessicaswell.com**). A blogger calling himself "a&mgrad" had posted a plaintive comment about the direction his party was going. "Seems all it takes to be called a Republican these days in Midland and elsewhere is to be against abortion and gay rights and be for tax cuts and 'the spread of Democracy in the world,' and to hell with everything else."

It is the absence of "everything else" that mainstream Republicans mourn. Not too long ago, when the

Democrats still ran the state, Republicans stood for a clear set of principles, among them limited government, fiscal restraint, free markets, private-property rights, local control, and individual liberty. But the realities of power and politics don't always mix so well with principle, and it doesn't take long to think of policies that violate each of the foregoing, right here in conservative Texas. Limited government? While the Legislature was wrestling unsuccessfully with school finance last summer, Senator Kyle Janek, of Houston, told me that the long fight had revealed to him how much politics had changed in the ten years since he had first won election to the House. "When I came here," he told me, "all the Republicans wanted to abolish the Texas Education Agency. Now I just voted for a bill to give the commissioner of education subpoena powers." Fiscal restraint? Not for Republican budget writers, who, as critics figure it, increased state spending by 20 percent compared with 2003–2004. Free markets? Not for electricity customers, who will have to pay higher rates because of a state mandate that utilities must supply a certain amount of power generated by wind. Private-property rights? Not if your property happens to be in the path of one of the mammoth toll roads Perry wants to build. Local control? Not if Republican ideologues, led by the governor, have their way and impose caps on the ability of cities and counties to raise and spend money. Individual liberty? Not if you want to have an abortion or you're gay and want to marry your partner.

I'm not charging Republicans with hypocrisy. When it comes to their own survival, politicians of all parties are the same: They talk the talk of philosophy, but sooner or later they walk the walk of expediency. The importance of the soul-searching going on among Republicans is that it highlights what happens when the outs become the ins and find themselves torn between the ideology that propelled them to power and their responsibility to govern. If Republicans had been successful in governing, their ideological civil war would be of little import. But they haven't been.

The question is straight out of a government textbook: Should our elected representatives serve as delegates—that is, rubber stamps for party power brokers and the legislative leadership carrying out an ideological agenda—or trustees who are empowered by their constituents to make up their own minds? The tradition in

Texas has been that the Legislature is not organized formally along party lines and that lawmakers act more like trustees than delegates. But as GOP activists seek to impose their definition of what a true conservative is on elected legislators, that tradition is in mortal danger.

Nearly a century ago, a sharp-penned journalist named Ambrose Bierce defined a "conservative" as "a statesman who is enamored of existing evils, as distinguished from the Liberal, who wishes to replace them with others." Bierce disappeared into revolutionary Mexico in 1913, never to be heard from again, but his observation about the role of ideology in politics retains its force. The search for the perfect doctrine, and the insistence that it be adhered to, is an exercise in futility. Ideological consistency is all but impossible in a system in which people who put politicians in office want them to address problems. Before Hurricane Katrina, no one wanted to federalize disaster relief at a cost running into the hundreds of billions of dollars. It's amazing how the sight of bodies floating in the streets of New Orleans will change your perspective.

Still, nothing will dissuade the purists from demanding ideological consistency. The most heated battle in Texas politics—far more intense than the gubernatorial smackdown between Perry and Strayhorn or the endless sniping of Dewhurst and Craddick—is the debate over whether the party's elected representatives have betrayed its principles and what the consequences for the heretics should be.

What's happening inside the Republican party today is an inevitable consequence of political success. To win elections, a party must become a big-tent organization. But each time a new person is brought inside the tent—or shows his way in—the likelihood of harmony diminishes. Today's GOP consists of social conservatives with ties to evangelical Christianity, fiscal conservatives who reiterate antitax activist Grover Norquist's injunction to "starve the beast" of government, business conservatives who want goodies from government but not regulation (unless it would work to their benefit), libertarians, and mainstream conservatives who are neither political activists nor ideologues but are attracted to what the party stands for—supposedly.

The conflicts are self-evident and unavoidable between social conservatives, who want to impose their ideas of morality on everything from cheerleading to marriage, and libertarians, who want government out of just about everything; between fiscal conservatives, who want to cut taxes and rein in spending on government services, and business conservatives, who want increased spending for some services, such as transportation and education, at all levels for their future workforce. Meanwhile, the mainstream conservatives are left to wonder what became of the party they once knew. I am reminded of what Karen Hughes, then the communications director for Governor George W. Bush, told me in 1996 when evangelical conservatives took control and refused to respect the unwritten rule that the governor gets to chair the state's delegation to the national convention. "It's my party, and I'll cry if I want to."

The recent legislative marathon, consisting of the regular session and two desultory special sessions on school finance, was suffused with doctrinal conflict. The issue that best exposed the fault lines between "starve the beast" ideologues and mainstream Republicans involved two Perry-backed proposals to choke off local governments' access to money. One measure was aimed at limiting "appraisal creep"—annual increases in the value of real estate, as calculated by local officials for property tax purposes—to 5 percent. (The current cap is 10 percent.) Appraisal creep enables cities, counties, school districts, and other taxing authorities to take in more money each year, so long as property values increase, without raising their tax rates. Another bill sought to achieve the same end by limiting the revenue available to local governments to the previous year's budget plus 3 percent. If a city or county wanted to exceed that limit, it would have to do so by raising the tax rate—but only with the approval of voters (the assumption being, of course, that the voters would never approve).

Appraisal creep is a legitimate concern; repeated property tax increases can become such a burden on homeowners that they may be forced to sell their homes. But the proponents of appraisal and revenue caps ran up against another principle straight out of traditional conservatism: local control, the idea that the government that governs best is the one that's closest to the people. When Republicans were out of power in Texas, they assailed Democrats for imposing mandate after mandate—often unfunded—on local government. Echoing Barry Goldwater, the godfather of modern conservatism ("I fear Washington and centralized government more than I do Moscow"), they rejected the idea that all wisdom flowed from Austin. If local control was a tried-and-true idea in Democratic Texas, then it ought to make even more sense in Republican Texas, where most GOP legislators represent cities, counties, and school districts whose elected officials are overwhelmingly Republican (although city and school elections are officially nonpartisan). Yet the caps were the ultimate mandate. Fred Hill, a longtime conservative stalwart from Richardson and a strong proponent of local control, led the fight against the caps and likened them to Proposition 13 in California, which devastated the ability of local governments to perform basic services. Of the 86 Republicans in the House, 35 voted for a Democratic amendment that killed appraisal caps. Only a Democratic blunder allowed revenue caps to pass the House; later, the proposal died in the Senate.

Another high-visibility issue that gave Republicans "heartburn"—the euphemism du jour for being scared to death of getting a primary opponent—was the increased level of state spending. The Republican leadership reached a rare (if unspoken) consensus that the Legislature should restore state services reduced or eliminated in 2003, when lawmakers faced a $10 billion revenue shortfall. Outside the Legislature, however, no such consensus existed. The Texas Public Policy Foundation was particularly unhappy; as budget writers were putting the finishing touches on the new spending bill last May, the TPPF's vice president, Michael Quinn Sullivan, warned in a press release that spending might increase as much as 15 percent (which turned out to be an underestimation) and urged lawmakers to exercise fiscal restraint. After lauding the Legislature for cutting spending in the face of the 2003 budget crisis, Sullivan lamented, "By all accounts that same discipline does not seem to be in place today." His concerns fell on deaf ears: Not one Republican senator voted against the budget, and only 11 House Republicans did so (along with 29 Democrats). Those on the inside understand that voting for the budget is part of the responsibility of being in power. But will Republican primary voters care about such nuances when a challenger accuses an incumbent of voting to increase spending by 20 percent? Jim Pitts, of Waxahachie, the much-admired chairman of the House Appropriations Committee, is about to find out: He has an announced primary opponent.

"They're clueless," says Senator Steve Ogden, of Bryan, the Senate's chief budget writer, of the critics of the new spending bill. "Go back to May of '03," he says. "We passed a bill that spent $118 billion. That's what the critics are comparing to $140 billion to justify saying that we increased spending twenty percent. But total state spending for the biennium, when you count the emergency appropriations bill we pass every session, was $127 billion. Then $140 billion really represents a ten percent increase, not twenty percent." Ogden is one of many lawmakers whose conservative credentials have previously been regarded as impeccable, only to have them challenged in the GOP's eat-your-young frenzy. This session, he stood up for budget savings against entrenched opposition, insisting on a plan, opposed by doctors, that is estimated to result in savings of $109 million per biennium for the costly Medicaid program and scotching a pork barrel program for a good cause (state universities), known as tuition revenue bonds, because it violated the state's pay-as-you-go rule. "It's a fiction," he told me, "just a way to issue general-obligation bonds without asking the people to vote on them."

Ogden owns up to following the course set by previous legislatures of resorting to budgetary legerdemain to make ends meet. But, he insists, "This is a fiscally responsible budget. It's a ten percent increase over a two-year period, corresponding roughly to the growth of the economy and still leaving enough unspent to have a $3 billion surplus. Grover Norquist, you're full of bull."

The central figure in the Republican drama is Speaker Craddick. So far there have been no casualties in the War Between Republicans, but he has suffered the most wounds. Craddick came to the Legislature in 1969, when there were only eight Republicans, and he has seen scores, maybe hundreds, of GOP colleagues come and go. He has close ties to only a few House members; his real loyalties lie with people outside the Capitol—Republican power brokers like Leininger, Louis Beecherl, of Dallas, and tort reformer Dick Weekley and lobbyists Bill Messer and Bill Miller. Hard to pin down ideologically, he is more of a traditional business and economic conservative—particularly if the business happens to be oil and gas or real estate, professions in which he has amassed a sizable fortune and which drive the economy of his hometown of Midland—than a social conservative. Nevertheless, he identifies with his party far more than any Democratic Speaker of memory ever did, and he regards it as his duty to push its agenda.

This is the source of his problems. As members have always seen it, part of the role of the Speaker is to protect them from no-win situations in which they make enemies regardless of how they vote. Appraisal caps and revenue caps were two such situations. Vote against them and you anger the ideologues (including Perry, who was pushing for the caps). Vote for them and you anger your local officials who are fellow Republicans and see your constituents every day while you are off in Austin. Neither proposal had the votes to pass without Craddick's twisting arms to get them. So he twisted arms, particularly on revenue caps. Every member understood what had happened: Their Speaker had cast his lot with the outside-the-Capitol crowd.

The same thing happened in the school finance battle. Grusendorf's bill was anathema to the education community, though it had support from fiscal conservatives and some educational reformers. Rather than try to find a middle ground, Craddick resorted to arm-twisting, once again putting his members in the position of going against superintendents and school board members back in their districts. In fairness to Craddick, he had to pass a school finance bill, but he didn't have to pass one that many Republicans hated. He had to pass a tax bill too; it was necessary to replace the revenue that would have been lost due to proposed property tax reductions, had they passed. But his favored method of raising revenue—allowing businesses to choose between a payroll tax, which many Republicans saw as a roundabout tax on income, and a tax on business partnerships, which *was* a tax on income—was sure to be controversial. (It was not lost on Republican members that these taxes were good for the oil and gas industry, leading some critics to call it the "Fair to Midland" plan.)

Sometimes GOP legislators found themselves facing a dilemma to which there was no safe answer—for example, a motion to kill a proposed increase in the tax on beer and other alcoholic beverages. Voting against killing the increase would anger the fiscal conservatives who oppose anything that smacks of a new tax. Voting for killing the increase would anger social conservatives—in particular, the Texas Eagle Forum—who oppose all sin. Thirty-three Republicans decided that the safer haven was to oppose sin. Sure enough, the vote was one of 25 chosen by the Eagle Forum ("Progress Through Preservation of Traditional Values") for its postsession conservative rating of all House members. Forum president Cathie Adams, while praising one of the most staunchly conservative members, provided this sorrowful jeremiad: "Of the 181 elected Texas legislators serving during the [Seventy-ninth] Legislative Session and special called sessions in Austin, only 11 legislators were commended for their conservative voting record."

Let's not feel too sorry for lawmakers who have to cast dangerous votes; that's part of the job. What particularly rankles members is that many of those voted were demanded of Republicans by their own leader. To make matters worse, Craddick had declared war on the education groups by blaming superintendents for the Legislature's inability to pass a school finance bill. "They just want money, and they don't want any changes in the system," the Speaker was quoted as saying by the *San Antonio Express-News* three days before the second special session expired. One San Antonio–area superintendent returned fire: "Those people, and the Speaker especially, see public education as a liability, not as an asset. . . . They want to find anything else that's cheaper." Craddick is not alone in his assessment of educators, inside or outside the Capitol, but many of his Republican members—particularly those from rural areas and newer suburbs—come from districts where the schools are well regarded and are the center of their communities. Yet they were pressured to vote against proposals that would have given their school districts more money.

And that's not the worst of it. Many suburban members also cast a series of votes undercutting the programs and values that are most important to their schools. One amendment proposed to protect funding for the master science and math teachers program. It was killed in a virtually straight party-line vote. Another proposal ensured that funding for advanced placement programs would not be cut. AP classes are filled with the kids of Republican primary voters who are desperate to get their children into top colleges. It didn't matter: Republicans voted no. How about allowing a child who is assaulted by another child to be kept away from him? Sorry, no. (A separate bill allowing the victim to transfer to another school was later passed.) This by no means exhausts the lists of such votes, but you get the idea. Why did Republicans cast such dangerous votes? Because Tom Craddick forced them to,

# Chapter 5

# The Politics of Elections

★ **Voting**

★ **Primary, General, and Special Elections**

SARGENT © 2001
*Austin American-Statesman.* Reprinted
with permission of
UNIVERSAL PRESS
SYNDICATE. All rights
reserved.

The fundamental principle on which every representative democracy is based is citizen participation in the political process. Yet, even as in the twentieth century the right to vote was extended to almost every citizen 18 years of age or older, participation declined throughout the century's final decades and into the twenty-first century. Citizen participation through elections, and the impact of that participation, are the subjects of this chapter. Ben Sargent's cartoon notes that even self-proclaimed patriots may not take time to vote.

## ★ Voting

The U.S. Supreme Court has declared the right to vote the "preservative" of all other rights.[1] For most Texans, voting is their principal political activity. For many, it is their only exercise in practicing Texas politics. Casting a ballot brings individuals and their government together for a moment and reminds people anew that they are part of a political system. We begin the study of the electoral process in the Lone Star State by focusing on voters and voting.

### Obstacles to Voting

The right to vote has not always been as widespread in the United States as it is today. **Universal suffrage,** by which almost all citizens 18 years of age and older can vote, did not become a reality in Texas until the mid-1960s. Although most devices to prevent people from voting have been abolished, their legacy remains.

Adopted after the Civil War (1861–1865), the Fourteenth and Fifteenth Amendments to the U.S. Constitution were intended to prevent denial of the right to vote based on race. But for the next 100 years, African American citizens in Texas and other states of the former Confederacy, as well as many Latinos, were prevented from voting by one barrier after another—legal or otherwise. For example, the white-robed Ku Klux Klan and other lawless groups used terrorist tactics to keep African Americans from voting. Northeast Texas was the focus of the Klan's operations in the Lone Star State.[2]

**Literacy Tests**    Beginning in the 1870s, as a means to prevent minority people from voting, some counties in Texas began requiring prospective voters to take a screening test that conditioned voter registration on a person's literacy. Texans who could not pass these **literacy tests** were prohibited from registering. Other counties required constitutional-interpretation or citizenship-knowledge tests to deny voting rights. These tests usually consisted of difficult and abstract questions concerning a person's knowledge of the U.S. Constitution or understanding of issues supposedly related to citizenship. In no way, however, did these questions measure a citizen's ability to cast an informed vote.

**Grandfather Clause**    Another device enacted by southern states to deny suffrage to minorities was the **grandfather clause**. Laws with this clause provided that persons who could exercise the right to vote before 1867, or their descendants, would be exempt from educational, property, or tax requirements for voting. Because African Americans had not been allowed to vote before adoption of the Fifteenth Amendment in 1870, grandfather clauses were used along with literacy tests to prevent African Americans from voting while assuring this right to many impoverished and illiterate whites. The United States Supreme Court, in *Guinn* v. *United States* (1915) declared the grandfather clause unconstitutional because it violated equal voting rights guaranteed by the Fifteenth Amendment.

**Poll Tax**    Beginning in 1902, Texas required that citizens pay a special tax, called the **poll tax,** to become eligible to vote. The cost was $1.75 ($1.50, plus $.25 that was optional with each county). For the next 62 years, many Texans—especially low-income persons, including disproportionately large numbers of African Americans and Mexican Americans—frequently failed to pay their poll tax during the designated four-month period from October 1 to January 31. This, in turn, disqualified them from voting during the following 12 months in party primaries and in any general or special election. As a result, African American voter participation declined from approximately 100,000 in the 1890s to about

---

**universal suffrage** Voting is open for virtually all persons 18 years of age or older.

**literacy test** As a prerequisite for voter registration, this test was designed and administered in ways intended to prevent African Americans and Latinos from voting.

**grandfather clause** Exempted people from educational, property, or tax requirements for voting if they were qualified to vote before 1867, or were descendents of such persons.

**poll tax** A tax levied in Texas from 1902 until a similar Virginia tax was declared unconstitutional in 1962; failure to pay the annual tax (usually $1.75) made a citizen ineligible to vote in party primaries or in special and general elections.

5,000 in 1906. With ratification of the Twenty-Fourth Amendment to the U.S. Constitution in January 1964, the poll tax was abolished as a prerequisite for voting in national elections. Then, in *Harper* v. *Virginia State Board of Elections* (1966), the U.S. Supreme Court invalidated all state laws that made payment of a poll tax a prerequisite for voting in state elections.

**All-White Primaries**   The so-called **white primary**, a product of political and legal maneuvering within the southern states, was designed to deny African Americans and some Latinos access to the Democratic primary.[3] Following Reconstruction, Texas, like most of the South, was predominately a one-party (Democratic) state. Between 1876 and 1926, the Republican Party held only one statewide primary in Texas. By contrast, the Democratic primary was the main election in every even-numbered year.

White Democrats nominated white candidates, who almost always won the general elections. The U.S. Supreme Court had long held that the Fourteenth and Fifteenth Amendments, as well as successive civil rights laws, provided protection against public acts of discrimination, but not against private acts. In 1923, the Texas Legislature passed a law explicitly prohibiting African Americans from voting in Democratic primaries. When the U.S. Supreme Court declared this law unconstitutional, the legislature enacted another law giving the executive committee of each state party the power to decide who could participate in its primaries. The State Democratic Executive Committee immediately adopted a resolution that allowed only whites to vote in Democratic primaries. This practice lasted from 1923 to 1944, when the U.S. Supreme Court declared it unconstitutional in *Smith* v. *Allwright*.[4]

**Racial Gerrymandering**   Gerrymandering is the practice of manipulating legislative district lines to underrepresent persons of a political party or group. "Packing" black voters into a given district or "cracking" them to make black voters a minority in all districts both illustrate **racial gerrymandering**. Today this term is associated with the creation of "majority-minority" districts that allow more racial minorities to elect candidates of their choice. In *Shaw* v. *Reno* (1993), the U.S. Supreme Court condemned two extremely odd-shaped, black-majority districts in North Carolina.

A controversial redistricting plan adopted by the Texas Legislature in 2003 to draw new U.S. congressional districts was challenged by both the Texas Democratic Party and by minority groups, contending it diluted minority voting strength. Although the primary purpose of the plan, as crafted by U.S. House Majority Leader Tom DeLay, was to increase the number of Republican representatives in the Congress, an internal memo from the U.S. Justice Department revealed that all of the attorneys in the department's voting section believed that the plan "illegally diluted black and Hispanic voting power in two congressional districts."[5] Despite these conclusions, senior-level administrators at the Justice Department approved the redistricting plan. Shortly after the plan was passed, it was challenged in court. However, by a 5-4 margin, the United States Supreme Court upheld most of the plan, which

**white primary** A nominating system designed to prevent African Americans and some Mexican Americans from participating in Democratic primaries from 1923 to 1944.

**racial gerrymandering** Drawing districts designed to affect representation of a racial group (e.g., African Americans) in a legislative chamber, city council, commissioners court, or other representative body.

altered the Texas congressional delegation from a 17-15 Democratic majority to a 21-11 Republican majority. The Court invalidated one GOP-held district in South Texas on the grounds that it violated the Voting Rights Act by removing approximately 100,000 Democrats of Latino origin.[6]

**Diluting Minority Votes**    Creating **at-large majority districts** (each electing two or more representatives) for state legislatures and city councils can prevent an area with a significant minority population from electing a representative of its choice. Under this scenario, the votes of a minority group can be diluted when combined with the votes of a majority group. Federal courts have declared this practice unconstitutional where representation of ethnic or racial minorities is diminished.[7]

## Democratization of the Ballot

In America, successive waves of democratization have removed obstacles to voting. In the latter half of the twentieth century the U.S. Congress enacted important voting rights laws to promote and protect voting nationwide.

**Federal Voting Rights Legislation**    The Voting Rights Act of 1965 expanded the electorate and encouraged voting. As since amended, this law (together with federal court rulings) now:

- Abolishes use of all literacy tests in voter registrations
- Prohibits residency requirements of more than 30 days for voting in presidential elections
- Requires states to provide some form of absentee or early voting
- Allows individuals (as well as the U.S. Department of Justice) to sue in federal court to request that voting examiners be sent to a particular area

The Voting Rights Act of 1975 also established new federal policies designed to increase voter turnout among Native Americans and Latinos. For example, states with a significant percentage of Spanish-speaking residents, such as Texas, must use bilingual ballots and other election materials.

In 1993, Congress passed the National Voter Registration Act, or **motor voter law**, which simplified voter registration by permitting registration by mail, or at welfare, disability assistance, and motor vehicle licensing agencies or at military recruitment centers. The new procedures allow persons to register to vote when they apply for, or renew, driver's licenses or visit a public assistance office. Texas citizens can also apply for voter registration or to update their voter registration data by mail, using an appropriate state or federal voter registration form. In addition to registration by mail, motor vehicle offices and voter registration agencies are required to provide voter registration services to applicants. If citizens believe their voting rights have been violated in any way, federal administrative and judicial agencies such as the U.S. Department of Justice are available for assistance.

**at-large majority district**  A district that elects two or more representatives.

**motor voter law**  Legislation requiring certain government offices (e.g., motor vehicle licensing agencies) to offer voter registration applications to clients.

Amendments to the U.S. Constitution have also expanded the American electorate. The Fifteenth Amendment prohibits the denial of voting rights because of race; the Nineteenth Amendment precludes denial of suffrage on the basis of gender; the Twenty-Fourth Amendment prohibits states from requiring payment of a poll tax or any other tax as a condition for voting; and the Twenty-Sixth Amendment forbids setting the minimum voting age above 18 years.

**Two Trends in Suffrage**    From our overview of suffrage in Texas, two trends emerge. First, voting rights have steadily expanded to include virtually all persons, of both sexes, who are 18 years of age or older. Second, there has been a movement toward uniformity of voting policies among the 50 states. However, democratization of the ballot has been pressed on the states largely by the U.S. Congress, by federal judges, and by presidents who have enforced voting laws and judicial orders.

## Voter Turnout

Now that nearly all legal barriers to the ballot have been swept away, the road to the voting booth seems clear for rich and poor alike, for historical minority groups as well as for the majority, and for individuals of all races, colors, and creeds. But universal suffrage has not resulted in a corresponding increase in voter turnout, either nationally or in Texas.

**Voter turnout** is the percentage of the voting-age population casting ballots. In Texas, turnout is higher in presidential elections than in nonpresidential elections. Although this pattern reflects the national trend, electoral turnout in Texas tends to be significantly lower than in the nation as a whole. The 2002 nonpresidential election yielded a 29.3 percent turnout in Texas. Even with President George W. Bush running for reelection in the 2004 election, Texas ranked below the national average in voter turnout of the voting age population at 44.3 percent, compared to the 55.3 percent national average. Few citizens believe their vote will determine an election outcome, but races have actually been won by a single vote. In local elections at the city or school district level, a turnout of 20 percent is relatively high. Among the five largest cities conducting city council elections in Texas in 2005, none yielded a turnout greater than 15 percent. These figures illustrate one of the greatest ironies in politics: that people are less likely to participate at the level of government where they can potentially have the greatest influence.

Low citizen participation in elections has been attributed to the influence of pollsters and media consultants, voter fatigue resulting from too many elections, negative campaigning by candidates, lack of information about candidates and issues, and feelings of isolation from government. In 2001 members of Texas's 77th Legislature determined that low voter turnout was caused by governmental entities holding too many elections. To cure "turnout burnout," they passed legislation that limits elections to four uniform election dates each

**voter turnout** The percentage of the voting-age population casting ballots in an election.

year.[8] However, the effects of this change have failed to yield a higher voter turnout as anticipated. Additionally, runoff elections, local option elections under the Alcoholic Beverage Code, bond or tax levy elections for school or community college districts, emergency elections, elections to fill vacancies in the two chambers of the Texas Legislature and Texas delegation to the U.S. House of Representatives, recall elections, and other elections specifically exempted by statute can be held on nonuniform dates.[9]

People decide to vote or not to vote in the same way they make most other decisions: on the basis of anticipated consequences. A strong impulse to vote may stem from peer pressure, self-interest, or a sense of duty toward country, state, local community, political party, or interest group. People also decide whether or not to vote based on cost measured in time, money, experience, information, job, and other resources.

Cultural, socioeconomic, and racial factors also contribute to the low voter turnout in the Lone Star State. As identified in the chapter "The Environment of Texas Politics," elements of Texas's political culture place little emphasis on the importance of voting.

Of all the socioeconomic influences on voting, education is by far the strongest. Statistics clearly indicate that as educational level rises, people are more likely to vote, assuming all other socioeconomic factors remain constant. Educated people usually have more income and leisure time for voting; moreover, education enhances one's ability to learn about political parties, candidates, and issues.

Income strongly affects voter turnout as well. Texas ranks sixth in the nation in the percentage of its population living in poverty. People of lower income often lack access to the polls, information about the candidates, or opportunities to learn about the system. Income levels and their impact on electoral turnout can be seen in the 2004 general election. For example, Starr County, with a median household income of less than $17,000, had a turnout of 34.6 percent of its registered voters. By contrast, Collin County, with a median income of more than $70,000, experienced a turnout of 66.36 percent of its registered voters.

Although far less important than education and income, gender and age also affect voting behavior. In the United States, women are slightly more likely to vote than men. Young people (ages 18–25) have the lowest voter turnout of any age group. Nevertheless, participation by young people increased in the 2004 presidential election. The highest voter turnout is among middle-aged Americans (ages 40–64).

Race and ethnicity also influence voting behavior. The turnout rate for African Americans remains substantially below that for Anglos. African Americans tend to be younger, less educated, and poorer than Anglos. Although Latino voter turnout rates in Texas are slightly below the state average in primaries and general elections, findings by scholars indicate that the gap is narrowing. Still, the voting rate for African Americans and Latinos in Texas is approximately 65 percent of the state average.

## Administering Elections

In Texas, as in other states, determining voting procedures is essentially a state responsibility. The Texas Constitution authorizes the legislature to provide for the administration of elections. State lawmakers, in turn, have made the secretary of state the chief elections officer for Texas but have left most details of administering elections to county officials.

All election laws currently in effect in the Lone Star State are compiled into one body of law, the **Texas Election Code**.[10] In administering this legal code, however, state and party officials must protect voting rights guaranteed by federal law.

**Qualifications for Voting**     To be eligible to vote in Texas, a person must meet the following qualifications:

- Be a native-born or naturalized citizen of the United States
- Be at least 18 years of age on election day
- Be a resident of the state and county for at least 30 days immediately preceding election day
- Be a resident of the area covered by the election on election day
- Be a registered voter for at least 30 days immediately preceding election day
- Not be a convicted felon (unless sentence, probation, and parole are completed)
- Not be declared mentally incompetent by a court of law[11]

Most adults who live in Texas meet the first four qualifications for voting, but registration is required before a person can vote. Anyone serving a jail sentence as a result of a misdemeanor conviction or not finally convicted of a felony is not disqualified from voting. The Texas Constitution, however, bars from voting anyone who is incarcerated, on parole, or on probation as a result of a felony conviction and anyone who is "mentally incompetent as determined by a court." A convicted felon may vote immediately after completing a sentence or following a full pardon. (For examples of misdemeanors and felonies, see Table 10.3 in the chapter "Laws, Courts, and Justice.")

**Voter registration** is intended to determine in advance whether prospective voters meet all the qualifications prescribed by law. Most states, including Texas, use a permanent registration system. Under this plan, voters register once and remain registered unless they change their mailing address and fail to notify the voting registrar within three years or lose their eligibility to register in some other way. Because the requirement of voter registration may deter voting, the Texas Election Code provides for voter registration centers in addition to those sites authorized by Congress under the motor voter law. Thus, Texans may also register at local marriage license offices, in public high schools, with any volunteer deputy registrar, or in person at the office of the county voting registrar.

Between November 1 and November 15 of each odd-numbered year, the registrar mails a registration certificate effective for the succeeding two voting

**Texas Election Code** The body of state law concerning parties, primaries, and elections.

**voter registration** A qualified voter must register with the county voting registrar, who compiles lists of qualified voters residing in each voting precinct.

years to every registered voter in the county. Postal authorities may not forward a certificate mailed to the address indicated on the voter's application form if the applicant has moved to another address; instead, the certificate must be returned to the registrar. This enables the county voting registrar to maintain an accurate list of names and mailing addresses of persons to whom voting certificates have been issued. Registration files are open for public inspection in the voting registrar's office, and a statewide registration file is available in Austin at the Elections Division of the Office of the Secretary of State.

The color of voter registration certificates mailed to eligible voters in November of odd-numbered years differs from the color of the cards sent two years earlier. The Office of the Secretary of State determines the color of voter registration certificates. Although voter registration certificates are issued after a person registers to vote, one can legally cast a ballot without a certificate by providing some form of identification (such as a driver's license) and signing an affidavit of registration at the polls.

**Voting Early: In Person and by Mail**    Opportunities to vote early in Texas are limited to in-person **early voting**, voting by mail, facsimile machine voting (for military personnel and their dependents in combat zones), and electronic voting for astronauts on space flights. Texas law allows voters to vote "early"—that is, during a 17-day period preceding a scheduled election or first primary and for 10 days preceding a runoff primary. Early voting ends, however, four days before any election or primary. In less-populated rural counties, early voting occurs at the courthouse. In more populous urban areas, the county clerk's office accommodates voters by maintaining branch offices for early voting. Polling places are generally open for early voting on weekdays during the regular business hours of the official responsible for conducting the election. If requested by 15 registered voters within the county, polling places must also be opened on Saturday or Sunday.

Registered voters who qualify may vote by mail during an early voting period. Voting by mail has been available to elderly Texans and those with physical disabilities for decades. Today, anyone meeting the following qualifications can vote by mail-in ballot:

- Will not be in his or her county of residence during the entire early voting period and on election day
- Is at least age 65
- Is or will be physically disabled on election day, including those who expect to be confined for childbirth on election day
- Is in jail (but not a convicted felon) during the early voting period and on election day
- Is in the military or a dependent of military personnel and has resided in Texas[12]

**early voting** Conducted at the county courthouse and selected polling places before the designated primary, special, or general election day.

Since early voting was first used in 1998, the percentage of early voters has consistently been about 20 percent in the general elections. Although such

In 1997, the Texas Legislature enacted a provision allowing people on space flights to vote electronically from space on election day.

**Points to Ponder**

measures make voting easier, at least one study indicates that states with longer early voting periods have experienced a greater decline in voter turnout than states with more restrictive election laws.[13]

Residents displaced by Hurricane Katrina, many living in Texas, cast more than 21,000 early, or absentee, votes in the 2006 New Orleans Mayoral election. Several of the 22 mayoral candidates traveled to Houston to campaign to thousands of displaced New Orleanians. During the early voting period, before the election, buses traveled from cities across Texas, including Houston and Dallas, carrying hundreds of voters to New Orleans to cast early ballots. Additionally, several thousand ballots were cast by mail.

**Voting Precincts**  The basic geographic area for conducting national, state, district, and county elections is the **voting precinct**. Each precinct usually contains between 100 and approximately 2,000 registered voters. Texas has more than 8,500 voting precincts, drawn by the 254 county commissioners courts (county judge and 4 commissioners). When a precinct's population exceeds a number prescribed by the Texas Election Code (3,000, 4,000, or 5,000, depending on the county's population), the commissioners court must draw new boundaries.[14] Citizens vote at polling places within their voting precincts or, if voting precincts have been combined for an election, at a polling place convenient to voters in each of the combined voting precincts. Municipal precincts must follow the boundary lines of county-designed voting precincts adjusted to city boundaries. Subject to this restriction, municipal and special-district voting precincts are designated by the governing body of each city and special district, respectively.

**Election Officials**  Various county and political party officials administer elections. Whereas party officials conduct primary elections, the county clerk or elections administrator prepares general- and special-election ballots based on certification of candidates by the appropriate authority (the secretary of state for state and district candidates and the county clerk or elections administrator for local candidates). Some counties have officials whose sole responsibility is election administration. In other counties, it is one of many responsibilities of the tax assessor-collector or (if designated by the county commissioners court) the county clerk. In 2006, less than 14 percent of the counties in Texas employed a full-time **elections administrator**. There is also a county election commission, which consists of the county judge, county clerk or elections administrator,

**voting precinct** The basic geographic area for conducting primaries and elections; Texas is divided into more than 8,500 voting precincts.

**elections administrator** Less than 12 percent of Texas counties employ a full-time elections administrator to supervise voter registration and voting.

# POINT/COUNTERPOINT

## Online Voting as a Means to Increase Voter Turnout

**THE ISSUE**   National voter turnout has decreased from 63 percent of the voting-age population in 1960 to approximately 55 percent in 2004. Declining participation at the polls increasingly frustrates public officials and interest groups. A proposal to increase voter turnout with online voting is gaining support in many circles. Voters would cast ballots from the comfort of their own homes or offices. Such proposals include voting from home via secure e-mail, from home or another location through a Web link to the ballot, and from a traditional polling place with Internet access.

### Arguments For Online Voting

1. *Convenience will increase turnout.* If people could vote from their home computers, inclement weather or long lines at the polls would not deter people from voting. Additionally, online voting at home would improve access dramatically for disabled voters. It also has the potential to attract many more voters in the 18-to-34 age group, those most likely to use technology.

2. *More informed electorate.* The Internet is the fastest and easiest way for people to gain access to information about candidates and their campaigns. This medium strengthens representative government by bringing candidates closer to the voters than could a 30-second television commercial and would provide more information about candidates and their policy positions.

3. *Quickest, cheapest, and most efficient way to administer elections.* Online voting would reduce the number of geographic polling places and consolidate the counting process. Currently, Texas's decentralized election system involves more than 3,200 local jurisdictions, each of which can use its own voting system. Ninety counties still use paper ballots counted by hand. Adopting a uniform system of online voting will make tabulation more efficient.

### Arguments Against Online Voting

1. *Would create a disadvantage for those without access to technology.* The "digital divide"—the gap between technological haves and have-nots—could widen and online voting could discourage from voting people who lack access to a computer or are not computer-savvy. It discriminates against minority and low-income voters, who are not as likely to have access to the Internet.

2. *Integrity of election will be lost.* Security breaches and fraud could threaten the integrity of elections conducted online. Election officials must determine that each person trying to vote is eligible, that each person has only one vote and that the vote is secret, and that tabulation is accurate. Online voting systems would require each voter to have a digital signature. Such technology is expensive, and questions about funding need to be addressed. Texas now has more than 11 million registered voters, each of whom would need a digital signature.

3. *Could not prevent unlawful electioneering.* Texas has laws prohibiting electioneering within a certain distance of a polling place. Voters may take voting material but not campaign material into a polling place. Someone could vote online while viewing a candidate's web site.

*Source:* This Point/Counterpoint is abridged and adapted from Rita Barr, "Voting on the Internet: Promises and Problems," *Interim News* 76 (3) (Austin: House Research Organization, Texas House of Representatives, 16 March 2000): 1–5. Reprinted by permission.

sheriff, and chairs of the two major political parties. Commission responsibilities include selecting polling places, printing ballots, and providing supplies and voting equipment.

County commissioners courts appoint one **election judge** and one alternate judge, each from different political parties, to administer elections in each precinct for a maximum term of two years. Furthermore, each county's commissioners court canvasses and certifies election results. The election judge selects as many clerks as will be needed to assist in conducting general and special elections in a precinct. Clerks must be selected from different political parties. In city elections, the city secretary appoints election judges.

**Voting Systems**  In general elections, Texas uses five voting systems: paper ballot, manually operated voting machine, optical scan (like Scantrons), punch-card, and direct-record electronic (or touchscreen). In every county, the county commissioners court determines which system will be used. Each has advantages and disadvantages in such matters as ballot and equipment costs, ease of use by voters, accuracy of counting, labor cost, and time required to count the votes. For example, paper ballots are relatively cheap and easy to use, but counting is a slow, laborious, and error-prone process. Some sparsely populated counties continue to use paper ballots, which must be counted by hand. Voting machines and some optical scan and direct-recording electronic voting systems automatically count each vote as the ballot is cast. Punch-card devices and some optical scan systems are electronically counted on delivery to the county clerk's office after the polls close. Mechanical and electronic voting equipment is expensive to purchase and store but can reduce election costs when many voters are involved.

After the controversial 2000 presidential election, in which the state of Florida and the U.S. Supreme Court questioned the accuracy of punch-card ballots, both federal and state elected officials evaluated various voting systems. A study conducted by the Office of the Secretary of State of Texas revealed that the 14 Texas counties that used punch-card ballots (including Harris County [Houston]) had many more overvotes (in which voters selected more than one candidate for the same office) than counties using any other balloting method. Likewise, these counties had many more undervotes (in which voters did not clearly select any candidate for a specific office).[15] In testimony before the House Elections Committee, then Secretary of State Henry Cuellar emphasized the need to replace punch-card ballots with more accurate equipment but urged caution in abandoning the system quickly. Although legislators and Cuellar preferred prohibiting the use of punch-card ballots, replacement cost was a factor. Harris County estimated the cost of replacing its punch-card ballot equipment at $20 million. Balancing cost and the need for more accurate voting systems, the Texas Legislature required counties to phase out the punch-card equipment. No new punch-card tabulating machines could be purchased after September 2001, except for early-voting purposes. Further, chads (the small pieces of paper punched out of the ballot) must be

**election judge**  Appointed by the county commissioners court to administer an election in a voting precinct.

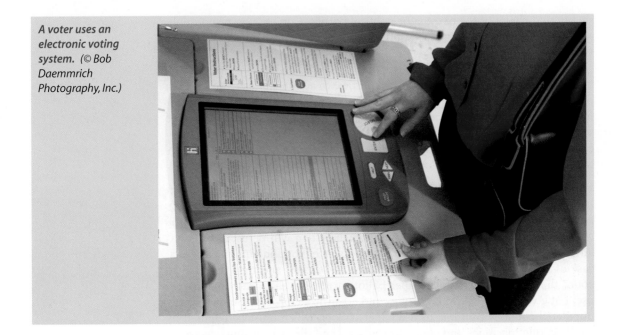

*A voter uses an electronic voting system.* (© Bob Daemmrich Photography, Inc.)

removed from tabulating machines before each election. By 2002, Harris County implemented an electronic voting system for all polling places.

On machine and punch-card ballot forms, a list of parties for straight-party-ticket voting appears first, followed by lists of candidates for national, state, district, and local offices, in that order. (Figure 5.1 shows a sample machine ballot used in the 2004 general election.) Punch-card ballots have space for names of write-in candidates on a detachable portion of the ballot card. A list of all write-in candidates who have filed an appropriate declaration is posted in each polling place on the day of election. The name of one of these candidates may be written in to indicate the voter's selection in the appropriate contest.

In some instances, candidates for nomination or election to an office may request a recount of ballots if they believe vote tabulations are inaccurate. Texas law is specific on how election officials determine a voter's intent if a punch-card ballot was used, but not punched through. Only one recount is allowed.[16] The Texas Election Code also provides detailed procedures for settling disputed elections. Since the 1960s, several changes in voting procedures have been made to encourage full, informed participation in elections.

As a result of the 1975 extension of the Federal Voting Rights Act, registration and election materials used in all Texas counties must be printed in both English and Spanish. Texas voters can also take voting guides, newspaper endorsements, and other printed material into the voting booth. In 1999, the Texas Legislature passed a series of laws ensuring disabled voters access to polling places and the opportunity to cast a secret ballot. The legislature

Vote Both Sides

*Vote en Ambos Lados de la Página*

November 2, 2004 Joint General and Special Elections
*el 2 de noviembre de 2004 Elecciónes General Junta y Especial*
Travis County
*Condado de Travis*
November 02, 2004 - *02 Noviembre 2004*

Precinct *Precinct* **467-TM**

**SPECIAL BALLOT INSTRUCTIONS:**
CAPITAL METRO REFERENDUM IS AT THE END OF THE BALLOT.
*INSTRUCCIONES ESPECIALES DE VOTACIÓN:*
*REFERENDUM DE CAPITAL METRO ESTÁ A FIN DE LA BOLETA.*

**INSTRUCTION NOTE:**
Use a BLUE or BLACK pen to mark your ballot. To vote, completely fill in the square to the left of your candidate or proposition choice. To vote for a write-in candidate, completely fill in the square to the left of "Write-in" and enter the name of the certified write-in candidate on the line provided.
*NOTA DE INSTRUCCION:*
*Marque su boleta con una pluma negra o azul. Para votar, llene completamenta el espacio cuadrado a la izquierda del nombre del candidato o selección de proposición de su preferencia. Para votar por un candidato por voto escrito, llene completamente el espacio cuadrado a la izquierda de "Voto Escrito" y escriba el nombre del candidato certificado en la linea provista.*

**STRAIGHT PARTY**
*PARTIDO RECTO*
To cast a vote for all the nominees of one party select the name of the party of your choice. Selecting a party automatically selects all candidates' names of that party, indicating a vote for those candidates.
If you cast a straight-party vote for all the nominees of one party and also cast a vote for an opponent of one of that party's nominees, your vote for the opponent will be counted as well as your vote for all the other nominees of the party of which the straight-party vote was cast.
*Para votar por todos los candidatos de un solo partido político marcar el nombre del partido deseado. Al seleccionar el partido, se marcarán automáticamente todos los nombres de los candidatos de ese partido, indicando un voto para esos candidatos.*
*Para votar "Straight Party" y también votar por un contrincante de un partido opuesto marcar el nombre del contrincante de un partido opuesto.*

☐ **REPUBLICAN**
*REPUBLICANO*
☐ **DEMOCRATIC**
*DEMOCRATA*
☐ **LIBERTARIAN**
*LIBERTARIO*

**PRESIDENT AND VICE PRESIDENT**
*PRESIDENTE Y VICE PRESIDENTE*
☐ George W. Bush/ Dick Cheney
REP
☐ John F. Kerry/ John Edwards
DEM
☐ Michael Badnarik/ Richard V. Campagna
LIB
☐ Write-in
*Voto Escrito*

**UNITED STATES REPRESENTATIVE, DISTRICT 25**
*REPRESENTANTE DE LOS ESTADOS UNIDOS, DISTRITO NÚM. 25*
☐ Rebecca Armendariz Klein
REP
☐ Lloyd Doggett
DEM
☐ James Werner
LIB

**RAILROAD COMMISSIONER**
*COMISIONADO DE FERROCARRILES*
☐ Victor G. Carrillo
REP
☐ Bob Scarborough
DEM
☐ Anthony Garcia
LIB

**JUSTICE, SUPREME COURT, PLACE 3**
*JUEZ, CORTE SUPREMA, LUGAR NÚM. 3*
☐ Harriet O'Neill
REP

**JUSTICE, SUPREME COURT, PLACE 5**
*JUEZ, CORTE SUPREMA, LUGAR NÚM. 5*
☐ Paul Green
REP

**JUSTICE, SUPREME COURT, PLACE 9**
*JUEZ, CORTE SUPREMA, LUGAR NÚM. 9*
☐ Scott Brister
REP
☐ David Van Os
DEM

**JUDGE, COURT OF CRIMINAL APPEALS, PLACE 2**
*JUEZ, CORTE DE APELACIONES CRIMINALES, LUGAR NÚM. 2*
☐ Lawrence "Larry" Meyers
REP
☐ Quanah Parker
LIB

**JUDGE, COURT OF CRIMINAL APPEALS, PLACE 5**
*JUEZ, CORTE DE APELACIONES CRIMINALES, LUGAR NÚM. 5*
☐ Cheryl Johnson
REP
☐ Tom Oxford
LIB

**JUDGE, COURT OF CRIMINAL APPEALS, PLACE 6**
*JUEZ, CORTE DE APELACIONES CRIMINALES, LUGAR NÚM. 6*
☐ Michael E. Keasler
REP
☐ J.R. Molina
DEM

**STATE REPRESENTATIVE, DISTRICT 49**
*REPRESENTANTE ESTATAL, DISTRITO NÚM. 49*
☐ Elliott Naishtat
DEM
☐ Robinson Butler "Bo" Howell
LIB

**JUSTICE, 3RD COURT OF APPEALS DISTRICT, PLACE 4**
*JUEZ, CORTE DE APELACIONES, DISTRITO NÚM. 3, LUGAR NÚM. 4*
☐ Bill Green
REP
☐ Jan Patterson
DEM

**Test Ballot**

201003071100

1000000041

25620300

Vote Both Sides

*Vote en Ambos Lados de la Página*

*Figure 5.1*    Sample Portion of Election Ballot for Travis County, Texas, 2004
Travis County, Texas ballot from The Hart Intercivic eSlate Voting System.

## How Do We Compare ... in Types of Primaries?

| Most Populous U.S. States | Primary Type | U.S. States Bordering Texas | Primary Type |
|---|---|---|---|
| California | Closed | Arkansas | Open |
| Florida | Closed | Louisiana | Jungle |
| New York | Closed | New Mexico | Closed |
| **Texas** | **Combination (open/closed)** | Oklahoma | Closed |

The Texas Election Code requires voters to identify their party affiliation at the time of voting, making Texas a combination of a closed primary state and an open primary state. Voter registration certificates are stamped with the party name when voters participate in a primary. Qualified voters may vote in the primary of any party, so long as they have not already voted in another party's primary or convention in the same year. The primary ballot contains the following restriction: "I am a Democrat (Republican) and understand that I am ineligible to vote or participate in another political party's primary election or convention during this voting year."[17] Violation of a party pledge is a misdemeanor offense punishable by a fine of $500.

**Administering Primaries**    In most states, political parties sponsor and administer their own primaries. The Texas Election Code allocates this responsibility to each political party's county executive committee. Political parties whose gubernatorial candidate received 20 percent or more of the vote in the preceding general election must nominate all of their candidates in direct primaries conducted in even-numbered years. In 2004, the first primaries and runoff (second) primaries were held on the second Tuesdays in March and April, respectively. But 20 other states conducted their presidential primaries earlier than Texas. As a result, by the date of Texas's first Republican and Democratic Party primaries (March 9), President George W. Bush and U.S. Senator John Kerry were already their party's de facto nominees for president.

A law passed by the 78th Texas Legislature in 2003 requires that Texas's first and runoff primaries must be conducted a week earlier—on the first Tuesdays of March and April. But some Texans argue that too much time elapses between March primaries and the November general elections. They explain that the electorate has little interest in early primaries and has lost all interest by November.

Individuals who want to run in a direct primary for their party's nomination for a multicounty district office or a statewide office must file the necessary papers with their party's state chair. The state chair certifies the names of these persons to each county chair in counties in which the election is administered. Prospective candidates who want their names placed on the primary ballot for a county or precinct office must file with the county chair of their party. County executive committees for each political party supervise the printing of primary ballots. If the parties conduct a joint primary, the county elections administrator or the county clerk administers the election. If each party conducts its own primaries, county chairs arrange for voting equipment and polling places in the precincts. With the approval of the county executive committee, the county chair obtains supplies and appoints a presiding judge of elections in each precinct. Together with the state executive committee, the county executive committee determines the order of names of candidates on the ballot and **canvasses** (that is, confirms and certifies) the vote tally for each candidate.

**Financing Primaries**    Major expenses for administering party primaries include renting facilities for polls (the places where voting is conducted), printing ballots and other election materials, and paying election judges and clerks. In recent years, approximately 30 percent of the cost of holding Texas primaries has come from filing fees paid by candidates. For example, candidates for the office of U.S. senator pay $5,000, and candidates for governor and all other statewide offices pay $3,750. Candidates for the Texas Senate and the Texas House of Representatives pay $1,250 and $750, respectively.[18]

In lieu of paying a fee, a candidate may file a nominating petition containing a specified number of signatures of people eligible to vote for the office for

**canvass** To scrutinize the results of an election and then confirm and certify the vote tally for each candidate.

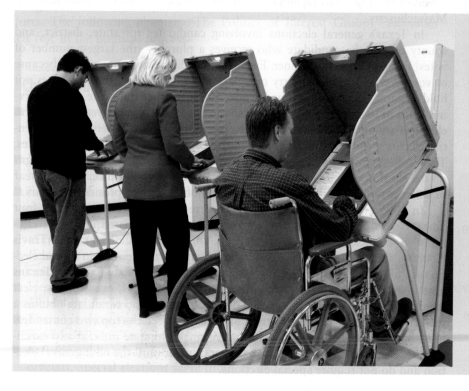

*Voters cast their ballots in the 2006 Texas primary election. (© Bob Daemmrich Photography, Inc.)*

## 5.1 In High-Tech E-Voting Age, Glitches Usually Low-Tech*

### *Laylan Copelin*

*As more counties in Texas convert to electronic voting systems, questions arise concerning the potential for error and fraud. This reading examines these criticisms as well as the need to train election workers in new technologies.*

Six thousand ballots were cast and counted electronically this spring [2006] before the first Travis County voter stepped into a voting booth. No, it was not the digital equivalent of Box 13, the "missing" South Texas ballot box that allowed a young Lyndon Johnson to squeak into the U.S. Senate in 1948. Instead, it was a test, just one of the many checks and balances that Travis County Clerk Dana DeBeauvoir uses to safeguard the ballot box in an electronic age.

"It's tedious and grueling," DeBeauvoir said of the process in which election workers cast thousands of test ballots over 12 hours. "But it's necessary."

Interest in ballot security has sizzled on the back burner this year as Texas passed a Jan. 1 federal deadline to put at least one electronic machine in every precinct. As some politicians, election lawyers, and critics of electronic voting—the self-proclaimed "black box" crowd—warn of voter fraud, the problems so far have been more of the low-tech variety. More times than not, it's the people—with a lack of training, a shortage of workers, or human error—at the root of problems.

The push to improve the speed and accuracy of voting came from the hanging chads of the 2000 Bush–Gore presidential standoff in Florida. But a primary purpose behind the federal Helping America to Vote Act is also to put at least one electronic voting machine in every precinct so people with disabilities can easily vote. Although Texas elections have sidestepped the major meltdown Florida experienced, not all vendors of electronic machines were prepared for this spring's elections at thousands of school districts, water districts, and counties waiting to join the e-vote revolution. In Williamson County, for example, the ballots for the new machines were not available until election day during the March primaries (the county used its old system for early voting). That's why DeBeauvoir insists that Travis County prepare its ballots instead of leaving it to the vendors. "It was almost like chaos for these vendors," she said. "Instead of talking to 254 county clerks and election administrators, they're talking to several thousand officials, some without a background in voting systems."

Even voter fraud in Texas still has a very low-tech approach. The most prevalent examples of voter fraud remain the manipulation of mail-in ballots for senior citizens, according to Attorney General Greg Abbott. Paid campaign workers befriend older voters, making sure they apply for mail-in ballots, and then return to "help" when the ballots are mailed, sometimes affecting local races.

### Criticisms of E-Voting

Even as more Texas counties are converting to electronic voting, detractors continue to question whether the systems are the best method. They collect examples of glitches throughout the country, circulate government and private reports critical of the systems, and generally fear that the machines can be programmed to add or subtract votes from candidates. "I don't trust any of the electronic systems," said Vicki Karp of Austin, a board member of BlackBoxVoting.org, a national organization that bills itself as consumer protection for elections.

There are four major manufacturers of electronic voting machines. Although they try to guard the secrets of their systems to protect their business, Karp said the

---

*From the *Austin American-Statesman*, 13 June 2006. Laylan Copelin is a reporter for the *Austin American-Statesman*. Copyright 2006, *Austin American-Statesman*. Reprinted with Permission.

programming codes of two manufacturers have been leaked on the Internet. Based on those unauthorized leaks, critics insist that the software can be compromised—an allegation the industry denies.

Bob Cohen, senior vice president with the Election Technology Council, a trade association, says that any problems can be traced to the nature of elections. "When you look at an election, it is an activity with a thousand moving parts," he said. "You have people, some who may be volunteers and new to the process, multiple processes, and technology that may be new to the workers and the voters."

Rice University professor Dan Wallach is a computer security expert who is skeptical of electronic voting. He said he has testified in election contests where he has found test votes—the kind Travis County used—wrongly included in election day totals. In another instance, Wallach said, election workers cleared out the electronic ballots from some machines to get ready for a runoff election, erasing the ability to double-check the election day returns. Wallach said the state has contributed to the problems by barring the public from attending the state's initial review of electronic voting systems.

Before a company may sell a voting system in Texas, it must be certified by the federal government and the state. Wallach said the hearings where examiners dissect the operating systems and programming codes should be open to the public but aren't. He argues that patent and copyright laws would protect the companies' proprietary interests while a public process would expose a system's flaws sooner. The industry cites trade secrets, competitive pressures, and security as reasons for limiting public knowledge about the machines and software. DeBeauvoir, the Travis County clerk, supports a larger panel of examiners but disagrees about opening up the hearings. "What good does it do to have a 14-year-old out there who knows everything about the software?" she asked.

## Travis County Model

The Travis County election system generally gets good marks, even from the harshest critics of electronic voting, because of the attention to security. "I'd give the machines a D-plus," Karp said. "I'd give (the election staff) an A-plus for their work."

DeBeauvoir said ballot security begins with low-tech solutions such as locks on doors, video cameras in secure areas, and a limit on access. And it extends to anticipating emergencies—for example, covering the machines with waterproof tarps in the warehouses in case the sprinkler system goes off.

Travis County's eSlate system, developed by Hart InterCivic of Austin, monitors any activity and checks its figures as it goes along. It also can shut itself down if there is a problem. Troubleshooters stand by on election day. The most prevalent problem? Loose cables. However, not all counties have the technical work force or the $5 million Travis County spent—largely reimbursed by the federal government—to purchase its election system. And skeptics remain. Buck Wood, an Austin elections lawyer, is one. "It's just a matter of time until we have a major scandal with a machine," he said.

One solution suggested is a paper copy of the electronic ballot, printed in the polling booth, reviewed by the voter and filed away for audits. You'd have the best of both worlds, proponents argue: the speed of electronic counting and the security of a paper ballot. "No matter how screwed up the computer is, you can always go back to check the paper ballot," Rice professor Wallach said.

But the hybrid would create its own problems, DeBeauvoir said. It's more expensive, it would slow down voting, and the printers are likely to jam and malfunction. Whatever the next generation of electronic machines looks like, DeBeauvoir predicted that Travis County's security efforts will become the norm. "Our approach is not white bread, but it will be," she said.

# How votes get counted

## Testing

Before early voting and again before election day, the county performs a public 'Logic and Accuracy' test on all eSlate equipment. Identical votes are cast on eSlate and on manual ballot. The results are compared and should be identical.

**Early voting**

Each day, law enforcement officers retrieve the Judge's Booth Controller from each early voting site and take it to election officials. The officials lock up the units, and the law enforcement officers keep the key. The process is reversed to set up the voting stations.

### 1 Votes are stored

Each ballot cast is stored on the voter's eSlate unit, the Judge's Booth Controller and the Mobile Ballot Box. The system is not networked externally and is not affected by power outages.

### 2 Polls close

After the polls close, election judges deliver the controllers to election officials at one of five substations. Election officials verify paperwork and check the integrity of the mobile box seals.

### 3 Cards removed

The presiding judge takes off the seal and removes the mobile boxes. The mobile boxes are placed in a special box and sealed again for delivery to the central counting station.

### 4 Cards delivered for counting

Law enforcement officers pick up the sealed boxes and deliver them to the presiding judge at the central counting station.

### 5 Votes are counted

The presiding judge removes the seal, removes the mobile boxes and places them in a special PC flash memory card reader. By law, the card reader may not be networked to any other equipment except a printer. The votes are counted using proprietary software, and reports are printed. Observers from the public are present during this process.

### If a recount is needed

For recounts, Travis County has several alternatives, including printing individual paper records for each 'Cast Vote Record' (stored in the mobile box, eSlate and controller) and performing a manual count. The 'Cast Vote Records' can be printed from any of the system's three separate memory devices.

Sources: Travis County, Hart InterCivic

**Mobile Ballot Box**
A PC memory card is sealed into the controller.

**eSlate**
Each eSlate has a built-in memory chip to store voting records.

**Judge's Booth Controller**
The controller is the precinct's control center. It has a built-in memory chip to store voting records.

**Mobile boxes**
PC memory cards

**Sealed boxes of mobile boxes**

**Stand-alone computer with PC flash memory card reader**

**Printer**

**Robert Calzada** AMERICAN-STATESMAN

*Source:* Copyright © 2006 Austin *American-Statesman*. Reprinted with permission.

## 5.2  Small Communities Can't Afford Required Voting Technology*

### Joe Conger

*The Texas Legislature passed a series of laws ensuring disabled voters access to polling places and the opportunity to cast secret ballots. However, some smaller counties lack the financial resources to purchase voting equipment to implement these laws. This reading explores the high cost of securing the right of disabled people to vote.*

### Small Communities Can't Afford Required Voting Technology

Lots of important issues are facing voters this Saturday, from school district elections to fire coverage for county residents. However, Saturday is also the first time taxpayers will shell out double, triple, even quadruple the cost to have an election.

The right to vote is one of America's most cherished freedoms. When a person reaches the age of 18 years, he or she can participate. Texas state law now requires polling sites to have a IV otronic machine, making it easier for the disabled to participate in elections.

"They must have one of these (machines) available at every poll site," Bexar County Elections Administrator Jacquelyn Callanen said.

However, KENS 5 Eyewitness News found that the machine costs $2,500, plus an additional $15,000 in software licensing. Some Texas communities say the costs are unaffordable and unnecessary.

Bob Kafka is excited to know his disability won't be holding him back from voting at the polls.

"It's an issue of independence and control. We have so many people who are promised to have equal participation in the community, and voting is one of those basic rights that we care so much about," he said.

In the past, disabled voters who were unable to vote on their own would typically have a family member fill out a mail-in ballot at home during early voting. Now, they have a choice.

The 2000 presidential election exposed many flaws in the election systems, and as a result, the Help America Vote Act, or HAVA, was signed into law. The law gives everyone the ability to cast a ballot in secret by privately using a relatively new technology.

Texas took the law and ran with it. State lawmakers mandated last year that not only federal elections, but every single election—right down to the local level—will comply with HAVA.

Texas counties received millions of dollars in federal grant money to purchase and operate these electronic voting machines, but the school districts and small towns who also have their own elections didn't receive anything. So how are the smaller areas going to comply? Some of the communities say lawmakers didn't think this one through.

"I don't think the Legislature was wrong in doing what they did. I think they were visionary, frankly," Texas Secretary of State Roger Williams said.

However, small towns and schools are left trying to envision where they will get the money. Their dilemma: Buy tens of thousands of dollars in electronic machines and software, or rent the equipment and people from Bexar County. For Saturday's elections, 28 government agencies decided to rent.

"As we say our little 'instant election in a box'—$3,811.23," Callanen said.

The cost of renting has caused local election costs to skyrocket.

"The programming of this electronic equipment is approximately $1,500. That was our budget prior to this," Helotes City Secretary Theresa Helbert said.

In Helotes, this year's election budget was bumped from $2,000 to $6,000.

In Fair Oaks Ranch, the 2005 budget of $1,145 was increased to $4,812 for 2006.

In Balcones Heights, last year's budget was $900. This year, it increased to $4,000.

And in Shavano Park, the budget increased from $420 in 2005 to $4,000 for 2006.

But if they have the talking machines, will the disabled show up to use them? That's the $4,000 question.

*"Small Communities Can't Afford Required Voting Technology," by Joe Conger. Copyright 2006 by *San Antonio Express-News*. Reproduced with permission of *San Antonio Express-News* in the format Textbook via Copyright Clearance Center.

"The expense is a great expense for something we would never use, a machine that we would normally never use," Helbert said.

KENS 5 Eyewitness News found that in some small towns, where only dozens of folks vote in each election, city clerks have decided to ignore the new law. The Texas Municipal League confirms that at least half a dozen communities can't afford the machines, or believe there are no disabled folks in town to use them.

"If they say that, they're not meeting the requirement of the law, but I don't believe we'll have that. That's not the Texas spirit," Williams said.

The Secretary of State's Office says it isn't aware of that problem, but why would it be? None of the municipalities ignoring the law would talk with KENS 5 on the record, for fear of potential lawsuits from disabled rights groups.

However, even Bexar County officials admit there's not a long line at the HAVA-required machines. Of the county's 900,000 registered voters, KENS 5 found only seven disabled citizens reportedly used the machines in the last election.

But activists say the small numbers aren't the issue.

"We want to be able to do the most basic thing in our country—vote by ourselves," Kafka said.

---

An extensive bibliography of books and articles for this chapter is posted on Selected Sources for Reading, available online at http://college.hmco.com/PIC/brownPTP13e. For use with any chapter, see Resources for Further Research online at http://college.hmco.com/PIC/brownPTP13e.

*Chapter 6*

# The Politics of Interest Groups

★ **Interest Groups in the Political Process**

★ **Organization of Interest Groups**

★ **Classification of Interest Groups**

★ **Interest Group Activities**

★ **Techniques of Interest Groups**

★ **Regulation of Interest Group Politics**

★ **Interest Group Power and Public Policy**

★ **Pinpointing Political Power**

© Tribune Media Service, Inc. All Rights Reserved. Used with permission.

Politics typically focuses on the nomination and election of individuals to public office. There is, however, much more to it than that. Politics is perhaps best understood as the process of influencing public policy decisions to protect and preserve a group, to achieve the group's goals, and to distribute benefits to the group's members. Organized citizens demand policies that promote their financial security, education, health, welfare, and protection.

Because government makes and enforces public policy decisions, it is not surprising that people try to influence the officials who make and apply society's rules or policies, nor is it surprising that one important approach is through group action. History shows that people who organize for political action tend to be more effective in achieving their goals than persons acting alone. This is particularly true if a group is well financed. Money plays a big role in state government and state elections, and groups that help politicians finance their campaigns often achieve their goals.

# ★ Interest Groups in the Political Process

When people attempt to influence political decisions or the selection of the men and women who make decisions, they usually turn either to political parties (examined in the chapter "Political Parties") or to interest groups (the subject of this chapter).

## What Is an Interest Group?

An **interest group** may be identified as a pressure group, special-interest group, or lobby. It is an organization whose members share common views and objectives. To promote their interests, such groups engage in activities designed to influence government officials and policy decisions. During the 2005 regular legislative session, the interest groups in action included the Independent Colleges and Universities of Texas (ICUT), which lobbied the legislature against cuts for the Texas Equalization Grants (TEG) and Texas Grants Scholarship programs for college students. Included also was the Texas Coalition to Abolish the Death Penalty, which continues to lobby actively for a moratorium on the death penalty. For the 2005 and 2006 special legislative sessions on school finance, parent groups, teacher organizations, and school board associations lobbied for more state money for the state's public schools.

## Political Parties and Interest Groups

Although political parties and interest groups both attempt to influence policy decisions by government officials, they differ in their methods. The principal purpose of party activity is to gain control of government to achieve party goals. In contrast, an interest group seeks to influence government officials (regardless of their party affiliation) to the advantage of the group. Interest groups try to influence policy decisions in the following ways:

- By using persuasion to mobilize members and supporters
- By attempting to sway public opinion
- By building coalitions with other groups with identical or closely related interests in one or more issues
- By obtaining access to key decision makers
- By influencing elections

Generally, an interest group wants government policies implemented in ways that benefit the group without necessarily placing its own members in public office. Economic groups (for example, the Texas Bankers Association) and professional groups (such as the Texas Trial Lawyers Association) serve as vehicles to make their policy preferences known to government officials. As intermediaries for people who share common interests but reside throughout the state, interest groups in effect supplement the formal system of geographic representation used for electing many officeholders. In essence, such organizations

**interest group** An organization that seeks to influence government officials and their policies on behalf of members sharing common views and objectives (e.g., labor union or trade association).

provide an internal system of functional representation. They offer a form of protection for such groups as businesspeople, laborers, farmers, Roman Catholics, Latinos, teachers, physicians, and college students across the state. These groups are composed of people who have similar interests but may not constitute a majority in any city, county, legislative district, or state.

## Factors Fostering Interest Group Formation

The growth and diversity of interest groups in the United States continue unabated. An increasingly complex society has much to do with the rate of proliferation of interest groups in the country and within states. Political scientists Burnett Loomis and Allan Cigler contend that these growing numbers, plus high levels of activity, distinguish contemporary interest group politics from previous eras.[1] Interest groups proliferate in Texas and throughout the country for several reasons.

**Legal and Cultural Influences**    In *NAACP* v. *Alabama* (1958), the U.S. Supreme Court recognized the **right of association** as part of the right of assembly granted by the First Amendment of the U.S. Constitution. This decision greatly facilitated the development of interest groups, ensuring the right of individuals to organize for political, economic, religious, and social purposes.

The nation's political culture has traditionally encouraged individuals to organize themselves into a bewildering array of associations—religious, fraternal, professional, and recreational, among others. Americans have responded by creating literally thousands of such groups. Social movements during the 1960s and 1970s also sparked interest group activity. New groups formed on issues surrounding civil rights, women's rights, and opposition to the Vietnam War. In Texas, controversies over social issues (e.g., ban on same-sex marriage) and education policy issues (e.g., school finance) have sparked new groups and revitalized existing interest groups.

**Decentralized Structures of Governance**    In a **decentralized government,** power is not concentrated at the highest level. Decentralization is achieved in two principal ways. First, the federal system divides power between the national government and the 50 state governments (as explained in the chapter "Federalism and the Texas Constitution"). In turn, each state shares its power with a wide variety of local governments, including counties, cities, and special districts. Second, within each level of government, power is separated into three branches or departments: legislative, executive, and judicial. This separation of powers is especially apparent at the national and state levels.

A decentralized structure increases the ability of interest groups to influence governmental activities. This structure provides different access points for groups to fight their battles at different levels of government and within different branches at each level. Dispersal of power within branches or departments of government enhances an interest group's chance of success. Divided power also makes public officials more vulnerable to the influence of interest groups.

**right of association**
The U.S. Supreme Court has ruled that this right is part of the right of assembly guaranteed by the First Amendment of the U.S. Constitution and that it protects the right of people to organize into groups for political purposes.

**decentralized government**    Decentralization is achieved by dividing power between national and state governments and separating legislative, executive, and judicial branches at both levels.

**Decentralized Party System and Deemphasized Ideologies**   Two other factors have precipitated interest group activity: a decentralized political party system and deemphasized ideologies. First, the absence of unified and responsible political parties magnifies opportunities for influential interest group action. A lack of strong, organized political parties can particularly affect policymakers (both state and local). By contrast, a united, cohesive party can provide policymakers with a concrete agenda and political strength to resist pressure from well-organized interest groups. In recent years, Texas has experienced stronger party competition, which should produce more party unity, but interest groups continue to exert heavy influence over state officials. Second, ideologies—well-developed systems of political, social, and economic beliefs—traditionally have not been strong factors in Texas politics. Texas voters do not typically act in accordance with their commitment to ideological beliefs, although recently conservative political ideas have increased in importance for many Texans, especially supporters of Republican candidates. The Christian Coalition and similar organizations have spurred this new wave of political activism among social conservatives.

---

**Learning Check 6.1**      **(Answers on p. 234)**

**1.** True or False: Similar to political parties, interest groups are interested in shaping public policy.
**2.** Name five factors that foster interest group formation.

---

# ★ Organization of Interest Groups

As defined, an interest group is an organization of individuals who seek to influence government decisions, usually without trying to place its members in public office. Individuals join an interest group for a variety of reasons, whether financial, professional, or social. In some cases, people join an interest group simply because they want to join a network of like-minded individuals working for a cause. The interest group often provides members with information and benefits and usually tries to involve them in the political process. Such a description suggests that any organization becomes an interest group when it influences or attempts to influence governmental decisions.

## Organizational Patterns

There are almost as many **organizational patterns** as there are interest groups. This variety arises from the fact that, in addition to lobbying, most interest groups carry on nonpolitical functions of paramount importance to their members. A religious organization, for example, emphasizes charitable and spiritual activities, but it may undertake political activity.

Some interest groups are highly centralized organizations that take the form of a single controlling body without affiliated local or regional units. An example of such a centralized group currently operating in Texas is the National Rifle

**organizational pattern**
Some interest groups have a decentralized pattern of organization (e.g., the AFL-CIO, with many local and unions). Others are centralized (e.g., the National Rifle Association, which is a national body without affiliated local or regional units).

Association (NRA). Other groups are decentralized, consisting of loose alliances of local and regional subgroups. Their activities may be directed at either the local, state, or national level. Many trade associations (such as the Texas Mid-Continent Oil and Gas Association) and labor unions (such as those affiliated with the American Federation of Labor–Congress of Industrial Organizations [AFL-CIO]) are examples of decentralized organizations active in Texas politics. Groups with national organizations, including the National Women's Political Caucus and Common Cause, usually have both state and local chapters in Texas.

### Membership and Leadership

Interest groups are composed chiefly of persons from professional and managerial occupations. These individuals tend to have greater resources than most people possess. For instance, members are more likely to be homeowners with high levels of income and formal education who enjoy a high standard of living. Participation, especially active participation, varies. Many citizens are not affiliated with any group, whereas others are members of several. One study found that more than two-thirds of all Americans belong to at least one group or association.[2]

An organized group of any size is usually composed of an active minority and a passive majority. As a result, decisions are regularly made by relatively few members. These decision makers may range from a few elected officers to a larger body of delegates representing the entire membership. Organizations generally leave decision making and other leadership activities to a few people. Widespread apathy among rank-and-file members and the difficulty of dislodging entrenched leaders probably account for limited participation in most group decisions.

Other factors influence **group leadership**. These include the financial resources of the group (members who contribute most heavily usually have greater weight in making decisions); time-consuming leadership duties (only a few people can afford to devote much of their time without compensation); and the personality traits of leaders (some individuals have greater leadership ability and motivation than others).

> **Learning Check 6.2**        **(Answers on p. 234)**
>
> **1.** True or False: In addition to lobbying, most interest groups also have nonpolitical functions.

## ⭐ Classification of Interest Groups

The increasing diversity of American interest groups at the national, state, and local levels of government permits them to be classified in several ways. Not only can they be studied by organizational patterns (as we discussed above), they can also be categorized according to the level or branch of government to which they direct their attention. Some groups exert influence at all levels of government and on legislative, executive (including administrative), and judicial officials. Others may try to spread their views among the general public

**group leadership**
Leaders of groups tend to have financial resources that permit them to contribute money and devote time to group affairs.

and may best be classified according to the subject matter they represent. Some groups do not fit readily into any category, whereas others fit into more than one. In the next section, various types of interest groups are examined—from economic groups, professional and government employee groups, and social groups to public interest groups.

### Economic Groups

Many interest groups exist primarily to promote their members' economic self-interest. These organizations are commonly known as **economic interest groups**. Traditionally, many people contribute significant amounts of money and time to obtain financial benefits. Thus, some organizations exist to further the economic interests of a broad group, such as trade associations, while others seek to protect the interests of a single type of business, such as restaurant associations. The Texas Association of Business and Chambers of Commerce is an example of a broader type of interest group, known as an umbrella organization. Then there are individual corporations, such as communications giant AT&T, that use the political process to promote a company's particular economic interests.

**Business Groups** Businesspeople understand they have common interests that may be promoted by collective action. They were among the first to organize and press national, state, and local governments to adopt favorable public policies. **Business organizations** typically advocate lower taxes, a lessening or elimination of price and quality controls by government, and minimal concessions to labor unions. At the state level, business organizations most often take the form of trade associations (groups that act on behalf of an industry). The newly formed Texas Gaming Association, as well as the Amusement and Music Operators of Texas (a trade group representing bars and taverns), were among interest groups that lobbied the state legislature in 2005 in support of gambling interests. Some of the many other Texas trade associations are the Texas Association of Builders, the Texas Good Roads and Transportation Association, and the Texas Coalition for Affordable Insurance Solutions. (See Table 6.1 for a partial list of Texas trade associations.)

In past legislative sessions, Texas businesses and their representatives succeeded in having many of their policy preferences enacted into law. Some reports indicate that the Texas Association of Business and Texans for Lawsuit Reform contributed more than $2.6 million to support Republican candidates in key legislative races in 2002. Subsequently, the GOP-controlled 78th Legislature passed several "business friendly" bills. One of these bills limited lawsuits against manufacturers, pharmaceutical companies, and retailers.[3] In 2005, the Texas Association of Business and Chambers of Commerce credited the Texas Legislature with providing a strong pro-business climate. During the special legislative sessions of that year, business groups successfully lobbied against tax reform proposals that would shift the cost of school finance from property taxes to increased business taxes.

**economic interest group** Trade associations and labor unions are classified as economic interest groups because they are organized to promote policies that will maximize profits and wages.

**business organization** An economic interest group, such a trade association (e.g., Texas Association of Builders) that lobbies for policies favoring Texas business.

*AFL-CIO rally in Texas* (Courtesy of Ed Sills, Director of Communications, Texas AFL-CIO)

**Government Employee Groups**   Officers and employees of state and local governments organize to obtain better working conditions, higher wages, more fringe benefits, and better retirement packages. The Texas State Employees Union, for instance, lobbies for legislation that prevents job cuts and increases pay and health care. Teacher groups made headway in the 76th legislative session, when Senate Bill 5 allocated $2 billion to fund a $3,000 pay raise for every public school teacher, librarian, and registered school nurse in Texas. Building on their momentum, teacher groups successfully pushed a plan to fully or partially fund state-supported health insurance for public school teachers and other school employees, both active and retired. But when the 78th Legislature faced a budget crisis in 2003, teacher groups unsuccessfully lobbied the legislature against cuts in education funding. These groups included the Texas State Teachers Association (TSTA), Texas Federation of Teachers (TFT), Texas Association of College Teachers (TACT), and Texas Community College Teachers Association (TCCTA). According to the Texas State Teachers Association, 39 bills that the organization opposed were defeated in the 2003 legislative session. During the 2005 regular legislative session and two special sessions, as well as in a 2006 special session, teacher organizations lobbied against school finance legislation they believed would provide inadequate new funding and would intrude on local control of school matters.

Among state government employees, the largest group is the Texas Public Employees Association (TPEA). City government groups include the Texas City

*Table 6.2*   Texas Professional and Occupational Associations

**Health Related**

Texas Dental Association
Texas Health Care Association
Texas Hospital Association
Texas Medical Association
Texas Ophthalmological Association

**Law Related**

Criminal Defense Attorneys Association
Texans for Lawsuit Reform
Texas Civil Justice League
Texas Trial Lawyers Association

**Education Related**

Texas Federation of Teachers
Texas Association of College Teachers
Texas Classroom Teachers Association
Texas Congress of Parents and Teachers
Texas Community College Teachers Association
Texas State Teachers Association

**Miscellaneous**

Association of Engineering Geologists
Cotton Growers Co-operative Association
Texas Family Planning Association
Texas Society of Architects
Texas Society of Certified Public Accountants
Texas Transportation Society

Management Association and the Texas City Attorneys Association. Through their organizational activities, **public officer and employee groups** resist efforts to reduce the size of state and local governmental bureaucracies (although not always with success). The County Judges and Commissioners Association of Texas and the Justices of the Peace and Constables Association of Texas, for example, have been instrumental in blocking measures designed to reform justice of the peace courts and county courts in Texas.

## Social Groups

Texas has a wide array of **social interest groups**. These include racial and ethnic organizations, civil rights organizations, gender-based organizations, religious-based organizations, and several public interest groups.

**public officer and employee group** An organization of city managers, county judges, or other public employees or officials that lobbies for public policies that protect group interests.

**social interest group** Included among groups concerned primarily with social issues are organizations devoted to civil rights, racial and ethnic matters, religion, and public interest protection.

**Racial and Ethnic Groups**    Leaders of **racial and ethnic groups** recognize that only through effective organizations can they hope to achieve their cherished goals. Examples of these goals include eliminating racial discrimination in employment, improving public schools, increasing educational opportunities, and obtaining greater representation in state legislatures, city councils, school boards, and other policymaking bodies of government.

One formidable group, the National Association for the Advancement of Colored People (NAACP), is an effective racial group. The organization has been successful in influencing public policies relating to school integration and local government redistricting. The NAACP also fought for hate crimes legislation that enhances penalties for crimes based on race, color, disability, religion, national origin, gender, or sexual preferences.[4] The organization continues to fight against racial profiling. Texas law defines racial profiling as an action by law enforcement based on an individual's race, ethnicity or national origin as opposed to the individual's behavior or information identifying the individual as engaged in criminal activity.

In Texas, Latino groups, especially Mexican American organizations, are more numerous than African American groups. The oldest Latino group, the League of United Latin American Citizens (LULAC), was founded in 1929. (See Selected Reading 6.1, "Unsung Hero of Civil Rights," for information on founder Alfonso S. Perales.) LULAC has worked for equal educational opportunities for Latinos, as well as full citizenship rights. It continues to advocate for adequate public-school funding, as well as the Ten Percent Rule to diversify institutions of higher education. More recently, LULAC pressed for state funds to open the new school of pharmacy at Texas A&M–Kingsville, named after the late state legislator and strong advocate for higher education, Irma Rangel. Another organization, the Mexican American Legal Defense and Education Fund (MALDEF), uses court action to obtain political equality and representation for Latinos. Both LULAC and MALDEF have been instrumental in addressing inequitable funding allocations for public schools serving Latino children and for state universities in South Texas.

MALDEF filed a case challenging the 2003 redrawing of congressional districts by the Republican-controlled state legislature. The case was heard by the U.S. Supreme Court in 2006. MALDEF charged that the new redistricting scheme had diluted the voting strength of Latinos and African Americans in violation of the Voting Rights Act. MALDEF, on behalf of the American G.I. Forum and LULAC, also filed a lawsuit against the Texas Education Agency for failing to adequately enforce Texas's bilingual education requirements.

On a different issue, a coalition composed of MALDEF, LULAC, and the NAACP lobbied against a 2005 congressional proposal that would require voters to present photo identification at polling places. Civil rights advocates claimed that the proposal would have the effect of intimidating the elderly, minorities, and first-time voters.

**Women's Groups**    The Women's Political Caucus of Texas is an example of a **women's organization** that promotes equal rights and greater participation by

**racial and ethnic groups** Organizations such as the National Association for the Advancement of Colored People and the League of United Latin American Citizens, which seek to influence government decisions affecting African Americans and Latinos, respectively.

**women's organization** A women's group, such as the League of Women Voters, that engages in lobbying and educational activities to promote greater political participation by women and others.

women in the political arena. The League of Women Voters of Texas is a non-partisan organization advocating greater political participation and public understanding of governmental issues. It also assists voters in becoming better informed by publishing *The Texas Voters Guide*, which provides information about elections, candidates, and candidates' positions on various issues.

The Texas Federation of Republican Women, a partisan interest group with about 170 local chapters in mid-2006, provides resources for women to influence government actions and policies. This organization actively encourages Republican women to run for public office. Other interest groups, such as the Hispanic Women's Network of Texas (HWNT) center on the concerns and needs of Hispanic women. HWNT is a statewide organization dedicated to advancing the interests of Hispanic women in the public, corporate, and civic arenas.

**Religious-Based Groups** The Christian Coalition is an example of a **religious-based group.** With millions of Texans identifying themselves as conservative Christians, the organization has emerged as one of the state's most influential political forces. This interest group engages in political action, primarily within the Republican Party. Issues that have precipitated the Christian Coalition's entrance on the political scene are abortion, homosexuality, limits on prayer in public schools, and the decline of the traditional nuclear family.[5]

In 1995, Cecile Richards (daughter of former governor Ann Richards) played a leading role in organizing the Texas Freedom Network to oppose the Christian Coalition. Others created a similar group, the Texas Freedom Alliance. Both organizations watch the activities of right-wing conservatives, muster liberal and mainstream voters, and provide an alternative voice on current political issues.[6] The Texas Faith Network, also formed in 1996, calls on religious leaders statewide to resist Christian Coalition tactics intended to influence political conservatives (usually Republicans). More recently, the Texas Freedom Network has been battling pro–school-voucher forces and advocates of intelligent design who promote teaching a competing theory to evolution theory in the public schools.

Another religious-based organization, the Texas Industrial Areas Foundation (IAF), operating in cities such as Dallas and in the Rio Grande Valley, supports increased funding for parent and teacher training and for making it easier for children to qualify for Medicaid benefits.[7] Valley Interfaith, made up primarily of churches and schools, has successfully lobbied the Brownsville school district to increase wages for employees and indirectly influenced other public institutions and companies to provide a living wage for their workers. In 2005, Valley Interfaith actively lobbied the state legislature demanding restoration of funds cut from the Children's Health Insurance Program, increases in Medicaid funding, and increases in state funding for public schools, as well as an equitable tax system that does not burden the poor. In addition, sister organizations in San Antonio—Communities Organized for Public Service (COPS) and Metro Alliance—successfully lobbied the 77th Legislature to pass a bill that allows cities to use sales tax revenue to create job training and early childhood development programs.[8]

**religious-based group**
An interest group such as the Christian Coalition or the Texas Faith Network that lobbies for policies promoting its religious interests.

Table 6.3    Texas Public Interest Groups

**Consumer**

Consumers Union
Texas Citizen Action
Texas Consumer Rights Action League

**Environmental**

Environmental Action for Texas Residents Against Petrochemical Encroachment
Texas Wildlife Association

**Public Participation**

Association of Community Organizations for Reform Now (ACORN)
Communities Organized for Public Service (COPS)
Public Citizen / Texas
Texas League of Women Voters

**Public Morality**

American Family Association
Mothers Against Drunk Driving (MADD)
National Organization for the Reform of Marijuana Laws (NORML)
Texas Right to Life Committee
Texas Abortion Rights Action League

## Public Interest Groups

Unlike most interest groups, **public interest groups** claim to promote the general interests of society rather than narrower private or corporate interests. Environmental, consumer, political participation, and public morality organizations are often identified as public interest groups.

Public interest organizations pursue diverse goals. Common Cause of Texas, for example, focuses primarily on governmental and institutional reform. It supports open-meeting laws, public financing of political campaigns, stricter financial disclosure laws, and recorded votes in legislative chambers. Texans for Public Justice supports efforts toward campaign finance reform, such as limitations on campaign contributions by political action committees and individuals. Likewise, the Texas League of Conservation Voters monitors the voting records of members in the state legislature that support environment-friendly "green" bills. (See Table 6.3 for a partial list of Texas public interest groups.)

**public interest group**
An organization claiming to represent a broad public interest (environmental, consumer, civil rights) rather than a narrow private interest.

## Texas Power Groups

Texas legislators readily identify the types of interest groups they consider most powerful: business-oriented trade associations (oil and gas, chemical industry, and insurance), professional associations (physicians, lawyers, and teachers), and labor unions. Other groups wielding considerable influence include brewers, truckers, automobile dealers, bankers, and realtors. Some of the most influential interests groups operating in Texas and nationwide are general business organizations (e.g., chambers of commerce), school teacher associations, utility companies, insurance companies and associations, hospital and nursing home associations, and bar associations for lawyers.[9]

Interest groups typified as **power groups** have several common traits. For one, these groups maintain strong linkages with legislators (whose policy decisions affect group interests) and with bureaucrats (whose regulatory authority controls activities of group members). They often are repeat players in Texas politics, meaning they have been influencing politics in consecutive legislative sessions over a long period of time.

Another indication of power-group influence is having headquarters in Austin. Many business-related associations, for example, own a headquarters building in the capital city. Others lease or rent buildings and office suites there. This proximity provides regular contact with state officials and gives such associations a path to influence in state government.[10] In some cases, according to watchdog organizations, interest groups have received free use of meeting rooms in the Texas Capitol for receptions.

Among the most influential business power groups operating in Texas are the Alliance for Responsible Energy Policy (representing the Texas Railroad Association), the Texas Mining and Reclamation Association, the Association of Electric Companies of Texas, and the Texas Taxpayers and Research Association. Other powerful interest groups include the Texas Conference for Homeowners' Rights, the Texas Bankers Association, the Independent Bankers Association of Texas, and the Texas Credit Union League.

Another increasingly influential group is the Texas Medical Association (TMA). With a well-organized grassroots network, a skilled lobbying team, and more than 40,000 physicians licensed in Texas, TMA is one of Texas's most powerful professional groups. According to the TMA's figures, the group succeeded in passing as much as 90 percent of their agenda items in the late 1990s.[11] In 2003, the TMA successfully lobbied for passage of Proposition 12 concerning medical malpractice lawsuits. Two years later, this association claimed success in defeating most bills that it opposed during the 79th regular session of the Texas Legislature.

---

**Learning Check 6.3**       **(Answers on p. 234)**

1. True or False: All interest groups have one aspect in common, to promote their self-interest.
2. Which are generally more powerful in Texas, business interest groups or labor groups?
3. Which religious organization has emerged as one of Texas's most influential political forces?

**power group** An effective interest group strongly linked with legislators and bureaucrats for the purpose of influencing decision making and having a continuing presence in Austin as a "repeat player" from session to session.

*Lobbyists huddle in the halls of the state Capitol in hopes of speaking with state legislators.   (Harry Cabluck / AP-Wide World Photos)*

state officials), their tool of influence is the information and research they convey to state legislators.

In addition, because the process requires careful strategy, the lobbyist chooses the most appropriate time and place to speak with an official and determines how best to phrase arguments to have a positive impact. For maximum effectiveness in using this technique, a lobbyist must select the proper target (for example, a key legislative committee chair, regulatory agency administrator, county commissioner, or city zoning board member). Successful lobbyists rely heavily on computers, calculators, pagers, cellular telephones, Internet communications, and other high-tech devices to store and communicate information. In fact, an important study of interest group politics in Texas has concluded that lobbying in the Lone Star State has shifted from an emphasis on personal argument to information-based communications.[13]

A former Texas legislator compared lobbyists to pharmaceutical salespeople who explain new medicines to doctors too busy to keep up with the latest developments. To perform their jobs effectively, successful lobbyists should clearly indicate the group they represent, define their interests, make clear what they want to do and why, answer questions readily, and provide enough information for politicians to make judgments. Successful lobbyists befriend as many legislators as possible, especially influential legislative leaders like committee chairs, and discover their interests and needs. Lobbyists also put pressure on sympathetic legislators to influence other legislators.

**Favors and Gifts**   Another lobbying technique involves providing favors for legislators and other government decision makers. Common favors include arranging daily or weekly luncheon and dinner gatherings; providing free liquor, wine, or beer; furnishing tickets for entertainment events, air transportation, and

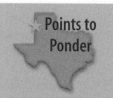
**Points to Ponder**

- At present, no effective laws prohibit former legislators (including former legislative officers) from becoming lobbyists and immediately lobbying former colleagues.
- During the 2003 regular session, 10 former lawmakers from the 2001 regular session served as "revolving-door lobbyists."
- Senator Bill Ratliff (R–Mount Pleasant), a prominent legislator and former acting lieutenant governor, resigned in 2004 and joined his son's lobbying firm.
- According to a report by Texans for Public Justice, five former lawmakers were hired as lobbyists in 2005 and 2006, in some cases by industries that benefited from their work as lawmakers.

athletic contests; and giving miscellaneous gifts. Campaign finance laws place limits on the value of gifts.

**Grassroots Activities**   Yet another influential technique is grassroots lobbying. Interest groups rely heavily on pressure from a grassroots network of organization members and sympathizers. Interest groups attempt to create an image of broad public support for a group's goals—mobilizing support when it is needed. They use such political campaign techniques as direct mailings, television and newspaper advertisements, rallies and demonstrations, and local group action. Recently, the Internet has emerged as a forum for grassroots lobbying. These communication methods are designed to generate information favorable to an interest group's cause and to spread it widely among legislators, other policymakers, and the general public. The Texas State Teachers Association (TSTA) and the National Rifle Association (NRA) are extremely effective at rallying grassroots support.

## Electioneering

Participating in political campaign activities, or **electioneering**, is widespread among interest groups. These activities usually center on particular candidates but may also revolve around issue advocacy. If a candidate who favors a group's goals can be elected, the group has a realistic expectation that its interests will be recognized and protected once the candidate takes office. Interest group participation in the election process takes various forms. Publishing or otherwise publicizing the political records of incumbent candidates is one of the simplest and most common forms of interest group participation. Providing favored candidates with group membership information and mailing lists is another valuable contribution that helps candidates solicit money and votes. Groups may also allow candidates to speak at their meetings, thus giving them opportunities for direct contact with voters and possible media coverage.

During the gubernatorial primary campaigns in 2006, various interest groups publicly endorsed specific candidates. For instance, Governor Rick Perry received endorsements from such groups as the Texas Medical Association (TMA), the

**electioneering** Active campaigning on behalf of a candidate; the total efforts made to win an election.

## POINT/COUNTERPOINT

### Should Campaign Contributions Be Limited?

**THE ISSUE**　Most observers of Texas politics would agree that money plays a big role in political campaigns. There is less agreement on whether or not Texas needs strict campaign finance laws. The following are some of the most common arguments that address this issue.

**Arguments For Limiting Campaign Contributions**

1. Current federal law requires caps on all campaign contributions by individuals and PACs for federal elections.
2. Without a cap on campaign contributions, money will control politics, and wealthy individuals and PACs will have tremendous influence in public policymaking.

   *"Wealthy individuals, businesses and lobby interests write the big checks that have thrown Lone Star democracy out of balance."*

   —Craig McDonald, Director for Texans for Public Justice

**Arguments Against Limiting Campaign Contributions**

1. Campaign contributions to political candidates are still considered a form of freedom of expression protected by the U.S. Constitution.
2. Campaign contributions to candidates and public officials guarantee only access, not policy outcomes.

   *"It never ceases to amaze that people are so cynical they want to tie money to issues, money to bills, money to amendments."*

   —Tom DeLay, former U.S. Representative

Texas Public Employees Association, the Texas Municipal Police Association, and the Texas State Association of Firefighters. In contrast, Democratic gubernatorial candidate Chris Bell gained support from various organizations, such as the Houston Federation of Teachers, the Mexican American Democrats of Texas, and Texas blogs such as the Jeffersonian, the Red State, and the Advocate. Carole Keeton Strayhorn, running as an Independent, received endorsement from the 65,000-member Texas State Teachers Association (TSTA); this was the first time the TSTA endorsed a Republican officeholder for another statewide office. In an effort to win the votes of public school teachers, Strayhorn advocated salary increases for educators and renounced her previous support for school vouchers. The Texas AFL-CIO endorsed Chris Bell in its 2006 state convention.

Another type of group participation in electioneering involves "getting out the vote"—the favorable vote. Typically, increasing favorable voter turnout entails mailing campaign propaganda, making telephone calls to members, registering voters, transporting voters to the polls, and door-to-door canvassing (soliciting votes). Group members may also volunteer their time to the campaigns of sympathetic candidates. Regarding the controversial constitutional amendment banning same-sex marriages, groups on both sides of the issue worked diligently in 2005 to get the vote out in their favor. The Liberty Legal

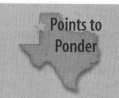

In 2005, a newly formed PAC centered on parents' concerns with the school funding system. Calling itself the Texas Parent PAC, the nonpartisan group endorses House and Senate candidates who support their principles, which include:

■ Adequate and equitable funding to meet state and national standards
■ Local control of public education
■ Quality teachers and educators for children
■ Public money for public schools
■ State testing and an accountability system for children

*Source:* Katherine Cromer Brock, "Group Will Evaluate State Candidates and Give Parents a Voice," *Fort Worth Star-Telegram,* November 26, 2005; Ellen Jones, "Proud of Texas Schools," *Dallas Morning News,* August 17, 2005.

**Points to Ponder**

Institute and the Texas Eagle Forum, for instance, supported the ban, while a coalition group calling themselves No Nonsense in November opposed the ban.

### Campaign Financing by Political Action Committees

Because political campaigns are becoming more expensive with each election, contributions from interest group members constitute an important form of participation. Although individuals continue to make personal financial contributions to candidates, more campaign funds are coming from **political action committees** (PACs). Texas statutes prohibit political contributions by corporations and labor unions to individual candidates. These and other groups, however, may form PACs composed of their employees or members. PACs have the task of raising funds and distributing financial contributions to candidates who are sympathetic to their cause. A PAC may also influence political campaigns involving issues that affect the group's vital interests. Currently, Texas imposes no limits on what PACs (or individuals for that matter) can raise or spend in the state. During the 2005 legislative session, a proposal to place a $100,000 limit on individual contributions to state candidates in each two-year election cycle was defeated. The proposal targeted the influence of wealthy "mega-donors" that account for a significant percentage of the money given during election campaigns.

PAC activities and their influence continue to increase. Close to 1,000 PACs were reported in Texas in 2002, and 850 PACs were reported in 2004.[14] (See Table 6.4 for a listing of some of the top Texas PACs.) During the congressional elections of 2004, Texas ranked third among the most populous U.S. states in overall PAC contributions (see "How Do We Compare"). Reports during the 2004 election cycle note that PAC contributions were dominated by business PACs (accounting for 67 percent of the total); ideological PACs (which emphasize liberal or conservative leanings, such as the Texans for a Republican Majority PAC); and single-issue PACs (such as All Children Matter, Texas) accounted for 26 percent, while PACs representing labor (such as the Fort Worth Firefighters)

**political action committee** An organizational device used by corporations, labor unions, and other organizations to raise money for campaign contributions.

### How Do We Compare . . . in Total PAC Contributions for the 2004 Congressional Election?

| Most Populous U.S. States | Total Contributions | Percentage Given to Democrats | Percentage Given to Republicans |
|---|---|---|---|
| California | $241,235,735 | 58.5 | 41 |
| Florida | 24,220,144 | 36.7 | 63 |
| New York | 178,666,489 | 68 | 31.5 |
| Texas | 130,844,852 | 30.5 | 69.3 |
| U.S. States Bordering Texas | | | |
| Arkansas | 12,131,791 | 43.4 | 56.4 |
| Louisiana | 25,405,562 | 39 | 60.9 |
| New Mexico | 10,462,520 | 56.6 | 42.9 |
| Oklahoma | 14,664,532 | 40.6 | 59.3 |

Source: **www.opensecrets.org/states**

accounted for only 7 percent of the total. In all, these PACs spent more than $68 million.[15]

Preliminary reports before the 2006 gubernatorial primaries in June showed Governor Rick Perry had raised over $24 million from special interests in energy and natural resources as well as other businesses. Democratic nominee Chris Bell had collected over $2 million in campaign contributions, primarily from lawyers and lobbyists. Independent candidate Carole Keeton Strayhorn reported over $12 million received from finance interests, as well as lawyers and lobbyists. Kinky Friedman, another independent candidate, had raised over $3 million from business interests.[16]

Perhaps the best indication of power among interest groups is the connection between the election campaign contributions of PACs and lobbying activities. It takes a coordinated effort on the part of an interest group to influence one part of the political process (the campaign) while also affecting policy decisions in another part (the legislative process). In this way, interest groups can exercise far greater control over the output of the Texas Legislature than their numbers would indicate.

### Bribery and Unethical Practices

Bribery and blackmail, although not common in Texas, nevertheless have taken place in state and local government. There were, for example, several well-publicized scandals in the 1950s involving Texas legislators. In the 1970s, the Sharpstown Bank scandal rocked the legislature. House Speaker Gus Mutscher (D-Brenham) and others were convicted of conspiring to accept bribes for passing deposit-insurance bills as requested by Houston banker Frank Sharp.

*Table 6.4*    Top Ten Texas PACs in Spending and by Interest Category, 2003–2004

| Donor | 2004 Spending | Category |
|-------|---------------|----------|
| Texans for Lawsuit Reform | $3,105,386 | Ideological |
| Texas Association of Realtors | $2,967,081 | Real Estate |
| Republican Party of Texas* | $1,927,676 | Ideological |
| Texas Democratic Party* | $1,922,185 | Ideological |
| Texas Medical Association | $1,919,026 | Health |
| Texans for Insurance Reform | $1,911,888 | Lawyers/Lobbyists |
| Associated Republicans of Texas | $1,688,087 | Ideological |
| Texas Trial Lawyers Association | $1,665,284 | Lawyers/Lobbyists |
| Valero Refining & Marketing | $1,607,132 | Energy/Natural Resources |
| SBC TX Employee PAC | $1,167,318 | Communications |

*Source:* Texans for Public Justice at **www.tpj.org/reports/txpacs04/Vbiggest.html**
*TPJ identifies political parties as an ideological interest category.

Following the scandal, the state legislature passed a law prohibiting speaker candidates from giving anything of value to a supportive legislator as a means of being elected as speaker. The law requires separate finance committees for election as a representative and for the speaker's race.

In February 1980, as revealed by an FBI investigation, House Speaker Billy Clayton (D-Springlake) accepted (but did not spend) $5,000 intended to influence the awarding of a state employee insurance contract. Because he had not cashed the checks, a federal district court found Clayton innocent of all bribery charges. In January 1981, he was elected to a fourth term as speaker of the House. After eight years as Speaker, Clayton left the House to become a lobbyist.

*Table 6.5*    PAC Spending by Interest Category, Ranked by No. of Active PACs, 2004

| Interest Category | No. of Active PACs | 2004 Spending |
|-------------------|--------------------|---------------|
| Ideological | 278 | $17,789,167 |
| Labor | 79 | $4,512,391 |
| Construction | 68 | $4,615,275 |
| Energy/Natural Resources | 54 | $5,539,115 |
| Health | 52 | $5,656,252 |
| Miscellaneous Business | 48 | $2,432,734 |
| Lawyers/Lobbyists | 44 | $11,487,862 |
| Finance | 38 | $3,167,020 |
| Real Estate | 33 | $4,801,603 |
| Agriculture | 27 | $1,504,376 |

*Source:* Texans for Public Justice at **www.tpj.org/reports/txpacs04/III_byinterest.html**

In 1991, five-time Speaker Gib Lewis (D–Fort Worth) was indicted on two misdemeanor ethics charges by a Travis County grand jury. Rather than face the possibility of a trial subjecting him to a stiffer penalty, Lewis agreed to a plea bargain, was fined $2,000, and announced his decision not to seek reelection to the House of Representatives in 1992. He became a successful lobbyist.

More recently, scrutiny centered on state Representative Tom Craddick (R-Midland). Although Texas law prohibits a speaker candidate from giving money to House candidates, in 2002 Craddick donated $20,000 from his reelection campaign to Campaigns for Republican Leadership (CRL), a political action committee. In turn, CRLPAC gave all of its $176,500 to eight GOP House candidates. After Republicans won a majority of House seats, Craddick was elected speaker in January 2003.[17]

Another political action committee, Texans for a Republican Majority (TRMPAC), was organized under the patronage of U.S. House member Tom DeLay (R–Sugar Land). In 2002, TRMPAC was involved in raising money for GOP candidates seeking seats in the Texas House. Later, in cooperation with DeLay, Speaker Craddick played a major role in the success of a 2003 congressional redistricting effort that resulted in the 2004 election of more Republicans in the Texas delegation to the U.S. House of Representatives.

Craddick was not charged with violation of any law, but DeLay and three associates involved with TRMPAC were indicted in 2005 by a Travis County grand jury for money laundering and conspiracy to launder $190,000 of campaign contributions from corporate contributors.[18] After indictment, DeLay was forced to step down as majority leader in the U.S. House of Representatives. Then in June 2006, while awaiting trial, DeLay resigned from his congressional seat. (For more details, see "Redistricting and Electoral Results in Texas in the Twenty-First Century," Selected Reading 7.2 in the following chapter.)

On another matter, in 2006, Governor Rick Perry and other Republican officials were criticized by Democrats in the Texas Legislature for hiring lobbyists with ties to Tom DeLay to represent the state's interest in Washington. Although the Texas Office of State and Federal Relations, a state government agency, is responsible for lobbying there, Perry claimed that Texas needed special help in pressing Congress for additional national disaster relief funds to cover expenses resulting from damage caused by Hurricanes Rita and Katrina in 2005. Some state legislators insisted, however, that these hired lobbyists were not needed because Texans in the U.S. Senate and U.S. House of Representatives hold responsibility for representing the state's interests in Congress.

### Learning Check 6.4    (Answers on p. 234)

1. Name two techniques lobbyists use to influence legislators.
2. Does Texas place limits on PAC contributions, as the federal government does?
3. True or False: At present, Texas forbids corporations to contribute campaign funds directly to state candidates.

## Regulation of Interest Group Politics

Prompted by media reports of big spending by lobbyists and a grand jury investigation into influence peddling, the 72nd Legislature created the eight-member **Texas Ethics Commission** to enforce new legal standards for lobbyists and public officials. This 1991 legislation increased the power of public prosecutors to use evidence that contributions to lawmakers by lobbyists and other individuals are more than mere campaign donations. The legislation also expanded disclosure requirements for lobbyists and legislators, and it put a $500 annual cap on lobbyist-provided food and drink for a lawmaker. The law also bans honoraria (gratuitous payments in recognition of professional services for which there is no legally enforceable obligation to pay) and lobby-paid pleasure trips (unless a legislator makes a speech or participates in a panel discussion). Although state law also requires public officials to disclose any gifts valued over $250 and include a description, the Texas Ethics Commission drew criticism in 2006 when it ruled that public officials need only disclose the existence of a monetary gift without revealing the dollar amount. Overall, there is no indication that campaign contributions from special interests have been reduced.

The ethics law defines any campaign contribution accepted with an agreement to act in the contributor's interest as a felony. The law also prohibits a candidate or official from receiving a contribution in the Capitol itself. The problem, however, is the difficulty in proving a candidate has intentionally accepted a campaign contribution from a particular interest group in exchange for policy benefits.

Detailed records of political contributions and how this money is spent must be filed between two and seven times each year with the Texas Ethics Commission. These records are open to the public and are available on the commission's web site. Candidates for legislative and statewide office are required to file electronic campaign disclosure reports, so that this information can be made instantly available. Current law requires that all candidates file semiannual reports. In contested elections, however, candidates must file itemized contribution and expenditure reports every six months, thirty days, and eight days before the election. Contributions and expenditures in the last two days need not be disclosed until the next semiannual report is due. A study by Texans for Public Justice reports that 102 candidates raised $18.7 million in the primary election of 2002, with $1.7 million comprising last minute contributions. The study also notes that more than $300,000 was contributed in the last two days before the election. Among the top donors were plaintiff attorneys, doctors, and the Republican National State Elections Committee. During the 2006 primary election, several legislative candidates benefited from contributions of a previously dormant PAC. According to political watchdog groups, the Texas Opportunity PAC contributed nearly $300,000 to six Republican house incumbent candidates in the last two weeks of the campaign.[19]

**Texas Ethics Commission** Enforces state standards for lobbyists and public officials, including registration of lobbyists and reporting of political campaign contributions.

On its web site, the Ethics Commission lists the names of lobbyists and their clients, as well as a range of payments received by each lobbyist. However, the commission's records do not give a complete picture. Lobbyists do not have to report exact dollar amounts for their contracts; payment at the top end can range from $200,000 to as much as $5 million.

In addition, the Texas Ethics Commission is authorized to hear ethics complaints against state officials, candidates for office, and state employees, though its budget allows only a limited number of reviews each year. Recent reports indicate that in the past decade 729 external sworn complaints were made to the commission. From 2002 to 2004, a total of 183 sworn complaints were made, and in 2005, there were 42 sworn complaints.[20] The majority of these infractions centered on penalties against campaign and PAC treasurers who failed to file or missed filing reports on contributions, earnings, or expenditures. Reform advocates and others, however, contend that staff members are restricted from investigating complaints because of strict confidentiality rules that expose them to possible criminal prosecution, fines, and jail time.

With ineffective laws in place, questionable connections between lobbyists and legislators are largely unchecked. Governor Rick Perry drew criticism when he first took office after issuing a "strict" revolving-door lobbying policy for his staff, preventing staff members from leaving their employment to become lobbyists. Shortly thereafter, however, he hired senior staff personnel who had been registered as lobbyists during the preceding legislative session. In *Texas Lobby Watch*, Texans for Public Justice concluded that special interests had entered the governor's office through a revolving back door.[21] Likewise, when Tom Craddick first became speaker, he received criticism from watchdog groups for selecting lobbyists with ties to the insurance industry as members of his transition team.

A study by political watchdog group Campaigns for People highlighted the continued relationship between corporate money and politics. Although Texas law prohibits corporate and union funds in political campaigns, "soft money" can be directed to state Republican and Democratic party coffers. These monies can be used for "administrative expenses." The study notes that 79 percent of the state's Republican funds came from corporations in the 2002 election, and 51 percent in the 2004 election. Among Democrats, corporate and union monies accounted for 9 percent of the party's total funding in the 2002 election, and 37 percent in the 2004 election.[22]

A powerful relationship continues between campaign contributions and policy decisions. Sam Kinch (a retired political reporter and founder of the political newsletter *Texas Weekly*) and Anne Marie Kilday (a former capitol correspondent for Texas newspapers) conclude that little has changed since creation of the Ethics Commission. The system is still set up to support incumbents.[23] All recent attempts to significantly reform campaign finance have been defeated. Proposed reforms included contribution limits for individuals and PACs in legislative and statewide races, and full disclosure laws. As columnist Molly Ivins points out, "Texas is the Wild Frontier of campaign financing."[24]

## How Do We Compare . . . in Campaign Finance Laws?

| Most Populous U.S. States | Overall Rankings & State Score[a] | Registration of Lobbyists[b] | Allow Revolving-Door Lobbyists | Lobby Lists Updated |
|---|---|---|---|---|
| California | 8 (71 score) | Yes | No | Daily |
| Florida | 32 (55 score) | Yes | No | Daily |
| New York | 5 (74 score) | Yes | No | Monthly |
| **Texas** | **12 (66 score)** | **Yes** | **Yes** | **Daily** |
| **U.S. States Bordering Texas** | | | | |
| Arkansas | 29 (56 score) | Yes | Yes | Daily |
| Louisiana | 32 (55 score) | Yes | No | Monthly |
| New Mexico | 26 (58 score) | Yes | No | Weekly |
| Oklahoma | 42 (47 score) | Yes | (no information) | Daily |

*Source:* The Center for Public Integrity at **www.publicintegrity.org/default.aspx**

[a]The state's score is determined by the responses to a state survey. Scores of 60 to 69 are classified as barely passing.
[b]The state requires lobbyists to fill out registration materials.

Following a 2002 review of the Ethics Commission by the Texas Sunset Advisory Commission, the 78th Legislature in 2003 passed H.B. 1606, which renewed the Ethics Commission until 2015. First and foremost, the law strengthened the enforcement powers of the commission. The law also provides stricter disclosure requirements. For example, legislators must disclose the occupation and employer of large donors. Furthermore, reports from elected officials concerning campaign cash on hand, as well as personal financial disclosure statements by municipal officers, are now required. Other features include disclosure reports of lawyer-legislators who seek trial postponements during a legislative session, along with broadened requirements for disclosing conflicts of interest.[25]

### Learning Check 6.5        (Answers on p. 235)

1. True or False: Texas's campaign finance laws often involve disclosure by public officials and lobbyists.

## Interest Group Power and Public Policy

The **political influence of interest groups** is determined by several factors. Some observers argue that a group with a sizable membership, above-average financial resources, knowledgeable and dedicated leadership, and a high degree of unity (agreement on and commitment to goals among the membership) will be able to exert virtually limitless pressure on governmental decision makers. Others point out that the more the aims of an interest group are consistent with broad-based public beliefs or stem from issue networks, the more likely the group is to succeed and wield significant power. They also observe that if interest groups are well represented in the structure of the government

**political influence of interest groups** This highly variable factor depends largely on the size of a group's membership, financial resources, quality of leadership, and degree of unity.

itself, their power will be enhanced materially. Also, it is noted that a structure of weak governments will ordinarily produce strong interest groups.

From a different point of view, others insist that factors external to the group are also highly relevant. Research indicates that a strong relationship exists between the larger socioeconomic conditions in a state and the power of interest groups. These findings have led some observers to conclude that states with high population levels, advanced industrialization, significant per capita wealth, and high levels of formal education are likely to produce relatively weak interest groups and strong political parties. Interestingly, despite a large population, wealth, and such, Texas is among the states with strong interest groups and relatively weak political parties. Compared to other states, scholars rank Texas as one of 26 states where interest groups dominate or fluctuate in power over time.[26]

Three circumstances explain why states such as Texas may not fit the expected pattern. First, many Texas interest groups are readily accepted because they identify with free enterprise, self-reliance, and other elements of the state's individualistic political culture. Most Texans are predisposed to distrust government and its agents but to trust interest groups and their lobbyists. Second, the century-long, one-party Democratic tradition in Texas, and the present one-party Republican trend, have rendered interparty competition negligible. The absence of strong parties and meaningful competition between parties has made Texas government vulnerable to the pressures of strong interest groups and their lobbyists. Finally, the Texas Constitution of 1876 and its many amendments have created state and local governments beset by weak, uncoordinated institutions. Faced with a government lacking sufficient strength to offer any real opposition, interest groups often obtain decisions favorable to their causes.

## ★ Pinpointing Political Power

Assessing the political power and influence that interest groups have in American government is difficult, and determining the extent of their power in Texas is especially complex. There is no simple top-down or bottom-up arrangement. Rather, political decisions (especially policy decisions) are made by a wide variety of individuals and groups. Some of these decision makers participate in local ad hoc (specific-purpose) organizations; others wield influence through statewide groups. Ascertaining which individuals or groups have the greatest influence often depends on the issue or issues involved.

The political influence of any interest group cannot be fairly calculated by looking at the distribution of only one political asset, whether it be money, status, knowledge, organization, or sheer numbers. Nevertheless, we may safely conclude that organized interest groups in Texas often put the unorganized citizenry at a great disadvantage when public issues are at stake.

## ⭐ Looking Ahead

Texas interest groups exert their influence over public policy decisions within local governments, the Texas Legislature, executive departments, the judiciary, and the state's bureaucracy. To be sure, students should be alert to evidence of interest group participation in all levels and branches of Texas government. Nothing better illustrates the power of interest groups in Texas politics than the power they wield in the legislative process, which is the subject of the next chapter, "The Legislature."

## ⭐ Chapter Summary

- Interest groups act in the interests of their members to influence policy decisions made by government officials. Various factors foster interest group formation, such as legal and cultural reasons, a decentralized government and party system, as well as deemphasized ideologies.
- Involvement in an interest group provides members with information and opportunities to become active in the political process.
- Interest groups vary by organizational pattern, membership, and leadership.
- Generally, all interest groups at all levels of government can be classified according to their interests, members, and the public policies they advocate.
- Interest groups are involved in all types and areas of political activity. They serve various functions, which include recruiting candidates for public office, shaping consensus on issues, and providing an outlet for concerned citizens.
- To influence policy decisions, interest groups use several techniques, including lobbying, personal communication, favors and gifts, grassroots activities, electioneering, campaign financing by political action committees (PACs), and in extreme cases resorting to bribery and other unethical or illegal practices.
- An eight-member Texas Ethics Commission is charged with enforcing legal standards for lobbyists and public officials.
- There are various ways to gauge an interest group's potential for political influence, such as the group's size of membership, financial resources, quality of leadership, and the degree of unity among members.
- Interest group participation influences public policy at all levels and within each branch (legislative, executive, judicial) of Texas government, and it allows all members to become a part of the political process.

## Key Terms

- interest group, *p. 207*
- right of association, *p. 208*
- decentralized government, *p. 208*
- organizational pattern, *p. 209*
- group leadership, *p. 210*
- economic interest group, *p. 211*
- business organization, *p. 211*
- labor organization, *p. 213*
- professional group, *p. 213*
- public officer and employee group, *p. 215*
- social interest group, *p. 215*
- racial and ethnic groups, *p. 216*
- women's organization, *p. 216*
- religious-based group, *p. 217*
- public interest group, *p. 218*
- power group, *p. 219*
- interest group techniques, *p. 220*
- lobbying, *p. 221*
- electioneering, *p. 223*
- political action committee, *p. 225*
- Texas Ethics Commission, *p. 229*
- political influence of interest groups, *p. 231*

## Learning Check Answers

### 6.1

1. True. Similar to political parties, interest groups are interested in shaping public policy. But, unlike political parties, interest groups do not necessarily field candidates to run for office.
2. Laws, cultural influences, a decentralized government, a decentralized political party system, and deemphasized ideologies all foster the formation of interest groups.

### 6.2

1. True. In addition to lobbying, most interest groups have nonpolitical functions.

### 6.3

1. False. Unlike most interest groups, public interest groups are interested in promoting the public interest.
2. In Texas, business groups are generally more powerful than labor groups.
3. The Christian Coalition has emerged as one of Texas's most influential political forces.

### 6.4

1. Lobbyists use personal communication as well as favors and gifts to influence legislators.
2. Unlike federal law, Texas law does not limit campaign contributions by PACs.
3. True. Texas law prohibits corporations and unions from directly contributing to campaigns.

**6.5**

1. True. Texas's campaign finance laws often involve disclosure by public officials and lobbyists, although critics would argue that current disclosure requirements are not sufficient to reform the system.

## Discussion Questions

1. What interest groups are you familiar with? If you are not already a member of an interest group, would you consider joining one?
2. Are interest groups beneficial in Texas politics? What are the advantages and disadvantages?
3. Do you think interest groups have too much power in Texas politics?
4. Do you think Texas should have stricter campaign finance law? Or do you think the disclosure laws we currently have suffice?
5. Do you think Texas law should place caps on campaign contributions for individuals and PACS in state elections?
6. What are your recommendations for increasing or decreasing the powers of the Texas Ethics Commission?

## Internet Resources

Common Cause Texas: **www.commoncause.org/states/texas**
League of Women Voters of Texas: **www.lwvtexas.org**
Mexican American Legal Defense and Education Fund (MALDEF):
   **www.maldef.org**
Professional Advocacy Association of Texas: **www.texasadvocacy.com**
Public Citizen/Texas: **www.citizen.org/texas**
Sierra Club, Lone Star Chapter: **texas.sierraclub.org**
Texans for Public Justice: **www.tpj.org/index.jsp**
Texas Community College Teachers Association: **www.tccta.org**
Texas Christian Coalition: **www.texascc.org**
Texas Ethics Commission: **www.ethics.state.tx.us**
Texas League of United Latin American Citizens: **www.txlulac.org**
Texas NAACP: **www.texasnaacp.org**
Texas Public Employees Association: **www.tpea.org**
Texas State Employees Union: **www.cwa-tseu.org**

## ★ Notes

1. Burdett Loomis and Allan Cigler, *Interest Group Politics*, 5th ed. (Washington: Congressional Quarterly Press, 1998), 2.
2. Steffen W. Schmidt, Mack C. Shelley II, and Barbara A. Bardes, *American Government and Politics Today* (Belmont, Calif.: Wadsworth, 1997), 248.

3. Christy Hoppe, "Business Lobby Flexes Muscle in Legislature," *Dallas Morning News*, 12 April 2003.

4. Peggy Fikac, "Perry Signs Hate Crimes Legislation," *San Antonio Express-News*, 12 May 2001.

5. For information on the role of the Christian Coalition, see James Lamare, Jerry L. Polinard, and Robert D. Wrinkle, "Texas: Religion and Politics in God's Country," in *The Christian Right in American Politics: Marching Toward the Millennium*, edited by John C. Green, Mark J. Rozell, and Clyde Wilcox (Washington, D.C.: Georgetown University Press, 2003), 59–78.

6. Peggy Fikac, "Alliance Formed to Monitor Radical Right," *Houston Chronicle*, 1 October 1995.

7. See Dennis Shirley, *Valley Interfaith and School Reform: Organizing for Power in South Texas* (Austin: University of Austin Press, 2002).

8. For a history of COPS, see Mark R. Warren, *Dry Bones Rattling: Community Building to Revitalize an American Democracy* (Princeton, N.J.: Princeton University Press, 2001).

9. Clive S. Thomas and Ronald J. Hrebenar, "2002 State Interest Group Power Update: Results and Tables," manuscript (June 12, 2003), 1, 2, as cited in Ann O'M. Bowman and Richard Kearney, *State & Local Government*, 6th ed. (Boston: Houghton Mifflin, 2005), 122.

10. H. C. Pittman, *Inside the Third House: A Veteran Lobbyist Takes a 50-Year Frolic Through Texas Politics* (Austin: Eakin Press, 1992), 219. See also John Spong, "State Bar," *Texas Monthly* (July 2003), 110–113, 148–149.

11. "Doctors' Orders: Medical Lobby Becomes a Powerhouse in Austin," *Wall Street Journal*, 19 May 1999.

12. "2006 Lobby Lists," Texas Ethics Commission at **www.ethics.state.tx.us/dfs/ loblists.htm**.

13. Keith E. Hamm and Charles W. Wiggins, "Texas: The Transformation from Personal to Informational Lobbying," in *Interest Group Politics in the Southern States*, edited by Ronald J. Hrebenar and Olive S. Thomas (Tuscaloosa: University of Alabama Press, 1992), 80.

14. Texans for Public Justice, "Texas PACs: 2004 Election Cycle Spending," *Texas PAC Reports* (13 September, 2005) at **www.tpj.org/reports/txpacs04/index.html**.

15. "Texas PACs 2004 Election Cycle: Comparing Business, Ideological, and Labor PACs," *Texas PAC Reports* (September 2005), **www.tpj.org**.

16. Texans for Public Justice, "Keeping Texas Weird: The Bankrolling of the 2006 Gubernatorial Race," Major Reports (Sept. 25, 2006) at **www.tpf.org/reports/ governor06/index.html**.

17. Texans for Public Justice, "Craddick-Tied PAC Cash Routed to Just 8 GOP House Candidates," *Lobby Watch*, 2 April 2004, at **www.tpj.org/publication_ list.jsp?typeid=2**

18. See Ralph Blumenthal and Carl Hulse, "Judge Lets Stand 2 of 3 Charges Faced by DeLay," *New York Times*, 6 December 2005; Gary Martin, "Texas Jury Indicts DeLay," *San Antonio Express-News*, 29 September 2005.

19. *The Morning After: Last-Minute Contributions in Texas' 2002 Primary Elections* (October 2002), **www.tpj.org/publications/reports/index.html**. See also Robert Garrett, "PAC's Late Aid Altered Races," *Dallas Morning News*, 10 March 2006.

20. See the web site for the Texas Ethics Commission and search for "sworn complaints."
21. Texans for Public Justice, "New Governor Hires Guns as He Hypes Lobby Ethics Code," *Lobby Watch* (5 January 2001).
22. Lisa Sandberg, "Watchdog Barks at Soft Money Practices," *San Antonio-Express News*, 3 June 2005.
23. See Sam Kinch, Jr. with Anne Marie Kilday, *Too Much Money Is Not Enough: Big Money and Political Power in Texas* (Austin: Campaigns for People, 2000). See also Lisa Sandberg and Kelly Guckian, "Lobbyists' Money Talks—Softly, But It's Heard," *San Antonio-Express News*, 12 April 2006.
24. Molly Ivins, "Who Let the PACs Out? Woof, Woof!" *Fort Worth Star-Telegram*, 18 February 2001.
25. "With Perry's Signature, Texas Campaign Law Will Get Boost They Need," *Austin American-Statesman*, 9 June 2003; Ginger Richardson, "Stronger Ethics Rules Hang on House Vote," *Fort Worth Star-Telegram*, 2 June 2003.
26. Clive S. Thomas and Ronald J. Hrebenar, "2002 State Interest Group Power Update: Results and Tables," manuscript (June 12, 2003), Table 2B, 1–3, as cited in Ann O'M. Bowman and Richard Kearney, *State & Local Government,* 6th ed. (Boston: Houghton Mifflin, 2005), p. 125.

## Selected Readings

## 6.1  Unsung Hero of Civil Rights: "Father of LULAC" a Fading Memory*

### Hector Saldana

*Mexican American civil rights leader Alonso S. Perales is all but a fading memory for most students of Texas politics. Attempts, however, are being made to preserve his collection of papers for students and scholars. This reading sheds light on a Texas hero and on efforts to preserve Perales's papers for an archival collection in a university depository.*

Though he was once hailed as the "Father of LULAC" and a civil rights giant, Alonso S. Perales today is a historical shadow figure, little more than a name frozen on an elementary school building on the West Side [of San Antonio]. Students pass by his portrait daily without much thought, says Perales Elementary School principal Dolores Mena. "The kids know what he looks like, but they don't know what he's done." "He was a most extraordinary man," recalls retired County Commissioner and Municipal Court Judge Albert Pena, a friend who says he is perplexed why such a historic leader is forgotten to a generation. "But he was very well known when I knew him." That was more than 40 years ago. Perales died in 1960 at the age of 61.

A self-made man, highly educated and erudite, Perales was a prolific writer of position papers and books on the second-class status of Mexican Americans, a newspaper columnist, a spokesman at rallies, a foreign diplomat and shaper of laws. He traveled the globe to promote his culture and to fight for its rights—"En defensa de mi raza." "He was the great intellectual of LULAC," says Ed Peña, former LULAC national president in Washington, D.C. "He was our Thomas Jefferson."

In the late 1920s, Perales founded the League of United Latin American Citizens in his image—working alongside other activist-philosophers such as J. T. Canales, Ben Garza, M. C. Gonzalez, Gus Garcia, Carlos Castañeda, George Sanchez, and Jose Luz Saenz to shape its goals.

Perales delineated that vision in a draft of LULAC bylaws: "To develop within the members of our race the best, purest, and most perfect type of true, loyal citizen of the United States." "We are going to show the world that we have just and legitimate aspirations, that we have self-pride, dignity, and racial pride; that we have a very high concept of our American citizenship; that we have a great love of our country," Perales said in a 1943 radio address. . . .

And as politico Romulo Munguia notes, Perales had the wisdom, guts, and skills to "fight the fight in English." Seventy-five years ago, he declared English "the official language" of LULAC and campaigned for Hispanics to be classified as "white" in the census—actions that rankle modern Latinos, many of whom accuse Perales of elitism in light of today's continuing struggle for equality. But the fiery speaker whose persuasive rhetoric often kept LULAC from splintering also considered certain Anglos the enemy, says one family member. Perales' language in 1929 is blunt: "We shall resist and attack energetically all machinations tending to prevent our social and political unification." He was the voice of calm, however. "We should pity and not despise those who are yet in darkness," Perales wrote. Perales was a bridge builder who never forgot where he came from, say those who knew him. His ideas were born of early struggle and poverty.

A dark-skinned Mexican American, Perales was born in Alice in 1898. Orphaned young, he picked cotton in the fields to earn a living and enlisted in the army during World War I. Through guts and determination, and the belief that education could overcome other handicaps, he graduated with a law degree from George Washington University. He passed the Texas State Bar exam in 1925 and became an early civil rights lawyer in San Antonio.

"He was a poor kid that had nothing and it's hard to visualize how he got from this point to that point. He had a vision; he had a dream. I want to say he was like Martin Luther King—but he preceded Martin Luther King," says Carrizales. To his nephew and namesake, Alonso M. Perales, 77, his uncle was down-to-earth "and a real Tejano."

---

*"Unsung Hero of Civil Rights! 'Father of the LULAC' a Fading Memory," by Hector Saldana from *San Antonio Express-News,* September 14, 2003. Copyright © 2003 *San Antonio Express-News.* Reprinted by permission.

In 1931, *La Prensa* called Perales the one American [who] defends Mexicans. His early radio speeches made clear that Mexicans were "thirsty for justice" and had a rightful place in the society they labored to support. By the mid-'40s, he had documented more than 150 towns in Texas with establishments that barred service to Hispanics and wrote about it in the book, "Are We Good Neighbors?" Throughout the '50s, Perales fought for a living wage for braceros. He opposed restrictive covenants that kept Mexican Americans out of certain neighborhoods; he fought the poll tax. His fight against segregation and for equal rights rivals the work of Martin Luther King, say historians and admirers....

Yet for all his work on behalf of Mexican Americans, Perales has all but faded from collective memory. "We don't know how to take care of our heroes," says Dallas attorney Jose Angel Gutierrez, co-founder of La Raza Unida and a guiding light of the Chicano Movement of the '60s and '70s, about Perales' modern obscurity—which he considers a travesty. "[Perales'] history is there for those who seek it out," Houston attorney Alfred J. Hernandez says. "This is a deep story about *nosotros*." It's a story that can be found in a cache of Perales' personal documents—and that has yet to see the light of day.

## Died Too Soon

They say that history belongs to those who write it. Perales' story rests in dozens of moldy boxes once coveted by his widow, a high-strung former opera singer who in later years vacillated between guarding that packaged legacy and threatening to burn the entire lot, says Perales' nephew. The boxes have collected dust since Perales died in 1960. When Marta Perales died a couple of years ago, heirs Raymond Perales and Martha Carrizales—Perales' adopted children—vowed to preserve their father's papers and restore his rightful image. But action has been slow. They eventually asked Henry Cisneros' politically savvy uncle, printer Ruben Munguia, to help sort mountains of pioneering material....

It was Ruben Munguia's last great undertaking, his brother says. He worked meticulously sorting the delicate treasure of documents at his draft table at his Buena Vista Street print shop "because he liked to be around all the action," says Ruben Munguia's daughter Mary Perales. Since his death earlier this year, the project has languished. Brother and sister do what they can in their spare time. As Carrizales pores over reams of her father's delicate documents, she gushes, "It's like learning about a character in history." Perales' collection is voluminous.... Historian and University of Texas associate professor Emilio Zamora agrees and urged the family to deposit the papers at the Mexican American Library Program at the University of Texas because of its "unmatched historical value." In 2001, he wrote to Carrizales: "I honestly believe that Perales is the most important Mexican American leader of the 20th century." Zamora cites Perales' prominence as an author, diplomat, and LULAC officer, and his ties to Latino organizations, civic service, and civil rights activism. "Not only within the Mexican American community, but I think he's a major civil rights leader of the nation," Zamora says.

That the materials are still out of the hands of researchers is a serious issue, he says. There is also a fear that the integrity of the collection could be unintentionally undermined and lose research value. "Anyone who's involved in archival collection will tell you that a collection of that immense value has to be deposited somewhere and processed and then made available for researchers," Zamora says. His hope is that UT gets them ("It's the natural home," he says) because Perales' contemporaries are archived there....

## Not Really 'Radical'

"My mother was a radical and marched with César Chavez," says Carrizales. "Of course, she could afford that. She was bourgeois. My father wouldn't have agreed with the '60s." Certainly Perales' words from the late '20s—"We shall oppose any radical and violent demonstration which may tend to create conflicts and disturb the peace and tranquility of our country"—had no place in the Chicano Movement. "He was a realist," says Chicano leader Gutierrez, who notes that the FBI's surveillance of LULAC started because of Perales' overseas activities. "It was very dangerous to be an activist Mexican at that time, very dangerous. You could lose your life, and people did. This was not a time to stand up and be radical, and what he was doing was perceived to be radical."

Zamora argues that Perales' great achievement was taking the cause of Mexican Americans to international forums. Perales spoke at international conferences; he appealed for nations to put pressure on the United States for Mexican American equal rights. Perales participated in founding meetings of the United Nations in 1945. "At that meeting, he again included the Mexican American in the deliberations of human rights," Zamora explains.

"He was an extraordinary man. If we had him today, I'm telling you, he'd be up in front. And he'd be shaking stuff," Zamora says. "He had conservative ideas, but some of his ideas for that time were pretty radical. He had so much courage and intellect. His stamina and sense of civic responsibility was just tremendous." Many say that the true value of the Perales papers is to put his "conservative" activism in perspective. "It was a very primitive democracy for us," LULAC historian Pena adds. "He was visible when there were very few (Mexican Americans) that were visible…."

He outlined his views in October 1931 in a position paper, "El Mexico Americano y la Politica del Sur Texas." "If we want to accelerate our political evolution, it's imperative that we change the system," wrote Perales, who argued that self-education on issues was more important than party affiliation.

In his eyes, pulling a voting lever blindly was akin to a sin: "It's one thing to vote and know what you're voting for, but it's another thing to do it because someone ordered you to do it and who to vote for," he wrote in Spanish. And though he fought against the poll tax, he urged Latinos to pay it and participate. Former Houston judge Hernandez says that Perales is responsible "for Mexican Americans coming of age" because he was willing to enter *un nido de viboras* (the viper's nest) of an often-racist Texas legal system….

## Lost History

It was only in the '70s that major universities became interested in collecting the papers of major Latino figures. In some cases, that was more than 50 years too late. "Man, I could tell you some stories that would make you cry about stuff we've lost," Zamora says from Austin. "We're lacking in the telling of the story because the historical record is not readily available," Zamora adds.

Sociologist and Mexican American studies expert Avelardo Valdez at the University of Houston says that Perales is "part of a constellation of lost figures" in the Mexican American experience. "It's highly significant and important that these kinds of papers are found, and that they be archived and that we have access to them," says Valdez, adding that the find will show "Perales' founding generation was much more progressive than our generation today. It took a lot of guts to be organizing political organizations in the 1920s and '30s in South Texas…."

Carrizales says her ultimate dream is that researchers will restore her father's legacy. "He was an activist for human dignity—like César Chavez, like Martin Luther King," Carrizales says. "He needs to be recognized, not glorified, for his efforts. History must do him justice. People need a full cup of information." Gutierrez says the Perales papers must be made public sooner rather than later. "It's a way to make him alive again," he said.

# 6.2   "Texas Capitol's Lobby Has a Revolving Door"*

### Lisa Sandberg

*Texans for Public Justice has been vigilant in investigating the role and influence of "revolving-door lobbyists" in the Texas Legislature. This reading highlights recent legislators-turned-lobbyists hired by interest groups to represent their interests.*

## The Path of the Superlobbyists

The day before Ray Allen resigned his seat as a state representative a week ago, he announced he was setting up shop as a lobbyist. By hanging out his shingle, he'll take the expertise and contacts amassed in his seven terms in office representing the public—and put them to work for private concerns. Allen, a Republican from Grand Prairie, is following a well-trampled path in Texas, a way for state lawmakers who are paid only $600 a month to cash in on their insider status. If he continues down the path of the so-

*"Texas Capitol's Lobby Has a Revolving Door" by Lisa Sandberg from *San Antonio Express-News* (January 29, 2006). Reproduced with permission of *San Antonio Express-News* in the format Textbook via Copyright Clearance Center.

called superlobbyists, he will complete the circle by returning to government. An ongoing scandal in Washington has focused on fancy meals and overseas trips for politicians arranged by a highly successful lobbyist, Jack Abramoff, who pleaded guilty this month to corruption and fraud charges. He's now cooperating with federal investigators targeting his former allies in Congress.

In Texas, watchdog groups say ethics reforms in the early 1990s largely have curtailed the wining, dining, and high-priced hotel stays provided by lobbyists and their clients. What those reforms didn't address, the watchdogs say, is the so-called revolving door that can entice public officials to put the priorities of their potential employers ahead of constituents. Over the past 18 months, five state lawmakers who lost or surrendered their elective posts have resurfaced as lobbyists, collectively amassing contracts worth up to $1.7 million from clients whose interests they once affected in the Legislature. Besides Allen, the list includes two former House Republicans, Arlene Wohlgemuth and Todd Baxter; and two former House Democrats, Jaime Capelo and Barry Telford. "They know the secrets that go on behind closed doors, they know the committee members, they know the arguments for and against, and they've got on-the-job training," said Tom "Smitty" Smith, director of the Austin-based Public Citizen. "Their value to (special interests) is enormous."

Andrew Wheat, research director of the watchdog group Texans for Public Justice, also in Austin, said the issue posed serious challenges for democracy. "What does that do to the public's faith in the integrity of their government? "The essential problem is wealthy special interests have better access and representation in Austin than does the general public," he said.

## Need the Money

Allen, 55, who resigned his seat Jan. 20, has said he's merely trying to make ends meets. "The reason is plain and simple: I simply cannot afford to serve on a $600-a-month salary with no other source of income with the prospect that we will soon be in special session until June," Allen, 55, told the Fort Worth *Star-Telegram* last week. Neither Allen, Wohlgemuth, Baxter, nor Capelo returned calls for comment. In a phone interview from DeKalb, where he lives and works part time as a propane dealer, Telford dismissed concerns about wealthy special interests benefiting unfairly by the revolving-door lobby. He said he wasn't ashamed of landing a contract worth as much as $150,000 with the Texas Retired Teachers Association after not seeking reelection in 2004. The private not-for-profit group's nearly 60,000 members have a keen interest in making sure the state's pension system for teachers is fully funded. The group also is working to raise teacher pensions. Telford served for years on the House Pensions and Investments Committee. "The only thing I do is go to the members of the Legislature and talk about things I know," he said.

Though not neutral, lobbyists supply factual information and that alone serves an important function, Telford said, adding he relied on them during his 18 years in office to verse him on the ins and outs of issues. "The people in the state of Texas are busy with their lives. If it hadn't been for the people who knew the issues ... we'd have had a helluva mess," he said. Telford took the lobbying job with the teachers association because he believed in its cause and because it came with the very thing the watchdog groups fear: money.

Lobbyists have been around for about as long as there have been people who want to influence government. They are hired guns used by virtually every industry and interest group in the country. Newspapers employ them, as do pharmaceutical, telecommunications, oil, grocery and auto companies, cities and counties, labor unions and professional associations. They are paid to convince lawmakers to back their clients' particular agendas and they do so with charm, research—and money, sometimes lots of it, often channeled into campaign coffers. Their expertise allows them to write bills, or portions of bills, if a lawmaker wants to help their cause but doesn't know enough about it to draft legislation. Across the country, a hodgepodge of regulation governs lobbyists' relationships with legislators. Texas doesn't ban lawmakers from accepting trips, gifts and fancy meals but it does require that they report any meals or travel worth more than $76.80 per day or gifts worth more than $50 per day. Some states don't require any disclosure. Federal law requires a one-year "cooling off" period before outgoing members of Congress can become lobbyists. According to the Washington-based Center for Public Integrity, Texas is one of 27 states with no such revolving-door ban on its legislators, although Gov. Rick Perry has a limited rule affecting his own senior staff. The other states have either a one- or two-year ban, the latter including Florida, Kentucky, and New York.

What's clear around the country is that reforms almost always follow scandal, said the center's Leah Rush. In Texas, some watchdog groups say the Abramoff mess isn't likely to be scandalous enough to convince state lawmakers to pass a new ethics bill. "I think they'll work in the dark to kill any meaningful reforms," Wheat said. "There are two huge, very powerful (forces)—lawmakers and lobbyists—who'll work to sabotage in the back room whatever might get proposed." Close to 1,400 lobbyists are registered in Texas, and more than 36,000 are registered around the country. Nationally, that works out to be about five lobbyists and almost $130,000 in expenditures per state lawmaker, according to the Center for Public Integrity. Texas has eight lobbyists per state lawmaker, more than most states, and it ranks second only to California in the total value of lobby contracts, according to Texans for Public Justice. The watchdog groups agree that in certain respects, Texas does a fair job of regulating lobbyists. They say the state's disclosure provisions have reined in the luxurious junkets that politicians—Texas House Speaker Gib Lewis among them—were caught taking from special interests in the late 1980s.

## Big Loopholes

But in other areas, Texas laws are weak, they complain. It's one of 42 states to require some disclosure of lobbyists' earnings, but contracts worth $200,000 or more can be disclosed as "$200,000 and more." "So is the contract worth $250,000, $500,000, a million dollars or 2 million dollars? Is that disclosure?" Wheat asked, noting that con-

tracts worth $200,000 or more have shot up from six in 1999 to 39 in 2005. The reforms were considered far-reaching when passed in 1991, Smith said. Today, his group is more concerned with the superconnected revolving-door lobbyist who joins other superconnected lobbyists in a team, Smith said. He refers to people like Mike Toomey, a onetime lobbyist who earlier this decade became Gov. Perry's chief of staff before returning to the Texas lobby group, where he picked up many of his old clients. Critics say the biggest beneficiaries were clients like Texans for Lawsuit Reform, which saw its interests prevail when Toomey served the governor. Four former members of Perry's staff worked as lobbyists both before and after their public service, according to Texans for Public Justice.

Like his predecessor, Perry bars senior staffers from lobbying his office for one year and one legislative session after they depart. The policy says nothing about lobbying the legislature, requires no "cooling off" period for lobbyists hired by the governor, and carries no criminal sanctions. Perry's spokeswoman, Kathy Walt, said hiring lobbyists to senior staff positions has been common practice among Texas governors and is "not something that's peculiar to Perry. The governor hires people he has confidence in and knows and who are good. It would not be good government to hire somebody who doesn't know anything about the Legislature."

If the Abramoff fallout is intense enough, Texas could see reforms in 2007, Smith said. But, he added, no matter how tight you make a loophole, someone will always find a way through. As for Telford, he said his contract with the Retired Teachers Association ends later this year. He's hoping it'll be extended.

---

An extensive bibliography of books and articles for this chapter is posted on Selected Sources for Reading, available online at http://college.hmco.com/PIC/brownPTP13e. For use with any chapter, see Resources for Further Research online at http://college.hmco.com/PIC/brownPTP13e.

# Chapter 7

# The Legislature

- ★ **A Preliminary View**
- ★ **Legislative Framework**
- ★ **Compensation**
- ★ **Membership**
- ★ **Powers and Immunities**
- ★ **Presiding Officers**
- ★ **Committee System**
- ★ **Legislative Caucus System**
- ★ **Procedure**
- ★ **Influences Within the Legislative Environment**

**Points to Ponder**

- A copy of the King James Bible (bearing desk number and state seal on its blue cover) is provided to each senator and representative.
- Some Texas legislators wear official rings and official lapel pins that they purchase at their own expense.
- To protect legislators and others, Department of Public Safety troopers patrol the Capitol and surrounding grounds with dogs trained to sniff for explosives.
- Hung behind the House speaker's rostrum during legislative sessions is the original San Jacinto battle flag, on which is painted a partially bare-breasted woman clutching a sword draped with a streamer proclaiming "Liberty or Death." When legislators are not in session, a reproduction of this flag is displayed, and the original is covered by a curtain.

*general assembly.* In the 49 states with bicameral legislatures, the larger chamber ranges in size from 40 members in Alaska to 400 members in New Hampshire. Texas has 150 members in its House of Representatives. The smaller legislative chamber is called the Senate. Alaska has the smallest senate, with 20 members; Minnesota has the largest, with 67. The Texas Senate has 31 members.

### Election and Terms of Office

Voters residing in representative and senatorial districts elect Texas legislators. Representatives are elected for two years. Senators are usually elected for four

*Floor of the Texas House of Representatives as viewed from the gallery behind the speaker's podium (Texas House of Representatives Photography Department)*

*Visitors watch Senate proceedings from the gallery. (Senate Media Services)*

years. Terms of office for members of both houses begin in January of odd-numbered years.

Legislative redistricting for both the House and the Senate occurs in the first odd-numbered year in a decade (for example, 2001). Voters elect a new House of Representatives in every even-numbered year. After redistricting, a new Senate is elected in the general election of the following year (for example, November 2002). In January of the next odd–numbered year (for example, 2003), Senators draw lots, using 31 numbered pieces of paper sealed in envelopes. The 16 who draw odd numbers get four-year terms, but the 15 who draw even numbers get

## How Do We Compare . . . in State Legislative Seats?

| Most Populous U.S. States | Senate Seats | House Seats* | U.S. States Bordering Texas | Senate Seats | House Seats | Mexican States Bordering Texas | Unicameral *Congreso* Seats |
|---|---|---|---|---|---|---|---|
| California | 40 | 80 | Arkansas | 35 | 100 | Chihuahua | 35 |
| Florida | 40 | 120 | Louisiana | 39 | 105 | Coahuila | 33 |
| New York | 62 | 150 | New Mexico | 42 | 70 | Nuevo León | 52 |
| **Texas** | **31** | **150** | Oklahoma | 48 | 101 | Tamaulipas | 32 |

*Sources: The Book of the States, 2006* (Lexington, Ky.: Council of State Governments, 2006), 72; and Gobiernos y Congresos Estatales de México at **www.cddhcu.gob.mx/virtual/gem/htm.**

*In California and New York, this chamber is called the Assembly.

only two-year terms. Subsequently, about half of the senators (that is, 15 or 16) will be elected in each even-numbered year.

A legislator may be expelled by a two-thirds majority vote of the membership of the legislator's chamber. If a member of the legislature dies, resigns, or is expelled from office, the vacancy is filled by special election. A 2003 constitutional amendment allows a legislator called to active military duty for longer than 30 days to retain the office if he or she appoints a constitutionally qualified temporary replacement of the same political party and if the replacement is approved by the appropriate chamber. As of mid-2006, three male representatives had been called to military duty. Each appointed his wife as a temporary replacement.[3]

### Sessions

A Texas law requires a **regular session** to begin on the second Tuesday in January of each odd-numbered year (for example, January 9, 2007 and January 13, 2009). In practice, these regular biennial sessions always run for the full 140 days authorized by the Texas Constitution (for example, through May 28, 2007 and June 1, 2009). Legislative sessions mean big money for many Austin businesses. Spending by legislators and lobbyists, along with people who work for them, boosts the Austin economy by an estimated $25 million or more during a regular session.

The governor may call **special sessions**, lasting no longer than 30 days each, at any time. Governor Perry called three special sessions on congressional redistricting in 2003, one on school finance in 2004, two on school finance in 2005, and one on school finance and property tax reform in 2006. (For the text of the governor's call for the 2006 special session, see Selected Reading 7.1, "Governor Rick Perry Calls a Special Legislative Session Commencing April 17, 2006.") During a special session, the legislature may consider only those matters placed before it by the governor. Such limits on sessions indicate a deep-seated popular distrust of legislators and a fear of change. Governor Bill Clements expressed his sentiments with the statement that "all kinds of bad things can happen when the legislature is in session." This attitude further reflects the individualistic political ideology of many Texans, who believe in limiting government control.

### Districting

Providing equal representation in a legislative chamber involves dividing a state into districts with approximately equal numbers of inhabitants. Population distribution changes constantly, owing to migration and to different birthrates and death rates. Therefore, legislative district boundaries must be redrawn periodically to ensure equitable representation. Such **redistricting** can be politically painful to a legislator. It may take away territory that has provided strong voter support; it may add an area that produces little support and much opposition; or it may produce a new district that includes the residences of two or more representatives or senators, only one of whom can be reelected to represent the district.[4]

**regular session** A session of the Texas Legislature that begins on the second Tuesday in January of odd-numbered years and lasts for a maximum of 140 days.

**special session** A legislative session called by the governor and limited to not more than 30 days.

**redistricting** Redrawing of boundaries following the federal decennial census to create districts with approximately equal population (e.g., legislative, congressional, and commissioners court districts in Texas).

Framers of the Texas Constitution of 1876 stipulated, "the legislature shall, at its first session after the publication of each United States decennial census, apportion the State into Senatorial and Representative districts." Nevertheless, in the decades that followed, the legislature sometimes failed to redivide the state's population and map new districts for legislators. Thus, some districts became heavily populated and greatly underrepresented; others experienced population decline or slow growth, resulting in overrepresentation.

In 1948, legislative districting inequities finally led to the adoption of a Texas state constitutional amendment designed to pressure the legislature to remedy this situation. Under the amendment, failure of the legislature to redistrict during the first regular session following a decennial (every ten years) census brings the Legislative Redistricting Board into operation. This board consists of the following five ex officio (that is, "holding other office") members: lieutenant governor, speaker of the House of Representatives, attorney general, comptroller of public accounts, and commissioner of the General Land Office. The board must meet within 90 days after the legislative session and redistrict the state within another 60 days.

Although the legislature drew new legislative districts after the federal censuses of 1950 and 1960, the Texas Constitution's apportionment formulas for the Texas House and Senate discriminated against heavily populated urban counties. These formulas were not changed until after the U.S. Supreme Court held in *Reynolds* v. *Sims* (1964) that "the seats in both houses of a bicameral state legislature must be apportioned on a population basis." This "one person, one vote" principle was applied first in Texas by a federal district court in *Kilgarlin* v. *Martin* (1965).

Redistricting by the Texas Legislature sparks complaints about **gerrymandering**. This practice involves drawing legislative districts to include or exclude certain groups of voters to favor one group or political party. The party in power often benefits in subsequent elections. Usually gerrymandered districts are oddly shaped rather than compact. The term "gerrymander" originated to describe irregularly shaped districts created under the guidance of Governor Elbridge Gerry in Massachusetts in 1812. Many state and federal court battles have been fought over the constitutionality of Texas's legislative districting arrangements.

Members of the Texas Senate have always represented **single-member districts**; that is, the voters of each district elect one senator. Redistricting according to the 2000 federal census provides for a population of about 673,000 in each senatorial district. Many of the 31 senatorial districts cover several counties. District 28, where Lubbock is the largest city, has the most, with 38 West Texas counties. A few big-city senatorial districts are formed from the territory of one county or part of a county. For example, Harris County, which includes Houston, has eight senatorial districts, some of which extend into adjoining counties. (See Figure 7.1.)

Until 1971, a Texas county with two or more seats in the House used **multimember districts** to elect representatives at large who represented the whole county. Thus, a voter in such a county could vote in all of the county's House

**gerrymandering**
Drawing the boundaries of a district (e.g., state senatorial district) to include or exclude certain groups of voters and thus affect election outcomes.

**single-member district**
An area that elects only one representative to serve on a policymaking body (e.g., city council, county commissioners court, state House and Senate).

**multimember district**
A district in which all voters participate in the election of two or more representatives to a policymaking body, such as a city council or a state legislature.

**Figure 7.1**    Texas State Senate Districts (used for electing state senators in 2002, 2004, and 2006)

races. In 1971, however, single-member districts were established in Harris, Dallas, and Bexar Counties. Four years later, the single-member districting system was extended to all other counties electing more than one representative. Today all representatives are elected on a single-member-district basis. The change to single-member districts was largely a result of court actions. Election results demonstrate that single-member districts reduce campaign costs and increase the probability that more African American and Latino candidates will be elected. As a result of the 2000 federal census, redistricting provided each state representative district with a population of approximately 139,000. District 88, in the Panhandle region of West Texas, covers 19 counties; but densely populated Harris County has 22 districts or parts of districts. (See Figure 7.2.)

In the year following each federal census, the Texas Legislature is supposed to draw new district lines for its U.S. congressional districts (from which

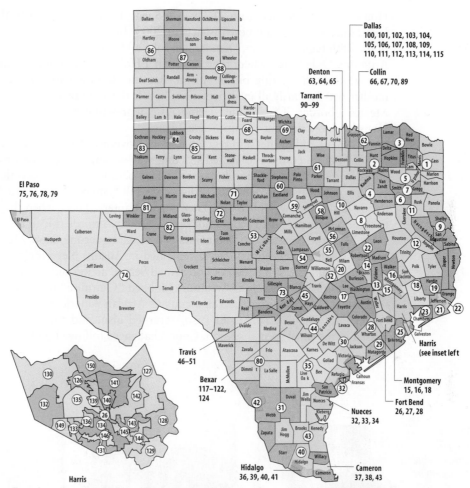

*Figure 7.2*    Texas State House Districts (used for electing state representatives in 2002, 2004, and 2006)

representatives to the U.S. House of Representatives are elected) and for its State Board of Education (SBOE) districts to make the number of people in each district equal. Results of the 2000 federal census indicated that each of Texas's 32 congressional districts should have a population of about 652,000. According to 2000 census figures, each of its 15 SBOE districts should have a population of about 1.4 million.

In 2001, the Texas Legislature failed to pass a bill to redistrict Texas's seats in the U.S. House of Representatives. Likewise, the legislature failed to draw new district lines for the SBOE. Because congressional and SBOE districting does not fall within the jurisdiction of the Legislative Redistricting Board, and because Governor Perry was opposed to calling a special session of the legislature, it fell to federal judges to carry out these redistricting tasks before the 2002 elections.[5]

In November 2002, Texas Republicans won 15 U.S. House seats, while Democrats won 17. Wanting more GOP representation in Washington, U.S.

House majority leader Tom DeLay (R–Sugar Land) insisted that the Texas Legislature should draw new districts in 2003. But in May 2003, near the end of the 78th regular session, Democrats broke a House quorum. Fifty-one fled to Ardmore, Oklahoma, where they stayed in a Holiday Inn until time ran out for voting on a redistricting bill in Austin. Because Representative Rene Olivera's mother was seriously ill in Brownsville, he left the state by crossing the nearby Mexican border. Three other Democratic representatives were absent from House proceedings but did not leave Texas.

After the end of the 78th regular session, Governor Perry called three special sessions before congressional redistricting was accomplished. The first session ended without Senate action because the Democratic minority used that chamber's two-thirds rule to prevent a redistricting bill from being considered (see the discussion of the two-thirds rule later in the chapter). Then, when they learned that the Senate president would not observe the two-thirds rule in a second session, 11 of the Senate's 12 Democrats fled to Albuquerque, New Mexico. Sen. Kenneth Armbrister from Victoria remained in Austin. Nevertheless, the quorum-busting flight of 11 senators prevented Senate action on a redistricting bill until Houston's Senator John Whitmire (dubbed "Quitmire" by critics) returned to Austin. Then the other 10 Democrats (2 African Americans, 7 Latinos, and Anglo Eliot Shapleigh from El Paso) returned also, and the redistricting bill passed in the third special session. Court challenges followed, but in November

*Representatives Martha Wong (R-Houston) and Debbie Riddle (R-Tomball) in 78th Regular Session (© Bob Daemmrich Photography, Inc.)*

2004, Republicans were elected to 21 of the state's 32 congressional seats. (For more details concerning procedures and consequences of legislative and congressional redistricting in the Lone Star State early in the current decade, see Selected Reading 7.2, "Redistricting and Electoral Results in Texas in the Twenty-First Century.")

---

**Learning Check 7.1**        **(Answers on p. 287)**

1. How many years make a full term for a representative?
2. True or False: In the year following each federal census, the Texas Legislature is supposed to divide the state into congressional districts.

---

# ★Compensation

Many states pay legislators ridiculously low salaries (for example, an average of $300 per year in Rhode Island and $100 per year in New Hampshire). In contrast, California pays legislators an annual salary of $110,880. That is more than any other state pays its legislators. Texas's legislators receive low pay, reasonable allowances, and a relatively generous retirement pension after a minimum period of service.

## Pay and Per Diem Allowance

Originally, Texas legislators' salaries and per diem (daily) personal allowances during a regular or special session were specified by the state constitution and could be changed only by constitutional amendment. Today, Texas voters retain the right to approve salary increases for legislators; but, as authorized by a constitutional amendment, the Texas Ethics Commission sets their per diem expense allowance. Additionally, this commission may recommend salary increases for legislators and even higher salaries for the speaker and the lieutenant governor; but the ultimate decision on a salary increase rests with voters. The $7,200 annual salary has not been increased since 1975.

For the 79th Legislature, which convened in January 2005, the per diem allowance to cover meals, lodging, and other personal expenses was $128 for senators, representatives, and the lieutenant governor. This amounted to a total of $17,920 per official for the 140-day regular session. (The maximum amount permitted as a federal income tax deduction by the Internal Revenue Service was $128 per day.) As explained below, legislators' office expenses are also funded by the state.

## Contingency Expense Allowances

Each chamber authorizes contingency expense allowances for its members' office expenses. For example, the House authorized every representative's operating account to be credited monthly, from January 2005 to January 2007, with $11,250. House members in the 79th Legislature could use money in this

## How Do We Compare ... in Salary of Legislators?
### Annual Salary of Legislators for the Year of the Last Regular Session

| Most Populous U.S. States | Annual Salary | U.S. States Bordering Texas | Annual Salary |
|---|---|---|---|
| California | $110,880 | Arkansas | $14,067 |
| Florida | $29,916 | Louisiana | $16,800 |
| New York | $79,500 | New Mexico | $0* |
| **Texas** | **$7,200** | Oklahoma | $38,400 |

Source:  *The Book of the States, 2006* (Lexington, Ky.: Council of State Governments, 2006), 84–86.

*Legislators in New Mexico receive mileage and a per diem allowance but no annual salary.

account to cover the cost of travel, postage, office operations, and staff salaries. Some representatives and senators use money from campaign contributions to supplement their assistants' salaries.

During the regular session of the 79th Legislature, Senate committee chairs were restricted to not more than $32,000 per month for secretarial and other office staff salaries and for staff travel within Texas. Other senators, not assisted by committee employees, had the slightly higher maximum monthly allowance of $36,000. Senate members, too, can supplement staff salaries with money from campaign contributions.

### Retirement Pension

Under the terms of the State Employees Retirement Act of 1975, legislators contribute 8 percent of their salaries to a retirement fund. Retirement pay for senators and representatives amounts to 2.3 percent of a district judge's annual salary, which was $125,000 in fiscal years 2006 and 2007 for each year served. Thus, when Senator Gonzalo Barrientos (D-Austin) retired at the beginning of 2007 after 32 years of legislative service (10 years in the House and 22 years in the Senate), his annual pension was more than $88,000. A legislator who serves a minimum of 8 years becomes eligible for a pension of more than $22,000 per year. Of course, many legislators do not serve long enough to qualify for a pension, but those who do can begin collecting payments while they are still relatively young. As a result of an unpublicized amendment slipped into a state employee benefits bill in 1991, legislators with 12 years of service may retire at age 50, and those with 8 years of service may retire at age 60.

### Learning Check 7.2      (Answers on p. 287)

1. True or False: Salary increases for legislators must be submitted to the state's voters for approval or disapproval.
2. True or False: Each chamber of the legislature authorizes contingency expense allowances for its members.

# Membership

Members of the Texas Legislature must meet specific state constitutional qualifications concerning citizenship, voter status, state residence, district residence, and age. Despite such restrictions, millions of Texans possess all the prescribed legal qualifications. As is true of the memberships in other state legislatures, however, the biographical data for members of recent Texas legislatures suggest informal qualifications that restrict opportunities for election to either of the two chambers.

## Qualifications of Members

The Texas Constitution specifies the formal qualifications for House and Senate members. All of these elected legislative officials must be citizens of the United States, qualified Texas voters, and residents of the districts they represent for one year immediately preceding a general election. In matters of state residence and age, however, qualifications differ between the two chambers (see Table 7.1).

A House candidate must have resided in Texas for two years before being elected, whereas a Senate candidate must have five years of state residence. To be eligible for House membership, a person must be at least 21 years of age; to serve in the Senate, a person must be at least 26. If a question arises concerning constitutional qualifications or a dispute over election returns, each legislative chamber determines who will be seated.

## Characteristics of Members

The typical Texas legislator is an Anglo Protestant male between 35 and 50 years of age, born in Texas, an attorney or a businessperson, and has served one or more previous terms of office. Such characteristics do not guarantee any predetermined reaction to issues and events, but legislators tend to be influenced by their experience and environment, both of which have policy consequences. Any study of the legislature must pay attention to the biographical characteristics of legislators. See Table 7.2 for data on political party affiliation, racial/ethnic classification, and gender of legislators from 1971 to 2005.

*Table 7.1* Constitutional Qualifications for Membership in the Texas Legislature

| Qualification | House | Senate |
|---|---|---|
| Citizenship | United States citizen | United States citizen |
| Voter status | Qualified Texas voter | Qualified Texas voter |
| Residence in district to be represented | 1 year immediately preceding election | 1 year immediately preceding election |
| Texas residence | 2 years immediately preceding election | 5 years immediately preceding election |
| Age | 21 years | 26 years |

*Source:* Constitution of Texas, Art. 3, Secs. 6 and 7.

Table 7.2 Some Characteristics of Texas Legislators at the Beginning of the 62nd Through the 79th Legislatures, 1971–2005

HOUSE OF REPRESENTATIVES

| No. of regular session | Year of regular session | Total member- ship | POLITICAL PARTY | | | | RACIAL/ETHNIC CLASSIFICATION | | | | | | | | GENDER | | | |
|---|---|---|---|---|---|---|---|---|---|---|---|---|---|---|---|---|---|---|
| | | | Democrates | | Republicans | | Anglos | | Latinos | | African American | | Asian American | | Man | | Woman | |
| | | | No. | % | No. | % | No. | % | No. | % | No. | % | No. | % | No. | % | No. | % |
| 62nd | 1971 | 150 | 140 | 93.33 | 10 | 6.67 | 137 | 91.33 | 11 | 7.33 | 2 | 1.33 | 0 | 00.00 | 149 | 99.33 | 1 | 0.67 |
| 63rd | 1973 | 150 | 133 | 88.67 | 17 | 11.33 | 131 | 87.33 | 11 | 7.33 | 8 | 5.33 | 0 | 00.00 | 145 | 96.67 | 5 | 3.33 |
| 64th | 1975 | 150 | 134 | 89.33 | 16 | 10.67 | 127 | 84.67 | 14 | 9.33 | 9 | 6.00 | 0 | 00.00 | 143 | 95.33 | 7 | 4.67 |
| 65th | 1977 | 150 | 132 | 88.00 | 18 | 12.00 | 119 | 79.33 | 18 | 12.00 | 13 | 8.67 | 0 | 00.00 | 140 | 93.33 | 10 | 6.67 |
| 66th | 1979 | 150 | 128 | 85.33 | 22 | 14.67 | 118 | 78.67 | 18 | 12.00 | 14 | 9.33 | 0 | 00.00 | 139 | 92.67 | 11 | 7.33 |
| 67th | 1981 | 150 | 114 | 76.00 | 36 | 24.00 | 119 | 79.33 | 18 | 12.00 | 13 | 8.67 | 0 | 00.00 | 139 | 92.67 | 11 | 7.33 |
| 68th | 1983 | 150 | 115 | 76.67 | 35 | 23.33 | 117 | 78.00 | 21 | 14.00 | 12 | 8.00 | 0 | 00.00 | 137 | 91.33 | 13 | 8.67 |
| 69th | 1985 | 150 | 98 | 65.33 | 52 | 34.67 | 118 | 78.67 | 19 | 12.67 | 13 | 8.67 | 0 | 00.00 | 135 | 90.00 | 15 | 10.00 |
| 70th | 1987 | 150 | 94 | 62.67 | 56 | 37.33 | 118 | 78.67 | 19 | 12.67 | 13 | 8.67 | 0 | 00.00 | 134 | 89.33 | 16 | 10.67 |
| 71st | 1989 | 150 | 93 | 62.00 | 57 | 38.00 | 118 | 78.67 | 19 | 12.67 | 13 | 8.67 | 0 | 00.00 | 134 | 89.33 | 16 | 10.67 |
| 72nd | 1991 | 150 | 92 | 61.33 | 58 | 38.67 | 117 | 78.00 | 20 | 13.33 | 13 | 8.67 | 0 | 00.00 | 131 | 87.33 | 19 | 12.67 |
| 73rd | 1993 | 150 | 91 | 60.67 | 59 | 39.33 | 110 | 73.33 | 26 | 17.33 | 14 | 9.33 | 0 | 00.00 | 125 | 83.33 | 25 | 16.67 |
| 74th | 1995 | 150 | 88 | 58.67 | 62 | 41.33 | 110 | 73.33 | 26 | 17.33 | 14 | 9.33 | 0 | 00.00 | 121 | 80.67 | 29 | 19.33 |
| 75th | 1997 | 150 | 82 | 54.67 | 68 | 45.33 | 108 | 72.00 | 28 | 18.67 | 14 | 9.33 | 0 | 00.00 | 120 | 80.00 | 30 | 20.00 |
| 76th | 1999 | 150 | 78 | 52.00 | 72 | 48.00 | 108 | 72.00 | 28 | 18.67 | 14 | 9.33 | 0 | 00.00 | 121 | 80.67 | 29 | 19.33 |
| 77th | 2001 | 150 | 78 | 52.00 | 72 | 48.00 | 108 | 72.00 | 28 | 18.67 | 14 | 9.33 | 0 | 00.00 | 120 | 80.00 | 30 | 20.00 |
| 78th | 2003 | 150 | 62 | 41.33 | 88 | 58.67 | 105 | 70.00 | 30 | 20.00 | 14 | 9.33 | 1 | 00.67 | 118 | 78.67 | 32 | 21.33 |
| 79th | 2005 | 150 | 63 | 42.00 | 87 | 58.00 | 104 | 69.33 | 30 | 20.00 | 14 | 9.33 | 2 | 1.34 | 119 | 79.33 | 31 | 20.67 |

| No. of regular session | Year of regular session | Total membership | POLITICAL PARTY | | | | RACIAL/ETHNIC CLASSIFICATION | | | | | | | | GENDER | | | |
| --- | --- | --- | --- | --- | --- | --- | --- | --- | --- | --- | --- | --- | --- | --- | --- | --- | --- | --- |
| | | | Democrates | | Republicans | | Anglos | | Latinos | | African American | | Asian American | | Man | | Woman | |
| | | | No. | % | No. | % | No. | % | No. | % | No. | % | No. | % | No. | % | No. | % |
| SENATE | | | | | | | | | | | | | | | | | | |
| 62nd | 1971 | 31 | 29 | 93.55 | 2 | 6.45 | 29 | 93.55 | 1 | 3.23 | 1 | 3.23 | 0 | 00.00 | 30 | 96.77 | 1 | 3.23 |
| 63rd | 1973 | 31 | 28 | 90.32 | 3 | 9.68 | 29 | 93.55 | 2 | 6.45 | 0 | 0.00 | 0 | 00.00 | 30 | 96.77 | 1 | 3.23 |
| 64th | 1975 | 31 | 28 | 90.32 | 3 | 9.68 | 29 | 93.55 | 2 | 6.45 | 0 | 0.00 | 0 | 00.00 | 30 | 96.77 | 1 | 3.23 |
| 65th | 1977 | 31 | 28 | 90.32 | 3 | 9.68 | 28 | 90.32 | 3 | 9.68 | 0 | 0.00 | 0 | 00.00 | 30 | 96.77 | 1 | 3.23 |
| 66th | 1979 | 31 | 27 | 87.10 | 4 | 12.90 | 27 | 87.10 | 4 | 12.90 | 0 | 0.00 | 0 | 00.00 | 30 | 96.77 | 1 | 3.23 |
| 67th | 1981 | 31 | 24 | 77.42 | 7 | 22.58 | 27 | 87.10 | 4 | 12.90 | 0 | 0.00 | 0 | 00.00 | 30 | 96.77 | 1 | 3.23 |
| 68th | 1983 | 31 | 26 | 83.87 | 5 | 16.13 | 26 | 83.87 | 4 | 12.90 | 1 | 3.23 | 0 | 00.00 | 31 | 100.00 | 0 | 0.00 |
| 69th | 1985 | 31 | 25 | 80.65 | 6 | 19.35 | 26 | 83.87 | 4 | 12.90 | 1 | 3.23 | 0 | 00.00 | 30 | 96.77 | 1 | 3.23 |
| 70th | 1987 | 31 | 25 | 80.65 | 6 | 19.35 | 23 | 74.19 | 6 | 19.35 | 2 | 6.45 | 0 | 00.00 | 28 | 90.32 | 3 | 9.68 |
| 71st | 1989 | 31 | 23 | 74.19 | 8 | 25.81 | 23 | 74.19 | 6 | 19.35 | 2 | 6.45 | 0 | 00.00 | 28 | 90.32 | 3 | 9.68 |
| 72nd | 1991 | 31 | 23 | 74.19 | 8 | 25.81 | 24 | 77.42 | 5 | 16.13 | 2 | 6.45 | 0 | 00.00 | 27 | 87.10 | 4 | 12.90 |
| 73rd | 1993 | 31 | 18 | 58.06 | 13 | 41.94 | 23 | 74.19 | 6 | 19.35 | 2 | 6.45 | 0 | 00.00 | 27 | 87.10 | 4 | 12.90 |
| 74th | 1995 | 31 | 17 | 54.84 | 14 | 45.16 | 24 | 77.42 | 5 | 16.13 | 2 | 6.45 | 0 | 00.00 | 27 | 87.10 | 4 | 12.90 |
| 75th | 1997 | 31 | 14 | 45.16 | 17 | 54.84 | 22 | 70.97 | 7 | 22.58 | 2 | 6.45 | 0 | 00.00 | 28 | 90.32 | 3 | 9.68 |
| 76th | 1999 | 31 | 15 | 48.39 | 16 | 51.61 | 22 | 70.97 | 7 | 22.58 | 2 | 6.45 | 0 | 00.00 | 28 | 90.32 | 3 | 9.68 |
| 77th | 2001 | 31 | 15 | 48.39 | 16 | 51.61 | 22 | 70.97 | 7 | 22.58 | 2 | 6.45 | 0 | 00.00 | 27 | 87.10 | 4 | 12.90 |
| 78th | 2003 | 31 | 12 | 38.71 | 19 | 61.29 | 22 | 70.97 | 7 | 22.58 | 2 | 6.45 | 0 | 00.00 | 27 | 87.10 | 4 | 12.90 |
| 79th | 2005 | 31 | 12 | 38.71 | 19 | 61.29 | 22 | 70.97 | 7 | 22.58 | 2 | 6.45 | 0 | 00.00 | 27 | 87.10 | 4 | 12.90 |

Sources: Texas Legislative Reference Library and Texas Legislative Council.

**Gender Classification**    Anglo males continue to dominate the Texas Legislature, but their number has declined in recent years. At the beginning of the 62nd Legislature's regular session in January 1971, the legislative rolls included just one woman, Senator Barbara Jordan (D-Houston).[6] Thirty-five years later, results of the 2006 general election indicated that there would be 37 women (4 senators and 33 representatives) in the 80th Legislature. Two of the female senators were Anglo Republicans; the other two were Latina Democrats. Eighteen of the female representatives were Democrats (6 Latinas, 8 African Americans, and 4 Anglos), and 15 were Anglo Republicans. Among the Anglo Republican representatives was Glenda Dawson, who was elected after her death in September. Dawson's name remained on the ballot because she did not die prior to the 74th day before the November election, and Governor Perry called a special election to fill the seat.

**Racial/Ethnic Classification**    Representation of members of historical racial/ethnic minorities increased substantially from the late 1960s through the early 1990s. Barbara Jordan, the first African American elected to the Texas Senate in the twentieth century, served from 1967 until she was seated in the U.S. Congress in 1973. At the beginning of the regular session of the 79th Legislature in 2005, Senate seats were held by 2 African Americans and 7 Latinos. In November

Rep. Yvonne Gonzalez Toureilles (D-Alice) shows her baby to Rep. Betty Brown (R-Terrell) and Rep. Doc Anderson (R-Waco) early in the 79th Regular Session. (Texas House of Representatives Photography Department)

2006, 2 African Americans and 6 Latinos were elected to serve in the Senate in the 80th Legislature. At the same time, 14 African American representatives and 31 Latino representatives were elected. Although both African Americans and Latinos have been under-represented in the Texas Legislature, total African American representation increased from 3 legislators in 1971 to 16 in 2005, and the number of Latino legislators grew from 12 to 37. Texas's first Asian American legislator was Thomas J. Lee (D–San Antonio, January 1965–January 1967). The state's second Asian American legislator was Martha Wong (R–Houston, January 2003–January 2007); the third, Hubert Vo (D–Houston) began his first term in January 2005 and was reelected in 2006 for a second term.

**Political Party Affiliation**    The 1960 election saw no Republicans seated in the 57th Legislature. But in 2006, Texans elected 20 Republican senators (one more than in 2004) and 81 Republican representatives (6 fewer then in 2004). Thus, during this 46-year period, the House political division shifted from a total of 150 Democrats and no Republicans to a majority of 81 Republicans and a minority of 69 Democrats. During that same period, the political lineup for the Senate changed from 31 Democrats and no Republicans to a minority of 11 Democrats (one less than in 2004) and a majority of 20 Republicans. Since January 2003, when Republicans began operating with comfortable majorities in both the House and the Senate, each chamber has seen more "party-line" votes, with Democrats voting one way on an issue and Republicans voting the other way.

Republican legislators and their counterparts (mostly African and Latino Democrats) tend to reside in metropolitan areas. Election patterns differ between urban areas and the suburbs. Central-city residents usually elect African American and Latino Democrats as their lawmakers, but Republican senators and representatives receive their strongest support from suburban Anglo voters. Because legislative districts in the area extending from South Texas to El Paso tend to have large numbers of Latinos in both rural and urban areas, voters in most of those districts elect Latino Democrats.

**Age**    Despite minimum age qualifications of 26 years for senators and 21 years for representatives, legislators are rarely younger than 30. In recent years, the average age has been in the late 40s for representatives and slightly higher for senators.

**Occupation**    Traditionally, Texas legislators have included a large number of attorneys and business owners or managers. Lesser numbers of real estate and insurance people, and some farmers and ranchers, have also served. Teachers, medical personnel, engineers, and accountants have held few legislative seats. Laborers have held almost none.

Lawyer-legislators may receive retainers (payments) from corporations and special-interest groups, with the understanding that legal services will be performed if needed. In some cases, these retainer payments appear intended to influence legislation rather than guarantee availability of legal counsel. It is also noteworthy that lawyer-legislators, some of whom represent defendants in courts, exercise a decisive influence in amending and revising the Penal Code and the Code of Criminal Procedure. Since 2003, a legislator may not represent a paying client before a state agency such as the Railroad Commission or the Alcoholic Beverage Commission.

Individuals and corporations desiring to delay justice may seek the services of lawyer-legislators because these attorneys are entitled to obtain a continuance (that is, a postponement) of any case set for trial during a period extending from 30 days before to 30 days after a legislative session. As a result of blatant abuse of this privilege, a law was enacted that allows a judge to deny a continuance when, within 10 days of the trial or any related legal proceeding, a lawmaker is hired to assist another lawyer handling a case. A legislator is required to disclose payment received for obtaining a continuance.

**Education**   In government, as in business, most positions of leadership call for college credentials. Thus, it is not surprising to find that nearly all members of recent Texas legislatures attended one or more institutions of higher education. Most of them could claim a bachelor's degree, and many had graduate degrees or professional degrees (especially in law).

**Religious Affiliation**   The Texas Constitution guarantees freedom of religion and prohibits use of public funds for the benefit of a sect or religious group. Since the era of the Texas Republic, Texans have tended to support separation of church and state, but this principle has become the subject of recent controversies. Because religion may play a critical role in the formulation of public policy, political analysts must take a legislator's denominational ties and church doctrines into consideration. These factors are especially important when considering legislation involving abortion, birth control, gambling, sale of alcoholic beverages, state aid to parochial schools, Sabbath observance, and other matters of vital concern to some religious groups. The religious affiliation of each legislator is not a matter of record, but it appears that Catholic senators and representatives are most numerous, followed (in order) by Baptists, Methodists, and Episcopalians.

**Legislative Experience**   In a legislative body, experience is measured in terms of turnover (first-termers replacing experienced members who have retired or lost an election) and tenure (years served in a legislative chamber). For the 8 recent Texas legislatures (72nd–79th), the average turnover in the House was 26 or about 17 percent of the membership every two years. In the Senate, it was 4.6 or about 15 percent. Turnover tends to be higher for the first legislature following redistricting. (For example, in 2003 it was 24 percent in the House and 23 percent in the Senate.)

The average length of service in the 8 legislatures identified above was more than 6 years in both the House and the Senate, but most senators had served first as representatives. In 2005, for example, 20 of the 31 senators in the 79th legislature had been representatives for four years or more before they became senators. After a term in office, an incumbent is more likely to win an election than is an inexperienced challenger.

As a general rule, lawmakers become most effective after they have spent two or more years learning procedural rules related to enacting legislation and working with constituents, bureaucrats, lobbyists, fellow legislators, and other elected officials. Many Americans believe, however, that long legislative tenure should be discouraged if not prohibited. To date, all efforts to propose term limits amendments to the Texas Constitution have been unsuccessful.

**Learning Check 7.3**      **(Answers on p. 287)**

1. What is the minimum age for a state representative as specified in the Texas Constitution?
2. True or False: The Texas Constitution disqualifies all lawyers from service in the legislature.

## Powers and Immunities

Although bound by restrictions found in few state constitutions, the legislature is the dominant branch of Texas government and the chief agent in making public policy. Legislators, for example, control government spending, which makes state agencies and personnel—and, to some extent, units of local government—dependent on them. In addition to their constitutional powers, lawmakers enjoy certain immunities designed to allow them to function freely.

### Legislative Powers

Using language reminiscent of George Orwell's *Animal Farm*, we may say that whereas all powers exercised by the Texas Legislature are, in a sense, legislative, some are more legislative than others. The more typical exercise of legislative power involves making public policy by passing bills and adopting resolutions. As explained below, each bill or resolution has a distinctive abbreviation that indicates the chamber of origin, and every legislative proposal is designated by a number indicating the order of introduction.

**Simple Resolutions**   Abbreviated H.R. (House Resolution) if introduced in the House and S.R. (Senate Resolution) if introduced in the Senate, a **simple resolution** involves action by one house only and is not sent to the governor. Adoption requires a simple majority vote (more than half) of members present. Matters dealt with by simple resolution include rules of the House and Senate, procedures for House and Senate operation, and invitations extended to nonmembers to address the chambers.

**Concurrent Resolutions**   After adoption by simple majority votes of members present in both the House and the Senate, a **concurrent resolution** (H.C.R. or S.C.R.) is sent to the governor, who has two options: sign it or veto it. Typical examples are resolutions requesting action by the U.S. Congress, demanding information from state agencies, establishing joint study committees composed of senators and representatives, or granting permission to sue the state.

**simple resolution**
A resolution that requires action by one legislative chamber only and is not acted on by the governor.

**concurrent resolution**
A resolution adopted by House and Senate majorities and then approved by the governor (e.g., request for action by Congress or authorization for someone to sue the state).

In addition, the chambers adopt a concurrent resolution to adjourn at the end of any legislative session. This measure does not require approval by the governor. In 2005, the 79th Legislature adopted 198 concurrent resolutions.

**Joint Resolutions**    Adoption of a **joint resolution** (H.J.R. or S.J.R.) requires approval by both houses but no action by the governor The nature of a joint resolution determines whether a simple majority or a two-thirds vote is required. Proposed amendments to the Texas Constitution are examples of joint resolutions requiring a two-thirds majority vote of the membership of each house. To date, all proposed amendments to the U.S. Constitution initiated by Congress, with the exception of the Twenty-First Amendment, have been submitted to state legislatures for ratification. The Texas Legislature ratifies a proposed U.S. constitutional amendment with a joint resolution adopted by simple majority votes of members present in both houses.

**Bills**    Before enactment, a proposed law is known as a **bill** (H.B. or S.B.). Each regular session brings forth an avalanche of bills, but only about one-fourth become law. In the regular session of the 79th Legislature in 2005, for example, 3,592 bills were introduced in the House and 1,892 in the Senate. Together, both chambers passed 876 House bills and 513 Senate bills. The governor vetoed 8 House bills and 11 Senate bills.

For purposes of classification, bills fall into three categories: special, general, and local. A special bill makes an exception to general laws for the benefit of a specific individual, class, or corporation. Of greater importance are general bills, which apply to all people or property in all parts of Texas. To become law, a bill must pass by a simple majority of votes of members present in both the House and the Senate, but a two-thirds majority vote of the membership in each chamber is required to pass an emergency measure that will take effect as soon as the governor signs it. A local bill creates or affects a single unit of local government (for example, a city, county, or special district). Such bills usually pass without opposition if sponsored by all legislators representing the affected area.

## Other Powers

The Texas Legislature exercises its principal powers by passing bills and adopting resolutions. Additionally, the House and Senate have other important powers. Some of these relate only indirectly to the lawmaking function.

**Constitutional Amendment Power**    Members of either chamber may introduce a joint resolution to amend the Texas Constitution. A proposal is officially made when the joint resolution is approved by a two-thirds majority vote of the total membership of each house. (The constitutional amendment process is covered in detail in the chapter "Federalism and the Texas Constitution.")

**Administrative Power**    The legislature defines the responsibilities of state agencies and imposes restrictions on them through appropriation of money for their

**joint resolution**  Must pass by a majority vote in each house when used to memorialize the U.S. Congress or to ratify an amendment to the U.S. Constitution. As a proposal for an amendment to the Texas Constitution, a joint resolution requires a two-thirds majority vote in each house.

**bill**  A proposed law or statute.

operation and through oversight of their activities. One form of administrative supervision involves requiring state agencies to make both periodic and special reports to the legislature. The state auditor, who provides information concerning irregular or inefficient use of funds by administrative agencies, is appointed by (and serves at the will of) the Legislative Audit Committee. This six-member committee is composed of the speaker, the chair of the House Appropriations Committee, the chair of the House Ways and Means Committee, the lieutenant governor, the chair of the Senate Finance Committee, and a senator appointed by the lieutenant governor. Another important instrument of control over state administration is the legislature's Sunset Advisory Commission, which makes recommendations to the House and Senate concerning continuation, merger, division, or abolition of nearly every state agency within a 12-year period (see the chapter "Public Policy and Administration" for more).

Most of the governor's appointments to boards and commissions that head state agencies must be submitted to the Senate and approved by at least two-thirds of the senators present. Thus, the Senate is in a position to influence the selection of many important officials. Moreover, the unwritten rule of **senatorial courtesy** requires that the Senate "bust" (reject) an appointment if the appointee is declared "personally objectionable" by the senator representing the district in which the appointee resides. Consequently, a governor will privately seek prior approval by that senator before announcing a selection.

**Investigative Power**   To obtain information about problems that may require legislation, the legislature has the power to subpoena witnesses to testify, administer oaths, and compel submission of records and documents. Such action may be taken jointly by the two houses as a body, by one house, or by a committee of either house. Refusal to obey a subpoena may result in prosecution for contempt of the legislature, which is a misdemeanor offense punishable by a jail sentence of from 30 days to a year and a fine ranging from \$100 to \$1,000. Legislative investigations that led to reforms include probes of higher education in South Texas, rural health care delivery, and the insurance industry.

**Impeachment Power**   The House of Representatives has the power to impeach judges of hundreds of district courts, justices of the 14 state courts of appeals and the Supreme Court of Texas, and judges of the Texas Court of Criminal Appeals. The House may also impeach executive officers, such as the governor, the attorney general, the comptroller of public accounts, and the commissioner of the General Land Office. Impeachment power is rarely used, however.

**Impeachment** involves bringing charges by a simple majority vote of House members present. It resembles the indictment process of a grand jury (see the chapter "Law, Courts, and Justice"). Following impeachment, the Senate conducts a proceeding that resembles a court trial, after which it renders judgment. Conviction requires a two-thirds majority vote of the Senate membership. The only punishment that may be imposed is removal from office and disqualification from holding any other public office under the Texas Constitution. If a crime

**senatorial courtesy** Before making an appointment, the governor is expected to obtain approval from the state senator in whose district the prospective appointee resides; failure to obtain such approval will probably cause the Senate to "bust" the appointee.

**impeachment** Process in which the Texas House of Representatives, by a simple majority vote, initiates action (brings charges) leading to possible removal of certain judicial and executive officials (e.g., the governor) by the Senate.

has been committed, the deposed official may also be prosecuted before an appropriate court like any other person.

### Immunities

In addition to their constitutional powers, state senators and representatives enjoy legislative immunities conferred by the Texas Constitution. First, they may not be sued for slander or otherwise held accountable for any statements made in a speech or debate during the course of a legislative proceeding. Of course, this protection does not extend to remarks made under other circumstances. Second, they may not be arrested while attending a legislative session or while traveling to or from the legislature's meeting place for the purpose of attending, unless charged with "treason, felony, or breach of the peace."

---

**Learning Check 7.4        (Answers on p. 287)**

1. What legislative measure is abbreviated as H.J.R.?
2. What is the unwritten rule that requires the Senate to reject an appointment if the appointee is "personally objectionable" to the senator representing the appointee's district?

---

## ★ Presiding Officers

Merely bringing 181 men and women together in the Capitol does not ensure the making of laws or any other governmental activity. Gathering people to transact official business requires organized effort. The Texas Constitution prescribes the basic organization of the legislature. For example, it designates the lieutenant governor as president of the Senate and provides for the election of a speaker to preside over the House of Representatives.[8]

### President of the Senate: The Lieutenant Governor

The most important function of the lieutenant governor of Texas is to serve as **president of the Senate**. Just as the vice president of the United States is empowered to preside over the U.S. Senate but is not a member of that national law-making body, so too the lieutenant governor of Texas is not a member of the state Senate. The big difference between them is that the lieutenant governor presides over most sessions and plays a leading role in legislative matters, whereas the vice president seldom presides or becomes involved in the daily business of the U.S. Senate.

    Chosen by the people of Texas in a statewide election for a four-year term, the lieutenant governor is first in line of succession in the event of the death, resignation, or removal of the governor. When the governor is absent from the state, the lieutenant governor serves as acting governor and receives the gubernatorial salary, which amounted to nearly $350 per day at the beginning of

**president of the Senate**
Title of the lieutenant governor in his or her role as presiding officer for the Texas Senate.

2007. Ordinarily, however, the lieutenant governor's salary is the same as those of senators and representatives: $7,200 per year, which amounts to less than $20 per day.

As president of the Texas Senate, the lieutenant governor:

- Appoints all Senate committee chairs and vice chairs
- Appoints Senate committee and standing subcommittee members
- Determines the Senate committee to which a bill will be sent after introduction
- Recognizes senators who wish to speak on the Senate floor or make a motion (for example, to take up a bill out of order of calendar listing)
- Votes to break a tie vote in the Senate
- Joint-chairs, with the speaker of the House, the Legislative Council (a research arm of the legislature)
- Joint-chairs, with the speaker of the House, the Legislative Budget Board
- Joint-chairs, with the speaker of the House, the Legislative Audit Committee

Because of his powers (most of which have been granted by the Senate rather than the Texas Constitution), the lieutenant governor is perhaps the most powerful officer in the state, especially when the legislature is in session.

At the beginning of each session, the Senate elects a president pro tempore, who presides when the lieutenant governor is absent or disabled. At the end of a session, a new president pro tempore is named for the interim period. Customarily, on the basis of seniority—that is, years of cumulative service as a member of the Senate—the office is passed among senators who have not yet served as president pro tempore. By custom, the governor and lieutenant governor arrange to be absent from the state on the same day during the president pro tempore's term so that official can serve as governor for at least one day. This event involves a swearing-in ceremony and celebration with friends, family members, and constituents. Lobbyists, who usually pay for the festivities, are also included.

## Speaker of the House

The presiding officer of the House of Representatives is the **speaker of the House,** a representative elected to that office for a two-year term in an open (not secret) vote by the House membership. Like the lieutenant governor in the Senate, the speaker controls proceedings in the House. Among the speaker's more important powers are the following:

- Appoints all chairs and vice-chairs of House substantive and procedural committees
- Appoints all members of House procedural committees
- Appoints House substantive committee members within limitations of the seniority rule (this rule does not apply to the House Appropriations Committee)

**speaker of the House**
The state representative elected by House members to serve as the presiding officer for that chamber.

- Recognizes members who wish to speak on the House floor or to make a motion
- Assigns bills and resolutions to House committees
- Joint-chairs, with the lieutenant governor, the Legislative Council
- Joint-chairs, with the lieutenant governor, the Legislative Budget Board
- Joint-chairs, with the lieutenant governor, the Legislative Audit Committee

House rules authorize the speaker to name another representative to preside over the chamber temporarily. The speaker may also name a member of the House to serve as permanent speaker pro tempore for as long as the speaker desires. A speaker pro tempore performs all the duties of the speaker when that officer is absent.[9]

Because of the speaker's power, filling this House office involves intense political activity. Lobbyists make every effort to ensure the election of a sympathetic speaker, and potential candidates for the position begin to line up support several months or even years before a speaker's race begins. Long before election of a speaker, anyone aspiring to that office will attempt to induce House members to sign cards pledging their support. House rules, however, prohibit soliciting written pledges during a regular session. Once elected, a speaker usually finds it easier to obtain similar pledges of support for reelection in future regular sessions.

A candidate for speaker must file with the Texas Ethics Commission before receiving loans or contributions and before spending money on a speaker's race. By state law, money from regular political contributions may not be spent in a campaign to win this House office. It is customary for speaker candidates to visit members in their districts to gain and keep their support.

When 88 Republicans won House seats in November 2002, it was apparent that the GOP would capture the speaker's office for the first time in more than 130 years. On 14 January 2003, House members elected Tom Craddick (R–Midland) as presiding officer in the House by a vote of 149–1. After casting the only dissenting vote, Representative Lon Burnam (D–Fort Worth) stated that he liked Craddick but explained, "I don't like the way he votes. I don't like his sense of ethics."[10] As did his three immediate, long-tenured predecessors (Bill Clayton, Gib Lewis, and Pete Laney), Craddick appointed both Republicans and Democrats as committee chairs—but not Burnam!

Craddick named Democrats to chair nearly one-third of all committees; however, his professed dedication to bipartisanship wore thin as the 78th regular session progressed in the early months of 2003. Party differences over the state budget and congressional redistricting were the two most divisive issues during that session, but party-line votes on other issues were common. Nationwide publicity given to the flights of Democratic representatives to Oklahoma and senators to New Mexico embarrassed and angered the speaker. As discussed earlier in the chapter, they fled from Austin to break quorums in the two chambers and thus delayed action on the redistricting plan pushed by Congressman Tom DeLay

*Rep. Jim Dunnam (D-Waco) makes an appeal to Speaker Tom Craddick (R-Midland) during the 79th Regular Session in 2005. (Texas House of Representatives Photography Department)*

(R–Sugar Land). Before the end of the 78th regular session in June 2003, bipartisanship was dead; and partisan conflict over school finance and other issues raged in subsequent sessions. Ronnie Earle, Travis County's Democratic district attorney, contributed to Craddick's discomfort when he investigated Craddick's relations with Congressman DeLay and the transmitting of questionable campaign funds to certain Republican legislative candidates in 2002.[11] But Craddick avoided indictment with skilled legal assistance from Roy Minton, an Austin attorney who is famous for defending prominent Texas politicians.

**Points to Ponder**

- For nearly a century after Texas became part of the Federal Union (1846–1931), speakers of the state House of Representatives were elected for a single two-year term (with only three exceptions, and none held this office for consecutive terms).
- In the 40 years from 1933 to 1973, 10 speakers were elected for 1 term and 5 were elected for 2 consecutive terms.
- In the 28 years from 1975 to 2003, only 3 representatives were elected as speaker: Bill Clayton (4 terms, 1975–1983), Gib Lewis (5 terms, 1983–1993), and Pete Laney (5 terms, 1993–2003).
- Tom Craddick was elected speaker in 2003 and again in 2005. Has a tradition of electing speakers for consecutive terms been established?

**Learning Check 7.5**        **(Answers on p. 287)**

1. True or False: The lieutenant governor's salary is the same as that of the governor.
2. True or False: The speaker of the House of Representatives presides over that body but cannot vote on a bill or resolution.

## ★ Committee System

Presiding officers determine the committees to which bills will be referred. (See Table 7.3 for committee titles and numbers of members for House and Senate committees in the 79th Legislature.) Because both House and Senate committees play important roles in the fate or fortune of all bills and resolutions, selection of committee members goes far toward determining the amount and type of legislative output during a session. Permanent staff members are available to assist legislators with committee work on a continuing basis. Usually, they also work on interim study committees created to examine legislative issues between regular sessions.

### House Committees

**substantive committee**
Appointed by the House speaker, a substantive committee considers bills and resolutions related to the subject identified by its name (e.g., House Agriculture Committee) and may recommend passage of proposed legislation to the appropriate calendar committee.

**procedural committee**
These House committees (e.g., Calendars Committee and House Administration Committee) consider bills and resolutions relating primarily to internal legislative matters.

**select committee**
Created independently by the speaker, a select committee may work on emergency legislation early in a session before substantive committees are appointed.

**Substantive committees** consider bills and resolutions relating to the subject identified by a committee's name (for example, elections or transportation). The speaker appoints all members of the Appropriations Committee, but seniority determines a maximum of half the membership for other substantive committees—exclusive of the chair and the vice chair. When a regular session begins, each representative, in order of seniority, designates three committees in order of preference. A representative is entitled to become a member of the committee of highest preference that has a vacant seniority position. The speaker appoints other committee members. Seniority does not apply to membership on the six **procedural committees**, each of which considers bills and resolutions relating primarily to an internal legislative matter (for example, the Calendars Committee, which determines when a bill will be considered by the full House). The speaker appoints all members of procedural committees. In 2005, Craddick departed from the practice of maintaining a Republican majority on each House committee. As the result of his appointments, the 7-member Agriculture Committee had 4 Democrats.

Although substantive and procedural committees are established under House rules adopted in each regular session, the speaker independently creates **select committees** and appoints all members. He may do so at the beginning of a session, so that the House can work on emergency legislation before appointments for House substantive committees have been made. In 2005, for example, Speaker Craddick created select committees on Election Contests and Public Education Reform.

To ensure that representatives' efforts are not divided among too many committees, membership is limited to no more than two substantive committees.

*Table 7.3*　Texas House and Senate Committees, 79th Legislature, January 2005–January 2007

| House Committees (number of members) 34 Substantive Committees | House Committees (number of members) 6 Procedural Committees |
|---|---|
| Agriculture and Livestock (7) | Calendars (11) |
| Appropriations (29) | General Investigating and Ethics (5) |
| Border and International Affairs (7) | House Administration (11) |
| Business and Industry (9) | Local and Consent Calendars (11) |
| Civil Practices (9) | Redistricting (15) |
| Corrections (7) | Rules and Resolutions (11) |
| County Affairs (9) | |
| Criminal Jurisprudence (9) | **2 Select Committees** |
| Culture, Recreation, and Tourism (7) | Election Contests (9) |
| Defense Affairs and State-Federal Relations (9) | Public Education Reform (5) |
| Economic Development (7) | |
| Elections (7) | **Senate Committees (number of members)** **15 Standing Committees** |
| Energy Resources (7) | |
| Environmental Regulation (7) | Administration (7) |
| Financial Institutions (7) | Business and Commerce (9) |
| Government Reform (7) | Criminal Justice (7) |
| Higher Education (9) | Education (9) |
| Human Services (9) | Finance (15) |
| Insurance (9) | Government Organization (7) |
| Judiciary (9) | Health and Human Services (7) |
| Juvenile Justice and Family Issues (9) | Intergovernmental Relations (5) |
| Land and Resource Management (9) | International Relations and Trade (7) |
| Law Enforcement (7) | Jurisprudence (7) |
| Licensing and Administrative Procedures (9) | Natural Resources (11) |
| Local Government Ways and Means (7) | Nominations (7) |
| Natural Resources (9) | State Affairs (9) |
| Pensions and Investments (7) | Transportation and Homeland Security (9) |
| Public Education (9) | Veterans Affairs and Military Installations (7) |
| Public Health (9) | |
| Regulated Industries (7) | |
| State Affairs (9) | |
| Transportation (9) | |
| Urban Affairs (7) | |
| Ways and Means (9) | |

*Sources: Texas Legislative Handbook, 2005–2006* (Austin: Texas State Directory Press, 2005); and web sites for the House (**www.house.state.tx.us**) and Senate (**www.senate.state.tx.us**).

*Representative Harold Dutton questions economist Milton Friedman at a meeting of the House Public Education Committee, 78th Regular Session, 18 March 2003. (Texas House of Representatives Photography Department)*

Chairs of the powerful Appropriations Committee (spending of state money), Ways and Means Committee (taxes), and State Affairs Committee (many of the important subjects that do not involve spending and taxing) may not serve concurrently on another substantive committee.

### Senate Committees

Senate rules provide for **standing committees** (but do not identify them as substantive or procedural committees) and **special interim committees** (for studying important policy issues between sessions). As president of the Senate, the lieutenant governor appoints all committee members and designates the chair and vice chair of each committee. This power of appointment also extends to the three 3-member standing subcommittees: Agriculture and Coastal Resources (within the Committee on Natural Resources), [Military] Base Realignment and Closure (within the Committee on Veterans Affairs and Military Installations), and Emerging Technologies and Economic Development (within the Committee on Business and Commerce). Also appointed by the lieutenant governor is one 6-member standing subcommittee: Higher Education (within the Committee on Education). A senator serves on a maximum of three standing committees and is restricted to holding not more than one standing committee chair. At the beginning of the 79th regular session in 2005, Lieutenant Governor David Dewhurst appointed Republicans to chair nine standing committees and Democrats to chair six. None of the committees had a Democratic majority.

**standing committee** A Senate committee appointed by the lieutenant governor for the purpose of considering proposed bills and resolutions prior to possible floor debate and voting by senators.

**special interim committee** A Senate committee appointed by the lieutenant governor to study an important policy issue between regular sessions.

### Learning Check 7.6    (Answers on p. 287)

1. The House Administration Committee is not a substantive committee. What kind of committee is it?
2. What term describes a Senate committee appointed to study an important policy issue between sessions?

# ★ Legislative Caucus System

With the House and Senate firmly controlled for several years by Speaker Gib Lewis (1983–1993) and Lieutenant Governor Bill Hobby (1973–1991), caucuses of like-minded members exercised limited influence on the Texas Legislature. Each of these presiding officers sought to absorb potential opponents within his team and to discourage caucuses, which are legislative organizations based on partisan, philosophical, racial, ethnic, or other special interests. Although increasingly important, **legislative caucuses** are prohibited from receiving public money and using state office space.[12]

## Party Caucuses

Students of American national government are aware of the importance of Democratic and Republican Party caucuses in both chambers of the U.S. Congress. In state legislatures, one finds strong party caucus organizations whenever two-party competition is keen. In the 1980s and 1990s, the growing importance of party caucuses in each chamber of the Texas Legislature was one indication that Texas was becoming a two-party state. The House Democratic Caucus was organized in 1981 with 37 members. In recent years, all Democratic legislators have been reported as belonging to their party's House or Senate caucuses. Under the leadership of Tom Craddick, the House Republican Caucus was organized at the beginning of the 71st regular session in 1989. Party caucuses take policy positions on important issues and promote unity among their members.

## Racial/Ethnic Caucuses

In the U.S. Congress and in many state legislatures, racial and ethnic minorities organize and form voting blocs to maximize their power. Because African Americans and Latinos constitute significant minorities in the Texas Legislature, it is not surprising that they have formed caucuses for this purpose. Composed of African American senators and representatives, the Legislative Black Caucus concentrates on issues affecting African American Texans, such as the 2001 hate crimes bill that became law. It increased punishment for violent acts committed against individuals based on the victim's race, ethnicity, or sexual orientation. In the 1980s, the House-based Mexican American Legislative Caucus successfully pushed legislation placing farm workers under state workers' compensation, unemployment compensation, and minimum wage protection. In the 1990s, pressure from this caucus produced larger appropriations for state universities in South Texas and the Mexican border area from El Paso to Brownsville and north to Corpus Christi and San Antonio. More recently, the caucus has been instrumental in obtaining authorization and funding for a school of pharmacy at Texas A&M University–Kingsville, for the Regional Academic Health Center to serve the Lower Rio Grande Valley, and for the

**legislative caucus** An organization of legislators who seek to maximize their influence over issues in which they have a common interest.

Rep. Helen Giddings (D-Dallas, member of the Legislative Black Caucus) and Speaker Tom Craddick (R-Midland) at the front of the House chamber, with the San Jacinto battle flag in the background. (Texas House of Representatives Photography Department)

Texas Tech University Health Services Center in El Paso. Both the Mexican American Legislative Caucus and the Senate Hispanic Caucus include a few Anglo and African American members who have large numbers of Latino voters in their districts.

### Ideological Caucuses

Two House-based ideological caucuses have emerged. A conservative organization attracts Republicans and conservative Democrats, and a liberal group appeals to many Democrats (including several who are also members of the Legislative Black Caucus and the Mexican American Legislative Caucus). As might be expected, the conservative and liberal caucuses reflect opposing views on taxing and spending as well as on public interest issues such as environmental protection, but a few representatives belong to both caucuses.

Organized in 1985, the Texas Conservative Coalition is composed of both Republicans and conservative Democrats. This organization owes its creation to an increased number of Republican legislators elected in the early 1980s and to dissatisfaction with education reforms and tax increases enacted during a special session in 1984. Membership in the Texas Conservative Coalition reached 69 in 1993 and climbed to 93 in 1997, but by 2005 it had fallen to 83 (76 Republicans and 7 Democrats). Sixty-nine were representatives, and 14 were senators. The Texas Conservative Coalition Research Institute claims to be independent of the Texas Conservative Coalition but was organized on the initiative of Coalition leaders. It does public policy research and works through the media to sell its ideas to the public.

Established in November 1993 with 42 charter members, the Legislative Study Group represents the liberal Democrats' response to the Texas Conservative Coalition. The Legislative Study Group has called for ethical conduct throughout state government, campaign finance reform, consumer and environmental protection, long-term solutions to problems involving public safety, and various changes in Texas's systems of public education, health and human services, and criminal justice. Membership during the 79th regular session in 2005 was 45. All members were Democrats (43 representatives and 2 senators).

---

**Learning Check 7.7**    **(Answers on p. 287)**

1. True or False: The House-based Mexican American Legislative Caucus includes some Anglo and African members.
2. What is the name of the ideological caucus that represents the views of liberal Democrats?

---

## ★ Procedure

Enacting a law is not the only way to get things done in Austin. Passing bills and adopting resolutions, however, are the principal means whereby members of the Texas Legislature participate in making public policy. The legislature conducts its work according to detailed rules of procedure.

### Rules

To guide legislators in their work, each chamber adopts its own set of rules at the beginning of every regular session. Usually, few changes are made to the rules of the preceding session. Whether a bill is passed or defeated depends heavily on the skills of sponsors and opponents in using House and Senate rules.

The lieutenant governor and the speaker, who wield the gavel of authority in their respective chambers, decide questions concerning interpretation of rules. Because procedural questions may be complex and decisions must be made quickly, each chamber employs a **parliamentarian** to assist its presiding officer. Positioned on the dais immediately to the left of the lieutenant governor or speaker, this Senate or House expert on rules is ever ready to provide answers to procedural questions.

### A Bill Becomes a Law

The Texas Constitution calls for regular legislative sessions divided into three periods for distinct purposes. The first 30 days are reserved for the introduction of bills and resolutions, action on emergency appropriations, and the confirmation or rejection of recess appointments—appointments made by the governor

**parliamentarian** An expert on rules of order who sits at the left of the presiding officer in the House or Senate and is ever ready to give advice on procedural questions.

which would probably be approved if brought up for a vote. This delaying action is called **chubbing**.

To limit legislative logjams and discourage uninformed voting in the final days of a regular session, House rules contain prohibitions against second and third readings for the following:

- Nonlocal House bills during the last 17 days
- Local House bills during the last 10 days
- Senate bills during the last 5 days

Other detailed restrictions apply to House actions on the 126th to 139th days of a regular session. On the 140th, or final, day, House voting is limited to correcting bills that have passed. The Senate has similar end-of-session restrictions on considering legislation.

**5. Third reading (House)**    On the third reading, passage requires a simple majority vote of members present. Amendments may still be added at this stage, but such action requires a two-thirds majority vote. Following the addition of an amendment, a copy of the amended bill is made, checked over by the chief clerk, and stamped "Engrossed."

**6. First reading (Senate)**    After a bill passes on the third reading in the House, the chief clerk adds a statement certifying passage and transmits the bill to the Senate (where the original House number is retained). In the Senate, the secretary of the Senate reads aloud the House bill's caption and announces the committee to which the bill has been assigned by the lieutenant governor. Unless a sponsor certifies that the bill has no effect on the Texas Public Information Act, the director of the Legislative Budget Board must compile an impact statement that indicates whether the proposed legislation would prevent access to a public record and thus violate the state's open records law.

**7. Senate Committee Consideration and Report**    Senate procedure differs somewhat from House procedure. A senator may tag any bill by filing a request with either the Senate secretary or the committee chair to notify the tagging senator 48 hours before a hearing will be held on the bill. A tag usually kills the bill if done during the last days of a session.

If a majority of the committee members wants a bill to pass, it receives a favorable report. Bills are listed on the Senate's Regular Order of Business in the order in which the secretary of the Senate receives them. Unlike the House, the Senate has no calendar committees to control the flow of bills from standing committees to the Senate floor. At the beginning of each session, however, the Senate Administration Committee "parks" a blocking bill (called a "blocker")—on which floor action is not intended—at the head of the line. Bills arriving later are designated "out of order," and a vote of two-thirds of senators present and voting is required to suspend the regular order (i.e., bypass the blocker bill) and bring the bill to the Senate floor for debate. This **two-thirds rule** enhances the power of a party or a bipartisan group that can control more than one-third of the votes (which would be 11 votes if all 31 senators were

**chubbing**  A practice whereby supporters of a bill engage in lengthy debate for the purpose of using time and thus prevent floor action on another bill that they oppose.

**two-thirds rule**  A procedural device to control bringing bills to the Senate floor for debate.

# POINT/COUNTERPOINT

## Should Record Votes Be Required on Bills and Amendments?

**THE ISSUE** In an article published in the *Abilene Reporter News*, April 3, 2004, Scripps Howard reporter Monica Wolfson stated: "[Texas] lawmakers make thousands of votes every session on a variety of legislation including second and third readings of bills, amendments to bills, adoption of conference committee reports and constitutional joint resolutions. In the 2003 legislative session the Texas House recorded 951 votes, an increase from 649 in 2001, but there were at least 3,200 votes that went unrecorded. The Texas Senate took 3,449 recorded votes, but at least 1,000 votes went unrecorded." Should the House and Senate be required to record votes?

### Arguments For Requiring Record Votes

1. At an estimated expense of $330,000 for each regular session, including additional costs of printing and labor for daily journals, recorded votes will be worth the price ($50 per House vote and $100 per Senate vote).
2. Record votes are not too time-consuming; 41 state legislatures operate successfully with such a requirement.
3. The quality of debate will improve when legislators know that measures debated will be the subject of record votes.
4. Voters will be educated concerning the work of their legislators and will be able to cast informed votes when senators and representatives seek reelection.

*"It's poor governance to permit legislators to conceal their votes by failing to require that they be documented."*

—*Dallas Morning News* editorial, April 29, 2004

### Arguments Against Requiring Record Votes

1. In a time of tight budgets, any additional expenditure is too much.
2. Time devoted to recording votes will reduce the amount of time available for more important matters.
3. Debate will be chilled when legislators worry about how every one of their votes could be the subject of politically motivated criticism.
4. Any House member may ask for a record vote; in the Senate, a record vote is conducted at the request of three members. Some actions automatically require a record vote.

*Texas legislators like Rep. Roberto Gutierrez invariably insist that their votes should be recorded, but he warns: "If we were to go to a record vote on every vote, it could cost the state a great deal of money."*

—Quoted by Alma Walzer, "Groups Look to Change Legislature's Voting Method," *McAllen Monitor*, June 8, 2004.

present for voting).[15] Bills without this level of support cannot make it to the Senate floor.

**8. Second reading (Senate)** As with second readings in the House, the Senate debates the bill and considers proposed amendments. During the debate, custom permits a senator to speak about a bill as long as physical endurance permits. This delaying tactic is known as **filibustering**. On one occasion in 1977, Senator Bill Meier (D-Euless) filibustered for a record-setting 43 hours. A filibuster is most effective if undertaken toward the end of a session when time is short. A computer on the desk of each senator displays the texts of proposed amendments.

**filibustering** A delaying tactic whereby a senator may speak, and thus hold the Senate floor, for as long as physical endurance permits.

When debate has ended, a roll call vote is called by the secretary of the Senate. Unless a senator holds up two fingers to indicate an intention to vote no, the presiding officer usually announces that the chamber unanimously approves the bill after only a few names are called. The vote is recorded if requested by three senators. A computer-controlled board at the front of the chamber shows how each senator has voted. A vote requires a quorum of 21 senators present, but a simple majority of "yea" votes is sufficient to pass a bill.

**9. *Third reading (Senate)*** If passed on the second reading, a bill can have its third reading immediately, assuming the rules have been suspended. This action is routinely taken in the Senate by the required four-fifths majority vote of members present. Amending a bill on the third reading requires a two-thirds majority vote of members present. A simple majority vote is required for passage.

**10. *Return to the House*** After passage by the Senate, a House bill returns to the chief clerk of the House, who supervises preparation of a perfect copy of the bill and delivers it to the speaker. When an amendment has been added in the Senate (as usually happens), the change must be voted on in the House. If the House is not prepared to accept the amended bill, the ordinary procedure is to request a conference. Otherwise, the bill will die unless one of the chambers reverses its position.

**11. *Conference committee*** When the two chambers agree to send the bill to conference, each presiding officer appoints five members to serve on the **conference committee**. Attempts are made to adjust differences and produce a compromise version acceptable to both the House and the Senate. At least three Senate members and three House members must agree before the committee can recommend a course of action in the two houses. The author of the House bill (usually but not necessarily) serves as conference committee chair.

**12. *Conference committee report*** The conference committee's recommended settlement of questions at issue must be fully accepted or rejected by a simple majority vote in each chamber. Most are accepted. Both chambers, however, may agree to return the report to the committee, or, on request of the House, the Senate may accept a proposal for a new conference.

**13. *Enrollment*** After both chambers have accepted a conference report, the chief clerk of the House prepares a perfect copy of the bill and stamps it "Enrolled." The report is then presented to the House.

**14. *Signatures of the Chief Clerk and Speaker*** When the House receives the enrolled bill and the conference committee report, the bill is read by number only. Subsequently, it is signed by the chief clerk, who certifies the vote by which it passed. Then the speaker signs the bill.

**15. *Signatures of the Secretary of the Senate and the Lieutenant Governor*** Next, the chief clerk of the House takes the bill to the Senate, where it is read by number only. After certifying a passing vote, the secretary of the Senate signs the bill. Then the lieutenant governor does likewise.

**16. *Action by the governor*** While the legislature remains in session, the governor has three options. The governor can sign the bill; allow it to remain unsigned

**conference committee**
A committee composed of representatives and senators appointed to reach agreement on a disputed bill and recommend changes acceptable to both chambers.

for 10 days, not including Sundays, after which time it becomes law without the chief executive's signature; or, within the 10-day period, veto the measure by returning it to the House unsigned, with a message giving a reason for the veto. The Texas Constitution requires a vote of "two-thirds of the membership present" in the first house that considers a vetoed bill (in this case, the House of Representatives) and a vote of "two-thirds of the members" in the second house (in this case, the Senate) to override the governor's veto.[16]

After a session ends, the governor has 20 days, counting Sundays, in which to veto pending legislation and file the rejected bills with the secretary of state. A bill not vetoed by the governor automatically becomes law at the end of the 20-day period. Since the legislature is no longer in session, the governor's postadjournment veto is of special importance because it cannot be overridden. Usually, relatively few bills are vetoed. (See the chapter "The Executive" for information on Governor Perry's vetoes.)

Ordinarily, an act of the legislature does not take effect as a law until 90 days after adjournment, or even later if specified in the bill. Exceptions to this rule include a general appropriations act (which takes effect when approved) and a measure containing the provision that it will take effect immediately or less than 90 days after adjournment. The latter is no longer required to contain an emergency clause, but it must pass each house by a two-thirds majority vote of the total membership (21 votes in the Senate and 100 votes in the House of Representatives).

---

**Learning Check 7.8**     (Answers on p. 287)

**1.** True or False: The reading clerk reads aloud the full text of a House bill before it is referred to a committee.

**2.** What is the term for pressing a voting button for an absent representative?

---

## ⭐ Influences Within the Legislative Environment

In theory, elected legislators are influenced primarily, if not exclusively, by their constituents (especially constituents who vote). In practice, however, many legislators' actions bear little relationship to the needs or interests of the "folks back home." To be sure, Texas senators and representatives are not completely indifferent to voters, but many of them fall far short of being genuinely representative. One problem is that large numbers of citizens are uninterested in most governmental affairs and have no opinions about how the legislature should act in making public policy. Others may have opinions but are inarticulate or unable to communicate with their legislators. Therefore, lawmakers are likely to yield not only to the influence of the presiding officers in the House and Senate, but also to pressure from the governor and other powerful political actors (especially lobbyists) seeking to win their voluntary support or force their cooperation.

### The Governor

The threat of executive veto has an important influence on legislative behavior. Even a bill popular with many senators and representatives may not pass, because of such a threat. Knowledge that the governor opposes the measure is often sufficient to discourage its introduction. A bill introduced despite the governor's opposition is likely to be buried in a committee, tabled (postponed without commitment to reconsider), or defeated on the House or Senate floor.

Each governor campaigns for office on a platform of promises and then feels compelled to promote certain policies after being elected. Thus, legislators must be influenced to ensure the success of the governor's plans for taxing, spending, building, and educating, among other things. And if any doubt arises as to what the governor wants, gubernatorial policies are outlined in messages from time to time. Popular support for the chief executive's ideas makes opposition difficult, even though the people in a legislator's district may be adversely affected.[17]

### Judges, the Attorney General, and the Comptroller of Public Accounts

An act may be politically expedient and even popular with constituents and yet conflict with provisions of the Texas Constitution or the U.S. Constitution. Thus, in their lawmaking, all legislators are influenced by what state and federal judges have done or could do about possible legislative action. Usually, senators and representatives wish to avoid spending time or investing political capital in legislative efforts that will be struck down by judicial decisions or opinions of the attorney general. Therefore, while considering a bill, the committee chair may turn to the attorney general for an opinion concerning its constitutionality.

The state comptroller exercises great influence by estimating how much money will be collected under current and projected revenue laws because the legislature must keep state spending within the limits of anticipated revenue. For example, after an appropriation bill has passed the House and Senate, it goes to the comptroller. If the comptroller determines that Texas won't collect sufficient revenue, the bill does not receive the comptroller's certification and cannot be enacted unless both houses approve it by a four-fifths majority vote.

### Lobbyists

Lobbying as an interest group tactic is discussed in the chapter "The Politics of Interest Groups." Opinions vary concerning lobbyists' influence on legislative behavior and public policy. In many minds, lobbying means corruption. Others see lobbyists as performing a useful role by supplying information and serving as links with organized groups of constituents. But it is a nagging fact that special-interest groups spend large amounts of money to induce legislative action (usually to kill a bill) that a legislator would not otherwise take on personal initiative or in response to constituent requests. In fact, many bills are written by lobbyists and "carried" by cooperative legislators.[18]

Lobbyists must register with the Texas Ethics Commission and make state-required lobbying reports to that agency. Both lobbyists and political action committees (PACs) contribute directly to the campaign funds that cover legislators' election expenses. These same influence-seekers pay for a wide range of political and officeholder expenses.[19]

### Research Organizations

Policymakers need reliable information. Most Texas legislators depend heavily on information provided by their staffs, by administrative agencies, and by lobbyists. In addition, legislators obtain information from three official research bodies:

- The Texas Legislative Council: **www.tlc.state.tx.us**
- The House Research Organization: **www.hro.house.state.tx.us**
- The Senate Research Center: **www.senate.state.tx.us/src/index.htm**

Two of Texas's more important independent providers of public policy research and analysis are the following:

- The Center for Public Policy Priorities: **www.cppp.org**
- The Texas Public Policy Foundation: **www.tppf.org**

**The Legislative Council**    Authorizing special research projects by its staff is one function of the Legislative Council. It is composed of the lieutenant governor (joint chair), the speaker of the House (joint chair), six senators appointed by the lieutenant governor, the chair of the House Administration Committee, and five representatives appointed by the speaker. The council's staff provides support to legislators, other state officials, and the public in various areas. During the 79th regular session in 2005, the Legislative Council's executive director supervised about 400 employees, who provided bill drafting, legislative counseling, legislative research and writing, interim study committee research support, demographic and statistical data compilation and analysis, computer mapping and analysis, publications, and computer services.

**The House Research Organization**    A bipartisan steering committee of 15 representatives—elected by the House membership for staggered four-year terms—governs the House Research Organization (HRO). In 2006, eight Republicans and seven Democrats served on the steering committee. Because the HRO is an administrative department of the House, its operating funds are included in the House Administration Committee's budget. The HRO employed 16 staff personnel during the 79th regular legislative session in 2005, and about half that number worked during the interim between regular sessions.

(TRMPAC) modeled after Americans for a Republican Majority founded by U.S. Representative Tom DeLay (R–Sugar Land).[1]

As president of TAB, former Texas House member Bill Hammond viewed the 2002 primaries and general election as steps toward a House GOP majority that would elect his friend Tom Craddick as Texas's first Republican speaker since the Reconstruction era. To do this, Hammond used his corporate contacts to raise big money, but it is a third-degree felony offense to give corporate funds directly to candidates. Hammond's strategy was to spend corporate contributions, such as those he solicited from the Texas insurance industry in August 2002, to "educate" voters by using TAB phone banks and direct mail for communicating positive or negative messages designed to influence voter behavior in selected districts.

A few weeks before the November 2002 election, lobbyist Mike Toomey began playing a major role in the effort to elect Republican legislative candidates. He was a member of TAB's governing board, former state representative, former chief of staff for governor Bill Clements, and long-time friend of Governor Perry. According to Austin journalist Laylan Copelin, Toomey raised funds for TAB's $1.7 million advertising campaign, supervised direct-mail efforts, and organized meetings attended by representatives of TRMPAC and Texans for Lawsuit Reform, business lobbyists and public relations specialists, and others who wanted to elect business-friendly legislators.[2]

As an example of TAB's operations, Representative Ann Kitchen (D-Austin) was targeted with negative "issue ads" mailed to voters in her district and by phone calls suggesting that Kitchen favored more government taxing and spending. Todd Baxter, her GOP opponent, denied that his election campaign was coordinated with TAB. As evidence that the defeated Democrats could have grounds for complaint, Hammond bragged that TAB "blew the doors off" the 2002 election by "educating" voters with 4 million mailings and spending $2 million on just 22 House contests and 2 Senate races. Hammond's boasting caught the attention of Travis County district attorney Ronnie Earle, who began a grand jury investigation.

Although TAB was indicted in Austin for using corporate money to influence elections, the case was thrown out by state District Judge Mike Lynch in June 2006. Lynch asserted that most common-sense people would view TAB's ads as "clear support for specific candidates," but he held that these ads did not expressly call for defeat or election of anyone. Earle indicated that he would appeal the decision and that he would proceed with another indictment charging TAB with making an illegal contribution to its own political action committee.

Earle investigated TRMPAC, too. Organized by Tom DeLay on September 1, 2001, this political action committee received $50,000 in start-up money from Americans for a Republican Majority. Jim Ellis, one of DeLay's top aides, became director of the Texas PAC. Bill Ceverha, a lobbyist and former GOP member of the Texas House, was made treasurer; and John Colyandro, executive director of the Texas Conservative Coalition in 2004, was hired as executive director.

How TRMPAC raised money that influenced the outcome of legislative elections in 2002 is documented in a typed memo obtained by the *Texas Observer* and first publicized by the *Houston Chronicle*. The memo features a list of executives with Houston businesses (e.g., Reliant Energy, Compass Bank, Maxxam, EOG Resources) who were visited on September 9, 2002, by Representative Beverly Woolley (R-Houston) and TRMPAC fundraiser Susan Lilly. Beside the names of these business executives are notes that indicate amounts of money promised and legislative matters in which donors were interested. A total of $53,000 was pledged that day, and campaign finance records indicate the pledges were paid shortly thereafter. On September 12, 2002, Lilly and Representative Dianne Delisi (R-Temple) made similar fundraising efforts in Dallas netting $35,000; but their itinerary for that trip does not indicate the legislative interests of the Dallas executives they visited.[3]

Results of the 2002 election caused most Republicans to be jubilant. GOP candidates won 88 of 150 state House seats and 19 of 31 Senate seats. At the same time, Republicans won the governor's race and all other statewide contests. Outcomes of congressional elections, however, were disappointing for DeLay and the GOP.

Across the Lone Star State, nearly 2,300,000 Republican votes were cast to elect fifteen U.S. representatives; but seventeen were elected with less than 1,900,000 Democratic votes. In part, these results were due to low voter turnout in Democrat-controlled districts with many Latino and African American residents. Furthermore, some Republican ticket-splitters and independent voters preferred incumbent Democratic representatives with seniority rather than less-experienced Republican candidates. (When seeking federal funds for projects within a congressional district, seniority helps to "bring home the bacon.")

## Congressional "Re-redistricting" in 2003

Traditionally, congressional redistricting in Texas and other states is done only once each decade, unless a districting plan is found to violate the U.S. Constitution or a statute. Nevertheless, DeLay was determined that the Republican-controlled 78th Legislature would "re-redistrict" Texas in 2003, and Texas Attorney General Greg Abbott ruled that it had such authority. Lieutenant Governor David Dewhurst was not enthusiastic about drawing new congressional districts, but Tom Craddick (R-Midland) had been elected speaker of the House in January 2003, and Craddick and Governor Perry agreed with DeLay. Nevertheless, a congressional redistricting bill failed to pass the House because 51 Democratic members broke the House quorum by fleeing to Ardmore, Oklahoma, and one crossed the border into Mexico. They stayed away until time ran out for House action in the regular session that ended on June 2, 2003.

In the first special session called by Governor Perry (June 30 to July 28), GOP efforts to pass a congressional redistricting bill were thwarted by the Senate rule requiring a two-thirds majority to bring a bill to the Senate floor. Just before the second special session was called, eleven of the Senate's twelve Democrats escaped to Albuquerque, New Mexico, when it became apparent that Lieutenant Governor Dewhurst would dispense with the two-thirds rule for that session (July 28 to August 26). Eventually, Senator John Whitmire (D-Houston) deserted his colleagues in Albuquerque and returned to Austin. This paved the way for the third special session (September 15 to October 12), when the two-thirds rule was not used and a congressional redistricting bill crafted under the personal direction of Congressman Tom DeLay was passed. This legislation adopted Plan 01374C for Texas's 32 congressional districts.

Democrats contended that Plan 01374C involved unconstitutional partisan and racial gerrymandering (some called it "perrymandering") and violated the Voting Rights Act. When submitted to the U.S. Department of Justice for preclearance by its Civil Rights Division, Plan 01374C was rejected in a 73-page confidential memorandum prepared by career staff in the Voting Section. Political appointees in the Department of Justice precleared the plan, however, and the memorandum was not made public until it was leaked to the press two years later. Meanwhile, early in 2004, a three-judge federal district court sitting in Austin responded to a Democratic challenge by deciding 2-1 to uphold the plan. Democrats

Tom DeLay grins as he strides down a Capitol hallway during congressional "re-redistricting" struggle in October 2003. *(Tom Reel/San Antonio Express/Zuma Press)*

*Table 2*    Tom DeLay Timeline

| | |
|---|---|
| **2001** | |
| September | Texans for a Republican Majority (TRMPAC) organized with start-up money from Tom DeLay's Americans for a Republican Majority (ARMPAC). |
| **2002** | |
| September | TRMPAC raises $190,000 in corporate donations that is sent to the Republican National Committee (RNC). |
| October | RNC sends $190,000 in noncorporate donations to 7 Republican candidates for Texas House. |
| **2003** | |
| May–October | DeLay urges Congressional "re-redistricting" by Texas Legislature. |
| **2004** | |
| September | Travis County grand jury indicts 3 of DeLay's associates and 7 corporations for activities involving corporate money-raising by TRMPAC. |
| October | U.S. House Committee on Standards of Official Conduct rebukes DeLay for golfing with executives from TRMPAC contributor Weststar Energy Corporation, while an energy bill supported by Weststar was pending in Congress. |
| **2005** | |
| September | DeLay steps down as U.S. House majority leader after a Travis County grand jury indicts him and 2 associates for conspiracy to violate election laws. Indictments dismissed later. |
| October | Another Travis County grand jury indicts DeLay and the same 2 associates for conspiracy and laundering $190,000 of TRMPAC's corporate donations through RNC. |
| **2006** | |
| March | DeLay wins Republican primary contest for U.S. House District 22 candidacy. |
| April | DeLay announces he will withdraw candidacy and resign from U.S. House. |
| June | DeLay resigns from U.S. House. |
| July | U.S. District Court rules DeLay can withdraw District 22 candidacy but Republicans cannot nominate a successor. |
| August | U.S. Circuit Court and U.S. Supreme Court Justice Antonin Scalia sustain the district court's ruling. |
| September | DeLay resigns District 22 seat. |
| November | Democrat Nick Lampson wins District 22 seat for 2007–2008. |

appealed this decision, but the U.S. Supreme Court refused to prevent the plan's use while the case was pending. Thus, the way was clear for using Plan 01374C to elect Texas's 32 U.S. representatives in November 2004.

## Elections of 2004

Because his old Piney Woods district was dismembered by the new congressional redistricting plan, U.S. Repre-

sentative Jim Turner (D-Crockett) did not seek reelection in 2004. Ralph Hall (D-Rockwall) saved his congressional skin by switching to the Republican Party and winning the District 4 nomination in the GOP's first primary. Chris Bell (D-Houston) was defeated in the Democratic Party's first primary by African American Al Green in District 9, a largely African American district. Democrats Eddie Bernice Johnson (Dallas, Dist. 30), Sheila Jackson Lee (Houston, Dist. 18), and Gene Green (Houston, Dist. 29) had no

Republican opponents in November. Democrats Charlie Gonzalez (San Antonio, Dist. 20), Solomon Ortiz (Corpus Christi, Dist. 27), Silvestre Reyes (El Paso, Dist. 16), and Ruben Hinojosa (Mercedes, Dist. 15) had GOP opponents but won their general election contests. Five incumbents did not face opposition in the second Democratic primary: Max Sandlin (Marshall, Dist. 1), Nick Lampson (Beaumont, Dist. 2), Chet Edwards (Waco, Dist. 17), Charlie Stenholm (Abilene, Dist. 19), and Martin Frost (Arlington, Dist. 32). All but Edwards were defeated in November when they ran in districts that had been drawn to the advantage of Republican candidates. Frost's opponent was U.S. Representative Pete Sessions (R-Dallas). Incumbent Ciro Rodriguez (San Antonio, Dist. 28) was named winner over Henry Cuellar in the first Democratic primary, but a recount turned Rodriguez's victory by a margin of 145 votes into a 203-vote loss that he challenged unsuccessfully in court. Cuellar won the District 28 seat by defeating Republican Jim Hopson in November. In the first Democratic primary, Lloyd Doggett (Austin, Dist. 25) defeated Leticia Hinojosa in a predominantly Hispanic-populated, "fajita-strip" or "bacon-strip" district stretching 300 miles from Austin to the Rio Grande. In November, Doggett retained his congressional seat by beating Republican Rebecca Armendariz Klein. GOP candidates in Republican-friendly districts won the remaining seats in the Texas delegation.

As a result of congressional redistricting in 2003, Texas's Republican representation in the U.S. House increased from 15 in that year to 21 in 2005, while Democratic representation fell from 17 to 11. But at what risks and what costs did DeLay and others engineer their redistricting feats and electoral triumphs?

## Legal Problems

As Ronnie Earle pursued grand jury investigations in 2003, Republican Party chair Tina Benkiser filed an open records request that produced hundreds of documents. Among the DA's records that were released were five advance drafts of an article by Dave McNeely, a long-time columnist for the *Austin American-Statesman,* concerning Craddick, Hammond, and DeLay. With one of these drafts sent to Earle and assistant district attorney Gregg Cox, McNeely wrote, "Appreciate it if you each give it a read and then let's

talk. Looking mostly to make sure I haven't screwed up anywhere or have some huge omission." Later, McNeely's long article, "Grand Old Politics," appeared in the July 20, 2003, issue of the *Austin American-Statesman.* The article's subheading declared: "Money paved the road to Republican dominance in the Legislature, and to no one's surprise, that road led straight to contributors' goals. But was it all legal?"

While Earle and a succession of Travis County grand juries conducted official investigations, researchers for the *Houston Chronicle* independently examined more than 10,000 pages of Republican and Democratic campaign records. A *Chronicle* article published on April 25, 2004, noted "no apparent violations of state laws" by the Texas Democratic Party. At the same time, it reported that in 2002 the Texas Republican Party raised $5.7 million from corporations and from national committees that solicit corporate donations. Most of these funds, according to the *Chronicle,* were then transferred to the Texas Republican Congressional Campaign Committee (TRCCC) and spent for nonadministrative purposes.

On June 15, 2004, Texas's congressional redistricting controversy became a national political issue. That was the day U.S. Representative Chris Bell announced he had filed a complaint with the U.S. House Committee on Standards of Official Conduct against House Majority Leader Tom DeLay. Seven years had passed since the committee's finding in another ethics case led the House to reprimand Speaker Newt Gingrich, fine him $300,000, and influence his departure from the U.S. Congress. Now Bell was striking back at DeLay, whose congressional redistricting scheme had forced Bell into a losing primary contest. His complaint charged that DeLay

- accepted $25,000 for TRMPAC, from Westar Energy Corporation, in return for promoting congressional legislation that would have benefited the Kansas-based energy company.
- used the Republican National Committee to launder $190,000 in corporate contributions to benefit GOP legislative candidates in Texas
- pressured federal agencies to locate Pete Laney's airplane and prevent its use to transport Texas representatives out of the state in an effort to prevent passage of a congressional redistricting bill.[4]

The bipartisan Committee on Standards of Official Conduct (5 Republicans and 5 Democrats) found Bell's complaint had merit. This meant that the committee would study it for a maximum of 45 days before deciding whether to undertake an investigation that could lead to fining DeLay or even expelling him from the House. Many Democrats and others were calling for appointment of an independent counsel to investigate Bell's charges against DeLay.

On September 21, 2004, DeLay's involvement with TRMPAC became national news when a Travis County grand jury returned indictments against three of DeLay's associates (Jim Ellis, John Colyandro, and Warren RoBold), seven corporations, and the Alliance for Quality Nursing Home Care. The corporations and the nursing home organization contributed to TRMPAC before the 2002 election. On September 22, 2004, it was revealed that Chris Winkle, CEO of Mariner Health Care, had given Speaker Tom Craddick the Alliance's $100,000 check for TRMPAC as they dined at Anthony's in Houston.

On October 6, the U.S. House Committee on Standards of Official Conduct rebuked DeLay for participating with Weststar Energy Corporation executives in a golfing fundraiser shortly after they contributed $25,000 to Texans for a Republican Majority and while an energy bill was before Congress. Although the ethics committee also criticized DeLay for seeking the Federal Aviation Administration's assistance in locating Speaker Pete Laney's private plane when Democratic legislators fled from Austin to Ardmore in 2003, it decided not to rule on Bell's money-laundering charge while legal actions were underway in Texas.

After nearly a year passed without further action by the U.S. House committee, DeLay faced a more serious problem in Austin. On September 28, 2005, DeLay, Jim Ellis, and John Colyandro were indicted by a Travis County grand jury for conspiracy to violate Texas election laws by using corporate donations to support state legislative candidates. This offense is a state jail felony punishable by a fine of $10,000 and confinement for six months to two years. When DeLay's lawyer challenged the indictments, Ronnie Earle sought money laundering indictments before a second grand jury on September 30. After this effort failed, Earle went before a third grand jury on October 3 and obtained criminal conspiracy (2nd degree

felony) and money laundering (1st degree felony) indictments against Delay, Ellis, and Colyandro. The charges involved sending a TRMPAC check for $190,000 raised from corporations to the director of the Republican National Committee (RNC) along with names of seven Texas House candidates. Punishment for a 2nd felony is a maximum fine of $10,000 and imprisonment for 2 to 20 years. A 1st degree felony is punished with the same maximum fine and imprisonment for 5 to 99 years.[5]

## League of United Latin American Citizens [LULAC] v. Perry

The U.S. Supreme Court responded to the 2005 appeal from Texas Democrats (noted above) by remanding the redistricting case to the three-judge district court with instruction to reconsider it in light of *Vieth* v. *Jubelirer* (2004), a Pennsylvania case in which the U.S. Supreme Court upheld (5 to 4) a Republican gerrymander. After reconsideration, the district court ruled again in favor of Texas Republicans. Subsequently, the U.S. Supreme Court decided to rehear the case. Thus, on March 1, 2006, *LULAC* v. *Perry* and three related Texas redistricting cases were argued in Washington. Four months later (on June 28, just one day before the end of the term) the court announced its decision.[6]

Multiple opinions were written on different parts of the case, but Justice Anthony M. Kennedy (supported by Chief Justice John G. Roberts, Jr. and Justices Samuel A. Alito, Antonin Scalia, and Clarence Thomas) rejected complaints by Democrats that the Texas redistricting plan was too partisan to be constitutional. On another issue, only Justices Kennedy and John Paul Stevens condemned mid-term redistricting. But Justice Kennedy (supported by Justices David M. Souter, Ruth Bader Ginsburg, John Paul Stevens, and Stephen G. Breyer) ruled that Congressman Henry Bonilla's District 23, stretching from Laredo to El Paso, had been drawn in violation of Section 2 of the Civil Rights Act. This section protects the right of minorities to "participate in the political process and to elect representatives of their choice." The problem was that the Republican-controlled 78th Texas Legislature had protected Bonilla by moving part of Webb County with about 100,000 Latinos from his district and adding an equal number of largely Republican Anglos in three Hill Country counties northwest of San Antonio. To remedy this vote dilution for Latinos, the district court was directed to act. It responded by inviting parties to the suit to submit redistricting plans for District 23 and, as necessary, for nearby counties. So, all Webb County was put in District 28, while four Hill Country counties were taken from Bonilla's district and south Bexar County added.

## Tom Delay in 200611

As required by rules of the U.S. House of Representatives, Tom Delay had to resign his office as majority floor leader after he was indicted. Nevertheless, in March 2006, he won a Republican primary contest for nomination as the GOP candidate in District 22. Then on April 4, DeLay announced that he had moved his residence to Virginia and would resign as a member of the House and would withdraw as a candidate for reelection. This announcement came amidst a growing scandal concerning Washington lobbyist Jack Abramoff and former DeLay aides who pled guilty to corruption charges.[7] Seeking to capitalize on DeLay's declining popularity and perceived loss of political power, Texas Democrats sued to prevent the Republican Party from naming another candidate. In July, U.S. District Judge Sam Sparks ruled that DeLay could withdraw his candidacy but that the GOP could not name a substitute. Republicans appealed the case to the U.S. Court of Appeals for the Fifth Circuit. Meanwhile, Democrat Nick Lampson, who had lost his District 2 seat in 2004, continued a well financed campaign to win the District 22 seat.

After the circuit court affirmed Judge Sparks's ruling, the case was appealed to the U.S. Supreme Court. That court would not convene until October, but Justice Antonin Scalia ruled in August that the Texas Republican Party could not nominate another candidate. After DeLay requested removal of his name from the November general election ballot, Republican leaders urged voters to cast write-in votes for Houston Councilwoman Shelley Sekula-Gibbs. She paid the $3,125 filing fee required of write-in candidates, and she filed also as a candidate in a special election to fill the District 22 vacancy for the two months (November and December) remaining in the term. Both elections were held on November 7.

Democrat Nick Lampson concentrated on his general election campaign and did not run in the special election race. Sekula-Gibbs won the special election, but Lampson won the general election. As for Tom DeLay, he was still awaiting trial when Lampson took office in January 2007. Meanwhile, District Attorney Ronnie Earle continued investigations in Austin, and Texas politicians speculated on the course of future elections and on redistricting following the federal census of 2010.

**Notes**

1. For biographical information and details concerning DeLay's involvement in Texas redistricting politics, see Lou Dubose and Jan Reid, *The Hammer, Tom DeLay: God, Money, and the Rise of the Republican Congress* (New York: Public Affairs Press, 2004). The updated edition of this book is *The Hammer Comes Down: The Nasty, Brutish and Shortened Political Life of Tom DeLay* (New York: Public Affairs Press, 2006). Details on the 2002 election cycle and the involvement of TAB and TRMPAC are covered by Jake Bernstein and Dave Mann in their critical article, "The Rise of the Machine: How a Small Group of Politicians and Corporations Bought Themselves a Legislature," *Texas Observer*, 29 August 2003, 4–11, 19, 28–30.

2. Laylan Copelin, "GOP Heavyweight Toomey Led Key Ad Effort," *Austin American-Statesman,* 16 May 2004.

3. For details concerning corporate money, lobbyists and campaign funding, see Jake Bernstein and Dave Mann, "Rate of Exchange: What Corporations Might Have Gotten from Their Investment in Craddick and DeLay," *Texas Observer*, 12 March 2004, 4–7, 18–19; and *The K Street Effect Hits Texas* (Austin: Texans for Public Justice, July 2006). For a controversial film made with the cooperation of District Attorney Ronnie Earle, see Mark Birbaum and Jim Schermbek, *The Big Buy: Tom DeLay's Stolen Congress*, Birbaum/Schermbek Films, DVD distributed by Brave New Films (Culver City, Calif.: 2006).

4. See Eunice Moscoso, "DeLay Targeted in Ethics Complaint," *Austin American-Statesman,* 16 June 2004; and Gary Martin, "DeLay Accused of Criminal Ethics Violations," *San Antonio Express-News,* 16 June 2004. For conflicting views, see U.S. Rep. Chris Bell, "DeLay Undermines Small 'd' Democracy," *Houston Chronicle,* 20 June 2004; and Rep. John Carter, "Bell's Frivolous Complaint Is a Bid to Demonize DeLay," *Austin American-Statesman,* 25 June 2004.

5. See Jake Bernstein's critical "Tommy and the $190,000: The Tale of the Money Transfer that

Toppled the House Majority Leader," *Texas Observer*, 21 October 2005, 12, 21.

6. *League of United Latin American Citizens* v. *Perry*, 126 S. Ct. 2594 (2006). The day after this decision was announced, all of Texas's major newspapers printed front-page stories on the ruling. For example, see Todd J. Gellman and Robert T. Garrett, "GOP Wins in Map Ruling," *Dallas Morning News*, 29 June 2006. See also Charles Backstrom, Samuel Krislov, and Leonard Robins, "Desperately Seeking Standards: The Court's Frustrating Attempts to Limit Political Gerrymandering," *PS: Political Science & Politics*, 39 (July 2006): 409–415.

7. See Paul Burka, "Without DeLay," *Texas Monthly*, May 2006, 112–117, 196, 198–207.

An extensive bibliography of books and articles for this chapter is posted on Selected Sources for Reading, available online at http://college.hmco.com/PIC/brownPTP13e. For use with any chapter, see Resources for Further Research online at http://college.hmco.com/PIC/brownPTP13e.

*Chapter 8*

# The Executive

★ **Looking Back**

★ **Overview of the Governorship**

★ **Powers of the Governor**

★ **The Plural Executive**

John Branch cartoon. Copyright © 2004 *San Antonio Express-News*. Reprinted with permission.

No other Texas officeholder is so widely recognized and receives as much media attention as the governor. Consider Governor Rick Perry's April 2004 proposal to raise additional revenue for public education, which focused on raising part of the money through a $1 increase per pack for the state cigarette tax, a $5 admission fee to places of so-called adult entertainment, and a state tax on video-lottery terminals (similar to slot-machines) at racetracks. Although many Texans reacted with disdain to some or all elements of Perry's revenue plan (see John Branch's cartoon) and the legislature ultimately rejected it, news media throughout the state gave much publicity to Perry's proposal. In 2006, however, the legislature did increase the cigarette tax by $1 per pack.

Given the level of attention and media coverage the office receives, you might be surprised to learn that, unlike the president of the United States, the Texas governor shares executive power. The president appoints (with Senate approval) and can independently remove members of a cabinet. In Texas, however, Article IV of the Texas Constitution establishes a multi-headed executive branch or plural executive within which the governor shares power with other *elected* executive officials and with appointed members of numerous boards and commissions created by the legislature (see Figure 8.1).

As you learn about the workings of the executive branch of Texas government, consider an observation that Professor Larry Sabato (University of Virginia) makes in a book widely read by political scientists and others for more than two decades: "Governors as a class have outgrown the description 'good time Charlie.'"[1] He observes that they are concerned about their work, have new powers that give them influence in state and national councils, are skilled negotiators and coordinators in dealing with officials at state and national levels, and are trained, effective leaders. In your opinion, is the governor of Texas a "good-time Charlie"? What about the other officials in Texas's executive branch?

## Looking Back

Several of Texas's political traditions and institutions stem from the state's experiences after the Civil War. Even today, the state's executive structure shows the influence of anti-Reconstruction reactions against Governor E. J. Davis's administration (1870–1874). Numerous abuses of power by state officials reporting directly to Governor Davis explain why many Texans still distrust the "strong" executive model of state government.

Written after the end of Reconstruction, the Constitution of 1876 provides for election of the governor, lieutenant governor, attorney general, comptroller of public accounts, and commissioner of the General Land Office. In addition, the legislature has provided for election of a commissioner of agriculture. The secretary of state is the only constitutional executive officer who is appointed by the governor, with approval by the Senate.

## Overview of the Governorship

Recent acts of the Texas Legislature have given the governor more power than earlier governors held, but Texas does not have a governor who merits the title "chief executive." Nevertheless, limited executive power does not discourage ambitious gubernatorial candidates who wage multimillion-dollar campaigns in their efforts to win this prestigious office.

### Gubernatorial Politics: Money and Media

After pumping millions of dollars into a winning gubernatorial election campaign, donors of large amounts of money are often appointed to key policy-making positions. The practice of buying influence with campaign contributions permeates American politics. Texas politics is no exception.

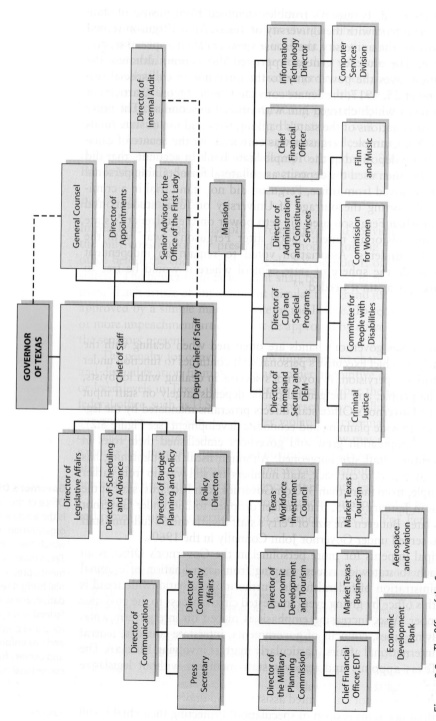

*Figure 8.2*    The Office of the Governor

a primary function of many staff assistants, particularly the press secretary and the director of appointments. All Texas governors have placed close friends and political associates in staff positions—persons who can be relied on for their loyalty to the chief executive. For example, Mike McKinney, Mike Toomey, and Rick Perry began serving in the House of Representatives in 1985. With two other conservative representatives, they became known as the "Pit Bulls" for their budget-cutting zeal. After Perry became governor, he appointed McKinney

## POINT/COUNTERPOINT

### Should Top Aides Receive Supplemental Pay from Campaign Funds?

**THE ISSUE**   "Pay Supplements to Top State Aides Let Lobby Buy Access, Critics Charge" is the title of journalist Ken Herman's article in the *Austin American-Statesman,* August 9, 2003. Explaining that annual salary supplements are paid from Governor Rick Perry's campaign fund, Herman provides the following data:

| Aide | State Salary | Salary Supplement |
|---|---|---|
| Mike Toomey, chief of staff | $135,000 | $107,000* |
| Bill Jones, general counsel | $134,160 | $13,842 |
| Deirdre Delisi, deputy chief of staff | $84,000 | $14,378 |
| Eric Bearse, speechwriter | $77,400 | $4,282 |

*Annualized calculation based on payments reported by Perry for the first six months of the year.
*Source:* Governor's Office and campaign finance reports.

**Arguments For Supplemental Pay**

1. Higher pay is needed to attract top talent to important jobs.
2. Supplemental pay is a bargain for taxpayers, because it does not come from the state treasury.
3. Top staff members do some political work, so it is appropriate they receive supplemental pay from campaign funds.

*In a letter seeking money to supplement primarily the salary of one top staff assistant for then comptroller Carole Keeton Rylander, fundraiser Len Mertz explained, "These professionals are necessary for the comptroller's office to provide the state of Texas with first-class service and would most likely not be in public service due to the disparity in wages compared with the private sector."*

—Quoted by Jay Root in "Campaign Raises Funds for Staffers," *Fort Worth Star-Telegram,* June 19, 2004

**Arguments Against Supplemental Pay**

1. Texas can afford to pay whatever compensation is needed for personnel who assist elected officials.
2. State employees at all levels should be beholden to taxpayers alone and not be beholden in part to big donors who contribute most of the campaign money raised by elected officials.
3. Supplemental pay for employees of the federal government is illegal, and this should be the model for Texas government.

*Tom "Smitty" Smith, director of the Texas branch of Public Citizen, commented that raising campaign funds to supplement the salaries of high-ranking staff personnel "…is a new twist in the annals of campaign fundraising and will lead to government of, for and by the contributors."*

—Quoted by Jay Root in "Campaign Raises Funds for Staffers," *Fort Worth Star-Telegram,* June 19, 2004.

his law enforcement career as a DPS Highway Patrol trooper in El Paso in 1975, served as Texas's first black Chief Ranger in 2004–2005.

**Budgetary Power**     Gubernatorial **budgetary power** is subordinated in part to the legislature's prerogative of controlling the state's purse strings. By statutory requirement, the governor (assisted by personnel in the Governor's Office of Budget, Planning and Policy) and the Legislative Budget Board each should prepare separate budgets for consideration by the legislature. Texas law requires distribution of the governor's budget to each legislator before delivery of the governor's State of the State message. Traditionally, both the House and the Senate have been inclined to give greater respect to the Legislative Budget Board's spending proposals.

In the fall of 2002, Governor Perry announced his intention to present a detailed budget to the 78th Legislature early in 2003. Perry and his budget assistants followed the comptroller's earlier estimate that the state would experience a $5.1 billion shortfall for the 2004–2005 biennium. But on January 13, the day before the legislature convened, Comptroller Carole Keeton Strayhorn shocked Perry and others with a new estimate indicating that the shortfall would be $9.9 billion. Subsequently, the governor ceased efforts to produce a detailed spending plan, and on January 17, he sent to the legislature a 400-page document filled with budget items followed by zeros. Perry explained that this "zero-based" budget would make legislators start from scratch and justify spending for every budget item. In his State of the State address delivered in February, Perry made suggestions for spending reductions totaling about $9.5 billion.[9]

The Texas governor's principal control over state spending comes from the constitutional power to veto an entire appropriations bill or to use the **line-item veto** to kill individual budget items. (See "Veto Power" below for more on this subject.) In June 2003, for example, Governor Perry used the line-item veto to cut $81.1 million from the state budget for fiscal years 2004 and 2005. In June 2005, his line-item vetoes reduced the state budget by $35.3 billion for all funds, including $33.8 billion for public education. In subsequent special sessions of the legislature, $33.2 billion was restored to the Texas Education Agency.

**Executive Orders and Proclamations**     One instrument of executive authority is the **executive order**. In his first five years as governor, Rick Perry issued 56 executive orders to set policy within the executive branch and to create or abolish various executive task forces, boards, commissions, and councils. In 2002, for example, he issued Executive Order 21, creating the Governor's Clean Coal Technology Council to advise him on preserving fuel diversity and on reducing emissions and increasing efficiency of coal-fired electric generation.[10] One of Perry's most controversial actions was Executive Order 47 issued in 2005. It directs school districts to use at least 65 percent of their revenue for direct classroom instructional purposes as defined by the National Center for Education Statistics.

Another instrument of executive authority is the **proclamation**, an official public announcement often used for ceremonial purposes (for example, pro-

---

**budgetary power** The governor is supposed to submit a state budget to the legislature at the beginning of each regular session. When an appropriation bill is enacted by the legislature and certified by the comptroller of public accounts, the governor may veto the whole document or individual items.

**line-item veto** Action by the governor to delete a line item while permitting enactment of other parts of an appropriation bill.

**executive order** The governor issues executive orders to set policy within the executive branch and to create task forces, councils, and other bodies.

**proclamation** A governor's official public announcement (e.g., calling a special election or declaring a disaster area).

claiming Pearl Harbor Remembrance Day or Disabilities Employment Awareness Month). In 2004, Governor Perry stirred up controversy when he rejected President Bush's recommendation that all governors observe October 24 as United Nations Day with "appropriate ceremonies and activities." Perry refused to issue a proclamation calling for the requested observance because of the UN's failure to support the U.S. government's Iraq policy. Important uses of proclamations include calling special sessions of the legislature and special elections, declaring a region to be a disaster area (qualifying some individuals, businesses, and local governments for financial assistance), and announcing the ratification of constitutional amendments.

**Economic Development**    After a series of mismanagement problems within the Texas Department of Economic Development, Governor Perry sought direct control over efforts to attract investment from other states and countries. In 2003, the 78th Legislature abolished the department and placed the state's economic development program within the Governor's Office. This action was taken after the department's failure to coordinate local and state efforts to persuade the Boeing Company to relocate its corporate headquarters from Seattle to the Dallas–Fort Worth area instead of selecting Chicago. To prevent a similar occurrence, Governor Perry intervened directly in efforts to bring a Toyota plant to San Antonio. Finally, with a $133 million incentive package for Toyota and $28.5 million for an 8-mile rail spur and other infrastructure improvements, the Toyota Motor Company announced on February 5, 2003 that it would build a pickup truck plant in San Antonio.[11]

At Perry's urging, the 78th Legislature established the Texas Enterprise Fund by taking $295 million from the state's "rainy day" fund (an account intended to pay for state operations in times of emergency) and using it to attract or retain industry in fiscal years 2004 and 2005. With approval of Speaker Craddick and Lieutenant Governor Dewhurst, by April 2004 about $195 million had been allocated to keep or create more than 9,000 jobs in Texas. Included were $40 million to keep Sematech in Austin; $35 million for Vought Aircraft Industries to consolidate two of its out-of-state facilities with operations in Dallas; $3.5 million for the Texas Energy Center at Sugar Land, near Houston; $50 million for engineering and computer science programs at the University of Texas at Dallas, as part of a deal for Texas Instruments to build a microchip factory nearby; and $5 million to the Citgo Petroleum Corporation to move its headquarters from Tulsa to Houston.[12]

In 2005, the 79th Legislature appropriated $182.3 for the Texas Enterprise Fund. Nearly $11 million of that money was given to Samsung, the South Korean computer chip maker, to build a second factory in Austin expected to employ 900 people. Other incentives for Samsung featured tax abatements by the Manor Independent School District (about $115 million over 10 years), the City of Austin ($62.9 million over 20 years), and Travis County ($44.7 million over 20 years).[13] (For more details concerning the Texas Enterprise Fund, see Selected Reading 8.2, "How Texas Plays 'Let's Make a Deal' for Jobs.")

To complement the Texas Enterprise Fund, Perry established TexasOne, a nonprofit, tax-exempt corporation with directors appointed by the governor. Its primary mission is to attract business from other states by marketing economic opportunities in Texas. Perry invited major companies and business-related groups to support the fund for three years with a range of annual tax-deductible contributions, which provided the following yearly benefits for donors:

1. $50,000 contribution: quail hunting with the governor at "one of Texas's premier ranches," a luncheon at the Governor's Mansion, and a seat on the TexasOne Round Table to advise on the use of marketing funds
2. $25,000 contribution: a TexasOne Round Table seat
3. $10,000 contribution: a donor's corporate logo placed on TexasOne marketing materials
4. $5,000 contribution: marketing name recognition
5. $1,000 contribution: an invitation to a business briefing hosted by Perry[14]

To recruit out-of-state companies, prospective contributors were informed that visiting executives would be given "red carpet treatment throughout; flight into Texas, limousine transportation, four-star hotel accommodations, reception on arrival evening with local and state leadership, one host assigned for each guest, tickets/box seats for enterainment event, personalized clothing (jackets, etc.) for each guest, gifts, etc."[15]

At the urging of Governor Perry, the 79th Legislature created the Texas Emerging Technology Fund (TETF) in 2005 and appropriated $200 million to cover fiscal years 2006 and 2007. Under the terms of H.B. 1765, TETF is designed to help small to midsize companies develop new technology for a range of industries. Included are semiconductors, computer and software technology, micro-electromechanical systems, nanotechnology, biotechnology, and "other pursuits" as determined by the governor in consultation with the speaker of the House of Representatives and the lieutenant governor. Assisting in administration of TETF are seven regional Centers of Innovation and Commercialization (CICs) and the statewide Texas Life Science CIC. These partnerships of universities, non-profit groups, and businesses review applications for funding and make rec-ommendations to the 17-member Texas Emerging Technology Committee. That committee makes its recommendations to the governor, lieutenant governor, and speaker, who determine which applications are approved. Royalties and revenue from products developed with TETF grants are shared with the state and deposited with the fund. Announced in February 2006, the first TETF investment was for $2 million to further Texas Tech University's partnership with Bayer CropScience and help start the International Center of Excellence in Agriculture Genomics and Biotechnology.

### Legislative Powers

Perhaps the most stringent test of a Texas governor's capacity for leadership involves handling of legislative matters. The governor has no direct law-

A 2005 bill-signing ceremony with Governor Rick Perry (center) flanked on the left by Representative Glenda Dawson (R-Pearland, deceased September 12, 2006) and on the right by Senator Judith Zaffirini (D-Laredo), 2005. (Texas House of Representatives Photography Department)

making authority, but **legislative power** is exercised through three major functions authorized by the Texas Constitution:

- Delivering messages to the legislature
- Vetoing bills and concurrent resolutions
- Calling special sessions of the legislature

However, the success of a legislative program depends heavily on a governor's ability to bargain with influential lobbyists and legislative leaders (particularly the speaker of the House of Representatives and the lieutenant governor).

**Message Power**  Article 4, Section 9, of the Texas Constitution requires the governor to deliver a State of the State address at the "commencement" (beginning) of each regular session of the legislature, but this is not interpreted to mean the first day of a session. In 2005, Governor Perry delivered his State of the State address on January 28, seventeen days after the beginning of the 79th regular session. On occasion, the governor may also present messages, either in person or in writing, to the legislature. A governor's success in using **message power** to promote a harmonious relationship with the legislature depends on such variables as the timing of messages concerning volatile issues, the support

**legislative power**  The governor's legislative power is exercised through messages delivered to the Texas Legislature, vetoes of bills and concurrent resolutions, and calls for special sessions of the legislature.

**message power**  The governor's State of the State address at the "commencement" of a legislative session and messages delivered in person or in writing are examples of gubernatorial exercise of message power to communicate with legislators and the public.

of the governor's program by the chairs of legislative committees, and the governor's personal popularity with the pubic.

**Veto Power**    The governor's most direct legislative tool is the power to veto legislation. A governor vetoes a bill by returning it unsigned (with written reasons for not signing) to the chamber in which it originated. If the legislature is no longer in session, the vetoed bill is filed with the secretary of state. **Veto power** takes different forms. For example, the line-item veto is restricted to spending measures. It allows the governor to kill one or more specific spending authorizations in an appropriation bill while permitting enactment of the remainder of the budget. Using the line-item veto power to refuse funding for a specific agency, the governor can effectively eliminate that agency, as Governor Perry did to six agencies in 2003. This line-item veto authority places the governor in a powerful bargaining position with individual legislators in the delicate game of pork-barrel politics. That is, the governor may strike a bargain with a senator or representative in which the chief executive promises not to deny funding for a lawmaker's pet project (the pork). In return, the legislator agrees to support a bill favored by the governor. The legislature can override the governor's veto by a two-thirds majority vote in both houses, but overriding a governor's veto has occurred only once since the administration of Governor W. Lee O'Daniel (1939–1941). In 1979, the House and Senate overrode a veto by Governor Clements. The strong veto power that the Texas Constitution gives to the governor and the governor's informal power of threatening to veto a bill are formidable weapons for dealing with uncooperative legislators.

Both the governor of Texas and the president of the United States have the prerogative of neither signing nor vetoing a bill within 10 days (Sundays excepted) after its passage, thus allowing the measure to become law without executive signature. But if the president "pockets" a bill passed within 10 weekdays before congressional adjournment, such failure to act kills the measure. Although not possessing pocket-veto power, the governor of Texas may exercise a **postadjournment veto** by rejecting any pending legislation within 20 days after a session has ended. Because most bills pass late in a legislative session, the postadjournment veto allows the governor to veto measures without threat of any challenge. It is therefore almost absolute.

Throughout most of the 77th Legislature's regular session in 2001, Governor Perry vetoed only a few bills. But in what some critics termed the "Father's Day Massacre," he exercised 78 postadjournment vetoes at 9 P.M. on the last possible day to do so (June 17). Perry's total of 82 vetoes in 2001 set a record, surpassing Governor Bill Clements' 59 vetoes in 1989. Two years later, Perry issued a total of 48 vetoes to kill bills passed during the regular session of the 78th Legislature. In 2005, he vetoed only 19 of the 79th Legislature's regular session bills.[16]

**Special-Sessions Power**    Included among the governor's powers is the authority to call special sessions of the legislature. The Texas Constitution places no restrictions on the number of special sessions a governor may call, but the length of a special session is limited to 30 days. During a special session, the

**veto power** Authority of the governor to reject a bill or concurrent resolution passed by the legislature.

**postadjournment veto** Rejection by the governor of a pending bill or concurrent resolution during the 20 days following a legislative session.

legislature may consider only those matters the governor specifies in the call or subsequently presents to the legislature. Exceptions to this limitation extend to confirmation of appointments and to impeachment proceedings without gubernatorial approval.

As with message power, a governor's success in using the power to call special sessions depends on timing and on rapport with legislative leaders. From 1991 through 1994, Governor Richards called four special sessions. Governor Bush called none, mainly because the state did not experience budget crises during his six years in office. In 2003, Governor Perry called three special sessions before a congressional redistricting bill was passed. In 2004, he called an unsuccessful special session on school finance, and in 2005 he called two special sessions on this subject. Finally, in April 2006, Perry called a special session on school finance and property tax reduction. It produced legislation he desired. (For discussion of this subject, see Chapter 11, "Finance and Fiscal Policy.")

## Judicial Powers

The governor exercises a few formal judicial powers. Included are powers to:

- Fill vacancies on state (but not county or city) courts
- Play a limited but outdated role in removing judges and justices
- Perform acts of clemency to lighten sentences given to some convicted criminals

**Appointment and Removal of Judges and Justices**   More than half of Texas's state judges and justices first serve on district courts and higher appellate courts through gubernatorial appointment to fill a vacancy caused by a judge's death, resignation, or removal from office. For example, in 2001 Wallace B. Jefferson became the first African American to serve on the Texas Supreme Court after Governor Perry appointed him to replace Justice Alberto Gonzales. Jefferson won election to a six-year term in 2002, and Perry appointed him as chief justice of the Supreme Court in 2004. Two years later, Jefferson did not have a Democratic opponent when he was elected as chief justice for a six-year term.

Most appointees to appellate courts have had prior judicial experience, but Governor Perry appointed Don Willett to the Texas Supreme Court in 2005. Willett had never held a judicial position, although he had served as an assistant attorney general and is a close friend of Mike Toomey, Perry's former chief of staff.[17]

According to Article XV, Section 8, of the Texas Constitution, the governor may remove any jurist "on address of two-thirds of each house of the Legislature for willful neglect of duty, incompetence, habitual drunkenness, oppression in office, or other reasonable cause which shall not be sufficient ground for impeachment." Governors and the legislature have not used this process for many years. They have left removal of state jurists to other proceedings and to voters. (See the chapter "Laws, Courts, and Justice" for a discussion of the disciplining and removal of judges and justices.)

**Acts of Executive Clemency**    Until the mid-1930s, Texas governors had extensive powers to undo or lessen punishment for convicted criminals through acts of clemency that set aside or reduced court-imposed penalties. Exercise of these powers led to charges of corruption, which are illustrated by the story about a man who stepped on a foot of Miriam A. Ferguson (governor, 1925–1927 and 1933–1935) after they entered an elevator in the Capitol. According to this apocryphal tale, the man said to the governor, "Pardon me." Her response was, "You will have to ask Jim." Whether or not Ma Ferguson and her husband, James E. Ferguson (governor, 1915–1917), sold pardons has been hotly debated. Nevertheless, a constitutional amendment adopted in 1936 reduced the clemency powers of the governor and established the Board of Pardons and Paroles, which is now a division of the Texas Department of Criminal Justice.

Release of a prisoner before completion of a sentence on condition of good behavior is called **parole**. The seven-member Board of Pardons and Paroles grants parole without action by the governor. However, the governor may perform various acts of executive clemency that set aside or reduce a court-imposed penalty through pardon, reprieve, or commutation of sentence. On recommendation of the Board of Pardons and Paroles, the governor may grant a full pardon or a conditional pardon. A **full pardon** releases a person from all consequences of a criminal act and restores rights enjoyed by persons who have not been convicted of crimes. In 2006, for example, Governor Perry pardoned Arthur Merle Mumphrey after DNA evidence proved he was wrongfully imprisoned for 18 years. (See Selected Reading 10.2, "Mumphrey Attorney Called Shining Star in Legal Arena.") Under a **conditional pardon**, the governor may withhold certain rights, such as being licensed to practice a selected occupation or profession. Acting independently, the governor may also revoke a conditional pardon if the terms of that pardon are violated.

The governor may also independently grant one 30-day **reprieve** in a death sentence case. A reprieve temporarily suspends execution of the penalty imposed by a court. Ann Richards refused nearly all requests for reprieve from the 48 condemned men executed during her four years as governor. She did, however, grant one reprieve in the highly publicized capital murder case of Gary Graham, who later requested a second 30-day stay of execution from Governor Bush. However, a Texas attorney general's opinion advised that only one 30-day reprieve could be issued in any given case. Graham was executed.

One reprieve was granted in a death-penalty case while Bush served as governor, but 150 men and two women failed in their attempts to obtain stays of execution.[18] After becoming governor, Perry granted no reprieves in death sentence cases during his first three and one-half years in office, but in 2004 he gave Frances Newton a temporary reprieve pending the retesting of a gun previously tested by the Houston Police Department's crime laboratory. Nevertheless, in 2005 Newton became the first African American woman to be executed in Texas since the Civil War.

**parole**  Release from prison before completion of a sentence; good behavior of the parolee is a condition of release.

**full pardon**  On recommendation of the Board of Pardons and Paroles, the governor may grant a full pardon. This act of executive clemency releases a convicted person from all consequences of a criminal act and restores rights enjoyed by others who have not been convicted of a crime.

**conditional pardon**  On recommendation of the Board of Pardons and Paroles, the governor may grant a conditional pardon. This act of clemency releases a convicted person from the consequences of his or her crime but does not restore all rights, as in the case of a full pardon.

**reprieve**  An act of executive clemency that temporarily suspends execution of a sentence.

The governor possesses two other clemency powers. If recommended by the Board of Pardons and Paroles, the governor may reduce a penalty through **commutation of sentence** and may remit (return) forfeitures of money or property surrendered as punishment. After having granted only one death-penalty commutation in his administration, in June 2005, Governor Perry commuted the sentences of 28 death-row inmates convicted of crimes committed when they were younger than age 18. Perry took this action after the U.S. Supreme Court ruled in *Roper* v. *Simmons* (2005) that people cannot be executed if they were minors at the time of the crime. The court held this would violate the Eighth Amendment's ban on cruel and unusual punishment.

## Informal Powers

A governor's ability to sway public opinion and to direct or influence the actions of other government officials depends on more than constitutional powers or powers conferred by the legislature. Informal powers are not based on law but stem from a governor's popularity with the public and on traditions, symbols, and ceremonies. Governor Rick Perry, who is a runner, uses his personal dedication to physical fitness to relate to Texans who share his interest and to challenge others to "fight the war on fat."[19]

In the eyes of most Texans, the governor's ceremonial office in the Capitol holds center stage. Although this room is used primarily for press interviews and public functions, its occupant is a symbol of the government of the Lone Star State. For routine daily work, the governor has another office in the Capitol, and staff members have offices in the State Insurance Building, located on San Jacinto Boulevard, one block east of the Capitol.

Of course, a governor cannot accept all invitations to deliver speeches or participate in dedications, banquets, and other public events. Within the limits of time and priorities, however, every governor does attempt to play the role of chief of state. The breadth and depth of this role cannot be fully measured, but its significance should not be underestimated in determining a governor's effectiveness.

Media relations are important. Responding to journalists' demands for information requires an efficient press secretary. Effective governors must be able to make impressive speeches, to remain at ease while communicating in interviews with newspaper and television reporters, and to express their views in articles (perhaps drafted by staff members) published in newspapers (especially the big-city press).[20] Public involvement of family members may also be a source of support. Laura Bush, for example, enhanced her husband's image as a governor committed to improving education. Her First Lady's Family Literacy Initiative Program was especially designed to improve the reading skills of children from lower-income families living in disadvantaged neighborhoods.

Anita Perry, with bachelor's and master's degrees in nursing and 17 years of experience in various fields of nursing, is often referred to by her husband as First Nurse as well as First Lady. Her public speeches on topics such as

**commutation of sentence** On the recommendation of the Board of Pardons and Paroles, the governor may commute (reduce) a sentence.

Alzheimer's disease, breast cancer awareness, and prevention of family violence have been a source of support for Governor Perry. In addition, Anita Perry has worked with her husband to host the annual Texas Conference for Women, at which women from all parts of Texas, as well as other states, meet to consider a wide range of women's interests, such as health care, personal growth, and professional development. Late in 2003, Anita Perry made history when she began work as a consultant, at $5,000 per month, for the Texas Association Against Sexual Assault. No wife of any earlier governor was employed while her husband was in office.[21]

---

**Learning Check 8.2**          **(Answers on p. 333)**

1. How is a special session of the legislature called?
2. True or False: Most gubernatorial appointments must be approved by a two-thirds vote of the House of Representatives.
3. True or False: The governor may independently grant one 30-day reprieve in a death sentence case.

---

## ★ The Plural Executive

Politically, the governor is Texas's highest-ranking officer, but in practice the governor shares executive power with other state officers. Although millions of Texans cannot readily identify by name the attorney general, the comptroller of public accounts, the land commissioner, and the agriculture commissioner, these elected executive officers oversee large departments with multimillion-dollar budgets. Determined by the legislature, their annual salaries for fiscal years 2006 and 2007 were budgeted at $125,000. Along with the governor, the lieutenant governor, and the appointed secretary of state, these state officials are referred to collectively as the **plural executive**.

**plural executive** The governor and elected department heads as provided by the Texas Constitution and statutes.

This structural arrangement contributes significantly to the state's long ballot, because these executive officials (except the secretary of state) are pop-

---

 **Points to Ponder**

Beginning in 1846, following annexation by the United States in 1845, Texas has had the following numbers of state officials (through December 2006):

- 62 governors
- 42 lieutenant governors
- 50 attorneys general
- 26 comptrollers of public accounts
- 28 commissioners of the General Land Office
- 11 commissioners of agriculture (office created by the legislature in 1907)
- 90 secretaries of state

*Source: Texas Almanac 2006–2007* (Dallas: Dallas Morning News, 2006), 417–423; Office of the Commissioner of Agriculture; and web sites for the executive departments.

ularly elected to four-year terms without limit on reelection. Elected department heads are largely independent of gubernatorial control; however, should one of these positions become vacant in an official's term of office, with the advice and consent of the Senate, the governor appoints a successor until the next general election. Each new governor appoints his or her own secretary of state. Individuals who hold this position often serve only a year or so. For example, Rick Perry had four secretaries of state in his first six years as governor. Unlike department heads in the federal government, those in Texas do not form a cabinet to advise the governor.

### The Lieutenant Governor

Considered by some political observers to be the most powerful official in Texas government, the **lieutenant governor** functions less in the executive branch than in the legislative branch. The Texas Constitution requires the Senate to convene

**lieutenant governor**
Popularly elected, serves as president of the Senate, and is first in the line of succession if the office of governor becomes vacant before the end of a term.

*Lieutenant Governor David Dewhurst*

*Attorney General Gregg Abbott*

*Comptroller of Public Accounts Susan Combs*

*Commissioner of the General Land Office Jerry Patterson*

*Commissioner of Agriculture Todd Staples (Senate Media Services)*

*Secretary of State J. Roger Williams (© Bob Daemmrich Photography, Inc.)*

within 30 days whenever a vacancy occurs in the lieutenant governor's office. Senators then elect one of their members (as in the case of Bill Ratliff in 2000) to fill the office as acting lieutenant governor until the next general election.

The annual state salary for the office of lieutenant governor is only $7,200, the same as that paid to members of the legislature. Like legislators, the lieutenant governor may also hold a paying job in private business or practice a profession. For example, from 1992 to 1998, Lieutenant Governor Bob Bullock was affiliated with the law firm of Scott, Douglas, Luton & McConnico LLP in Austin.

As president of the Senate, the lieutenant governor is the presiding officer for that chamber. In that role, this official exercises great influence on legislation. (See Chapter 7, "The Legislature.") Also, because the lieutenant governorship is regarded as a possible steppingstone to the governorship or other high positions, competition is intense among candidates for that office.

Many Texas lobbyists and members of the business community supported John Sharp, a Democrat and former comptroller of public accounts, in the 2002 race for lieutenant governor. But multimillionaire Republican David Dewhurst, the state's commissioner of the General Land Office at that time, won the November general election. To finance his campaign, Dewhurst used more than $10 million of his own money plus another borrowed $13 million. After his victory, Dewhurst recouped some of this money at fundraising events where Sharp's former supporters "caught the late train" by making postelection contributions to Dewhurst.[22] In 2006, Dewhurst won a second term by defeating Democratic candidate Maria Luisa Alvarado, an Air Force veteran and social/health research analyst.

### The Attorney General

One of Texas's most visible and powerful officeholders is the **attorney general**. Whether suing tobacco companies, arguing affirmative action questions, or try-

**attorney general** The constitutional official elected to head the Office of the Attorney General, which represents the state government in lawsuits and provides legal advice to state and local officials.

ing to resolve redistricting disputes, the state's chief lawyer is a major player in making many important public policy decisions. This officer gives advisory opinions to state and local authorities and represents the state in civil litigation.

With more than 4,000 employees, the Office of the Attorney General gives advice concerning the constitutionality of many pending bills. The governor, heads of state agencies, and local government officials also request opinions from the attorney general on the scope of their jurisdiction and the interpretation of vaguely worded laws. Although neither judges nor other officials are bound by these opinions, the attorney general's rulings are considered authoritative unless overruled by court decisions or new laws. Another power of the attorney general is to initiate, in a district court, quo warranto proceedings that challenge an official's right to hold public office. Such action may lead to removal of an officeholder who lacks a qualification set by law or is judged guilty of official misconduct. Among its many functions, the Office of the Attorney General enforces child-support orders issued by state courts; and it administers the Crime Victims' Compensation Fund.

The election of Democratic candidate Dan Morales as attorney general in 1990 gave him the distinction of being the first Latino elected to head an executive department under the Texas Constitution of 1876. Morales's low-key style during his first term as attorney general (1991–1995) contrasted sharply to the high-profile lawsuits his office handled, especially Texas's multibillion-dollar suit against the country's biggest tobacco companies. In 1994, Morales won a second term by defeating Republican rival Don Wittig, a Houston state district judge. He did not seek a third term, but in 2002 Morales challenged Tony Sanchez for nomination as the Democratic Party's gubernatorial candidate. After losing the primary contest with Sanchez, he endorsed Republican candidate Rick Perry in the general election. Later, however, Morales pled guilty to federal charges of filing a false income tax return and committing mail fraud related to lawyer's fees for his friend, attorney Marc Murr, in Texas's $17.3 billion tobacco settlement. Morales was sentenced to imprisonment for four years.[23]

Morales was replaced as attorney general by San Antonio lawyer John Cornyn, a Republican and former Texas Supreme Court justice. When Cornyn decided to run for a seat in the U.S. Senate in 2002, the Republican Party nominated Supreme Court Justice Greg Abbott for attorney general. In the November election of 2002, Abbott defeated Democrat Kirk Watson, a former Austin mayor. Before Abbott began his elected term in January 2003, Governor Perry appointed him to serve for a few weeks in that office following Cornyn's resignation in November 2002.

Upon his appointment, Abbott declared that he was "philosophically very committed to open government" and that he would enforce the state's open records laws for the benefit of the public and the media. This statement was welcomed by the press and public interest groups that had complained about lack of access to information concerning government operations.[24] In 2005,

Attorney General Abbott influenced the legislature to enact S.B. 286. This law requires public officials to undergo at least one to two hours of open records training and one to two hours of open meetings training not later than 90 days after taking office. Training videos are posted on the attorney general's web site, but there is no penalty for failure to comply with the training law. Abbott won a second term when he defeated Democratic candidate David Van Os, a San Antonio lawyer, in the 2006 general election.

### The Comptroller of Public Accounts

One of the most powerful elected officers in Texas government is the **comptroller of public accounts**, the state's chief accounting officer and tax collector. After a biennial appropriation bill passes by a simple majority vote in the House and Senate, the Texas Constitution requires the comptroller's certification that expected revenue will be collected to cover all of the budgeted expenditures. Otherwise, an appropriation must be approved by a four-fifths majority vote in both houses. One of the comptroller's duties is to designate hundreds of Texas financial institutions (mostly banks, but also a few savings and loan companies and credit unions) to serve as depositories for state-collected funds.

Bob Bullock left the comptroller's post in 1990 to become lieutenant governor. Democrat John Sharp, a former state legislator and member of the Texas Railroad Commission, succeeded him. Sharp won a second term in 1994 when he defeated Republican Theresa Doggett. Sharp was succeeded by Carole Keeton Rylander. She resigned her Texas Railroad Commission seat to become Texas's first woman state comptroller after defeating Democrat Paul Hobby, son of former lieutenant governor Bill Hobby, in 1998. Four years later Rylander won another term by defeating Democratic candidate Marty Akins, a former lawyer, rancher, and All-American quarterback for the UT Longhorns. In January 2003, at the swearing-in ceremony for her second term, the self-styled "tough grandma" presented her third husband, announced that Strayhorn would be her new surname, and took personal pride in her weight loss of more than 100 pounds.[25]

During the legislature's 78th regular session in 2003, Strayhorn clashed with Governor Perry and legislative leaders concerning her budget estimates. Then, in the third special session, the legislature transferred the comptroller's school district audit and performance review programs to the Legislative Budget Board. In addition, the state auditor was given authority to review contested tax cases settled by the comptroller. This permits the auditor to compare the comptroller's campaign finance reports with tax settlements to determine if a relationship exists between tax refunds and political contributions. While stating that there was no implication of wrongdoing, a state auditor's report issued in 2005 noted that for 1999-2004 about half of Strayhorn's $1.7 million in campaign contributions from taxpayer representatives came from Ryan and Company. It is one of the businesses that help people resolve their tax disputes with the Comptroller's Office.

**comptroller of public accounts** This elected constitutional officer is responsible for collecting taxes, keeping accounts, estimating revenue, and serving as treasurer for the state.

In 2004, Strayhorn loudly criticized the Perry school finance plan and changes in the Children's Health Insurance Program (CHIP) that cut enrollment. When Strayhorn concluded that she could not defeat Perry in the 2006 Republican primary, she announced that she would run for governor as an independent candidate. Strayhorn lost the 2006 general election and was succeeded as comptroller of public accounts by Susan Combs, former commissioner of agriculture. Combs won the office by defeating Democratic candidate Fred Head, an Athens lawyer and former state legislator.

## The Commissioner of the General Land Office

Although less visible than other elected executives, the **commissioner of the General Land Office** is an important figure in Texas politics. Since the creation of the General Land Office under the Constitution of the Republic of Texas (1836), the commissioner's duties have expanded to include awarding oil, gas, and sulfur leases for lands owned by the state; serving as chairman of the Veterans Land Board; and sitting as an ex-officio member of other boards responsible for managing state-owned lands. With more than 600 employees, the General Land Office also oversees growth of the Permanent School Fund. This fund is financed by oil and gas leases, rentals, and royalties that annually provide more than $700 million for public school funding.

When Democrat Garry Mauro left the land commissioner's post to make an unsuccessful bid for the governorship in 1998, his decision afforded Republicans an opportunity to win a state office. Houston businessman David Dewhurst seized that moment, spending more than $5 million in winning his first political office. Arguably, Dewhurst's election was helped by Governor George W. Bush's popularity.

After Dewhurst decided to run for lieutenant governor in 2002, lobbyist and former state senator Jerry Patterson became the GOP candidate for land commissioner. Patterson defeated the Democratic candidate, state senator David Bernsen. When he took the oath of office in January 2003, Patterson declared that he would serve out his term and seek reelection in 2006. He kept his word and won reelection in November 2006 by defeating the Democratic candidate, VaLinda Hathcox, an attorney in Sulphur Springs.

Environmentalists have been unhappy with Patterson's plan to increase oil and gas production by reducing drilling restrictions along the Gulf Coast, including the Padre Island National Seashore.[26] Because the General Land Office administers vast land holdings for the state, the commissioner is involved in many legal disputes. In November 2003, Patterson became involved in a controversy with then Agriculture Commissioner Susan Combs about negotiations between Patterson and Rio Nuevo, Ltd., for the lease of rights to water under state-owned land in West Texas. Patterson insisted that such leasing and piping of water to other areas would bring millions of dollars into the Permanent School Fund, but Combs was concerned about the loss of water needed for agriculture and other purposes in that arid region. In 2006, the

**commissioner of the General Land Office** As head of Texas's General Land Office, this elected constitutional officer oversees the state's extensive land holdings and related mineral interests, especially oil and gas leasing for the benefit of the Permanent School Fund.

General Land Office issued rules for licensing state groundwater rights to water companies through direct negotiation or sealed bid procedure. In that same year, Patterson announced other revenue-raising projects involving the lease of thousands of acres of submerged Gulf of Mexico land within 10 miles offshore for erecting huge windmills to convert coastal wind into electric power.[27]

### The Commissioner of Agriculture

By law, the **commissioner of agriculture** is supposed to be a "practicing farmer." This criterion is vague enough to qualify anyone who owns or rents a piece of agricultural land. Name recognition by the state's voters (most of whom live in suburbs or central cities) is the principal requirement for winning the office.

In 1998, Susan Combs, a former state representative from Austin, became Texas's first woman to be elected agriculture commissioner. This state officer is responsible for enforcing agricultural laws and for providing service programs to Texas farmers, ranchers, and consumers. Control over the use of often-controversial pesticides is exercised through the Department of Agriculture's Pesticide Programs Division. This division restricts the use of high-risk chemicals and licenses dealers and commercial applicators as well as private applicators who use pest control chemicals on their own farms and ranches. Other enforcement actions of the department include inspections to determine the accuracy of commercial scales, pumps, and meters.

Combs won a second term by defeating Democrat Tom Ramsay in 2002. Subsequently, she gained widespread publicity with demands that Mexico repay its water debt by releasing more water into the Rio Grande. Other matters that attracted her attention were childhood obesity and diabetes. Combs used her authority to curb sale of junk food in Texas schools and to prohibit sodas in elementary schools during the school day, in middle schools before the end of the last lunch period, and in high schools during meal periods in areas where cafeteria lunches are served and consumed. Some school districts set policies that control soda sales further.[28]

After Combs announced that she would run for the office of comptroller of public accounts in 2006, Senator Todd Staples sought and won nomination as the Republican candidate for commissioner of agriculture. His credentials for the office include a degree from Texas A&M University with a major in agricultural economics, experience as a rancher and real estate broker, and 12 years of service in the Texas Legislature. In November 2006, Staples won the office by defeating Democrat Hank Gilbert, also a Texas A&M University graduate, with experience as rancher and high school agriculture teacher.

### The Secretary of State

The only constitutional executive officer appointed by the governor is the **secretary of state**. This appointment must be confirmed by a two-thirds vote of

**commissioner of agriculture** The elected official who heads Texas's Department of Agriculture, which promotes the sale of agricultural commodities and regulates pesticides, aquaculture, egg quality, weights and measures, and grain warehouses.

the Senate. The secretary of state serves a four-year term concurrent with that of the governor. As a department head, the secretary of state oversees a staff of about 250 people and is the chief elections officer of Texas. Principal responsibilities of the office include the following:

- Administering state election laws in conjunction with county officials
- Tabulating election returns for state and district offices
- Granting charters to Texas corporations
- Issuing permits to outside corporations to conduct business within Texas
- Processing requests for extradition of criminals to or from other states for trial and punishment

With these diverse duties, the secretary of state is obviously more than just a record keeper. How the office functions is determined largely by the occupant's relations with the governor.

George W. Bush's first secretary of state, and first Latino appointee, was Tony Garza, a former Cameron County judge. When the Brownsville attorney resigned to win a seat on the Texas Railroad Commission, he was succeeded as secretary of state by Houston attorney Alberto Gonzales. Later, Bush appointed Gonzales to fill a vacancy on the Supreme Court of Texas; and after Bush became president, he named Gonzales as White House counsel and then U.S. attorney general.[29] Reaching out to Democrats, Bush chose Insurance Commissioner Elton Bomer, a former Democratic state representative from East Texas, as his third secretary of state. When Rick Perry succeeded Bush as governor, he appointed another Democrat, Representative Henry Cuellar from Laredo, to fill this office. After Cuellar resigned, Perry named Republican Gwyn Shea as secretary of state in January 2002. She resigned in July 2003 and was replaced by Geoffrey S. Connor. Before his appointment by Perry, Connor served for two years as assistant secretary of state.

During his 15 months as secretary of state, Connor, at Governor Perry's direction, made several international trips to promote Texas products abroad and to attract foreign investment in Texas.[30] Early in 2005, Perry replaced Connor with J. Roger Williams, a wealthy entrepreneur with businesses in Weatherford (Roger Williams Auto Mall) and Fort Worth (Vestry Financial Corporation). A former Texas Christian University baseball player, professional player in the Atlanta Braves farm system, and coach at TCU, Williams is well known among Republican leaders as a fundraiser for President Bush and Governor Perry.[31] In 2006, Williams's annual state salary was $117,516.

**Learning Check 8.3**    **(Answers on p. 333)**

1. True or False: An opinion issued by the attorney general is authoritative unless overruled by a new law or a court decision.
2. Which elected official is the state's chief accounting officer?
3. True or False: The secretary of state is an elected official.

**secretary of state** The state's chief elections officer, appointed by the governor for a term concurrent with that of the governor.

## Discussion Questions

1. Is the governor compensated adequately?
2. Should changes be made in the governor's removal powers?
3. How does the governor exercise influence over legislation?
4. How does the governor exercise influence over judicial matters?
5. Should executive department heads be popularly elected or appointed by the governor?
6. Which executive department head appears to have the greatest potential for affecting your personal life and career?

## Internet Resources

Office of the Attorney General: **www.oag.state.tx.us**
Office of the Comptroller of Public Accounts: **www.window.state.tx.us**
Office of the Governor: **www.governor.state.tx.us**
Office of the Lieutenant Governor: **www.ltgov.state.tx.us**
Office of the Secretary of State: **www.sos.state.tx.us**
Texas Department of Agriculture: **www.agr.state.tx.us**
Texas General Land Office: **www.glo.state.tx.us**

## ★ Notes

1. Larry Sabato, *Good-bye to Good-time Charlie*, 2d ed. (Washington, D.C.: CQ Press, 1983), 2.
2. Robert Bryce, "The Pols He Bought," *Texas Observer*, February 5, 1999, 11. For Dr. Leininger's account of political spending, see his interview by Evan Smith, "Money Talks," *Texas Monthly*, June 2006, 138–141, 268–269.
3. "Perry Links Funding for Medical Facilities to Reform Legislation," *Houston Chronicle*, January 11, 2003.
4. See Carolyn Barta, *Bill Clements: Texian to His Toenails* (Austin: Eakin Press, 1996); and Bill Minutaglio, *First Son: George W. Bush and the Bush Family Dynasty* (New York: Times Books, 1999).
5. Jim Nicar, "A Summer of Discontent," *Texas Alcalde*, September/October 1997, 83.
6. For more about Toomey and other actors on the Texas political stage, see Patricia Kilday Hart, "The Enforcer," *Texas Monthly*, May 2003, 128–131, 175–177; Wayne Slater and James Moore, *Bush's Brain: How Karl Rove Made George W. Bush Presidential* (New York: Wiley, 2003); and Lou Dubose, Jan Reid, and Carl Cannon, *Boy Genius: Karl Rove, the Brains Behind the Remarkable Triumph of George W. Bush* (New York: Public Affairs, 2003).
7. Mike West, "Group Raising Money for Perry Interns," *Austin American-Statesman*, July 28, 2004.

8. *Governor Bush's Well-Appointed Texas Officials* (Austin: Texans for Public Justice, 2000); and *Governor Perry's Patronage* (Austin: Texans for Public Justice, 2006). Both reports are online at **www.tpj.org/index.jsp**.

9. Ken Herman, "Governor Unveils Budget Recipe," *Austin American-Statesman*, February 12, 2003.

10. For praise of this order, see David Sibley, "Perry's Coal Initiative Important Step," *Waco Tribune-Herald*, January 27, 2003. Sibley, a lobbyist and former state senator, played a leading role in lobbying for this executive order.

11. See T. A. Badger, "Perry Proposes $15 Million for Rails to Entice Toyota," *Fort Worth Star-Telegram*, December 19, 2003; and L. A. Lorek, "Luring Plant Was a Texas-Size Job," *San Antonio Express-News*, February 9, 2003.

12. See Jenalia Moreno and L. M. Sixel, "Citgo Headquarters Moving to Houston," *Houston Chronicle*, April 27, 2004; and Monica Wolfson, "Some Lawmakers Unhappy with State Enterprise Fund," *Wichita Falls Times Record News*, April 2, 2004.

13. Kirk Ladendorf, "Samsung Says 'Yes' to Austin Plant," *Austin American-Statesman*, April 14, 2006. For criticism of Governor Perry's use of the Texas Enterprise Fund, see Paul Sweeney, "Texas: The Corporate Welfare State," *Texas Observer*, April 15, 2005, 6–9, 28; and Mike Ward, "Enterprise Funds Need Oversight, Critics Say," *Austin American-Statesman*, January 30, 2005.

14. See Ken Herman, "Lunch and Hunt with Perry for $150,000," *Austin American-Statesman*, November 5, 2003; Clay Robison, "Perry's Perks Go to Big Spenders," *Houston Chronicle*, November 5, 2003; and W. Gardner Selby, "Critic Pans Perry's Bid for Funds as 'Greedy and Seedy,'" *San Antonio Express-News*, November 5, 2003.

15. Quoted by Wayne Slater, "Perry Criticized for Soliciting Funds," *Dallas Morning News*, November 5, 2003.

16. See *Vetoes of Legislation*, 77th, 78th, and 79th Legislatures, Focus Reports No. 77–10, No. 78–11, and No. 79–9 (Austin: House Research Organization, Texas House of Representatives, 2001, 2003, and 2005).

17. Editorial Board, "Bad Judgment: Perry Proves Texas Needs New Way to Appoint Judges," *Waco Tribune-Herald*, January 3, 2005.

18. For a critical report on the 57 requests for reprieve considered and rejected by Governor Bush while Alberto R. Gonzales served as his legal counsel, see Alan Berlow, "The Texas Clemency Memos," *Atlantic Monthly*, July 2003, 91–96. Bush describes his clemency actions and the work of the Texas Board of Pardons and Paroles in the widely publicized murder cases of Karla Faye Tucker and Henry Lee Lucas in *A Charge to Keep* (New York: Morrow, 1999), 146–166.

19. William Pack, "Governor Fires 1st Volley in War on Fat," *San Antonio Express-News*, November 21, 2003.

20. For example, see Rick Perry, "A Look Behind the Headlines Reveals Texas' Bright Future," *Austin American-Statesman*, November 11, 2003.

21. Ken Herman, "First Lady of Texas Takes a New Job," *Austin American-Statesman*, November 7, 2003. For Anita Perry's responses to questions about her life in politics, see her interview by Evan Smith, "Anita Perry," *Texas Monthly*, September 2005, 178–180, 182, 184.

22. Michele Kay and Gary Susswein, "Supporters Gave Millions in 'Late Train' Donations," *Austin American-Statesman*, January 16, 2003.

administrative minds in Texas," Wheat said. "Clearly these people serve to pleasure the governor and the governor rewards people who contribute to his campaign." Indeed, you have to wonder why, exactly, construction equipment magnate—and San Antonio Spurs owner—Peter Holt merited a spot on the Texas Parks and Wildlife Commission. Holt has contributed $206,000 to Perry since 2000.

Other big donors such as Donna Stockton-Hicks (total: $163,160), occupy prestigious but less consequential posts on organizations like the Poet Laureate, State Musician, and State Artists Committee (universally known as the PLSMSAC). Stockton-Hicks runs a design warehouse in Austin.

In at least one case, Perry donors got their own state agency. In 2003, the Legislature created the Texas Residential Construction Commission, at the governor's behest, ostensibly to regulate the home-construction industry. Homebuilders, however, have dominated the agency from the start. Seven of the nine agency commissioners appointed by Perry have direct ties to home-

builders. That includes Commissioner John Krugh, corporate counsel for Perry Homes—the building company owned by GOP mega-donor Bob Perry. Perry Homes has contributed $690,000 to Gov. Perry (no relation) since 2000. In all, employers of the governor's appointees have donated more than $3 million.

By law, candidates are required to disclose the employers and occupations of individuals who donate $500 or more. Curiously, the Perry campaign seems to have trouble identifying the occupation of the governor's own political appointees. For instance, under a $25,000 donation from Erle Nye—chairman of TXU Corp. and a Perry appointee to the Texas A&M Board of Regents—the campaign left blank Nye's occupation. For a $20,000 contribution from William F. Scott—whom Perry once appointed to the Jefferson and Orange County Pilot Commission—the campaign listed Scott's occupation as "best efforts," meaning the campaign didn't know. Others were left blank or simply labeled "retired" or "self." Here's a suggestion: how about "money bags"?

## 8.2  How Texas Plays "Let's Make a Deal" for Jobs*

### Mike Ward

*One of Governor Rick Perry's most highly publicized economic development tools is the Texas Enterprise Fund. It features use of state government money to attract industries to Texas and to retain Texas industries that threaten to move elsewhere. The primary objective of this government intervention is to create and maintain jobs for Texans. Journalist Mike Ward describes positive features of the fund and notes changes that critics recommend.*

When the phone rang in the governor's office three months ago, the caller was to-the-point: If the state could chip in $2 million or so, it might cinch Michigan-based Stryker Corp.'s proposed expansion in Texas. Stryker, one of the world's largest makers of medical devices, was thinking about moving an office from California to the Dallas area,

where it already had employees. The deal could mean up to 200 new employees over several years.

Days after Stryker's application was filed, state officials conducting a background check discovered that the company already had signed a lease on 75,000 square feet of office space north of Dallas. Game over. Stryker was turned down. "We don't fund companies who already are planning to move to Texas," said Phil Wilson, Gov. Rick Perry's deputy chief of staff, who oversees Texas Enterprise Fund activities.

Given a peek into Texas' covert world of economic development, the *Austin American-Statesman* has found that of the 123 companies that have applied for money from the Enterprise Fund, only 17 have received any. That is proof, Perry's office says, that the fund is properly managed. Of those that have been turned down, some were faltering businesses seeking a bailout. Others were ideas seeking a venture capital source. Others had bad business plans. Another wanted Texas taxpayers to retool its manufacturing plant.

*"How Texas Plays 'Let's Make a Deal' for Jobs," by Mike Ward from the *Austin American-Statesman*, February 21, 2005. Mike Ward is a reporter for the *Austin American-Statesman*. Copyright 2005, Austin American-Statesman. Reprinted by Permission.

Top aides to Perry say the rejections highlight the stringent checks and balances that have been built into the largely secret process of choosing which companies or projects will get Enterprise Fund money. Critics are adamant that the fund is viewed by companies as free money and that more regulations governing its use need to be written into law.

The Enterprise Fund was created in 2003 with $295 million that the Legislature took from the state's rainy day fund. It is overseen by Perry's Economic Development and Tourism Office and is to be used to close deals so that businesses will expand in Texas or move here. When it was set up, it was the largest such cash fund in the country. With $212.4 million committed so far, Perry is seeking from lawmakers $300 million to establish the Enterprise Fund and $300 million to establish an Emerging Technology Fund that would also be administered by his office.

Texas' Enterprise Fund economic development program is among hundreds nationwide, a pool estimated to be as big as $50 billion. And although Texas ranked poorly a few years ago in accountability for its economic development programs, before the Enterprise Fund was created, several experts suggest that has changed. Now, said Greg LeRoy, director of Good Jobs First, a Washington-based advocacy group that studies incentive programs, "It sounds like the state is kicking the tires and trying to be careful about who they fund. . . . We promote those kinds of safeguards in those programs."

## Competition Sensitive

"We approach each of the applications from a business standpoint: Is it a sound investment? Will it grow jobs? Does it meet the proper criteria? Is it good for the State of Texas?" said Mike Chrobak, chief financial officer for the office that oversees the Enterprise Fund. "We scrub every application to make sure it's a good deal."

For the biggest single project awarded Enterprise Fund money, scrubbing began just after state officials were alerted that Countrywide Financial Corp. was considering expanding to Texas. Officials say the deal, which was announced in December and is expected to add 7,500 Texas jobs in five years, demonstrates how the process works. Project FS, they called it, for financial services.

In the world of Eco Devo, as those in the business incentive industry refer to themselves, competitive edge means everything. Interest from corporations is a closely held secret. Negotiations are conducted with top-secret confidentiality. Every project in Texas is assigned a code name that officials use in discussions and memos until a deal is signed. "Competition Sensitive," all documents are marked.

Project FS began with a phone call to the governor's office in October 2003, Wilson said. The California-based company, which had about 5,000 of its 34,200 employees in Plano, was planning to expand its financial services operations during the next five years. It was sending out requests to several states to see what incentives might be available. Within days, Texas' economic development staff members had compiled a detailed initial assessment of what the deal could mean to the Lone Star State: $200 million in capital investment over seven years, plus the payroll. Average wage? $38,000, expected to increase to $42,795 by 2010. Potential Texas locations for the expansion: 14 cities, including Austin, San Marcos, New Braunfels, and San Antonio. Competitors: Louisiana, Oklahoma, and Colorado.

In most cases, the companies select the Texas locations they are interested in. Although most Enterprise Fund applications come from companies that contact state or local officials, Perry's office is actively marketing Texas as a great place to do business—at trade shows, in mailings to corporate executives, in contacts with consultants whom companies use to scout sites.

Within a few more weeks, state officials had completed a detailed assessment of Countrywide—its management, legal, and work force issues and corporate history, among other details—and a comparison of the incentives Texas was proposing and those of the competing states, gleaned through inquiries and networking within the economic development community. Also included was a study of the costs of doing business here and in the competitor states and an analysis of the financial services industry in Texas to measure how Countrywide might fit in.

An outside consultant assessed the economic and fiscal effects. Bottom line: The state could recoup the $20 million investment sought from the Enterprise Fund in six years. Local and state incentives could be recouped in 20 years. Separate analyses were subsequently completed to determine what "clawback provisions" would need to be included in any contract to ensure that money was doled out only as jobs were created. "By using the analyses and background we had developed, we knew exactly what we needed to make this work from our standpoint," said Wilson, a point man on the negotiations.

## Game On

In January 2004, Perry invited a number of corporate leaders, including Angelo Mozilo, the Countrywide board chairman and chief executive officer, to attend the Super Bowl in Houston with him. At a private dinner at Pappas Bros. Steak House two nights before the big game, Perry and Mozilo quickly established a rapport. A few months later, Mozilo invited Perry to present Texas' pitch at a meeting of the Countrywide board of directors, where they quizzed him about tort reform, workers compensation and taxes, among other issues. "They were looking at this as a business deal that would be beneficial to them," Wilson said. "We were looking for the same thing."

Next came the waiting. On a Sunday afternoon in October, almost a year after the first contact by Countrywide, Wilson got a call at home on his cell phone. Game on. A final offer was approved by Perry, Lt. Gov. David Dewhurst, and House Speaker Tom Craddick. On Nov. 29, they signed a letter to Countrywide outlining the proposed deal. With a contract finalized two weeks later, the deal was announced Dec. 14 in Richardson—selected as home base for the expansion. Other offices would be in Fort Worth, Plano, and other Texas cities, probably including Craddick's hometown of Midland.

A similar process has taken place for each of the other 122 applications for Enterprise Fund money, officials said. Only 17 were accepted by Perry, Dewhurst, and Craddick. One vote against and the deal is off, Wilson said. "So far, 31 projects have received no consensus," Wilson said. An additional 43 have not located in Texas, such as Boeing Co., which was offered $45 million to come to the Rio Grande Valley, and Union Tank Car Co., which was offered a $2 million package to expand in the Houston area.

Among the 17 projects approved, 24,446 jobs are to be created during the next decade—about $8,700 each for the state's expenditure of $212.4 million. Perry aides note that the return on that will be $6.3 billion in capital investment in Texas. "That's a great return," Wilson said.

Critics say that although safeguards may be a part of the review process, enhanced accountability and public disclosure are needed and other measures for review should be added. "The Texas Enterprise Fund has the opportunity to travel a 'high road' economic development path, paving the way towards transparency, rigorous compliance, higher wages, and guaranteed health insurance coverage," said a recent report by the Center for Public Policy Priorities, an Austin advocacy group. "Or it could continue to pursue a 'low road' economic development approach—limiting public disclosure and reporting while subsidizing companies that don't pledge to create high-quality jobs."

To illustrate its point, the group cites:

- The Minnesota Business Subsidy Accountability Law, which requires detailed public disclosure on every deal.
- The North Carolina Job Development Investment Grant Program, which mandates thorough wage reporting and post-award compliance.
- The Oklahoma Quality Jobs Program, which requires participating employers to provide basic health-care insurance to all new employees, with at least 50 percent of the cost paid by the company, and minimum-wage requirements.
- The Virginia Opportunity Fund, which provides grants or loans to localities, instead of companies, to complement their efforts to attract jobs and business investment.

Other programs mandate environmental protection and geographic diversity in the incentives, according to the report. Supporters of the Enterprise Fund say the current process addresses most of those issues. Like other states, they say, the details in Texas come out only after a deal is done. "Our program is as successful as it is because it has a great amount of flexibility," Wilson said. "You can't negotiate these in public." He said 27 applications for Enterprise Funds are under review: two "very large" proposals involving thousands of jobs, the rest much smaller.

Each is being analyzed just like Countrywide's, aides to Perry say.

If Texas must play the corporate incentive game, some lawmakers say, the safeguards are welcome. But, said state Sen. Eliot Shapleigh, D–El Paso, there's a better way to attract business: "The state ought first to invest in education, its work force, and infrastructure before subsidizing corporate entities."

---

An extensive bibliography of books and articles for this chapter is posted on Selected Sources for Reading, available online at http://college.hmco.com/PIC/brownPTP13e. For use with any chapter, see Resources for Further Research online at http://college.hmco.com/PIC/brownPTP13e.

# Chapter 9

# Public Policy and Administration

SARGENT © 2003 *Austin American-Statesman.* Reprinted with permission of UNIVERSAL PRESS SYNDICATE. All Rights Reserved.

Public policy doesn't just happen. It is the result of a long process involving a multitude of people and decisions. Interest groups and state agencies fight for the policies they want, some of which the legislature passes and funds. When a bill passes, a state agency receives the authority to implement the policy and must decide how to interpret the law and spend the money. Finally, state employees must actually apply these decisions in concrete cases. Following a uniform set of rules, they must decide such things as whether you or I qualify for benefits or are in compliance with a state regulation. When the budget is tight, some decisions are harsh, as is illustrated by Ben Sargent's cartoon above. Understanding the nature of this process and the situation of those who implement public policy helps us better understand the policies they produce.

One good way to see what is important in public policy is to follow the money. For many years in Texas, the state government has spent the lion's share of the budget on four areas. For example, in the 2006–2007 biennium (two-year budget cycle), the legislature appropriated $138.2 billion as follows:

- Education 40%
- Health and human services 35%
- Business and economic development 14%
- Public safety and criminal justice 6%
- Everything else 6%[1]

Regulation costs the government little (0.4% of the total in 2006–2007) but can put heavy costs on those being regulated by requiring more and better care in nursing homes, scrubbers to reduce pollution from smokestacks, better processing of city sewage, and so on.

This chapter's focus is twofold: (1) the situation of Texas's public employees and the nature of the agencies in which they work, and (2) the implementation of policy in four major areas—education, health and human services, business and economic development, and environmental issues. The other big-ticket item in Texas state government, public safety and criminal justice, is covered in the chapter "Laws, Courts, and Justice." More detail on state spending is provided in the chapter "Finance and Fiscal Policy." The impact of agencies and their funding extends to all who pay taxes, study for diplomas and degrees, purchase goods and services, breathe the state's air, drink its water, and live within its borders.

## Role of State Agencies

In addition to agencies headed by the elected officials discussed in the chapter "The Executive," more than 200 boards, commissions, and departments implement state laws and programs in Texas. Most boards and commissions are appointed by the governor, but once individuals are appointed to a board, the governor must rely on persuasion and personal or political loyalty to exercise influence. Fragmentation of the state executive into so many largely independent agencies was an intentional move to avoid centralized power. Administering state programs through boards was also thought to keep partisan politics out of public administration. Unfortunately, this also makes it difficult to hold the agencies responsible to the public and to coordinate efforts.

Boards appointed by the governor usually meet quarterly or more frequently. A board-appointed executive director oversees day-to-day agency operation. Although boards usually make general policy and leave much of the detail to the executive director, some are much more active and involved. In recent years, the influence of the governor has increased through the ability to name a powerful executive director for two major agencies—the Health and Human Services Commission and the Texas Education Agency. Two important boards are elected—the Railroad Commission (which regulates the gas and oil industry) and the State Board of Education.

Some agencies were created in the Texas Constitution. Others were created by the legislature, either as directed by the state constitution or independent of it. As problems emerge that elected officials believe government must address, they look to existing state agencies or create new ones to provide solutions. Sometimes, citizen complaints force an agency's creation. For example, citizen outrage at rising utility rates resulted in creation of the Public Utilities Commission to review and limit those rates. Lobbying is also important in the creation of agencies. The most famous Texas case is oil and gas industry lobbying in the early twentieth century to have the Railroad Commission create a system of regulation to reduce economic chaos in the fledgling industry. In 2003 the legislature created the Texas Residential Construction Commission in response to lobbying by home-builders. But consumer advocates complain that the agency serves primarily to protect the builders from homeowner suits alleging shoddy construction.

There is also a process to abolish or change existing state agencies. At least every 12 years, each agency must participate in a **sunset review process** whereby the agency is systematically studied and then abolished, merged, reorganized, or retained. This examination is conducted by the Sunset Advisory Commission, composed of 10 legislators (5 from each chamber) and 2 public members. It has a staff of about 30 employees. In 2005–2007, the commission reviewed 24 agencies, including the Texas Education Agency (discussed later in this chapter), the Texas Department of Criminal Justice (the prison system), and the Alcoholic Beverage Commission. The Sunset Advisory Commission makes recommendations to the legislature. Whether an agency lives or dies is determined by majority votes in the Texas Senate and House of Representatives.

It is not surprising that regulated groups (often enjoying cozy relationships with friendly administrators and legislators) and state employees (fighting for their jobs) wage vigorous campaigns to preserve agencies and continue business as usual. From the Sunset Advisory Commission's beginning in 1979 through 2005, 81 percent of state agencies were retained, 9 percent abolished outright, and 9 percent reorganized in major ways (such as combining two or more agencies). Of those retained, over a fourth had changes such as adding public members (people not from the regulated industry) on governing boards or improved procedures. From 1982 to 2005, the sunset process saved the state $784 million, or about $36 for every dollar spent by the Sunset Advisory Commission.[2]

**sunset review process**
Over a cycle of 12 years, each state agency is studied, and then the legislature decides whether to abolish, merge, or retain it.

# ★ State Employees

For most people, the face of state government is the governor, legislators, and other top officials. And, certainly, they are critical decision makers. However, most of the work of Texas state government (called **public administration**) is in the hands of people in agencies headed by elected officials and appointed boards. These **bureaucrats** (public employees), although often the subject of criticism or jokes about inefficiency and "red tape," are responsible for delivering governmental services to the state's residents. The public may see them in action as a clerk taking an application, a supervisor explaining why a request was turned down, or an inspector checking a nursing home. They are the focus of this section.

The nature of bureaucracy is both its strength and its weakness. Large organizations such as governments and corporations need many employees doing specialized jobs with sufficient coordination to achieve the organization's goals (profits for a company, service for a government). That means employees must follow set rules and procedures so that they can provide relatively uniform results. When a bureaucracy works well, it harnesses many individual efforts to achieve the organization's goals. But along the way, "red tape" (the rules the bureaucrats must follow) slows the process and prevents employees from making decisions that go against the rules. State rules should mean the same in Dallas as in Houston, but making the decisions may seem slow, and the "street level" bureaucrat may not have the authority to make adjustments for differences in local conditions. Thus, bureaucracies are necessary but sometimes frustrating.

## Bureaucracy and Public Policy

We often think of public administrators as simply implementing the laws passed by the legislature, but the truth is that they must make many decisions not clearly specified in the law. Not surprisingly, their own views, their bosses' preferences, and their agency's culture make a difference in how they apply laws passed by the legislature. Agencies also want to protect or expand their turf (their jobs and the size, power, and responsibility of the agency). Lobbyists know this and work just as hard to influence agency decisions as they work to influence legislation.

Public agencies also must build good relations with top state leaders (such as the governor), key legislators, and their staff members, because these determine how much money and authority the agency receives. Dealing with the legislature often involves close cooperation between state agencies and lobbyists for groups the agencies serve or regulate. For example, the Texas Good Roads/Transportation Association (mostly trucking companies and road contractors) and the Texas Department of Transportation have long worked closely, and relatively successfully, to lobby the legislature for more highway money.

In Texas, three factors are particularly important in determining agencies' success in achieving their policy goals: the vigor and vision of their leadership, resources, and elite access. Many Texas agencies define their job narrowly and

**public administration**
The implementation of public policy by government employees.

**bureaucrats** Public employees.

make decisions on narrow technical grounds without considering the broader consequences of their actions. In the past, this passive approach typified most Texas environmental agencies, which is one reason for Texas's many environmental problems. Other agency heads take a proactive approach. Beginning in 1975, for example, three successive activist comptrollers transformed the Texas Comptroller's Office into a major player in Texas government, a more aggressive collector of state taxes, a problem-solver for other agencies, and under Comptroller Strayhorn, a focus of controversy. It appears that elected agency heads, such as the comptroller and attorney general, have more clout (and perhaps incentive) to be proactive about their agency's job than do appointed agency heads.

Historically, Texas government agencies have had minimal funds to implement policy. Consider the example of nursing homes, which are big business today and mostly run for profit. In the words of one commentator,

> While costs for nursing homes are going up, there's less money coming in from state Medicaid programs. With state budgets so tight, Medicaid rates have been stagnant, Texas' Medicaid rates for nursing homes rank 49th in the country.... Because the vast majority of nursing home residents rely on Medicaid to pay their way, these trends make it increasingly difficult for nursing homes to make money. The less scrupulous for-profit nursing homes boost earnings by curtailing staff and services.[3]

Nursing homes residents are generally weak and unable to leave if the service is bad or threatens their well-being. Therefore, they depend heavily on government inspectors to ensure that they are treated well. Unfortunately, the number of nursing home inspectors in Texas has been like a rollercoaster—sometimes up, sometimes down. When the legislature cut the number of inspectors in 2001, inspections dropped and abuse increased. Even when there are enough inspectors, connections between nursing-home company executives and lobbyists and top agency administrators often ensure that infractions result in a slap on the wrist and a promise to do better. (This is called **elite access**.) Over the years, both the Health and Human Services Commission and the state attorney general have been criticized for their lack of vigor in pursuing nursing home violations.

As this example illustrates, elite access and lack of resources make policy less effective and abuse more common in Texas nursing homes. One study found that in 1999–2003 Texas had more severe and repeat violations of federal patient care standards than any other state. Results can include neglect, physical and verbal abuse, injury, and death. The study also found that for-profit nursing homes were more likely to have serious and repeat actions harmful to residents than were government and nonprofit homes.[4]

## Number

Governments are Texas's biggest employers. In 2003, the equivalent of 266,000 Texans drew full-time state paychecks. Put another way, Texas had

**elite access** The ability of the business elite to deal directly with high-ranking government administrators to avoid meeting regulations.

120 full-time state employees for every 10,000 citizens. This sounds like a lot, but Texas ranked 45th out of the 50 states in number of state employees per 10,000 citizens. As you can see in the table "How Do We Compare... In Number of State Employees," Texas is following a national pattern. As populations grow, most states, including Texas, are hiring proportionately fewer employees. From 1993 to 2003, the number of state employees has declined relative to the population in both Texas and the nation. One reason Texas ranks so low is that the state government passes a great deal of responsibility to local governments. Texas local governments employed 987,000 workers, or 447 per 10,000 residents in 2003. That placed them 6th among the 50 states. Moreover, like local governments in other states, local government employment in Texas is increasing faster than the population.

### Competence, Pay, and Retention

Most public administrators do a good job, but some are less effective. Many observers believe that bureaucratic competence improves with a civil service system and good pay and benefits. In the first century of our nation, many thought that any fool could do a government job, and as a result, many fools worked in government. From local to national levels, government jobs were filled through the **patronage system.** Government officials hired friends and supporters with little regard for whether or not they were competent. The idea was that "to the victor goes the spoils." **Merit systems,** on the other hand, require officials to hire, promote, and fire government employees based on objective criteria such as tests, education, experience, and performance. If a merit system works well, it tends to produce a competent bureaucracy. But a system that provides too much protection makes it difficult to fire the incompetent and gives little incentive for the competent to excel.

Texas has never had a merit system covering all state employees, and in 1985, the partial state merit system was abolished. What replaced it was a

**patronage system** Hiring friends and supporters as government employees without regard to their abilities.

**merit system** Hiring, promoting, and firing on the basis of objective criteria such as tests, degrees, experience, and performance.

### How Do We Compare ... in Number of State Employees?

*Full-Time Equivalent State Employees (FTE) and Number per 10,000 Population*

| Most Populous U.S. States | Number of FTE Employees 2003 | Number per 10,000 of State Population 1993 | Number per 10,000 of State Population 2003 | U.S. States Bordering Texas | Number of FTE Employees 2003 | Number per 10,000 of State Population 1993 | Number per 10,000 of State Population 2003 |
|---|---|---|---|---|---|---|---|
| California | 389,000 | 110 | 110 | Arkansas | 54,000 | 190 | 198 |
| Florida | 187,000 | 120 | 110 | Louisiana | 90,000 | 209 | 201 |
| New York | 248,000 | 146 | 129 | New Mexico | 46,000 | 262 | 247 |
| **Texas** | **266,000** | **136** | **120** | Oklahoma | 66,000 | 210 | 187 |
| All 50 States | 4,191,000 | 150 | 144 | | | | |

*Source:* U.S. Census Bureau, *Statistical Abstract of the United States, 2006,* **www.census.gov**.

highly centralized compensation and classification system covering most of the executive branch but not the judicial and legislative branches and higher education. Individual agencies are free to develop their own systems for hiring, promotion, and firing (so long as they comply with federal standards where applicable). Critics worried that the result would be greater turnover and lower competence. However, a survey of state human resource directors indicates that agencies have developed more flexible personnel policies that provide some protection for most employees. Moreover, patronage appointments have not become a major problem in state administration. In the words of one observer, "It's not uncommon for state agencies to become repositories for campaign staff or former officeholders, . . . But there are no wholesale purges" when new officials are elected.[5]

While each agency determines its own personnel policies, the legislature sets salaries, wage scales, and other benefits. Despite employee incentive options, state employee turnover is consistently high. The state government's turnover rate was 15 percent in fiscal year 2004 compared to 9 percent for Texas's local governments and the national average of 10 percent. The State Auditor's Office (SAO) estimates that turnover cost the state $345 million that year. One reason for turnover is low pay. The SAO study found that the average state employee's pay was 17 percent less than the pay of workers doing similar jobs in other Texas governments and private business.[6] In 2006, as an example, a newly hired computer operator in the Texas Department of Criminal Justice received an annual salary of only $21,792. As the state economy improves, higher pay outside of government is expected to increase state employee turnover.

*Table 9.1*   Texas Minorities and Women in State Government Compared to the Total Civilian State Workforce, 2004 (in percentage)[a]

| Job Category | African American | | Hispanic American | | Female | |
|---|---|---|---|---|---|---|
| | Govt. | Total Workforce | Govt. | Total Workforce | Govt. | Total Workforce |
| Official, Administrator | 9 | 7 | 12 | 15 | 47 | 44 |
| Professional | 12 | 8 | 16 | 14 | 57 | 54 |
| Technical | 15 | 10 | 19 | 20 | 53 | 48 |
| Administrative Support | 18 | 10 | 28 | 23 | 89 | 62 |
| Skilled craft | 9 | 5 | 23 | 34 | 4 | 7 |
| Service & Maintenance | 28 | 9 | 24 | 33 | 50 | 40 |
| **TOTALS** | **17** | **11** | **20** | **33** | **56** | **45** |

*Source:* Compiled from Texas Workforce Commission, Civil Rights Division, February 2005.

[a]State Agencies Workforce (including executive agencies and higher education) and Statewide Civilian Workforce (including both private and public workers) for calendar 2004.

**Note on interpretation:** The first cell indicates that 9 percent of Texas government officials and administrators are African American; the next cell shows that 7 percent of the officials and administrators in the state's total economy are African American.

Other, nonfinancial factors help to attract state employees. Studies consistently show that large numbers of government employees have a strong sense of service and thus find being a public servant rewarding. Three "perks" also increase the attractiveness of public employment: paid vacations, state holidays, and sick leave.

Another incentive for employment can be equitable treatment. For many years, Texas state government has advertised itself as an "equal opportunity employer," and evidence indicates that it has been, albeit imperfectly. Women constitute more than half of state employees, and are more likely to hold higher ranking positions in government than in the private economy. Table 9.1 shows that women make up a higher proportion of employees in government than in the total state economy in every job category except skilled craft workers. African Americans also fare better in government employment than in the private economy—in all categories. Hispanic Texans, on the other hand, are more likely to be employed in the private economy than in government in most job categories. In both public and private arenas, all three groups are underrepresented in the top employment category compared to their numbers in the state population. Data on newly hired state employees indicate that these patterns will probably continue.

### How Do We Compare ... in State Employee Compensation?

*Average Monthly Pay per Full-Time-Equivalent (FTE) Employee, 1993 and 2003*

| Most Populous U.S. States | 1993 | 2003 | U.S. States Bordering Texas | 1993 | 2003 |
|---|---|---|---|---|---|
| California | $3,644 | $4,892 | Arkansas | $2,261 | $3,041 |
| Florida | $2,266 | $3,298 | Louisiana | $2,242 | $3,171 |
| New York | $3,335 | $4,404 | New Mexico | $2,223 | $2,964 |
| Texas | $2,426 | $3,382 | Oklahoma | $1,897 | $3,083 |

Source: U.S. Census Bureau, *Statistical Abstract of the United States, 2006,* **www.census.gov**.

### Learning Check 9.1      (Answers on p. 373)

1. True or False: Public administrators simply implement the laws passed by the legislature without making any changes.
2. What three factors are particularly important in determining how successful agencies are in Texas?
3. Have women been more successful in finding higher-ranking positions in Texas government or the private sector?

## Education

In 2003, after a legislative hearing on health problems along the Mexican border, Representative Debbie Riddle (R-Tomball) asked an *El Paso Times* reporter,

"Where did this idea come from that everybody deserves free education, free medical care, free whatever? It comes from Moscow, from Russia. It comes straight out of the pit of hell."[7] Indeed, education and social services are controversial in Texas.

## Public Schools

Texas's commitment to education began with its 1836 constitution, which required government-owned land to be set aside for establishing public schools and "a University of the first class." Later, framers of the Constitution of 1876 mandated an "efficient system of public free schools." What continues to perplex state policymakers is how to advance public schools' efficiency while seeking equality of funding for students in districts with varying amounts and values of taxable property. (See the chapter "Finance and Fiscal Policy" for a discussion of school finance issues.)

Today, approximately 1,040 independent school districts (ISDs) shoulder primary responsibility for delivery of educational services to more than 4 million students. (The chapter "Local Governments" discusses the organization and politics of local schools.) Although local districts have somewhat more independence today, they are part of a relatively centralized system in which state authorities substantially affect local decisions, from what is taught to how it is paid for.

**State Board of Education**    Oversight of Texas education is divided between two bodies: the elected **State Board of Education (SBOE)** and the commissioner of education, who is appointed by the governor to run the Texas Education Agency. Over the years, the extreme ideological positions taken by many SBOE members have embarrassed the legislature and caused it to whittle away the board's authority. For years, the board was even made appointive rather than elective. Today, the greater power over state education is in the hands of the commissioner of education through control of the Texas Education Agency, but the SBOE remains important and highly controversial.

Among the board's most significant powers are curriculum approval for each subject and grade; textbook selection for the public schools;[8] approval of State Board for Educator Certification rules; and management of the Permanent School Fund. (Interest from the $22 billion fund is an important source of revenue for public schools.)

Representing districts with approximately equal population (about 1.4 million), the 15 elected board members serve without salary for overlapping terms of four years. The governor appoints, with Senate confirmation, a sitting SBOE member as chair for a two-year term.

Deep ideological differences divide the board. The ideological lines also follow partisan and ethnic lines. The socially conservative members tend to be Anglo Republicans, while the moderate and liberal members are commonly African American and Latino Democrats. Openly hostile debates on subjects such as textbook adoption and public criticism surrounding possible conflict of

**State Board of Education (SBOE)**
A popularly elected 15-member body with limited authority over Texas's K-12 education system.

**Points to Ponder**

Over time, education has become increasingly important to individuals and the nation as a whole. Not surprisingly, both leaders and ordinary citizens regularly speak about the importance of education. But how serious are we? The numbers below suggest that Texas may not yet be seeking or achieving the excellence in education that it could.

| Texas Public Schools | | | Texas Higher Education | | |
|---|---|---|---|---|---|
| Indicator | Amount | Rank Among the 50 States | Indicator | Amount | Rank Among the 50 States |
| Expenditure per pupil, 2005 | $7,142 | 40 | Per capita state & local government expenditure for higher education, 2002 | $575 | 26 |
| Average teacher salary, 2005 | $41,009 | 33 | Average tuition & fees at public universities, 2003-04 | $3,579 | 36 |
| Student to teacher ratio, 2005 | 14.9:1 | 26 | Average salary of an associate professor at a flagship university, 2004 | $64,900 | 25 |
| No. students per instructional computer, 2003 | 3.5 | 37 | Percent of population 25 & older with a bachelor's degree, 2004 | 24.5 | 35 |
| Public library visits per capita, 2002 | 3.0 | 46 | African Americans & Hispanics as percentage of age 15–34 population, 2005 | 55 | NA |
| High school graduation rate, 2004 | 67.5 | 36 | African Americans & Hispanics as percentage of higher ed. students, 2005 | 36 | NA |
| Percent age 25 & older with high school diploma, 2004 | 78.3 | 50 | Number universities ranked in top 100, 2006 (4 private and 2 public) | 6 | 4 |
| Percent age 25 & older with 8th grade education or less, 2000 | 11.5 | 2 | | | |
| Average Math SAT, 2005 | 502 | 46 | | | |
| Average Verbal SAT, 2005 | 493 | 49 | | | |

*Sources:* Legislative Budget Board, *Texas Fact Book, 2006,* **www.lbb.state.tx.us**; Higher Education Coordinating Board, *Texas Higher Education Facts—2006,* **thecb.state.tx.us**; Texas Comptroller, *Texas: Where We Stand,* February 2006, **window. state.tx.us**; and *Chronicle of Higher Education,* April 27, 2004.

interest in the selection of investment managers and independent financial consultants for the Permanent School Fund have led some legislators to advocate reforming board procedures and others to threaten elimination of the SBOE.

Probably the most contentious issue facing the SBOE is its periodic review of textbooks for the state textbook adoption lists. The SBOE may decide whether to reject a book or to place it on either a "conforming" or a "nonconforming" adoption list. Books on both lists must meet the SBOE's physical specifications (for example, quality of binding and paper) and be free of factual errors. Critics charge that some board members have interpreted the latter requirement to mean that expressions of theories and interpretations that conflict with their views are errors.[9] To be included on the conforming list, a book must cover all of the essential elements in the Texas Essential Knowledge and Skills (TEKS) curriculum for its subject and grade. Inclusion on the nonconforming list requires coverage of at least half of a curriculum's elements.

As an incentive, the state will pay 100 percent of the cost if local school districts use books on these lists but not more than 70 percent for books not on the adoption lists. Because most districts want the state to pay the full cost, textbook publishers want their books on one of the adoption lists (preferably the conforming list). Because Texas, California, and Florida purchase huge numbers of textbooks, publishers cater to these markets. Other states complain that their textbook options tend to be limited to books published for one or more of the three big "adoption-state" markets.

Chase Untermeyer, a Houston Republican who served on the SBOE for four years, including two years as chair, has summed up the SBOE dilemma:

> What we now have is a body with partial powers, not enough to help Texas education but sufficient to get into trouble. That is because state lawmakers have two conflicting minds with regard to the board: They lack confidence in it, but they also lack the desire to do away with it. As long as this situation continues, the board—regardless of who serves on it or how it is chosen—will take actions that upset the Legislature and the educational establishment.[10]

**Texas Education Agency**   Which level of government should make educational policy? The local level, according to many Texans. Local officials know local needs, and most parents and citizens believe that they should have a say. But many who study education, along with many public officials, believe that the broader, more professional perspective found at the state or national level encourages higher educational standards. Texas responds to both of these views. Local school boards and superintendents run the schools, but almost all of their decisions are shaped by state and, to a much smaller extent, federal rules and procedures. At the federal level, the U.S. Department of Education, with nearly 5,000 employees, provides federal aid, requires nondiscrimination, and, under President Bush's No Child Left Behind program, requires extensive testing.

In the Lone Star State, the **Texas Education Agency (TEA)**, headquartered in Austin, is staffed with about 600 full-time employees. Created by the legislature in 1949, the TEA today is headed by the **commissioner of education**, appointed by the governor to a four-year term with Senate confirmation. The TEA has the following powers:

- Oversee development of the statewide curriculum
- Accredit and rate schools (Exemplary, Recognized, Academically Acceptable, or Academically Unacceptable)
- Monitor accreditation: Whenever a local school district fails to meet state standards, TEA officials can assume control of that district, after

**Texas Education Agency (TEA)** Administers the state's public school system of more than 6,300 schools.

**commissioner of education** The official who heads the TEA.

approval by the U.S. attorney general, until acceptable reforms are made. In 2005, for example, the TEA removed the elected school board and appointed managers for the Wilmer-Hutchins Independent School District in the Dallas area.

- Oversee the testing of elementary and secondary school students
- Serve as a fiscal agent for the distribution of state and federal funds (administers about three-fourths of the Permanent School Fund and supervises the Foundation School Program, which allocates state money to independent school districts [ISDs])
- Monitor compliance with federal guidelines
- Grant waivers to schools seeking charter status and exemptions from certain state regulations
- Manage the textbook adoption process
- Administer a data collection system on public school students, staff, and finances and operate research and information programs
- Handle the administrative functions of the State Board of Educator Certification (placed under TEA in 2005 as part of the Sunset Process)

**Charter Schools**    In 1995, the legislature authorized the State Board of Education to issue charters to schools less limited by TEA rules in hopes that with greater flexibility, they could deal more effectively with at-risk students. Charter schools are public schools but draw students from across district lines, use a variety of teaching strategies, and are exempt from many rules such as state teacher certification requirements. The experiment is still developing. Despite early problems with corruption and lack of evidence that charter schools were improving student learning, almost 200 were operating by 2005. Charter school students are somewhat more economically disadvantaged (63 percent) than the state average (53 percent) and more African American (39 percent versus the state average of 14 percent). Hispanics are slightly underrepresented in charter schools (41 to 44 percent), although their enrollment numbers are increasing. The state provides most of the funding ($4,500 per student in fiscal year 2005). Other money must be obtained from federal and private sources. Charters are granted to nonprofit corporations that in turn create a board to govern the school. The particular organization varies from school to school.[11]

**Testing**    Educators are sharply divided about how to assess student progress and determine graduation standards. Nevertheless, testing as a major assessment tool is now federal and state policy. Texas began to rely heavily on testing in 1990 with the Texas Academic Assessment of Skills (TAAS). In 2003, the TAAS was replaced by the **Texas Assessment of Knowledge and Skills (TAKS)**. This new testing program for grades 3 through 11 was developed as a better and more difficult measure of students' mastery of the Texas Essential Knowledge and Skills (TEKS), a core curriculum required by the legislature.

Ordinarily, a student who fails to pass a test on three attempts must repeat the grade. For eleventh-graders, the TAKS is an exit-level test that covers language arts, mathematics, science, and social studies. Passing grades in all four areas are required for a diploma upon completion of the twelfth grade, but

**Texas Assessment of Knowledge and Skills (TAKS)** A standardized test covering a core curriculum.

failing students are allowed to retake tests even after leaving school. The TEA also uses TAKS results to evaluate the performance of schools, and legislation passed in 2006 created a merit pay plan for teachers based largely on student test results.

From its beginning, the statewide testing program drew cries of protest from many parents and educators. Social conservatives argue that this state-mandated testing program intrudes excessively into local school operations, while African American and Latino critics charge that the tests are discriminatory. Over time, scores for ethnic minorities and the economically disadvantaged have increased but still average lower than the scores of Anglos and more affluent students. Educational critics complain that "teaching to the test" raises scores on the test but causes neglect of other subjects and does not seem to raise scores on other, national tests. Supporters of testing argue that it holds schools and teachers responsible for increasing student learning and point to the improved scores of most groups of students since the program began.[12]

## Colleges and Universities

Texas has many colleges and universities—101 public and 42 private institutions of higher education, serving 1.2 million students. The large number reflects several factors: the early tradition of locating colleges away from the "evils" of large cities, the demand of communities for schools to serve their needs, and the desire to make college education accessible to students. Most potential Texas students live within commuting distance of a campus. The public institutions include 31 four-year universities, 7 two-year institutions, 9 health-related institutions, 50 community college districts, and the Texas Technical College System. All receive some state funding and, not surprisingly, state regulation.

The two "flagship" universities are the University of Texas at Austin and Texas A&M University in College Station. Both have evolved into large systems with multiple campuses spread across the state. They have traditionally been the most prestigious academically and the most powerful politically. Four universities are independent (for example, Texas Woman's University), and the rest are part of three other university systems (for example, the Texas State University System). Schools aggressively seeking funding and status as part of the state's unofficial second tier of universities include Texas Tech, North Texas, the University of Houston, four universities from the University of Texas system (Dallas, Arlington, El Paso, and San Antonio), and most recently Texas State University–San Marcos.

**Boards of Regents**   Texas's public independent universities, university systems, and the Texas Technical College System are governed by boards of regents. The regents are appointed by the governor for six-year terms with Senate approval. The board makes general policy, selects each university's president, and provides general supervision of the universities in their system. Day-to-day operation is in the hands of the individual university's top officials (commonly the president and the academic vice president, although terminology varies). The governance of community colleges is by local boards discussed in the chapter "Local Governments."

**Texas Higher Education Coordinating Board**   The **Texas Higher Education Coordinating Board** (THECB) is not a super board of regents, but it does provide some semblance of statewide direction for all public community colleges and universities. The coordinating board must approve new academic programs, degrees, universities, community colleges, and technical colleges. To force greater use of campus facilities (which means more afternoon classes), the THECB has long refused new construction permits to schools with low use of existing classrooms. Students who have problems transferring course credits from one Texas college or university to another may appeal to the board. Membership on the board was reduced to 9 in 2007. The members receive no pay and are appointed by the governor to six-year terms with Senate approval. Gubernatorial power also extends to designating two board members as chair and vice chair, with neither appointment requiring Senate confirmation.

**Higher Education Issues**   Two sets of issues have challenged Texas higher education in recent years: funding and affirmative action. Funding and the sharp increase in tuition rates are discussed in the chapter "Finance and Fiscal Policy," but we address affirmative action in the section below.

Improving the educational opportunities of Texas's ethnic minorities and economically disadvantaged is a controversial issue. Texas's long history of official and private discrimination still has consequences today. While many Latinos and African Americans have made it into the middle class since the civil rights changes of the 1960s and 1970s, both groups remain overrepresented in the working class and the ranks of the poor and underrepresented in Texas higher education. Latinos and African Americans represented 55 percent of the state's 15 to 34 age group but only 36 percent of college students in 2005–2006.

Texas colleges and universities commonly describe themselves as equal opportunity/affirmative action institutions. **Equal opportunity** simply means that the school takes care that its policies and actions do not discriminate. **Affirmative action** means that the school takes positive steps to attract women and minorities. For most, this means such noncontroversial steps as making sure that the school catalog has pictures of all groups—Anglos and minorities, men and women—and recruiting in predominantly minority high schools, not just Anglo schools. However, some selective-admission schools have actively considered race in admissions and aid, and other schools have had scholarships for minorities. This side of affirmative action has created controversy.

Some Anglo applicants denied admission or scholarship benefits challenged these affirmative action programs in the courts. In the case of *University of California* v. *Bakke* (1978), the U.S. Supreme Court ruled that race could be considered as one factor along with other criteria to achieve diversity in higher education enrollment; however, setting aside a specific number of slots for one race was not acceptable.[13] Relying on the *Bakke* decision, the University of Texas Law School then created separate admission pools based on race and ethnicity, a practice the U.S. Fifth Circuit Court of Appeals declared unconstitutional in

**Texas Higher Education Coordinating Board** An agency that provides some direction for the state's community colleges and universities.

**equal opportunity** Takes care that policies and actions do not discriminate.

**affirmative action** Takes positive steps to attract women and minorities; may include using race in admission or hiring decisions.

*Hopwood* v. *Texas*.[14] Subsequently the U.S. Supreme Court issued two rulings on affirmative action in 2003: in the Michigan case of *Grutter* v. *Bollinger*, the court ruled that race could constitute one factor in an admissions policy designed to achieve student body diversity;[15] then, in another Michigan case, *Gratz and Hamacher* v. *Bollinger*, the court condemned the practice of giving a portion of the points needed to guarantee admission to every single "unrepresented minority" seeking admittance.[16] In the years ahead, both the *Grutter* and *Gratz* rulings will provide guidance to legislators and university officials as they formulate admissions policies for Texas's institutions of higher education.

After the *Hopwood* ruling, Texas schools looked for ways to maintain minority enrollment. In 1997, Texas legislators mandated that the **top 10 percent** of every high school graduating class could be admitted to tax-supported colleges and universities of their choosing, regardless of test admission scores.[17] Thus, the best students at Texas's many high schools, including those heavily minority, economically disadvantaged, or in small towns, can gain admission. The policy has been moderately effective in helping all three groups. The practice, however, is controversial, especially among applicants from competitive high schools denied admission to the state's flagship institutions—UT–Austin and Texas A&M. In fall 2005, 72 percent of students admitted to UT–Austin, for example, qualified based on top 10 percent ranking, a situation that leaves little room for students to be admitted based on high scores or other talents.

Each legislative session sees one or more bills introduced to change the **top 10 percent rule**, but through 2006, none had passed. The University of Texas at Austin reintroduced affirmative action in its admission policy in 2005, while in 2004 Texas A&M said that it would not use race in admission but would increase minority recruiting and provide more scholarships for first-generation, low-income students. ("First generation" students are the first in their family to attend college.) All Texas institutions of higher education are under mandate from the Higher Education Coordinating Board to actively recruit and retain minority students under its Closing the Gap initiative.

---

**Learning Check 9.2**    **(Answers on pp. 373–374)**

**1.** Which two state government entities are most important for public schools?
**2.** True or False: Almost all observers consider Texas's testing program a success.
**3.** What is the most important entity for governing Texas colleges and universities?
**4.** What is the "top 10 percent rule" in Texas higher education?

---

# ★ Health and Human Services

Most people think of Texas as a wealthy state, and indeed there are many wealthy Texans and a large middle class. But Texas also has long been among the states with the largest proportion of its population in poverty. Texas's 2004 poverty rate was the fifth highest in the nation—16.5 percent. This was slightly worse than in 1980, when the rate was 15.7 percent. Poverty is particularly high

**top 10 percent rule**
Texas law gives automatic admission to any Texas public college or university to those graduating in the top 10 percent of their Texas high school class.

## POINT/COUNTERPOINT

**Should Texas Continue to Use the "Top 10 Percent Rule"?**

**THE ISSUE**  To promote diversity in Texas colleges and universities without using race as an admission criterion, the state legislature in 1997 passed a law guaranteeing admission to any public college or university in the state for Texas students who graduate in the top 10 percent of their high school class. The law sought to promote greater geographic, socioeconomic, and racial/ethnic diversity. It has had its greatest effect on the two flagship universities—UT–Austin and Texas A&M—Tier 1 schools that limit admission. It has increased minority representation at both schools but more so at UT–Austin.

**Arguments For the Top Ten Percent Rule**

1. It is doing what it was designed to do—increase diversity among highly qualified students.
2. Virtually all top 20 percent students from competitive high schools who choose UT or A&M actually succeed in enrolling there.
3. The problem is not that Texas has too many students entering schools under automatic admission. Rather, there are too few flagship universities to accommodate the number of qualified students.

**Arguments Against the Top Ten Percent Rule**

1. It unfairly disadvantages students who attend high schools with rigorous standards. Thus, they are tempted to take lighter loads or attend less-demanding high schools.
2. So many students are admitted under this one criterion that the universities have too little discretion, and students with other talents (such as music and the arts) are left out.
3. The rule is creating a brain drain; many top students are leaving Texas to attend college in other states, where they often stay.

For more information, see *Should Texas Change the Top 10 Percent Law?* Focus Report No. 79–7 (Austin: House Research Organization, Texas House of Representatives, February 25, 2005), **www.hro.house.state.tx.us/frame4.htm#fac**.

for children and ethnic minorities, as can be seen in detail in Table 9.2. Even more Texans are low income, meaning they earn an income above the poverty line but insufficient for many "extras" such as health insurance. (A common measure of this is an income up to twice the poverty level. Just over one in five Texans meets this measure—between 101 and 200 percent of the poverty level.)

Texans also suffer from a multitude of health problems—old-age infirmities, inadequate health care, malnutrition, physical disabilities, mental illness, and life-threatening diseases such as AIDS. In recent decades, health insurance has become an important gatekeeper dividing those who can receive adequate medical care and those who cannot. Unfortunately, Texas has led the nation in the proportion of people without health insurance since at least 1988—about one in four Texans compared to one in six in the nation.[18] We also lead in the proportion of uninsured children.

*Table 9.2*   Who's in Poverty in Texas and the United States? (2004)

| | TEXAS | | U.S. |
| --- | --- | --- | --- |
| | % | Number (million) | % |
| Individuals | 17 | 3.7 | 13 |
| Anglos | 8 | 0.8 | 9 |
| Hispanics | 26 | 2.2 | 22 |
| African Americans | 22 | 0.5 | 25 |
| Children Under 18 | 23 | 1.5 | 18 |
| Age 65 and Over | 12 | 0.3 | 10 |

*Source:* U.S. Census Bureau, **www.census.gov**, and Center for Public Policy Priorities, "Texas Poverty 101," September 2005, **www.cppp.org**.

Since the Great Depression of the 1930s, state and national governments have gradually increased efforts to address the needs of the poor, the elderly, and those who cannot afford adequate medical care. The national government has taken responsibility for relatively popular social welfare programs such as Social Security, Medicare, and aid to the blind and disabled. The states, on the other hand, have responsibility for less popular programs with less effective lobbying behind them such as Medicaid, Food Stamps, and Temporary Assistance for Needy Families (TANF). The federal government pays a significant part of the cost of state social welfare programs, but the state administers them, makes eligibility rules, and pays part of the tab.

Health and human services programs are at a disadvantage in Texas for two reasons. First, the state's political culture values individualism and self-reliance; thus, anything smacking of welfare is difficult to fund at more than the most minimal level. In addition, the most needy Texans are not organized to compete with the special-interest groups representing the business elite and the middle class. The Lone Star State has responded with social service agencies that provide assistance for millions of needy Texans, but at relatively low benefit levels. And many are left out. Poor and low-income people are Texas politicians' most underserved constituencies.

The Health and Human Services Commission (HHSC) coordinates social service policy. Sweeping changes were launched in 2003 when the 78th Legislature consolidated functions of 12 social service agencies under the **executive commissioner of the Health and Human Services Commission**. The legislation also began a process of privatizing service delivery, creating more administrative barriers to services, and slowing the growth of expenditures.

The executive commissioner is appointed by the governor for a two-year term and confirmed by the Senate. Health and human services not controlled directly by the executive commissioner are supervised by commissioners heading each of four agencies: Department of State Health Services, Department of Aging and Disability Services, Department of Assistive and Rehabilitative Services,

**executive commissioner of the Health and Human Services Commission** Appointed by the governor with Senate approval, this executive commissioner administers the HHSC, develops policies, makes rules, and appoints (with approval by the governor) commissioners to head the commission's four departments.

and Department of Family and Protective Services. These commissioners receive their appointments from the executive commissioner with approval of the governor. (See Figure 9.1 for the commission's organization chart.) The HHSC handles centralized administrative support services, develops policies, and makes rules for all agencies. In addition, the commission determines eligibility for food stamps, the Children's Health Insurance Program (CHIP), Medicaid, and long-term care services.

The new organization went through substantial changes during its first years, and problems arose. A change that provoked widespread opposition involved replacing many local offices and caseworkers with call centers operated by private contractors rather than staffed by state employees. Applicants for social services would be encouraged to use telephone and Internet communication to establish eligibility for social services. Not surprisingly, state employees complained of the loss of 2,900 jobs. Then, in April 2006, implementation stalled a second time because of problems with the private contractor. Clients in the pilot program had complained of long waits and problems receiving benefits for which they were eligible. During three months of the transition, about 100,000 children lost medical benefits.[19] For more discussion see Selected Reading 9.1 "Privatized Services Stumbling."

### Human Services

The Health and Human Services Commission administers a variety of programs. But three have long received a great deal of attention and controversy—TANF, food stamps, and Medicaid. All are administered by the executive commissioner within federal guidelines and are paid for by the federal government and to a lesser extent by the state.

The executive commissioner has direct responsibility for the **Temporary Assistance for Needy Families (TANF)** program. This program provides limited support for poor families with income below the poverty level, $20,000 for a family of four in 2006. Caretakers must sign a "personal responsibility agreement" requiring them either to work or to enroll in a job-training program. Children may continue to receive benefits if their caretaker seeks but fails to find employment. Caretakers must be U.S. citizens or legal residents. According to HHSC, the "most common" TANF caretaker is a woman about 30 years old with 1–2 children under age 11. She is unemployed and has no other income, and receives a TANF grant of $208 or less per month for less than 12 months.

A second federal-state program administered by the executive commissioner is the **food stamp program**. It makes food available to elderly or disabled people, families, and single adults who qualify because of low income. About 80 percent of those who benefit from food stamps receive no TANF support. Benefits vary, depending on income and the number of people in a household. In September 2006, for example, a qualified Texas household composed of four people with a maximum combined monthly income of $2,097 could obtain groceries costing up to $506 each month. To reduce fraud, the program has

**Temporary Assistance for Needy Families (TANF)** Replaced Aid for Families with Dependent Children (AFDC) in an attempt to help poor people move from welfare to the workforce.

**Food stamp program** Joint federal-state program administered by the state to provide food to low-income people.

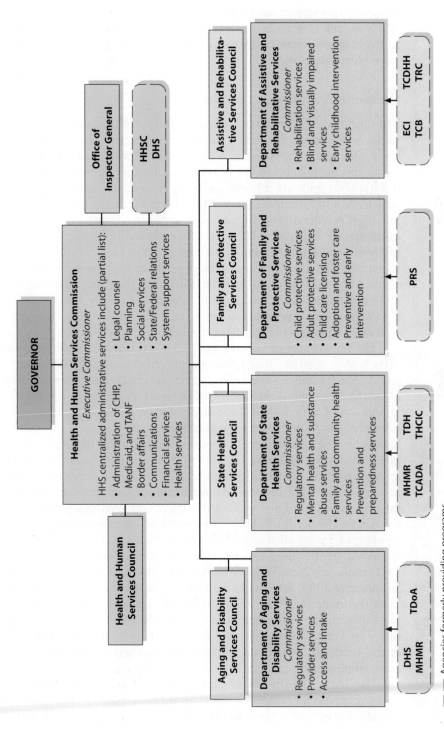

**GOVERNOR**

**Office of Inspector General**

HHSC
DHS

**Health and Human Services Commission**
*Executive Commissioner*

HHS centralized administrative services include (partial list):

- Administration of CHIP, Medicaid, and TANF
- Border affairs
- Communications
- Financial services
- Health services
- Legal counsel
- Planning
- Social services
- State/Federal relations
- System support services

**Health and Human Services Council**

**Aging and Disability Services Council**

**Department of Aging and Disability Services**
*Commissioner*
- Regulatory services
- Provider services
- Access and intake

DHS
MHMR
TDoA

**State Health Services Council**

**Department of State Health Services**
*Commissioner*
- Regulatory services
- Mental health and substance abuse services
- Family and community health services
- Prevention and preparedness services

MHMR　TDH
TCADA　THCIC

**Family and Protective Services Council**

**Department of Family and Protective Services**
*Commissioner*
- Child protective services
- Adult protective services
- Child care licensing
- Adoption and foster care
- Preventive and early intervention

PRS

**Assistive and Rehabilita-tive Services Council**

**Department of Assistive and Rehabilitative Services**
*Commissioner*
- Rehabilitation services
- Blind and visually impaired services
- Early childhood intervention services

ECI　TCDHH
TCB　TRC

──── Agencies formerly providing programs

*Figure 9.1*　The Consolidated Texas Health and Human Services System

*Source:* Texas Health and Human Services Commission, January 2006, www.hhsc.state.tx.us.

replaced paper stamps used for such purchases with a plastic "Lone Star Card," which resembles a credit or debit card. For these and other benefits, log on to the State of Texas Assistance and Referral System at **www.txstars.net** and **www.hhsc.state.tx.us**.

### Health and Mental Health Services

The third major federal-state program administered by the executive commissioner is **Medicaid**. Part of President Lyndon B. Johnson's Great Society initiatives in the 1960s, Medicaid is designed to provide medical care for persons whose income falls below the poverty line. Resources not counted against the poverty-level limit are a home, personal possessions, and a low-value motor vehicle. Not to be confused with Medicaid is **Medicare**, another Great Society initiative. A federal program providing medical assistance to qualifying applicants age 65 and older, Medicare is administered by the U.S. Department of Health and Human Services without use of state funds. Because Medicaid is considered welfare and serves the poor, it has much less political clout than Medicare, which serves a more middle class clientele. Medicaid has much more difficulty gaining funding, and benefits for clients and service providers tend to be lower. Benefits are so low, in fact, that some doctors refuse Medicaid patients, and nursing homes have trouble covering their costs.

The Department of State Health Services performs a wide variety of functions, including public health planning and enforcement of state health laws. As with public assistance, state health policies are closely tied to several federal programs. One example is the Special Supplemental Nutrition Program for Women, Infants, and Children (WIC), a delivery system for food packages, nutritional counseling, and health care screening. Because diseases are a constant threat to human life and a drain on the economy, the Department of State Health Services is responsible for educating Texans about infectious diseases. Texas invests significant resources in making the public aware of high-risk behavior that spreads sexually transmitted diseases. Acquired immunodeficiency syndrome (AIDS), the principal killer of men in their thirties, is unrivaled as a public health problem. Caused by the deadly human immunodeficiency virus (HIV) and commonly transmitted by sexual contact (both homosexual and heterosexual) and contaminated needles used by drug addicts, AIDS is an international epidemic. Texas trails only New York, California, and Florida in numbers of cases. At the beginning of 2006, Texas had a cumulative total of just under 92,000 HIV/AIDS cases reported, 36,000 of whom had died. A related problem is the 100,000 cases of sexually transmitted diseases other than HIV/AIDS reported in Texas each year. Persons between 15 and 24 years of age account for about two-thirds of this total, but it is common knowledge that many cases go unreported by personal physicians.

The Texas Department of State Health Services provides public mental health programs for persons unable to afford private therapy for emotional problems. However, Texas's per capita funding for mental health programs ranks 47th

**Medicaid** Funded in largest part by federal grants and in part by state appropriations, Medicaid is administered by the state. It provides medical care for persons whose incomes fall below the poverty line.

**Medicare** Funded entirely by the federal government and administered by the U.S. Department of Health and Human Services, Medicare provides medical assistance to qualified applicants age 65 and older.

among the 50 states. This means that many people must wait years before receiving treatment in one of Texas's ten state hospitals. As a result, thousands of untreated, mentally ill Texans are detained in jails, incarcerated in the state's penitentiaries, or living on city streets. Like most states, Texas relies heavily on community out-patient services for mental health treatment. In 2006, the state had only 41 community mental health centers, and they were hard pressed to meet the demand for help. About 20,000 state employees are involved in providing mental health services throughout Texas.[20]

## Employment

In 1995, the state legislature consolidated several job-training programs under the **Texas Workforce Commission (TWC)**. The TWC also matches unemployed workers with employers offering jobs. The agency is directed by three salaried commissioners appointed by the governor, with consent of the Senate, for overlapping six-year terms. One member represents employers, one represents labor, and one represents the general public. The TWC collects an employee payroll tax paid by employers, which funds weekly benefit payments to unemployed workers covered by the Texas Unemployment Compensation Act. The amount paid depends on wages earned in an earlier quarter (three months). In 2006, the maximum weekly compensation was $328 and the minimum was $53.

---

**Learning Check 9.3**     **(Answers on p. 374)**

1. Compared to other states, is poverty high or low in Texas?
2. Why are health and human services programs at a disadvantage in Texas?
3. What program provides limited cash benefits to poor families?
4. Which program is better funded, Medicaid or Medicare?

---

## ★ Economic Policies

Have you ever complained about a high telephone bill, a big automobile insurance premium, or the cost of a license to practice a trade or profession for which you have been trained? Welcome to the Lone Star State's regulatory politics! For businesses seeking to boost profits or professional groups trying to strengthen their licensing requirements, obtaining changes in regulations can be costly but also rewarding. Less-organized consumers and workers often believe they are left to pick up the tab for higher bills and fees, and, on occasion, inferior service.

### Business Regulation

The **Railroad Commission of Texas (RRC)** and the state's Public Utility Commission (PUC) are among Texas's most publicized agencies. This is because the former regulates the oil and gas industry, which has a declining but still important influence on the Texas economy, and the latter affects the telephone and electric power bills paid by millions of Texans.

**Texas Workforce Commission (TWC)** A state agency headed by three salaried commissioners who oversee job training and unemployment compensation programs.

**Railroad Commission of Texas (RRC)** A popularly elected, three-member commission primarily engaged in regulating natural gas and petroleum production.

Railroad Commissioner Victor Carillo (right) being sworn in by Texas Chief Justice Wallace Jefferson (left) in January 2005. Looking on are Carillo's wife, Joy, and two daughters. (© Bob Daemmrich Photography, Inc.)

**Oil and Gas**    The three popularly elected Railroad Commission (RRC) members function in several capacities, most of which have nothing to do with railroads. Today, the commission no longer "busts" railroad monopolies; rather, the RRC is primarily involved in granting permits for drilling oil and gas wells and performing other regulatory duties designated by the legislature. For example, the RRC regulates natural gas rates in rural areas and hears appeals of municipally set gas rates for residential and business customers. Other important functions of this agency include preventing waste of valuable petroleum resources, ensuring pipeline safety, and overseeing the plugging of depleted or abandoned oil and gas wells.

Textbooks often cite the RRC as the classic case of "agency capture," a situation in which the regulated industry exerts excessive influence over the agency intended to regulate it. The RRC has long seen its major function as maintaining the profitability of the state's oil and gas industry, although that industry's relative decline and the state's greater economic diversity have reduced industry dominance somewhat.

**Public Utility Commission (PUC)**
A three-member body with regulatory power over the electric and telephone companies.

**Public Utilities**    State regulation of Texas's utility companies did not begin until 1975 with the creation of the **Public Utility Commission (PUC)**. Its three

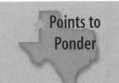

**Points to Ponder**

In 2006, Texas had 142 miles of toll roads, but motorists drove without charge on:

- 78,648 miles of city streets
- 142,477 miles of county roads
- 79,645 miles of state-maintained roads and highways that include:
- 40,986 miles of farm-to-market roads
- 16,256 miles of state highways
- 12,101 miles of U.S. highways
- 6,719 miles of frontage roads
- 3,233 miles of interstate highways
- 339 miles of park roads

Texans drive an average of 627 million miles a day. While state-maintained roads make up only a fourth of total roadways, they carry three-fourths of the vehicle miles traveled.

*Source:* Texas Department of Transportation, *Annual Summary, 2004,* 35, and *Pocket Facts, 2006,* **www.dot.state.tx.us.**

members are appointed by the governor, with Senate approval, to overlapping six-year terms.

The PUC's responsibility for overseeing telecommunications within Texas is limited by national policies. Federal law allows the Federal Communications Commission (FCC) to preempt state regulation of telephone companies. Ultimately, determining whose regulations apply is a matter for courts to decide.

Today, Public Utility Commission operations exemplify recent trends in regulatory policies nationwide. Business practices formerly controlled by government agency rules are now governed more by market conditions. This industry-backed policy is known as **deregulation**. Its objective is to free businesses from governmental restraints and to depend largely on competition to protect the public interest.

Over the past decade, the Texas Legislature has caused the PUC to shift from setting rates telephone and electric power companies may charge to a policy of deregulation that emphasizes competition. Allowing consumers to choose their telephone service supplier, for example, is expected to result in reasonable telephone bills and reliable service from companies that must compete for customers. According to critics, however, deregulation of electricity has made Texas rates among the highest in the nation—"a reversal of at least a decade of relatively cheap electricity under the state's old regulated system."[21] In 2005, Texas ranked 40th among the 50 states on affordability of electricity.

**Insurance**    The **commissioner of insurance** heads the Texas Department of Insurance, which regulates to some degree the more than $70 billion insurance industry in the Lone Star State. The Office of Public Insurance Counsel represents consumers in rate disputes.

**deregulation** The elimination of government restrictions to allow free-market competition to determine or limit the actions of individuals and corporations.

**commissioner of insurance** Appointed by the governor, the commissioner heads the Texas Department of Insurance, which is responsible for ensuring the industry's financial soundness and protecting policyholders.

At the beginning of 2003, Texans owning homes and automobiles were paying the highest insurance rates in the country. Rates for 95 percent of homeowners and 30 percent of automobile owners were unregulated and rising rapidly. In response to a public outcry against high insurance rates, Governor Perry declared insurance reform to be an emergency matter requiring fast action by the 78th Legislature. Although the Senate and the House moved slowly, a law was enacted giving the commissioner of insurance authority to regulate all home insurers doing business in Texas.

Home insurance companies posted record profits in 2004, and despite the destruction by Hurricane Rita, most companies posted large earnings in 2005. The loss ratio is considered the key component in insurance company profitability. It is what a company pays in benefits as a percentage of the premium money it receives. In 2005, the statewide average for the insurance companies was 57 percent, leaving 43 percent for profits and other expenses.

On December 1, 2004, Texas began a largely deregulated "file-and-use" system for auto and homeowners insurance. Insurers are free to set their rates, but the commissioner of insurance is authorized to order reductions and refunds if rates are determined to be excessive. Advocates of this system expected it to produce reasonable rates by promoting competition among insurance companies; but as of 2006, it remained to be seen whether the results would be significant competition, lower premiums, and more satisfied consumers.

### Business Promotion

Some cynical observers contend that the business of Texas government is business. Others argue that boosting business strengthens the Texas economy and creates jobs that benefit the lives of all Texans. Certainly, Texas's political culture and the strength of business lobbyists make most of Texas government highly responsive to business. State agencies in at least three policy areas—transportation, tourism, and licensing—are administered to promote and protect economic interests.

**Highways**    The **Texas Department of Transportation (TxDOT)** has constructed and maintains almost 80,000 miles of state highways. This agency is headed by a five-member commission appointed by the governor, with Senate concurrence, to six-year overlapping terms. Drawing no state salary, each commissioner must be a "public" member without financial ties to any company contracting with the state for highway-related business. Commission appointees must reflect Texas's diverse population groups and regions and include at least one commissioner who resides in a rural area. TxDOT has almost 15,000 full-time-equivalent employees.

**Texas Department of Transportation (TxDOT)** Headed by a three-member commission, the department maintains almost 80,000 miles of roads and highways and promotes highway safety.

Texans operate about 19 million registered vehicles, most of them concentrated in metropolitan areas. One result is growing congestion and increased accidents. Part of the cost of Texas's overcrowded highways is time spent commuting. A more serious cost is the annual death toll of more than 3,500 drivers and passengers, half of which are alcohol related. Nevertheless, most Texans want more and better highways, and some want better rail and public transportation as well. In 2003, the 78th Legislature enacted the Trans Texas Corridors plan pushed by Governor Perry. When completed, it will provide a 4,000-mile network of toll roads, utility lines, and rail lines. Public transportation has less state support. Only a few Texas cities have light rail for public transportation; 95 percent of public transportation is by bus. The state's eight Metropolitan Transit Authorities (MTAs) provide 90 percent of Texans' public transit trips. The MTAs are local regional governments, and TxDOT has little role in their planning, finance, or operation. Meanwhile, vehicle traffic on existing highways grows more congested and dangerous.

**Tourism and Trade**    Responsibility for preserving Texas's natural habitats and for providing public recreational areas lies with the **Texas Parks and Wildlife Department**. The nine members of its governing commission are appointed by the governor with senatorial approval. The governor also designates the chair of the commission from among the members. The commission sets fees for fishing and hunting licenses, and entrance fees for state parks. The department's game wardens enforce state laws and departmental regulations that apply to hunting, fishing, and boating.

Tourism is the third-largest industry in the Lone Star State. It involves promoting recreational travel and providing camping and hiking opportunities for Texas residents. In addition, tourism attracts visitors with money to spend from other states and countries. The state park system attracts 10 million visitors a year and, according to the state, generates $1.2 billion for the economy. However, with Texas ranked 49th in state money spent on parks, Texas state parks are suffering deterioration in quality and services. Fewer employees and less money to maintain facilities have forced parks to cut hours, campgrounds, and electricity. Some parks have been downgraded to wildlife management areas, several parks have been transferred to cities and universities, and commissioners even considered selling off part of Big Bend Ranch State Park to a private developer. Fewer and poorer quality parks are, of course, a loss to middle- and working-class Texans who depend on public parks for recreation. But they are also bad for business.

Most likely, the park system's decline will reduce out-of-state tourism. South Texas businesses, for example, fear loss of the "snow birds," people who winter in warmer areas such as South Texas. The park system's poor condition also hurts Texas's ability to lure new businesses. Quality of life, including parks, is considered second only to an educated workforce when major companies evaluate potential locations. In 2001, for example, Dallas–Fort Worth outbid other areas in tax breaks but lost Boeing's new headquarters to Chicago, in significant part because Chicago has more park space.[22]

**Certification of Trades and Professions**    More than 40 occupational groups are certified (licensed) to practice their respective skills by state boards and commissions. Reflecting Texas's shift to a service economy, half of the state's certifying agencies are health-care related. As a result of combined legislative and public

**Texas Parks and Wildlife Department**
Texas agency that runs state parks and regulates hunting, fishing, and boating.

*Ruins at Fort McKavett State Historical Park. (Picture courtesy of Jim Carter.)*

pressure, each licensing board and commission now has at least one "public" member (not from the regulated occupation). All members are appointed to six-year terms by the governor, with approval by the Senate. Thus, from plumbers and electricians to physicians and nurses, occupational and professional standards are affected by the politics of gubernatorial appointments and senatorial confirmations or rejections.

---

**Learning Check 9.4**          **(Answers on p. 374)**

1. True or False: Business regulation in Texas tends to be tough on the businesses.
2. Is the movement in Texas toward more regulation or deregulation?
3. What are two costs of Texas highways other than money?
4. Are Texas state parks improving or in decline?

---

##  Environmental Issues

The Lone Star State's growing population requires more jobs. However, among Texas's many public policy concerns, none draws sharper disagreements than how to maintain and nurture all forms of life while advancing business development that will provide jobs for Texas workers and profits for businesses. For years, Texas has been among the most polluted states. Texas industries, for example, produce more toxic contaminants (chemical waste) than do those of any other state. (The chapter "The Environment of Texas Politics" lists eight areas in which Texas is the leading polluter among the 50 states.) This grim reality is part of an increasingly complex problem that confronts local, state, and national policymakers. Federal policies give impetus to state environmental initiatives. Examples include rulings by the U.S. Environmental Protection Agency (EPA) and congressional directives in the Clean Air and Clean Water Acts.

Texas business people, who often complain about governmental red tape, usually support state policies designed to forestall federal regulations. Tracking corporate Texas's every step, however, is a growing army of public "watchdogs" (such as the Sierra Club) who do much to inform the public concerning environmental problems.

### Air and Water

The **Texas Commission on Environmental Quality (TCEQ)**, commonly called "T-sec," coordinates the Lone Star State's environmental policies. Six full-time, salaried commission members, an executive director, and about 3,000 employees oversee environmental regulation in Texas.

State policymakers maintain a continual balancing act as they respond to federal directives, local business pressures, and demands of individuals and environmental groups seeking stronger regulation of polluters. Texas's air pollution problems extend beyond the millions of motor vehicles on its roadways daily. Petrochemical and cement plants, refineries, smelters, and a large variety of factories dot cityscapes statewide. Combined, these and other sources of pollution put the health of millions of Texans at risk.[23] Even the sparsely populated Big Bend National Park in West Texas has polluted air. For that reason, it is now designated as one of the 10 most endangered national parks in the United States.

Water contamination is another major area of TCEQ's responsibilities. Working with local prosecutors, the commission hears cases involving individuals and corporations alleged to have dumped toxic waste and other contaminants into the state's waterways. A growing problem is contamination from corporate agriculture, for example the large chicken farms operated by or under contract with the major poultry processors. The waste from the large concentration of chickens has contaminated numerous waterways. As with actions of other regulating bodies, TCEQ's decisions can be appealed to state courts.

Water will remain an important resource in a state that is primarily arid. The six-member Texas Water Development Board (TWDB) and its staff develop strategies for water conservation. In addition, they collect water-related data and administer grants and loans from funds established to support water supply, wastewater treatment, and flood control projects.

### Hazardous Waste

Hazardous waste is a fact of modern life. From hospitals using low-level radioactive materials to diagnose disease, to industries producing plastics and chemicals on which we have come to depend, the state and the nation generate large quantities of dangerous waste. This waste ranges in danger from

**Texas Commission on Environmental Quality (TCEQ)** The state agency that coordinates Texas's environmental protection efforts.

high-level radioactive material with potential toxicity for thousands of years to nonradioactive hazardous waste. Those who produce hazardous materials want to get rid of them as cheaply as possible, and they have the money and incentive to succeed. Environmental groups in Texas have grown in power and political skill but generally can only delay and modify actions favored by pollution producers. For its part, much of the public simply says "Not in my backyard." The result has been a series of political skirmishes stretching back to at least the 1970s, a lack of a coordinated plan, and a growing amount of waste. Several West Texas counties (noted for sparse populations, undeveloped land, and little political clout) have been targeted by private companies and state and federal officials looking for places in which to dispose of industrial and residential waste. Increased accumulation of the nation's waste will only intensify the demand for dumpsites in the years to come.

Generated largely by Texas's petrochemical industry, nonradioactive hazardous waste stored in landfills presents another environmental dilemma. Housing and commercial land developers covet landfill sites for their building projects. Pressured to relax regulations for cleaning up dumpsites in land-scarce cities, TCEQ has angered environmentalists with its tendency to approve less restrictive guidelines for dealing with this problem. As the state's population increases in the years ahead, even greater demands will be placed on the quality of its air, water, and land. Texans will continue to balance economic interests and environmental safety in making these decisions.

---

**Learning Check 9.5**        **(Answers on p. 374)**

**1.** How does Texas compare with other states on levels of pollution?
**2.** What state agency coordinates environmental policies?
**3.** What are some demands state environmental policymakers must balance?

---

## ★ Homeland Security

Following the terrorist hijackings of four commercial passenger planes on September 11, 2001, federal, state, and local officials throughout the United States began giving more attention to preparations for preventing or coping with terrorist actions. Texas's experience with Hurricanes Katrina and Rita in 2005 heightened state and local government awareness of the need for preparation and coordinated effort. In Texas, the Governor's Office provides emergency response resources and information concerning disaster preparedness. Within the Texas Department of Public Safety, a counterterrorism intelligence unit handles reports of suspicious or criminal activities in which terrorists may be involved. The threat of bioterrorism has caused the Texas Department of State Health Services to compile information on that subject, and the Texas Department of Agriculture has done the same for diseases that terrorists could spread among the state's livestock. (The chapter "Finance and Fiscal Policy" addresses financial implications of disaster preparedness.)

# ★ Looking Ahead

Five trends appear likely to continue in Texas's approach to state administration. First, resources are likely to be increasingly scarce as demands increase. State agencies will have to do more with less. Whether or not this approach will overcome the many challenges facing Texans in the twenty-first century remains to be seen.

Second, accountability will continue to be an important watchword. Increasingly, the legislature has required state agencies to document progress in education, human services, and other public policy areas. Driven by business principles of profit motive and cost effectiveness, the state's leaders are sending at least one clear message: Agencies must show that they are achieving their goals and doing so efficiently if they want to compete for the limited funds available.

Third, and likely to continue regardless of who sits in the White House or the Governor's Mansion, is devolution, whereby the federal government turns over more of its work to the state governments.

Fourth, the Republican legislative leadership will push legislation to give the governor more control over state agencies not headed by elected officials.

Finally, state policies that conflict with national programs will continue to be shaped by judicial decisions. While Texas state courts are not as likely to hand down broad policy decisions as are the federal courts, they have played a major role in educational finance, and under Republican leadership, they have tilted toward business interests and away from plaintiffs. Texas courts are likely to continue to be important political and policy actors. The chapter "Laws, Courts, and Justice" describes Texas's judicial system and its many roles.

# ★ Chapter Summary

- Most of the state budget is spent on four areas: education, health and human services, business and economic development, and public safety and corrections.
- The sunset process requires periodic review of state agencies by the legislature. While producing no major changes in state government, it has had positive effects.
- The state's 200-plus agencies provide a variety of services to Texans, including public and higher education, social services, and business regulation and promotion.
- State agencies and their employees (bureaucrats or public administrators) carry out laws passed by the legislature but add their influence through interpreting and applying the laws to specific situations.
- The success of agencies in Texas is influenced by the vigor of their leaders, the lack of resources for most agencies, and elite access.

- State employees are Texas's largest work group.
- Texas state government has done better than the private sector in providing access to women and African Americans but not to Latinos.
- Whether in boardrooms of public school districts and institutions of higher education or in legislative chambers, policymakers face the challenge of achieving educational excellence at a price that Texas taxpayers can pay and that voters will support.
- The State Board of Education is weak and highly controversial. The greater state role in education is handled by the commissioner of education, who heads the Texas Education Agency.
- Testing remains a major tool for trying to improve education in the state. It is also a source of great controversy.
- The Texas Higher Education Coordinating Board oversees all institutions of higher education; boards of regents govern universities; and local boards make policy for community colleges.
- Affirmative action and the top 10 percent rule have been major issues in college admission.
- Devolution of public assistance programs will continue to place demands on Texas's social service agencies to provide financial help for needy families and to assist impoverished people who are physically or mentally ill, or who are aged or disabled.
- Health and human services programs in Texas are politically weak and poorly funded.
- Health and human services programs are coordinated by the Health and Human Services Commission.
- It remains to be seen whether deregulation (the current direction of regulators) will be more effective than regulation in protecting the public interest; meanwhile, Texas consumers demand low-cost utilities, safer drinking water, and cleaner air.
- Texas regulators tend to be protective of the industries they are charged to regulate.
- The recent deterioration of state parks through funding shortages may cause Texas to lose tourist dollars and new business locations.
- Texas has long had major pollution problems and public policies that did little to improve the environment. Challenges to polluters are increasing, but change is slow.
- Texas has responded to the terrorist threat by seeking grants of federal money for homeland security, compiling information, and seeking more coordination and planning.

## Key Terms

- sunset review process, *p. 345*
- public administration, *p. 346*
- bureaucrats, *p. 346*
- elite access, *p. 347*
- patronage system, *p. 348*
- merit system, *p. 348*
- State Board of Education (SBOE), *p. 351*
- Texas Education Agency (TEA), *p. 353*
- commissioner of education, *p. 353*
- Texas Assessment of Knowledge and Skills (TAKS), *p. 354*
- Texas Higher Education Coordinating Board, *p. 356*
- equal opportunity, *p. 356*
- affirmative action, *p. 356*
- top 10 percent rule, *p. 357*
- executive commissioner of the Health and Human Services Commission, *p. 359*
- Temporary Assistance for Needy Families (TANF), *p. 360*
- food stamp program, *p. 360*
- Medicaid, *p. 362*
- Medicare, *p. 362*
- Texas Workforce Commission (TWC), *p. 363*
- Railroad Commission of Texas (RRC), *p. 363*
- Public Utility Commission (PUC), *p. 364*
- deregulation, *p. 365*
- commissioner of insurance, *p. 365*
- Texas Department of Transportation (TxDOT), *p. 366*
- Texas Parks and Wildlife Department, *p. 367*
- Texas Commission on Environmental Quality (TCEQ), *p. 369*

## Learning Check Answers

**9.1**

1. False. Public administrators must make many decisions not clearly specified in the law. Their own views, their bosses' preferences, and their agency culture make a difference in how they apply laws passed by the legislature.
2. The vigor of agency leaders, resources, and elite access are particularly important in determining how successful agencies are in Texas.
3. Women been more successful at finding higher-ranking positions in Texas government than in the private sector.

**9.2**

1. The State Board of Education and the commissioner of education (who runs the Texas Education Agency) are the most important entities for public schools.
2. False. Texas's testing program is highly controversial, supported by some and opposed by others.

3. The Higher Education Coordinating Board is the most important entity for governing Texas colleges and universities.
4. According to the 10 percent rule, Texas students graduating in the top 10 percent of their high school class must be admitted to the public college or university of their choice.

**9.3**

1. Compared to other states, poverty in Texas is high.
2. Health and human services programs are at a disadvantage in Texas because of the state's political culture and the lack of organization of those needing the services.
3. Temporary Assistance for Needy Families (TANF) provides limited cash benefits to poor families.
4. Medicare is better funded than Medicaid.

**9.4**

1. False. Regulation of business in Texas tends not to be tough on the businesses (consider the RRC, for example).
2. The movement in Texas is toward deregulation (consider the PUC and the commissioner of insurance, for example).
3. Traffic deaths and time lost commuting are two costs of Texas highways other than money.
4. Texas state parks are in decline.

**9.5**

1. Texas is one of the country's most polluted states.
2. The state agency responsible for coordinating environmental policies is the Texas Commission on Environmental Quality (TCEQ).
3. State environmental policymakers must balance federal directives, business pressures, and demands from environmental groups.

## Discussion Questions

1. What services should Texas's government provide to the state's residents?
2. In what ways are public administrators involved in politics?
3. What are some advantages and disadvantages of employment in Texas state government agencies?
4. Does Texas need its State Board of Education? Why has the board faced criticism and controversy?
5. Is Texas's emphasis on testing students a good thing? Why?
6. How are Texas's state universities governed? What is the role of the Texas Higher Education Coordinating Board?

7. Discuss the impact of *Hopwood* v. *Texas* on Texas colleges and universities, and explain why you support or oppose affirmative action programs in institutions of higher education. Is the 10 percent rule a good solution?

8. Why are some health and human services programs better supported than others?

9. Explain why AIDS is a serious health problem in Texas, and suggest ways that state and local governments should deal with it.

10. State regulators seem to be moving toward deregulation. Which agencies are doing this, and is it a good idea? Who benefits and who loses from deregulation?

11. The state parks system is deteriorating from lack of resources. What are the consequences of this? What are possible solutions?

12. What are Texas's principal environmental problems? Which government agencies deal with these problems and what do they do?

## Internet Resources

Center for Public Policy Priorities: **www.cppp.org**
Department of Public Safety of the State of Texas: **www.txdps.state.tx.us**
Office of Public Utility Counsel: **www.opc.state.tx.us**
Public Utility Commission of Texas: **www.puc.state.tx.us**
Railroad Commission of Texas: **www.rrc.state.tx.us**
State Board of Education: **www.tea.state.tx.us/sboe**
State Board of Educator Certification: **www.sbec.state.tx.us**
Sunset Advisory Commission: **www.sunset.state.tx.us**
Texas Commission on Environmental Quality: **www.tceq.state.tx.us**
Texas Comptroller of Public Accounts: **www.window.state.tx.us**
Texas Department of Human Services: **www.dhs.state.tx.us**
Texas Department of Insurance: **www.tdi.state.tx.us**
Texas Department of Transportation: **www.dot.state.tx.us**
Texas Education Agency: **www.tea.state.tx.us**
Texas Food Stamp Outreach: **www.lonestarcard.org**
Texas Health and Human Services Commission: **www.hhs.state.tx.us**
Texas Higher Education Coordinating Board: **www.thecb.state.tx.us**
Texas Parks and Wildlife Department: **www.tpwd.state.tx.us**
Texas Public Policy Foundation: **www.tppf.org**
Texas State Employees Retirement System: **www.ers.state.tx.us**
Texas Water Development Board: **www.twdb.state.tx.us**
Texas Workforce Commission: **www.twc.state.tx.us**
U.S. Census Bureau: **www.census.gov**

## 9.1  Privatized Services Stumbling*

### *Robert T. Garrett*

*Social services have long been controversial in Texas, but disagreements intensified when the 2003 legislature decided to privatize the delivery of many of these services. (Privatization involves government hiring private companies to provide specific public services.) As the following article spells out, problems implementing the newly privatized programs only added to the controversy.*

Texas's health and welfare agencies are undertaking the most sweeping and rapid privatization of social services in the country, but the experiments are plagued with problems. Tens of thousands of aid recipients can't get through to privately run call centers. Thousands more poor families are complaining that their children were wrongly denied health insurance. At state hospitals and schools for the mentally impaired, head nurses must slog through new and burdensome online payroll duties.

Conservative policymakers who championed privatization predicted it would save money and make services more efficient. But so far, the state has had to dial back its savings estimates and rescind planned layoffs of hundreds of eligibility workers.

Liberal policy analysts and advocates for the poor say Texas rushed into outsourcing without a good plan or enough testing. Some lawmakers in both parties vow to reevaluate the push, especially before the state begins next year to privatize a highly sensitive task—caring for abused and neglected children.

Others, such as conservative commentators and Albert Hawkins, Gov. Rick Perry's point man on social services, defend privatization. They insist change will be worth the initial pain as private firms help the state trim administrative fat, verify recipients are eligible, and better serve the needy. And, they note, privatization is here to stay, because Republican legislative leaders won't go back to—or pay for—old ways of checking eligibility and running programs.

"It makes so much sense that the only reason that someone would be opposed to this is that they're beholden to state employees," said former Rep. Arlene Wohlgemuth, R-Burleson. She pushed through the 2003 law that strongly encouraged using privately run call centers and other cost-cutting techniques. Ms. Wohlgemuth said she's "absolutely astounded" that critics "would like to take this system back to the dark ages," when employed adults had to take off work to go to field offices and wait in lines to apply for benefits for their children.

Celia Hagert, an expert on food stamps who monitors the call-center push for the progressive Center for Public Policy Priorities, said the state has actually had to spend more to determine eligibility. The state cancelled 1,000 layoffs this month and has sent managers and workers to various cities to fix glitches, she said. "We've deployed an untested, badly performing system that's causing people to lose benefits," Ms. Hagert said, noting that 108,000 fewer children are enrolled in health insurance programs than were six months ago. State agencies "are asking the Legislature for more money to keep the administrative functions afloat. The exact opposite of what they promised is what's happening now."

Mr. Hawkins, the state health and human services commissioner, has acknowledged the problems. But he and conservative supporters say they are temporary, the result of the transition to privatization. Other analysts are concerned the problems will only grow as more state functions are outsourced....

"What Texas is attempting to do is a radical transformation of service delivery," said Stacy Dean, a former federal budget official who monitors privatization efforts for the liberal Center on Budget and Policy Priorities in Washington. She said the state ignored warnings that fast changes would be a technological and human gamble.

Florida spent fours years testing a similar though mostly state-run system, and Pennsylvania, Washington,

---

*"Privatized Services Stumbling," by Robert T. Garrett, from *Dallas Morning News,* May 28, 2006. Reprinted by permission. Robert T. Garrett is an Austin reporter for the *Dallas Morning News.*

and Utah bit off only small chunks of the job for starters, she said. But Texas officials tried to award an $899 million contract and convert the whole state in 14 months. "They thought they could pull it off without testing the waters," Ms. Dean said. "It's that sort of Lone Star bravado—'we can do it when nobody else can, and experience from other states isn't relevant.'"

But Jason Turner of the conservative Heritage Foundation describes Texas as an innovative defender of taxpayers.

"Looking beyond the government service-delivery monopoly for improvements ... has a long and well-established pedigree," said Mr. Turner, who favored private competition as a designer of former Wisconsin Gov. Tommy Thompson's welfare overhauls and as former New York Mayor Rudolph Giuliani's welfare commissioner. The early bumps in Texas are no surprise, Mr. Turner said. "When major systems undergo a changeover from public to private, start-up failures of various kinds always occur," he said.

## 9.2  Dallas Region's Reservoir Plans Irk East Texas*

### *Thomas Korosec*

*Water regulation and distribution is a major issue in Texas, largely because agriculture in the western half of the state and metropolitan areas throughout the state need large amounts of water not readily available. For years, the state has experienced hard political fights over creation of reservoirs and movement of water to areas in need. Opposition comes particularly from those who lose their land and jobs to the reservoirs and from those concerned with the environmental damage caused by the new water sources. The Texas Water Development Board plays a major role in this struggle when it approves regional water plans and submits a statewide plan to the legislature every five years. The following article highlights one recent conflict over water availability.*

The name *Dallas* has become a fighting word in some quarters of East Texas. As the Dallas-Fort Worth region moves ahead on long-range plans to build two new reservoirs in East Texas, landowners, environmentalists, and timber interests have united in opposition, pulling many local politicians along. Miffed at the prospect of job losses in the timber industry and destruction of choice wildlife habitat, opponents have begun calling Dallas a spoiled and selfish bully that wants its swimming pools and green lawns, even in droughts, and has the political muscle to do as it pleases.

"We have about 400,000 people to their 5 million. When we go down to Austin, it's kind of embarrassing,"

said John Bradley, a timber grower from Jefferson and former vice chairman of the North East Texas Water Planning Group. "Last time we were down there, the state water board sounded like the Dallas water board." His reference was to a 5–1 vote last month by the Texas Water Development Board in favor of a Dallas-Fort Worth area plan that calls for building the reservoirs as part of a 50-year plan to provide water for the region. The plan calls for the 68,000-acre Marvin Nichols reservoir to be built on the Sulphur River near Mount Pleasant and the 24,000-acre Lake Fastrill to be built on the Neches River near Jacksonville.

The prospect of Fastrill flooding the U.S. Wildlife Service's proposed 25,000-acre Neches River National Wildlife Refuge as well as an antique railroad has sparked considerable opposition from loggers and conservation groups since it was proposed last year. But opponents of the Marvin Nichols reservoir, which was first proposed in 2001, have had several more years to organize, and even the regional water planning group governing the area in which the reservoir would be built opposes the project.

On Tuesday, the North East Texas planning group gets its turn before the state panel, and its long-range plan recommends that Marvin Nichols not be built. Whatever the outcome, it will be merely another step in what promises to be a decade-long fight. "Sentiment is overwhelmingly against it," said Jim Thompson, chairman of North East Texas Water Planning Group and an executive with Ward Timber Ltd., a major timber producer in the

*From *Houston Chronicle*, May 14, 2006, B1, B10. Copyright 2006 Houston Chronicle Publishing Company. Reprinted with permission. All rights reserved. Thomas Korosec is News Bureau Chief of the *Houston Chronicle*.

Texarkana area. "Any benefit we might get in terms of water is outweighed by the harm to our economy." In a recent letter to the state planning panel, Thompson said the Marvin Nichols reservoir clashed with state law requiring water plans to be "consistent with the long-term protection of the state's water, agricultural and natural resources."

## Threat to Timber

Dallas' proposal makes no mention of the reservoir's impact on the timber industry, even though it is a major agricultural crop in the area, Thompson said. He said plans for the reservoir also clash with a state law that allows transfer of water between river basins only if the user is employing the highest level of conservation.

If it gets approved, the Marvin Nichols reservoir is scheduled to go on line in 2030 and begin shipping water 115 miles west. By that time, the Dallas-Fort Worth area will be using 202 gallons of water per day per person, the highest usage of any region in the state and a few gallons less per day from its current rate. "I don't know why I should lose my heritage so Dallas can have St. Augustine lawns," said Max Shumake, who along with other family members owns 797 acres of farmland in Red River County that would be flooded by the reservoir. Shumake, a 57 year-old retired electrician who founded the Sulphur River Oversight Society, is often credited with turning local opinion against the project. "We never dreamed it was going to take our farms and knock down the timber industry," he said.

A study by the Texas Forest Service, a state agency, estimated that Marvin Nichols would lead to the loss of 417 to 1,334 jobs in the area—most in the timber industry. The range depends on how much land beyond the reservoir is set aside to mitigate the flooding of the river and how strictly it is managed for wildlife. Under federal law, sensitive environmental areas such as the bottomland hardwoods along the Sulphur River, considered prime habitat for songbirds and other animals, must be replaced with similar lands when a reservoir is built.

The industry's ally in this case is its frequent opponent, a constellation of environmental groups led by the Texas Committee on Natural Resources. "It will not only flood highly valued land for wildlife and waterfowl, but

you will alter downstream flows," said Janice Bezanson, the group's executive director. She said downstream effects will be particularly troublesome below Fastrill, which would be completed in 2050 under the plan. Below it on the Neches are four wildlife preserves or wilderness areas, including the Big Thicket National Preserve. Bezanson predicted that both reservoirs will face lawsuits.

## Effects of Development

Jim Parks, chairman of the Region C Water Planning Group, the official name of the Dallas-Fort Worth water planning body, concedes the proposals are controversial. "Very little can be built in Texas that doesn't affect someone in a positive or negative way," he said. Parks also is a former director of the North Texas Municipal Water District, which supplies the fast-developing suburbs north of Dallas. It is one of three chief water wholesalers in the Dallas-Fort Worth region. "There's no opposition here (in the cities) because people remember we had a drought of record in the 1950s," he said. "Dallas almost ran out of water. The city said to its staff, 'We can't let that happen again.'" He said new reservoirs included in the region's long-range plans will account for only 18 percent of supplies. Far more will come from conservation and reuse and by drawing on existing reservoirs and water rights.

In 1950, Parks said, there were eight reservoirs in the state. Over the next 55 years, 29 more were built. "We plan to build only four more over the next 55 years, so it doesn't appear to me that we have gone overboard on reservoir construction." Because viable reservoir sites have all been used in the Dallas-Fort Worth region, the only place to turn is East Texas, he said.

"Unless we start telling people where they can live, you have to move water around the state to meet the needs," Parks said. "This is the bottom line." He said it is impossible to predict the projects' future. The Marvin Nichols and Fastrill reservoirs would cost $2.1 billion and $569 million, respectively. "Until you get into the permitting process, where you get engineering details and concerns are addressed by other governmental agencies, you don't have the answers," he said, referring to federal environmental impact reviews.

Parks said he is wary of assertions by critics that the reservoirs will not be needed. "At the population trends we are seeing now, there's a possibility that by 2040 we will have 5.5 million more people here than we are planning for." His plan predicts that the 16-county north-central Texas region will more than double its population by 2060—reaching 13 million. Given the size and long timelines for these major reservoirs, state water planners appear to be in no rush to rule them in or out.

The state board is expected to approve the North East group's plan, which opposes the Marvin Nichols reservoir, but leave the Dallas plan intact as well, said Thompson, the regional chairman. "We think there's a conflict between the plans, but they say there isn't."

Carla Daws, a spokeswoman for the state water development board, said under its rules there is a conflict between two regions only in cases where "two regions have identified the same supply." Thompson said his group had wanted the issue to be resolved. "But it's one of those things that's going to be a long battle," he said. "We only have to stop it once, and down the line I think we will."

---

An extensive bibliography of books and articles for this chapter is posted on Selected Sources for Reading, available online at http://college.hmco.com/PIC/brownPTP13e. For use with any chapter, see Resources for Further Research online at http://college.hmco.com/PIC/brownPTP13e.

# Chapter 10

# Laws, Courts, and Justice

SARGENT © 1997
*Austin American-
Statesman.* Reprinted
with permission of
UNIVERSAL PRESS
SYNDICATE. All Rights
Reserved.

On August 24, 1993, the State of Texas executed Ruben Cantu for capital murder. Evidence against him included eyewitness testimony by Juan Moreno, who sustained nine gunshot wounds during a robbery in which Moreno's friend was murdered, allegedly by Cantu and a codefendant. In 2005, Juan Moreno recanted his testimony, saying intimidation by San Antonio police officers caused him to misidentify Cantu. This admission, an affidavit from the codefendant saying Cantu was not with him the night of the murder, and Cantu's claims that he was framed all point to his possible innocence. These factors embody an anxiety expressed by many death penalty opponents: that innocent people will die.

Ben Sargent's opening cartoon renaming the Texas death house to "express check-out" reflects an attitude some suggest represents Texas's willingness to implement the death penalty more than any other state. Others argue that adequate procedures are in place to ensure that only the guilty receive the ultimate punishment. They share President

George W. Bush's confidence, when he asserted, "As far as I'm concerned there has not been one innocent person executed since I've become governor."[1] (Bush was governor of Texas from 17 January 1993 through 21 December 2000.) By mid-2006 facts pointed to the possible innocence of two other executed inmates—Carlos de Luna, executed in 1989, convicted in part on dubious eyewitness testimony, and Cameron T. Willingham, executed in 2004, convicted in part on questionable evidence of arson.

Concern about death penalty fallibility is only one of many issues facing Texas's justice system in the first decade of the twenty-first century. Incompetent representation of indigent defendants, inadequate access to attorneys and courts for poor people, excessive malpractice insurance premiums for doctors, wrongful incarceration of innocent people, allegations of racial profiling, a politicized judiciary, and a judicial system that is much less ethnically diverse than the population it serves are also characteristics of the Texas justice system. Technology now regularly confirms that some innocent people have been punished for crimes they did not commit. These faults erode confidence, yet a democratic society depends on a justice system that is respected by and responsive to its citizens. Legal theorists such as Professor David Kairys suggest that the very survival of a justice system in a representative democracy depends on citizens' belief in the legitimacy of its authority. Growing mistrust by people of color of state justice systems caused the American Bar Association's Commission on the 21st Century Judiciary to declare that the "systems are in great jeopardy."[2] This chapter examines both the civil and criminal justice systems of Texas. As you read, consider whether the criticisms and fears expressed above are reasonable.

## ⭐ An Introduction to Texas's Justice System

Texans have given substantial power to their justice system. The Texas Constitution and state statutes grant government the authority, under appropriate circumstances, to take a person's life, liberty, or property. Significant connections between politics and justice in the Lone Star State result from state constitutional requirements that judicial officials (except municipal court judges) be popularly selected in partisan elections. Many Texas judges, however, first obtain their offices when appointed to fill a vacancy caused by a judge's death or retirement until the next general election. Such appointments, as well as elections, are usually influenced by political party affiliation. Although judges are involved in the policymaking process, they attract less public attention than do state legislative and executive officials; yet, their decisions affect Texans every day. It is therefore important that the state's residents understand the role of the judicial branch.[3]

# State Law in Texas

With more than 3,000 justices and judges, and almost that many courts, Texas has one of the largest judicial systems in the country. Counting the traffic violations dealt with in lower courts, millions of cases are handled each year. Texas courts deal with cases involving **civil law** (for example, disputes concerning business contracts, divorces and other family issues, and personal injury claims). They also hear cases involving **criminal law** (proceedings against persons charged with committing a **misdemeanor**, such as using false identification to purchase liquor and punishable by a fine and jail sentence, or a **felony**, such as armed robbery punishable by a prison sentence and a fine). A court's authority to hear a particular case is its **jurisdiction**. The law creating a particular court fixes the court's jurisdiction; it may be civil, criminal, or both. In addition, some courts have **original jurisdiction** only, meaning they are limited to trying cases being heard for the first time. Other courts are restricted to hearing appeals from lower courts and thus have only **appellate jurisdiction**. Still other courts exercise both original and appellate jurisdiction.

## Sources of Law

Regardless of their jurisdiction, Texas courts interpret and apply state law. These laws include statutes enacted by the legislature, the provisions of the Texas Constitution, and judge-made common law based on custom and tradition dating back to medieval England. A court may apply a statute, constitutional provision, and common law all in the same case. Procedures for filing a case, conducting a trial, and appealing a judgment depend on whether the case is civil or criminal.

Newly enacted laws passed in each legislative session are compiled by the Office of the Secretary of State and published under the title *General and Special Laws of the State of Texas*. For easier reference, these laws are arranged by subject matter. Many of these statutes may be found in *Vernon's Annotated Revised Civil Statutes of the State of Texas*, available from the West Group and on the Internet.

## Code Revision

In 1963, the legislature charged the Texas Legislative Council with the responsibility of reorganizing Texas laws related to specific topics (such as education or taxes) into a systematic and comprehensive arrangement of legal codes. More than 40 years later, the Council continues to work on this project. Completed codes are found in *Vernon's Texas Codes Annotated*. In addition to piecemeal changes resulting from routine legislation, on occasion the legislature undertakes extensive revision of an entire legal code.

**civil law** The body of law concerning noncriminal matters, such as business contracts and personal injury.

**criminal law** The body of law concerning felony and misdemeanor offenses by individuals against other persons and property.

**misdemeanor** Classified as A, B, or C, a misdemeanor may be punished by fine and/or jail sentence.

**felony** A serious crime punished by fine and prison confinement.

**jurisdiction** A court's authority to hear a particular case.

**original jurisdiction** The power of a court to hear a case first.

**appellate jurisdiction** The power of a court to review cases after they have been tried elsewhere.

**Points to Ponder**

Laws enacted in 2005:

- Allow cities to provide "fitness incentive pay" to police officers and firefighters as encouragement to stay in shape (H.B. 1213)
- Bar Texans from suing food companies, food producers, and restaurants for injuries related to obesity or weight gain (H.B. 107)
- Provide for an automatic six-month suspension of the driver's license of anyone over age 21 convicted of purchasing or supplying alcohol for or to a minor (H.B. 1357)

## ★ Courts, Judges, and Lawyers

Article V of the Texas Constitution is titled "Judicial Department." This article provides that all state judicial power "shall be vested in one Supreme Court, in one Court of Criminal Appeals, in Courts of Appeals, in District Courts, in County Courts, in Commissioners Courts [which have no judicial authority, as discussed in the chapter "Local Governments"], in Courts of Justice of the Peace and in such other courts as may be provided by law." In exercising its constitutional power to create other courts, the Texas Legislature has created municipal courts, county courts-at-law, and probate courts (all of which are described below). These courts are referred to as statutory courts.[4]

The Texas Legislature continues to add specialized courts to meet specific needs of the state's residents. Among these specialized courts are "cluster courts," traveling courts that adjudicate only Children's Protective Services cases. Major metropolitan areas are now required to have drug courts that focus on treatment options rather than incarceration for substance abusers

Texas's judicial system is complex. (See the structure of the current judicial system presented in Figure 10.1.) A court may have both exclusive and concurrent jurisdiction. A court that has **exclusive jurisdiction** is the only court with the authority to decide a particular type of case. **Concurrent jurisdiction** means that more than one court has authority to try a specific dispute. In that instance, a plaintiff selects the court in which to file the case. The same court may have original and appellate jurisdiction. Further distinctions are made regarding whether a court resolves criminal matters, civil disputes, or both.

Qualifications and compensation for judges vary among the different courts, as shown in Table 10.1. Although many judges receive $100,000 or more in annual pay, which seems ample when compared with salaries for most jobs, in fact they are well below amounts earned by many attorneys. For example, in 2005, first-year associates at Dallas law firm Thompson & Knight received a total of $125,000 in salary (the same amount as a district judge) and signing bonuses.[5]

### Local Trial Courts

The courts with which Texans are most familiar are municipal courts and justice of the peace courts. Together, these local trial courts handle, among other

**exclusive jurisdiction**
Authority of only one court to hear a particular type of case.

**concurrent jurisdiction**
The authority of more than one court to try a case (e.g., a civil dispute involving more than $500 but less than $5,000 may be heard in either a justice of the peace court, a county court, or a district court).

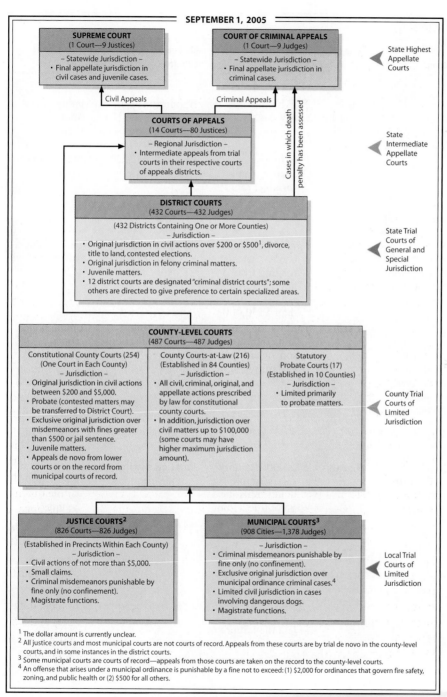

**Figure 10.1**   Court Structure of Texas

*Source:* Office of Court Administration, *Judicial Branch: Structure and Operation* (2005 Annual Statistical Report) available at <www.courts.state.tx.us/oca/Public Info/AR200>.

*Table 10.1*    Texas Judges and Justices

| Court | Judicial Qualifications | Term of Office | Annual Salary | Method of Selection | Unexpired Terms Filled by |
|---|---|---|---|---|---|
| **Local Courts** | | | | | |
| Municipal Courts | Varies; set by each city | Varies; set by each city | Paid by the city; highly variable | Appointment or election, as determined by city charter | Method determined by city charter |
| Justice of the Peace Courts | None | 4 years | Paid by the county; highly variable, ranging from $1 to $100,000 | Partisan precinct-wide elections | Commissioners court |
| **County Courts** | | | | | |
| Constitutional County Courts | Must be "well informed" in Texas law; law degree not required | 4 years | Paid by the county; highly variable, ranging from a few thousand dollars to more than $130,000 | Partisan countywide elections | Commissioners court |
| Statutory County Courts (courts-at-law and probate courts) | At least 25; licensed attorney with at least 4–5 years' experience depending on statutory requirements; 2 years county residence | 4 years | Paid by the state and county; somewhat variable | Partisan countywide elections | Commissioners court |
| **State Courts** | | | | | |
| District Courts | Ages 25–74; licensed attorney with at least 4 years' experience; 2 years county residence | 4 years | $125,000; county salary supplements; must be $5,000 less than court of appeals justices' salaries | Partisan district-wide elections | Governor with advice and consent of Senate |
| Courts of Appeals | Ages 35–74; licensed attorney with at least 10 years experience | 6 years | $137,500 (justices); $140,000 (chief justices); county salary supplements; must be $5,000 less than Supreme Court justices' salaries | Partisan districtwide elections | Governor with advice and consent of Senate |

Table 10.1   Continued

| Court | Judicial Qualifications | Term of Office | Annual Salary | Method of Selection | Unexpired Terms Filled by |
|-------|------------------------|----------------|---------------|---------------------|---------------------------|
| Court of Criminal Appeals | Ages 35–74; licensed attorney with at least 10 years experience | 6 years | $150,000 (judges); $152,500 (presiding judge) | Partisan statewide elections | Governor with advice and consent of Senate |
| Supreme Court | Ages 35–74; licensed attorney with at least 10 years' experience | 6 years | $150,000 (justices); $152,500 (chief justice) | Partisan statewide elections | Governor with advice and consent of Senate |

*Sources:* Compiled from Office of Court Administration, *Annual Statistical Report for the Texas Judiciary, Fiscal Year 2005* (Austin: Office of Court Administration, 2005), and Texas Legislature Online available at **www.capitol.state.tx.us/**.

types of cases, charges involving Class C misdemeanors, the least serious category of criminal offenses. Both municipal judges and justices of the peace serve as magistrates of the state. In this capacity, they issue warrants for the arrest of suspects and conduct hearings to determine whether a person charged with a criminal act will be jailed pending further court action or released on bail.

**Municipal Courts**   Judicial bodies in more than 900 incorporated cities, towns, and villages in Texas are known as municipal courts. Although mayors of a general-law city have the authority to serve as municipal judges, unless the city council provides for election or appointment of someone to perform this function, only 2 percent of municipal judges are mayors. Usually, municipal court judges of home-rule cities are named by city councils for two-year terms. These individuals are not required to be licensed attorneys (unless presiding over a municipal court of record, discussed below); however, approximately 40 percent of Texas's almost 1,400 municipal judges have this professional qualification. The city council determines the number of judges and sets judicial salaries.

Municipal courts have limited civil jurisdiction in cases involving owners of dangerous dogs. They have no appellate jurisdiction. Their original and exclusive criminal jurisdiction extends to all violations of city ordinances, and they have criminal jurisdiction concurrent with justice of the peace courts over Class C misdemeanors committed within city limits. Municipal court judges are authorized to impose maximum fines of $2,000 in cases involving violations of some municipal ordinances (for example, regulations governing fire safety and public health). The maximum fine for violations of other city ordinances and state criminal laws is $500. If an individual is dissatisfied with the result of a municipal court ruling, the case can be appealed to the county court or a county court-at-law. Appeals are filed in only about 1 percent of municipal court cases.

If a city has a municipal **court of record** (a court with a court reporter or electronic device to record the testimony and proceedings), a transcript of the municipal trial is made, and any appeal at the county level is based on that record of the case. Otherwise, appealed cases receive a trial de novo (a completely new trial). All incorporated cities are authorized to maintain municipal courts of record. Few Texas municipalities have such courts because of the expense involved.

**Justice of the Peace Courts**   A justice of the peace, often called the JP, is elected by voters residing in a precinct with boundaries created by the county court. The number of precincts per county (one to eight) is mandated according to population by the Texas Constitution. The number of JPs (one or two) per precinct is also directed in part by that same document.

The position requires neither previous legal training nor experience. Approximately 6 percent of Texas's JPs (usually in large cities) are lawyers and may engage in private legal practice while serving as a justice of the peace. Within a year after election, a justice of the peace who is not a lawyer must by law complete a 40-hour course in performing the duties of that office. Thereafter, the JP is supposed to receive 20 hours of instruction annually. Because failure to complete the training is a violation of a JP's duties under the law, arguably a noncomplying JP could be removed from office for official misconduct. However, such removal is highly unlikely.

In urban areas being a justice of the peace is a full-time job, whereas justices in many rural precincts hear few cases. In addition to presiding over the justice court, a justice of the peace serves as an ex officio notary public and, like other Texas judges and justices, may perform marriages. A JP also functions as a coroner, determining cause of death when the county commissioners court has not named a county medical examiner. Justice of the peace courts have both criminal and civil jurisdiction. In all cases, their jurisdiction is original. In criminal matters, these local courts try Class C misdemeanors, but any conviction may be appealed to the county court or a county court-at-law for a new trial.

A constable, who is a peace officer with full law enforcement authority, is elected for a four-year term in each JP precinct. Constables primarily serve writs (for example, a subpoena requiring appearance in court) and other processes issued by trial courts. A precinct with a large population may have one or more deputy constables to assist the constable. Although justices of the peace depend on precinct constables to handle any courtroom disruption, most constables leave law enforcement and crime detection to local police and the county sheriff's department.

Exclusive civil jurisdiction of JP courts is limited to cases in which the amount in controversy is $200 or less, not including interest. Concurrent civil jurisdiction is shared with county courts and district courts (discussed below) if the amount in controversy exceeds $200 but is not more than $5,000. Appeals from a JP court of cases involving $20 or more are taken to the county level, where cases are tried de novo. For cases involving less than $20, the JP court is the court of last resort, the highest state court that can render a judgment in the

**court of record**  Has a court reporter or electronic device to record testimony and proceedings.

matter. Interestingly, the only court to which such a decision could be appealed, if a constitutional matter were at stake, is the U.S. Supreme Court. It is highly unlikely that such an appeal would be accepted.

**Small-Claims Courts**   Did the cleaners damage your sweater and then refuse to replace it? Did you work last week and now your boss is withholding your wages? **Small-claims court,** also administered by the JP, is where you should seek justice. Presided over by the justice of the peace, a small-claims court can hear almost any civil dispute in which the damages claimed are for $5,000 or less, except for divorces, slander, or suits affecting title to land. Plaintiffs must pay a fee of approximately $70 to bring a case against one individual. Additional amounts will likely be charged if the case has more than one defendant. Because these proceedings are informal, parties to the suits often represent themselves. When the amount in controversy exceeds $20, the losing party may appeal to a county-level court.[6]

### County Trial Courts

Every Texas county has a county court as prescribed by the state constitution, and some have one or more additional county-level courts created by statute. All are courts of record. The county commissioners court fills a vacancy on a county-level court.

**Constitutional County Courts**   Under the Texas Constitution, each of the state's 254 counties has a county judge. If these officials perform judicial functions, they must take Supreme Court–approved courses in court administration, procedure, and evidence, along with judges of county courts-at-law, district courts, and appellate courts. Less than 15 percent of Texas's constitutional county court judges are licensed attorneys.

Most constitutional county courts have original and appellate jurisdiction as well as probate, civil, and criminal jurisdiction. In some instances, however, the legislature has created county courts-at-law to exercise such jurisdiction. **Probate** matters include establishing the validity of wills, guardianship proceedings, and mental competency determinations. Original civil jurisdiction of a constitutional county court is limited to cases involving between $200 and $5,000. Original criminal jurisdiction includes all Class A and Class B misdemeanors.

Appellate criminal jurisdiction extends to cases originating in JP courts and municipal courts. A constitutional county court's appellate jurisdiction is final with regard to criminal cases involving fines of $100 or less. For cases in which greater fines are imposed, the plaintiff may appeal to a court of appeals. Civil cases are heard on appeal from JP courts, and the county court's decision is final with regard to those cases in which the amount in controversy does not exceed $100.

**County Courts-at-Law**   In counties with large populations, the burden of presiding over the county commissioners court and handling many administrative responsibilities has left the judges of constitutional county courts with little or

**small-claims court**
Presided over by a justice of the peace, a small claims court offers an informal and inexpensive procedure for handling damage claims of $5,000 or less.

**probate** Probate cases involving wills and guardianships fall under the jurisdiction of county courts and probate courts.

no time to try civil, criminal, and probate cases. Thus, to relieve constitutional county court judges of some or all courtroom duties, the legislature has authorized more than 200 statutory courts, most commonly called county courts-at-law, in more than 80 counties. With few exceptions, the criminal jurisdiction of county courts-at-law is limited to misdemeanors. Civil jurisdiction of most county courts-at-law is limited to controversies involving amounts of $200 to $100,000.

**Probate Courts**   Some constitutional county courts share jurisdiction with statutory county courts over guardianship and competency proceedings, as well as the admission of wills to probate. These courts are in ten counties located in six of the most populous metropolitan areas in Texas. In the authorizing statutes creating each probate court, the legislature restricts their jurisdiction to hearing probate cases only.

### State Trial Courts

Texas's principal trial courts are composed of 432 district-level courts of general and special jurisdiction (as of 2006). The 79th Legislature authorized the creation of an additional seven courts effective January 1, 2007. Most state trial courts are designated simply as district courts, but a few are called criminal district courts. Each district-level court has jurisdiction over one or more counties. Heavily populated counties may have several district courts with countywide jurisdiction.

**District Courts**   Most district court judges are authorized to try both criminal and civil cases, although a statute creating a court may specify that the court give preference to one or the other. All criminal jurisdiction is original. Except for cases transferred from constitutional county courts, misdemeanor jurisdiction is limited to offenses involving misconduct by government officials while acting in an official capacity. Felony jurisdiction extends to all types of felonies. Appeal following a capital felony conviction is taken directly to the Court of Criminal Appeals. Other criminal convictions are appealed to an intermediate appellate court.

District courts have exclusive original jurisdiction over civil cases involving divorce, land titles, contested elections, contested wills, slander, and defamation of character. They have original civil jurisdiction in controversies involving $200 or more (however, one court of appeals held the minimum amount to be $500). Thus, concurrent jurisdiction with lower courts begins at this level; above the maximum "dollar-amount" jurisdiction of those courts, district courts exercise exclusive civil jurisdiction. Appeals of civil cases go to courts of appeals.

**Drug Courts**   All counties with populations of 550,000 or greater are required to establish drug courts. These courts focus on rehabilitation and court monitoring of nonviolent drug offenders rather than imprisonment. By 2005, Texas had 44 such courts to work with adult drug offenders, juveniles, and families. Advocates argue that treatment of low-level substance abusers through drug court sentencing is more successful than incarceration. Both national- and state-level research seems to support these claims, although it should be noted that offenders are prescreened for likelihood of success before they are allowed to participate. Each of the three courts studied in Texas experienced significantly lower rearrest rates for drug court graduates when compared to users who had not been through the program.[7] A lack of state funding for court operations and concerns that rehabilitation gives the appearance of being "soft on crime" may limit the success of this program.

## Appellate Courts

The Lone Star State's appellate courts consist of 14 courts of appeals, the Court of Criminal Appeals, and the Supreme Court of Texas. Each of these courts has three or more judges or justices. Terms are staggered so that one-third of the members are elected or reelected every two years. This arrangement helps ensure that at any given time—barring death, resignation, or removal from office—each appellate court will have two or more judges with prior experience on that court. Decisions are reached by majority vote of the assigned judges after they examine the written record of the case, review briefs (written arguments) prepared by the parties' attorneys, and hear oral arguments by the attorneys. The Supreme Court of Texas and the Court of Criminal Appeals are authorized to answer questions about Texas law asked by federal appellate courts (for example, the U.S. Supreme Court).

**Courts of Appeals**   The legislature has divided Texas into 14 state court of appeals districts and has established a court of appeals in every district. Each of these intermediate appellate courts is composed of a chief justice and from 2 to 12 justices. These courts hear appeals of civil and criminal cases from district courts and county courts (but not those involving capital punishment or DNA forensic testing appeals for individuals sentenced to death). Final jurisdiction includes cases involving divorce, slander, boundary disputes, and elections held for purposes other than choosing government officials (for example, bond elections). Courts must hear appeals in panels of at least three justices. A decision requires a majority vote of a panel of justices.

**Court of Criminal Appeals**   Texas and Oklahoma are the only states in the Union that have bifurcated (divided) court systems for dealing with criminal and civil appeals. In Texas, the highest tribunal with criminal jurisdiction is the Court of Criminal Appeals. This nine-judge court hears criminal appeals exclusively. Noncapital criminal cases are appealed from the courts of appeals. Capital punishment cases are appealed directly to the Court of Criminal Appeals from district courts. Texans continue to resist the creation of a unified judicial system, which would have a single appellate court of last resort for both criminal felony and complex civil cases.[8]

Members of the Court of Criminal Appeals, including one whom voters elect as presiding judge, are chosen in partisan elections on a statewide basis for

### How Do We Compare ... in Salaries of Highest Court Justices and Judges?

**Annual Salaries of Highest Court Justices and Judges (in dollars as of 2005)**

| Most Populous U.S. States | Chief Justice/Judge | Associate Justice/Judge | U.S. States Bordering Texas | Chief Justice/Judge | Associate Justice/Judge |
|---|---|---|---|---|---|
| California | $199,000 | $182,000 | Arkansas | $139,000 | $128,000 |
| Florida | $155,000 | $155,000 | Louisiana | $124,000 | $118,000 |
| New York | $156,000 | $151,000 | New Mexico | $109,000 | $107,000 |
| Texas[a] | $152,500 | $150,000 | Oklahoma | $118,000 | $114,000 |

Source: *Survey of Judicial Salaries: Setting Judge Salaries* 30, no. 1 (April 2005) **www.ncsconline.org**.

[a]Judicial salaries increased to these amounts on December 1, 2005.

six-year terms. Presiding Judge Sharon Keller has headed the Texas Court of Criminal Appeals since 2000 when she became the first woman elected to this position. As of 2006, three of the other eight judges were women. There are currently (2006) no Hispanics or African Americans on the Court of Criminal Appeals. All members of the court are Republicans.

**Supreme Court**    Officially titled the Supreme Court of Texas, the state's highest court with civil jurisdiction has nine members elected statewide on a partisan basis: one chief justice and eight justices. No Democrats have served on the Texas Supreme Court since Justice Raul Gonzalez resigned in 1998. As of 2006, two African Americans were serving on the court. Chief Justice Wallace Jefferson, the first African American to join this body, was appointed by Governor Rick Perry in 2001. Perry elevated him to the position of chief justice in 2004. Justice Dale Wainwright became the first African American ever to win election to the court in 2002. In 2004, Governor Perry appointed Justice David Medina from Houston to the court, making him the fourth Hispanic in history to serve in this position. As of 2006, he was the only Hispanic on the court. At the same time, the only female member of the court was Justice Harriet O'Neill.

Without criminal jurisdiction, this high court is supreme only in cases involving civil law. Because it has severely limited original jurisdiction (for example, issuing writs and hearing cases involving denial of a place on an election ballot), nearly all of the court's work involves appeals of cases that it determines must be heard based on statutory provisions. Much of the Supreme Court's work involves handling applications for a writ of error, which can be requested by a party who argues that a court of appeals made a mistake on a question of law. If as many as four justices favor issuing a writ, the case is scheduled for argument in open court. Of the 805 petitions for review filed in 2005, the Supreme Court granted 109 of them, or 13.5 percent, representing the highest percentage of petitions accepted by the court since 1996.

In addition to hearing motions and applications and deciding cases, the Supreme Court performs other important functions. It is responsible for formulating the rules of civil procedure, which set out the manner in which civil cases are to be handled by the state's trial courts and appellate courts. The Supreme Court also has the authority to transfer cases for the purpose of equalizing workloads (cases pending on the dockets) of courts of appeals. The chief justice can temporarily assign district judges outside their administrative judicial regions and assign retired appellate justices (with their consent) to temporary duty on courts of appeals. Early in each regular session of the Texas Legislature, the chief justice is required by law to deliver a "State of the Judiciary" message, either orally or in written form, to the legislature. Chief Justice Jefferson devoted about half of his 2005 address to urging judicial pay increases.[9]

## Disciplining and Removing Judges and Justices

Each year, a few of Texas's judges and justices commit acts that warrant discipline or removal. Traditionally, the most common method of dealing with erring judges was to vote them out of office at the end of a term. Situations involving the most serious judicial misconduct were handled through trial by jury for judges at all levels and by legislative address or impeachment for state court judges. Although all of these methods are still available, the State Commission

*District Court Judge Cynthia Kent of Tyler confers with attorneys during a capital murder trial. (D. J. Peters /AP-Wide World Photos)*

on Judicial Conduct now plays the most important role in disciplining the state's judiciary. This 13-member commission is composed of 6 judges, each from a different-level court; 2 attorneys; and 5 nonattorney private citizens.

The commission considers cases in which a judge is accused of failure to follow rules adopted by the Texas Supreme Court, incompetence, inappropriate conduct, or violation of the Texas Code of Judicial Conduct. Judicial behavior viewed as sexual discrimination and gender bias has been a source of complaint. Selected Reading 10.1 is a publication from the State Bar of Texas designed to assist judges in creating gender-neutral courtrooms, thus avoiding this type of complaint. The goal of the Code of Judicial Conduct is to set ethical standards for judges that reinforce the public's confidence in the judicial system.

The State Commission on Judicial Conduct has several options for the manner in which it deals with judges who come before it, ranging from private reprimands to recommending removal of the judge (although actual removal can only be decided by a seven-judge tribunal appointed by the Texas Supreme Court). In addition, the commission oversees Amicus Curiae, an employee assistance program that locates service providers for judges suffering from substance abuse or mental or emotional disorders. In fiscal year 2004, the commission resolved in excess of 1,100 complaints. Disciplinary action was taken in 65 cases. Summaries of public sanctions are available on the commission's web site.

### Lawyers

Both the Texas Supreme Court and the State Bar of Texas play roles in regulating legal practice in the state. The Supreme Court is involved with issues relating to the training and licensing of lawyers. Although accreditation of law schools is largely a responsibility of the American Bar Association, the Supreme Court appoints the eight-member Board of Law Examiners. That board supervises administration of the bar exam for individuals seeking to become licensed attorneys, and it certifies the names of successful applicants to the court. The State Bar of Texas oversees the state's lawyers.

**State Bar of Texas**    To practice, a licensed attorney must be a member of the State Bar of Texas and pay dues for its support. Although the state bar is well known for its high-pressure lobbying activities, the organization promotes high standards of ethical conduct for Texas lawyers and conducts an extensive program of continuing legal education. As an administrative agency of the state, it is authorized to discipline, suspend, and disbar attorneys. One of the primary purposes of the state bar is to maintain public confidence in the integrity of lawyers in the Lone Star State.

In 2006, Texas had about 70,000 attorneys. Of that number approximately 43,000 worked as private practitioners, which means they were not employed by corporations or governmental entities and could be hired to represent clients. This means 1 attorney is available for every 519 residents. Although nearly 50 percent of Texans are Hispanics and African Americans,

In 2004:

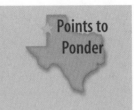

**Points to Ponder**

■ Harris County had the most attorneys engaged in private practice—12,472.
■ The ratio of private attorneys to citizens was highest in Travis County—1:209.
■ Twenty-one counties had no attorneys engaged in private practice.

*Source:* State Bar of Texas Department of Research and Analysis, *Private Practitioner Attorney Population by County Density Report, 2004–05,* September 2005.

they represent only 11 percent of licensed attorneys. Almost 30 percent of the state's attorneys are female.

It is possible to research an attorney's qualifications. Many lawyers are rated by their fellow attorneys in the areas of legal ability and ethics in the *Martindale-Hubbell Legal Directory*. Information about an attorney's professional disciplinary record is also available from the Find-A-Lawyer link on the state bar's web site.

**Legal Services for the Poor**    Under the Bill of Rights in the Texas Constitution and the Sixth Amendment to the U.S. Constitution, individuals accused of a crime are entitled to be represented by an attorney. Courts must appoint attorneys for criminal defendants who establish that they are indigent (too poor to hire a lawyer). These attorneys are paid by the county. No assistance is available for cases brought by prisoners that challenge the constitutionality of their incarceration (habeas corpus proceedings), unless the defendant has been sentenced to death. Programs such as the American Bar Association's Death Row Penalty Representation Project provide attorneys to a limited number of death row inmates by recruiting large civil law firms to handle appeals for persons sentenced to capital punishment.

If these same individuals were seeking legal help for a civil matter, little or no free assistance would be available. People who have suffered bodily injury may be able to hire an attorney on a **contingency fee** basis in which the lawyer is paid from any money recovered in a lawsuit. Representation in legal matters such as divorce, child custody, or contract disputes, however, requires the client to make direct payment to the attorney at the time services are performed. Despite an abundance of lawyers, nationally less than 20 percent of the civil legal matters of the poor actually receive attention from an attorney.[10] When legal assistance is available, it is often through an attorney with the Legal Services Corporation, more commonly referred to as Legal Aid. To qualify, an individual must meet federal poverty guidelines (not more than $11,963 in individual annual income in 2005). Almost 4 million Texans met this income standard in 2005. While in the same year the nation had 1 legal aid attorney per 6,861 poor persons, in Texas the ratio was 1 legal aid attorney per 11,762 eligible individuals.

Many attorneys and judges agree that access to the justice system is critical for all Texans, regardless of income level. The Texas Access to Justice Commission, created by the Texas Supreme Court, works to coordinate and increase delivery of legal services to the state's poor. The 15-member commission

**contingency fee**
A lawyer's compensation paid from money recovered in a lawsuit.

includes judges, lawyers, and private citizens. The State Bar of Texas and the Texas Equal Access to Justice Foundation support and collaborate with these efforts. Funding for legal services for the poor represents a combination of sources, including governmental appropriations, court fees, assessments on attorneys, interest on some client trust accounts, and donations Yet, this funding remains inadequate to meet the needs of a state with a growing population, many of whom are poor.

The state bar works to fill the legal-services gap through attorney volunteers. Recommending that attorneys donate 50 hours per year assisting needy clients, the organization asks them to report volunteer hours when paying their annual dues. According to former State Bar President Kelly Frels, in 2004, Texas lawyers provided almost 900,000 hours in pro bono (free) legal services and approximately 700,000 hours of work at reduced fees.[11]

Another source of legal assistance can be found at **TexasLawHelp.org**, a web site maintained by the Texas Equal Access to Justice Foundation. Low- and no-cost legal service providers are linked to the site. In addition, the site offers information on topics such as elder law, disaster relief, and family law. In some instances, the site includes legal forms that an individual can complete. A "Protective Order Kit" can be accessed with complete instructions on how to complete the forms and obtain a protective order in cases of domestic violence. Instructions are available in English, Spanish, and Vietnamese.

**Self-Help Legal Software**    For-profit companies are also in the business of furnishing self-help materials in response to rising legal costs and, arguably, help make the law accessible to middle-income individuals. Some of the sites include lawyer referrals in the event customers decide they want assistance. It is possible to purchase interactive software, such as that offered by Standard Legal Software, and legal self-help books, such as those published by Nolo Press, that will allow a person to write a will, obtain a divorce, or create a corporation. Legal documents that would cost hundreds, and sometimes thousands, of dollars if prepared by an attorney can be completed at little or no cost by using self-help products.

In addition, legal forms are available on the Internet. Some companies offer forms and then direct the client to an attorney. Others have the user answer questions on the web site, and software is programmed to complete all forms. The user then files the documents with the court, and no attorney is involved. Some enterprising attorneys provide forms directly through their own web sites along with phone, fax, and e-mail assistance to the client. Internet providers and some lawyers claim these services are low-cost and efficient. Others argue that "you get what you pay for" in quality and assistance.

| Learning Check 10.1        (Answers on p. 428) |
| --- |

1. True or False: All judges in Texas must be lawyers.
2. A court must have jurisdiction to hear a case. What does this mean?
3. True or False: Texas has a single appellate court of last resort for both criminal felony and complex civil cases.

#  Juries

A jury system lets citizens participate directly in the administration of justice. Texas has two types of juries: grand juries and trial juries. The state's Bill of Rights guarantees that individuals may be charged with a felony only by grand jury indictment. It also provides that anyone charged with either a felony or a misdemeanor has the right to trial by jury. If requested by either party, jury trials are required in civil cases.

## Grand Jury

A **grand jury** is composed of twelve citizens who may be chosen at random or selected by a judge from a list of fifteen to twenty county residents recommended by a judge-appointed grand jury commission. Members of a grand jury must have the qualifications of trial jurors and are paid like trial jurors (see the following "Trial Jury" section). The district judge appoints one juror to serve as presiding juror or foreman of the jury panel. A grand jury's life lasts for a district court's term, which varies from three to six months, although a district judge may extend a grand jury's term. During this period, grand juries have authority to inquire into all criminal actions but devote most of their time to felony matters.

A grand jury works in secrecy. Jurors and witnesses are sworn to keep secret all they hear in grand jury sessions. If, after investigation and deliberation (often lasting only a few minutes), at least nine grand jurors decide there is sufficient evidence to warrant a trial, an indictment is prepared with the aid of the prosecuting attorney. The indictment is a written statement accusing some person or persons of a particular crime (for example, burglary of a home). An indictment is referred to as a true bill; failure to indict constitutes a no bill.

Individuals may be subject to multiple grand jury investigations. In 2005, for example, U.S. Representative Tom DeLay was investigated by three grand juries for allegedly conspiring with two of his associates to (1) donate money contributed by corporations to several Republican candidates for the state legislature in violation of the state's election laws and (2) launder money. The first grand jury issued an indictment on the last day of its term, after a six-month investigation. That indictment dealt only with election code violations. The second grand jury refused to indict DeLay when asked to do so on the final day of its term. A third grand jury issued an indictment covering both charges within hours of being impaneled on the first day of its term.[12]

Grand jury indictments are authorized but not required for misdemeanor prosecutions. On the basis of a complaint, the district or county attorney may prepare an information. This document formally charges the accused with a misdemeanor offense.

## Trial Jury

Although relatively few Texans ever serve on a grand jury, almost everyone can expect to be summoned from time to time for duty on a trial jury (**petit jury**).

**grand jury** Composed of 12 persons with the qualifications of trial jurors, a grand jury serves from three to six months while it determines if sufficient evidence exists to indict persons accused of committing crimes.

**petit jury** A trial jury of 6 or 12 members.

Official qualifications for jurors are not high, and many thousands of jury trials are held in the Lone Star State every year. To ensure that jurors are properly informed concerning their work, the court gives them brief printed instructions (in English and Spanish) that describe their duties and explain basic legal terms and trial procedures. In urban counties, these instructions are often shown as a video in English and other languages common to segments of the county's population, such as Spanish or Vietnamese.

**Qualifications of Jurors**    A qualified Texas juror must be:

- A citizen of the United States and of the state of Texas
- 18 years of age or older
- Of sound mind
- Able to read and write (with no restriction on language), unless literate jurors are unavailable
- Neither convicted of a felony nor under indictment or other legal accusation of theft or of any felony

Qualified persons have a legal responsibility to serve when called, unless exempted or excused. Individuals exempted from jury duty:

- Are age 70 or older
- Have legal custody of a child or children under age 10
- Are enrolled in and attending a university, college, or secondary school
- Are the primary caregivers for invalids
- Are employed by the legislative branch of state government
- Have served as petit jurors within the preceding three years (only in counties with populations of more than 250,000)

Judges retain the prerogative to excuse others from jury duty in special circumstances. A person who is legally exempt from jury duty may avoid reporting to the court as summoned by filing a signed statement with the court clerk at any time before the scheduled date of appearance. In urban counties, prospective jurors can complete necessary exemption forms on the Internet.

In addition, anyone summoned for jury duty is entitled to reschedule the reporting date one time, so long as the new date is within six months. Subsequent rescheduling requires an emergency that could not have been previously anticipated, such as illness or a death in the family. A failure to report or falsely claiming an exemption is punishable as contempt of court and a guilty individual can be fined up to $1,000.

**Selection of Jurors**    A **venire** (panel of prospective jurors) is chosen by random selection from a list provided by the secretary of state. The list includes the county's registered voters, licensed drivers, and persons with identification cards issued by the Department of Public Safety. A trial jury is composed of six or twelve individuals, one of whom serves as foreman or presiding juror: six in a justice of the peace court, municipal court, or county court; twelve in a district court. A jury panel generally includes more than the minimum number of jurors.

**venire** A panel of prospective jurors drawn by random selection. These prospective jurors are called veniremen.

Attorneys question jurors through a procedure called **voir dire** (which means "to speak the truth") to identify any potential jurors who cannot be fair and impartial. An attorney may challenge for cause any venire member suspected of bias. If the judge agrees, the prospective juror is excused from serving. Some individuals try to avoid jury duty by answering voir dire questions in a way that makes them appear biased.

An attorney challenges prospective jurors either by peremptory challenge (up to fifteen per side, depending on the type of case, without having to give a reason for excluding the venire members) or by challenge for cause (an unlimited number). In 2002, Governor Rick Perry was eliminated from a jury panel in Travis County through a peremptory challenge. The defendant, who was representing himself on a charge of speeding, said he excluded Perry because "Governors of Texas are known to be kind of strict on the law."[13] Jurors may not be eliminated on the basis of race or ethnicity. For a district court, a trial jury is made up of the first twelve venire members who are neither excused by the district judge nor challenged peremptorily by a party in the case. For lower courts, the first six venire members accepted form a jury.

When jurors are impaneled, a district judge may direct the selection of four alternates, and a county judge may require the selection of two alternates. If for some reason a juror cannot finish a trial for either a civil or a criminal case, an alternate juror may be seated as a replacement. Even if no alternate has been selected and a juror cannot complete service, the Texas Court of Criminal Appeals has ruled that in criminal cases once a jury has been impaneled, it must proceed to trial and judgment with only 11 members.

**Compensation of Jurors**    Daily pay for venire members and jurors varies from county to county. Under provisions adopted by the legislature in 2005, counties must now pay jurors a minimum amount of $6 for all or part of the first day of jury duty and $40 for each subsequent day of service, without a maximum amount. This increase represented the first adjustment of minimum juror pay in more than 50 years in the Lone Star State. Counties fund the first $6 each day, and the state reimburses the counties up to $34 for each subsequent day of service. The law now requires anyone convicted of an offense, other than for a pedestrian or parking violation, to pay an additional court fee of $4, which the state comptroller uses to fund county reimbursements. Attorneys from Vinson & Elkins, one of the state's most prestigious law firms, led the juror-pay reform effort. Other supporters included leaders of the State Bar of Texas and elected officials from both political parties. Although employers are not required to pay wages to an employee summoned or selected for jury duty, they are prohibited by law from discharging permanent employees for such service.

**Juror Diversity**    One of the principal arguments for increasing juror pay was to encourage members of historical minority groups to appear and serve on juries. Assuring that jury pools reflect the ethnic and racial diversity of a community is important for two reasons. First, the U.S. Supreme Court's interpretation of the

**voir dire** Courtroom procedure whereby attorneys question prospective jurors to identify any who cannot be fair and impartial.

Sixth Amendment in the case of *Taylor v. Louisiana*, 419 U.S. 522 (1975), guarantees a criminal defendant a jury representative of a cross-section of the surrounding community. Laws that permit systematic exclusion of members of a particular group are therefore unconstitutional. Those supporting an increase in juror pay argued that the state had created a system that in practice excluded low-wage workers, and, in particular, members of historical minority groups. Second, public confidence in the judicial system requires involvement of all groups, not just a privileged few.

Does low pay for jury service discourage involvement of members of historical minority groups? Research suggests the answer may be yes. Many of these individuals work for hourly wages, arguably the kinds of jobs for which an employer would withhold pay from a worker who honored a jury summons. The $6 per day that most counties paid frequently did not even cover parking and food costs, much less lost wages. In studies conducted in Dallas and Harris Counties, researchers determined that although Hispanics represented 30 percent of the population eligible for jury service, they comprised less than 10 percent of jury pools. In Harris County, those from affluent, white areas were 7 times as likely to appear for jury service as those from predominantly low-income, African American and Hispanic neighborhoods.[14] El Paso County raised its minimum juror pay to $40 per day prior to passage of the state law. Officials reported an immediate increase in the number of Hispanics who answered their jury summons. If jury pools become more diverse, juries will reflect this change, as veniremen cannot be excluded from a jury based on race or ethnicity. Whether El Paso County's experience is repeated across the state and whether increased participation translates into increased confidence in the judicial system remain open issues.

---

**Learning Check 10.2**        (Answers on p. 428)

1. True or False: A grand jury indictment means a criminal defendant is guilty.
2. Can someone convicted of a felony serve as a juror in a civil case?
3. How much are jurors paid?

---

## ★ Judicial Procedures

Many Texas residents, as well as people from outside the state, appear in court as litigants or witnesses. As a litigant, for example, a person may become a party to a civil case arising from an automobile accident or from a divorce. A person would become a party in a criminal case when accused of a crime such as theft. Witnesses may be summoned to testify in any type of case brought before the trial courts of Texas, but a court pays each witness only $10 per day for court attendance. In still another capacity, a citizen (even someone without legal training) may be elected to the office of county judge or justice of the peace. For these reasons, Texans should understand what happens in the state's courtrooms.

## Civil Justice System

As used in Texas, the term *civil law* generally refers to matters not covered by criminal law. The following are important subjects of civil law: **torts** (for example, unintended injury to another person or a vehicle in a traffic accident); contracts (for example, agreements to deliver property of a specified quality at a certain price); and domestic relations or family law (such as marriage, divorce, and parental custody of children). Civil law disputes usually involve individuals or corporations. In criminal cases, a person is prosecuted by the state. It is possible for a single incident to result in a civil suit for personal damages and prosecution on a criminal charge.

The state legislature frequently changes both criminal and civil law. In recent years, recoveries in tort cases have been greatly limited by state lawmakers, through changes in statutes, and by the people of Texas, as the result of constitutional amendments.[15] In civil cases plaintiffs may be eligible for three different types of damages:

- Economic damages, which include lost wages and actual expenses (for example, hospital bills)
- Noneconomic damages, which include a loss in quality of life such as disfigurement, mental anguish, and emotional distress
- Exemplary or punitive damages, intended to punish the defendant.

As originally written, the law allowed juries to determine the maximum amount of money judgments. Over time, the legislature has exercised more control over recovery amounts. Changes in Texas's liability law are shown in Table 10.2.

A major justification for limiting recoveries in tort cases is that individuals and businesses must pay high liability insurance premiums for protection against the risk of lawsuit judgments. After limitations were placed on recoveries in medical malpractice cases, many insurers reduced their malpractice insurance rates. Skeptics argued that rate decreases did not equate to a reduction in incidents of medical negligence or even necessarily to the results of tort reform. Others maintained that rate declines and the increased number of insurers willing to issue policies to Texas doctors were the direct result of capping damage awards.

## Civil Trial Procedure

The Supreme Court of Texas makes rules of civil procedure for all courts with civil jurisdiction. These rules, however, cannot conflict with any general law of the state. Rules of civil procedure are enacted unless they are rejected by the legislature.

**Pretrial Actions**   Civil cases normally begin when the **plaintiff** (injured party) files a petition, a written document containing the plaintiff's complaints against the **defendant** and the remedy sought—usually money damages. This petition is filed with the clerk of the court in which the lawsuit is contemplated, and the

**tort**  An unintended injury to another person or to a person's property.

**plaintiff**  The injured party who initiates a civil suit or the state in a criminal proceeding.

**defendant**  The person sued in a civil proceeding or prosecuted in a criminal proceeding.

*Table 10.2*    Changes in Tort Law Recoveries (1990–2005)

| Year | Type of claims limited | Limitations | Dollar limitation | Constitutional or statutory change |
|---|---|---|---|---|
| 1995 | All claims, whether contract or tort, except those resulting from felonies | Legislative caps on exemplary or punitive damages | Greater of $200,000 or amount equal to twice economic damages plus noneconomic damages not to exceed $750,000 | Statutory |
| 1995 | All torts | Ability to recover against defendants | Plaintiff cannot sue if more than 50% responsible for damages. Defendants liable for only their pro rata share unless more than 50% responsible for damages | Statutory |
| 2003 | Medical malpractice and all other claims, whether contract or tort | Legislature can set limitations on recovery amounts for all but economic damages | To be set by legislature | Constitutional |
| 2003 | Medical malpractice | Legislative caps on recovery amounts | $250,000 for noneconomic damages against health care providers; $250,000 for noneconomic damages against any medical institution; and no more than $500,000, no matter how many medical institutions | Statutory |

clerk issues a citation. The citation is delivered to the defendant, directing that person to answer the charges. If the defendant wants to contest the suit, he or she must file a written answer to the plaintiff's charges. The answer explains why the plaintiff is not entitled to the remedy sought and asks that the plaintiff be required to prove every charge made in the petition.

Before the judge sets a trial date (which may be many months or even years after the petition is filed), all interested parties should have had an opportunity to file their petitions, answers, or other pleas with the court. These written instruments constitute the pleadings in the case and form the basis of the trial. Either party has the option to have a jury determine the facts. If no one demands a jury, the trial judge decides all facts and applies the law. When a jury determines the facts after receiving instructions from the judge, the judge's only duty is to apply the law to the jury's version of the facts.

**Trial and Appeal of a Civil Case**    As a trial begins, lawyers for each party make brief opening statements. The plaintiff's case is presented first. The defendant has the opportunity to contest the relevance or admissibility of all evidence introduced and may cross-examine the plaintiff's witnesses. After the plaintiff's case has been presented, it is the defendant's turn to offer evidence and the testimony of witnesses. The plaintiff may challenge this evidence and testimony. The judge is the final authority as to what evidence and testimony may be introduced by all parties, although objections to the judge's rulings can be used as grounds for appeal.

After all parties have finished their presentations, in a jury trial, the judge writes a charge to the jury, submits it to the parties for their approval, makes any necessary changes they suggest, and reads the charge to the jury. In the charge, the judge instructs the jury on the rules governing their deliberations and defines various terms. After the charge is read, attorneys make their appeals to the jurors, at which point the jury retires to elect one of its members as the foreman and to deliberate.

The jury must answer a series of questions that will establish the facts of the case. These questions are called **special issues**. The judgment will be based on jurors' answers to these special issues. They will not be asked directly whether the plaintiff or the defendant should win. To decide a case in a district court, at least 10 jurors must agree on answers to all of the special issues. Five must agree in a county court or JP court. If the required number of jurors cannot reach agreement, the foreman reports a hung jury. If the judge agrees, the jury is discharged. Either party may then request a new trial, which will be scheduled unless the case is dismissed. If the judge disagrees, jurors continue to deliberate.

A jury's decision is known as a **verdict**. If there is no jury, the judge arrives at a verdict. The judge prepares a written opinion, known as the **judgment** or decree of the court. Either party may then file a motion for a new trial based on the reason or reasons the party believes the trial was not fair. If the judge agrees, a new trial will be ordered; if not, the case may be appealed to a higher court. In each appeal, a complete written record of the trial is sent to the appellate court. The usual route of appeals is from a county or district court to a court of appeals and then, in some instances, to the Supreme Court of Texas.

## Criminal Justice System

The State of Texas has identified more than 1,900 crimes as felonies. Less serious offenses are classified as misdemeanors. Features of the Texas Penal Code include **graded penalties** for noncapital offenses and harsher penalties for repeat offenders. Also provided is a two-step procedure for establishing whether a crime punishable by death (a **capital felony**) has been committed and, if so, whether a death sentence should be ordered.

**Graded Penalties**   First-, second-, and third-degree felonies may involve imprisonment and fines in cases involving the most serious noncapital crimes. Some lesser offenses (especially those involving alcohol and drug abuse) are defined as state jail felonies (so-called fourth-degree felonies) and are punishable by fines and confinement in jails operated by the state. The three classes of misdemeanors (A, B, and C) may involve county jail sentences and/or fines. (See Table 10.3

**special issues**
Questions a judge gives a trial jury to answer to establish facts in a case.

**verdict** A jury's decision about a court case.

**judgment** A judge's written opinion based on a verdict.

**graded penalties**
Depending on the nature of the crime, felonies are graded as first, second, and third degree; misdemeanors are graded as A, B, and C.

**capital felony** A crime punishable by death or life imprisonment.

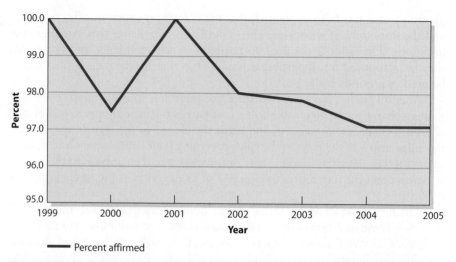

*Figure 10.2*    Death Sentences Affirmed by Court of Criminal Appeals    *Source:* Office of Court Administration, *Annual Statistical Report for the Texas Judiciary: Fiscal year 2005* (Austin : Office of Court Administration): p. 24. Although convicted capital felons have an automatic right of appeal to the Court of Criminal Appeals, the likelihood their conviction will be overturned is unlikely.

for categories of noncapital offenses and ranges of penalties.) People who engage in organized criminal activity, repeat offenders, and those who commit hate crimes (anyone motivated by bias against a person's race, ethnicity, religion, age, gender, or sexual preference) are punished as though they had committed the next higher degree of felony. This practice is called enhanced punishment.

**Capital Punishment**    The issue of capital punishment remains controversial. Over the last three decades, no state in the union has executed more capital felons than Texas (376 men and 2 women from January 1982 through November 2006). In addition to questions of possible innocence of some of these individuals, concerns about the method used to impose the death penalty keep this matter before the public. Currently (2006), Texas prison officials use a lethal injection comprised of a series of three drugs: the first to render the inmate unconscious, the second to induce paralysis and collapse the lungs and other organs; and the third to stop the heart. The U.S. Supreme Court held in *Hill* v. *McDonough* (126 S. Ct. 2096 [2006]) that inmates may raise a claim that this method represents cruel and unusual punishment. Whether the practice is cruel and unusual and thus violates the Eighth Amendment of the U.S. Constitution has not been determined.

Under the Texas Penal Code, a person commits murder if there is evidence of intent to kill or cause serious bodily harm to the victim. The presence of additional circumstances makes the crime a capital felony, for which the death penalty may be applied. Murder becomes a capital felony if the victim was under the age of six, a peace officer, firefighter, or a prison employee. In addition, mur-

*Table 10.3*     Selected Texas Noncapital Offenses, Penalties for First Offenders, and Courts Having Original Jurisdiction

| Selected Offenses | Offense Category | Punishment | Court |
|---|---|---|---|
| Murder<br>Theft of property valued at $200,000 or more | First-degree felony | Confinement for 5–99 years/life<br>Maximum fine of $10,000 | District Court |
| Theft of property valued at $100,000 or more but less than $200,000<br>Aggravated assault, including a spouse | Second-degree felony | Confinement for 2–20 years<br>Maximum fine of $10,000 | District Court |
| Theft of property valued at $20,000 or more but less than $100,000<br>Unlawfully taking a weapon to school | Third-degree felony | Confinement for 2–10 years<br>Maximum fine of $10,000 | District Court |
| Theft of property valued at $15,000 or more but less than $20,000<br>Illegal recruitment of athletes if the value of benefits exceed $1,500 but are less than $20,000 | State jail felony | Confinement for 180 days–2 years<br>Maximum fine of $10,000 | District Court |
| Theft of property valued at $500 or more but less than $1,500<br>Manufacture, sale, or possession of a counterfeit disabled parking placard | Class A misdemeanor | Confinement for 1 year<br>Maximum fine of $4,000 | Constitutional county court and county court-at-law |
| Theft of property valued at $20 or more but less than $500<br>Engaging in computer-assisted hunting if the animal is in Texas | Class B misdemeanor | Confinement for 180 days<br>Maximum fine of $2,000 | Constitutional county court and county court-at-law |
| Theft of property valued at less than $20<br>Advertising, preparing, or selling term papers and reports used by others | Class C misdemeanor | No confinement<br>Maximum fine of $500 | Justice of the peace court and municipal court (if offense committed within city limits) |

ders become capital felonies when they occur during the commission of another felony or a prison escape or are retaliation against a judge. Also, murder for hire, serial murders (including killing an unborn child), or inmate-on-inmate murder are capital felonies.

After a jury has found a defendant guilty of a capital offense, it must unanimously answer two questions to impose the death penalty:

1. Is there a probability that the defendant will commit criminal acts of violence that would constitute a continuing threat to society?
2. Is there mitigating evidence in the defendant's background, such as child abuse or mental retardation, that warrants a sentence of life imprisonment rather than death?

The minimum sentence for a capital felony is life imprisonment without parole. If the state seeks the death penalty, all jurors must agree to the sentence. Assessment of the death penalty has declined across the United States and in Texas in recent years. Both Illinois and New Jersey have placed moratoriums on the practice, and the American Bar Association is actively encouraging other states with death penalty laws to do the same. In the 79th Legislature meeting in 2005, Representative Ruth McClendon (D-San Antonio) sought to amend the Constitution to declare a moratorium for some convicted capital felons. This effort failed.

Further, some capital defendants are exempt from the death penalty. As the result of U.S. Supreme Court decisions and state law, the death penalty cannot be used as punishment for anyone who was under the age of 18 when committing a capital crime (*Roper* v. *Simmons*, 543 U.S. 551 [2005]) or any individual who is mentally retarded (*Atkins* v. *Virginia*, 536 U.S. 304 [2002]). The death penalty cannot be assessed if a defendant is found to have been mentally incompetent at the time of committing a capital crime. In addition, the death penalty cannot be carried out on a convicted individual who is mentally ill. The death certificate of someone who has been executed reflects the cause of death as "Death caused by judicially ordered execution."

### Criminal Trial Procedure

Rules of criminal procedure are made by the legislature. The Texas Code of Criminal Procedure is written to comply with U.S. Supreme Court rulings regarding confessions, arrests, searches, and seizures. Additional rules of procedure have been adopted to promote fairness and efficiency in handling criminal cases.

**Pretrial Actions**    It is likely that millions of illegal acts are committed daily in Texas. For example, many people drive faster than official speed limits allow or drive while under the influence of alcohol. After an arrest and before questioning, suspects must be given a Miranda warning informing them of their rights. When a prosecuting attorney files charges, a suspect must appear before a judicial officer (usually a justice of the peace) who names the offense or offenses charged and provides information concerning the suspect's legal rights. A person charged with a noncapital offense may be released on personal recognizance (promising to report for trial at a later date), released on bail by posting personal money or money provided for a charge by a bail bond service, or denied bail and jailed.

People who cannot afford to hire a lawyer must be provided with the services of an attorney in any felony or misdemeanor case in which conviction may result in a prison or jail sentence. Research from Harris County indicates that those with appointed attorneys are twice as likely to serve time in jail or prison as defendants who hire attorneys. The Texas Fair Defense Act (2001) established minimum attorney qualifications and standards for the appointment of counsel for indigent defendants charged with capital crimes.

Under Texas law, the right to trial by jury is guaranteed in all criminal cases. Except in death penalty cases, defendants may waive jury trial (if the prosecuting attorney agrees) regardless of the plea—guilty, not guilty, or nolo contendere (no contest). To expedite procedures, prosecuting and defense attorneys may engage in plea bargaining, in which the accused pleads guilty in return for a promise that the prosecutor will seek a lighter sentence or will recommend community supervision. Usually, a judge will accept a plea bargain. If the defendant waives a trial by jury and is found guilty by a judge, that judge also determines punishment.

**Trial of a Criminal Case**   After the trial jury has been selected, the prosecuting attorney reads an information (misdemeanor) or an indictment (felony). The jury is thus informed of the basic allegations of the state's case. The defendant then enters a plea.

As plaintiff, the state begins by calling its witnesses and introducing any evidence supporting the information or the indictment. The defense may challenge the truth or relevance of evidence presented and is allowed to cross-examine all witnesses. Next, the defense may present its case, calling witnesses and submitting evidence that, in turn, is subject to attack by the prosecution. After all evidence and testimony have been presented, the judge charges the jury, explaining the law applicable to the case. Both prosecuting and defense attorneys then address final arguments to the jury before it retires to reach a verdict.

**Verdict, Sentence, and Appeal**   The jury must reach a unanimous decision to return a verdict of guilty or not guilty. If jurors are hopelessly split and the result is a hung jury, the judge declares a mistrial and discharges the jurors. When requested by the prosecuting attorney, the judge orders a new trial with another jury.

If a jury brings a verdict before a court, the judge may choose to disregard it and order a new trial on grounds that the jury has failed to arrive at a verdict that achieves substantial justice. In a jury trial, the jury may fix the sentence if the convicted person so requests; otherwise, the judge determines the sentence. A separate hearing on the penalty is held, at which time the person's prior criminal and/or juvenile record, general reputation, and other relevant factors may be introduced, such as facts concerning the convicted person's background and lifestyle as determined by a presentence investigation.

A convicted defendant has the right to appeal on grounds that an error in trial procedure occurred. All appeals (except for capital punishment cases) are heard first by the court of appeals in the district in which the trial was held, and ultimately by the Texas Court of Criminal Appeals. Death penalty appeals are made directly to the Texas Court of Criminal Appeals.

| Learning Check 10.3 | (Answers on p. 428) |
|---|---|

1. What are the parties to a civil lawsuit called?
2. Which is the most serious level of criminal offense—a misdemeanor, a felony, or a state-jail felony?
3. To which court is a capital felony for which the defendant received the death penalty appealed?

## Correction and Rehabilitation

Confinement in a prison (either a penitentiary or a state jail) or a county or municipal jail is designed to punish lawbreakers, deter others from committing similar crimes, and isolate offenders from society, thus protecting the lives and property of citizens who might otherwise become victims of criminals. Ideally, while serving a sentence behind bars, a lawbreaker will be rehabilitated and, after release, will obey all laws, find employment, and make positive contributions to society. In practice, approximately 30 percent of convicted criminals violate the conditions of their release or commit other crimes after being released, for which they are re-sentenced to prison.

The number of Texans either imprisoned or supervised by local and state criminal justice authorities is larger than in any other state. In 2004 (the most recent year for which information is available), more than 650,000 Texans were incarcerated, on parole, or under community supervision (formerly known as probation). In response to high crime rates in the early 1990s, the Texas Legislature lengthened prison sentences. In addition, the Texas Board of Pardons and Paroles and the legislature tightened the procedures and circumstances under which inmates could be granted parole. The minimum number of years of incarceration before qualifying for parole was increased. An increase in the number of prisoners and a corresponding decrease in those receiving parole continue to place Texas's incarceration rates among the highest in the country.

### How Do We Compare . . . in Prison Incarceration Rates?

#### Number of Prisoners per 100,000 State Residents (as of December 2004)

| Most Populous U.S. States | Number of Prisoners per 100,000 Residents | U.S. States Bordering Texas | Number of Prisoners per 100,000 residents |
|---|---|---|---|
| California | 456 | Arkansas | 495 |
| Florida | 486 | Louisiana | 816 |
| New York | 331 | New Mexico | 318 |
| **Texas** | **694** | Oklahoma | 649 |

*Source:* Paige M. Harrison and Allen J. Beck, Ph.D., *Bureau of Justice Statistics Bulletin: Prisoners in 2004* (Washington, D.C.: U.S. Department of Justice, October 2005), at **www.ojp.usdoj.gov**.

## The Texas Department of Criminal Justice

The principal criminal justice agencies of the state are organized within the Texas Department of Criminal Justice (TDCJ). This department is headed by the nonsalaried Texas Board of Criminal Justice, composed of nine members appointed by the governor (with advice and consent of the Texas Senate) for overlapping six-year terms, including one member selected as chair by the governor. The board employs a full-time executive director, who hires directors of the department's divisions. Each division director is responsible for hiring division personnel. TDCJ employed about 40,000 Texans in 2004 (the most recent year for which official figures are available). Of that number, approximately 25,000 were correctional officers. These employees are responsible for a prison population that exceeded 150,000 inmates in 2006.

The Correctional Institutions Division supervises the operation and management of state prisons, state jails, and other specialized facilities. Older prison units are largely in East Texas, but since the 1990s additional units have been located throughout Texas. State jail facilities, located across the state, are designed for nonviolent offenders. Private contractors operate seven prisons, five state jails, and various pre-release, work, substance abuse, and intermediate sanctions facilities. Figure 10.3 shows the location of prison and state jail units in Texas.

Two agencies are responsible for convicted criminals who serve all or a part of their sentences in the community. The Community Justice Assistance Division establishes minimum standards for county programs involving community supervision and community corrections facilities (such as a boot camp or a restitution center). The Parole Division manages Texas's statewide parole and mandatory supervision system for convicted felons. The seven-member Board of Pardons and Paroles recommends acts of clemency (such as pardons) to the governor and grants or revokes paroles.

## State Correctional Institutions for Adults

Adult offenders sentenced to confinement on misdemeanor convictions are housed in a county jail or another type of community corrections facility. An adult sentenced to prison following a felony conviction is supposed to be incarcerated in a state penitentiary or state jail within forty-five days. When Texas prisons become overcrowded, they cannot accept convicted felons in a timely manner, which may result in overcrowded county jails.

**The Prison**   Correcting or modifying the behavior of convicted felons is a goal of TDCJ's Correctional Institutions Division. Training and instructional programs are used to rehabilitate inmates and equip them with a means for self-support after release. Discipline and education are the primary means of combating **recidivism** (criminal behavior resulting in reimprisonment after release). Every prisoner must be given a job but may elect not to work. These prisoners' labor saves the state money and, in some instances, generates revenue. Prisoners repair

**recidivism** Criminal behavior that results in reincarceration after a person has been released from confinement for a prior offense.

*Figure 10.3*    Facilities of the Texas Department of Criminal Justice, February 2006

engines; perform all types of agricultural labor; manufacture furniture (see photo on p. 413), including maroon mattresses for Texas A&M University; and even make the wooden gavels used by the presiding officers of the Texas Legislature.

More than half of Texas prisoners are enrolled in vocational and academic classes offered through the prison system's Windham Independent School District. In addition, some prisoners take community college and university courses. In 2004, approximately 2,000 prisoners received certificates of technology from community colleges. Another 500 graduated with degrees ranging from associates to masters. Almost 70 percent of Texas prisoners have less than a high school education, one-third are functionally illiterate, and approximately 7 percent are classified as mentally retarded, having scored less than 70 on an IQ test. (Only 3 percent of the general population tests as being mentally retarded.) According to

*Among the items manufactured by inmates are university dormitory room furnishings. (Texas Department of Criminal Justice, Public Information Office)*

estimates by TDCJ officials, between 85 and 90 percent of prisoners committed crimes while under the influence of narcotics, were drug users, or were convicted of drug-trafficking crimes. The profile of Texas prisoners in Table 10.4 highlights characteristics of the state's incarcerated population.

**Prison Problems**    At the beginning of the twenty-first century, Texas prisons face many challenges. Recurring concerns about overcrowding force continued assessment of the number of prison beds needed, incarceration rates, and parole policies. Low pay and difficult working conditions produce a turnover rate of approximately 25 percent annually for correctional officers. An aging prison population adds to the cost of incarceration because of extra health care expenses. In a post–September 11, 2001, world, the state's correctional officers are engaged in the war on terrorism. Prison officials monitor inmate behavior and correspondence (especially letters written in Arabic, Farsi, and other Middle Eastern languages) in an effort to identify any attempts to recruit prisoners for terrorist groups or activities. Several gangs exist within the prison system.

Approximately 10,000 violent inmates and gang members are held in administrative segregation cells. Here, they have little or no contact with anyone other than corrections officers. There is increased concern about how these individuals will integrate into society upon release. In 2004, the Rehabilitation and Reentry Programs Division of the Texas Department of Criminal Justice

*Table 10.4*    Some Characteristics of Texas's Prison Population (2004)

| Characteristic | Measurement |
| --- | --- |
| *Gender* | |
| Male | 94% |
| Female | 6% |
| *Race* | |
| African American | 39% |
| White | 31% |
| Hispanic | 30% |
| *Type of Offense Leading to Incarceration* | |
| Violent | 54% |
| Property | 17% |
| Drugs | 17% |
| Other | 12% |
| *IQ* | |
| Average | 90.7 |

*Source:*  Texas Department of Criminal Justice.

developed a program to facilitate the transition of these isolated prisoners into the "free world" after release. Both in-cell and post-release programs provide training, support, socialization skills, and employment in an attempt to ease reentry and reduce recidivism.

**State Felony Jails**   The Texas Penal Code provides for a system of state jails to house people convicted of state jail felonies. State jails are rehabilitation-oriented. Allowing judges to sentence offenders to "up-front" time (a period of incarceration preceding community supervision), the law also provides for substance abuse treatment and other support programs. Advocates argue that they significantly reduce recidivism rates for treated individuals and that the cost of treatment is significantly less than the cost of reincarceration.

### Local Government Jails

Unlike the state felony jails, which are funded through appropriations by the Texas Legislature, county and city jails are financed largely by county and municipal governments, respectively. Like penal institutions of the TDCJ, however, local government jails are used to control lawbreakers by placing them behind bars. These facilities often must deal with complaints of overcrowding and unsafe conditions.

**County Jails**   All but 17 Texas counties maintain a jail. Some counties have contracted with commercial firms to provide "privatized" jails, but most counties maintain public jails operated under the direction of the county sheriff.

These penal institutions were originally established to detain persons awaiting trial (if not released on bail) and to hold individuals serving sentences for misdemeanor offenses. Jail facilities vary in quality and usually do not offer rehabilitation programs.

The Texas Commission on Jail Standards is responsible for establishing minimum standards for county jails, requiring an annual jail report from each county sheriff, reviewing jail reports, and arranging for on-site inspections. The commission determines appropriate population and staffing levels, and issues remedial orders to enforce its standards. In the case of an ongoing failure to comply with commission rules, a jail may be closed, or the commission, represented by the attorney general, may take court action against the county. In the commission's 30-year history, only one jail, located in Calhoun County, has been permanently closed (due to mold in the facility).[16]

**Municipal Jails**   Texas has more than 300 municipal jails. Some are used primarily as "drunk tanks" to detain people for a few hours after they have been arrested for public intoxication. In large cities these facilities often house hundreds of inmates who have been arrested for a variety of offenses ranging from Class C misdemeanors to capital murder. Those charged with more serious crimes are usually held temporarily until they can be transferred to a more secure county jail. The quality of municipal jail facilities varies greatly. A city jail is not subject to regulation by the Texas Commission on Jail Standards, unless it is managed by a private vendor or houses out-of-state prisoners.

### Private Prisons

Both state and local governments have dealt with their prison crises by contracting with private companies to construct and operate prisons and direct prerelease programs. Texas now has more privately operated facilities than any other state. More than 20 percent of all U.S. prisoners housed in private prisons are in the Lone Star State. Private penitentiary facilities are under the supervision of the Correctional Institutions Division of the TDCJ. The Texas Commission on Jail Standards supervises privatized county and municipal units. The Texas Youth Commission oversees private contract facilities that house juvenile offenders. In addition to prisons and jails, private contractors also provide substance abuse treatment programs and halfway houses, where state and county prisoners are incarcerated in privately operated units. Some also house out-of-state convicts and federal offenders. After several successful escapes in which state and local officials spent taxpayer dollars to apprehend the escaped inmates, legislators passed a law requiring operators of private facilities to reimburse the state for such assistance. Table 10.5 provides a breakdown of the approximate 30,000 jail and prison beds in the state that are under private contract.

### Supervision of Released Offenders

Although Texas prisons and jails are usually successful in isolating lawbreakers, the quality of their rehabilitation efforts has been more disappointing.

Table 10.5    Privately Operated Correctional Facilities in Texas (2006).

| Vendor | Regulator | Number of Units | Number of Beds |
|---|---|---|---|
| Bobby Ross Group | TCJS | 1 | 515 |
| CiviGenics | TCJS | 8 | 2,865 |
| Cornell Corrections | TYC | 2 | 246 |
| Cornell Corrections | TDCJ | 1 | 500 |
| Cornell Corrections | TCJS | 1 | 300 |
| CCA | TDCJ | 10 | 10,990 |
| Emerald | TCJS | 2 | 1,120 |
| GEO | TCJS | 10 | 5,753 |
| GEO | TDCJ | 6 | 3,890 |
| GEO | TYC | 1 | 200 |
| LCS | TCJS | 2 | 1,285 |
| MTC | TDCJ | 2 | 1,070 |
| MTC | TCJS | 1 | 540 |
| Total Number of Privatized Jail and Prison Beds | | | 29,274 |

Sources: Texas Department of Criminal Justice (TDCJ), Texas Commission on Jail Standards (TCJS), Corrections Corporation of America (CCA), Global Expertise in Outsourcing (GEO), and Management and Training Corporation (MTC).

Confinement is expensive for taxpayers and often produces embittered criminals rather than rehabilitated, law-abiding citizens. As a result, criminal justice reform measures in recent years have emphasized supervision of released offenders and more effective rehabilitation.

**Community Supervision**   In cases involving adult first-time offenders convicted of misdemeanors and lesser felonies, jail and prison sentences are commonly commuted to community supervision. This punishment was formerly termed adult probation. These convicted persons are not confined if they fulfill certain court-imposed conditions.

**Parole**   The Board of Pardons and Paroles grants, denies, and revokes paroles to the state's sentenced felons. Seven full-time salaried members are appointed for six-year terms by the governor with the advice and consent of the Senate. The board's presiding officer employs and supervises twelve commissioners. A three-member panel comprised of parole board member(s) and commissioner(s) reviews inmate applications and decides whether to grant or deny parole. If a parolee violates any conditions of release, a board panel determines whether to revoke parole.

Prisoners who have served some portion of their sentences may be eligible for parole. Felons who commit serious, violent crimes, such as rape or murder, must serve 30 to 40 years of "flat time" (without the possibility of having prison time reduced for good behavior). Other offenders may apply for parole after serving one-fourth of a sentence or 15 years, whichever is less (minus good-time credit, time off for good behavior). Prisoners who file two or more frivolous lawsuits against the state in a year, as determined by a court, can lose up to six months of good-time credit, thus lengthening the period until they are eligible for parole.

Parole can range from regular, with no electronic monitoring requirements, to superintensive, in which parolees wear GPS monitoring systems so officials know their physical location at all times. The Board of Pardons and Paroles may also attach any conditions that a judge has ordered in probating convicted felons' sentences. These restrictions include psychological counseling, substance abuse treatment, prohibiting access to areas in which children congregate, or any other measure deemed appropriate to rehabilitate a felon or keep the community safe.

**Reentry Issues**   During 2005, approximately 115,000 Texans were convicted of felonies in the state's district courts. Another 43,000 took deferred adjudication for their offenses, in which they were not convicted of a crime, but were placed under community supervision. All of these individuals will bear the designation of felon for the remainder of their lives, and their punishment will not terminate when their criminal sentences end. Although the state restores the right to vote to convicted felons once they have completed their sentences, many barriers remain to successful reentry to society.

Among the civil rights felons lose are:

- The right to serve on juries
- The right to hold elected office
- The right to administer the estate of a deceased person

Among impediments to employment are:

- Employers' right to disqualify applicants with felony or misdemeanor convictions
- Exclusion from jobs in education, health care services, child and elder care, financial services, and transportation
- Enhanced liability for employers providing delivery and home-services who hire individuals convicted of indecency or crimes against persons or property
- Inability to obtain required licenses for jobs such as attorneys or cosmetologists

In fact, more than 100 state laws restrict and otherwise regulate convicted felons and different kinds of jobs. (See the Point/Counterpoint feature for the arguments for and against the need to change some of these laws.) Those convicted of drug-related offenses endure additional problems, which include being:

- Barred for life from receiving TANF benefits (felony only)
- Barred for life from obtaining food stamps (felony only)
- Denied state student aid until two years after sentence completion (felony or misdemeanor)
- Denied a driver's license (felony or misdemeanor)

# POINT/COUNTERPOINT

## Should Texas Make Reentry Easier?

**THE ISSUE**   Most individuals convicted of a crime believe that when they have finished serving their sentences, they will have paid their debt to society. Yet, conviction as a felon is a lifelong sentence. Some argue that this "invisible punishment" is unfair. Others believe that a prison sentence is only part of the punishment for someone who violates the law.

### Arguments For Modifying Current Laws

1. These individuals have paid their debt to society, especially those who committed nonviolent crimes, and should have the opportunity to be reintegrated fully into society.
2. Because members of historical minority groups and the poor are overrepresented in prisons, laws that make reentry more difficult keep them at the margins of society in disproportionate numbers.
3. One of the best predictors of recidivism is the inability of an individual to find work. Limiting meaningful employment opportunities increases the likelihood that convicted felons will commit other crimes.
4. Not only do convicted felons suffer when employment, housing, and welfare benefits are unavailable, so do family members, including children.

"[T]hese punishments have become instruments of 'social exclusion,' they create a permanent diminution in social status of convicted offenders, a distancing between 'us' and 'them.'"

—Jeffrey Travis, "Invisible Punishment: An Instrument of Social Exclusion"

### Arguments Against Modifying Current Laws

1. These individuals have chosen to violate the social contract by violating the law and therefore should suffer the consequences of their actions.
2. The lifelong stigma of being a convicted felon will deter others from similar conduct.
3. Members of society should have the right to avoid contact with someone who has engaged in felony criminal behavior.
4. Texas has sufficient social service agencies, parole officers, and state agencies to help these individuals find jobs and make a successful reentry into society.

"[E]very malefactor, by attacking the social right, becomes by his crimes a rebel and a traitor to his country, by violating its laws, he ceases to be a member of it, and, in fact, wages war upon it.... The proceedings and the judgment announced in consequence are the proofs and the declaration that he has broken the social treaty, and, consequently, that he is no longer a member of the State."

—Jean Jacques Rousseau, *The Social Consequence or Principal of Political Right*

Convicted felons face other issues as well: difficulty in obtaining housing, since both public housing authorities and private owners can bar convicted felons; possible domestic upheaval, as a felony conviction is grounds for divorce; and, for sex offenders, forced registration and public disclosure of their offenses for the rest of their lives. As tens of thousands of released inmates return to society each year, researchers and public officials express increasing concern about these barriers to reentry and their impact on recidivism rates.[17]

Although convicted felons may have these disabilities removed if they receive a pardon from the governor of Texas, this action is highly unlikely. The governor can grant a pardon only if it is recommended by the Board of Pardons and Paroles. In 2005, Governor Rick Perry granted 14 pardons, two for felony convictions that were disproved by subsequent DNA evidence and the remaining 12 to individuals convicted of minor offenses in their teens and early twenties, ten or more years before being pardoned.

---

**Learning Check 10.4**        **(Answers on p. 429)**

1. What is the punishment for a capital felon who does not receive the death penalty?
2. True or False: All prisons and jails in Texas are operated by the state or local governments.
3. What are the two most common problems for the majority of Texas's prison inmates?

---

# ⭐Juvenile Justice

Texas's juvenile justice system clearly distinguishes between youthful pranks and violent, predatory behavior. Generally, young Texans at least 10 years of age but under age 17 are treated as "delinquent children" when they commit acts that would be classified as felonies or misdemeanors if committed by adults. Children are designated as "status offenders" if they commit noncriminal acts such as running away from home, failing to attend school, or violating a curfew established by a city or county.

## State and Local Agencies

Under Texas law, each county is required to have a juvenile probation board that designates one or more juvenile judges, appoints a chief juvenile probation officer, and makes policies carried out by a juvenile probation department. Overseeing these county departments is the Texas Juvenile Probation Commission (TJPC). Its nine members are appointed by the governor with the consent of the Senate. The TJPC allocates state funds to county juvenile boards, trains and certifies juvenile probation officers, and sets standards for local detention and probation facilities. Supervising the rehabilitation and training of delinquent youths is the responsibility of the Texas Youth Commission (TYC). The governor appoints the seven members of the TYC with Senate approval.

## Procedures and Institutions

Although juvenile offenders are arrested by the same law enforcement officers who deal with adult criminals, they are detained in separate facilities. Some, along with their parents, are merely warned by police officers not to engage in delinquent behavior. Many are held in short-term residential detention facilities until they are released to their families pending a hearing on the charges against them. Others remain in detention until disposition of the case against them, if a judge determines there is a need to continue holding them.

Counseling and probation are the most widely used procedures for dealing with juvenile offenders. An increasing number of delinquent youths, however, are placed on probation in local boot camps and residential treatment centers or committed to facilities operated by the TYC. An arresting officer has the discretion to release a child or refer the case to a local juvenile probation department. Other referrals come from public schools, victims, and parents. More than 100,000 Texas youths enter the state's juvenile justice system each year.

**Court Procedures**    Trials in juvenile courts are termed *adjudication hearings.* Juvenile courts are civil rather than criminal courts; therefore, any appeal of a court's ruling will be made to the appropriate court of appeals. Ultimately a few cases are appealed to the Texas Supreme Court.

A Juvenile Determinate Sentencing Law covers about twenty serious offenses. Under this sentencing provision, juveniles who commit offenses such as capital murder and aggravated sexual assault can be transferred to adult prisons when they reach age 18 and held there for as long as 40 years. In addition, some juveniles who commit violent offenses are ordered to stand trial as adults and their cases are transferred to a district court. In 2003, the most recent year for which information is available, courts certified 139 juveniles to stand trial as adults, most frequently for the crimes of murder or robbery. Any incarceration is in the state's adult prison system.

**Texas Youth Commission Facilities**    Juveniles who violate terms of probation or are found delinquent for a serious criminal offense may be confined to TYC training schools and boot camps located across the state. As of year end 2004, almost 5,000 youths were incarcerated in these facilities for an average of 21 months. TYC programs focus on behavioral changes in youths prone to criminal activity. Efforts are targeted to specific types of offenses or needs.

The likelihood that juvenile felony offenders will return to confinement within three years of release has declined in recent years, but remains at approximately 50 percent. Programs achieving the greatest success in diverting youth from continued criminal behavior are those addressing sexual behavior and mental health. State officials argue that the greater length of these treatment periods may be a strong contributing factor to their success.[18]

Education is a critical element in the successful reintegration of youthful offenders. All TYC-operated units provide academic instruction with teachers employed by the agency. According to assessment tests administered when juveniles are committed to TYC, most individuals are four to five years below grade level. Nonetheless, high-school-age inmates must develop graduation plans and are placed in courses tailored to their learning needs.

The commission also operates halfway houses for juveniles who need minimum supervision. These facilities partner directly with local school districts to furnish instruction. They contract with privately operated, community-based residential programs that provide vocational training, drug treatment, General Equivalency Diploma (GED) preparation, and other services.

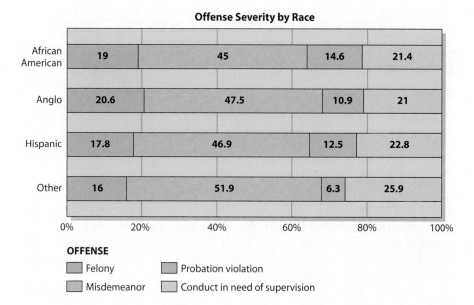

**Offense Severity by Race**

| | Felony | Misdemeanor | Probation violation | Conduct in need of supervision |
|---|---|---|---|---|
| African American | 19 | 45 | 14.6 | 21.4 |
| Anglo | 20.6 | 47.5 | 10.9 | 21 |
| Hispanic | 17.8 | 46.9 | 12.5 | 22.8 |
| Other | 16 | 51.9 | 6.3 | 25.9 |

**OFFENSE**
- Felony
- Misdemeanor
- Probation violation
- Conduct in need of supervision

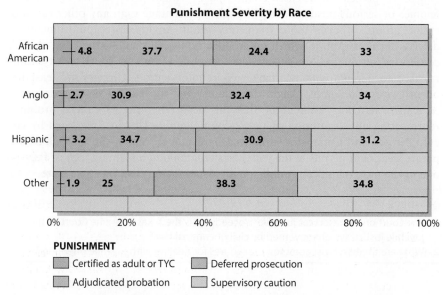

**Punishment Severity by Race**

| | Certified as adult or TYC | Adjudicated probation | Deferred prosecution | Supervisory caution |
|---|---|---|---|---|
| African American | 4.8 | 37.7 | 24.4 | 33 |
| Anglo | 2.7 | 30.9 | 32.4 | 34 |
| Hispanic | 3.2 | 34.7 | 30.9 | 31.2 |
| Other | 1.9 | 25 | 38.3 | 34.8 |

**PUNISHMENT**
- Certified as adult or TYC
- Adjudicated probation
- Deferred prosecution
- Supervisory caution

*Figure 10.4* Comparison of Offenses and Punishment by Race (2003)   *Source:* Calculated from Texas Juvenile Probation Commission, *The State of Juvenile Probation Activity in Texas–2003* (Austin: Texas Juvenile Probation Commission, August 2005).

*Table 10.6*    Comparison of Texas's Juvenile Population (ages 10–16) with Juvenile Offenses by Race and Ethnicity (2003)

| Race or Ethnicity | % of Juvenile Population | % of Juvenile Offenses |
|---|---|---|
| African American | 13.4 | 22.6 |
| Anglo | 42.9 | 31.8 |
| Hispanic | 40.5 | 44.5 |
| Other | 3.2 | 1.0 |

*Source:* Texas Juvenile Probation Commission, *The State of Juvenile Probation Activity in Texas, 2003* (Austin: Texas Juvenile Probation Commission, August 2005).

**Racial and Ethnic Issues**    As in the state's adult criminal justice system, a disproportionate number of African American and Hispanic youth are represented in the juvenile justice system. Table 10.6 compares the percentage of the total juvenile population of each racial or ethnic group with the number of juvenile offenses in each demographic category.

Once in the justice system, members of historical minority groups are likelier to receive more severe punishment, as illustrated in Figure 10.4. Although almost 70 percent of offenses committed by Anglo juveniles are classified as felonies or serious misdemeanors, a higher percentage than any other racial or ethnic group, officials more frequently grant Anglos lesser punishments of deferred prosecution, in which no adjudication occurs unless the child violates conditions of release, or supervisory caution, in which youth are typically released to parents with no further court intervention. Charges are least frequently dropped against Anglo defendants, and most often dismissed against African Americans. Some argue that this occurrence suggests racial profiling, representing an assumption of wrongdoing against African Americans by law enforcement authorities not supported by evidence. Similar allegations of disparate treatment permeate the justice system, making a seeming lack of fairness one of the most significant public policy issues facing the Lone Star State.

**Learning Check 10.5**    **(Answers on p. 429)**

1. The court of last resort for juvenile proceedings is the Texas Supreme Court. Is the juvenile justice system governed by civil or criminal law?
2. What are the two most common procedures for dealing with juvenile offenders?

## ★ Problems and Reforms: Implications for Public Policy

Throughout the late twentieth century, Texas's criminal justice system experienced a series of crises resulting from an increase in violent crimes and stiffer sentences for criminals. The state's civil justice system dealt with similar pressures from litigants using courts to resolve their disputes. The legislature responded (often slowly) with authorizations for more courts and judges and alternative means to resolve lawsuits. Legislators, however, refused to propose changes to judicial selection procedures. While these nineteenth- and twentieth-century problems have not yet been fully addressed, the legislature must also deal with the twenty-first century issues of technology and changing demographics. A special Advisory Commission on Criminal Justice appointed by Governor Rick Perry in 2005 recommended, among other matters, that the state improve access to DNA testing for accused criminals, establish a public defender system to represent capital felony defendants, and assess the accuracy of eyewitness testimony.

### Coping with Crowded Dockets

In recent years, the state has adopted several methods to encourage litigants to resolve their disputes without going to trial. To reduce workloads, speed the handling of civil disputes, and cut legal costs, each county is authorized to set up a system for **alternative dispute resolution (ADR)**. Two frequently used ADR procedures are mediation (in which an impartial mediator facilitates communication between the parties in a conference designed to allow them to resolve their dispute) and arbitration (in which impartial arbiters hear both sides and make an award that is binding or nonbinding, depending on the parties' previous agreement).

Collaborative divorce is another method for resolving disputes outside the courtroom. The couple and their attorneys agree in writing to settle all disputes in a nonadversarial manner. If either spouse elects to litigate after the process begins, both attorneys must resign.

### Judicial Selection

Texas remains one of only four states in which all judges (except municipal court judges) are chosen in partisan elections and then reelected through the same procedure. The other three states are Alabama, Louisiana, and West Virginia.[19] Critics of this method argue that requiring candidates to run from particular political parties and expensive election campaigns, financed largely by lawyers and special-interest groups, taint the justice system. They tend to favor a merit selection model such as those used in Missouri and most other states. The **Missouri Plan** features a nominating commission that recommends a panel of names to the governor whenever a judicial vacancy is to be filled. The appointee then serves for a year or so before the voters decide, based on his or her judicial performance record, whether to give the new judge a full term or allow the nominating commission and the governor to make another appointment on a similar trial basis. Others favor an **appointment-retention system** for all courts of record, in which the governor appoints a judge and the voters determine whether to retain the appointee. Reform proposals have consistently failed in the Texas Legislature.

Problems of perceived bias in judges' political partisanship became a central focus in Congressman Tom DeLay's pre-trial proceedings regarding campaign contribution law violations (more fully discussed in Selected Reading 7.2,

**alternative dispute resolution (ADR)** Use of mediation, conciliation, or arbitration to resolve disputes among individuals without resorting to a regular court trial.

**Missouri Plan** A judicial selection process in which a commission recommends a panel of names to the governor, followed by a one-year or so appointment before voters determine whether the judge will be retained for a full term.

**appointment-retention system** A merit plan for judicial selection, whereby the governor appoints to fill a court vacancy for a trial period after which the judge must win a full term in an uncontested popular election.

"Redistricting and Electoral Results in Texas in the Twenty-first Century"). The first judge scheduled to try the case, Judge Bob Perkins, a Democrat, was removed because of donations to MoveOn.org, a liberal political organization, and Democratic presidential candidate John Kerry. The judge who removed Perkins, Judge B. B. Shcraub, was not allowed to appoint a replacement because he had donated to Republican candidates. Finally, Chief Justice Wallace Jefferson named retired judge Pat Priest to preside over the trial. In the process, it was disclosed that Justice Jefferson shared a campaign treasurer and a consultant with Texans for a Republican Majority, a political action committee connected to DeLay. Information about Judge Priest indicated he had made small donations to Democratic candidates.[20] Although the charges and countercharges regarding who would serve as a judge in this case attracted brief attention, it is unlikely that Texas will change the manner in which judges are selected.

### Technology

From Internet divorces to video cameras at stoplights, technology now touches every aspect of the civil and criminal justice systems. Evidence found only in science fiction a few years ago is now commonplace in Texas courtrooms. One subject that has gained significant attention in recent years is DNA evidence. The use of biological evidence in criminal cases became increasingly important after geneticist Alec Jeffreys invented DNA testing in the early 1980s.[21] This testing can help identify a suspect, as well as exonerate the innocent. The 79th Legislature authorized creation of a DNA database in the state, and TDCJ and TYC are now required to collect DNA samples of all inmates convicted of a felony. Crime-scene evidence can then be tested against database samples to seek DNA matches with previously convicted felons. Postconviction analysis may be available for certain inmates tried and convicted before the development of DNA testing. It is required for cases in which these test results could make a difference in establishing innocence.

Although DNA evidence has proved almost conclusive in establishing the guilt or innocence of accused criminals, high levels of police and juror confidence in the accuracy of biological test results can be devastating if that trust is misplaced. In 2003, for example, complaints surfaced about the quality of DNA testing conducted by the Houston Police Department's crime lab. Several inmates were released after retesting verified that their DNA did not match crime scene DNA. State law now requires all public crime labs to be accredited and DNA evidence to be held for retesting.

As further protection against the miscarriages of justice that resulted from deficiencies in crime labs across the state, the 79th Legislature created the Texas Forensic Science Commission to investigate charges of negligence and misconduct at crime lab facilities. Members are appointed by the governor, lieutenant governor, and attorney general. The 11-member commission includes attorneys, scientists, and professors from across the state. Confidence in the judicial system depends on evidence that can be relied on to convict the guilty and exonerate the innocent.

## Exoneration Issues

The Fourteenth Amendment to the U.S. Constitution guarantees that no state can "deprive any person of life, liberty, or property without due process of law." Texas's court system and the many rules and procedures that must be followed in criminal cases are specifically designed to protect people from losing their lives, liberty, or property from arbitrary acts by the government. And yet, despite all of these protections, innocent people continue to lose their liberty, their property, and perhaps even their lives. According to the Innocence Project at New York's Cardozo Law School, 187 inmates across the nation were exonerated between 1989 and November 2006 after DNA analysis proved their innocence. Twenty-one of those individuals were from Texas. (For the story of the exoneration of one such individual, see this chapter's Selected Reading, 10.2, "Mumphrey Attorney Called Shining Star in Legal Arena.")

Although DNA test results have contributed to the release of innocent prisoners, this evidence is not the panacea that will eliminate all wrongful imprisonment. In fact, Ruben Cantu, whose story opened this chapter, had no DNA evidence to exonerate him. He was, however, the victim of the most common reason people are wrongfully convicted, according to case histories collected by the Innocence Project: mistaken eyewitness identification, another form of evidence jurors consider highly reliable. Research now indicates several flaws in this type of evidence:

- Likelihood of individuals overlooking differences in facial features of people of a different race from them
- Ability of police to sway an eyewitness in the way they structure line-ups and photo identifications (For example, police officers showed Ruben Cantu's photo to Juan Moreno on three separate occasions before Moreno identified him.)
- Possibility of transference in which someone seen by a victim in another setting is misidentified as the criminal
- Interference with the ability to see detailed features of an attacker, such as a witness's visual impairment or quality of light
- Alteration of a victim's recall of events and facial features due to the stress of the experience[22]

Although most people convicted of a crime are guilty, the probability of exoneration is remote even for the innocent. The political reality is that to obtain a pardon and be fully exonerated requires the joinder of district attorneys, judges, the Board of Pardons and Paroles, and the governor. As Governor Perry noted in granting two felony pardons in 2005:

> I believe that a full pardon for innocence must be supported by strong evidence, such as forensic DNA tests. In both of these cases, new DNA evidence proves that these men are innocent. The recommendations of the district attorney, judges, the Dallas County Sheriff, the Dallas Chief of Police and the Board of Pardons and Paroles also were very important factors in my decision.[23]

The state of Texas compensates individuals wrongfully incarcerated. Someone found innocent after being imprisoned is entitled to $25,000 for each year he or she was wrongly incarcerated up to a total of $500,000. Programs at several of the state's law schools including Texas Tech, the University of Houston, and the University of Texas, engage law students in researching and assisting those convicted of crimes who present arguments supporting their claims of innocence. These efforts and continued technological advances will likely result in the release of more innocent prisoners.

### Racial and Ethnic Diversity

Changes in the state's demography have begun to affect its justice system. The underrepresentation of African Americans and Hispanics in elected and appointed leadership positions is matched by their overrepresentation in the criminal justice system. If many Texans believe the laws are unfair or unfairly applied, as noted at the beginning of this chapter, the justice system is jeopardized. In this environment, if the race or ethnicity of those enforcing the law is consistently different from those against whom the law is enforced, the system has even less credibility.

The Texas Criminal Justice Reform Coalition, the American Civil Liberties Union of Texas, the NAACP of Texas, and Texas LULAC reached similar conclusions when they commissioned research on traffic stops and searches.[24] The studies found racial profiling present in approximately 85 percent of Texas law enforcement agencies and an increasing trend in the practice of stopping and searching African Americans and Hispanics at significantly higher rates than Anglos. Interestingly, in many urban jurisdictions, searches of Anglos were more likely to reveal incriminating evidence than searches of any other group. Instances of racial and ethnic bias are the subject of growing concern as Texas has evolved into a state in which two historical minority groups, African Americans and Latinos, will soon comprise the majority population, and the state's Latino population continues movement toward becoming the majority.

---

**Learning Check 10.6**    **(Answers on p. 429)**

1. True or False: Test results from any crime lab are admissible in Texas courts.
2. How much does the State of Texas compensate someone who was wrongfully incarcerated?
3. Which ethnic or racial group is most likely to have incriminating evidence when searched during a traffic stop in Texas?

---

## ⭐Looking Ahead

The Texas legal system is indeed confusing. From sorting out overlapping court jurisdictions to decide which court should hear a case to identifying elected judges and justices—the system appears to be shrouded in mystery and anonymity. Often understood only by those who use the system daily—Texas lawyers—decisions of criminal and civil court judges affect every Texan. It is therefore critical that Texans understand this complex system. Whether the state's residents consider the justice system as fair and responsive or biased and closed depends in part on their knowledge of it. This understanding, plus changing demographics, rising costs, and greater reliance on science and technology, will influence not only the Lone Star State's justice system but also the way politics is practiced in Texas in the twenty-first century.

Costs of maintaining a justice system continue to rise. These increases affect the amount of money state government needs and how it budgets and spends those funds. We consider services, spending, and other financial processes in the chapter "Finance and Fiscal Policy."

## ★ Chapter Summary

- Public confidence in the judicial system is critical to its effectiveness.
- Texas state law includes both civil law and criminal law. Texas courts and judges apply and interpret the state's constitution, its statutes, and the common law.
- Both constitutional and statutory laws have been used to create the state's court system. Courts may have original or appellate jurisdiction, or both. Texas has local, county, trial, and appellate courts. Judges and lawyers are subject to regulation and discipline.
- There are two types of juries: grand juries (which determine if adequate cause exists to bring a defendant to trial in a criminal case) and petit juries (which determine the facts in criminal and civil cases).
- The civil justice system includes contract cases, tort cases, family law matters, and juvenile justice cases. Significant reforms have occurred in recent years in tort law, as the Texas Legislature has limited the amount of punitive and noneconomic damages in tort cases.
- Criminal law regulates many types of behavior. Less severe crimes are classified as Class A, B, or C misdemeanors and result in fines or detention in a county jail. More severe crimes include state jail felonies; first-, second-, and third-degree felonies; and capital felonies.
- More than 650,000 Texans were under the supervision of a state judicial or correctional officer in 2004.
- The juvenile justice system is administered through the Texas Family Code. Youths between the ages of 10 and 16 are subject to its provisions. In recent years, more juveniles have been placed in detention facilities operated by the Texas Youth Commission.
- Issues that remain problematic for the Texas justice system include crowded court dockets, the popular, partisan election of judges, technological and scientific advances, the probable innocence of some inmates (including several who were executed), and possible racial and ethnic bias in the justice system.

## Key Terms

- civil law, *p. 385*
- criminal law, *p. 385*
- misdemeanor, *p. 385*
- felony, *p. 385*
- jurisdiction, *p. 385*
- original jurisdiction, *p. 385*
- appellate jurisdiction, *p. 385*
- exclusive jurisdiction, *p. 386*
- concurrent jurisdiction, *p. 386*
- court of record, *p. 390*
- small-claims court, *p. 391*
- probate, *p. 391*
- contingency fee, *p. 397*
- grand jury, *p. 399*
- petit jury, *p. 399*

- venire, *p. 400*
- voir dire, *p. 401*
- tort, *p. 403*
- plaintiff, *p. 403*
- defendant, *p. 403*
- special issues, *p. 405*
- verdict, *p. 405*
- judgment, *p. 405*
- graded penalties, *p. 405*
- capital felony, *p. 405*
- recidivism, *p. 411*
- alternative dispute resolution (ADR), *p. 423*
- Missouri Plan, *p. 423*
- appointment-retention system, *p. 423*

## Learning Check Answers

### 10.1

1. False. Judges of some municipal courts, justices of the peace, and county judges need not be lawyers.
2. Jurisdiction means that the court must have the authority to hear a particular kind of case. Jurisdiction may be granted in the Constitution or in the statute creating a court.
3. False. Texas has a bifurcated court system. The Court of Criminal Appeals has jurisdiction over criminal appeals and the Supreme Court of Texas decides civil appeals.

### 10.2

1. False. A grand jury indictment means sufficient evidence exists for the case to proceed to trial. An indicted defendant might then be found guilty or not guilty by a trial jury.
2. No. Anyone convicted of a felony or under indictment or other legal accusation of theft or a felony is barred from serving as a juror in any court.
3. Jurors receive $6 for the first day of service and $40 for all subsequent days of service.

### 10.3

1. The parties to a civil lawsuit are the plaintiff, who is the injured party bringing the lawsuit, and the defendant, who is the person being sued.
2. Felonies are the most serious crimes and are punishable with imprisonment in state penitentiary.
3. A capital felony for which the defendant received the death penalty is appealed to the Court of Criminal Appeals.

**10.4**

1. A capital felon who does not receive the death penalty gets life without parole.
2. False. Many prisons and jails in Texas are operated by private companies.
3. The two most common problems for the majority of Texas's prison inmates are a lack of education and substance abuse.

**10.5**

1. The juvenile justice system is governed by civil law.
2. Counseling and probation are the two most common procedures used with juvenile offenders.

**10.6**

1. False. Only evidence from certified labs approved by the Director of the Texas Department of Public Safety is admissible in Texas courts.
2. Someone who was wrongfully incarcerated receives $25,000 per year (up to a total of $500,000) from the State of Texas.
3. Anglos are most likely to have incriminating evidence when searched during a traffic stop in Texas.

## Discussion Questions

1. Is Texas's justice system fair?
2. What are the advantages and disadvantages of Texas's court system?
3. What can be done to make the legal system accessible to more Texans?
4. What are the advantages and disadvantages of the death penalty?
5. What are possible reforms to the method of selecting judges in Texas?

## Internet Resources

Death Penalty Institute: **www.deathpenaltyinfo.org**
Innocence Project: **www.innocenceproject.org**
State Bar of Texas: **www.texasbar.com**
State Commission on Judicial Conduct: **www.scjc.state.tx.us**
Texas Law Help: **www.texaslawhelp.org**
Texans for Public Justice: **www.tpj.org**
Texas Department of Criminal Justice: **www.tdcj.state.tx.us**
Texas Department of Public Safety: **www.txdps.state.tx.us**
Texas Judiciary Online: **www.courts.state.tx.us**
Texas Youth Commission: **www.tyc.state.tx.us**

## ★ Notes

1. "George W. Bush on Crime," *Issues 2000*, at **www.issues2000.org/Celeb/ George_W_Bush_Crime.htm**.

2. American Bar Association, Commission on the 21st Century Judiciary, *Justice in Jeopardy: Report of the American Bar Association Commission on the 21st Century Judiciary* (2003) at **www.manningproductions.com/ABA263/ finalreport.pdf**, i. Also, see Nate Blakeslee, *Tulia: Race, Cocaine, and Corruption in a Small Texas Town* (New York: Public Affairs, 2005). For a discussion of the roles of political empowerment and political reality in shaping attitudes, see L. Marvin Overby, Robert D. Brown, Charles E. Smith, Jr., and John W. Winkle, III, "Race, Political Empowerment, and Minority Perceptions of Judicial Fairness," *Southwestern Social Science Quarterly* 86, no. 2 (2005): 444–462.

3. Of special interest to young college and university students is lawyer L. Jean Wallace's *What Every 18-Year-Old Needs to Know About Texas Law*, rev. ed. (Austin: University of Texas Press, 1997). Another easy-to-understand book that explains Texas law is Richard Alderman, *Know Your Rights: Answers to Texans' Everyday Legal Questions*, 7th ed. (Dallas: Taylor, 2005). For a discussion of criminal law, see Ken Anderson, *Crime in Texas: Your Complete Guide to the Criminal Justice System*, rev. ed. (Austin: University of Texas Press, 2005).

4. Annual statistics and other information on the Texas judicial system are available from the Texas Judicial Council and the Office of Court Administration.

5. Brenda Sapino Jeffreys, "Thompson & Knight Raises Associates' Base Salaries," Law.Com, 9 August 2004, available at **www.law.com/jsp/article.jsp? id=1090180304226**.

6. The State Bar of Texas web site includes a how-to manual for prosecuting a claim in small-claims court (*How to Sue in Small Claims Court*). Available at **www.texasbar.com/Template.cfm?Section=Legal_and_Judicial_System& CONTENTID=3869&TEMPLATE=/ContentManagement/ContentDisplay.cfm**.

7. Senate Criminal Justice Committee, *Interim Report to the 79th Legislature* (December 2004), 25–27. Of the three counties studied (Dallas, Jefferson, and Travis), Dallas County drug court graduates fared the best with a 10.2 percent recidivism rate compared to a 51 percent re-arrest rate for those not going through this process.

8. For an excellent discussion of the development and adoption of the constitutional amendment granting courts of civil appeals criminal appellate jurisdiction, see former Chief Justice Joe R. Greenhill, "The Constitutional Amendment Giving Criminal Jurisdiction to the Texas Courts of Civil Appeals and Recognizing the Inherent Power of the Texas Supreme Court," *Texas Tech Law Review* 33, no. 2 (2002): 377–404.

9. Chief Justice Wallace B. Jefferson, "The State of the Judiciary in Texas," February 23, 2005, available at **www.supreme.courts.state.tx.us/advisories/ STATE_OF_THE_JUDICIARY_2005.pdf**.

10. Legal Services Corporation, *Documenting the Justice Gap in America: The Current Unmet Civil Legal Needs of Low-Income Americans* (Washington, D.C.: Legal Services Corporation, September 2005.)

11. "Supreme Court of Texas Revisits Status of Legal Services," *Texas Bar Journal*, 67, no. 9 (2004), 736–737.

12. Laylan Copelin, "Prosecutor Reveals Third Grand Jury Had Refused DeLay Indictment," *Austin American-Statesman*, October 4, 2005.

13. "Governor's Day in Court," *New York Times*, August 29, 2002. The defendant, Stenson Hutcherson, was still convicted.

14. Andrew Tilghman, "Turnout Skews Juries' Makeup," *Houston Chronicle*, March 6, 2005.

15. For a discussion of the history of tort reform in Texas, see Mimi Swartz, "Hurt? Injured? Need a Lawyer? Too Bad!" *Texas Monthly* (November 2005), 164–169, 218–234, 254–258.

16. Steve McVicker and Bill Murphy, "County Jail Conditions Condemned in Report," *Houston Chronicle*, July 16, 2005.

17. Ann del Llano and Ana Yàñez-Correa, *Proven Pro-family Criminal Justice Policies That Save Families, Save Tax Payers' Money, and Improve the Safety of Our Community* (Austin: Texas League of United Latin American Citizens, August 2004) at **www.txlulac.org**.

18. Texas Youth Commission, "2004 Review of Agency Treatment Effectiveness," at **www.tyc.state.tx.us/research/TxmtEffect/index.html**.

19. American Judicature Society, *Judicial Selection in the States: Appellate and General Jurisdiction Courts* (Des Moines, IA: American Judicature Society, 2004). For a discussion of issues related to an elected judiciary, see Kyle Cheek and Anthony Champagne, *Judicial Politics in Texas: Partisanship, Money, and Politics in State Courts* (New York: Peter Lang, 2005).

20. Laylan Copelin, "In Rapid Motions Judge Picked for DeLay Case," *Austin American-Statesman*, November 4, 2005; Ralph Blumenthal, "DeLay Case Turns Spotlight on Texas Judicial System," *New York Times*, November 8, 2005.

21. Howard Safir and Peter Reinharz, "DNA Testing: The Next Big Crime-Busting Breakthrough," *City Journal* 10, no. 1 (Winter 2000): 49–57 at **www.city-journal.org/html/issue10_1.html**.

22. Colin G. Tredoux, Christian A. Meisner, Roy S. Malpass, and Laura A. Zimmerman, "Eyewitness Identification," *Encyclopedia of Applied Psychology*, vol. 1, ed. C. D. Spielberg (New York: Elsevier Academic Press, 2004), 875–887.

23. Office of the Governor, "Gov. Rick Perry Grants Two Pardons for Innocence," December 22, 2005 at **www.governor.state.tx.us/divisions/press/pressreleases/PressRelease.2005-12-22.5914**.

24. Steward Research Group, "Racial Profiling: Texas Traffic Stops and Searches" (Austin: Texas Criminal Justice Reform Coalition, February 2004) at **www.protex.org/criminaljustice**; and Dwight Steward and Molly Totman, "Racial Profiling: Don't Mind if I Take a Look, Do Ya?: An Examination of Consent Searches and Contraband Hit Rates at Texas Traffic Stops" (Austin: Texas Criminal Justice Coalition, February 2005) at **www.criminaljusticecoalition.org**.

## Selected Readings

# 10.1  Guidelines for Practicing Gender Neutral Courtroom Procedures[*]

### The Supreme Court of Texas Gender Bias Task Force

*The Texas Supreme Court created the Gender Bias Task Force to identify and eliminate gender-biased treatment in Texas courtrooms. In 2004, the task force released its* Guidelines for Practicing Gender Neutral Courtroom Procedures *and called on Texas lawyers and judges to implement its recommendations. The following excerpt suggests ways to reach this goal.*

## Some Suggested Ways to Avoid Gender Bias

1. **Address all persons in the courtroom by last names and appropriate title.**

■ Counsel or attorney
■ Mr./Ms. (unless Miss or Mrs. is requested)
■ Dr. or Officer or Representative/Senator
■ Jurors or Juror
■ Presiding Juror

To avoid differential treatment or even the appearance of differential treatment, address both women and men in the same formal or professional manner. Always use a consistent form of address such as "Attorney X" and "Attorney Y." In private conversation or social settings, first names and other informal address may convey a friendly or casual attitude; in the public settings where courthouse business takes place they suggest a lack of respect.

2. **Address mixed groups of women and men with gender neutral or gender inclusive terms.**

■ Colleagues
■ Members of the jury
■ Members of the bar
■ Counselors
■ Ladies and gentlemen

Conversation that creates an exclusively masculine or feminine atmosphere should be avoided so that everyone is included in the justice system.

3. **Use gender neutral language in all court correspondence and jury instructions.**

Use "Dear Counsel" when not using the individual's name and where appropriate include reference to he/she, him/her. The plural (witnesses/they) is helpful.

4. **Avoid terms of endearment and diminutive terms in courthouse interaction, as such terms imply a lower status.**

■ honey, sweetie, dear, doll, babe
■ little lady, pretty girl, young lady, lady lawyer (in reference to adult women)
■ boy, son (in reference to adult men)

These terms can demean or offend even if the speaker does not intend to do so. Courtroom protocol requires the highest degree of professionalism and courtesy.

5. **Avoid comments on or references to physical appearance, such as:**

■ body parts
■ pregnancy
■ dress style
■ hair style

Comments on physical appearance can be seen as demeaning and put people at a disadvantage by drawing attention to their gender rather than the reason for their presence in the court. Comments appropriate in a social setting often are inappropriate in a professional setting. For example, complimenting a female attorney on her appearance or drawing attention to her pregnancy while she is conducting business may undermine how others perceive her. Avoid using opposing counsel's gender as a litigation tactic either inside or outside the courtroom.

---

[*]Reprinted by permission of the State Bar of Texas. Online at **www.supreme.courts.state.tx.us/rules/GenderNeutralCourtroomProcedures-NoCovers.pdf**.

6. **Jokes and remarks with sexual content, or jokes and remarks that play on sexual stereotypes, are out of place in the courthouse setting.**

Everyone in the courthouse must protect the dignity and integrity of the court and show respect for every other person. Sexual, racial, and ethnic jokes and remarks are improper in the courthouse and in the administration of justice.

7. **Avoid comments, gestures, and touching that can offend others or make them uncomfortable.**

Because touching people may offend them, it should be avoided. They may not feel free to interrupt or complain, especially when the person doing the touching is in a position of authority, such as a supervisor touching an employee or a court employee touching a litigant, witness, juror, or attorney.

Sexually suggestive comments, gestures, and touching, as well as sexual advances, undermine the dignity of the court. Such acts may constitute sexual harassment, which is prohibited by law and subject to sanction pursuant to court policy. Harassment to provoke an emotional response is inappropriate under all circumstances.

8. **Treat women and men with dignity, respect, and attentiveness, mindful of their professional accomplishments.**

The Task Force found that women lawyers are much more likely than men to be asked if they are attorneys. Do not inquire of a woman regarding her professional status when you would not ask the same question of a man. To avoid this, use a question that applies to everyone, such as, "**Will all attorneys please identify themselves to the court?**"

---

## 10.2 Mumphrey Attorney Called Shining Star in Legal Arena[*]

### *Renée C. Lee*

*Obtaining an exoneration for someone convicted of a violent sexual assault is a difficult process. Yet, attorney Eric J. Davis did just that in his representation of Arthur Mumphrey, who was released from prison in 2006. The following article about Davis provides insight into his dedication and effectiveness.*

In his 12 years as a criminal law attorney, Eric J. Davis has had many courtroom successes, but none compares to his latest victory—getting an innocent man out of prison. The Houston attorney became the center of national headlines last month [January 2006] when his client, Arthur Mumphrey, gained his freedom after spending 18 years in prison on a sexual assault conviction. DNA evidence recovered with Davis' persistence and new testing not available when the crime occurred in February 1986 cleared Mumphrey as one of two attackers of a 13-year-old girl.

Those who know Davis or have worked with him say it comes as no surprise that he prevailed in the challenging

case. He's a man who believes in defending people's rights and who will search under every stone when trying a case, they said. Fellow attorneys see him as a shining star in the legal arena, destined to become a judge someday. His clients often speak of him as the attorney who cares about those he represents.

Davis, reserved and soft-spoken outside the courtroom, takes the compliments in stride. He says his motivation is simply to ensure that justice is done. "I question the government," Davis said. "I think we as a people should. Our government is based on people who asked questions and questioned authority. Part of my job is not to go with the status quo."

A licensed attorney since 1994, Davis, 36, says he has tried about 70 cases as both a former prosecutor and a private attorney. Some of his notable victories include:

- A federal religious discrimination suit against the Texas Department of Criminal Justice in 2002. The jury awarded his client, a prison employee and

*From the *Houston Chronicle*, February 8, 2006, B1. Copyright 2006 Houston Chronicle Publishing Company. Reprinted with permission. All rights reserved. Renée C. Lee is a *Houston Chronicle* reporter.

*Attorney Eric. J. Davis looks on as his exonerated client, Arthur Mumphrey, meets the press. (James Nielsen)*

Jehovah's Witness, $500,000 in damages plus $44,000 in attorney fees. The employee claimed she suffered retaliation after she complained about a warden requiring employees to pray with him during monthly meetings.

- A 2004 criminal case in which a prison guard faced two cases of sexual assault against two inmates. The jury found the prison guard not guilty in both cases in which the state introduced two sets of DNA evidence and the testimony of the two alleged victims.

- And a case that resulted in the removal of Port Arthur Justice of the Peace Thurman Bartie from office, barring him from ever holding a judicial office in Texas. The case was heard before a Review Tribunal in April 2004.

Seana Willing, executive director of the State Commission on Judicial Conduct, recalls how impressed she was with Davis, who served as a special counsel for the commission on the Bartie case. The commission had recommended Bartie's removal because he used obscene language in the courtroom, failed to follow the law, and used corporal punishment in a truancy matter.

"He's not a big-name attorney, but he should be," Willing said of Davis. "You could tell he just had the right stuff as far as his skill, his professionalism and manner in dealing with people. . . . These days you're more often to run into legal terrorists who use the rules to gain advantages that aren't fair. He's not that kind of lawyer."

## Pro Bono Assignment

Bill Torrey, who worked as a staff attorney for the commission at the time of the Bartie case, recommended Davis for the pro bono assignment. He had worked with Davis two years earlier on a drug case in Victoria. He said he admired his integrity and intensity in the courtroom.

"He's very laid-back, but in the courtroom he shifts into overdrive and you can feel it," Torrey said. "You can see the street fighter in him."

On Bartie's appeal, Davis was so effective that the group of appellate judges returned a unanimous affirmation in two hours, Torrey said. "I've never heard of that in my life. It usually takes a month," said Torrey, who has practiced law for 29 years and is now in private practice.

Davis, the youngest of three children, grew up in New Orleans' lower 9th Ward, an area ravaged by Hurricane Katrina. Davis said he always knew he wanted to help people for a living. Just before graduating from high school, he narrowed his career choices to medicine and law. He studied political science and chemistry at Howard University, a historically black college in Washington, D.C., and graduated magna cum laude in 1991. He earned his law degree at Tulane University Law School in New Orleans, where he graduated cum laude in 1994. He landed his first job with the State Attorney's Office in Jacksonville, Fla., prosecuting felony cases for three years.

Rick Alexander, who worked with Davis as a prosecutor, described Davis as "a good student of the court" because he studied the judges' rulings and pet peeves, a habit that helped him win cases against some seasoned lawyers.

Duval County Circuit Judge Jack Schemer presided over many of Davis's cases in the criminal division. He described Davis as confident, even as a novice. He said he recalls Davis being reasonable and fair in his recommendations and plea bargains.

Alexander, now a trial lawyer in Jacksonville, said he'd be surprised if Davis had enemies. "He was tough, but he never railroaded anybody," he said.

## Knack for Negotiating

Looking back, childhood friend Sheldon Jones said Davis always had a knack for negotiating and bartering. "He likes competition, and he loves to argue," said Jones, who still lives in New Orleans. "That's just in him. He's a good-hearted person. He likes for people to be done right by."

Davis moved to Houston in 1997 with his wife, Caria, who had a job offer here. Davis worked full time at defunct Western Indemnity Insurance Co. for three years and tried criminal cases on the side before opening his own firm, Davis and Associates, in 2000. The two-attorney firm handles mostly criminal cases and some labor and employment cases. Much of his business comes from repeat clients and referrals, he said. Mumphrey came to him as a referral from another inmate also serving time at the Rufe Jordan Unit in Pampa.

Davis has never had a case like Mumphrey's. He said he had no reason not to believe Mumphrey's claims of innocence when he reopened the case three years ago. "I just knew it was a case that could be defended," he said. He meticulously researched the case and in early 2005 found what he needed to clear Mumphrey's name—DNA evidence.

## Request for DNA Denied

The challenge came in getting the evidence. Davis said initially officials with the Texas Department of Public Safety crime lab in Houston said the agency had the evidence. Davis quickly filed a motion for DNA testing in early 2005, but a state district judge denied it when the Montgomery County District Attorney's Office said DPS officials told them there was no evidence. Stunned by DPS's reversal, Davis kept pushing for answers until he got one from a lab supervisor.

## Frozen Samples Located

The supervisor wrote a letter dated Aug. 18, 2005, informing Davis that he had located the frozen DNA samples, consisting of a vaginal swab, the victim's panties, and blood and saliva from the victim and Mumphrey. Davis filed another motion in the fall, and the judge granted the testing. Although the system failed Mumphrey, Davis said he does not believe it is broken. "It's easy to judge the whole system on a case-by-case basis, but in a lot of cases it works out OK," he said. "I'd be lying to you if I said it should be scrapped and thrown away."

---

*An extensive bibliography of books and articles for this chapter is posted on Selected Sources for Reading, available online at http://college.hmco.com/PIC/brownPTP13e. For use with any chapter, see Resources for Further Research online at http://college.hmco.com/PIC/brownPTP13e.

# Chapter 11

# Finance and Fiscal Policy

★ **Fiscal Policies**

★ **Revenue Sources**

★ **Budgeting and Fiscal Management**

★ **Future Demands**

©2005 Mike Luckovich. All rights reserved. Published originally in the *Atlanta Journal-Constitution*. Reprint rights granted by Mike Luckovich and Creators Syndicate.

On August 29, 2005, Hurricane Katrina roared ashore just east of New Orleans, Louisiana. Shortly thereafter the levees surrounding the city were breached and overflowing water submerged more than 80 percent of the city. The Mississippi Gulf coast also sustained significant damage. The hurricane and subsequent flooding sent approximately 500,000 storm evacuees to Texas, many planning to stay. The Lone Star State did not need Old Father Time's cautionary reminder not to forget the disaster, as seen in Mike Luckovich's cartoon. Agencies, cities and small towns across the state recalled the hurricane's impact each day as they worked to meet the emergency needs of this new population, much of which went beyond food, water, and shelter.

At the state level, agencies provided many key services:

- The Texas Forest Service distributed water, ice, and food in Louisiana and provided security services support in Houston.

- The staff of the Texas Department of Insurance assisted evacuees in completing insurance claim forms.
- The Texas Department of Criminal Justice provided supervision to evacuated probationers and parolees.
- The Texas Department of Assistive and Rehabilitative Services provided medical equipment and interpreter and other services to disabled evacuees.
- The Texas Department of Family and Protective Services helped unite displaced children with their parents and legal guardians and worked to connect shelter residents with social services.
- The Health and Human Services Commission agencies assisted more than 120,000 families in obtaining food stamps.
- The Texas Workforce Commission helped evacuees complete unemployment insurance claims and secure new jobs.
- The Department of Public Safety offices gave free identification cards to those temporarily displaced to Texas.

In addition, agencies that supply social and emergency services created and staffed phone banks in the initial weeks after the disaster to assist those affected. State web sites furnished information specific to Hurricane Katrina victims. Licensing agencies, such as the State Board of Dental Examiners, Board of Nurse Examiners, Board of Barber Examiners, and the State Bar of Texas, adopted provisional rules so that displaced individuals' requiring a license to practice their trade or profession could do so in Texas.

Local governments also provided aid for the evacuees. Texas public schools absorbed as many as 60,000 additional students. An estimated cost of $7,500 per pupil brought the total expenditure to $450 million during 2005–2006. Cities and counties incurred significant costs in housing, feeding, transporting, and providing security for evacuees. The City of Houston, which housed the most evacuees in the state, estimated its initial cost at $44.5 million.

All of these additional services drew heavily on the human and financial resources of Texas's state and local governments, and many communities looked to the federal government for aid. President George W. Bush declared Texas a federal disaster area on September 2, 2005. The federal

*Hurricane Katrina evacuees obtain assistance from FEMA in Houston. (Ed Edah/FEMA)*

government created a funding pool to cover the required state match for Medicaid funding, and provided immediate promises that school districts would be reimbursed for the costs of temporary classrooms, transportation, and computers for evacuees. Governor Rick Perry assured Texans that the state, its cities, and counties would receive reimbursement for the cost of aid each provided to the evacuees. However, existing federal law did not cover reimbursement for teachers and textbooks for out-of-state students. The Federal Emergency Management Agency (FEMA) could reimburse only amounts spent to save lives, protect public health and safety, and prevent damage to public and private property. The total cost to the state, its counties, and cities remained a concern for many Texans.

Less than a month after Katrina, Hurricane Rita made landfall near Port Arthur, forcing a second evacuation into the interior of the state and causing millions of dollars in damage. Months after these two catastrophic events, many individuals remained dependent on government support. As the Lone Star State and its local governments continued to provide for those in need, the federal government often delivered less than full reimbursement for these services. Texans saw firsthand how difficult it is to balance what we expect of our government with what we are willing to pay. This chapter examines this balance between costs and services and provides an overview of the Lone Star State's fiscal policies, budgeting processes, and most costly public policy areas, all of which will have a significant impact on twenty-first century Texans.

## ⭐ Fiscal Policies

During fall 2005 and spring 2006, Texas's traditional, low-tax approach to **fiscal policy** (public policy that concerns taxes, government spending, public debt, and management of government money) faced key challenges. As noted above, one major hurdle was the devastation caused by Hurricanes Katrina and Rita. While local communities absorbed as many as 500,000 Louisiana and Mississippi evacuees (with approximately 400,000 still in Texas six months later), Governor Rick Perry and local governmental officials continued to negotiate with the federal government regarding reimbursement for services furnished to evacuees ranging from education to health care to housing. The first-year cost estimate was $1.6 billion to the state of Texas and $1.3 billion to local governments. Ongoing expenditures for the state were estimated at $550 million annually. Officials anticipated federal aid to offset first-year expenses would be between $600 and $900 million, but Texas taxpayers would be responsible for the balance.

Yet, when Governor Perry testified before Congress requesting funding in March 2006, Senator Christopher "Kit" Bond from Missouri captured the reaction of others on Capitol Hill when he advised Texans to "[get] back to being a good neighbor and not a paid companion."[1] Bond noted, as had others, that in addition to bearing costs, Texas had received benefits. For example, sales tax revenue increased significantly during late 2005 and early 2006 as residents of the Beaumont-Port Arthur area began to rebuild after the devastation of Hurricane Rita. Evacuees from Katrina were also consumers who purchased goods from Texas retailers and contributed to the state's economy. Damage to Gulf of Mexico and Louisiana oil rigs and petrochemical plants drove the price of oil and gas upward throughout the fall of 2005, and as an owner of mineral interests, the Lone Star State benefited from added royalty income. Increases in product consumption and land revenue meshed perfectly with Texas's tax system. Partly because of these benefits, it remained unclear just how much additional money Texas would receive from Washington.

Meanwhile, as financial negotiations between Texas and the federal government continued, another challenge to Texas's traditional fiscal policy emerged. The Texas Legislature faced the ongoing need to restructure the state's public school finance system. When the Texas Supreme Court declared the existing system unconstitutional in November 2005, the necessity of finding new revenue sources became immediate.

**fiscal policy** Public policy that concerns taxing, government spending, public debt, and management of government money.

Many politicians confirmed what some observers had said for years: the source of Texas's school finance problem, and its revenue problems in general, was a nineteenth-century land- and product-based tax system no longer appropriate to the knowledge- and service-based economy of the twenty-first century.[2] They noted that local and state governments relied heavily on real estate taxes for local revenue and on sales taxes at the state level, while business activities of **service-sector** employers, including those in utilities trade, finance, and the professions, were often tax-free. State government's increasing dependence on the sales tax as a major source of state revenue ignores the need to tax the core businesses and assets of the service sector. The political involvement of service-sector business people, as voters, campaign donors, and lobbyists, provided one explanation for their limited tax liability. Changes in Texas's economy, without corresponding changes in its tax system, had eroded the tax base so that the part of the economy generating the greatest amount of revenue paid the least amount in taxes.

Yet, even with a declining tax base and an increasing demand for government services, Texans remain committed to pay-as-you-go government spending. The Lone Star State's fiscal policy has not deviated from its nineteenth-century origins. Today, the notion of a balanced budget, achieved by low tax rates and low-to-moderate government spending levels, continues to dominate state fiscal policy. Consequently, state government, its employees, and its taxpayers face the daily challenge of meeting higher demands for services with fewer resources.

The state's elected officials appear to adopt the view expressed by economist Milton Friedman that "the preservation of freedom requires limiting narrowly the role of government and placing primary reliance on private property, free markets and voluntary arrangements." The state legislature and other state leaders have repeatedly demonstrated a willingness to reduce services, outsource governmental work to decrease the number of employees on the state's payroll, and maintain or lower tax rates as solutions to the state's fiscal problems. A comparison of per capita taxing and spending rates (see "How Do We Compare?") illustrates these policies.

## Taxing Policy

Texans have traditionally opposed mandatory assessments for public purposes, or **taxes**. Residents have pressured their state government to maintain low taxes. When additional revenues have been needed, Texans have indicated in poll after poll their preference for **regressive taxes** that favor the rich and fall most heavily on the poor ("the less you make, the more government takes"). Under such taxes, the burden decreases as personal income increases. Figure 11.1 illustrates the impact of regressive taxes on different levels of income. The poorest 20 percent of Texans pay almost three and one-half times as much of their income for taxes as the wealthiest 20 percent.

Texas lawmakers have developed one of the most regressive tax structures in the nation. A general sales tax and selective sales taxes have been especially

**service sector**
Businesses that provide services such as finance, health care, food service, data processing, or consulting.

**tax** A compulsory contribution exacted by a government for a public purpose.

**regressive tax** A tax in which the effective tax rate falls as the tax base (e.g., individual income, corporate profits) increases.

### How Do We Compare . . . in Taxes and Spending?
#### Per Capita Taxes and Spending

| Most Populous U.S. States | Per Capita State Taxes (FY2004) | Per Capita State Expenditures (FY2003) | U.S. States Bordering Texas | Per Capita State Taxes (FY2004) | Per Capita State Expenditures (FY2003) |
|---|---|---|---|---|---|
| California | $2,388 | $5,765 | Arkansas | $2,027 | $4,430 |
| Florida | $1,769 | $3,313 | Louisiana | $1,777 | $4,157 |
| New York | $2,384 | $6,635 | New Mexico | $2,103 | $5,680 |
| **Texas** | **$1,367** | **$3,456** | Oklahoma | $1,824 | $4,314 |

Source: The Tax Foundation, *Facts & Figures: How Does Your State Compare?* (Washington, D.C.: Tax Foundation, 2006).

popular. **Progressive taxes** (taxes whose impact increases as income rises—"the more you make, the more government takes") have been unpopular. Texas officials and citizens so oppose state income taxes that the state constitution requires a popular referendum before an income tax can be levied. Newspaper columnists often observe that any elected official who proposes a state income tax commits political suicide.

To finance services, Texas government depends heavily on sales taxes, which rank among the highest in the nation. In addition, the Lone Star State has a dizzying array of other taxes. For example, Texas imposes taxes on bingo

**progressive taxes** A tax in which the effective tax rate increases as the tax base (e.g., individual income, corporate profits) increases.

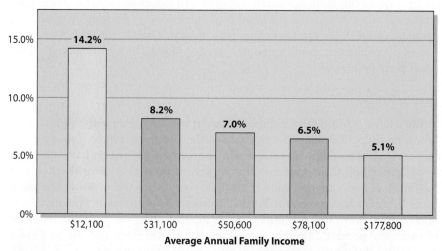

*Figure 11.1*    Percent of Income Paid in Local and States Taxes by Average Annual Family Income
*Source:* Dick Lavine, "Who Pays Texas Taxes?" Austin: Center for Public Policy Priorities, 9 February 2005. Reprinted by permission.

games, sulfur production, and oil and gas well servicing. Yet the sales tax remains the most important source of state revenue.

In addition, the state funds many activities through special fees and assessments, which are not called taxes, but represent money state residents pay to government. Texas legislators, reluctant to raise taxes, have often assessed these fees and surcharges on the state's residents to finance government. Is a **fee**, defined as "a fixed sum charged, as by an institution or by law, for a privilege"[3] different from a tax? Some argue these assessments represent an artful use of words, not a refusal to raise taxes. For example, every year attorneys pay an attorney occupation tax (required since 1991) and a legal services fee (required since 2003), in addition to their mandatory dues to the State Bar of Texas (an administrative agency and their professional organization discussed in the chapter "Law, Courts, and Justice"). Each of these amounts must be paid by an attorney to maintain the right to practice law in the state. Whether assessments are called dues, taxes, or fees, they represent money an attorney must pay to finance government.

### Budget Policy

Hostility to public debt is demonstrated in constitutional and statutory provisions designed to force the state to operate on a pay-as-you-go **balanced budget.** The Texas Constitution prohibits the state government from borrowing money "except to supply casual deficiencies of revenue, repel invasion, suppress insurrection, and to defend the state in war." The comptroller of public accounts must submit to the legislature in advance of each regular session a sworn statement of cash on hand and revenue anticipated for the succeeding two years. Appropriation bills enacted at that particular session, and any subsequent special session, are limited to not more than the amount certified unless a four-fifths majority in both houses votes to ignore the comptroller's predictions or the legislature provides new revenue sources.

Despite these constitutional provisions, casual deficits (unplanned shortages) occur periodically. These deficits usually arise in the **General Revenue Fund** (the fund available to the legislature for general appropriations). Although only one of nearly 400 funds in the state treasury, it is the critical fund in that maze of accounts. Like a thermometer, the General Revenue Fund measures the state's fiscal health. If the fund shows a surplus, fiscal health is good; if a deficit occurs, fiscal health is poor. Less than one-half of the state's expenditures come from the General Revenue Fund. The remainder comes from other funds and is restricted to specific uses.

Restriction on use has not prevented the state legislature from manipulating certain accounts to satisfy the mandate for a balanced budget. In 2005, the 79th Legislature refused to appropriate portions of several dedicated funds to give the appearance of a balanced budget. Among the frozen funds were those derived from the sale of animal-friendly license plates and dedicated to support spaying and neutering programs and telephone fees dedicated to supplementing funding for 911 services, and a sporting goods tax intended to finance the state's parks

**fee** A fixed sum charged by government for a privilege.

**balanced budget** A budget in which total revenues and expenditures are equal, producing no deficit.

**General Revenue Fund** An unrestricted state fund which is available for general appropriations.

(see Selected Reading 11.1). State lawmakers justified these actions by noting that the high cost of Medicaid forced them to freeze these balances. This accounting trick made money appear available on paper that in fact was not available to fund Medicaid.[4]

In more direct efforts to reach dedicated funds, the legislature diverted funds for state parks (see Selected Reading 11.1) and eliminated a program designed to assist low-income households with their electricity bills. In August 2005, the Public Utility Commission notified eligible individuals that the Low-Income Telephone and Electric Utilities Program, LITE-UP Texas, had been "discontinued due to a lack of funding."[5] In fact, electric utility ratepayers continue to pay a monthly fee that funded the program, but payments are now diverted to the General Revenue Fund.

## Spending Policy

Historically, Texans have shown little enthusiasm for state spending. Consequently, public expenditures have remained low relative to those of other state governments. Texas has consistently ranked forty-ninth or fiftieth in state spending per capita. Further, the state's voters have indicated their willingness to spend for highways, roads, and other public improvements; but they have demonstrated much less support for welfare programs, recreational facilities, and similar social services.

Hurricanes Katrina and Rita challenged Texans to consider the appropriate role for government in dealing with a natural disaster. School finance issues focused attention on what constitutes a desirable level of services. When House of Representatives speaker Tom Craddick observed that people want to spend more money for education, "but if you ask if [they] want more taxes to pay for it, they'll say 'no,'"[6] he may have correctly described the attitudes of Texas taxpayers. Yet, when former Lieutenant Governor Bill Ratliff testified that, because of inadequate funding, any increased demand for services or standards from the public schools would be like "asking people to make bricks without straw,"[7] he likewise may have offered an accurate assessment of the situation. Texans' fiscal priorities will shape the state, its residents, and its economic future in the twenty-first century.

---

**Learning Check 11.1**       (Answers on p. 476)

1. To finance services, on what taxes does Texas government depend heavily?
2. What are three characteristics of Texas's fiscal policy?
3. The state of Texas relies heavily on the sales tax to fund state government. It does not have a state income tax. Is Texas's tax structure an example of a regressive or a progressive tax system?

---

## ★ Revenue Sources

Funding for government services primarily comes from those who pay taxes. In addition, the state derives revenue from fees for licenses, sales of assets, investment income, gambling, and borrowing. When revenue to the state declines, elected officials have only two choices: increase taxes or other sources of revenue or decrease services. When faced with budget shortfalls, the legislature's first response has often been to decrease services.

## The Politics of Taxation

According to generally accepted standards, each tax levied and the total tax structure should be just and equitable. Of course, there are widely varying notions of what kinds of taxes and what types of structures meet these standards. Conflicts became most apparent as state officials struggled to lower real estate taxes for the state's property owners between 2003 and 2006. Because these property taxes funded public schools, any reduction in revenue had to be replaced by the state to comply with the constitutional mandate to provide "an efficient system of public free schools." Table 11.1 provides a list of the various taxes and fees proposed to meet this requirement.

A review of Table 11.1 discloses that the governor and the legislature considered raising almost every type of tax used by the state to generate revenue. Pressure from special interest groups made the imposition of taxes on those in the professions or business difficult. Proposed increases in the sales tax brought criticism from groups that worked with the poor. Although some legislators and several public policy groups called for the imposition of an income tax, elected

*Table 11.1*  Proposed Taxes and Fees in School Finance Plans (2003–2006)

| | Legislative Session | | | | | |
|---|---|---|---|---|---|---|
| Type of Tax/Fee | 78th Regular Session | 78th Fourth Special Session | 79th Regular Session | 79th First Special Session | 79th Second Special Session | 79th Third Special Session |
| General Sales | X | X | X | X | X | |
| Franchise | | X | X | X | X | X* |
| Motor Vehicle | X | | | X | X | X* |
| Payroll | | X | | | | |
| Tobacco | | X | X | X | | X* |
| Entertainment | | X | | | | |
| Snack Foods | | | X | | | |
| Alcohol | | | X | X | | |
| Boats | | | | X | X | |
| Professional Licensing Fees | | | | X | | |
| Income | X | X | X | X | X | X |
| Environmental | | | | | | X |

*Adopted into law.

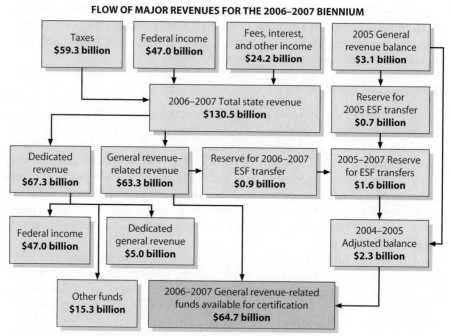

**FLOW OF MAJOR REVENUES FOR THE 2006–2007 BIENNIUM**

Taxes $59.3 billion

Federal income $47.0 billion

Fees, interest, and other income $24.2 billion

2005 General revenue balance $3.1 billion

2006–2007 Total state revenue $130.5 billion

Reserve for 2005 ESF transfer $0.7 billion

Dedicated revenue $67.3 billion

General revenue–related revenue $63.3 billion

Reserve for 2006–2007 ESF transfer $0.9 billion

2005–2007 Reserve for ESF transfers $1.6 billion

Federal income $47.0 billion

Dedicated general revenue $5.0 billion

2004–2005 Adjusted balance $2.3 billion

Other funds $15.3 billion

2006–2007 General revenue-related funds available for certification $64.7 billion

Note: Totals may not sum because of rounding.

*Figure 11.2*    Sources of State Revenue, 2006–2007    *Source:* State Comptroller, *Biennial Revenue Estimate 2006–2007* available at <www.window.state.tx.us/tax.bud/bre2006/revenue.html>.

officials consistently refused to consider this issue, allowing any proposed legislation to languish in the House Ways and Means Committee and never reach the full House for a vote. (See the chapter, "The Legislature.") In the end, despite resistance from several large law firms, the legislature modified and expanded the franchise tax (discussed below). It also imposed an additional $1 tax on cigarettes, increased taxes on other tobacco products (except cigars), and required buyers to pay a tax on used cars at their presumptive value as determined by publications such as *Kelley Blue Book*. The legislature also used a portion of an $8.2 billion revenue surplus to increase state funding for public schools.

**general sales tax**  At the rate of 6.25 percent of a sale, the general sales tax is Texas's largest source of tax revenue. It is applied largely to the sale price of tangible personal property and "the storage, use, or other consumption of tangible personal property purchased, leased, or rented."

**Sales Taxes**  By far the most important single source of tax revenue in Texas is sales taxation. (See Figure 11.2 for the sources of state revenue.) Altogether, sales taxes accounted for more than 55 percent of state tax revenue and 25 percent of all revenue in fiscal years 2006–2007. The burden that sales taxes impose on individual taxpayers varies with their particular patterns of spending and their income level, because they are regressive taxes.

For more than 40 years, the state has levied and collected two kinds of sales taxes: a general sales tax and several selective sales taxes. First imposed in 1961, the limited sales, excise, and use tax (commonly referred to as the **general sales tax**) has become the foundation of the Texas tax system. The current (2006) statewide rate of 6.25 percent is one of the nation's highest (ranking as the seventh-highest rate among the 45 states that imposed a sales tax as of mid-year 2006).

The base of the tax is the sale price of "all tangible personal property" and "the storage, use, or other consumption of tangible personal property purchased, leased, or rented." Among exempted tangible property are the following: receipts from water, telephone, and telegraph services; sales of goods otherwise taxed (for example, automobiles and motor fuels); food and food products (but not restaurant meals); medical supplies sold by prescription; nonprescription drugs; animals and supplies used in agricultural production; and sales by university and college clubs and organizations (so long as the group has no more than one fundraising activity per month).

Two other important items exempt from the general sales tax are goods sold via the Internet and most professional and business services. As the volume of untaxed cybersales increases, one study projected that Texas's sales tax revenue will decrease approximately 10 percent per year by 2008, based on 2003 tax collections.[8] According to U.S. Supreme Court decisions, a state cannot require businesses with no facilities in the state to collect sales taxes for it because the practice interferes with interstate commerce. Therefore, when a student buys a textbook from an on-line seller such as Amazon, no sales tax is collected. The book is, however, subject to a use tax, which requires the purchaser to file a form with the comptroller's office and pay taxes on items purchased out-of-state for use in Texas. Because the cost of enforcing such a provision on individual consumers is prohibitive, these transactions remain largely untaxed. Some on-line merchants, such as kitchen retailer Williams-Sonoma, Inc., voluntarily collect sales taxes for the states. Other sellers argue that multiple rates and definitions of products subject to state sales taxes create a collection nightmare. Through the **Streamlined Sales Tax Project**, many states, including Texas, are devising a uniform tax system that would overcome these arguments. If the U.S. Congress grants states the authority to force out-of-state retailers to collect sales taxes on their behalf, Texas could experience a significant increase in tax revenue.[9]

Because the general sales tax primarily applies to tangible personal property, many services are untaxed. A sales tax is charged for dry cleaning, football tickets, and parking; however, accountants, lawyers, architects, and consultants provide their services tax-free. Proposals that would require these groups to charge and collect a sales tax have been strongly resisted. Because professional service providers and business represent some of the most powerful and well-organized interests in the Lone Star State, it is unlikely services provided by these groups will be subject to a sales tax. (See the chapter "The Politics of Interest Groups.")

Since 1931, when the legislature first imposed a sales tax on cigarettes, many items have been singled out for **selective sales taxes**. For convenience of analysis, these items may be grouped into three categories: highway user taxes, sin taxes, and miscellaneous sales taxes. Highway user taxes include taxes on fuels for motor vehicles that use public roads and registration fees for the privilege of

**Streamlined Sales Tax Project** A voluntary effort by a number of states to simplify collection and administration procedures of the sales tax for sellers so that sales tax can be collected on Internet and catalog purchases.

**selective sales taxes** These are quantity-based consumption taxes on specific products.

operating those vehicles. The principal **sin taxes** are those on cigarettes and other tobacco products, alcoholic beverages, and mixed drinks. Sin taxes are among the easiest to increase in the state and, in 2004, became the centerpiece of Governor Rick Perry's proposal to fund the state's public schools. The governor sought to increase taxes on cigarettes and impose a tax on admission fees paid to "gentlemen's clubs." Effective January 1, 2007, taxes on tobacco products (except cigars) increased. Additional items subject to selective sales taxes include hotel and motel room rentals (also called a "bed tax") and retail sales of boats and boat motors.

**Business Taxes**    As with sales taxes, Texas imposes both general and selective business taxes. A general business tax is assessed against a wide range of business operations. Selective business taxes are those levied on businesses engaged in specific or selected types of commercial activities.

Commercial enterprises operating in this state have historically paid three general business taxes:

- Sales taxes, because businesses are consumers
- Franchise taxes, because many businesses operate in a form that attempts to limit personal liability of owners (i.e., corporations, limited liability partnerships, and similar structures)
- Unemployment compensation payroll taxes, because most businesses are also employers

The **franchise tax**, which has been levied on business for almost 100 years, is imposed on businesses for the privilege of doing business in Texas. As a part of the restructuring of the state's school finance system, the legislature expanded the franchise tax to include all businesses operating in a format that limited the personal liability of owners. Effective January 1, 2008, an additional 200,000 businesses became liable for payment of franchise taxes. Sole proprietorships, general partnerships wholly owned by natural persons, passive investment entities, and businesses that make $300,000 or less in annual income or owe less than $1,000 in franchise taxes remain exempt. The tax is levied on a business's taxable margin which is its total income less either (1) the cost of goods sold or (2) compensation paid to employees, not to exceed $300,000 per employee. To gain support from the Texas Medical Association, the law allows health care providers to deduct amounts collected from government-sponsored programs such as Medicaid and Medicare and the cost of uncompensated medical care. This tax is estimated to produce about $6 billion in state revenue each fiscal year, approximately three times the amount generated by the corporate franchise tax used by the state through December 31, 2007.

All states have unemployment insurance systems supported by **payroll taxes**. The payroll tax is levied against a portion of the wages and salaries paid to individuals to insure employees against unemployment. These amounts are paid into the Unemployment Trust Fund in the U.S. Treasury. Benefits are distributed to workers who lose their jobs.

**sin tax** A selective sales tax on items such as cigarettes, other forms of tobacco, and alcoholic beverages.

**franchise tax** This tax is levied on the annual receipts of businesses organized to limit the personal liability of owners.

**payroll tax** A tax levied against a portion of the wages and salaries of employees to provide funds for payment of unemployment insurance benefits to these people when they lose their jobs.

The most significant of the state's selective business taxes are levied on the following:

- Oil and gas production
- Insurance company gross premiums
- Public utilities gross receipts

These selective business taxes accounted for about 16 percent of the state's tax revenue in 2005, representing significant increases in taxes on oil and gas production.

One of the more important selective business taxes is the severance tax. Texas has depended far more than other states on **severance taxes,** which are levied on a natural resource, such as oil or natural gas, when it is removed from the earth. Texas severance taxes are based on the quantity of minerals produced or on the value of the resource when removed. The Texas crude oil production tax and the gas-gathering tax were designed with two objectives in mind: to raise substantial revenue and to help regulate the amount of natural resources mined or otherwise recovered. Each of these taxes is highly volatile, reflecting dramatic increases and decreases as the price and demand for natural resources fluctuate. For example, revenue from severance taxes tumbled 50 percent between fiscal year FY2001 and FY2002. When natural gas and oil prices rose dramatically in 2005, state revenue from this tax more than doubled over collections in FY2002, increasing from $966 million to $2.4 billion.

**Death Tax**   Because of changes to federal law, no death tax is due on the estates of individuals dying on or after January 1, 2005. Some states have enacted laws imposing a tax on estates. It is unlikely Texas will do so.

**Tax Burden**   The U.S. Census Bureau places Texas well below the national average for the tax burden imposed on its residents. In 2005, when state taxes alone were considered, the Lone Star State ranked 49th among the 50 states. A candidate's "no new taxes" pledge remains an important consideration for many Texas voters and will likely result in state officials' continuing to choose fewer services over higher taxes to balance the state budget.

**Tax Collection**   As Texas's chief tax collector, the comptroller of public accounts collects more than 90 percent of state taxes, including those on motor fuel sales, oil and gas production, cigarette and tobacco sales, and franchises. Amounts claimed due by the comptroller's office can be challenged through an administrative proceeding conducted by that office. Taxpayers dissatisfied with the results of that hearing can appeal the decision to a state district court. (See the chapter, "Laws, Courts, and Justice.")

Other agencies also collect taxes on behalf of the state. The Department of Transportation collects motor vehicle registration and certificate-of-title fees through county tax collectors' offices; the State Board of Insurance collects insurance taxes and fees; and the Department of Public Safety collects driver's license, motor vehicle inspection, and other such fees. The Texas Alcoholic Beverage

**severance tax**  An excise tax levied on a natural resource (e.g., oil or natural gas) when it is severed (removed) from the earth.

*A staff member in the Office of the Comptroller of Public Accounts reviews tax-payer records to determine taxpayer liability. (Courtesy of Texas State Comptroller)*

Commission collects state taxes on beer, wine, and other alcoholic beverages. Although taxes represent the largest source of state revenue, Texas has other funding means.

### Revenue from Gambling

Texas receives revenue from three types of gambling operations: horse racing and dog racing, a state-managed lottery, and bingo games. In addition, the Kickapoo nation, a Native American tribe near Eagle Pass, operates a casino, which does not pay state taxes on its operations. Because Texas has highly restrictive gambling laws, the tribe's gambling operations only allow players to compete against each other in games of chance. They cannot compete against the house as one would do in a Las Vegas casino. The state's other two tribes (the Alabama-Coushatta in East Texas and the Tigua near El Paso) are prohibited from operating casinos because of state law and the wording of their treaties with the United States. Gambling proponents continue to argue for legalization of more games of chance. Both social conservatives and many Democrats oppose their efforts.

**Racing**    Pari-mutuel wagers on horse races and dog races are taxed. This levy has never brought Texas significant revenue. In most years (including 2004, the most recent year for which information is available), the Racing Commission

# ◀ POINT/COUNTERPOINT ▶

## Should Texas Expand Gambling Operations?

**THE ISSUE**   Does gambling represent "get-rich quick schemes" that lure the poor and unwary into using the baby's milk money to place bets against incredible odds of winning? Or, do casinos and other gambling operations make valuable contributions to a state's economic development by providing much-needed jobs and revenue? As state lawmakers search for ways to increase revenue without raising taxes, they continue to hear many arguments for and against expanding gambling operations. Some groups support modifying the law to allow video lottery terminals (VLTs), similar to slot machines, at racetracks across the state. Others encourage installation of VLTs in additional sites such as bingo halls and bars. Still other gambling proponents argue for legalization of casino gambling in the state.

### Arguments For Expanding Gambling Operations

1. Expanding gambling operations only to VLTs would increase revenue to the state by as much as $1.8 billion per year. Further, having access to VLTs at racetracks will increase the winning purses that can be offered in horse races and dog races, and thus improve the quality of these events and attract even more bettors. Casinos would generate additional revenue for Texans.

2. Texas is losing money to other states as the state's residents go to casinos in Louisiana, Oklahoma, and New Mexico to gamble. Losses on VLTs alone are about $1 billion per year. There are more than 35 gambling operations within 50 miles of the Texas border in surrounding states. Recently expanded gambling opportunities in Mexican border cities could add to this outflow.

3. Increasing the kinds of gambling operations will have a direct benefit for the Texas economy by creating jobs, bringing in tourism dollars, and aiding other industries such as farming and ranching.

*"We are completely surrounded by states that have casinos, horse racing, you name it. It doesn't make sense to me why we would drive billions of dollars across state lines when we could keep that money right here in Texas."*

—Bill Stinson, a lobbyist representing Fort Worth Stockyards, a group seeking to develop a hotel and casino in Fort Worth, as quoted in John Moritz, "Casino Gambling Fight Expected in Spring," *Fort Worth Star-Telegram,* February 12, 2006

### Arguments Against Expanding Gambling Operations

1. Gambling proponents have consistently overestimated the revenue benefit to the state and underestimated the costs, which include the expense of regulating this industry; diversion of money from retailers and other entertainment businesses to gambling; and the social costs of crime, addiction, and related societal problems.

2. Because the poor spend greater percentages of their income on gambling than the wealthy, expansion of operations represents an increase in regressive taxes.

3. The more reliant the state becomes on gambling revenue, the greater likelihood that it will promote, rather than regulate, gambling.

*"The social costs are very high. It [gambling] brings with it addiction, bankruptcy and crime. In this industry, addiction is not incidental; it's essential to the business."*

—Suzii Paynter, Texas Baptist Christian Life Commission

collects less than its operating expenses. Texas has four types of horse racing permits ranging from Class 1 with no limit on the number of race days per year to Class 4 limited to 5 race days annually. As of mid-2006, the Lone Star State had seven permitted horse racing tracks and three dog tracks providing live and simulcast racing events on which people could wager legal bets.

**Lottery**    Texas operates one of 40 state-run lotteries. Chances for winning the jackpot are 1 in 26 million. A major competitor for lottery players' money is the multistate lottery, Mega Millions. Texas is one of 12 states participating in this lottery, which has offered prizes as large as $365 million. Chances for winning are 1 in 135 million. Between December 2003, when Texans became eligible to play Mega Millions, and September 2006, the state has had two jackpot winners, one for $101 million in October 2004 and a second for $112 million in March 2005.

The Texas Lottery Commission administers the state's lottery. Among its functions are determining the amounts of prizes, overseeing the printing of tickets, advertising ticket sales, and awarding prizes. Because this three-member commission also oversees bingo operations, one member must have experience in the bingo industry.

All profits from the lottery are dedicated to public education spending, rather than to the General Revenue Fund. In 2006, the Texas Lottery Commission began a public awareness campaign to let Texans know how lottery proceeds were spent. In 2005, approximately $1 billion went to the Texas Foundation School Fund. That amount constituted a small portion of the state's annual budgeted expenditure of more than $17 billion on public education in that same year. Unclaimed prizes from the Texas Lottery revert to the state 180 days after a drawing. These funds are transferred to hospitals across the state to reimburse them for unfunded indigent medical care.

**Bingo**    State law allows bingo games to benefit charities (for example, churches, veterans' organizations, and service clubs). There is a tax of 5 percent on bingo prizes, of which the state receives half and local governments the other half. The state's revenue from bingo taxes remains low. Local charities do benefit from these games, as a portion of the proceeds must be distributed to them. In 2005, these donations exceeded $30 million.

### Nontax Revenues

Less than 50 percent of all Texas state revenue comes from taxes and gambling operations; therefore, other nontax revenues are important sources of funds. The largest portion of these revenues (approximately two-thirds in the 2006–2007 biennium) is derived from federal grants, but state business operations (such as interagency sales of goods) and borrowing also are significant sources of revenue. Growth in federal funding during the opening years of the George W. Bush administration (Texas's former governor) has been dramatic,

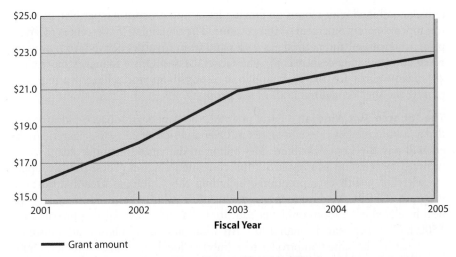

*Figure 11.3*    Annual Federal Grants to Texas (FY2001–FY2005) (in billions)    *Source:* Office of the Comptroller of the State of Texas, "Texas Revenue History by Source, 1973–2005," available at www.window.state.tx.us/taxbud/revenue.html

increasing by more than 40 percent or almost $7 billion per year as illustrated by Figure 11.3.

**Federal Grants-in-Aid**    Gifts of money, goods, or services from one government to another are defined as **grants-in-aid**. Federal grants-in-aid contribute more revenue to Texas than any single tax levied by the state. More than 95 percent of federal funds are directed to three programs: health and human services, business and economic development (especially highway construction), and education. For the 2006–2007 biennium, federal funds, including grants, were expected to account for more than $47 billion in revenue. These calculations do not include any additional funding received for damage from Hurricane Rita or reimbursement of costs of Hurricane Katrina evacuees.

State participation in federal grant programs is voluntary. States choosing to participate must:

■ Contribute a portion of program costs (varying from as little as 10 percent to as much as 90 percent)
■ Meet performance specifications established by federal mandate

Funds are usually allocated to states on the basis of a formula. Factors commonly used in deriving a formula include lump sums (made up of identical amounts to all states receiving funds) and uniform sums (based on items that vary from state to state: population, area, highway mileage, need and fiscal ability, cost of service, administrative discretion, and special state needs).

**Land Revenues**    Texas state government receives substantial nontax revenue from public land sales, rentals, and royalties. Sales of land, sand, shell, and

**grant-in-aid** Money, goods, or services given by one government to another (e.g., federal grants-in-aid to states for financing public assistance programs).

gravel, combined with rentals on grazing lands and prospecting permits, account for approximately 3 percent of this revenue. The remaining 97 percent is received primarily from oil and natural gas leases and from royalties derived from mineral production on state-owned land. The General Land Office manages more than 20 million acres for the state and has responsibility for selling, leasing, and renting the surface and minerals of the property.

**The Tobacco Suit Windfall**    Early in 1998, the American tobacco industry settled a lawsuit filed by the state of Texas. Over a period of 25 years, cigarette makers will pay the Lone Star State $18 billion in damages for public health costs incurred by the state as a result of tobacco-related illnesses. These funds support a variety of health care programs, including the Children's Health Insurance Program (CHIP), Medicaid, tobacco-education projects, and endowments for health-related institutions of higher education. Payments averaged approximately $500 million per year through 2007. An additional $2.3 billion is administered as a trust by the state comptroller to reimburse local governments (cities, counties, and hospital districts) for unreimbursed health care costs. In 2005, these political subdivisions received more than $50 million from this fund.

Business groups and others have suggested selling bonds, backed by future payments from the tobacco settlement funds, to private investors. This practice is called **securitization**. The major advantage of these bond sales would be an immediate cash payment to the state. A serious disadvantage is that the bond prices would be heavily discounted because the private investors risk that settlement payments will not be made, and this discount decreases the total cash the state would receive. Pressure to sell the funds will likely rise whenever the economy weakens.

**Miscellaneous Sources**    Fees, permits, and income from investments are major miscellaneous nontax sources of revenue. Fee sources include those for motor vehicle inspections, college tuition, student services, state hospital care, and certificates-of-title for motor vehicles. The most significant sources of revenue from permits are those for trucks and automobiles; the sale of liquor, wine, and beer; and cigarette tax stamps. Income from fees and permits approximated $6 billion per year in 2005.

It is easier to generate revenue by increasing fees than by raising taxes. One of the most popular methods has been by increasing **"losers' fees."** These amounts represent surcharges added to items such as traffic tickets, given to the few who get caught for violations many commit.

At any given moment, Texas actually has on hand billions of dollars invested in securities or on deposit in interest-bearing accounts.[10] Trust funds constitute the bulk of the money invested by the state (for example, the Texas Teacher Retirement Fund, the State Employee Retirement Fund, the Permanent School Fund, and the Permanent University Fund). Investment returns closely track fluctuations in the stock market. The Texas state comptroller is responsible for overseeing the investment of most of the state's surplus funds. Restrictive money-management laws limit investments to interest-bearing negotiable order with-

**securitization**  Sale of bonds backed by anticipated future payments of tobacco settlements.

**losers' fees**  A surcharge added to assessments against the few who get caught disobeying a law violated by many.

Although the fine for a broken taillight in the city of Houston is $30, those caught receive a $93 ticket. The state adds twenty further surcharges totaling $63, including:

- $5 to cover the cost of the officer who wrote the ticket
- $15.05 for the Crime Victim's Compensation Fund
- $0.48 for the Correctional Management Institute at Sam Houston State University
- $30 split between the General Revenue Fund ($20) and the state's trauma care centers ($10)
- $4 fee to cover judicial pay raises granted in 2005

drawal (NOW) accounts, treasury bills (promissory notes in denominations of $1,000 to $1 million) from the U.S. Treasury, and repurchase agreements (arrangements that allow the state to buy back assets such as state bonds) from banks. Conservative investment strategies have resulted in low returns for these funds in recent years. Interest and investment income provided less than 3 percent of the General Revenue Fund in 2005.

The University of Texas Investment Management Co. (UTIMCO) invests the Permanent University Fund and other endowments for the University of Texas and the Texas A&M University systems. Its investment authority extends to participating in venture capital partnerships that fund new businesses. Board members for UTIMCO include the chancellor and three regents from the University of Texas, one regent from Texas A&M, and four outside investment professionals. This nonprofit corporation is the first such investment company in the nation affiliated with a public university.

### The Public Debt

When expenditures exceed income, governments finance shortfalls through public borrowing. Such deficit financing is essential to meet short- and long-term crises and to pay for major projects involving large amounts of money. Most state constitutions, however, severely limit the authority of state governments to incur indebtedness.

For more than 50 years, Texans have sought, through constitutional provisions and public pressure, to force the state to operate on a pay-as-you-go basis. Despite those efforts, the state is allowed to borrow money by issuing general obligation bonds (borrowed amounts repaid from the General Revenue Fund) and revenue bonds (borrowed amounts repaid from a specific revenue source, such as college student loan bonds repaid by students who received the funds). Commercial paper and promissory notes also cover the state's cash flow shortages. General obligation bonds and commercial paper borrowings must have voter approval; other forms of borrowing do not require voter approval. **Bonded debt** that must be repaid from the General Revenue Fund has increased by almost 500 percent since 1988, with a total debt outstanding of more than $21 billion as of FY2005. Thus, many Texas voters approve both a balanced

**bonded debt** Borrowings obtained through sale of revenue bonds and general obligation bonds.

budget and bond amendments that authorize the state to increase its debt by borrowing money.

**Bond Review**    Specific projects to be financed with bond money require legislative approval. Bond issues also must be approved by the Texas Bond Review Board. This board is composed of the governor, lieutenant governor, speaker of the House, and comptroller of public accounts. It approves all borrowings with a term in excess of five years or an amount in excess of $250,000.[11]

**Economic Stabilization Fund**    The state's Economic Stabilization Fund (popularly called the **"rainy day" fund**) operates like an individual's savings account. It is intended for use when the state faces an economic crisis, primarily to prevent or eliminate temporary cash deficiencies in the General Revenue Fund. The "rainy day" fund is financed with any excess money remaining in the General Revenue Fund at the end of a biennium and with oil and natural gas taxes that exceed 1987 collections (approximately $1.3 billion in that year). This fund has provided temporary support for public education and the criminal justice system, as well as financed Texas's Enterprise Fund, designed to attract new businesses to the state. In 2005, the 79th Legislature authorized the creation of the Emerging Technology Fund, financed in part with money from the "rainy day" fund. This account is intended for use by companies engaging in work with new technologies likely to produce medical or scientific breakthroughs. Because of current budget needs and directives in the FY2006–2007 budget, the legislature authorized the transfer of more than $1.9 billion out of the "rainy day" funds in 2005.

---

**Learning Check 11.2        (Answers on p. 476)**

**1.** What problem is the Streamlined Sales Tax Project designed to address?
**2.** On what government service must lottery profits be spent?
**3.** What is the stated purpose of the "rainy day" fund?

---

**"rainy day" fund** A fund used for stabilizing state finance when revenue is insufficient to cover state-supported programs.

**budget** A plan indicating how much revenue a government expects to collect during a period (usually one or two fiscal years) and how much spending is authorized for agencies and programs.

## Budgeting and Fiscal Management

The state's fiscal management process begins with a budget and ends with an audit.[12] Other phases of the process include tax collection, investment of public funds, purchasing, and accounting. Each activity is important if the state is to derive maximum benefit from the billions of dollars it handles each year.

### Budgeting Procedure

A plan of financial operation is usually referred to as a **budget**. In modern state government, budgets serve a variety of functions, each important in its own right. A budget is a plan for spending that shows a government's financial condition at the close of one fiscal, or budget, year and the anticipated condition at the end of the next year. It also makes spending recommendations for the coming fiscal year. In Texas, the fiscal year begins on September 1 and ends on

August 31 of the following year. When referring to a budget year, the ending year is the one used, preceded by the initials FY for "fiscal year." For example, FY2006 began on September 1, 2005 and ended on August 31, 2006.

Texas is one of only seven states that have biennial (every two years) legislative sessions and budget periods. Many political observers argue that today's economy fluctuates too rapidly for this system to be efficient. Voters, however, have consistently rejected proposed constitutional amendments requiring annual state appropriations. Officials from other states, including California, view Texas's performance-based, biennial budgeting cycle as a model that forces strategic planning, allows for program evaluation, and permits agencies to spend less time on budgeting and more time on delivering services.[13]

**Legislative Budget Board**    By statute, the **Legislative Budget Board** (LBB) is a 10-member joint body of the Texas House of Representatives and the Texas Senate. Its membership includes as joint chairs the lieutenant governor and the speaker of the House of Representatives. Assisted by its director and staff, the LBB prepares a biennial (two fiscal years) current-services-based budget. This type of budget projects the cost of meeting anticipated service needs of Texans over the next biennium. The comptroller of public accounts furnishes the board with an estimate of revenue that will be available over the same time period to meet projected expenses. The comptroller's revenue projections establish spending limits.

The board's staff also helps draft the general appropriation bill for introduction at each regular session of the legislature. Furthermore, if requested by a legislative committee chair, staff personnel prepare fiscal notes that assess the economic impact of a bill or resolution. The LBB also assists agencies in developing performance evaluation measures and audits and conducts performance reviews.

**Governor's Office of Budget, Planning and Policy**    Headed by an executive budget officer who works under the supervision of the governor, the Governor's Office of Budget, Planning, and Policy (GOBPP) is required by statute to prepare and present a biennial budget to the legislature. Traditionally, the governor's plan is policy based. It presents objectives to be attained and a plan for achieving them. As a result of this dual arrangement, two budgets, one legislative in origin and the other executive, should be prepared every two years. In the closing decades of the twentieth century, governors often did not submit separate budgets; but Governor Rick Perry submitted budgets in 2001, 2003, and 2005. His 2003 budget proposal, however, allocated $0 for every spending category and neither set spending priorities nor recommended reductions. By this dramatic action, he sought to force the legislature to deal with a significant budget shortage. Striking a more positive note in the improved economic conditions of 2005, Perry's proposal was entitled *An Era of Possibility*.

**Budget Preparation**    Compilation of each budget begins with the preparation of forms and instructions by the LBB and the GOBPP. (See Figure 11.4 for

**Legislative Budget Board (LBB)** A 10-member body co-chaired by the lieutenant governor and the speaker of the House, this board and its staff prepare a biennial current-services budget. In addition, the LBB assists with the preparation of a general appropriation bill at the beginning of a regular legislative session; and, if requested, it prepares fiscal notes that assess the economic impact of a proposed bill or resolution.

a diagram of the budgeting process.) These materials are sent to each spending agency early in every even-numbered year. For about six months thereafter, representatives of the budgeting agencies work closely with operating agency personnel to prepare proposed departmental requests.

Each operating agency requesting appropriated funds must submit a five-year strategic operating plan to the GOBPP and to the LBB. These plans must incorporate the state's mission and philosophy of government developed by the governor in cooperation with the LBB. (For the mission and vision for FY2006-2007, see Selected Reading 11.2, "The Mission and Philosophy of Texas State Government.") Agency plans are then combined by the GOBPP and LBB into a long-term strategic plan composed of three phases:

1. Statewide functional goals (for example, increasing access to higher education for students with disabilities) and proposed measures of specific government performance
2. Strategic priorities (for example, a commitment to achieve the goal in the immediate future) and external and internal factors that might affect the agency's ability to meet the goal
3. Strategic policies or implementation strategies (for example, installation of elevators in all buildings and other facilities where higher education services are provided)

An agency's request must be organized according to the strategies the agency intends to use in implementing its strategic plan over the next two years. Each strategy, in turn, must be listed in order of priority and tied to a single statewide functional goal.

By early fall, state agencies submit their departmental estimates to the LBB and GOBPP. These budgeting agencies then carefully analyze all requests and hold hearings with representatives of spending departments to clarify details and supply any additional information needed. At the close of the hearings, usually in mid-December, budget agencies traditionally compile their estimates of expenditures into two separately proposed budgets.

Thus, during each regular session, legislators normally face two sets of recommendations for all state expenditures for the succeeding biennium. Since the inception of the **dual budgeting system**, however, the legislature has shown a marked preference for the recommendations of its own budget-making agency, the LBB, over those of the GOBPP and the governor.

By custom, the legislative chambers rotate responsibility for introducing the state budget between the chair of the Senate Finance Committee and the chair of the House Appropriations Committee. In subsequent months, the legislature debates issues surrounding the budget before approving it and sending it to the governor. The comptroller certifies the budget before signature.

The governor has the power to veto any spending provision in the budget through the line-item veto (rejecting only a particular expenditure in the budget). Through the exercise of the line-item veto in the 2006–2007 budget, Governor Perry vetoed all funding to the Texas Education Agency for the operation of Texas's public schools. In his veto proclamation Perry stated that he did so because

**dual budgeting system**
The compilation of separate budgets by the legislative branch and the executive branch.

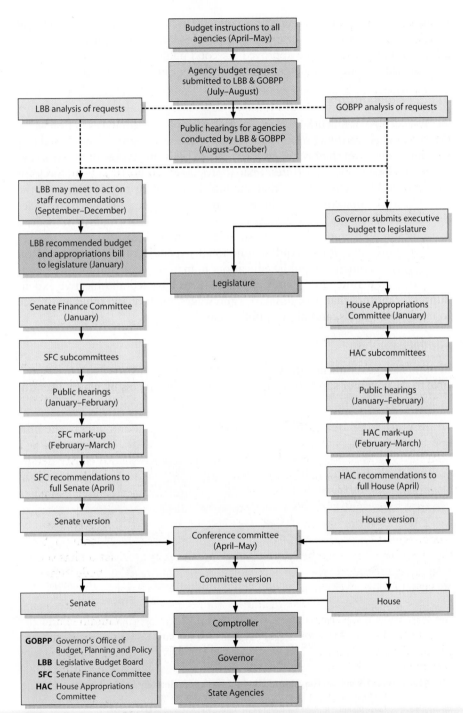

*Figure 11.4*  Texas Biennial Budget Cycle    *Source:* "Texas Biennial Budget Cycle" from Senate Research Center, *Budget 101: A Guide to the Budget Process in Texas* (Austin: Senate Research Center, January 2005).

of the legislature's failure to include accountability measures and incentives that he believed were necessary. In the first special session of the 79th Legislature in 2005, the House and Senate approved a second public education budget, which Perry signed. It contained neither accountability nor incentive measures.

### Budget Expenditures

Analysts of a government's fiscal policy look at public expenditures in two ways. One method is according to function—that is, the services being purchased (for example, education, highways, welfare, health, and protection of persons and property). Figure 11.5 illustrates Texas's proposed functional expenditures for fiscal years 2006–2007. The other method is according to the object of the expenditure, or objective expenditures (goods and services purchased to render the functional services, such as wages and salaries of public employees, medical assistance to needy individuals, and supplies and materials).

For more than four decades, functional expenditures have centered on three principal functions: public education, human services, and highway construction and maintenance. Similarly, three items have led all objective expenditures for most of that period: salaries and wages, medical and other assistance to needy individuals, and aid to public schools.

### Budget Execution

In most state governments, the Governor's Office or an executive agency responsible to the governor supervises **budget execution** (the process by which a central

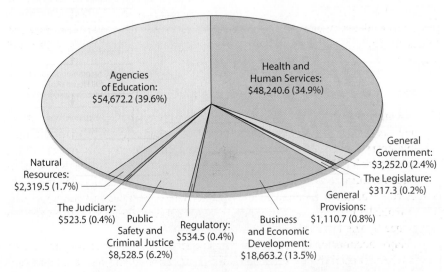

**budget execution** The process whereby the governor and the Legislative Budget Board oversee (and in some instances modify) implementation of the spending plan authorized by the Texas Legislature.

**TOTAL = $138,161.9 billion. The adopted budget was approximately $117 billion.**
*Note:* Excludes interagency contracts. Totals may not add because of rounding.

*Figure 11.5*    Texas Biennial Budget for Fiscal Years 2006–2007    *Source:* House Research Organization, *Texas Budget Highlights Fiscal 2006–07* State Finance Report No. 79-3 (Austin: Texas House of Representatives, 30 January 2006).

authority in government oversees implementation of a spending plan approved by the legislative body). The governor of Texas and the Legislative Budget Board have limited power to prevent an agency from spending part of its appropriations, to transfer money from one agency to another, or to change the purpose for which an appropriation was made. Any modification the governor proposes must be made public, after which the Legislative Budget Board may ratify it, reject it, or recommend changes. If the board recommends changes in the governor's proposals, the chief executive may accept or reject the board's suggestions.

The proper functioning of Texas's budget execution system requires a coordinated effort among the state's political leadership. Although the board met twice in 2004, it held no meetings in 2005 and 2006.

### Purchasing

Agencies of state government must make purchases through or under the supervision of the Texas Building and Procurement Commission. Depending on the cost of an item, agency personnel may be required to obtain competitive bids. This commission places greater emphasis on serving state agencies for which it purchases goods than on controlling what they purchase. It also provides agencies with administrative support services such as mail distribution, photocopying, and similar services. The governing board of the commission has seven members. Three are appointed by the governor, two are nominated by the speaker of the House but appointed by the governor, and two are appointed by the lieutenant governor. The commission also provides building and property management services for state facilities, including the Texas State Cemetery. The six-member Council on Competitive Government, chaired by the governor, is required to determine exactly what kinds of services each agency currently provides that might be supplied at less cost by private industry or another state agency.

### Accounting

The comptroller of public accounts oversees the management of the state's money. Texas law holds this elected official responsible for maintaining a double-entry system, in which a debit account and a credit account are maintained for each transaction. Other statutes narrow the comptroller's discretion by creating numerous special funds or accounts that essentially designate revenues to be used for financing identified activities. Because this money is usually earmarked for special purposes, it is not subject to appropriation for any other use by the legislature.

Major accounting tasks of the Comptroller's Office include preparing warrants (checks) used to pay state obligations, acknowledging receipts from various state revenue sources, and recording information concerning receipts and expenditures in ledgers and other account books. Contrary to usual business practice, state accounts are set up on a cash basis rather than an accrual basis. In cash accounting, expenditures are entered when the money is actually paid rather than when the obligation is incurred. In times of fiscal crisis the practice of creating obligations in one fiscal year and paying them in the next allows a budget to appear balanced. Unfortunately, it complicates the task of fiscal planning by failing to reflect an accurate picture of current finances at any given moment. The comptroller issues annual and quarterly reports that include general statements of revenues and expenditures.

### Auditing

State accounts are audited (examined) under direct supervision of the state auditor, who is appointed to a two-year term by the Legislative Audit Committee with approval by two-thirds of the Senate. The auditor may be removed by the committee at any time without the privilege of a hearing. With the assistance of approximately 200 staff members, the auditor provides random checks of financial records and transactions after expenditures. Auditing therefore involves reviewing the records and accounts of disbursing officers and custodians of all state funds. Another important duty of the auditor is to examine the activities of each state agency to evaluate the quality of its services, determine whether duplication of effort exists, and recommend changes. The agency conducts audits in order of priority, reviewing activities most subject to potential or perceived abuse first. Its stated mission is to provide elected officials with information to improve accountability in state government.

---

**Learning Check 11.3**        (Answers on p. 476)

1. What is a fiscal year?
2. Texas has a dual budgeting system. What does this mean?
3. Who has the authority to transfer money from one agency to another after a budget has been approved?

---

## ★ Future Demands

Elected officials have worked to keep taxing levels low. As a result, Texas has also kept its per capita spending levels among the lowest in the nation. Some observers believe that this limited funding is merely deferring problems in the areas of education and social services. Additionally, public safety concerns and homeland security demands strain the state's human and fiscal resources. A growing population, additional social service needs, an outdated infrastructure, changing views of the role of government, and federal mandates are among the problems facing Texans, their government, and its agencies in the twenty-first century.

### Public Education

The state, together with local school districts, is responsible for providing a basic education for all Texas school-age children. Public education was the Lone Star State's second most expensive public service in the 2006-2007 biennium, accounting for almost 30 percent of the state's expenditures (approximately $17 billion

**Points to Ponder**

- In 2004–2005, Texas ranked 33rd in the nation in average teacher salaries ($41,009 per year [Texas] versus $47,808 [national average])[a]
- In 2003–2004, Texas ranked 36th in student per capita revenue available for education ($8,208 [Texas] versus $9,407 [national average]).[a]
- Texas ranked 48th in the nation on average SAT scores in 2005 (995 [Texas] versus 1028 [national average]).[b]

*Sources:* [a]National Education Association; and [b]The College Board.

per year). That amount of state funding covered less than 40 percent of the actual cost of public education. The balance was paid with local taxes and federal grants.

This hybrid arrangement may account for some of the difficulties in operating and financing Texas's schools. Is public education a national issue deserving of federal funding, attention, and standards, similar to the interstate highway system, where the federal government pays for a road system that connects all parts of the nation? Or should education be a state function similar to the state's role in building and maintaining state highways so that all Texans are entitled to drive on the same quality of paved roads? Or is public education a local responsibility more akin to city streets so that towns with more money have better quality streets than their poorer neighbors? Although education appears to integrate all three levels of government into one system, confusion and conflict surround the fiscal responsibility and role of each in the state's educational system. Figure 11.6 illustrates the fluctuating funding levels of each level of government. State officials noted that by 2008, state funding would increase to 50 percent with a corresponding decline in local funding. This change reflected the results of school finance restructuring discussed below.

A continuing decline in state funding through 2006 became problematic for school districts, and by that year, school finance was the most pressing issue facing Texas. The public school finance dilemma rested on three prongs:

- The Texas Supreme Court's decision in *Neeley et al.* v. *West Orange-Cove Consolidated Independent School District, et al.*,[14] which declared state limitations on local property taxes unconstitutional as a violation of the prohibition against a statewide property tax
- The need to generate more state revenue for public education
- Increasing reliance on federal grants, a discretionary, and therefore unpredictable, revenue source

As a further complication, local taxpayers resented ever-increasing property taxes. Yet many special interests opposed new or additional taxes that would affect their business or industry. Located within this funding web were the school children of Texas. They demonstrated continued improvement on national measures such as the National Assessment of Educational Progress, given to randomly selected fourth- and eighth-graders across the United States, and remained near the bottom on tests such as the SAT.

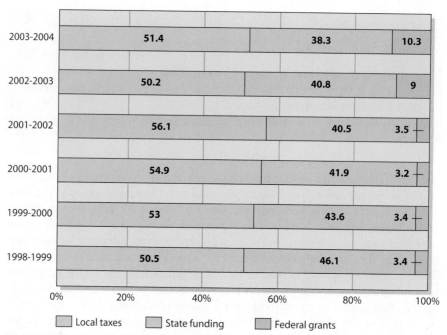

| | Local taxes | State funding | Federal grants |

**Figure 11.6**  Comparison of Funding Sources for Public Education (1998–2004)    *Source:* Texas Education Agency, *Pocket Edition: Texas Public School Statistics.*

**Sources of State Funding**    Texas state government has struggled with financing public education for more than 30 years. Court decisions, the Texas Constitution, and statutes have established funding sources and shaped the ways in which those sources are administered. In promoting public education, Texas state government has usually confined its activity to establishing minimum standards and providing basic levels of financial support. School districts and state government share the cost of three elements—salaries, transportation, and operating expenses. Local funding of school systems relies primarily on the market value of taxable real estate within the school district, because local schools raise their share primarily through property taxes. Average daily attendance of pupils in the district, types of students (for example, elementary, secondary, or disabled), and local economic conditions determine the state's share.

Money to finance the state's Foundation School Program is allocated to each school system from the Foundation School Fund. This fund receives its money from four sources. These sources include: (1) the Available School Fund (revenue received from a variety of state taxes and income from the Permanent School Fund), (2) the School Taxing Ability Protection Fund (money appropriated by the legislature to offset revenue reduction incurred by rural school districts), (3) the Texas Lottery, and (4) the General Revenue Fund.

In 2006, the legislature created the Property Tax Relief Fund. This new account receives all revenue generated from changes to the franchise tax (discussed previously) and the tobacco tax. In addition, taxes paid on the presumptive market value of used vehicles (also discussed above) are earmarked for this fund. Amounts in the fund must be used to reduce school district property taxes and to equalize funding among school districts.

**Funding Equalization** A continuing controversy surrounding public school finance in Texas has been court-mandated funding equalization. The legislatively enacted wealth equalization plan, labeled the **"Robin Hood plan"** by its critics, requires wealthier districts (those with a tax base equal to $319,500 or more per student) to transfer money to poorer school districts. These wealthier school districts are known as "Chapter 41 districts," referring to the Education Code chapter that designates them. Despite court challenges, the "Robin Hood plan" has been found constitutional. One-third of the state-administered Property Tax Relief Fund may be used to equalize funding among districts, and thus, reduce funding demands on "Chapter 41 districts."

At the heart of the dispute regarding how to achieve equalized funding is whether all students in the state are entitled to receive the same quality of education. In a series of cases arising in the Edgewood Independent School District in San Antonio,[15] the Texas Supreme Court has consistently answered yes. The Texas Education Agency has created a system to measure educational quality by reviewing characteristics such as test score results from the Texas Assessment of Knowledge and Skills (TAKS) test administered to students each year, drop-out rates, and completion rates. Both individual schools and their districts are rated. In addition, the agency reviews results from each population subgroup (Hispanic, Anglo, African American, Native American, Asian/Pacific Islander, and economically disadvantaged) by campus and district. School districts are rated as exemplary, recognized, academically acceptable, or academically unacceptable. Districts receive an academically unacceptable rating if they perform below state standards in some area or with some population subgroup. School districts must meet accreditation standards established by the Texas Education Agency in which each district is assessed on its academic and financial accountability performance. Loss of accreditation results in a loss of state funding and closure. In addition, individual campuses rated academically unacceptable must achieve an academically acceptable rating within four years. Failure to do so results in the school's being closed or being transferred to a nonprofit organization or another school district.

Table 11.2 examines the 9 public school districts in Texas that met the TEA's exemplary standard and the 14 districts that failed to meet minimum state standards in 2005. The remaining 1,014 districts were either recognized or academically acceptable. Academically unacceptable districts that fail to improve may be consolidated with another district or taken over by the state.

**Restructuring School Finance** Under court order issued in *Neeley et al.* v. *West Orange-Cove Consolidated ISD, et al.*, the Texas Legislature was forced to restructure the state's school finance system. Although legislators have the

**Robin Hood plan** A plan for equalizing financial support for school districts by transferring tax money from rich districts to poor districts.

*Table 11.2*    Selected Characteristics of Exemplary and Academically Unacceptable Public School Districts (2004–2005)

| Exemplary Districts | | | Academically Unacceptable Districts | | |
|---|---|---|---|---|---|
| **District** | **District Enrollment** | **Chapter 41 District** | **District** | **District Enrollment** | **Chapter 41 District** |
| Divide ISD | 16 | Yes | Burton ISD | 332 | Yes |
| Doss Consolidated CSD | 31 | Yes | Calvert ISD | 244 | No |
| Highland Park ISD | 6,166 | Yes | Humble ISD | 28,159 | No |
| Lovejoy ISD | 1,122 | Yes | Kendleton ISD | 107 | No |
| Malta ISD | 143 | No | Kennard ISD | 379 | No |
| Nazareth ISD | 220 | No | Megargel ISD | 66 | No |
| Patton Springs ISD | 130 | No | Morgan ISD | 172 | No |
| Red Lick ISD | 397 | No | Penelope ISD | 187 | No |
| Walcott ISD | 167 | No | Ramirez CSD | 50 | No |
| | | | San Felipe–Del Rio CSD | 10,364 | No |
| | | | Star ISD | 97 | No |
| | | | Waelder ISD | 235 | No |
| | | | Walnut Springs ISD | 266 | No |
| | | | Wilmer-Hutchins ISD | 2,916 | No |

*Source:*  Compiled from information available from the Texas Education Agency, **www.tea.state.tx.us**.

authority to set the maximum tax rate a local government may assess against property. By constitutional prohibition, Texas cannot have a statewide property tax. All property tax rates must be set and collected by local governmental officials. When numerous school districts across the state reached the maximum amount that could be assessed as set by the legislature ($1.50 for each $100 in value through FY2006), the Supreme Court held that the legislature had effectively created a statewide property tax. In November 2005, the court issued an injunction set to become effective on June 1, 2006 prohibiting state funding of public schools under the existing system.

With these limitations, an impending deadline, and pressure from taxpayers to lower property taxes, the legislature returned to Austin on April 17, 2006 for a sixth attempt to restructure Texas's school finance system. In late 2005, Governor Perry had appointed a business-dominated Tax Reform Commission to conduct hearings across the state regarding possible taxes that could replace the property tax. Their recommendations included an expansion of the franchise tax to include more businesses, a $1-per-pack tax increase on cigarettes, stricter enforcement of the sales and use tax on used cars, and closing any funding gap with a portion of the $8.2 billion surplus the state had on hand. These funds were to be used to reduce property taxes assessed by local school districts. By the time the legislature convened, several business groups had endorsed the proposal, including the Greater Houston Partnership (an organization that includes the local Chamber of Commerce) and the Texas Association of Business & Chambers of Commerce. As a result, all of the Commission's proposals became law. These amounts funded the reduction of property taxes due to public school districts by one-third. In addition the legislature raised teacher salaries $2,000 per year and allocated funding for a merit-bonus program. A court dismissed the injunction prohibiting state funding of public education on May 25, 2006.[16]

Conflict erupted between State Comptroller Carole Keeton Strayhorn and Governor Rick Perry immediately. Strayhorn certified spending proposals for FY2007, but she argued the legislation for subsequent years represented "a hot check."[17] Even the Legislative Budget Board reflected an anticipated funding gap of $4.7 billion in FY2008, the first year in which all new taxes were to be assessed. This gap represents the difference between the expected new revenue and public school funding needs. Strayhorn also accused Perry of overstating the amount homeowners would save on their property tax bills. Governor Perry maintained that the comptroller failed to account for business growth in her calculations. Within three weeks of this exchange, the Legislative Budget Board and the Governor's Office of Budget, Planning, and Policy notified all state agencies to reduce their requests for FY2008 and FY2009 funding by 10 percent. The only exceptions were public schools, federal entitlement programs such as Medicaid, and the adult prison system. The amount of public school funding that must be financed by budget reductions from other state agencies and public higher education remains open.

## Public Higher Education

The state's public higher education system, like its public schools, suffers from the dual pressures of increasing enrollment and declining state support. The Texas Higher Education Coordinating Board's Closing the Gaps initiative requires all public institutions to participate actively in increasing the number of Texas college students by 630,000 over year 2000 enrollment levels by the year 2015. At a time when Texas legislators, and other state legislatures across the nation, work to balance state budgets by reducing funding to higher education, the Closing the Gaps initiative, if successful, will place additional demands on colleges and universities for faculty, staff, and facilities. Further, the success of this effort depends on more economically disadvantaged students enrolling in institutions of higher education. State financial aid remains inadequate to meet current demand. To solve some of these problems, the state has developed financial rewards and punishments, rewarding those who move quickly through their academic programs and punishing those who dawdle. Increasing enrollments and low levels of state funding have meant students are bearing more of the cost of their educations by paying higher tuition and taking out more loans.

**Community College Funding**   State financing of public community or junior colleges is based on a "contact hour of instruction" rate for vocational-technical and academic courses. This rate is determined by calculating the hours of

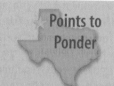

- Students at public universities who attempt more than 30 credit hours above those required for a baccalaureate degree in their major (typically 120 credit hours) can be charged out-of-state tuition rates (on average a difference of approximately $8,000 per year). Hours attempted include any courses in which a student remains enrolled after the twelfth class day.
- Students who earn a baccalaureate degree and attempt no more than 3 credit hours beyond the number required for the degree are eligible for a $1,000 tuition rebate upon graduation.
- Recipients of B-on-Time loans from the Texas Higher Education Coordinating Board can have their loans forgiven if they graduate with a "B" average within four calendar years of college enrollment (five years for certain programs and two years from a community college).
- Students at private universities must take at least 24 credit hours each year and maintain a 2.5 GPA to remain eligible for a Tuition Equalization Grant.

Points to Ponder

contact between an instructor and students. In addition, these two-year institutions use local property tax revenues, tuition, fees, gifts, and state and federal grants to finance their operations. Contact-hour funding to community colleges remains significantly below 1998 funding levels. During that same time period, costs increased. This gap in funding has been financed by students and local taxpayers.

**University Funding**   The 35 state universities and the Texas State Technical College System obtain basic financing from legislated biennial appropriations from the General Revenue Fund. They also obtain money from fees other than tuition, such as student service and computer use fees (which are deposited in the General Revenue Fund), auxiliary services income (for example, rent for campus housing and food service fees), grants, gifts, and special building funds. The University of Texas and the Texas A&M University systems share revenue from the Permanent University Fund (PUF) investments, with the University of Texas System receiving two-thirds of the money and the Texas A&M University System receiving one-third.

**Tuition Deregulation**   In late 2002, the University of Texas System led an effort to eliminate legislative caps on tuition and fees. According to university officials, funding limitations threatened the University of Texas at Austin's ability to remain a premier research institution. Despite fears that escalating tuition and fees would limit access to higher education for Texas's lower income students, the proposal became law in 2003.

Public community colleges and universities quickly moved to raise tuition. Both the dollar increase in tuition and the rate of increase have been dramatic. Figure 11.7 illustrates tuition rates before and after tuition deregulation. Study committees created by the Texas Senate reviewed the impact of these increases. No changes were made. Further, in 2005, the State Auditor's Office audited

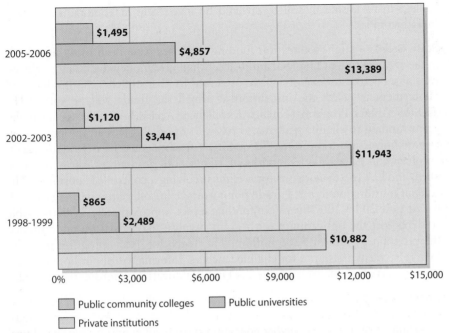

| | | | | |
|---|---|---|---|---|

**2005-2006**
$1,495
$4,857
$13,389

**2002-2003**
$1,120
$3,441
$11,943

**1998-1999**
$865
$2,489
$10,882

0%   $3,000   $6,000   $9,000   $12,000   $15,000

☐ Public community colleges    ☐ Public universities
☐ Private institutions

*Figure 11.7*   Tuition Rates for Selected Years (FY1999 through FY2006)   *Source:* Calculated from Texas Higher Education Coordinating Board, *College Student Budgets:* FY1999 to FY2006, available at **www.txhighereddata.org**

tuition increases at the state's four largest universities (University of Texas at Austin, Texas A&M University, University of Houston, and Texas Tech University) and found them all to be reasonable. By the spring of 2006, universities moved to raise tuition rates for academic year 2006–2007. State support of universities and community colleges rose at lower levels than tuition increases. These public institutions were included in the state's 10 percent budget reduction request discussed above.

A portion of the increased tuition dollars at public universities and community colleges must be set aside and awarded on a priority basis to meet financial needs of middle-class students who have unmet financial need and do not qualify for grant assistance. Of those eligible in 2004–2005, more than 62,000 students did not receive the assistance for which they qualified. University officials noted that identifying these priority-need students was difficult within the time constraints of financial-aid decisions.[18]

**Texas Tomorrow Funds**   The Texas Guaranteed Tuition Plan and Tomorrow's College Investment Plan comprise the Texas Tomorrow Funds. The Tuition Plan provides a way for parents to save for their children's education and to lock in the cost of tuition and fees at the state's public colleges and universities. The program is backed by the full faith and credit of the state of Texas. As tuition and fees began to rise during late 2003, the state closed the funds to new participants.

College living costs can still be covered by investment in Tomorrow's College Investment Plan.

**State Grants**    Higher-education funding increases have been most significant in the area of student financial aid. Rather than give money directly to colleges, legislators across the country have preferred to give students the funding and allow them to select the institution at which the funds will be spent. The **TEXAS Grants Program** (Toward Excellence, Access, and Success) provides grant funding to eligible students to pay all tuition and fees at any public college or university in the state. To qualify, a student must be a Texas resident, enroll in college within 16 months of high school graduation, show financial need, and have no convictions for a crime involving a controlled substance. The student must maintain a 2.5 grade point average in college to continue to qualify. At state 2006–2007 biennium funding levels, approximately 54,000 eligible students lost the opportunity for a grant because the legislature underfunded the program by almost $200 million. The Teach for Texas program provides loan repayment assistance for eligible teachers. Information about both of these programs is available from the Texas Higher Education Coordinating Board.

### Public Assistance

Enrolling more students in higher education is one way in which Texas's political leaders hope to address the issue of poverty. Income disparity between the wealthiest 20 percent of Texans and the poorest 20 percent is surpassed only by the gap between these two groups in the state of New York. A higher percentage of Texans lack health insurance than residents of any other state. The number of children without coverage also ranks as the highest in the nation, both in percentage and sheer numbers. Poverty levels remain above the national average (15.8% for Texas versus 12.1% for the nation as a whole) and are even more pronounced for young children (23% for Texas versus 18% for the nation as a whole) and the elderly (17.3% for Texas versus 10.2% for the nation as a whole). According to the Center for Public Policy Priorities, an advocacy group for low- and moderate-income people, access to public assistance benefits is more restricted in Texas than most other states because of eligibility requirements and lower levels of support.[19]

Rising health-care costs present significant challenges to state government. The percentage of the total state budget dedicated to health and human services (35 percent in FY2006–FY2007) now exceeds the amount of state funding available to public education (27 percent in FY2006–FY2007). Government welfare spending limits and restrictions on the amount of time individuals can qualify for Temporary Assistance to Needy Families (TANF) benefits will remain among the most pressing issues Texans and their government will confront in the years ahead.

Texas has little or no control over many of these policy matters. The federal–state partnership that exists in the TANF and Medicaid programs limits state responses. Federal law also continues to shift greater monetary responsibility for public assistance services to the states through devolution, even as the federal government issues mandates for these programs. Texas's economy

**TEXAS Grants Program**
"Toward Excellence, Access, and Success," the program provides funding for qualifying college and university students.

## How Do We Compare . . . in Tuition and Fees?

### Average Tuition and Fees for Academic Year 2005–2006

| Most Populous U.S. States | Private | Public University | Public Community College | U.S. States Bordering Texas | Private | Public University | Public Community College |
|---|---|---|---|---|---|---|---|
| California | $21,430 | $4,140 | $ 810 | Arkansas | $12,150 | $4,700 | $1,810 |
| Florida | $15,410 | $3,100 | $1,910 | Louisiana | Not reported. | $3,500 | $1,900 |
| New York | $21,760 | $4,950 | $3,490 | New Mexico | $21,380 | $3,310 | $1,470 |
| **Texas** | **$13,980** | **$4,830** | **$1,510** | Oklahoma | $13,420 | $3,430 | $2,260 |

*Source:* The College Board.

*Note:* Tuition rates are for in-state students at public universities and community colleges.

reacts to national and international economic conditions. Market conditions control the cost of health care services and other benefits. Natural disasters, such as Hurricanes Katrina and Rita, impact need forcing even more poor children and adults to rely on government to meet basic human needs of food, health care, and shelter. A review of Texas's fiscal policies provides insight into how the state will likely address these issues in the future.

For the past three biennia, the cost of Medicaid and the **Children's Health Insurance Program (CHIP)** exceeded budget allocations, even though many formerly eligible children are no longer covered. Some observers estimate that of the 1.4 million uninsured children in Texas in 2005, at least half, or 700,000, qualified for Medicaid or CHIP. Statutory changes and outsourcing by the Health and Human Services Commission had a dramatic impact on the number of children enrolled in these programs. From a high of 500,000 children insured by CHIP in 2003, the number plummeted to 295,000 by May 2006. Changing eligibility standards, requirements of recertification every six months, and reduced benefits accounted for much of this reduction. When Texas Access Alliance, under the leadership of Accenture, a Bermuda-based outsourcing firm and former consulting arm of now-defunct Arthur Andersen, took over enrollment responsibilities in 2005, membership in the program declined even more. One explanation offered by a Health and Human Services staff member was that about 20 percent of those previously covered by CHIP now qualified for Medicaid. However, an additional 79,000 children lost Medicaid benefits between November 2005 and May 2006. Problems with computer conversions and implementing a new eligibility system were cited as possible reasons for these declines. In May 2006, Health and Human Services Commissioner Albert Hawkins announced that the state would continue to employ state workers, and pay them retention bonuses to remain on the job and assist the transition to the private contractor. No date for the full transfer of responsibility had been announced as of September 2006.

Denying CHIP and Medicaid benefits to eligible children lowers the state's obligation to pay for benefits, but at what cost? For every dollar paid by the state, Texas receives an additional $1.50 for Medicaid and $2.60 for CHIP from the federal government, so reducing the state contribution also means giving up federal

**Children's Health Insurance Program (CHIP)** A program that provides medical insurance for children of low-income families.

money. Also, research conducted by the Robert Wood Johnson Foundation disclosed that uninsured children are ten times less likely to receive medical attention when they need it than are insured children.[20] Therefore, uninsured children are likely to have more severe symptoms and disease by the time they receive treatment. Much of the cost and care burden for uninsured residents, both children and adults, has shifted to local governments, hospitals, and the insured. Hospitals must subsidize unreimbursed costs for treating the uninsured by charging higher rates to the insured, which translates into higher insurance premiums.[21] Analysts project a continuing increase in indigent health care costs in the years to come. The ability of local entities to meet the social service needs of the state's low-income residents is one of the key challenges of the twenty-first century.

### Other Needs

In addition to demands for education, health, and human services, Texans look to state government to meet other needs. The state of Texas has a responsibility to provide a highway system for its residents. Public safety concerns are important to those who live here. Further, federal mandates regarding Homeland Security and the obligations of a state with a 1,254-mile long border with Mexico require both human and financial resources.

**Transportation**    Consistent with Texas's pay-as-you-go budget system is its pay-as-you-ride system of financing construction and maintenance of roads and highways. Historically, Texas roads have been financed through a combination of motor fuel taxes, motor vehicle registration fees, and the Federal Highway Trust Fund, to which certain federal highway user taxes are allocated. As increases in construction costs have exceeded funding, much of this expense has been transferred to users in the form of tolls. The reality of financing new highway construction with tolls was perhaps best expressed by Texas Transportation Commission Chair Ric Williamson when he described the policy as, "It's the no road, the toll road, or the slow road."[22] Increasing costs have required borrowing concessions, authorized by Texas voters by constitutional amendment. The Texas Mobility Fund allows the state to issue bonds and use the proceeds for road construction. A section of Texas 130, a toll way designed to provide an alternative north-south route around Austin, is the first project financed with these funds. Bonds will be repaid from tolls collected for roadway usage.

The **Trans-Texas Corridor** represents a private sector–public sector partnership intended to transform the transportation system of the Lone Star State. This 50-year development plan includes the potential acquisition of more than 548,000 acres of land, primarily from private landowners across the state, and the creation of more than 4,000 miles of new rights-of-way. It is anticipated that private contractors will build, maintain, and operate this system under the supervision of the Texas Department of Transportation. The rights-of-way will often be more than 300 yards wide and will include highways, rail lines, and utility easements. The only access will be from interstate, U.S., and some state highways, although the Texas Department of Transportation provides assur-

**Trans-Texas Corridor** A 50-year development plan to provide more than 4,000 miles of new rights-of-way in Texas that will include highways, railways, and utility easements.

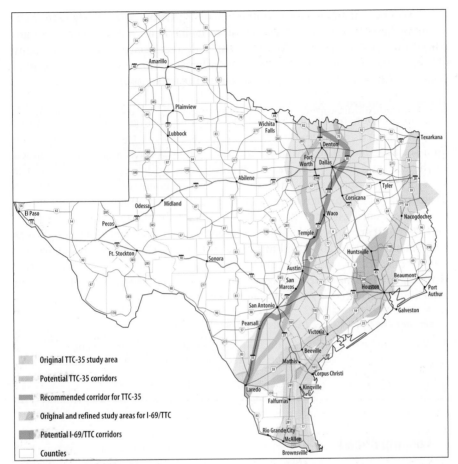

*Figure 11.8* Proposed Routes for Trans-Texas Corridor (March 2006)  Reprinted by permission of the Texas Department of Transportation.

ances on its web site that it will work with local officials to place entrance and exit ramps to towns along the way. Some private landowners, whose property may be subject to eminent domain claims by the state, oppose this program. Figure 11.8 shows the projected location of the corridor as of 2006.

**Public Safety Programs**   Historically, responsibility for protecting persons and property and providing other public safety programs was delegated to local governments. Today, various state agencies share the responsibility. The Department of Public Safety, for example, furnishes routine highway patrol functions, assists local law enforcement authorities in handling major crimes, and coordinates statewide efforts against lawlessness. For confinement of convicted felons, the Texas Department of Criminal Justice operates a system of prison units and state felony jails. (See the chapter "Laws, Courts, and Justice.")

After years of increasing the number of prison beds and passing laws that lengthened prison sentences, the legislature recognized the economic realities of these policies in the twenty-first century. State legislators now closely review the economic impact of proposed legislation to define new crimes or enhance punishment for existing felonies. An economic analysis convinced them that in many situations the cost of housing a felon for a longer term exceeded any potential benefit. With limited resources, prioritization became critical.

**Homeland Security**   Since September 11, 2001, federal, state, and local officials throughout the United States have given more attention to preparations for preventing or coping with terrorist actions. Most of the impetus for homeland security derives from the federal government. Yet, the states bear much of the cost and must perform and finance these unfunded mandates. As the United States continues to operate in an environment of heightened threat, Texas can anticipate increasing demands on the state budget for prevention and protection. Residents of the Lone Star State should also expect less monetary support from the federal government. Natural disasters like Hurricanes Katrina and Rita in 2005 will also add cost. There is, however, no guarantee that Texans will be safer than they were in 2001 or more secure from catastrophes. Safety is not appreciated unless an attack is experienced, plans for an attack are uncovered, or a hurricane makes landfall.

---

**Learning Check 11.4**         (Answers on p. 476)

1. What tax did state legislators reduce when they restructured school finance?
2. True or False: Tuition deregulation resulted in lower tuition at the state's public colleges and universities.
3. What is the Trans-Texas Corridor?

---

## ⭐ Looking Ahead

In the years ahead, Texas's governmental agencies will be forced to respond to the competing stresses of increasing demand and decreasing revenue. Doing more with less will be critical. In addition, taxpayers want better (at least from a business perspective) results for their money. This view is reflected in *Limited Government, Unlimited Opportunity* (2003), a study issued by Republican comptroller Carole Keeton Strayhorn. It concluded that Texas faced a "spending crisis, not a budget crisis" and that the Lone Star State's policymakers face the basic challenge of making government "smaller, smarter, and faster." Whether this government model will overcome the many challenges facing the state in the twenty-first century remains to be seen.

---

## ⭐ Chapter Summary

- Hurricanes Katrina and Rita created significant financial burdens for Texas and also provided additional revenue in the form of sales taxes and oil and gas royalty payments.

- Texas has one of the most regressive state tax systems in the United States because the Lone Star State relies so heavily on the sales tax and has no state income tax. Inability to tax Internet purchases and failure to tax most services cost the state significant revenue.
- Rather than raise taxes, Texas's elected officials often increase fees, fines, and other assessments.
- Texas operates with a pay-as-you-go budget.
- Each biennium, the Legislative Budget Board and the Governor's Office of Budget, Planning, and Policy are required to prepare proposed budgets. Tax collection, investment of the state's surplus funds, and overseeing management of the state's money are responsibilities of the comptroller of public accounts. The state auditor is responsible for examining all state accounts to ensure honesty and efficiency in agency spending of state funds.
- State revenue pays for services to Texas's residents. Most state money pays for public education (including higher education) and public assistance.
- Restructuring of the state's school finance system exposed weaknesses in the state's land- and property-based tax system.
- Texans who use services such as higher education and roads now must provide a greater portion of their funding.
- Unfunded mandates and devolution are federal policies that increase spending at the state level.

## Key Terms

- fiscal policy, *p. 440*
- service-sector, *p. 441*
- tax, *p. 441*
- regressive taxes, *p. 441*
- progressive taxes, *p. 442*
- fee, *p. 443*
- balanced budget, *p. 443*
- General Revenue Fund, *p. 443*
- general sales tax, *p. 446*
- Streamlined Sales Tax Project, *p. 447*
- selective sales taxes, *p. 447*
- sin tax, *p. 448*
- franchise tax, *p. 448*
- payroll tax, *p. 448*
- severance tax, *p. 449*

- grant-in-aid, *p. 453*
- securitization, *p. 454*
- "losers' fees," *p. 454*
- bonded debt, *p. 455*
- "rainy day" fund, *p. 456*
- budget, *p. 456*
- Legislative Budget Board (LBB), *p. 457*
- dual budgeting system, *p. 458*
- budget execution, *p. 460*
- Robin Hood plan, *p. 465*
- TEXAS Grants Program, *p. 470*
- Children's Health Insurance Program (CHIP), *p. 471*
- Trans-Texas Corridor, *p. 472*

## Learning Check Answers

### 11.1

1. Texas government depends heavily on sales taxes to finance services.
2. Texas requires a balanced budget, favors low taxes, and spends at low-to-moderate levels.
3. Texas has a regressive tax system, which means that poor people pay a higher percentage of their incomes in taxes than do wealthier residents.

### 11.2

1. States are attempting to devise a uniform sales tax system so Congress will allow state governments to force sellers, especially on-line merchants, to collect sales taxes on items they sell.
2. Lottery profits must be spent on public education.
3. The "rainy day" fund is to be used when the state faces an economic crisis.

### 11.3

1. A fiscal year is a budget year. In Texas it begins on September 1 and ends on August 31 of the following calendar year.
2. A state with a dual budgeting system requires both the executive branch and the legislative branch to prepare and submit proposed budgets to the legislature. In Texas, both the governor and the Legislative Budget Board submit proposed budgets.
3. The governor must request a transfer from one agency to another. That transfer must be approved by the Legislative Budget Board.

### 11.4

1. State legislators reduced the tax on real estate and other property, collected by local school districts, when they restructured school finance. They increased state taxes to replace the lost revenue from reduced property taxes.
2. False. Since tuition deregulation, student tuition has risen dramatically at public colleges and universities.
3. The Trans-Texas Corridor is a 50-year development plan to provide more than 4,000 miles of new rights-of-way in Texas that will include highways, railways, and utility easements.

## Discussion Questions

1. What services should Texas's government provide to the state's residents?
2. What are the advantages and disadvantages of a pay-as-you-go balanced budget requirement?
3. Should goods sold on the Internet be taxed?
4. What is the procedure for developing and approving a state budget?
5. What are some benefits and some disadvantages of the "Robin Hood" plan for public schools?
6. Who should pay more for higher education—the state's taxpayers or students?

## Internet Resources

Center for Public Policy Priorities: **www.cppp.org**
Legislative Budget Board: **www.lbb.state.tx.us**
Office of the Texas Comptroller of Public Accounts: **www.window.state.tx.us**
State Auditor's Office: **www.sao.state.tx.us**
Texas Education Agency: **www.tea.state.tx.us**
Texas Higher Education Coordinating Board: **www.thecb.state.tx.us**
Texas Lottery Commission: **www.txlottery.org**
Trans-Texas Corridor: **www.keeptexasmoving.com**

## ★ Notes

1. Michael Hedges, "Missouri Senator Urges Texas to Stop Seeking Katrina Funds," *Houston Chronicle*, March 9, 2006.
2. Billy Hamilton, "An Epic 100 Years Changes Texas," *Fiscal Notes* (December 1999): 1.
3. *The American Heritage Dictionary of the English Language*, 3d ed., ed. Anne H. Soukhanov (Boston: Houghton Mifflin, 1996), 669.
4. Jason Embry, "State Stashes Away Programs' Cash," *Austin American-Statesman*, August 5, 2005.
5. Polly Ross Hughes, "Poor in Texas to See Higher Power Bills," *Houston Chronicle*, August 9, 2005.
6. "Poll Finds Sales Tax Increase Opposed," *San Antonio Express-News*, February 21, 2005.
7. Clay Robison, "Court Has Spoken: School System on Verge of Collapse," *Houston Chronicle*, November 27, 2005.
8. Donald Bruce and William F. Fox, "State and Local Sales Revenue Losses from E-Commerce: Estimates as of July 2004." (Knoxville, TN: University of

Tennessee Center for Business and Economic Research, 2004), available at **www.newrules.org/retail/Ecommerceupdates.pdf.**

9. The Executive Committee Task Force on State and Local Taxation of Telecommunications and Electronic Commerce, National Council of State Legislatures, at **www.ncsl.org/programs/fiscal/tctelcom.htm.**

10. W. Gardner Selby, "Billions Out of Reach in Austin," *San Antonio Express-News*, February 21, 2005.

11. For excellent discussions regarding the process for issuing bonds in Texas, see various references on the Texas Bond Review Board web site, at **www.brb.state.tx.us,** including "Bonds 101" and the posted *Annual Reports*.

12. For excellent descriptions of the Texas budgeting process, see *Budget 101: A Guide to the Budget Process in Texas* (Austin: Senate Research Center, January 2005) and *Writing the State Budget: 79th Legislature*, State Finance Report No. 79–1 (Austin: House Research Organization, February 2005).

13. California Performance Review, "Biennial Budgeting Should Be Adopted," (Sacramento: Office of the Governor, 2004).

14. 176 S.W. 3rd 746 (Texas 2005). Justice Nathan Hecht's opinion in this case provides an excellent history of the school finance issues in Texas.

15. For an informative discussion of the holdings in the four cases arising in the Edgewood district, see Sharon Hope Weintraub, *School Daze and Legal Maze: Constitutional Challenges to Public School Finance in Texas* (Austin: Senate Research Center, September 2003).

16. For an excellent discussion of the school refinance bills and other legislation related to education adopted by the 79th Legislature, see House Research Organization, *Schools and Taxes: A Summary of Legislation of the 2006 Special Session*. Focus Report 79–13 (Austin: House Research Organization, Texas House of Representatives, May 25, 2006).

17. Clay Robison and Janet Elliott, "Across Finish Line, Perry Defends Plan," *Houston Chronicle*, May 16, 2006.

18. Polly Ross Hughes, "Priority Tuition Aid Missing the Mark," *Houston Chronicle*, September 8, 2005.

19. Lynsey Kluever, *Texas Poverty 101* (Austin: Center for Public Policy Priorities, February 2005), 3.

20. State Health Access Data Assistance Center and the Urban Institute, *Going Without: America's Uninsured Children* (Washington, D. C.: Robert Wood Johnson Foundation, August 2005), 11.

21. Office of the Comptroller, *The Uninsured: A Hidden Burden on Texas Employers and Communities* (Austin: Office of the Comptroller, April 2005).

22. Patrick Driscoll, "Gas Taxes Can't Fuel All Road Projects," *San Antonio Express-News*, 4 December 2005.

## Selected Readings

# 11.1  Put This Effort in Drive*

### Fort Worth Star-Telegram

*Do you enjoy camping and hiking in the state's parks? So do out-of-state tourists. Yet, chronic underfunding has jeopardized the Lone Star State's outdoor heritage, resulting in closures of portions of some parks, sales of some park lands, and disrepair of facilities. The following editorial highlights findings of the Texas State Parks Advisory Committee and calls on the Texas Legislature to act.*

Should Texans let their money-starved state parks system continue to rot? Or should we be good stewards of the system and dedicate ourselves to maintaining it properly?

A 17-member Texas State Parks Advisory Committee has delivered what should be the obvious answer: We should increase parks funding dramatically so as to not only maintain but improve and expand a great state asset that will become even more precious as our population swells and open space shrinks.

The committee, in a report released [August 24, 2006], said the system needs an additional $85 million annually. The money should be provided by dedicating all revenue from an existing sales tax on sporting goods to the parks, the panel said. Revenues from the tax, originally intended to be earmarked for parks, instead have been largely diverted to other expenditures. The tax raises about $105 million annually, but the parks system gets only about one-fifth of that.

The committee recommended spending an additional $45.4 million annually for operational and equipment needs and grants to local parks. It also advocated a 10-year capital program for major repairs and park acquistion that the Legislature could finance on a "pay-as-you-go" basis (at about $40 million annually) or through long-term debt (about $34.3 million annually).

The committee also called for releasing the rest of $101 million in bond money previously approved by

Texas voters for major park repairs. The parks system has received only about half that money. The recommendations would more than double annual spending on parks.

Texans recently were enraged to learn that millions of dollars raised from "conservation" license plates, such as the ones featuring Texas bluebonnets or horned lizards, aren't funding state parks even though motorists who agree to pay an additional $30 for the plates are told that's where the money is going. This deception of the public is fraudulent and must end.

Since 1990, the parks system has been receiving a shrinking share of the state budget. As a result, many facilities have been grossly neglected and are in disrepair. Some parks have been sold and parts of others shut down for lack of staffing. Texas now ranks 49th among the 50 states in per capita funding for state parks, and it shows.

At the local level in Tarrant County, the Texas Parks and Wildlife Department and the General Land Office should find a way to preserve the entirety of a 400-acre site bordering Eagle Mountain Lake in northwest Tarrant County for public parkland. Parks and Wildlife bought the site for a park in the 1980s but then did nothing with it. As a result, the General Land Office now has the property up for sale, and it could be snatched up by developers.

The Tarrant Regional Water District and Tarrant County have offered to buy the property, create a nature-oriented park and operate it. The Parks and Wildlife Commission and state Land Commissioner Jerry Patterson can expect an outpouring of public wrath if any portion of this property is sold to developers.

Patterson also could determine the fate of more than 1,900 acres of prairie in southwest Tarrant County that some are seeking to preserve in a natural state. In the case of both Tarrant County properties, Patterson is allowing parks and open-space advocates a limited period of time to see whether arrangements can be made to spare the properties from development.

Unless they're living under a rock, state officials should be getting the not-so-subtle message that residents not

*From "Put this effort in drive," *Fort Worth Star-Telegram*, August 27, 2006. Copyright 2006 by Knight Ridder Tribune Business News. Reproduced with permission of Knight Ridder Tribune Business News in the format Textbook via Copyright Clearance Center.

only in North Texas but throughout the state greatly value the parks system and other open space. The state parks advisory committee headed by former state Sen. John Montford should be commended for doing a fine job. And Parks and Wildlife Commission Chairman Joseph Fitzsimons deserves praise for selecting a caring, knowledgeable panel.

The state parks—stretching from swampy Caddo Lake in Northeast Texas to the rugged Big Bend region in far West Texas—are, first, an irreplaceable quality-of-life asset that all Texans can enjoy. Even in their current tattered condition, the parks also are an economic asset. They draw more than 10 million visitors annually and have an economic impact of nearly $800 million.

It's up to the Legislature to reverse its sad history of indifference toward the parks system. It must not only greatly increase parks funding but see that the state quits deceiving Texans by diverting money intended for parks to other purposes.

## 11.2  The Mission and Philosophy of Texas State Government*

### The Governor's Office of Budget, Planning and Policy, and the Legislative Budget Board

*As the chief executive officer of Texas, one of the governor's responsibilities, in collaboration with the Legislative Budget Board, is to furnish the guiding vision for government in the state. The state's mission and philosophy statements answer two questions about state government: What principles guide us? Why are we here? The following reading provides insight into the responses.*

March 2006

Fellow Public Servants:

The old adage remains true: If you fail to plan, you plan to fail. We must plan for prosperity. Strategic planning is critical to ensuring a future of opportunity and prosperity. We must always be willing to critically reexamine the role of Texas State Government and the efficiency of its operations. This document specifies our mission and priorities, reflects my philosophy of limited government and my belief in personal responsibility, and it is to be used as your agencies prepare their Strategic Plans. While the role of government must remain limited, governmental endeavors must be done with maximum efficiency and fairness.

Our endeavors must always have an eye first for the needs of our clients—the people of Texas.

Throughout the strategic planning process and the next legislative session, policymakers will endeavor to address our state's priorities and agencies will be asked to provide great detail about their operations. I encourage you to provide not only open and complete information but also your innovative ideas about how better to deliver government services.

Working together, I know we can accomplish our mission and address the priorities of the people of Texas. My administration is dedicated to creating greater opportunity and prosperity for our citizens, and to accomplish that mission, I am focused on the following critical priorities:

> *Assuring open access to an educational system that not only guarantees the basic core knowledge necessary for productive citizens but also emphasizes excellence and accountability in all academic and intellectual undertakings;*
>
> *Creating and retaining job opportunities and building a stronger economy that will lead to more prosperity for our people and a stable source of funding for core priorities;*
>
> *Protecting and preserving the health, safety, and well-being of our citizens by ensuring healthcare is accessible and affordable and by safeguarding our neighborhoods and communities from those who intend us harm; and*

*Governor's Office of Budget, Planning and Policy, and the Legislative Budget Board, *Instructions for Preparing and Submitting Agency Strategic Plans for Fiscal Years 2007–11* (March 2006), 31–33. Online at **www.governor.state.tx.us/divisions/bpp/files/2007splaninst.pdf**.

*Providing disciplined, principled government that invests public funds wisely and efficiently.*

I appreciate your commitment to excellence in public service.
RICK PERRY

## The Mission of Texas State Government

Texas State Government must be Limited, Efficient, and Completely Accountable. It should Foster Opportunity and Economic Prosperity, Focus on Critical Priorities, and Support the Creation of Strong Family Environments for our Children. The Stewards of the Public Trust must be men and women who Administer State Government in a Fair, Just, and Responsible Manner. To Honor the Public Trust, State Officials must seek new and Innovative ways to meet State Government Priorities in a Fiscally Responsible Manner.

*Aim High … We are not here to Achieve Inconsequential Things!*

## The Philosophy of Texas State Government

The task before all state public servants is to govern in a manner worthy of this great state. We are a great enterprise, and as an enterprise we will promote the following core principles:

- First and foremost, Texas matters most. This is the overarching, guiding principle by which we will make decisions. Our state, and its future, is more important than party, politics, or individual recognition.
- Government should be limited in size and mission, but it must be highly effective in performing the tasks it undertakes.
- Decisions affecting individual Texans, in most instances, are best made by those individuals, their families, and the local government closest to their communities.
- Competition is the greatest incentive for achievement and excellence. It inspires ingenuity and requires individuals to set their sights high. Just as competition inspires excellence, a sense of personal responsibility drives individual citizens to do more for their future and the future of those they love.
- Public administration must be open and honest, pursuing the high road rather than the expedient course. We must be accountable to taxpayers for our actions.
- State government has a responsibility to safeguard taxpayer dollars by eliminating waste and abuse, and providing efficient and honest government.

Finally, state government should be humble, recognizing that all its power and authority is granted to it by the people of Texas, and those who make decisions wielding the power of the state should exercise their authority cautiously and fairly.

---

An extensive bibliography of books and articles for this chapter is posted on Selected Sources for Reading, available online at http://college.hmco.com/PIC/brownPTP13e. For use with any chapter, see Resources for Further Research online at http://college.hmco.com/PIC/brownPTP13e.

# Glossary

*affirmative action*  Takes positive steps to attract women and minorities; may include using race in admission or hiring decisions.

*African American*  A racial classification indicating African ancestry.

*alien*  A person who is neither a national nor a citizen of the country where he or she is living.

*alternative dispute resolution (ADR)*  Use of mediation, conciliation, or arbitration to resolve disputes among individuals without resorting to a regular court trial.

*Anglo*  A term commonly used in Texas to identify non–Latino white people.

*annex*  To make an outlying area part of a city. Within a city's extraterritorial jurisdiction, the city can annex unincorporated areas without a vote by those who live there.

*appellate jurisdiction*  The power of a court to review cases after they have been tried elsewhere.

*appointive power*  The authority to name a person to a government office. Most gubernatorial appointments require Senate approval by two-thirds of the members present.

*appointment-retention system*  A merit plan for judicial selection, whereby the governor appoints to fill a court vacancy for a trial period after which the judge must win a full term in an uncontested popular election.

*Asian American*  A term used to identify people of Asian ancestry (e.g., Chinese, Japanese, Korean).

*at-large election*  Members of a policymaking body, such as some city councils, are elected on a citywide basis rather than from single-member districts.

*at-large majority district*  A district that elects two or more representatives.

*attorney general*  The constitutional official elected to head the Office of the Attorney General, which represents the state government in lawsuits and provides legal advice to state officials.

*balanced budget*  A budget in which total revenues and expenditures are equal, producing no deficit.

*Basin and Range Province*  An arid region in West Texas that includes the Davis Mountains, Big Bend National Park, and El Paso.

*bicameral*  Term describing a legislature with two houses or chambers (e.g., Texas's House of Representatives and Senate).

*bill*  A proposed law or statute.

*Bill of Rights*  Composed of 30 sections in Article 1 of the Texas Constitution, it guarantees protections for people and their property against arbitrary actions by state and local governments. Included among these rights are freedom of speech, press, religion, assembly, and petition. The Texas Bill of Rights is similar to the one found in the U.S. Constitution.

*block grants*  Congressional grants of money that allow the state considerable flexibility in spending for a program, such as providing welfare services.

*bond*  A certificate of indebtedness issued by a borrower to a lender that constitutes a legal obligation to repay the principal of a loan plus accrued interest. In Texas, both state and local governments issue bonds under restrictions imposed by state law.

*bonded debt*  Borrowings obtained through sale of revenue bonds and general obligation bonds.

*budget*  A plan indicating how much revenue a government expects to collect during a period (usually one or two fiscal years) and how much spending is authorized for agencies and programs.

*budget execution*  The process whereby the governor and the Legislative Budget Board oversee (and in some instances modify) implementation of the spending plan authorized by the Texas Legislature.

*budgetary power*  The governor is supposed to submit a state budget to the legislature at the beginning of each regular session. When an appropriation bill is enacted by the legislature and certified by the comptroller of public accounts, the governor may veto the whole document or individual items.

*bureaucrats*  Public employees.

*business organization*  An economic interest group, such as a trade association (e.g., Texas Association of Builders) that lobbies for policies favoring Texas business.

*Campaign Reform Act*   Enacted by the U.S. Congress and signed by President Bush in 2002, this law restricts donations of "soft money" and "hard money" for election campaigns, but it has been challenged in federal courts.

*canvass*   To scrutinize the results of an election and then confirm and certify the vote tally for each candidate.

*capital felony*   A crime punishable by death or life imprisonment.

*caucus*   A once-used nominating process involving selection of candidates by an informal committee of party leaders; also, a group of legislators organized according to party, racial/ethnic, ideological, or other identity.

*Children's Health Insurance Program (CHIP)*   A program that provides medical insurance for children of low-income families.

*chubbing*   A practice whereby supporters of a bill engage in lengthy debate for the purpose of using time and thus prevent floor action on another bill that they oppose.

*civil law*   The body of law concerning noncriminal matters, such as business contracts and personal injury.

*closed primary*   A primary in which voters must declare their support for the party before they are permitted to participate in the selection of its candidates.

*colonia*   A low-income settlement, typically located in South Texas and especially in counties bordering Mexico, that lacks running water, sewer lines, and other essentials.

*combined statistical area*   A geographic entity consisting of two or more adjacent core-based statistical areas.

*commission form*   A type of municipal government in which each elected commissioner is a member of the city's policymaking body, but also heads an administrative department (e.g., public safety with police and fire divisions).

*commissioner of agriculture*   The elected official who heads Texas's Department of Agriculture, which promotes the sale of agricultural commodities and regulates pesticides, aquaculture, egg quality, weights and measures, and grain warehouses.

*commissioner of education*   The official who heads the TEA.

*commissioner of insurance*   Appointed by the governor, the commissioner heads the Texas Department of Insurance, which is responsible for ensuring the industry's financial soundness and protecting policyholders.

*commissioner of the General Land Office*   As head of Texas's General Land Office, this elected constitutional officer oversees the state's extensive land holdings and related mineral interests, especially oil and gas leasing for the benefit of the Permanent School Fund.

*commissioners court*   A Texas county's policymaking body, with five members: the county judge, who presides, and four commissioners representing single-member precincts.

*commutation of sentence*   On the recommendation of the Board of Pardons and Paroles, the governor may commute (reduce) a sentence.

*companion bill*   Filed in one house but identical or similar to a bill filed in the other chamber, a companion bill speeds passage because committee consideration may take place simultaneously in both houses.

*comptroller of public accounts*   This elected constitutional officer is responsible for collecting taxes, keeping accounts, estimating revenue, and serving as treasurer for the state.

*concurrent jurisdiction*   The authority of more than one court to try a case (e.g., a civil dispute involving more than $500 but less than $5,000 may be heard in either a justice of the peace court or a county court).

*concurrent resolution*   A resolution adopted by House and Senate majorities and then approved by the governor (e.g., request for action by Congress or authorization for someone to sue the state).

*conditional pardon*   On recommendation of the Board of Pardons and Paroles, the governor may grant a conditional pardon. This act of clemency releases a convicted person from the consequences of his or her crime but does not restore all rights, as in the case of a full pardon.

*conference committee*   A committee composed of representatives and senators appointed to reach agreement on a disputed bill and recommend changes acceptable to both chambers.

*conservative*   Someone who advocates minimal intervention by government in social and economic matters and who gives a high priority to reducing taxes and curbing public spending.

**constitutional amendment process** Article XVII, Section 1, of the Texas Constitution stipulates that an amendment must be proposed by a two-thirds vote of members in each chamber of the legislature and approved by a simple majority of voters in a general or special election.

**constitutional guarantees** Included among the U.S. Constitution's guarantees to members of the Union are protection against invasion and domestic violence, territorial integrity, a republican form of government, representation by two senators and at least one representative in the U.S. Congress, and equitable participation in the constitutional amendment process.

**constitutional history of Texas** Texas constitutional history began with promulgation of the Constitution of Coahuila y Tejas within the Mexican federal system in 1827 and the Constitution of the Texas Republic in 1836. Texas has since been governed under its state constitutions of 1845, 1861, 1866, 1869, and 1875.

**constitutional revision** Extensive or complete rewriting of a constitution.

**constitutional revision convention** A body of delegates who meet to make extensive changes in a constitution or to draft a new constitution.

**contingency fee** A lawyer's compensation paid from money recovered in a lawsuit.

**council of governments (COGs)** A regional planning body composed of governmental units (e.g., cities, counties, special districts); functions include review and comment on proposals by local governments for obtaining state and federal grants.

**council-manager form** A system of municipal government in which an elected city council hires a manager to coordinate budgetary matters and supervise administrative departments.

**county** Texas is divided into 254 counties that serve as an administrative arm of the state and provide important services at the local level, especially within rural areas.

**county attorney** An individual elected to represent the county in civil and criminal cases, unless a resident district attorney performs these functions.

**county auditor** A person appointed by the district judge or judges to check the financial books and records of other officials who handle county money.

**county chair** Elected by county party members in the primaries, this key party official heads the county executive committee.

**county clerk** An individual elected to perform clerical chores for the county court and commissioners court, keep public records, maintain vital statistics, and administer public elections, if the county does not have an administrator of elections.

**county convention** A party meeting of precinct delegates held on the second Saturday after precinct conventions; it elects delegates and alternates to the state convention.

**county executive committee** Composed of a party's precinct chairs and the elected county chair, the county executive committee conducts primaries and makes arrangements for holding county conventions.

**county judge** An individual popularly elected to preside over the county commissioners court and, in many counties, to hear civil and criminal cases.

**county sheriff** An individual popularly elected as the county's chief law enforcement officer; the sheriff is also responsible for maintaining the county jail.

**county tax appraisal district** The district appraises all real estate and commercial property for taxation by units of local government within a county.

**county tax assessor-collector** This elected official no longer assesses property for taxation but does collect motor vehicle license fees.

**county treasurer** An elected official who receives and pays out county money as directed by the commissioners court.

**court of record** Has a court reporter to record testimony and proceedings.

**criminal law** The body of law concerning felony and misdemeanor offenses by individuals against other persons and property.

**crossover voting** A practice whereby a person participates in the primary of one party, then votes for one or more candidates of another party in the general election.

**cumulative voting** When multiple vacancies occur in more than 40 at-large city councils in Texas, voters cast one or more of the specified number of votes for one or more candidates in any combination. It is designed to increase representation of minorities.

**dealignment** Citizens abandon allegiance to a political party and become independent voters.

*decentralized government* Decentralization is achieved by dividing power between national and state governments and separating legislative, executive, and judicial branches at both levels.

*defendant* The person sued in a civil proceeding or prosecuted in a criminal proceeding.

*delegated powers* Specific powers entrusted to the national government by Article 1, Section 8, of the U.S. Constitution (e.g., regulate interstate commerce, borrow money, and declare war).

*deregulation* The elimination of government restrictions to allow free-market competition to determine or limit the actions of individuals and corporations.

*devolution* Devolution exists when the federal government's financial and administrative responsibilities shift to state and local governments, especially in the area of social services.

*direct primary* A nominating system that allows voters to participate directly in the selection of candidates for public office.

*district convention* Held on the second Saturday after the first primary in counties that have more than one state senatorial district. Participants elect delegates to the party's state convention.

*district executive committee* Composed of county chairs within a district that elects a state senator, representative, or district judge, this committee meets to fill a vacancy created by the death, resignation, or disqualification of a nominated candidate.

*dual budgeting system* The compilation of separate budgets by the legislative branch and the executive branch.

*early voting* Conducted at the county court house and selected polling places before the designated primary, special, or general election day.

*economic interest group* Trade associations and labor unions are classified as economic interest groups because they are organized to promote policies that will maximize profits and wages.

*electioneering* Active campaigning on behalf of a candidate; the total efforts made to win an election.

*election judge* Appointed by the county commissioners court to administer an election in a voting precinct.

*elections administrator* Less than 12 percent of Texas counties employ a full-time elections administrator to supervise voter registration and voting.

*elite access* The ability of the business elite to deal directly with high-ranking government administrators to avoid meeting regulations.

*equal opportunity* Takes care that policies and actions do not discriminate.

*exclusive jurisdiction* Authority of only one court to hear a particular type of case.

*executive commissioner of the Health and Human Services Commission* Appointed by the governor with Senate approval, this executive commissioner administers the HHSC, develops policies, makes rules, and appoints (with approval by the governor) commissioners to head the commission's four departments.

*executive order* The governor issues executive orders to set policy within the executive branch and to create task forces, councils, and other bodies.

*extraterritorial jurisdiction (ETJ)* The limited authority a city has outside its boundaries. The larger the city's population size, the larger the reach of its ETJ.

*federal grants-in-aid* Money appropriated by the U.S. Congress to help states provide needed facilities and services.

*fee* A fixed sum charged by government for a privilege.

*felony* A serious crime punished by fine and prison confinement.

*filibustering* A delaying tactic whereby a senator may speak, and thus hold the Senate floor, for as long as physical endurance permits.

*fiscal policy* Public policy that concerns taxing, government spending, public debt, and management of government money.

*food stamp program* Joint federal-state program administered by the state to provide food to low income people.

*franchise tax* This tax is levied on the annual receipts of businesses organized to limit the personal liability of owners.

*frontier experience* Coping with danger, physical hardships, and economic challenges tested the endurance of nineteenth-century Texans and contributed to the development of individualism.

*full faith and credit clause* It means that most government actions of another state must be officially recognized by public officials in Texas.

*full pardon* On recommendation of the Board of Pardons and Paroles, the governor may grant a full pardon. This act of executive clemency releases a convicted person from all consequences of a criminal act and restores rights enjoyed by others who have not been convicted of a crime.

*general election*  Held in November of even-numbered years to elect county and state officials from among candidates nominated in primaries or (for small parties) in nominating conventions.

*General Revenue Fund*  An unrestricted state fund which is available for general appropriations.

*general sales tax*  At the rate of 6.25 percent of a sale, the general sales tax is Texas's largest source of tax revenue. It is applied largely to the sale price of tangible personal property and "the storage, use, or other consumption of tangible personal property purchased, leased, or rented."

*general-law city*  Municipality with a charter prescribed by the legislature.

*gerrymandering*  Drawing the boundaries of a district (e.g., state senatorial district) to include or exclude certain groups of voters and thus affect election outcomes.

*ghost voting*  A prohibited practice whereby one representative presses the voting button of another House member who is absent.

*government*  A public institution with authority to allocate values by formulating, adopting, and implementing public policies.

*Governor's Office*  The Office of the Governor is the administrative organization through which the governor of Texas makes appointments, prepares a biennial budget recommendation, administers federal and state grants for crime prevention and law enforcement, and confers full and conditional pardons on recommendation of the Board of Pardons and Paroles.

*graded penalties*  Depending on the nature of the crime, felonies are graded as first, second, and third degree; misdemeanors are graded as A, B, and C.

*grand jury*  Composed of 12 persons with the qualifications of trial jurors, a grand jury serves from three to six months while it determines if sufficient evidence exists to indict persons accused of committing crimes.

*grandfather clause*  Exempted people from educational, property, or tax requirements for voting if they were qualified to vote before 1866 or 1867, or were descendents of such persons.

*grant-in-aid*  Money, goods, or services given by one government to another (e.g., federal grants-in-aid to states for financing public assistance programs).

*Great Plains*  A large area in West Texas extending from Oklahoma to Mexico, the Great Plains is an extension of the Great High Plains of the United States.

*group leadership*  Leaders of groups tend to have financial resources that permit them to contribute money and devote time to group affairs.

*Gulf Coastal Plains*  Stretching from the Louisiana border to the Rio Grande, Texas's Gulf Coastal Plains area is an extension of the Gulf Coastal Plains of the United States.

*hard money*  Campaign money contributed directly by individuals.

*high technology*  Technology that applies to research, development, manufacturing, and marketing of computers and other electronic products.

*home-rule city*  Municipality with a locally drafted charter.

*impeachment*  Process in which the Texas House of Representatives, by a simple majority vote, initiates action (brings charges) leading to possible removal of certain judicial and executive officials (e.g., the governor) by the Senate.

*implied powers*  Powers inferred by the constitutional authority of the U.S. Congress "to make all laws which shall be necessary and proper for carrying into execution the foregoing [delegated] powers, and all other powers vested by this Constitution in the government of the United States, or in any department or officer thereof."

*independent candidate*  A candidate who runs in a general election without party endorsement or selection.

*independent school district (ISD)*  Created by the legislature, an independent school district raises tax revenue to support its public schools. Voters within the district elect a board that hires a superintendent, determines salary schedules, selects textbooks, and sets the property tax rate for the district.

*individualistic culture*  This culture looks to government to maintain a stable society but with minimum intervention in the lives of the people.

*initiative*   A citizen-drafted measure proposed by a specific number or percentage of qualified voters, which becomes law if approved by popular vote. In Texas, this process occurs only at the local level, not at the state level.

*interest group*   An organization that seeks to influence government officials and their policies on behalf of members sharing common views and objectives (e.g., labor union or trade association).

*interest group techniques*   These actions include lobbying, personal communication, favors and gifts, grassroots activities, electioneering, campaign financing by political action committees, and, in extreme instances, bribery and other unethical practices.

*intergovernmental relations*   Relationships between different governments. They may be on the same or different levels.

*Interior Lowlands*   This region covers the North Central Plains of Texas extending from the Dallas–Fort Worth Metroplex westward to the Abilene area and northward to the Wichita Falls area.

*Jim Crow*   "Jim Crow" laws were ethnically discriminatory laws that segregated African Americans and denied them access to public services for many decades after the Civil War.

*joint resolution*   Must pass by a majority vote in each house when used to memorialize the U.S. Congress or to ratify an amendment to the U.S. Constitution. As a proposal for an amendment to the Texas Constitution, a joint resolution requires a two-thirds majority vote in each house.

*judgment*   A judge's written opinion based on a verdict.

*jungle primary*   Louisiana conducts a jungle primary in which candidates from all parties compete in a single election. A candidate who receives 50 percent or more of the vote is elected; otherwise, a runoff between the top two candidates must be held.

*junior college or community college district*   Establishes one or more two-year colleges that offer both academic and vocational programs.

*jurisdiction*   A court's authority to hear a particular case.

*labor organization*   A union that supports public policies designed to increase wages, obtain adequate health insurance coverage, provide unemployment insurance, promote safe working conditions, and otherwise protect the interests of workers.

*Latino*   This is an ethnic classification of Mexican Americans and others of Latin American origin. When applied to females, the term is *Latina*.

*Legislative Budget Board (LBB)*   A 10-member body co-chaired by the lieutenant governor and the speaker of the House, this board and its staff prepare a biennial current-services budget. In addition, the LBB assists with the preparation of a general appropriation bill at the beginning of a regular legislative session; and, if requested, it prepares fiscal notes that assess the economic impact of a proposed bill or resolution.

*legislative caucus*   An organization of legislators who seek to maximize their influence over issues in which they have a common interest.

*legislative power*   The governor's legislative power is exercised through messages delivered to the Texas Legislature, vetoes of bills and concurrent resolutions, and calls for special sessions of the legislature.

*liberal*   One who favors government regulation to achieve a more equitable distribution of wealth.

*lieutenant governor*   Popularly elected, serves as president of the Senate, and is first in the line of succession if the office of governor becomes vacant before the end of a term.

*line-item veto*   Action by the governor to delete a line item while permitting enactment of other parts of an appropriation bill.

*literacy test*   As a prerequisite for voter registration, this test was designed and administered in ways intended to prevent African Americans and Latinos from voting.

*lobbying*   Communicating with legislators or other government officials on behalf of an interest group or a corporation for the purpose of influencing the decision-making process.

*local government*   The Texas Constitution authorizes these units of local government: counties, municipalities, school districts, and other special districts. These "grassroots governments" provide a wide range of services that include rural roads, protection of persons and property, city streets, and public education.

*losers' fees*   A surcharge added to assessments against the few who get caught disobeying a law violated by many.

*maquiladora*   An assembly plant that uses cheap labor and is located on the Mexican side of the U.S.–Mexican border.

*martial law* Temporary rule by military authorities when civil authorities are unable to handle a riot or other civil disorder.

*Medicaid* Funded in largest part by federal grants and in part by state appropriations, Medicaid is administered by the state. It provides medical care for persons whose incomes fall below the poverty line.

*Medicare* Funded entirely by the federal government and administered by the U.S. Department of Health and Human Services, Medicare provides medical assistance to qualified applicants age 65 and older.

*merit system* Hiring, promoting, and firing on the basis of objective criteria such as tests, degrees, experience, and performance.

*message power* The governor's State of the State address at the "commencement" of a legislative session and messages delivered in person or in writing are examples of gubernatorial exercise of message power to communicate with legislators and the public.

*metro government* Consolidation of units of local government within an urban area under a single authority.

*metropolitan division* County or group of counties within a core based statistical area that contains a core with a population of at least 2.5 million.

*metropolitan statistical area* A freestanding urban area with a minimum total population of 50,000.

*metropolitanization* Concentration of people in urban centers that become linked.

*micropolitan statistical area* An area that has at least one urban cluster with a population of at least 10,000, but less than 50,000.

*misdemeanor* Classified as A, B, or C, a misdemeanor may be punished by fine and/or jail sentence.

*Missouri Plan* A judicial selection process in which a commission recommends a panel of names to the governor, followed by a one-year or so appointment before voters determine whether the judge will be retained for a full term.

*moralistic culture* This culture influences people to view political participation as their duty and to expect that government will be used to advance the public good.

*motor voter law* Legislation requiring certain government offices (e.g., motor vehicle licensing agencies) to offer voter registration applications to clients.

*multimember district* A district in which all voters participate in the election of two or more representatives to a policymaking body, such as a city council or a state legislature.

*municipal bonds* General obligation bonds (redeemed from city tax revenue) and revenue bonds (redeemed from revenue obtained from the property or activity financed by the sale of the bonds) are authorized under Texas law.

*municipal government* A local government for an incorporated community established by law as a city.

*national supremacy clause* Article VI of the U.S. Constitution states: "This Constitution, and the Laws of the United States which shall be made in Pursuance thereof; and all Treaties made, or which shall be made, under the Authority of the United States, shall be the supreme Law of the Land. . . ."

*Native American* A descendent of the first Americans, who were called *indios* by Spanish explorers and Indians by Anglo settlers who arrived later.

*neoconservatism* A political ideology that reflects fiscal conservatism but accepts a limited governmental role in solving social problems.

*neoliberal* A political view that advocates less government regulation of business but supports more governmental involvement in social matters.

*noneducation special districts* Special districts other than school districts or community college districts, such as fire prevention or crime control districts, that are units of local government and may cover part of a county, a whole county, or areas in two or more counties.

*nonpartisan blanket primary* A nominating process whereby voters indicate their preferences by using a single ballot on which are printed the names and respective party labels of all persons seeking nomination.

*nonpartisan election* An election in which candidates are not identified on the ballot by party label.

*North American Free Trade Agreement (NAFTA)* An agreement among the United States, Mexico, and Canada designed to expand trade among the three countries by reducing and then eliminating tariffs over a 15-year period.

*off-year or midterm election* A general election held in the even-numbered year following a presidential election.

*open primary*   A primary in which voters are not required to declare party identification.

*ordinance*   A local law enacted by a city council or approved by popular vote in a referendum election.

*organizational pattern*   Some interest groups have a decentralized pattern of organization (e.g., the AFL-CIO, with many local unions). Others are centralized (e.g., the National Rifle Association, which is a national body without affiliated local or regional units).

*original jurisdiction*   The power of a court to hear a case first.

*parliamentarian*   An expert on rules of order who sits at the left of the presiding officer in the House or Senate and is ever ready to give advice on procedural questions.

*parole*   Release from prison before completion of a sentence; good behavior of the parolee is a condition of release.

*patrón system*   A type of boss rule that has dominated areas of South Texas.

*patronage system*   Hiring friends and supporters as government employees without regard to their abilities.

*payroll tax*   Levied against a portion of the wages and salaries of employees to provide funds for payment of unemployment insurance benefits to these people when they lose their jobs.

*permanent party organization*   In Texas, the precinct chairs, county and district executive committees, and the state executive committee form the permanent organization of a political party.

*petit jury*   A trial jury of 6 or 12 members.

*physical region*   An area identified by unique geographic features, e.g., the Gulf Coastal Plains and the Great Plains.

*plaintiff*   The injured party who initiates a civil suit or the state in a criminal proceeding.

*platform*   A document that sets forth a political party's position on issues such as an income tax, school vouchers, or public utility regulation.

*plural executive*   The governor and elected department heads as provided by the Texas Constitution.

*political action committee (PAC)*   An organizational device used by corporations, labor unions, and other organizations to raise money for campaign contributions.

*political culture*   Attitudes, habits, and general behavior patterns that develop over time and affect the political life of a state or region.

*political inefficacy*   The inability to influence the nomination and election of candidates and the decision making of governing bodies. In Texas, this has been a major problem for minorities and low-income groups.

*political influence of interest groups*   This highly variable factor depends largely on the size of a group's membership, financial resources, quality of leadership, and degree of unity.

*political party*   An organization influenced by political ideology whose primary interest is to gain control of government by winning elections.

*politics*   The process by which individuals and political parties nominate and elect public officials and formulate public policy.

*poll tax*   A tax levied in Texas from 1902 until a similar Virginia tax was declared unconstitutional in 1962; failure to pay the annual tax (usually $1.75) made a citizen ineligible to vote in party primaries or in special and general elections.

*population shifts*   Within Texas, changes in population density have featured demographic movements from rural to urban areas and from large cities to suburbs and back.

*postadjournment veto*   Rejection by the governor of a pending bill or concurrent resolution during the 20 days following a legislative session.

*power group*   An effective interest group strongly linked with legislators and bureaucrats for the purpose of influencing decision making and having a continuing presence in Austin as a "repeat player" from session to session.

*precinct chair*   The party official responsible for the interests and activities of a political party in a voting precinct; typical duties include supervising party volunteer workers, encouraging voter registration, and getting out the vote on election day.

*precinct convention*   At the lowest level of political party organization, voters convene in March of even-numbered years to adopt resolutions and to name delegates to a county convention.

*president of the Senate*   Title of the lieutenant governor in his or her role as presiding officer for the Texas Senate.

*presidential preference primary*   A primary in which the voters indicate their preference for a person seeking nomination as the party's presidential candidate.

*primary election*   A preliminary election conducted within the party to select candidates who will run for public office in a subsequent general election.

*privileges and immunities*   Article IV of the U.S. Constitution guarantees that "citizens of each state shall be entitled to the privileges and immunities of citizens of the several states." According to the U.S. Supreme Court, this means that citizens are guaranteed protection by government, enjoyment of life and liberty, the right to acquire and possess property, the right to leave and enter any state, and the right to use state courts.

*probate*   Probate cases involving wills and guardianships fall under the jurisdiction of county courts and probate courts.

*procedural committee*   These House committees (e.g., Calendars Committee and House Administration Committee) consider bills and resolutions relating primarily to internal legislative matters.

*proclamation*   A governor's official public announcement (e.g., calling a special election or declaring a disaster area).

*professional group*   An organization of physicians, lawyers, accountants, or other professional people that lobbies for policies beneficial to members.

*progressive taxes*   A tax in which the effective tax rate increases as the tax base (e.g., individual income, corporate profits) increases.

*property tax*   A tax property owners pay according to the value of their homes and businesses. At the local level, property owners pay this tax to the city, the county, the school district, and often other special districts.

*public administration*   The implementation of public policy by government employees.

*public interest group*   An organization claiming to represent a broad public interest (environmental, consumer, civil rights) rather than a narrow private interest.

*public officer and employee group*   An organization of city managers, county judges, or other public employees or officials that lobbies for public policies that protect group interests.

*public policy*   Government action designed to meet a public need or goal as determined by a legislative body or other authorized officials.

*Public Utility Commission (PUC)*   A three-member body with regulatory power over the electric power and telephone companies.

*racial and ethnic groups*   Organizations such as the National Association for the Advancement of Colored People and the League of United Latin American Citizens, which seek to influence government decisions affecting African Americans and Latinos, respectively.

*racial gerrymandering*   Drawing districts designed to affect representation of a racial group (e.g., African Americans) in a legislative chamber, city council, commissioners court, or other representative body.

*Railroad Commission of Texas (RRC)*   A popularly elected, three-member commission primarily engaged in regulating natural gas and petroleum production.

*"rainy day" fund*   A fund used for stabilizing state finance when revenue is insufficient to cover state-supported programs.

*realignment*   Occurs when members of one party shift their affiliation to another party.

*reapportionment*   States get seats in the U.S. House of Representatives in proportion to their population. After the 2000 census Texas was apportioned 32 seats.

*recall*   A process for removing elected officials through a popular vote. In Texas, this power is available only at the local level, not at the state level.

*recess appointment*   An appointment made by the governor when the Texas Legislature is not in session.

*recidivism*   Criminal behavior that results in reincarceration after a person has been released from confinement for a prior offense.

*redistricting*   Redrawing of boundaries following the federal decennial census to create districts with approximately equal population (e.g., legislative, congressional, and commissioners court districts in Texas).

*referendum*   A process by which issues are referred to the voters to accept or reject. Voters may also petition for a vote to repeal an existing ordinance. In Texas, this process occurs at the local level. At the state level, bonds secured by taxes and state constitutional amendments must be approved by the voters.

*regressive tax*   A tax in which the effective tax rate falls as the tax base (e.g., individual income, corporate profits) increases.

*regular session*   A session of the Texas Legislature that begins on the second Tuesday in January of odd-numbered years and lasts for a maximum of 140 days.

*religious-based group*   An interest group such as the Christian Coalition or the Texas Faith Network that lobbies for policies promoting its religious interests.

*removal power*   Authority to remove an official from office. In Texas, the governor's removal power is limited to staff members, some agency heads, and (only with the consent of the Senate) to other appointees.

*reprieve*   An act of executive clemency that temporarily suspends execution of a sentence.

*reserved powers*   The Tenth Amendment of the U.S. Constitution declares that "The powers not delegated by the Constitution, nor prohibited by it to the States, are reserved to the States, respectively, or to the people." Although not spelled out in the U.S. Constitution, these reserved powers include police power, taxing power, proprietary power, and power of eminent domain.

*right of association*   The U.S. Supreme Court has ruled that this right is part of the right of assembly guaranteed by the First Amendment of the U.S. Constitution and that it protects the right of people to organize into groups for political purposes.

*Robin Hood plan*   A plan for equalizing financial support for school districts by transferring tax money from rich districts to poor districts.

*runoff primary*   Held a month after the first primary to allow party members to choose a candidate from the first primary's top two vote-getters.

*secretary of state*   The state's chief elections officer, appointed by the governor for a term concurrent with that of the governor.

*securitization*   Sale of bonds backed by anticipated future payments of tobacco settlements.

*select committee*   Created independently by the speaker, a select committee may work on emergency legislation early in a session before substantive committees are appointed.

*selective sales taxes*   These are quantity-based consumption taxes on specific products.

*senatorial courtesy*   Before making an appointment, the governor is expected to obtain approval from the state senator in whose district the prospective appointee resides; failure to obtain such approval will probably cause the Senate to "bust" the appointee.

*separation of powers*   The assignment of lawmaking, law-enforcing, and law-interpreting functions to separate branches of government.

*service sector*   Businesses that provide services such as finance, health care, food service, data processing, or consulting.

*severance tax*   An excise tax levied on a natural resource (e.g., oil or natural gas) when it is severed (removed) from the earth.

*simple resolution*   A resolution that requires action by one legislative chamber only and is not acted on by the governor.

*sin tax*   A selective sales tax on items such as cigarettes, other forms of tobacco, and alcoholic beverages.

*single-member district*   An area that elects only one representative to serve on a policymaking body (e.g., city council, county commissioners court, state House and Senate).

*small-claims court*   Presided over by a justice of the peace, a small claims court offers an informal and inexpensive procedure for handling damage claims of $5,000 or less.

*social interest group*   Included among groups concerned primarily with social issues are organizations devoted to civil rights, racial and ethnic matters, religion, and public interest protection.

*soft money*   campaign money donated to national political parties rather than to candidates.

*sound bite*   A 15-second statement of a candidate's theme communicated by radio or television.

*speaker of the House*   The state representative elected by House members to serve as the presiding officer for that chamber.

*special election*   An election called by the governor to fill a vacancy (e.g., U.S. congressional or state legislative office) or vote on a proposed state constitutional amendment or local bond issue.

*special interim committee*   A Senate committee appointed by the lieutenant governor to study an important policy issue between regular sessions.

*special issues*   Questions a judge gives a trial jury to answer to establish facts in a case.

*special session*   A legislative session called by the governor and limited to not more than 30 days.

*Spindletop Field*   Located near Beaumont, this oil field sparked a boom in 1901 that made Texas a leading petroleum producer.

*standing committee*   A Senate committee appointed by the lieutenant governor for the purpose of considering proposed bills and resolutions prior to possible floor debate and voting by senators.

*State Board of Education (SBOE)*   A popularly elected 15-member body with limited authority over Texas's K-12 education system.

*state convention* Convenes every even-numbered year to make rules for a political party, adopt a party platform and resolutions, and select members of the state executive committee; in a presidential election year it elects delegates to the national convention and names members to serve on the national committee.

*state executive committee* Composed of a chair, vice chair, and two members from each senatorial district, this body is part of a party's permanent organization.

*straight-ticket voting* Voting for all the candidates of one party.

*stratarchy* A political system wherein power is diffused among and within levels of party organization.

*Streamlined Sales Tax Project* A voluntary effort by a number of states to simplify collection and administration procedures of the sales tax for sellers so that sales tax can be collected on Internet and catalog purchases.

*strong mayor-council form* A type of municipal government with a separately elected legislative body (council) and an executive head (mayor) elected in a citywide election with veto, appointment, and removal powers.

*substantive committee* Appointed by the House speaker, a substantive committee considers bills and resolutions related to the subject identified by its name (e.g., House Agriculture Committee) and may recommend passage of proposed legislation to the appropriate calendar committee.

*suburbanization* Growth of relatively small towns and cities, usually incorporated but outside the corporate limits of a central city.

*suffrage* The right to vote.

*sunset review process* Over a cycle of 12 years, each state agency is studied, and then the legislature decides whether to abolish, merge, or retain it.

*superdelegate* An unpledged party official or elected official who serves as a delegate to a party's national convention.

*tax* A compulsory contribution exacted by a government for a public purpose.

*tax reinvestment zone (TRZ)* Municipal tax incentives are offered to encourage businesses to locate in and contribute to the development of a blighted urban area. Commercial and residential property taxes are frozen.

*Temporary Assistance for Needy Families (TANF)* Replaced Aid for Families with Dependent Children (AFDC) in an attempt to help poor people move from welfare to the workforce.

*temporary party organizations* Primaries and conventions that function briefly to nominate candidates, pass resolutions, adopt a party platform, and select delegates to party conventions at higher levels.

*Tenth Amendment* The Tenth Amendment of the U.S. Constitution declares that "the powers not delegated by the Constitution, nor prohibited by it to the States, are reserved to the States, respectively, or to the people." Although not spelled out in the U.S. Constitution, these reserved powers include police power, taxing power, proprietary power, and power of eminent domain.

*term limits* Restriction on the number of terms officials can serve in a public office.

*Texas Assessment of Knowledge and Skills (TAKS)* A standardized test covering a core curriculum.

*Texas Commission on Environmental Quality (TCEQ)* The state agency that coordinates Texas's environmental protection efforts.

*Texas Constitution of 1876* Texas's lengthy, much-amended constitution, a product of the post-Reconstruction era.

*Texas Department of Transportation (TxDOT)* Headed by a three-member commission, the department maintains almost 80,000 miles of roads and highways and promotes highway safety.

*Texas Education Agency (TEA)* Administers the state's public school system of more than 6,300 schools.

*Texas Election Code* The body of state law concerning parties, primaries, and elections.

*Texas Equal Legal Rights Amendment (ELRA)* Added to Article 1, Section 3, of the Texas Constitution, it guarantees that "Equality under the law shall not be denied or abridged because of sex, race, color, creed or national origin."

*Texas Ethics Commission* Enforces state standards for lobbyists and public officials, including registration of lobbyists and reporting of political campaign contributions.

*Texas Grange* Known as the Patrons of Husbandry, this farmers' organization was well represented in the constitutional convention that produced the Constitution of 1876.

*TEXAS Grants Program* "Toward Excellence, Access, and Success," the program provides funding for qualifying college and university students.

*Texas Higher Education Coordinating Board* An agency that provides some direction for the state's community colleges and universities.

*Texas Parks and Wildlife Department* Texas agency that runs state parks and regulates hunting, fishing, and boating.

*Texas Water Development Board (TWDB)* A board that conducts statewide water planning as mandated by state law.

*Texas Workforce Commission (TWC)* A state agency headed by three salaried commissioners who oversee job training and unemployment compensation programs.

*third party* A party other than the Democratic Party or the Republican Party. Sometimes called a "minor party" because of limited membership and voter support.

*top 10 percent rule* Texas law gives automatic admission to any Texas public college or university to those graduating in the top 10 percent of their Texas high school class.

*tort* An unintended injury to another person or to a person's property.

*traditionalistic culture* A product of the Old South, the traditionalistic culture uses government as a means of preserving the status quo and its leadership.

*Trans-Texas Corridor* A 50-year development plan to provide more than 4,000 miles of new rights-of-way in Texas that will include highways, railways, and utility easements.

*undocumented alien* A person who enters the United States in violation of federal immigration laws.

*unicameral* Term describing a one-house legislature (e.g., the Nebraska Legislature).

*universal suffrage* Voting is open for virtually all persons 18 years of age or older.

*urbanization* Migration of people from rural areas to cities.

*venire* A panel of prospective jurors drawn by random selection. These prospective jurors are called veniremen.

*verdict* A finding of guilty or not guilty by a jury.

*veto power* Authority of the governor to reject a bill or concurrent resolution passed by the legislature.

*voir dire* Courtroom procedure whereby attorneys question prospective jurors to identify any who cannot be fair and impartial.

*voter registration* A qualified voter must register with the county voting registrar, who compiles lists of qualified voters residing in each voting precinct.

*voter turnout* The percentage of the voting-age population casting ballots in an election.

*voting precinct* The basic geographic area for conducting primaries and elections; Texas is divided into more than 8,500 voting precincts.

*weak mayor-council form* A type of municipal government with a separately elected mayor and council, but the mayor shares appointive and removal powers with the council, which can override the mayor's veto.

*white primary* A nominating system designed to prevent African Americans and some Mexican Americans from participating in Democratic primaries from 1923 to 1944.

*women's organization* A women's group, such as the League of Women Voters, that engages in lobbying and educational activities to promote greater political participation by women and others.

# Index